There's been a lot of hype about the World Wide Web being an e[illegible] publishing medium and providing a new way of doing business. Although the Web is quite new in terms of organization, navigation, and quick access to information and media, the effect the Web has on marketing a product, defining a company, or launching a business depends upon the implementation of the technology for a specific commercial use.

Creating commercial Web pages is quite different from creating personal home pages. For one thing, a commercial Web site normally requires a variety of different pages assembled on one site. To achieve this, you need to develop an entire plan for a site that best reflects the needs of your particular business, and keep that in mind as you work through the process of designing and managing your pages. You have to learn how to design and create the text and graphic elements that will give your Web pages a consistent look and feel and allow you to deliver your message coherently in the most cohesive manner possible. You need to view this process as you would if a customer or client visited your physical company: you want them to be dazzled and impressed, informed, and persuaded.

This book walks you through everything creating commercial Web pages entails, and it shows you some of the many options that are available for using the Web to create connections with new and old customers alike. Combining knowledge and examples of HTML and commercial pages in this book with your knowledge of your own business, you should be able to create Web pages that sell products, perform customer service, and more.

Good luck and enjoy!

Laura Lemay
`lemay@lne.com`
`http://www.lne.com/lemay/`

y ear.

tores!

**LAURA LEMAY'S**
WEB WORKSHOP

# Creating Commercial Web Pages

# LAURA LEMAY'S WEB WORKSHOP

# CREATING COMMERCIAL WEB PAGES

Laura Lemay

Brian K. Murphy

Edmund T. Smith

201 West 103rd Street
Indianapolis, Indiana 46290

# Copyright © 1996 by Sams.net Publishing

FIRST EDITION



International Standard Book Number: 1-57521-126-2

Library of Congress Catalog Card Number: 96-68246

99 98 97 96 4 3 2 1

Interpretation of the printing code: the rightmost double-digit number is the year of the book's printing; the rightmost single-digit, the number of the book's printing. For example, a printing code of 96-1 shows that the first printing of the book occurred in 1996.

*Composed in Frutiger and MCPdigital by Macmillan Computer Publishing*

*Printed in the United States of America*



President, Sams Publishing: Richard K. Swadley

Publishing Manager: Mark Taber

Managing Editor: Cindy Morrow

Marketing Manager: John Pierce

Assistant Marketing Managers: Kristina Perry, Rachel Wolfe

**Acquisitions Editor**
*Beverly M. Eppink*

**Development Editor**
*Fran Hatton*

**Software Development Specialist**
*Bob Correll*

**Production Editor**
*Tonya R. Simpson*

**Copy Editors**
*Bart Reed*
*Kristen Ivanetich*
*Ryan Rader*

**Indexer**
*Tim Griffin*

**Technical Reviewers**
*Bill Vernon*
*Raj Mangal*

**Technical Writers**
*Myra H. Immell*
*Bill Vernon*

**Editorial Coordinator**
*Bill Whitmer*

**Technical Edit Coordinator**
*Lorraine Schaffer*

**Resource Coordinator**
*Deborah Frisby*

**Formatters**
*Lynn Everett*
*Frank Sinclair*

**Editorial Assistants**
*Carol Ackerman*
*Andi Richter*
*Rhonda Tinch-Mize*

**Cover Designer**
*Alyssa Yesh*

**Book Designer**
*Alyssa Yesh*

**Copy Writer**
*Peter Fuller*

**Production Team Supervisor**
*Brad Chinn*

**Production**
*Carol Bowers, Mona Brown, Chris Livengood, Paula Lowell, Timothy Osborn, Janet Seib, Mark Walchle*

# Dedication

To Cheryl, Mallory, and Jack, my constant inspirations.

— Brian K. Murphy

# Overview


Introduction ........ xxiv

**Part I Fast Track to Commercial Web Pages 1**

1 Selecting and Using Tools for Page Creation ........ 3

2 Developing a Plan for Design and Site Management ........ 21

**Part II Basic Business Pages—Web Site Building Blocks 39**

3 Corporate Presence Pages ........ 41

4 Creating News, Reference, and Content Pages ........ 59

5 Employee Directories and Biographies ........ 83

6 Online Catalogs and More: Presenting Your Products and Services ........ 101

7 Real-Life Examples: Putting the Basics Together ........ 123

**Part III Taking Your Pages (and Your Business) Beyond the Basics 137**

8 Gathering Information: Web-Based Surveys and Questionnaires ........ 139

9 Customer Support Pages: Boards and Beyond ........ 155

10 Advanced Information Pages: Tying Data to the Web ........ 173

11 Searching Your Site ........ 203

12 Real-Life Examples: Advancing Your Site ........ 225

**Part IV Creating Commerce in Cyberspace: Online Ordering and Advertising Techniques 241**

13 Advanced Catalogs ........ 243

14 Web Shopping Carts ........ 267

15 Web Cash Registers: Taking and Making Money on the Net ........ 283

16 Providing Content for a Price on the Web ........ 305

17 Setting Up Advertising-Supported Web Sites ........ 319

18 Order and Shipment Tracking on the Web ........ 339

19 Real-Life Examples: Doing Business on the Web ........ 363

**Part V Putting It All Together 377**

20 Marketing Your Web Pages ........ 379

21 Web-Site Administration and Management ........ 399

22 Real-Life Examples: Touting and Managing Your Site ........ 413

Part VI Appendixes 427

A Online Resources ........ 429

B HTML 3.2 Reference ........ 435

C What's on the CD-ROM? ........ 469

Index ........ 475

# Contents

Introduction ........ xxiv

Part I Fast Track to Commercial Web Pages 1

1 **Selecting and Using Tools for Page Creation** ........ 3
- About HTML Editors ........ 4
  - HotDog ........ 4
  - Microsoft FrontPage ........ 5
  - Netscape Gold ........ 7
  - Internet Assistant for Microsoft Word ........ 8
- About Web Page Utilities and Accessories ........ 9
- About Online Resources for Web Creation Tools and Design ........ 10
- Task: Creating a Basic Web Page ........ 12
- About Templates ........ 14
- Task: Creating a Basic Web Page Template ........ 15
  - Determining Text Elements ........ 15
  - Dealing With Graphic Elements ........ 15
  - Creating the Template Page ........ 16
  - Saving the Template ........ 17
- Task: Customizing Your First Web Page Template ........ 18
- Workshop Wrap-Up ........ 18
  - Next Steps ........ 19
  - Q&A ........ 19

2 **Developing a Plan for Design and Site Management** ........ 21
- About Creating a Web Page Theme ........ 22
- Task: Creating Horizontal Rules ........ 23
- Task: Creating a Large Graphic Banner ........ 26
- Task: Developing Navigational Buttons and Controls ........ 27
- Task: Creating Graphical Bullet Icons ........ 28
- About Color Schemes ........ 30
  - Anatomy of the <BODY> Tag ........ 32
- Task: Pulling Together the Color Scheme ........ 32
- About Style Sheets ........ 34
- Developing a Plan for Web Page Updating and Management ........ 35
- Workshop Wrap-Up ........ 36
  - Next Steps ........ 36
  - Q&A ........ 37

## Part II Basic Business Pages—Web Site Building Blocks 39

3 **Corporate Presence Pages** .......... 41
Laying the Groundwork .......... 42
Task: Creating a No-Wait Welcome Page .......... 44
The Importance of Speed .......... 45
Shrinking Your Graphics .......... 45
Using Progressive Images To Be the Quickest Draw .......... 46
Opening an Image File .......... 47
Task: Creating a Menu Bar .......... 50
Designing the Menu Bar .......... 51
Adding a Button Style Menu .......... 51
The What's New or News Link .......... 55
Quick Contacts .......... 55
Workshop Wrap-Up .......... 56
Next Steps .......... 56
Q&A .......... 57

4 **Creating News, Reference, and Content Pages** .......... 59
About Press Release Archives .......... 60
Task: Creating Navigational Tools .......... 61
Task: Writing and Placing Clickable Headings .......... 63
Writing Headings .......... 63
Placing Headings .......... 64
Task: Creating Links .......... 65
Designing and Creating a Press Release Format .......... 67
Task: Adding Links in Press Releases .......... 69
Task: Creating a Reference Page from Links .......... 70
Finding the Links .......... 71
Creating the List of Links .......... 72
Creating the Links .......... 73
Task: Inserting an Image .......... 73
Task: Finishing the Reference Page .......... 74
Task: Creating an Original Content Page .......... 75
Creating the Content .......... 76
Designing the Page .......... 76
Task: Creating Pages That Will Get You Bookmarked .......... 80
Workshop Wrap-Up .......... 81
Next Steps .......... 82
Q&A .......... 82

5 **Employee Directories and Biographies** .......... **83**
Creating an Employee Directory .......... 84
Task: Creating a Frame Layout .......... 85
Task: Creating the Alphabetical Employee Listing .......... 86
Creating a Default Employee Directory Page .......... 91
About Individual Web Pages .......... 93
A Sample Employee Directory Page .......... 95
Task: Making Provisions for Frameless Browsers (and Users) .......... 97
Workshop Wrap-Up .......... 98
Next Steps .......... 98
Q&A .......... 99
6 **Online Catalogs: Presenting Your Products and Services** .......... **101**
What You Need to Know Up-Front: Catalog Design Tips .......... 102
Creating "Layers" of Pages for a Web Catalog .......... 102
Offline and Online Are Not the Same .......... 102
A Product/Price List .......... 103
Task: Creating a Basic Layout Using Tables .......... 104
Determine Table Proportions .......... 105
Task: Adding and Formatting Product and Price Information .......... 108
To Add the Product and Price Information .......... 108
Formatting Table Text .......... 109
Task: Hyperlinking Product Names to Product Pages .......... 111
Creating Product Pages .......... 111
Linking Up the Product Pages .......... 113
Task: Adding Table and Background Formatting .......... 114
Adding a Border .......... 115
Adding to Background Colors .......... 116
Adding Table Headings .......... 116
Give the Text Some Space .......... 118
Task: Adding Information in Nested Tables .......... 118
Task: Adding Product Images .......... 120
Workshop Wrap-Up .......... 120
Next Steps .......... 121
Q&A .......... 121
7 **Real-Life Examples: Putting the Basics Together** .......... **123**
Example 1: Arachnid WorldWide .......... 124
Basic Welcome Page and Menu Bar .......... 124
Constructive Criticism .......... 126
Reference and Original Content Pages .......... 126

Example 2: Autometric, Inc. .... 127
Press Release Archive .... 128
Constructive Criticism .... 129
Example 3: ProMetrics, Inc. .... 129
Employee Directory Index and Default Page .... 130
Constructive Criticism .... 131
Basic Employee Page .... 131
Constructive Criticism .... 131
A Creative Employee Page .... 132
Example 4: Computer Parts & Pieces .... 132
Main Catalog Index Page .... 133
Product/Price List Page .... 133
Individual Product Page .... 134
Workshop Wrap-Up .... 135
Next Steps .... 136
Q&A .... 136

Part III Taking Your Pages (and Your Business) Beyond the Basics 137

8 **Gathering Information: Web-Based Surveys and Questionnaires .... 139**
About HTML Forms .... 140
Selecting an Approach to Implement Your Forms .... 140
Using `Mailto:` .... 141
Using CGI Scripting .... 142
Task: Setting Up a Separate Page for Each Form .... 142
Task: Getting the Information You Need Using Forms .... 145
Task: Designing the Form .... 148
The Value of Web Surveys .... 150
Task: Formatting and Managing Form Results .... 150
Formatting Your Results .... 150
Managing Your Results .... 151
Workshop Wrap-Up .... 152
Next Steps .... 152
Q&A .... 153

9 **Customer Support Pages: Boards and Beyond .... 155**
Create a FAQ List and Answer Database .... 156
Creating Product FAQs .... 156
Creating the Individual FAQ Pages .... 157
Answer Databases .... 161
Task: Set Up a Customer Support Web Bulletin Board .... 162
Usenet Without the Flames .... 162
Setting Up the Boards: A Script for Success .... 163

Use Multimedia to Answer Questions ... 167
Choose and Use Only Popular Formats ... 168
Task: Setting Up a Web Phone to Provide Support ... 168
Selecting a Web Phone to Support (For Support) ... 169
Setting Up the Web Phone on Your Web Page ... 169
Workshop Wrap-Up ... 171
Next Steps ... 172
Q&A ... 172

**10 Advanced Information Pages: Tying Data to the Web ... 173**

Product Databases ... 174
Static Database Pages ... 177
Task: Building a Database with Internet Assistant for Microsoft Access ... 180
Task: Using mSQL, a Shareware Database ... 182
Installing mSQL on Your Server ... 183
W3-mSQL ... 184
OBDC Databases ... 189
Task: Using SQL ... 189
Creating Web-Database Applications ... 192
Financial Spreadsheets ... 194
Task: Writing a Simple CGI Spreadsheet ... 195
Task: Creating Static Spreadsheets ... 199
Creating an HTML Page from an Excel Spreadsheet ... 199
Investor Relations Pages ... 200
Workshop Wrap-Up ... 201
Next Steps ... 202
Q&A ... 202

**11 Searching Your Site ... 203**

Creating a Site Index and Table of Contents ... 204
Site Indexes ... 205
Task: Creating a Table of Contents ... 205
Text Editors ... 206
HTML Editors ... 207
Task: Using an Indexing Program ... 207
Task: Making a Site Map ... 210
`cmap` ... 211
Task: Setting Up a Search Engine for Your Site ... 214
A Simple Search Script ... 214
Task: Setting Up an Advanced Search Engine ... 218
Site Searching and Navigation: Some Design Tips ... 221
Multiple Tables of Contents ... 221

Separate Table of Contents Page ..... 221
Navigation from Any Page ..... 221
Tables and Frames ..... 221
Site Search Engine ..... 222
Workshop Wrap-Up ..... 223
Next Steps ..... 223
Q&A ..... 223

**12 Real-Life Examples: Advancing Your Site ..... 225**
Example 1: Customer Forms and Surveys ..... 226
Business on the Move ..... 226
Rolling Hills Golf, Inc. ..... 228
Example 2: Customer Support Elements ..... 229
Microsoft Gaming Zone FAQ ..... 229
Medtronic's FAQ and Answer Database ..... 231
Mutual Funds Interactive ..... 232
Example 3: Tying Data to the Web ..... 234
The Internet Shopping Network ..... 234
Example 4: Searches and Tables of Contents ..... 234
The Faxon Company ..... 235
VMF Sales ..... 236
Attachmate SupportWeb! ..... 236
Enteract ..... 237
Workshop Wrap-Up ..... 239
Next Steps ..... 239
Q&A ..... 239

## Part IV Creating Commerce in Cyberspace: Online Ordering and Advertising Techniques 241

**13 Advanced Catalogs ..... 243**
Different Catalogs for Different Customers ..... 244
Separate Catalog Pages ..... 245
Task: Creating Catalogs on the Fly ..... 246
Set Up the Database ..... 246
Main Menu or Index ..... 246
Catalog Templates ..... 248
Task: Working with Text-Only Catalogs ..... 250
Task: Customizing Product Presentations ..... 252
Creating Separate Pages ..... 252
On-the-Fly Product Pages ..... 254
Multimedia and Interactive Catalogs ..... 256
Multimedia ..... 256
Interaction ..... 260

Workshop Wrap-Up ........ 264
Next Steps ........ 265
Q&A ........ 265
**14 Web Shopping Carts ........ 267**
Shopping Carts: How'd They Do That? ........ 268
Task: Preparing the Shopping Cart Files and Directory ........ 269
Edit the `cart.conf` Configuration File ........ 271
Customizing the Shopping Cart Header (`head.html`) ........ 272
Customizing the Shopping Cart Footer (`foot.html`) ........ 274
Task: Creating an Online Store ........ 275
The Rule of Threes ........ 275
Form-ulating Stores and Aisles ........ 276
OopShop in Action ........ 279
Workshop Wrap-Up ........ 281
Next Steps ........ 281
Q&A ........ 282
**15 Web Cash Registers: Taking and Making Money on the Net ........ 283**
Presenting Payment Options ........ 284
Task: Securing Transactions on Your Site ........ 286
Common Sense Security ........ 287
Secured Server ........ 287
Task: Preparing for Third-Party Transactions ........ 289
Jumbling the Data ........ 290
Taking Digital Cash ........ 291
Ecash ........ 291
Task: Providing Both Online and Offline Ordering ........ 294
Online Ordering ........ 294
Offline Ordering ........ 301
Workshop Wrap-Up ........ 303
Next Steps ........ 303
Q&A ........ 303
**16 Providing Content for a Price on the Web ........ 305**
Task: Identifying Premium Content ........ 306
Task: Setting Up Registration Forms ........ 308
The Registration Form ........ 309
Task: Gathering Payment Information for a Free Trial ........ 314
After the Trial: Making Real Money ........ 315
Pay Per View/Use/Download Services ........ 315
A Sample Pay-Per-Use Site ........ 316
Workshop Wrap-Up ........ 317
Next Steps ........ 318
Q&A ........ 318

17 **Setting Up Advertising-Supported Web Sites** ..... **319**
To Advertise or Not To Advertise? ..... 320
Advertising Basics: Placements, Charges, and Tracking ..... 321
A Place for Every Ad and Every Ad in Its Place ..... 321
Setting a Rate Scale ..... 323
Tracking Web Advertisements ..... 323
Task: Creating an Animated Banner Advertisement ..... 324
The Animated GIF Format ..... 325
Using the GIF Construction Set ..... 325
Task: Inserting the Banner Advertisement in Your Page ..... 328
Task: Creating Ads with the BillBoard Applet ..... 329
Task: Using the Commonwealth Network ..... 331
What Is the Commonwealth Network? ..... 332
Managing Your Page Portfolio ..... 334
Getting and Using the Banner Advertisement HTML Code ..... 336
Workshop Wrap-Up ..... 337
Next Steps ..... 337
Q&A ..... 338
18 **Order and Shipment Tracking on the Web** ..... **339**
Customer Order Information ..... 340
Order Data ..... 340
Additional Customer Data ..... 341
Collecting Customer Data ..... 342
Data Analysis ..... 344
Task: Setting Up the Saletrak Program ..... 346
Installation ..... 346
Configuration ..... 346
Specifying the Configuration File ..... 349
Customer Confidentiality ..... 350
Inventory and Order Tracking ..... 352
Inventory Tracking ..... 352
Task: Using Indirect Database Input ..... 354
Order Tracking ..... 356
Task: Using Stattrak for Providing Status ..... 357
Shipment Tracking Options ..... 359
Workshop Wrap-Up ..... 360
Next Steps ..... 361
Q&A ..... 361
19 **Real Life Examples: Doing Business on the Web** ..... **363**
Example 1: Jigowat Jewelry Catalog ..... 364
Example 2: Discovery Channel Catalog ..... 365

Example 3: Let's Talk Cellular Catalog ... 366
Example 4: Steve Dahl & Company Catalog ... 369
Example 5: NetBeat Catalog ... 370
Example 6: SportsLine ... 371
Example 7: Commonwealth Network Site ... 372
Example 8: Package Tracking Services ... 373
Workshop Wrap-Up ... 375
Next Steps ... 375
Q&A ... 376

Part V Putting It All Together 377

20 **Marketing Your Web Pages ... 379**
Netiquette: Know It Now or Know It Later ... 380
Where to Find the Online Rules of the Road ... 381
The Netiquette Home Page ... 382
Putting Your Page on a Web Index ... 383
Task: Getting Listed on Yahoo! ... 385
Picking Your Categories ... 386
Adding Title, Descriptions, and More ... 386
Task: Using Submit It! ... 387
Making Your Commercial Web Pages "Search Friendly" ... 389
Determine the "Key Words" for Your Page ... 389
Task: Create a Spider Web Page To Improve Search Results ... 390
Spreading the Word Via Usenet ... 391
Avoid the Flames ... 392
Post Where You're Welcome ... 392
Helping Others Can Help Yourself ... 392
Linking Your Pages ... 393
The Internet Link Exchange ... 393
Using Offline Techniques for Online Results ... 394
Generating Media Exposure ... 395
Workshop Wrap-Up ... 396
Next Steps ... 396
Q&A ... 396

21 **Web Site Administration and Management ... 399**
HTML Code and Link Verification ... 400
HTML Verifiers ... 400
Task: Using Weblint To Clean Your Pages ... 401
Setting Up Weblint on Your Server ... 401
Task: Using a Weblint Gateway ... 403
Link Checkers ... 404
The Doctor Is In: Using Doctor HTML ... 405

Managing Your Pages: Tools and Techniques ... 406
Web Management Tools ... 406
Management Techniques Without Tools ... 408
Task: Organizing a Site ... 408
Creating Directories ... 408
Moving Your Files ... 409
Resetting Links and Code ... 409
Security Considerations ... 410
Workshop Wrap-Up ... 411
Next Steps ... 411
Q&A ... 411

**22 Real-Life Examples: Touting and Managing Your Site ... 413**
Example 1: Making Your Site "Findable" ... 414
Yahoo! ... 414
Submit-It! ... 415
Example 2: Linking Up ... 416
Internet Link Exchange ... 416
Example 3: Using Usenet To Spread the Word ... 417
A Usenet Announcement ... 418
A Signature Ad ... 418
Example 4: Checking and Validating HTML ... 419
Weblint on Microsoft ... 420
Example 5: Checking Your Links ... 421
Doctor HTML ... 421
Example 6: Management Techniques Without Tools ... 423
Organizing Your Site ... 423
Workshop Wrap-Up ... 424
Next Steps ... 424
Q&A ... 424

## Part VI Appendixes 427

**A Online Resources ... 429**
Graphics Sites ... 429
General Business Reference ... 430
HTML Authoring Tools ... 430
HTML Design and Authoring ... 431
HTML Authoring Newsgroups ... 431
Web Searching and Indexes ... 431
CGI Scripts ... 432
Subscription and Pay-Per-View Web Services ... 433
Web Page Marketing ... 433
Multimedia ... 434

**B HTML 3.2 Quick Reference ............ 435**
HTML Tags ............ 435
Comments ............ 436
Structure Tags ............ 436
Headings and Title ............ 439
Paragraphs and Regions ............ 439
Links ............ 439
Lists ............ 441
Character Formatting ............ 442
Other Elements ............ 442
Images, Sounds, and Embedded Media ............ 444
Forms ............ 448
Tables ............ 451
Frames ............ 458
Scripting and Applets ............ 459
Marquees ............ 461
Character Entities ............ 462
**C What's on the CD-ROM ............ 469**
Windows Software ............ 469
ActiveX ............ 470
CGI ............ 470
GNU ............ 470
GZIP ............ 470
HTML Tools ............ 470
Java ............ 471
Graphics, Video, and Sound Applications ............ 471
Perl ............ 471
Explorer ............ 471
Utilities ............ 471
Electronic Books ............ 472
Macintosh Software ............ 472
Java ............ 472
HTML Tools ............ 472
Graphics, Video, and Sound Applications ............ 472
Electronic Books ............ 473
About Shareware ............ 473
**Index ............ 475**

# Acknowledgments

The only way I could have written this book was with a wife and family that tolerated a summer of lost weekends and a sleep-deprived zombie living in their midst. Cheryl, Mallory, and Jack are my constant inspiration for everything I do, and this book is no exception. I'd also like to thank my mom and dad for being such wonderful parents (and grandparents), the root of all success.

Special thanks to Beverly Eppink at Sams.net for giving me the opportunity to write this and every other book I have worked on. Her support, patience, and insight kept this project moving and on track from beginning to end. Also, to Mark Taber and Fran Hatton, who were essential to the formation of the ideas and words that follow. Thanks also to Mike Blanche at Digiserve and Charlie Ward at Enteract for helping me set up the book's Web page and keeping my lifeline to the Web alive and well at the most critical moments.

Thanks to Ed Smith, Myra Immell, and Bill Vernon for contributing to and enhancing the book and responding to the call for help.

Finally, to Laura Lemay who conceived and oversaw this and all the other titles in the *Web Workshop* series. It was an honor to work on a project associated with the undisputed Queen of HTML how-to books.

— Brian K. Murphy

# About the Authors

**Brian Murphy** (murph@murphnet.com) holds a law degree from the Ohio State University College of Law and a degree in film from Columbia College in Chicago. He was responsible for establishing the first Web home page for an inmate on death row, Girvies L. Davis, which was one of the 1,001 best Internet sites according to *PC Computing Magazine*. Brian was a contributing author for Sams.net Publishing's *Web Page Wizardry* and *Netscape 2 Unleashed*. He has discussed the impact and power of the Internet through television and radio interviews with ABC, CBS, NBC, CNN, BBC, CBC, and NPR. He has also appeared in *People* and been quoted on Internet issues by the *New York Times*, *Washington Post*, *The Economist*, *NetGuide* magazine and the Associated Press. Brian makes his home in Naperville, Illinois, with his wife Cheryl and their two children, Mallory and Jack. He is a practicing attorney with the law firm of Jenner & Block in Chicago.

**Ed Smith** (ets@edbo.com) is an Internet consultant and Web Site Developer in York County, Pennsylvania. He owns his own company, E.T. Smith Associates, which develops, establishes, and maintains Internet sites for businesses and organizations specializing in highly interactive sites. A former armored cavalry officer, Ed had worked in the electric utility industry as an engineer for 11 years before leaving to start his own Internet business. Ed enjoys travelling and motorcycle riding. He's ridden his Harley Softail through the U.S., to the top of the Colorado Rockies, and gone 2,000 miles in a couple of days to meet friends for a Thunder Run. However, he most enjoys his time with his wife, two daughters, and his wife's pit bull Katie (he's really good to the wife).

# Tell Us What You Think!

As a reader, you are the most important critic and commentator of our books. We value your opinion and want to know what we're doing right, what we could do better, areas in which you'd like to see us publish, and any other words of wisdom you're willing to pass our way. You can help us make strong books that meet your needs and give you the computer guidance you require.

Do you have access to CompuServe or the World Wide Web? Then check out our CompuServe forum by typing `GO SAMS` at any prompt. If you prefer the World Wide Web, check out our site at `http://www.mcp.com`.

**NOTE:** If you have a technical question about this book, call the technical support line at (800) 571-5840, ext. 3668.

As the team leader of the group that created this book, I welcome your comments. You can fax, e-mail, or write me directly to let me know what you did or didn't like about this book—as well as what we can do to make our books stronger. Here's the information:


FAX: 317/581-4669

E-mail: `newtech_mgr@sams.mcp.com`

Mail: Mark Taber
Publishing Manager
Sams.net Publishing
201 W. 103rd Street
Indianapolis, IN 46290

# Introduction

You can't turn on the television or open a newspaper or magazine today without hearing or reading about the latest and greatest Web pages available on the Internet. In little more than three years, the World Wide Web has become a widely accepted mass medium for digital information, entertainment, and commerce.

Every day, thousands of new Web pages are being created and put online with the fervent pace of a virtual gold rush. The majority of these new pages are commercial Web pages supported by and intended to promote products and businesses of virtually every category across the spectrum. For most businesses today, the question of whether to create a Web page has shifted from if to when. The next time you read a magazine or watch some television commercials during your favorite program, take a mental note of the number of URLs that appear in advertisements right now. This is only the beginning of a relatively infant technology.

The process of creating a Web page seems like a daunting task for the uninitiated. Even if you've conquered the basic confusion of HTML by reading Laura Lemay's *Teach Yourself Web Publishing with HTML in A Week*, the prospect of creating a commercial Web page raises a bevy of advanced design and implementation issues that you probably have neither thought about nor worked with before now.

The point of this book is to take you through the process of creating a commercial Web page and to show you some of the many options that are available for using the Web to create connections with new and old customers alike. One of the most critical things to remember in creating any Web page is that this is an evolutionary process. You should consider this book a springboard to your commercial Web pages, but you'll need to always look for ways to extend the examples and samples in new and creative ways to serve your specific customers and products. Combining the knowledge of HTML and commercial pages in this book with your knowledge of your own business, you should be able to create Web pages that sell products, perform customer service, and more.

The book is obviously designed to function as a workshop, as the title states. A good way to work with the book is with your laptop or desktop system nearby and warmed up and ready to go. You'll probably get the urge to work through many of the examples and sample code that are provided throughout these chapters. The best way to learn to create Web pages is by doing, and this book (and the entire *Laura Lemay's Web Workshop* series) was designed and written with that in mind.

The book follows a logical progression of HTML authoring capabilities from simplest to most advanced. Thus, the examples used in the first section of the book require the most basic HTML coding while the last section of the book requires more advanced techniques and knowledge. Depending on your skill level, you can simply refer to chapters that will help you with a specific task or you can work through the entire book and by the later chapters you will have acquired the HTML skills necessary to accomplish those tasks.

Here is just a sampling of the areas you'll cover as you work through the various sections and chapters:

- Selecting and using HTML editors and tools for Web page creation
- Developing and designing Web site themes for your business and products
- Creating basic welcome pages and Web page navigation menus
- Designing information sources and press release archives
- Implementing an employee directory
- Basic and advanced online catalogs for selling your company's products and services
- Using and creating forms and surveys to gather customer information
- Developing Web-based customer service and support options
- Using Web shopping carts and payment systems to generate online sales and revenue
- Using the Web to sell online content and information

For a comprehensive listing of the contents of the *Laura Lemay's Web Workshop: Creating Commercial Web Pages* CD-ROM, turn to Appendix C, "What's on the CD-ROM." You'll find out about all the sample Web pages, programs, and files that have been included to make the task of creating a commercial Web page even easier. Appendix A, "Online Resources," contains a reference for online authoring resources and Appendix B, "HTML 3.2 Reference," provides a quick and easy HTML creation.

Now it's time to start the workshop. I can't wait to see your pages.

# How to Read This Book

Margin notes tell you more about the current topic, as well as give you cross references to places in the book where you can find further information about a specific subject.

The following examples show how this book's tips, notes, and cautions help guide you through information you will need to know.

**TIP:** Tips offer important (or at least interesting) hints and suggestions related to the topic at hand.

**NOTE:** Notes provide you with interesting, added information about the subject at hand.

**CAUTION:** Cautions prompt you with gentle warnings to help you stay out of trouble.

CD-ROM notes alert you to programs and files on the CD-ROM at the back of this book that help with the topic at hand.

# PART I

# Fast Track to Commercial Web Pages


**Chapter 1** Selecting and Using Tools for Page Creation

**2** Developing a Plan for Design and Site Management

CHAPTER

ONE

# Selecting and Using Tools for Page Creation

Have you ever tried to do a home improvement project or assemble a piece of furniture or a child's toy when you don't have the right tools? If you have, you know all too well that without those tools you are doomed to hours of frustration that, in the end, result in a lot of valuable time lost and a not-too-great job overall.

Keep that "construction" experience in mind before you actually undertake the building of your Web pages. Start your Web project the same way you would any construction project—by selecting the tools you're going to use. When it comes to those tools, you'll find that you have an overabundance from which to pick. The good news is that virtually all Web creation software is available, often in a trial form, for free on the Internet. You can try one or many to find the one that best suits your needs and tastes. You certainly can't do that with circular saws.

## In this chapter, you

- ❑ Explore HTML editors
- ❑ Explore Web page utilities and accessories
- ❑ Learn about online resources for Web creation tools and design
- ❑ Create a basic Web page
- ❑ Create a basic Web page template
- ❑ Customize a Web page template

## Tasks in this chapter:

- ❑ Creating a Basic Web Page
- ❑ Creating a Basic Web Page Template
- ❑ Customizing Your First Web Page Template

This chapter introduces the tools you'll need to start building the Web pages demonstrated in this book. In fact, many already are at your disposal on the accompanying CD-ROM. If a tool is not on the CD-ROM, you can access it quickly by downloading it through direct links from this book's companion Web site: `http://www.murphnet.com`. I'll keep the online site updated so that as new tools and versions become available, you can be among the first to take them for a test drive.

This chapter takes you through the process of selecting your Web-creation tools and then using them to bring into being your first basic Web pages and templates.

# About HTML Editors

In the past, if you wanted to create a Web page you manually entered the appropriate code into a simple text editor as basic as the Windows Notepad. This process was extremely tedious and time-consuming, and when your pages didn't turn out as expected, troubleshooting wasn't always easy.

Today, as in the past, the HTML editor is the most important Web creation tool you will have to select. But we're a lot luckier now because there is a plethora of options available in the way of HTML editors. These editors provide a broad range of support for complex page creation and advanced HTML specifications. Some of them even offer WYSIWYG (wiz-e-wig: What-You-See-Is-What-You-Get) capabilities so that you can edit and design your page on-the-fly. Your level of experience with HTML, need for complex Web coding, and budget will determine which editor (or editors) best fill your needs.

## HotDog

Hot Dog, featured in Figure 1.1, provides an inexpensive, solid HTML editor that furnishes the vast majority of advanced HTML tags for both Netscape Navigator and Microsoft's Internet Explorer. Basically, it enables you to manipulate and format text in much the same way you would with your word processor. As long as you have a basic familiarity with HTML, getting up to speed on using the HotDog editor should not be a problem.

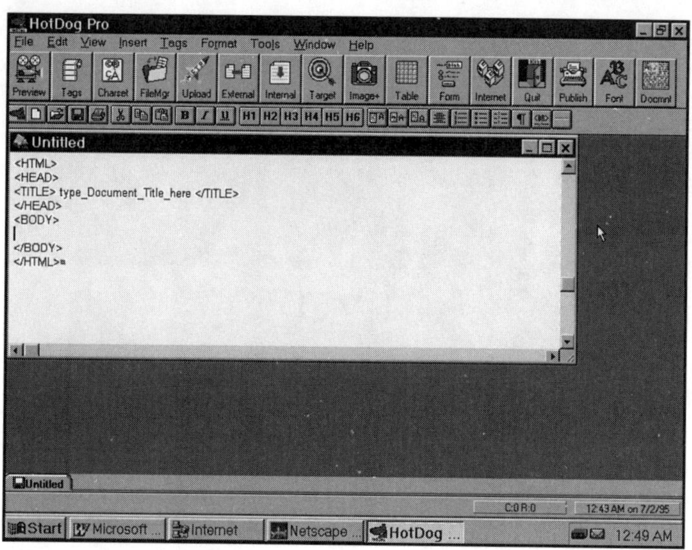


**Figure 1.1.**
*The HotDog HTML editor is one of the most popular Web editors on the market.*

Sausage Software offers a variety of advanced tools, such as its Egor Java applet creator, that can be used in conjunction with HotDog. You can view the entire line of Sausage Software Web-editing products at `http://www.sausage.com`.

Need a crash course or a refresher in HTML? Read Laura Lemay's *Teach Yourself Web Publishing with HTML 3.0 in a Week, Second Edition,* published by Sams.net.

If you have any problems with or questions about using HotDog as you work with the editor on your pages, you can always seek advice using Usenet. A good place to post your HotDog questions is at `comp.infosystems.www.html.authoring`.

HotDog comes in two flavors—Standard and Pro. Both enable you to configure them to load the current document into your default browser by selecting the Preview button. The major difference between the two, besides price, is that the Pro edition comes with ROVER, a real-time output viewer that lets you view the results of your edits to HTML code as they are made.

**NOTE:** I've found that the best way to work with HotDog, as well as most other Web editors, is to save the Web page I'm working on almost immediately after having filled in the `<TITLE>` tag. Then, with the saved document still open in the HotDog editor, I open my favorite browser and load the saved document. As I make edits in HotDog and want to see the results, I save the document, switch to the browser, and hit the Refresh or Reload button. Almost immediately, the browser brings up the Web page with the updated edits. Doing this should go a long way toward making you confident about what your page will look like when it's completed.

## Microsoft FrontPage

Like HotDog, Microsoft FrontPage provides a WYSIWYG interface. This interface makes creating Web pages even simpler than creating a normal document using your favorite word processor. FrontPage, however, extends beyond the basics of most HTML editors by providing an environment in which you can creatively edit and manipulate Web pages as you view how they will look when posted to the Web. Figure 1.2 offers an example of how FrontPage enables you to do this.

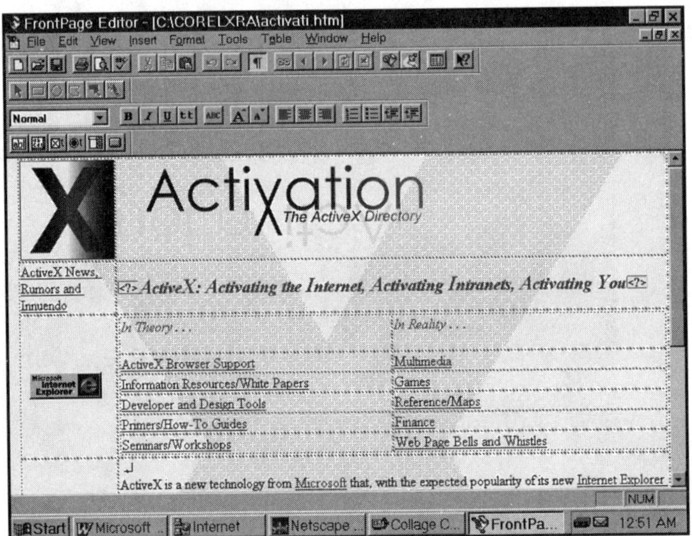


**Figure 1.2.**
*Microsoft's FrontPage provides you with a WYSIWYG environment for editing Web pages.*

Microsoft FrontPage is one of the most exciting pieces of Web creation software I have ever seen. The ease with which even new users can create complex Web pages without even seeing HTML code is astounding.

FrontPage, however, does not support all features for both editing and viewing purposes. Frames, for example, is supported for editing only, so you still need to use a browser such as Internet Explorer or Netscape Navigator to view your output for some pages.

One of the most radical advancements contained in the FrontPage package is its bots—short for "Robots"—which provide advanced Web page features that you couldn't have used before unless you knew how to use CGI scripts. For example, FrontPage enables you to drop a bot into a Web page that makes it possible for users to input a search request that will scan the entire Web site and display a list of results. And, with FrontPage's advanced technology, you can create interactive Web-based bulletin boards in minutes—without any CGI scripting.

**NOTE:** Even though I tend to use HotDog as my editor of choice, FrontPage or Netscape Gold have advantages or features that you might prefer to use. If you decide to use one of these products instead of HotDog as your primary HTML editor, grab a copy of the Sams.net publications *FrontPage Unleashed, Laura Lemay's Web Workshop: Microsoft FrontPage, or Laura Lemay's Web Workshop: Netscape Navigator Gold* to use in conjunction with this book. This will provide you with all the information you'll need to create attractive and interactive Web pages.

Before you can use these advanced features of FrontPage, your Web server must have specialized Web server extensions installed. These extensions are available free from Microsoft. If you rent Web space from a provider instead of running your own server, you'll probably have to ask about or request the server extensions. The Web hosting service I use, Digiserve (`http://www.digiserve.com`), provides support for FrontPage extensions on an account with a small additional charge.

Another great feature of FrontPage is its wizards. Intended to enable you to create Web pages quickly using preconfigured standard formats, there are numerous wizards—to create tables, to build custom pages and backgrounds, to generate custom frame grids, to guide you through the creation of webs and threaded discussion bulletin boards, and so on. The wizards are a good starting point for putting together professional-looking pages fast. Even so, it's really worth the time it might take to go beyond the basics so that your pages are unique. If you stick to the wizards exclusively, you run the risk of your pages mimicking those of every other site that used FrontPage.

Price used to be one of the biggest drawbacks associated with FrontPage, but recently Microsoft dropped that dramatically.

As FrontPage becomes more and more popular (which is sure to happen if it is included with Microsoft's Office 97), you should have little problem locating a hosting service that provides the server support you need to access all of FrontPage's advanced features with your pages.

FrontPage server extensions provide cross-platform support for most major hardware platforms, operating systems, and Web server software. For more information, check out the FrontPage home page at `http://www.microsoft.com/msoffice/frontpage/`.

## Netscape Gold

Netscape Gold is from the same folks who created the Netscape Navigator browser—the most popular Web browser available. Using Netscape Gold as your Web editor, you can create and edit Web pages using the exact same interface that you use to browse the Web. Even though Netscape Gold, as shown in Figure 1.3, is a commercial product, a new beta version that you can download for free always seems to be available on Netscape's Web site at `http://home.netscape.com`.

*Laura Lemay's Web Workshop: Netscape Navigator Gold* extensively covers the editor and how to use it to create Web pages.

Netscape is always striving to improve its products, so features that might not be available on Netscape Gold as I write this might be incorporated into the product by the time you read this.

One of the best features I've found in Netscape Gold is the ability to browse a Web page and then click the pencil icon to edit the HTML code for that page in a WYSIWYG environment. This means that if you come across a page whose style and layout you really like, you can instantly use Netscape Gold to edit the HTML code, adding your own information and graphics and saving the document locally for use on your Web site.

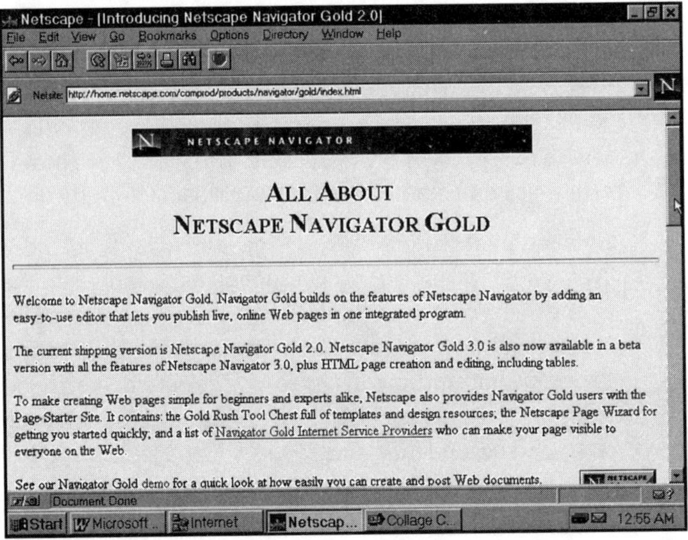


**Figure 1.3.**
*Netscape Gold is a WYSIWYG HTML editor that is available for downloading from* `http://home.netscape.com`.

**NOTE:** Remember that using someone else's Web pages as a jumping-off point for your designs is one thing. Effectively co-opting them and simply plugging in your company name is quite another. No matter which editor you use, use common sense when you borrow design techniques from others, and always give credit where credit is due for any innovative methods.

## Internet Assistant for Microsoft Word

If you use Microsoft Word as your word processor, Internet Assistant for Microsoft Word is a great HTML editing tool. Simply install it and Word becomes a full-fledged HTML editor that also enables you to view Web pages. Of course, you must have a copy of Microsoft Word and a fairly robust system to run it—at least 16MB of RAM. You can't beat the cost of this editor—it's free. This is probably one of its biggest selling points.

Internet Assistant for Microsoft Word has form-creation features that are particularly useful, so you might want to use it when you design and edit pages that implement forms. If you want to know more about these features, check out Chapter 8, "Gathering Information: Web-Based Surveys and Questionnaires," which includes examples that use forms extensively.

**NOTE:** Microsoft has also released a variety of Internet assistants for the other products in its Office suite—Excel, PowerPoint, and Schedule+—that you might find useful for programming different types of information into your commercial Web pages. Each of these Internet assistants easily takes information from the program's native format and converts it into Web-read HTML code.

# About Web Page Utilities and Accessories

The CD-ROM that accompanies this book is chock full of Web page programs and utilities. Check Appendix C, "What's on the CD-ROM," for a complete listing.

Although HTML editors are becoming more and more versatile, there are still several other programs that you'll need to consider and probably use when you create your Web pages.

For the latest-breaking news on these tools, you might want to check out some of the excellent resources referenced in Appendix A, "Online Resources."

- Stroud's Consummate Winsock Apps, at `http://www.cwsapps.com`, will give you a good amount of detail about what Web utilities are available, what they can accomplish, and where you can download them.
- The Ultimate Collection of Winsock Software (TUCOWS), at `http://www.tucows.com`, is another good resource.
- Cool Tool of the Day, at `http://www.cooltoll.com`, brings you the best of Web-oriented tools without regard to platform.

The Web became so wildly popular in great part because of its capability to present information in a graphically stimulating environment. It only stands to reason, then, that if you want to create a commercial Web page worth browsing, you'll need to work with graphics. The following are just a few of the tools you can use:

- Paint Shop Pro 3.12, included on the CD-ROM, is an excellent tool. As shown in Figure 1.4, Paint Shop Pro has a great interface for working with a broad range of graphics files. Figure 1.4 shows the program in action.

  Paint Shop Pro, which has a great interface for working with a broad range of graphics files, truly works with virtually every graphics format imaginable and enables you to manipulate the image in a variety of ways. Considered a poor man's Adobe Photoshop, a more powerful and expensive commercial graphics editor, you'll find that it will serve most of your basic needs for the majority of the Web pages discussed in this book.

**Figure 1.4.**
*Paint Shop Pro combines power with ease of use for manipulating graphics for your Web pages.*

- Map This!, included on the accompanying CD-ROM, is an image map editor. Image maps are images that have different links associated with them according to where on the image a user clicks. Map This! enables you to take images and assign links to different areas of the picture. You can create either client- or server-side image maps.

  Before advancements in HTML, you had to create image maps that called a CGI script to perform its functions. Now, several Web browsers support client-side image mapping. Client-side image maps offer some benefits. They are faster, easier to implement, and easier for Web surfers to use.

## About Online Resources for Web Creation Tools and Design

Many sites have libraries of graphics that can be used for backgrounds, buttons, horizontal dividers, and more. Sites like the ones that follow can save you time and money when it comes to putting together a slick presentation:

- Microsoft Internet Workshop, the focus of Figure 1.5, is a banner Web site for Web page developers and authors. At `http://www.microsoft.com/workshop`, it contributes a great deal of reference information and offers a nice library of royalty-free images packaged into themes that can be downloaded and used on Web pages.

**Figure 1.5.**
*Microsoft's Internet Workshop is an excellent (and free) resource for Web page designers.*

The themes, which cover a broad range of subjects or moods, range from old-time advertising to outer space. The graphic images that comprise each theme can be used for backgrounds, horizontal lines, navigational buttons, menu headers and footers, and even sounds and inline animations. What better way to quickly and cheaply add a high-priced look to your Web pages?

- `Webreference.com`, available at `http://www.webreference.com`, is the perfect online resource for all your Web design and authoring needs, complete with pointers to articles, file libraries, and more. Its well-organized and extensive set of links makes it a virtual reference library where most Web authors can find answers and ideas for a multitude of design problems.
- Randy's Icon and Image Bazaar, featured in Figure 1.6 and available at `http://www.infi.net/~rdralph/icons/`, is the place to go for icons and images, especially if you're looking for a background or some buttons. The site is filled with a variety of standard backgrounds, buttons, and icons, all of which can easily be incorporated in a relatively conservative-style Web page.

**NOTE:** There are a lot of background libraries on the Web. Unfortunately, you'll find most of them useless for your commercial Web pages unless you plan on creating some sort of psychedelic tribute to the Grateful Dead in order to sell your T-shirts to the tie-dyed market.

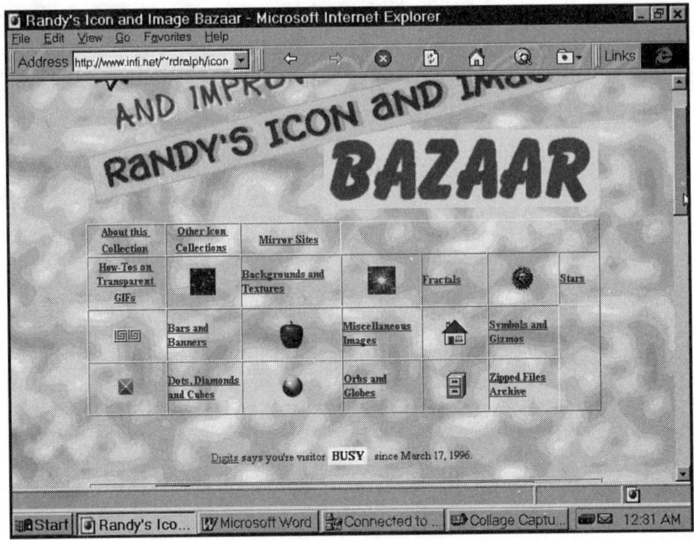


**Figure 1.6.**
*Randy's Icon and Image Bazaar is a treasure trove of backgrounds, buttons, and icons that can be added to any commercial Web page.*

- Usenet Newsgroups can be one of the Web's best—or worst—resources. Several of the Newsgroups are extremely popular with Web developers and others and generate a lot of traffic on a daily basis. Posting a question in these forums will definitely get you an answer quickly. Of course, there's always the risk of getting even more than you wanted. The following are three of the forums you might find helpful:

  `comp.infosystems.www.authoring.html` covers the broadest range of topics for Web authors. You can post general questions or comments here about HTML code and how it works with various browsers. This is also a good group to monitor for advancements in HTML and for how those advances can be integrated into your Web pages.

  `comp.infosystems.www.authoring.cgi` covers CGI scripts, which are addressed before this workshop comes to an end. When you get to the point where you'll be using CGI scripts for forms and other interactive elements of your page, this can be a time saver.

  `comp.infosystems.www.authoring.images` deals with graphical images—the very essence of the World Wide Web. Come to this forum if you want to locate graphical artists to create customized graphics to include in your Web pages.

## Creating a Basic Web Page

Creating a new Web page with HotDog is a simple process. To help you get comfortable with the HotDog editor, you'll create a fairly simple and straightforward page that contains contact information for Baby Makes Three, a mythical infant and toddler clothing store. Contact information can include such information as addresses, phone numbers, fax numbers, and e-mail information. Creating this page will give you a chance to get comfortable with the HotDog editor.

1. Give the page a title by selecting File | New and working with a Normal template in the editor. HotDog will automatically generate the HTML code basics like `<BODY>` and `<TITLE>` tags. I'll replace the default title text with what I want to appear in the browser's title bar for this page, Contacting Baby Makes Three.
2. Place the standard Baby Makes Three graphic logo at the top of the page. To do this, go to Insert | Image, select the open folder icon, and browse for the Baby Makes Three logo in a directory I've dedicated for this Web site's graphics.

   Select the `logo.gif` file and enter an alternate description so that the non-graphics browser will see text when it pulls up this page. People using Microsoft's Internet Explorer will see this alternate description in a tooltip window when they pass their mouse over the graphic. Highlight the entire `<IMG>` tag. Select Center from the Format menu to make the image appear in the center at the top of the page.
3. Enter the basic contact information, including address, telephone and fax numbers, and different e-mail addresses for different functions within the company. To apply varied styles to each line or word, use HotDog 's Format | Font command. Enter a `<BR>` tag after each line of the address and a `<P>` tag to start a new paragraph, thus placing a line between the text.
4. Use the `mailto:` command to make links so that users will be able to click on the company e-mail addresses and instantly send messages from the page. To establish different `mailto:` links that correspond to each address, select the External Hypertext Link on the toolbar or choose Insert | Launch and Internet Service.
5. Make sure the page isn't a dead end by creating a link back to your main Web page. Without this link, you might lose new users unfamiliar with the back button on a Web browser. To create this link, enter text such as `Back To Baby Makes Three` and use HotDog's External Hypertext Link button to make the connection.
6. Use the File | Save As command to create the Web page. Be sure to give your page a logical name—for this example, `contact.htm`. The file extension must be `.htm` or `.html` so that every Web browser knows that this is an HTML document. Figure 1.7 shows how the finished product for this example will look when viewed with Netscape.

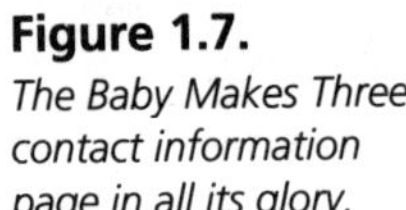

**Figure 1.7.**
*The Baby Makes Three contact information page in all its glory.*

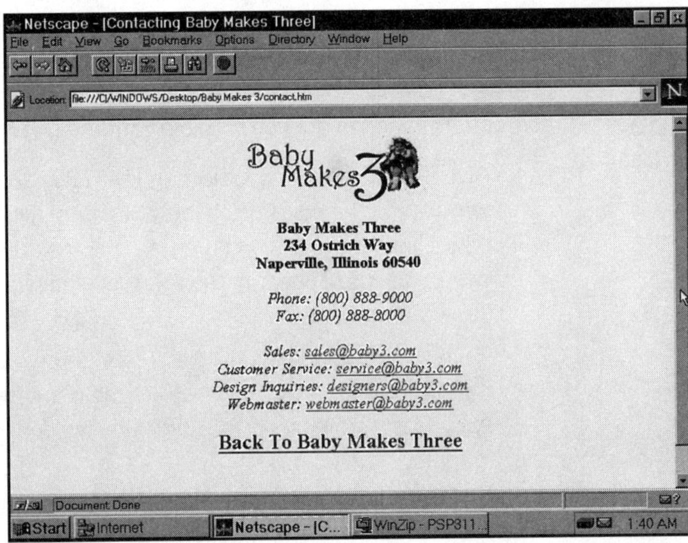


7. Copy the page to your Web server. You're finished for now, but remember that you'll have to create the rest of the Web site that will point to this document.

# About Templates

A Web page *template* is basically a skeleton document that can easily be customized at a later time to generate new Web pages. HotDog enables you to create a Web page and then save it as a template. This is an important function. Because HotDog requires you to save the new document under a different name, you can use the template to create future Web pages in the same format without worrying about overwriting the original template document.

When you create a Web page template, you have to use a placeholder—a filename or text that identifies the place in the Web page where later the template can be customized. If, for example, you place an `<IMG>` tag referring to `logo.gif`, when you use the template later you can replace the `logo.gif` filename with the actual name of a graphics file that you want to use.

**NOTE:** Keep in mind when you create a Web page template that the text will not stay the same—all will be replaced later. So be sure to include explicit directions that will allow for easier customization. For example, where a user will need to enter his or her e-mail address, you might put in a placeholder that says ***`youraddress`***`@megacorp.com`.

Templates are great for Web pages that must be consistent and that will be created in high volume on your Web site. Suppose, for example, that a large diverse corporation called Acme Rings, Inc. is going to provide an employee Web page for each member of its vast organization. Because the pages should be consistent and the volume will be high, a template is the ideal solution.

To learn more about employee Web pages, read the section titled "About Individual Web Pages" in Chapter 5, "Employee Directories and Biographies."

A Web page template will enable Acme's Webmaster to quickly create individual employee pages based on the same basic layout. Or, if the Webmaster prefers, she can distribute the template to company employees to customize on their own and return to her to include on the Web site. Either of these alternatives results in a significant time savings in HTML coding.

# Creating a Basic Web Page Template

The basic Acme Rings employee page is going to involve

- A logo
- A picture of the employee
- The employee's position within the company
- A link to the employee's e-mail address
- A section for the employee's hobbies and interests
- Links that the employee finds of interest
- Links to important other pages on the Acme Web site

Acme Rings wants to keep its employee pages as consistent as possible. At the same time, however, the pages can't be bland.

## Determining Text Elements

The first step in designing and creating a template is to determine what text elements are going to remain constant and what elements are going to be customized on a page-by-page basis. The key is to be sure to clearly identify the elements to be customized. Do this by placing a # symbol before and after each text placeholder. This will make it easy for you (or a user) to quickly identify those areas within the template that require customized information.

## Dealing With Graphic Elements

There are two ways to deal with graphic elements in a template:

- Insert a fake filename for the image. Then place a # symbol before and after it.

- Suppose, for example, you have inserted the fake filename `photo.gif` and are ready to customize the template. Simply change the image file to the placeholder's filename. For example, if I had an employee's photo saved in the file `bob.gif`, I would change its name to `photo.gif` and place it in the appropriate directory in which the Web page was located. Use this method only if you or someone else familiar with the template will be customizing the pages and if each page will have its own directory on the Web server.

## Creating the Template Page

The key to creating a template page is to treat it as if you were creating a typical Web page like the one we just worked with. Actually, the only difference in the template page is that the content in some sections will be generic placeholder text. Enter the placeholder text and format the document, including the generic text, as you want it to ultimately appear. Because the HTML places tags at the beginning and end of text to implement its formatting, the formatting will remain constant when customized text is filled in where the placeholder is.

Figure 1.8 shows the template page created for Acme Rings' employee pages. The logo at the top of the page, the graphical horizontal rules, the basic company contact information, and the categories for each employee's page are universal properties, or constants, for the page. Did you notice the broken picture graphic? It results from an invalid filename—in this case, one of our placeholders for a picture of the employee.

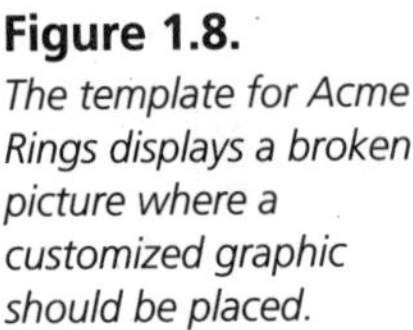

**Figure 1.8.**
*The template for Acme Rings displays a broken picture where a customized graphic should be placed.*

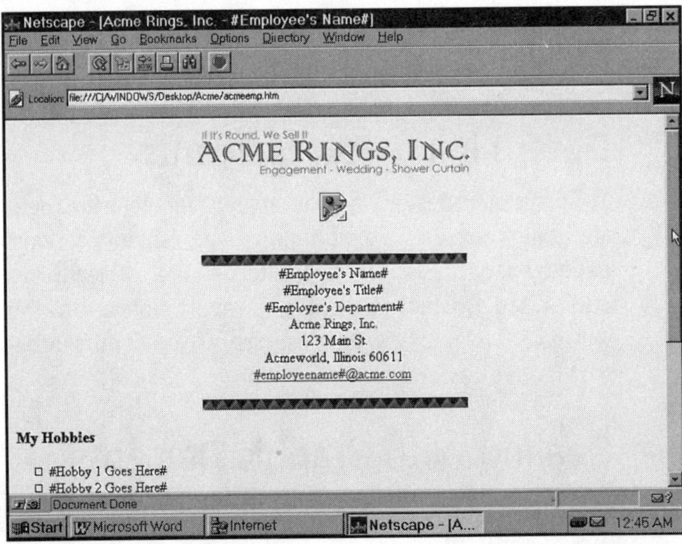

The following is an excerpt of the HTML code used to create the template. Notice that the # symbol convention was used for both text and graphic elements. Also note that descriptive placeholder text was used to help employees throughout the Acme Rings organization understand how they could customize their pages. The entire HTML code used to create the template is available on the accompanying CD-ROM.

**Listing 1.1. HTML document ACMEtplet.HTM (Figure 1.8).**

```
<HEAD><TITLE>Acme Rings, Inc. - #Employee's Name#</TITLE>
</HEAD>
<CENTER><IMG SRC="acmelogo.gif" ALT="Acme Rings, Inc."></CENTER>
<P><CENTER><IMG SRC=#employee photo.gif#" ALT="#Employee's Name#"
➥WIDTH=360 HEIGHT=360><BR>
<HTML>
<BODY>
<P><IMG SRC=" hruler02.jpg"><BR>
#Employee's Name#<BR>
#Employee's Title#<BR>
#Employee's Department#<BR>
Acme Rings, Inc.<BR>
123 Main St.<BR>
Acmeworld, Illinois 60611<BR>
<A HREF="mailto:#employeename#@acme.com">
#employeename#@acme.com</A>
<P><IMG SRC="hruler02.jpg"><BR></CENTER>
</BODY>
</HTML>
```

As you can see, it's easy to pick out the items that need to be changed simply by looking for the # symbol. Another way to locate placeholders within the template is to use the Edit | Find command in HotDog or any other HTML or text editor.

## Saving the Template

Most HTML editors provide a mechanism to save a Web page as a template. If you're using HotDog, go to the Tools | Make Template from Document menu to use this option. In HotDog, when you save a page as a template, you are presented with the option of using that template each time you create a new page. Template files in HotDog are given the extension `.tpl` so they are not confused with normal Web page documents.

You can always just save the Web page as a regular HTML document and give it a name like `template1.html`. If you do this, you must use the Save As command to avoid overwriting the template file. Be sure to keep a backup copy of your templates in a separate directory. If you have an unexpected accident, you'll be glad to have that backup copy to pull up.

# Customizing Your First Web Page Template

If you've followed instructions and taken the correct steps to create your Web page template, customizing it is the easy part of the process. All you have to do is get together the information and replace the text and image placeholders with the individual data.

1. Use HotDog to start a new file.
2. From the presented list of options, select the template you just saved.
3. For this example, use Billy Bob Briggs, an Acme sales manager in the shower curtain ring division. Using the saved template you just selected, input Briggs' information. You should come up with the following HTML:

```
<HTML>
<HEAD></TITLE>Acme Rings, Inc. - Billy Bob BriggsTITLE>
</HEAD>
<BODY>
<CENTER><IMG SRC="acmelogo.gif"
➥ALT="Acme Rings, Inc."></CENTER>
<P><CENTER><IMG SRC="briggs.gif" ALT="Billy Bob Briggs"
➥WIDTH=360 HEIGHT=360><BR>
<P><IMG SRC="hruler02.jpg"><BR>
Billy Bob Briggs<BR>
Sales Manager<BR>
Shower Curtain Rings Division<BR>
Acme Rings, Inc.<BR>
123 Main St.<BR>
Acmeworld, Illinois 60611<BR>
<A HREF="mailto:briggs@acme.com">briggs@acme.com</A>
<P><IMG SRC="hruler02.jpg"><BR></CENTER>
</BODY>
</HTML>
```

4. The template has places for Briggs' favorite hobbies—golf, stamp collecting, and NASCAR—as well as for his favorite links on the Web. Customize the template to include all this information by replacing the placeholders.

When the customized template is completed, Billy Bob Briggs will have the personalized Web page.

# Workshop Wrap-Up

All of the sample files and HTML code are on the accompanying CD-ROM.

Now you know that you're not alone out there and that creating a commercial Web page is not rocket science. You have a vast variety of tools and resources to help you accomplish your task and make your Web page everything you want it to be. You've been introduced to the basic tools you will need—an HTML editor and Web page utilities and accessories. You even have an idea of where to go on the Net for online resources that will help you.

Take your time selecting your tools and learning how they work. Then, practice with them. Create a trial basic Web page and Web page template. Take the next step and customize the template. When you're comfortable with the tools and have experimented with pages and templates, you'll be one step closer to creating the actual templates and pages that will bring customers to your organization and help it—and you—grow.

## Next Steps

You've learned enough in this chapter to have gained confidence in your ability to create a Web page and template. Essentially, you have "learned" the most basic of the basics. But it's a start. Now...

- ❑ To learn how to create a theme and page layout for your Web site, see Chapter 2, "Developing a Plan for Design and Site Management."
- ❑ To extend your ability to work with graphics when you create Web pages, see Chapter 3, "Corporate Presence Pages."
- ❑ To build an employee directory page, see Chapter 5, "Employee Directories and Biographies."
- ❑ To get design tips and know-how on creating HTML forms for your Web site, see Chapter 8, "Gathering Information: Web-Based Surveys and Questionnaires."

## Q&A

**Q: What is the single most important tool I will need to create my commercial Web pages?**

**A:** Without a doubt, the most important tool you will need is an HTML editor. A solid HTML editor, such as HotDog, which is on the CD-ROM, will literally save you hours in creation time for your pages. Editors like HotDog and Microsoft's FrontPage also enable you to implement advanced HTML functions like tables without detailed knowledge of how to code each particular HTML tag.

**Q: I thought you said I should try to be original. So why should I use Web page templates?**

**A:** Templates should not do anything to strip away your creativity in designing your commercial Web pages. The point of a template is to enable you (or others) to rapidly create Web pages that require a high degree of consistency. If, for example, you are going to set up your pages so that each product in your line has a separate page, you can use a template to ensure that the presentation is consistent no matter what product a user pulls up.

CHAPTER

TWO

# Developing a Plan for Design and Site Management

## In this chapter, you

- ❑ Create a theme for your Web pages
- ❑ Turn a theme into graphic elements
- ❑ Formulate a color scheme
- ❑ Are introduced to cascading style sheets
- ❑ Learn procedures for developing a plan for page updating and management

## Tasks in this chapter:

- ❑ Creating Horizontal Rules
- ❑ Creating a Large Graphic Banner
- ❑ Developing Navigational Buttons and Controls
- ❑ Creating Graphical Bullet Icons
- ❑ Pulling Together the Color Scheme

You wouldn't start a new business before you had put together a business plan, so why create a commercial Web page without a plan for your Web site? Taking time now to think through some of the fundamental requirements of your Web pages will save you a lot of headaches later.

Take design, for example. How many times have you visited a Web site and, as you moved through the pages, started to wonder if you were still at the same site? The pages just don't look like they belong together. Chances are pretty good that you haven't gone astray. It's just that every page of the site probably was designed and developed by a different author without regard for style continuity. You want to be sure when users move through your Web site that they have no doubts about whether they are still on your site—even if the company name or logo isn't on every page.

Creating commercial Web pages is a little different from creating personal home pages because, for a commercial Web site, normally you build a variety of different pages and then assemble them on one site. It's much easier to misstep in development. What better reason to plan and prepare properly?

This chapter walks through the initial steps of creating Web pages. You learn how to design and create the text and graphic elements that will give your Web pages a consistent look and feel and enable you to deliver your message coherently in the most cohesive manner.

The examples to which you'll be referring and with which you'll be practicing in this chapter are for Knowall Cuisine Culinary Institute, a small, mythical cooking school. Don't be put off by the fact that the specifics of what you develop and work with for the example might be different than for your own business. The ideas are the same, so the tasks you perform in the chapter will go a long way toward preparing you for development work for your own pages.

# About Creating a Web Page Theme

Creating a theme, the first step in the Web design process, is a multistep operation. It involves both creative and practical steps, each of which will help you to develop Web pages unique in character but consistent in style.

To be most effective, your theme must work with the business or product you are trying to sell or present through your Web pages. At the same time, however, it ought to have an attractive quality to it. In other words, although content should always be the key, you must present that content in an inviting fashion. That's where the theme comes in.

Theme, concept, and message are pretty much interwoven. You can't really have one without the other. In fact, you might even say that they are synonymous. So before you do much of anything else, sit down and figure out exactly what message you want to deliver to Web surfers. Is yours a "we're on the cutting edge of technology" message or a "we're an old friend you can trust" message? Or is it a very different message from both of these? The Web page themes that would go with the first and second concepts, for example, are radically different from one another. The concept on which you decide will steer the selection and creation of the graphic elements you'll use throughout your Web pages.

In developing your theme concept, you might want to think about how you are going to market your Web pages. Need some insights? Check out Chapter 20, "Marketing Your Web Pages."

**NOTE:** If you just can't seem to come up with a viable concept on your own, go to `http://www.murphnet.com`, the Web site companion to this book. It contains a set of links in a variety of theme categories and might give you the "jump" you need to get your creative juices flowing.

To put all this into perspective, think about the needs and wants of Knowall Cuisine Culinary School. As a cooking school, it provides instruction on a variety of cooking styles and categories. In its classes, though, the school emphasizes cooking for health, so it wants its Web pages to focus mostly on fresh, light, and healthy foods. A good concept, then, for the Knowall Web pages might be "fresh and healthy food."

Later in this chapter, in the section titled "About Color Schemes," you discover why the concept you develop now is important when you start thinking about a color scheme.

When you have your theme, you can start thinking of ways to turn it into graphic elements that can be used throughout your Web pages. For this, you can use a graphics editor like the one on the accompanying CD-ROM—Paint Shop Pro 3.12—or you can use the image or icon archives available on the Internet.

Turning a theme into graphic elements is not difficult—there's just a lot to remember because you should create a small stable of images and icons consistent with the theme. To make it easier, we'll consider the creation of each element a task of its own and use the Knowall Culinary Cuisine School as an example.

# Creating Horizontal Rules

When it comes to creating horizontal guidelines, here are a few things you should keep in mind:

Refer to Chapter 1, "Selecting and Using Tools for Page Creation," for pointers to Web sites with excellent archives of horizontal rules and buttons that you can download.

1. Have available at least two styles of horizontal rules—a large (wide) one and a smaller (thinner) one. This will give you the flexibility you'll want to break up Web page contents. Use the larger one when you begin a significant new section or area on a page. Use the smaller one when you simply want to break up the page for organizational or presentation purposes.
2. Use the HTML tag <HR> to insert a horizontal rule, and specify the size you want the rule to be in pixels.
3. Instead of the plain Jane <HR> tag, add a graphical flair to your pages by inserting an image-based horizontal rule like the one shown in Figure 2.1.

**TIP:** If nothing else, you can always simply create solid-color horizontal rules using the drawing tools available in Paint Shop Pro or the Windows Paint application. A solid-color rule that goes well with your theme is better than nothing at all. Just be sure to save the graphic you create in the GIF or JPEG format so that it can be viewed inline by most browsers.

4. To create a smaller horizontal rule, open a larger image in a program like Paint Shop Pro. Use the editing tools to cut out a small sliver of the picture. Save the sliver as its own graphic file. The rule shown in Figure 2.2, for example, is the vegetable banner from Microsoft's Multimedia Gallery.

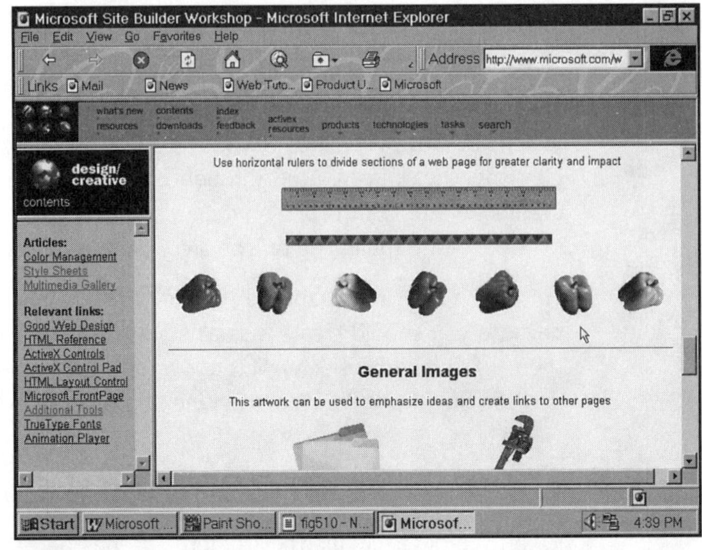


**Figure 2.1.**
*A string of vegetables can make an appealing horizontal rule.*

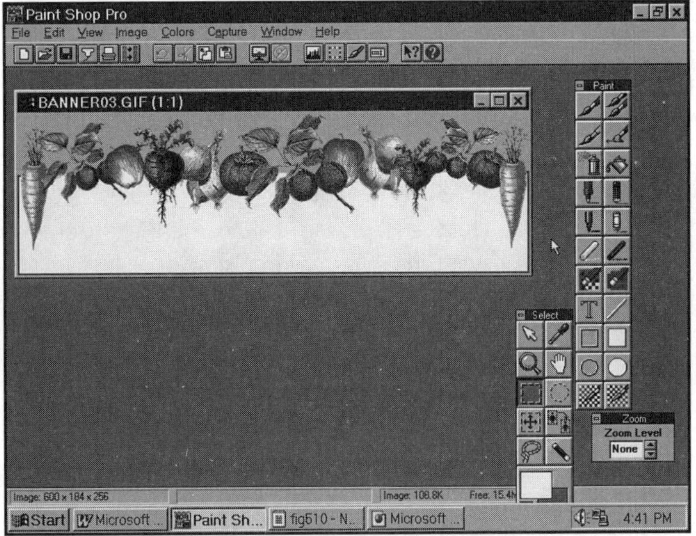


**Figure 2.2.**
*This vegetable banner from Microsoft's Multimedia Gallery can be used as more than a banner.*

Make sure you have a backup copy of your original graphic file before you start trying to create a smaller graphic from it.

Using Paint Shop Pro, open the vegetable banner, and use the rectangular selection tool to select a small sliver of the picture. As Figure 2.3 shows, a dotted line appears around the portion of the picture that you want to make your new horizontal rule. Select the Copy command from the Edit menu.

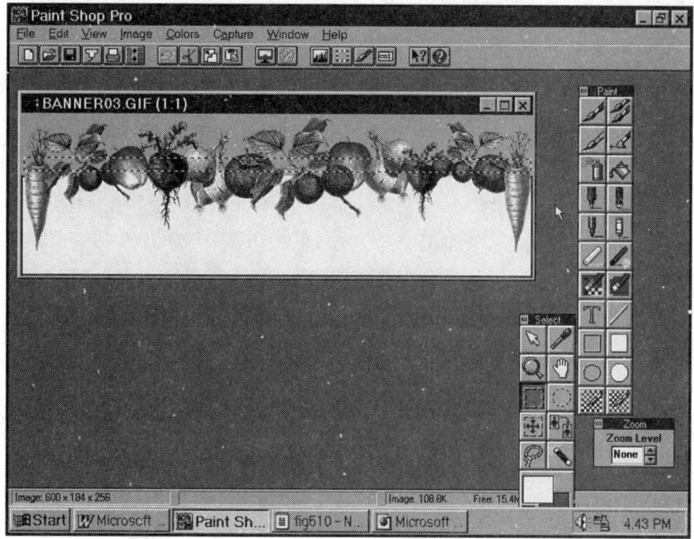


**Figure 2.3.**
*You can use Paint Shop Pro to create a small horizontal rule from virtually any graphic.*

5. Save the selected portion of the image as its own file by going to the Edit menu, selecting Paste, and then selecting As New Image. Look at Figure 2.4. You can see the new image window within Paint Shop Pro that you have created. Now you have two files—this new one and the original file from which you copied it. Select File | Save As. You now have a small horizontal rule to use when you develop a Web page.

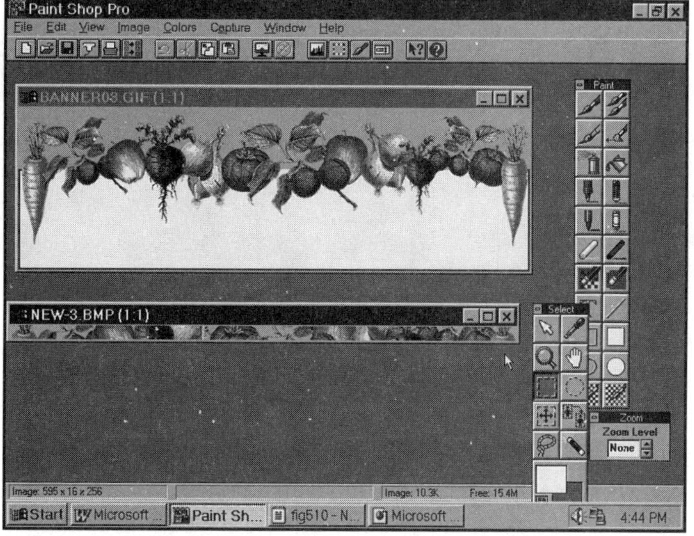


**Figure 2.4.**
*Using Paint Shop Pro's Paste As New Image command opens a new window within the application.*

# Creating a Large Graphic Banner

As the following steps clearly indicate, creating and saving a large graphic banner is an easy process:

1. Have available for your theme a large rectangular graphic like the vegetable graphic you used in the horizontal rule task. You can use it as a banner at the top of some of your Web pages as a standard header in lieu of or in addition to your company logo. Most banners will have a large open space where you can place text, as shown in Figure 2.3, or a lightly shaded area on top of which text can be placed.
2. You can use a banner in two different ways:
   - Save the banner as its own image, and then open the banner in Paint Shop Pro. Lay in text for each Web page as in Figure 2.5. Save the banner with the text as a new graphic image file with a new name.

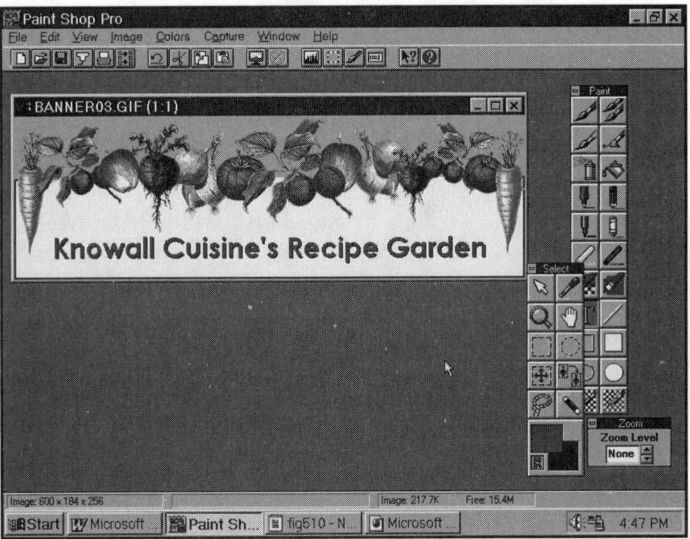


**Figure 2.5.**
*You can customize large graphic banners using Paint Shop Pro.*

   - At the top of a Web page, create a table that consists of one large cell. Set the background of the cell to be the banner graphic. Add text to the cell and format and align it using standard HTML coding.

**CAUTION:** Not all Web browsers support background images for table cells. You might want to use the previous method to make your banner available on as wide a number of platforms as possible.

# Developing Navigational Buttons and Controls

For more information on setting the background properties of a table cell, see Chapter 6, "Online Catalogs and More: Presenting Your Products and Services."

Navigational buttons and controls are those graphics on which you can click to go backward or forward through a Web site or home to the site's home page. The most common ones are arrows and little houses. Everyone seems to expect to see controls like these at the bottom of Web pages.

**TIP:** Don't spend a lot of time trying to develop radical new navigational buttons for your site. Many resources on the Web already provide vast libraries of them that you can download and use for free or for a minimal charge. A good index of these resources is available at `http://www.webreference.com`.

1. Be particularly careful when you develop navigational buttons and controls. Web users are quick to complain about confusing or illogical buttons they encounter on Web pages. Avoid confusion by adding to each button graphic a little text that explains what the button does. Most of the time, one word—Front, Back, Home—will do it.

Remember to check out Chapter 1 for pointers to resources for such graphical elements as icons and buttons.

2. Look at the sampling in Figure 2.6 of the type of creative graphical buttons you can use on a Web page. Notice how the graphics fit in with Knowall's theme. What better match for "fresh and healthy food" than a red pepper and two carrots? Don't get so caught up in the match that you forget what you started out to do—place the selected images at the bottom of each page on your Web site.
3. Create the links to the images so that when users select the graphical button they end up where you want them to go. To make the link (actually, the blue line) invisible, set the `BORDER` attribute within the `<IMG SRC>` tag to `0`.

**NOTE:** If your controls are part of one large graphic, such as the ones provided on the Microsoft Multimedia Gallery site, you can break them up into individual graphics using the same method you used to create a sliver graphic for the horizontal rule. Another option is to use the Map This! program on the accompanying CD-ROM to turn the graphic into a client-side image map.

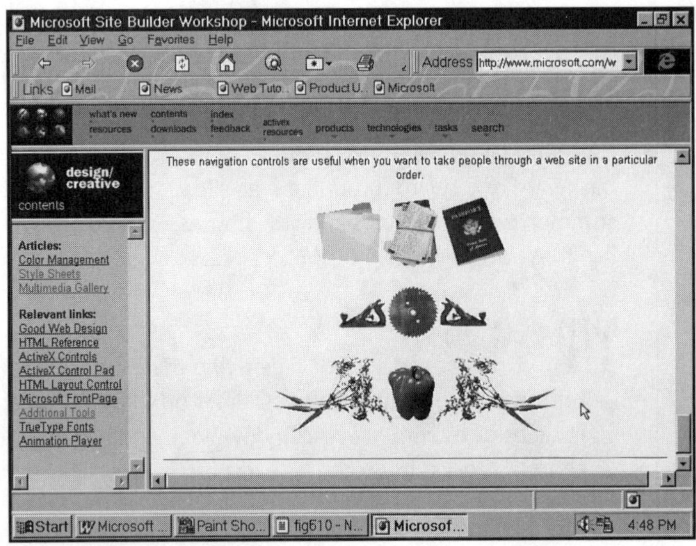


**Figure 2.6.**
*A sampling of some navigational controls that can be used on a Web page.*

# Creating Graphical Bullet Icons

The small added touches really make a difference, hold your pages together, and make them stand out from all the rest. Small graphic icons that you can use as bullets are one of those touches. Develop your theme by placing graphical bullet icons in a list of items on the various pages of your Web site. They're sure to help reinforce your message.

See Chapter 4, "Creating News, Reference, and Content Pages," for an example of graphical bullet icons used in a Web page.

1. Stick with the Knowall theme and the vegetables that you've been forced to see so much of recently. To provide maximum consistency on the Knowall pages, you'll take the red pepper image that is part of the control buttons and shrink it down to size for use as a bullet icon.
2. Use Paint Shop Pro to shrink the graphic. Don't forget that normally you should make a backup copy of your graphic before you start to make changes that will significantly alter its appearance. Shrinking the graphic is a very simple process:
   - ❑ Open the graphic image file (in this case, `redpepp.gif`).
   - ❑ From the menu, select Image | Resize.
   - ❑ In the Resize dialog box shown in Figure 2.7, select Custom Size.
   - ❑ In the first box on the left under Custom Size, enter the height of the new icon. Make sure that the height is no greater than 30 (pixels) and that the Maintain Aspect Ratio box is checked. The appropriate width will be calculated and filled in automatically by Paint Shop Pro.

Don't worry about making backups when you are working with this example, because all of the original files are on the accompanying CD-ROM.

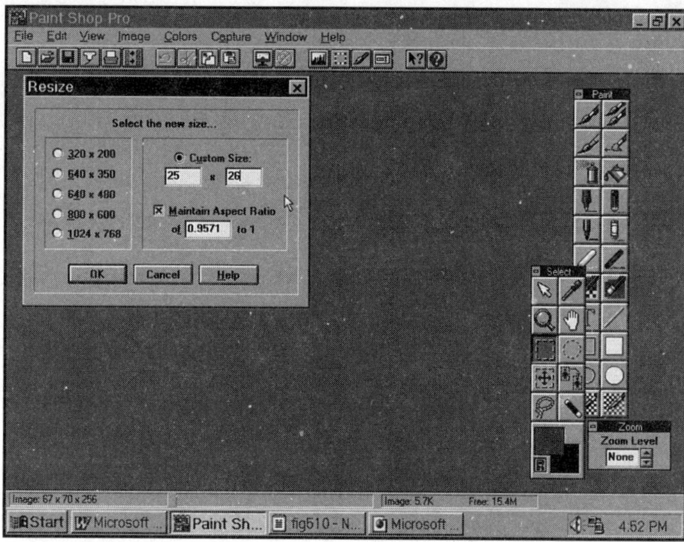


**Figure 2.7.**
*When you resize images in Paint Shop Pro, make sure that the Maintain Aspect Ratio box is checked.*

- ❑ Save the bullet icon graphic under a new name (for example, `redbull.gif`) by selecting File | Save As.

3. Use `redbull.gif` as a replacement for the standard black bullet whenever you create a bulleted list using the `<UL>` and `<LI>` tags in your (or Knowall's) Web pages.

**TIP:** Want to get a practical idea about what creating a Web page is all about? Go to Microsoft's Multimedia Gallery at

`http://www.microsoft.com/workshop/design/mmgallry/mmgallry.htm`

for exactly what elements you need to create a Web page theme. You'll find Web page themes in about 16 different categories, including Space, Gothic, and Old-Time Advertising. In fact, the images for Knowall's Web page come from some of Microsoft's themes and other icon archives on the Internet. The files we've used are also available from the Web site at `http://www.murphnet.com` and from the accompanying CD-ROM. You probably won't be able to use any of the Multimedia Gallery themes entirely, but you'll get a better feeling for exactly what elements you need to create a Web page theme.

# About Color Schemes

Gone are the days when your choice of background colors for Web pages was gray and you could have any text color you wanted as long as it was black. Now you can make your pages' colors as psychedelic (and annoying) as your brain and eyes will allow.

Unless you want to hire a graphic designer to make color decisions for you, you'll have to rely on your own sense of style and taste to determine what colors apply to the various elements on your pages. It doesn't matter that you're not Picasso or Rembrandt—you don't have to be to come up with a color scheme for your Web pages. Formulating a color scheme is just an extension of implementing the appropriate theme for your particular Web site.

If you want a good color sampler, check out Invented Worlds' online color selector at `http://www.enterprise.net/iw/cbrowser.html`. If you want to save some coding time before you decide on colors, use the JavaScript color match page.

Using the JavaScript color match page to help you try different variations of background and text colors will save you some coding time before you decide on colors. An online color selector is available at

`http://www.enterprise.net/iw/cbrowser.html`

Know exactly how to get the color you want before you start setting color properties for various attributes in the <BODY> tag of your documents. Most browsers support one of two ways of identifying colors for the various attributes—common name or hexadecimal.

**CAUTION:** Remember that many users will be viewing your pages with a 16-color setting. Before you let yourself get too exotic in your color scheme, test your pages on a 16-color setting so that you know what some users will see when they pull up your page.

- Common name: When it comes to colors, common names are much simpler to use than hexadecimal. You just don't have as broad a range of colors to pick from. If you use one of several common names available, many browsers, including Netscape Navigator and Internet Explorer, will support color attributes identified in the <BODY> tag. Valid common color names include Black, White, Red, Green, Blue, Yellow, Magenta, Cyan, Aqua, Fuchsia, Lime, Maroon, Navy, Olive, Gray, Silver, and Teal.

  If the color you want isn't available, you can create custom colors. To do this, however, you must enter in the corresponding hexadecimal value.

Look in Chapter 6 to see how to use these common names when you are setting background properties for tables.

- Hexadecimal: No one says that setting color values by hexadecimal values is simple, but if you're one of those people who has to have precise control over the colors available to you, hexadecimal is the option you will have to take.

OK, here goes. The format for custom colors is *#rrggbb*, where *rr* is the hexadecimal value for the red color component, *gg* is the green color component, and *bb* is the blue color component. In addition, each color component has its own actual hexadecimal value, with possible parameters going from a minimum of 00 to a maximum of FF; the value 88 is the median. Therefore, the color white is #FFFFFF, the color black is #000000, the color red is #FF0000, the color green is #00FF00, and the color blue is #0000FF.

**TIP:** An excellent site for selecting colors and finding their corresponding hexadecimal values is shown in Figure 2.8. Check it out on the Net at the Invented Worlds site at

```
http://www.enterprise.net/iw/cbrowser.html
```

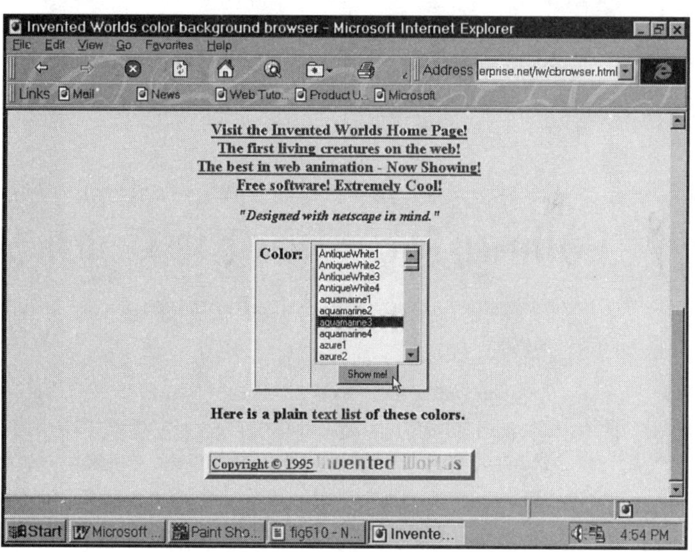


**Figure 2.8.**
*This and other Web sites can help you determine the correct hexadecimal value for custom background colors.*

Remember what you learned in grade school about black and white? The color white is the blending of all colors, and black isn't really a color because it is the absence of all colors.

If you're a numbers-type person (or a very determined individual), you'll probably enjoy playing with the values and (hopefully) coming up with an array of customized colors suited to your particular tastes. Be aware, though, that you'll save yourself a lot of valuable Web development time by using one of the common name colors or consulting one of the hexadecimal color resources mentioned previously.

## Anatomy of the <BODY> Tag

Most of the major portions of the color scheme for your Web pages will be entered as attributes within the <BODY> tag at the beginning of each HTML document. This tag contains properties, such as the following, that allow for custom color selection to put your color scheme in place.

- `BGCOLOR =` The page's background color
- `TEXT =` The text color on the page
- `LINK =` The color of the hyperlinks
- `ALINK =` The color of a selected (active) link
- `VLINK =` The color of a visited hyperlink

Even though you must enter the value of each of these one at a time, you need to decide all of the colors in conjunction with one another. In short, implementing the color scheme is relatively simple. Getting colors that work together is not.

**TIP:** Always get a second (or third or fourth) opinion on your color scheme. You don't want a color scheme that turns off users because inevitably it will prevent some people from exploring your site. With a million choices on the Web, few users will have the patience to read aqua-colored text on a blue background.

## Pulling Together the Color Scheme

Pulling together a color scheme is a multistep process, but it's not difficult. Just follow these steps:

1. Set the background color. A word of warning first—background colors can be a very dangerous thing in the wrong hands. The Web is filled with garish examples of colors you should not use for your background. Picking your background color or image is the one area in developing your Web pages in which you want to be conservative. Once again, Knowall is a good example. The background part of the color scheme is pretty much a no-brainer. White provides a nice clean background that gives a fresh look to any page—and the theme Knowall is trying to achieve is "fresh and healthy food." White is the way to go.

**NOTE:** Users can set their browsers to override any custom colors you specify for your pages. Don't drive them to resort to this option because you chose an incredibly bad color scheme.

2. Normally the next step would be to set the text color. For now, though, leave it as the default—black. Black on white might seem boring, but you'll be hard pressed to find a more readable combination. Besides, you can always change it later if you feel the need. To alter the color of any text (except links) within your Web pages, place a `<FONT COLOR>` tag immediately in front of the text.

**TIP:** When you want to de-emphasize the links on a page, set the text color on the page to the same color as your hyperlink. The only difference between the text and links will be that the links are underlined.

3. Choose your link colors. This is important if you want your Web pages to have a look and feel that present a style all your own. People get tired of seeing the same old blue (unvisited) and purple (visited) links in their Web browsers. Shake users out of the doldrums by changing the link default colors.

   What color combinations do you think would work for the links on the Knowall pages? Before you respond, think about which links might be the most common—on their page and on yours. The most common will probably be the unvisited links, followed by the visited links, followed by the activated links.

   If your Web page is good enough, visited links can move to the top of this list.

   Think about Knowall's ever-present theme—fresh and healthy food. That places a few colors at the head of the pack for developing the color scheme. First and foremost is green—not just because it's my favorite color, but because nothing conveys healthy food like green. Another good color to use here is orange. Orange and red are colors that supposedly increase your appetite (look at Burger King), and neither clashes with the color green. In fact, the colors green and orange bring to mind the image of a carrot. So, set the `<BODY>` tag properties to make unvisited links green, visited links orange, and the active link red. This color scheme should attract and encourage hungry Web-surfer appetites.

4. Assemble all of the color options we've looked at, and place them in a `<BODY>` tag with the appropriate attributes and settings. The following HTML code implements the color scheme developed for Knowall:

```
<BODY BGCOLOR="white" LINK="green" ALINK="red" VLINK="orange">
```

5. Open the Notepad application in Windows and save the piece of HTML code in a directory dedicated to various color schemes. You can save it using a descriptive term such as `food.htm`, open the file, and cut and paste the code into any document to which you want to apply that particular color scheme.

**TIP:** As indicated in Chapter 1 you can make your color schemes part of any Web page template that you create.

Currently, only Microsoft's Internet Explorer supports style sheets, but Netscape has pledged support for the standard. Meanwhile, as Figure 2.9 clearly shows, you can pick up a wealth of information on style sheets at the Microsoft Site Builder Workshop on the Net at `http://www.microsoft.com/workshop/`.

# About Style Sheets

Thanks to a new advancement in HTML, you can more carefully plan and design multiple Web pages on your site at one time without repetitive HTML coding or cutting and pasting. The tool that enables this is the cascading style sheet. Looking at a simple example will help you get a clearer idea of what the sheets are all about. For this example, you'll create a cascading style sheet that implements the color scheme you created earlier in this chapter.

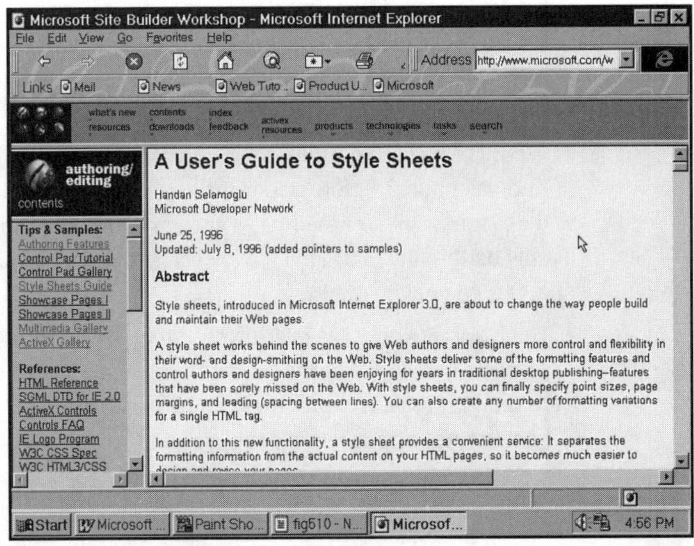


**Figure 2.9.** *Microsoft's Web pages can fill you in on the cascading style sheet standard.*

A full explanation of cascading style sheets is beyond the scope of this chapter. For a fairly detailed review of the various settings and properties for style sheets, consult the HTML reference in Appendix B, "HTML 3.2 Reference."

Style sheets can be used in a variety of different contexts. Potentially, however, the most useful one is to link to an external style sheet by entering a simple HTML tag within a document. Then, whenever you alter the style sheet, each document to which it is linked will change. The following is an example of the HTML code needed to do this:

```
<HEAD>
<TITLE>Your Great Commercial Web Page</TITLE>
<LINK REL=STYLESHEET HREF="http://www.company.com/colors.css" TYPE="text/css">
</HEAD>
```

**CAUTION:** Users whose servers don't have the proper MIME type registered for `text/css` might encounter problems using style sheets. Microsoft, however, might have resolved the problem by the time you read this book. For the latest information, check out

`http://www.microsoft.com/workshop/author/howto/css-f.htm`

Style sheets use brackets { } instead of the arrows < > used in HTML to contain various property settings. For the most up-to-date details on what elements of cascading style sheets have been approved and included in the latest version of HTML, visit `http://www.w3c.org`.

A simple style sheet, saved as `colors.css`, that enables you to instantly implement and change from a single file the color scheme for an entire Web site might look like this:

```
{background: white}
A:link {color: green}
A:visited {color: orange}
A:active {color: red}
```

# Developing a Plan for Web Page Updating and Management

An important task that many people who create Web pages often neglect, unfortunately, is site management and updating—making sure that the Web pages are kept up-to-date and correct. Nothing is more annoying to a user than to find a page that contains outdated, often erroneous or useless, information. To make sure this doesn't happen to your Web pages, schedule a period of time daily or weekly that you will use exclusively to make changes to your Web pages and to validate all the content and links.

A good site management and updating plan should make provisions for the following procedures:

- ❑ Adding new content and information
- ❑ Updating existing content and information
- ❑ Verifying file locations (for example, image files)
- ❑ Verifying internal Web links to your pages
- ❑ Verifying external Web links to other pages

Creating a plan up front for accomplishing these tasks helps ensure that you don't go to a lot of trouble creating great commercial Web pages that then fall into disrepair from neglect or mismanagement.

**TIP:** Users like to know that a Web page has recently been updated, so always place a small text indication on the first page of your Web site that gives the date of the last time the pages were revised.

# Workshop Wrap-Up

Don't underestimate the importance of theme concepts and color schemes. If you don't know what concept your organization wants to project, no one else will either. And, if the user doesn't get the message loud and clear, you can be pretty sure that he or she will not bother to make a return visit to your Web site—or buy your service or product.

Colors schemes are equally important. How often have you bought or not bought an article of clothing because it wasn't the "right" color? In a book store or library, how many times have you ignored a title because the cover color didn't catch your eye or the design was "too busy?" Your color scheme should be an integral part of your theme, one that clearly reflects the mood and clientele you want your product or service to inspire.

And don't write off style sheets either because they seem a little difficult to comprehend at first. Mastering them is well worth the effort in the long run. They will prove to be a great time-saver when it comes to consistency and another vital part of the Web page development scenario—site management and updating.

## Next Steps

After you've designed your Web pages and have created a workable plan for site management, think about moving on and finding out how to use your pages effectively. Now...

- ❑ To get ideas on how to develop an employee directory that will sell your people and your business, jump to Chapter 5, "Employee Directories and Biographies."
- ❑ To discover how to sell your products in addition to your people, turn to Chapter 6, "Online Catalogs and More: Presenting Your Products and Services."
- ❑ To see a real-world example of themes, color schemes, and style sheets in action, turn to Chapter 12, "Real-Life Examples: Advancing Your Site."

## Q&A

**Q: Do all my pages need to have the same color scheme and page elements?**

**A:** Not necessarily, although it does help provide consistency and familiarity across your pages. Of course, there are exceptions to every rule. Good uses can arise for breaking from your standard stable of elements and colors in developing certain portions of your Web site.

**Q: Why can I change the color of individual words using the `<FONT COLOR>` tag, but I don't seem to be able to change the color of different links on the same page?**

**A:** Good question. Unfortunately, I don't have a very good answer. The main reason is that link colors are set as part of the `<BODY>` tag, which applies to the entire document, and neither Netscape nor Microsoft has really pushed this type of change into the HTML standard.

**Q: If Netscape doesn't yet support cascading style sheets, will Netscape Navigator users be able to view my pages that rely on style sheets?**

**A:** Yes. Netscape plans support for style sheets in version 4 of its Navigator product. Users of older versions or other browsers that don't support cascading style sheets will be presented with a page that will use browser defaults and will lack all of the specialized styles you have applied in your style sheet.

PART

# II Basic Business Pages—Web Site Building Blocks

**Chapter** **3** Corporate Presence Pages

**4** Creating News, Reference, and Content Pages

**5** Employee Directories and Biographies

**6** Online Catalogs and More: Presenting Your Products and Services

**7** Real-Life Examples: Putting the Basics Together

CHAPTER THREE

# Corporate Presence Pages

## In this chapter, you

- Acquire and create basic Web graphics and titles
- Create a basic welcome page
- Reduce graphic sizes and speed page loading
- Create a menu bar for navigation

## Tasks in this chapter:

- Creating a No-Wait Welcome Page
- Creating a Menu Bar

The odds are good that when you set up a Web page for the first time, you're not going to want to spend hundreds of hours concocting a radically advanced interactive site filled with Java, ActiveX, and real-time multimedia files. You'll probably want to go slowly and stay out of the deep water before committing yourself, and your company, to more extravagant pages and endeavors on the Web.

Yet you're totally aware that the first step onto the Web is a critical one. First impressions always mean a great deal, and when you're in a medium with literally millions of choices, they mean even more. It stands to reason, then, that even though your first Web page doesn't have to be fancy, it does have to be good. Don't worry. With careful planning, design, and execution, you can lay the groundwork with a basic Web page that not only establishes your company's presence on the Web but also garners respect and appreciation.

In this chapter, you explore basic elements necessary for welcome pages that could be considered the online equivalent to business cards and brochures. While in and of themselves they might not seem to bring sales or increase market share, they are fundamental tools that every business should have because they provide many people with their first impression of your company or business.

All of the pages in this and subsequent chapters require simple knowledge of HTML and can be created and manipulated easily with an HTML editor such as Hot Dog, which is included on the accompanying CD-ROM.

**NOTE:** It's often difficult to fully understand examples of Web pages and how they work when presented on the printed page. All of the examples in this chapter and throughout the book have been included on the CD-ROM and can be accessed online through the companion Web site for this book: `http://www.murphnet.com`.

# Laying the Groundwork

As I said in Chapter 1, "Selecting and Using Tools for Page Creation," it's important to have all your tools and materials together before you start constructing your commercial Web pages. Let's put it all in perspective.

Start with what you already have on the accompanying CD-ROM—Hot Dog or W3c, a pair of HTML editors, and excellent utilities like Paint Shop Pro3.12. Next, make sure you have the graphic elements that you want to include on your Web pages. You can acquire these elements in one of two ways—create them yourself or hire a graphic artist to create them for you.

Refer to Chapter 1, "Selecting and Using Tools for Page Creation," for more information on finding and selecting tools to help you build your commercial Web pages.

If you're like me and couldn't get admitted to one of those by-mail art schools because you couldn't draw that duck in their magazine ad, you may want to seriously consider getting someone with artistic talent to help with your Web graphics. Be aware, though, that some Web page design startup companies charge big bucks for their services. Still, I don't think you can go wrong in spending your money on the work of a graphic artist to help design and create images for your pages. After all, the Web is a visual medium, so it's probably worth it to get a visual artist to help you accomplish the design goals of your Web pages. Adding the professional touches of graphic artists can pay big dividends.

**NOTE:** The Web is filled with talented graphic and visual artists. A good place to start on your search is Yahoo! at

`http://www.yahoo.com/Business_and_Economy/Companies/Graphic_Design/`

You've got a good chance of finding someone here among the literally hundreds of options for individuals and companies that provide graphic design and creation services. For recommendations, you can also post an inquiry to

`comp.infosystems.authoring.html.images`

Many sites on the Web also have graphics you can download and use on your Web page with absolutely no charge. For example, Microsoft provides the Multimedia Gallery (shown in Figure 3.1), which contains many Web page elements that you can check out at `http://www.microsoft.com`.

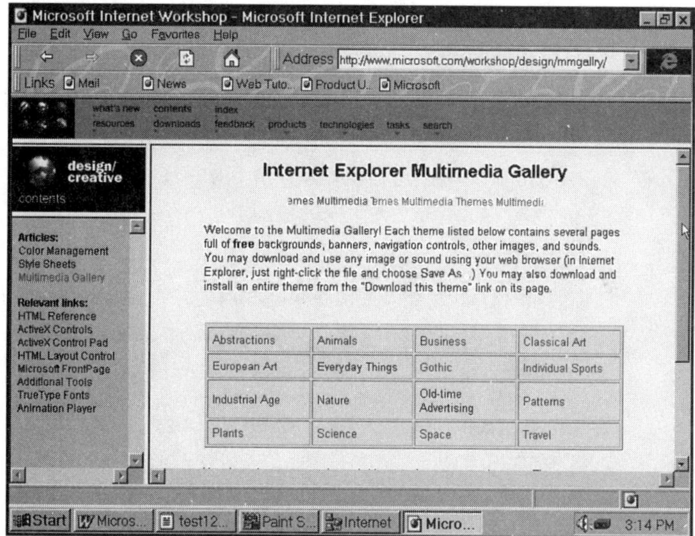


**Figure 3.1.**
*Microsoft's free Multimedia Gallery is an excellent graphics resource, and you can't beat the price.*

Again, the newsgroup `comp.infosystems.authoring.html.images` and Yahoo! can help you uncover many of these resources. Also, a set of links to Web sites offering free images for downloading from the Web site at `http://www.murphnet.com`.

Want pointers to resources on the Web for finding graphic elements to include in your Web page design? Check out the graphics section of the online resource directory in Appendix A, "Online Resources."

**NOTE:** If you want to create your own graphics or navigational buttons, you can start by using Paint Shop Pro, an advanced and powerful graphics program that you'll find located on the CD-ROM. Paint Shop Pro is an excellent program for working with graphics you may already have, to add either text or graphic effects. You can also use Paint Shop Pro to create some very basic graphics. For a more detailed and comprehensive discussion of creating Web graphics, check out *Laura Lemay's Web Workshop: 3D Graphics and VRML 2.0* from Sams.net Publishing.

TASK

## Creating a No-Wait Welcome Page

The process of creating a welcome page with fast-loading graphics and text involves relatively simple HTML, but can be a little confusing because there are many mini-tasks involved with putting it all together into a truly no-wait page. The following is a brief overview of what you'll be doing in this task, a simple to-do list you can always refer back to:

1. Create or convert graphics in JPEG or GIF format (the most popular file types on the Web).
2. Use progressive properties of the JPEG or GIF format for all your images (for example, buttons, bars, or icons).
3. Reduce the number of colors used in all of your graphics.
4. Design your pages to a maximum file size to ensure fast downloading.
5. Add properties for image height and width to reduce page loading times for text.

When you create a brochure about your business, it probably has a cover page. When people come to your office, they probably first go to a reception area. These types of conventions are used to handle your customers, and the information they receive, in an organized fashion. Your Web site should mimic this through the use of a basic welcome page that can direct users to other pages that are of particular interest to them.

Here are the main purposes behind creating a welcome page for your Web site:

- ❑ Making a good (and fast) first impression
- ❑ Providing easy navigation to key pages
- ❑ Highlighting the most important news or changes
- ❑ Allowing customers to quickly contact you

## The Importance of Speed

When a customer (or potential customer) types `www.yourcompany.com`, you need to make sure that the time it takes for him or her to see your Web page is as minimal as possible. Your goal should be to create a welcome page that loads in under 30 seconds in most browsers. I'll spare you the math; this works out to be a Web page that is approximately 50,000 KB or less. For a quick reference on file sizes and download speeds, look at Table 3.1.

**Table 3.1. Variables in files sizes and access speed can alter just how long a user has to wait for your page.**

| *Speed* | *2 MB* | *1MB* | *500KB* | *100KB* | *50KB* | *25KB* |
|---|---|---|---|---|---|---|
| 14.4 Kbps | 24 min. | 12 min. | 6 min. | 1.25 min. | 45 sec. | 20 sec. |
| 28.8 Kbps | 12 min. | 6 min. | 3 min. | 45 sec. | 20 sec. | 10 sec. |
| 64 Kbps | 5 min. | 3 min. | 1.5 min. | 20 sec. | 8 sec. | 4 sec. |
| 128 Kbps | 2.5 min. | 1.5 min. | 45 sec. | 10 sec. | 4 sec. | 2 sec. |
| T1 (1.5 Mbps) | 12 sec. | 6 sec. | 3 sec. | 1 sec. | 1 sec. | 1 sec. |

**TIP:** Java and ActiveX are outstanding Internet technologies that definitely should find a place on your Web site, but that place is most certainly not your welcome page. Most users access the Internet using a dial-up modem at 28.8 Kbps or less. Java applets and ActiveX controls can take a long time to download over these connections. Also, some browsers will not support one or both of these technologies. If you're a caffeine addict, make an ActiveX- and Java-free (decaffeinated?) page the default and provide a link to the enhanced version.

The 30-second goal can be and should be accomplished. You will see when you finish this task just how easy (and effective) this is to do. As you prepare your welcome page, just keep these simple tricks in mind and your page will be the quickest draw on the Web.

## Shrinking Your Graphics

Your welcome page should have a graphic image of your company's logo and possibly some other graphics dealing with your main product or highlighting some new promotion or special. You may also have buttons or other navigational helpers that are made with graphic image files. The easiest way to speed up (and shrink down) a

Web page with graphics is to use a progressive image format and to make the number of colors in each graphic as small as possible. First, let's talk about the progressive file formats.

## Using Progressive Images To Be the Quickest Draw

In the next section, you learn how to lay out graphic images, such as a logo and navigational buttons, on your welcome page.

When you save your images, such as a logo, using Paint Shop Pro, a dialog box, as shown in Figure 3.2, will show you a variety of options for file formats in which you can save your image. You should select the GIF or JPEG format only when you save images that you want to present as part of your Web pages. In addition, by specifying a certain subset of that file type, you can have an image that will slowly be rendered on the page as it is downloaded, almost like an image being brought into focus through the lens of a video camera.

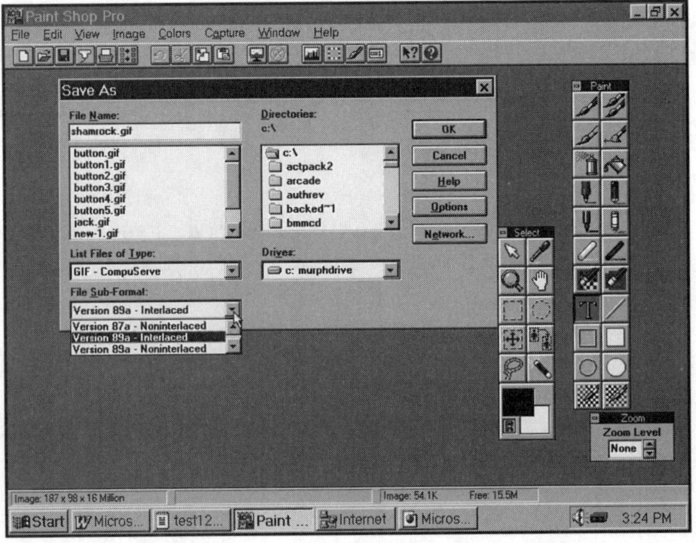


**Figure 3.2.**
*Paint Shop Pro can save to many formats, but you should select GIF or JPEG only for your Web pages.*

Browsers that do not support the progressive rendering of interlaced GIFs will be unaffected by your use of the file subformat. They will still load the image as a normal GIF file when it has been completely loaded into the browser.

The most popular progressively rendering file format is GIF 89a Interlaced. When you save your images using Paint Shop Pro, select "GIF - CompuServe" from the list of file types and then select "Version 89a - Interlaced" as the file subformat. Browsers that support interlaced GIFs, such as Netscape and Internet Explorer, will then progressively render your images as your page is loaded.

**NOTE:** A standard also exists for a progressive JPEG file format. The latest version of Paint Shop Pro supports progressive JPEGs and GIFs. Browser support for this standard is nowhere near as widespread as it is for interlaced (and standard) GIFs. Until progressive JPEG becomes a widely used and available format, stick with interlaced GIFs on your welcome page.

In order to speed up your Web page and slim down your graphics, you need to take four quick, simple steps:

1. Start Paint Shop Pro (or your own graphics editor such as Adobe Photoshop).
2. Open the graphic image file.
3. Decrease the Color Depth of the image to a maximum of 256 colors.
4. Save the image under a new filename.

I'll walk you through this process using a graphic image file enclosed on the CD-ROM. You will be using this image to build the sample welcome page for a fictitious software company, Shamrock Software, Inc.

## Opening an Image File

Paint Shop Pro is an excellent shareware graphics utility that can be used to create and manipulate virtually all types of graphic files. A copy of Paint Shop Pro is included on the accompanying CD-ROM. You should install it prior to working with the examples in the book.

The examples used here are all based on the assumption that you are running the Windows 95 operating system.

You'll need to run Paint Shop Pro to work through this example. You can either select the program icon from the Start | Programs | Paint Shop Pro menu or you can start it manually by running the file `psp.exe` in the `c:\psp` directory, if you used the default settings when installing the program.

Select the File | Open command in Paint Shop Pro and select the file `shamrock.bmp` from the Graphics directory of the CD-ROM. You will see the Shamrock Software logo in all its glory (see Figure 3.3). By looking at the lower-left side of the screen, you'll see how big the image is in terms of height, width, and color depth.

**TIP:** It's a good idea to save your image file under a different name immediately after opening it in your graphics editor. Once you reduce the color depth of an image, it will be impossible to restore it to the previous depth. You wouldn't want to reduce the color depth and accidentally save the new image over your original.

You can see that the `shamrock.bmp` file is a high resolution (16-bit) image containing 16 million colors. At this color depth, `shamrock.bmp` takes up 54,000 KB of space. Select the File | Save As command and save the high resolution image under a different name—`shamlow.gif`, for example. Now you're ready to start working with the image.

**Figure 3.3.**
*The lower-left corner of the main screen in Paint Shop Pro tells you the size of the graphic you're working on.*

Go to the Colors menu in Paint Shop Pro and select the Decrease Color Depth option. You'll be presented with several options for decreasing the depth of your image, as shown in Figure 3.4. First, start by selecting 256 Colors. This is the maximum resolution you should have for images on your welcome page.

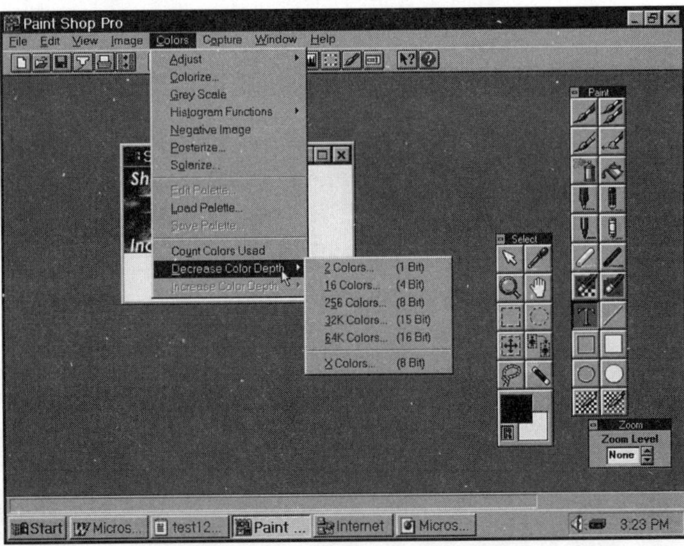


**Figure 3.4.**
*Paint Shop Pro enables you to decrease color depth of images and increase download speed as a result.*

Speed is critical when programming your welcome page, so 256 colors should be your maximum image size. Once users are into your site, they might tolerate longer downloads, so you should feel free to use larger images where appropriate on the other pages of your Web site.

Select File | Save and save the `shamlow.gif` image at the 256 color depth setting. Now, the file that was 54,000 KB is 34,000 KB in size. This means that the image will now take 17 seconds to download instead of 28 seconds for most Web users.

**NOTE:** Remember that the majority of Internet users will be viewing your Web pages on a video card and monitor that have been set for a maximum of 256 colors and that the GIF format cannot handle more than this. As a result, by reducing the color depth you'll not be taking away a significant benefit from most users. Keep this in mind when determining what is an acceptable degradation in image quality.

After you've saved the file at the 256 color depth setting, you can experiment and try to go even lower, to a color depth of 16 colors. You may find 16 colors sufficient for text-oriented graphics such as logos or navigation buttons. Don't try to decrease your image's color depth to anything below 16 colors. At that point, image quality generally becomes so poor that, although the download may be faster, it would be worth the little extra wait for a better image.

**CAUTION:** Be careful when you reduce the color depth of photographic images below 256 colors. You'll probably find with photographs that reducing the color depth to 16 colors yields a reduction in quality that is a greater detriment than the increase in speed is a benefit.

Always design your welcome page for someone with the patience of an average two-year-old and you should be fine. Two-year-olds would probably take longer to hit the stop button on their browser than the average Web surfer.

You can repeat the preceding procedures for each of the images that you plan on including on your welcome page. Remember you want to keep the size of this page under 50KB, and including a large number of images might nullify all the work you've done to keep each of them small. Refer to Table 3.1 for an excellent overview and reference for optimizing file sizes for downloading.

## Noting the Size of Your Images

As long as you have Paint Shop Pro open and are decreasing the color depth of your images, you can use it to help you increase the loading of your page even more on many browsers.

If you use Hot Dog, which is included on the accompanying CD-ROM, as your HTML editor, you can skip this step.

Netscape's Navigator and Microsoft's Internet Explorer, the two most popular browsers on the market, will both present the text of your welcome page almost instantaneously if the graphic images on your page contain their height and width dimensions in the `<IMG>` tag of your HTML code. If no height and width are specified in the <IMG> tag, the browser might not load any of the text of your page until *all* images on the page have been completely loaded. Netscape Navigator, particularly versions prior to 3.0, will be significantly slower in displaying your page when this information is not provided.

Appendix B, "HTML 3.2 Reference," gives you a complete HTML reference guide and serves as an excellent resource for refreshing your memory on the various tags as well as the associated variables and settings that are possible for each of them.

Here is an example of a typical <IMG> tag that could be used to place the Shamrock Software logo onto a welcome page:

```
<IMG SRC="shamlow.gif" WIDTH=187 HEIGHT=98 ALT="Shamrock Software, Inc.">
```

The `WIDTH` and `HEIGHT` parameters of the `IMG` tag specify, in number of pixels, exactly how much space your image file will take up when fully loaded into the browser. Using Paint Shop Pro, this information is provided in the lower-left status bar (in the same place that the color depth is shown). For example, in Figure 3.3 you can see that the size of the `shamlow.gif` image is 187 pixels wide and 98 pixels high. The first number shown by Paint Shop Pro is the width in pixels of the image and the second number is the height in pixels of the image.

**TIP:** Many HTML editors, including Hot Dog, will automatically fill in the `HEIGHT` and `WIDTH` attributes of the <IMG> tag when you use the editor to place the image into your HTML document.

Jot down the height and width of each of the images that you plan on incorporating into your Web pages. Notepad works well for this basic task, or even a sticky note if you want to go low-tech. Then simply insert the appropriate numbers into the <IMG> tag of your HTML code for each graphic on your page.

TASK

# Creating a Menu Bar

The old cliché for real estate is that there are only three important things to remember: location, location, and location. A similar rule applies to using your online real estate, but here the three most important things are navigation, navigation, and navigation. If users can't get around your site quickly and easily, they're not going to get around your site, and that would be a bad thing.

Using a consistent menu bar throughout your Web pages will make users more comfortable and your information more accessible.

You can make your site easy to navigate by using the following guidelines and procedures. Your goal is to create a simple, functional interface that welcomes and guides users of your Web pages. The best way to accomplish this is by providing a menu bar on your welcome page that will also appear on all the pages throughout your Web site.

In this task, you work through the following steps:

1. Consider design elements for a menu bar.
2. Create a button style menu bar.
3. Use ALT tags to enhance the menu bar's functionality.
4. Place the menu bar on each page of your site.

## Designing the Menu Bar

Think of your menu bar as the top-level directory of your Web site. It should highlight and provide links to five or six different pages or areas of your Web site from where your users can continue to explore your site in greater detail.

See Chapter 1 for resources on the Web where you can find graphics to use in constructing a menu bar for your welcome page.

**NOTE:** The menu bar I'll show you how to create is made up of a series of smaller images, each with its own link to another Web page on your site. You may be familiar with image maps, which you could use to perform similar functions. However, I think you'll see that with creative use of HTML you can accomplish the same thing—and even more, without the need to resort to either server- or client-side image maps.

## Adding a Button Style Menu

A popular and easy-to-create format for your menu bar is a series of graphical buttons, each with text and a corresponding hyperlink to other pages on your Web site. Normally, these buttons have a three-dimensional look and feel to them. You should design and use buttons that keep with the theme of your site.

The Web is overloaded with resources for graphical buttons that you could use for creating a menu bar. You can easily use one of the many available graphical buttons and then use a utility such as Paint Shop Pro to add text for each button and then save each individually under a different filename.

Refer to Appendix A for places on the Web for great design resources where you can locate buttons and other Web page elements.

**TIP:** One of the big benefits to using individual images to comprise your menu bar rather than an image map is the ability to use specific ALT tags for each button or selection on the bar. Thus, those with nongraphical browsers can still view the selections. Also, remember that Microsoft's Internet Explorer (and soon probably Netscape, too) displays the ALT text in a tooltip window when you place your mouse over a graphic, as shown in Figure 3.5.

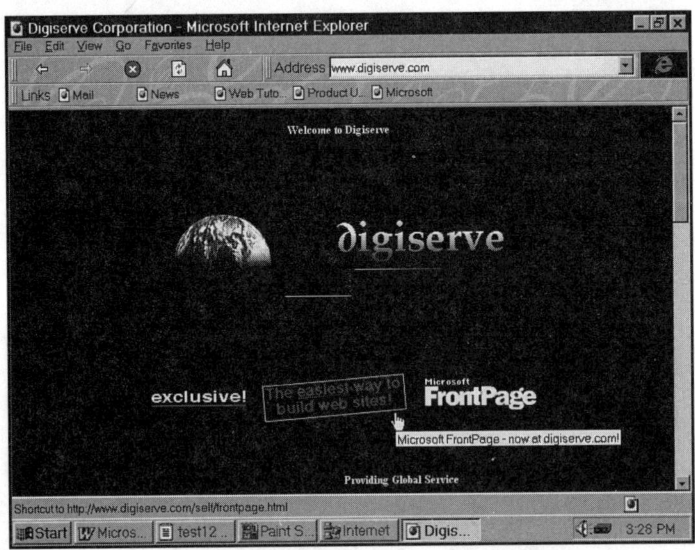


**Figure 3.5.**
*Microsoft's Internet Explorer presents alternative text for images in a tooltip window.*

For this example, you can create a faux three-dimensional button using Paint Shop Pro that works nicely in a menu bar. To do this, simply follow these steps:

1. Open a new image with the dimension of 100 pixels wide and 50 pixels high. Make sure you have the image set to at least 16.7 million colors.
2. Use the square drawing tool (non-fill) and create an empty square that fills the entire image area.
3. Select Image | Special Filters | Emboss.
4. Select Colors | Decrease Color Depth | 16 Colors.
5. Save to the filename `button.gif`.

Now you'll need to go back and open the image `button.gif` in Paint Shop Pro and edit the image by adding a layer of drop shadow text and saving it under a different filename (for example, `button1.gif`, `button2.gif`, and so on) for each selection you want to appear on the menu bar. Figure 3.6 shows the `button.gif` image opened in Paint Shop Pro.

**CAUTION:** Make sure that the text on each button is aligned with all the others. A good way to do this is to leave the saved images in an open window in Paint Shop Pro when you're creating the new buttons. (See Figure 3.7.)

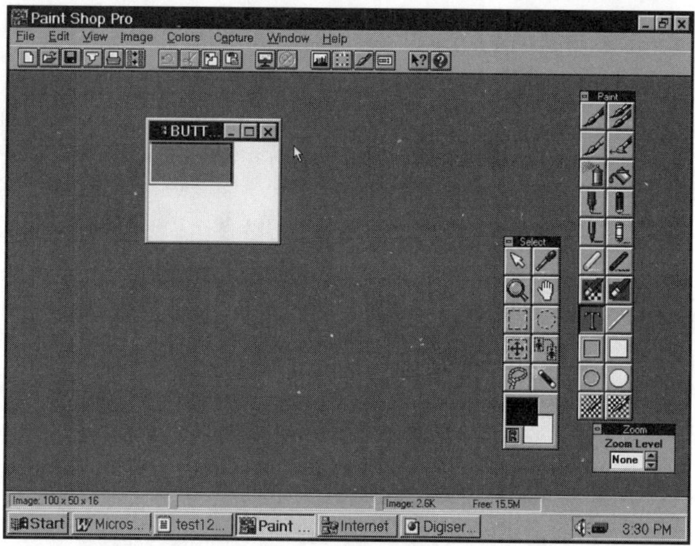


**Figure 3.6.**
*Paint Shop Pro's simple drawing tools and emboss filter can create buttons in no time.*

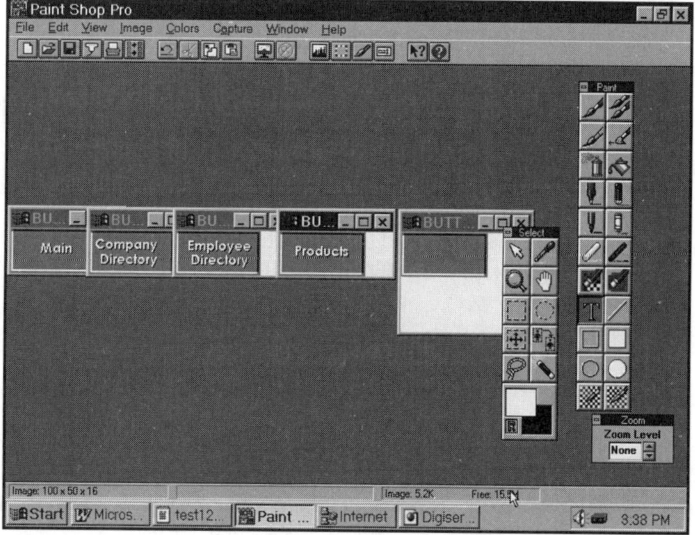


**Figure 3.7.**
*Keeping all your button images open enables you to properly line up the text.*

Shamrock Software is going to have five selections on its main button menu bar. Accordingly, you'll need to create buttons using the `button.gif` file for the following categories:

- ❑ Main
- ❑ Company Directory
- ❑ Employee Directory

- ❑ Products
- ❑ News

To add text to the `button.gif` image, simply select the text tool and choose a font, style, size, and type in the appropriate heading. Paint Shop Pro warns you if what you typed will not fit on the image. You can always use two lines of the image by placing the text on different lines, using the text tool twice.

When you've finished creating the buttons, you're ready to do the coding that will lay them out as a menu bar that can then be placed on every page throughout your site. This will give your users a coherent and consistent navigational tool.

All the sample files created in this book, including the button images, are available on the accompanying CD-ROM.

Placing the buttons in the proper order is a very simple HTML task. Simply place the `<IMG SRC>` tags for each button continuously in the document with no breaks or paragraph tags. In this example, you'll also center the menu bar on the page. Thus, the HTML code for the button bar should look like this:

```
<center><IMG SRC="button1.gif" ALT="Main Page>
<IMG SRC="button2.gif" ALT="Company Directory">
<IMG SRC="button3.gif" ALT="Employee Directory">
<IMG SRC="button4.gif" ALT="Products">
<IMG SRC="button5.gif" ALT="News"></center><br>
```

The next step, of course, is to add links to these images so that when a user "pushes" a button, he or she is taken somewhere on your Web site. For most menu bars you won't want any garish blue or other colored hyperlinks surrounding the beautiful buttons you've just created. Therefore, when you add your link's tag to each image, you'll also need to add `BORDER=0` to each `<IMG SRC>` tag so that the link is invisible on the page. Here's the HTML code you should end up with:

```
<A HREF="main.htm"><IMG SRC="button1.gif" ALT="Main Page" BORDER=0></A>
<A HREF="company.htm"><IMG SRC="button2.gif" ALT="Company Directory"
➥BORDER=0 </A>
<A HREF="employees.htm"><IMG SRC="button3.gif" ALT="Employee Directory"
➥BORDER=0></A>
<A HREF="products.htm"><IMG SRC="button4.gif" ALT="Products" BORDER=0></A>
<A HREF="news.htm"><IMG SRC="button5.gif" ALT="News" BORDER=0></A><br>
```

You can see from Figure 3.8 that what you've created is a menu bar that gives quick access to the key portions of Shamrock's Web site. You may be wondering why you've placed a selection on the menu bar for the very page, `main.htm`, that is your welcome page and where this menu bar is intended to be placed. The key to the menu bar is that you should place it on every page of your Web site. Thus, having the Main button there makes it easily portable across all your pages.

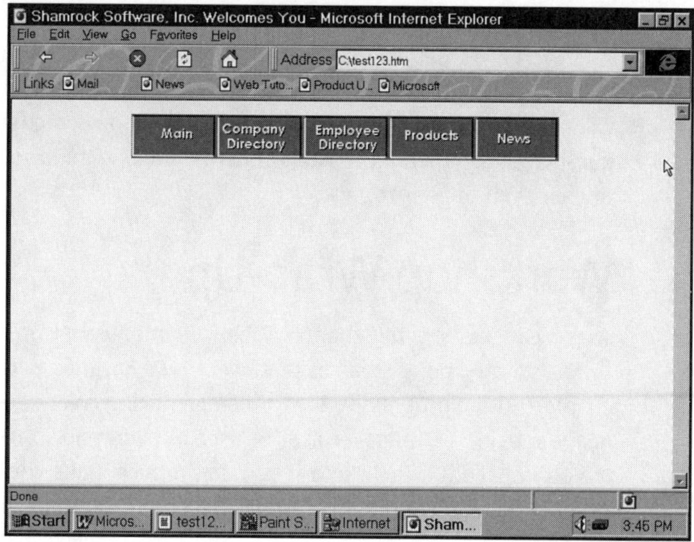


**Figure 3.8.**
*Each button is a link to another Web page, but by setting the border to `0`, you can't see the hyperlink.*

**NOTE:** Many of your pages will require users to scroll down their Web browsers to the bottom of a page. If most of your pages are of this type of length, you may want to consider placing a copy of your menu bar at the top and bottom of each page. The less your users have to scroll, the happier they will be.

## The What's New or News Link

You can see from the example that one of the links on the menu bar is News. One of the most important items you can have on your welcome page is a link to the latest news or information about your business or products. You should always allow your users to be, at most, one click away from finding out the latest on your company.

Frequent visitors to your Web site will appreciate a link on your welcome page to the latest information.

In Chapter 4, "Creating News, Reference, and Content Pages," you see how you can create the news and content behind these types of links and the different options for integrating them with the rest of your site. For now, it's just important for you to remember that a News or What's New link is a vital part of any well designed menu bar and welcome page.

## Quick Contacts

I would be remiss if I didn't tell you that another critical element of your welcome page should be a simple e-mail link at the bottom of the page for users to quickly contact the person responsible for the Web site or designated to handle online inquiries.

This simple line of HTML code,

```
<A HREF="mailto:yourname@yourdomain.com">Contact Us</A>
```

will save users a lot of aggravation from having to search for who to contact with a question or comment. It will also generate the one thing you can't get enough of out of your Web site—feedback.

# Workshop Wrap-Up

As you can see from this chapter, when it comes to welcome pages, size matters, and the size should be as small as possible. However, the techniques you utilized in this chapter—using progressive file formats, reducing color depth of graphics, specifying image sizes in HTML tags—can all be used on every page on your Web site. Web surfers are an impatient bunch, and if you can reduce waits you have a better chance of keeping them in your neck of the Web.

Ultimately, your welcome page should be a pleasant and useful opening to your site. By designing menu bars and using basic elements like What's New links and a quick contact link, you'll be able to provide a familiar interface to both new and old customers.

## Next Steps

Now...

- ❑ If you want to keep filling out your basic Web site, move on to Chapter 4, "Creating News, Reference, and Content Pages," where you learn how to create press release archives, company background pages, and other fundamental parts of a commercial Web site.
- ❑ If you're impatient and want to start putting your products on the Web right away, jump to Chapter 6, "Online Catalogs and More: Presenting Your Products and Services," where you learn how to create basic online catalogs for several different types of businesses.
- ❑ If you want to see how the elements you worked with here have been implemented in the real world, turn to Chapter 7, "Real-Life Examples: Putting the Basics Together."

## Q&A

**Q: If the welcome page is the first page people are going to see, shouldn't I load it up with information so I can get my message across in case they don't go elsewhere on my Web site?**

**A:** If users are overloaded with information as soon as they get to your welcome page, you run the risk of them not being prepared to distill this windfall of information and quickly pointing to another site. The Web is not television, and you don't need to try to squeeze a lot of information into a little window. By presenting a well organized and somewhat minimalist welcome page, you empower users to take their own course through your Web pages.

**Q: Java has become really popular and most browsers support it, so why do you think I should avoid using Java on my welcome page when I want it to look "cutting edge"?**

**A:** While most current browsers support Java, many older browsers do not. If you use Java, some portion of your potential customer base or audience will be unable to see it or get the message. It's probably not going to cost you any customers if you're talking about an animation or other Web page whistle. But be leery of presenting substance that a significant portion of users might miss out on. Remember that many options exist (for example, animated GIFs) that can accomplish some of the things that Java applets do.

CHAPTER FOUR

# Creating News, Reference, and Content Pages

If you've completed the tasks in Chapter 3, "Corporate Presence Pages," you've created a welcome page that will be quickly loaded into any browser complete with a well-designed menu bar that will facilitate easy navigation of all your Web pages. Now you have to create the content that will go behind some of those menu bar options and other links on your Web pages.

When you generate content for your pages, imagination and creativity are important. However, you have to include some old standards as well—basic building blocks that lay a solid foundation for any commercial Web endeavor. In this chapter, you find out how to rapidly assemble some of these "old standards" and integrate them onto your Web site.

## In this chapter, you

- ❑ Create a press release archive
- ❑ Create a set of reference links
- ❑ Create an original content page
- ❑ Learn what it takes to get bookmarked

## Tasks in this chapter:

- ❑ Creating Navigational Tools
- ❑ Writing and Placing Clickable Headings
- ❑ Creating Links
- ❑ Adding Links in Press Releases
- ❑ Creating a Reference Page from Links
- ❑ Inserting an Image
- ❑ Finishing the Reference Page
- ❑ Creating an Original Content Page
- ❑ Creating Pages That Will Get You Bookmarked

Remember that all the example files for this book are on the accompanying CD-ROM and at the Web site at `http://www.murphnet.com`.

This chapter covers some pages that might not seem too flashy or exciting—such as a press release archive—but users seem to want them, so you've got to have them. Basic pages like these can accomplish big things if they're well thought out, well targeted, and properly executed. The more exciting pages, such as interactive catalogs, might be more fun, but first you've got to give users enough information about your company and products to make them feel comfortable about dealing with you online.

So, roll up your sleeves, break open a 12-pack of Coke or some other caffeine provider, and start coding pages.

# About Press Release Archives

No matter how large or small an organization, its commercial Web site should have a press release archive. Press releases serve a dual purpose. Alone, they enable you to deliver a tailor-made pitch on a new product or development. As part of an archive, they serve as a living company chronology.

**NOTE:** Actually, for smaller businesses, the Internet in general makes the prospect of using press releases more realistic. E-mail can be used to target the releases to select members of the media who might have a particular interest in a specific business or product. In the past, if you wanted to get out a press release, you generally had to hire a public relations firm to do it for you. Even if you were brave enough or talented enough to create your own, you probably had to invest in an expensive fax or pay mailing charges. Now, thanks to the Web, you can send out press releases on your own quickly and inexpensively.

The press release archive is an excellent candidate for inclusion on your Web site's main menu bar. To find out how to design and implement a menu bar, see Chapter 3.

Putting together all the pieces of a Web-based press release archive is not a one-step process. You'll have to go through a whole series of steps that includes

- Creating a main listing page
- Writing clickable headings
- Keeping the archive on theme
- Creating a press release Web format
- Adding links to releases

For more information on how to contact the media and market your Web site, refer to Chapter 20, "Marketing Your Web Pages."

**TIP:** Effectively use the Web for press releases by sending a "teaser" e-mail release to media members. Include a URL to the full version of the press release on your Web site. Most people will be more inclined to read a sentence or two—even if it does direct them to someone's Web pages—than they will be to read a three-page e-mail. More often than not, long unsolicited e-mails find their way quickly into the Deleted folder. Be as creative as you can, though, to make sure the press release teaser actually teases.

TASK

## Creating Navigational Tools

Remember the "Task: Creating a Menu Bar" you completed in Chapter 3? The purpose of the bar was to have a menu that you could include on all the Web pages on your site to facilitate navigation. Well, think of the press release archive as a sort of sub-Web site all its own, one that requires its own navigational tools.

Design your press release archive using the same types of navigation tips explained in Chapter 3.

When you develop your archives, forget the two objectives foremost in your mind when you create most other Web pages—"be original" and "target your message on a particular page." As to the first objective, a certain unwritten standard has evolved on the Web for press release archives, and users seem to be comfortable using this basic format and layout. As for the second objective, when users pull up your press release page, they should be presented with a listing to all your press releases, with each listing hyperlinked to the full text of the corresponding release.

**NOTE:** Web page design can tax your creativity to its limits. Although a press release archive is an important element of your Web site, it's not a catalog and doesn't require the same kind of advanced design and layout as a catalog to make it effective. Your time would be better spent thinking about other pages on your site rather than trying to come up with a new way to present your press releases.

**CAUTION:** At some point in time, your main press release page might get too large. "Too large" generally means it has a total file size of more than 50KB. When you reach this point, combine older press releases onto a subpage, which can then be linked to the main page (I guess you could call it an archive within the archive). Hopefully, because the main page will be mostly text, you won't run into this problem very soon.

Begin with the listing page. At the top, place the menu bar that you created for your site in Chapter 3. Figure 4.1 shows you exactly where it should go and how it should look. Putting the menu bar here serves two purposes. It enables users who started on your main page to get back to where they started. At the same time, it opens the offerings of your entire Web site to the media and others who pull up the page directly from a URL you provided in a "teaser" or other message.

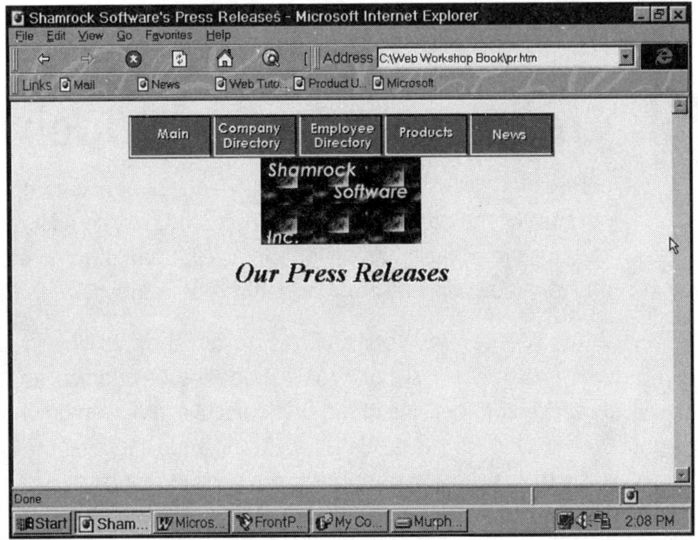


**Figure 4.1.**
*The press release archive page should contain the menu bar for your Web site.*

**NOTE:** Avoid using any of the advanced type of HTML tags and technology on your press release archive page. Java applets, ActiveX controls, even frames, are not necessary for a good presentation of press releases. You'll have plenty of other pages on which to use those cool technologies. Remember that in press releases in particular, you want everyone—including journalists with 386 computers—to be able to access all of the information.

Now, directly below the menu bar, add a small company logo. The logo in Figure 4.1 is a good example. Don't use large graphics because they'll just delay the loading of the listing. You want visitors to spend time reading your press releases, not downloading and viewing your logo.

Later in this example, you'll see how to provide additional materials for the media and others to use in conjunction with your press releases.

**TIP:** Background graphics can be an interesting enhancement to add to some of your Web pages, but neither your press releases nor the main page are one of these. On these pages, more than virtually anywhere else on your site, you need to emphasize text over all else. Background graphics might look cool online, but they can take away from the visibility of some text and create confusion. Press releases are ideal Web pages for printing out. Leave them clean, simple, and quick to print out.

# Writing and Placing Clickable Headings

Your archive page will need to include headings that describe the press releases in your archive. Want an example? Look at the three headings in Figure 4.2. Each heading is linked to the full text, so you must make the headings descriptive enough for users to know exactly what they're clicking on.

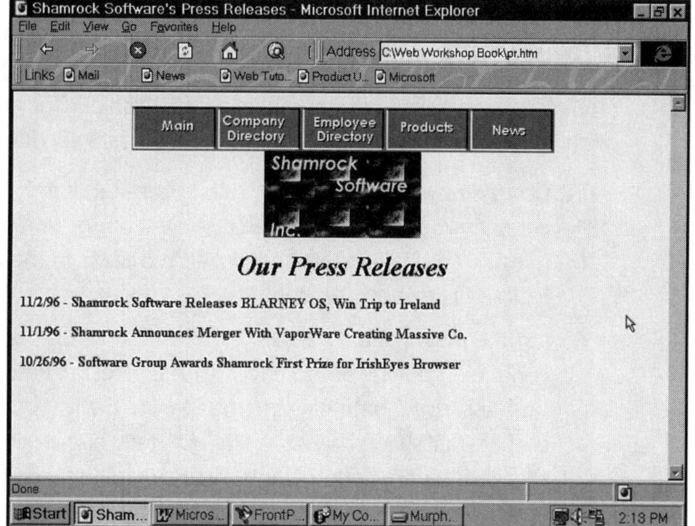


**Figure 4.2.** *Each heading in your press release listing should provide a lot of information in a little space.*

## Writing Headings

Generate a brief—no more than 10 or 12 words—but descriptive heading that includes the following:

- The date of the press release. Put this at the beginning of the heading. For example, 11/1/96 - Shamrock Announces....

- An action verb. Use an action word that describes the purpose of the press release. It should describe in a word what's happening with the product or company. For example, announcements or releases.
- The product or business affected. Prominently place the product or business most directly affected by the press release. For example, Software Group Awards Shamrock....
- Tease language. Include a brief tease or promo that will pique the interest of casual users and media types alike. For example, Win Trip to Ireland.

These might seem basic, but you'd be surprised how often people forget the basics. Don't forget that you have to put a lot of information (and punch) in the wording of the heading.

You'll be working with Shamrock Software's press release page throughout this section.

The heading you create should compare favorably with this listing from Shamrock Software's press release page, which has all the requisite elements and conveys a good deal of information in a very little amount of space:

```
11/2/96 - Shamrock Software Releases BLARNEY OS, Win Trip to Ireland
```

The promotion accompanying the release of the software product serves as a clever tease. Anyone who has any desire to visit Ireland will select the link and read the press release.

## Placing Headings

You must lay out your headings in an orderly fashion. There is no magic formula, but then laying out headings isn't rocket science. Just keep it clean and simple.

1. Use the bullet list format with either the standard bullet or a small graphic. For Shamrock Software, using a small shamrock graphic as the bullet was a natural, and it definitely added a little pizzazz to the page with extremely limited file size overhead.
2. List the press releases, beginning at the top with the most recent release and continuing downward to end with the oldest release. If yours is a young business, use month headers to separate the listing. If you have an older, more established business, using quarterly or even yearly headers as separators might work better. Using these separators will make it easier for you if and when you need to create subarchives of older press releases.

**TIP:** Create a simple subarchive for older months by placing a link on the name of the month to a new Web page created by cutting and pasting the HTML code for that month's press release headings.

3. Place a horizontal rule (the `<HR>` tag) directly below the most recent press release to set it apart from the less current ones. Many people who pull up

your press release page will be looking for your most recent release, and this helps make it stand out from the crowd.

Consult Chapter 1, "Selecting and Using Tools for Page Creation," to find out how to develop a design theme for all your Web pages.

If you developed a theme for your Web site, you probably have one or two standard horizontal rules that you can insert. For example, to keep with Shamrock Software's Irish theme, insert the horizontal rule graphic, `green.gif`, which is a simple solid-colored thin green line. As you can see in Figure 4.3, added touches like the horizontal rule and the graphic bullets spice up a press release archive page substantially.

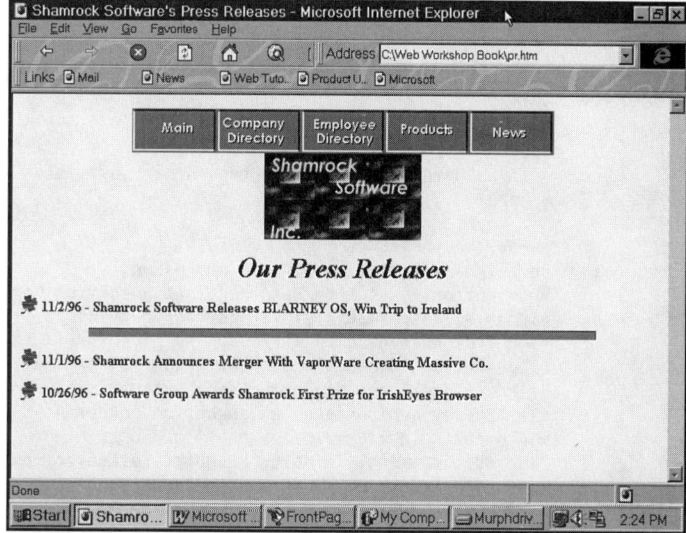


**Figure 4.3.**
*Adding elements from your Web site theme, such as graphical buttons and horizontal rules, can customize a page.*

# Creating Links

Creating links from the header listing to the accompanying press release is a critical step in the creation of your press release page. Follow these steps to create the links:

To find out how using a style sheet can help you effectuate this kind of design choice throughout all your Web pages, see the "About Style Sheets" section in Chapter 2, "Developing a Plan for Design and Site Management."

1. Place all your press releases in their own subdirectory for easier site and page management.
2. Put an `<A HREF>` tag around each heading.
3. Accentuate your site's style and theme by using the `LINK` attribute in the `<BODY>` tag to define the color of links. For example, make the links for Shamrock Software appear green by specifying `<BODY LINK="#008040">`.

Check out Chapter 21, "Web Site Administration and Management," to learn some of the basics involved in managing and administering a Web site and pages.

To get the full effect of the colored links and graphics, check out the press release archive listing page on the Web at `http://www.murphnet.com`.

**TIP:** Be sure to place the <A HREF> tag around graphics bullets so users who select the graphic itself will be taken to the corresponding link for that line. Every little bit of navigation assistance you can provide will give your pages an edge that can keep surfers coming back.

Figure 4.4 shows you the completed press release archive page. Listing 4.1 shows the HTML code that creates this page and implements all the design elements you've looked at.

### Listing 4.1. Shamrock Software press release list.

```
<html>

<head>
<title>Shamrock Software's Press Releases</title>
</head>

<body link="#008040">
<p align=center><a href="main.htm"><img
src="button1.gif" alt="Main Page" align=bottom border=0
width=100 height=50></a> <a href="company.htm">
<img src="button2.gif" alt="Company Directory"
align=bottom border=0 width=100 height=50 A> </a>
<a href="employees.htm"><img src="button3.gif"
alt="Employee Directory" align=bottom border=0
width=100 height=50></a> <a href="products.htm">
<img src="button4.gif" alt="Products" align=bottom border=0
width=100 height=50></a> <a href="news.htm"><img
src="button5.gif"
alt="News" align=bottom border=0 width=100 height=50></a><br>
<img src="SHAMLOW.gif" align=bottom
width=187 height=98></p>
<p align=center><font size=6><em>
<strong>Our Press Releases</strong></em></font></p>
<p align=left><a href="112pr.htm">
<img src="SHAMROCK.gif" align=bottom width=20 height=22>
<font size=3><strong>11/2/96 - Shamrock Software Releases BLARNEY OS,
Win Trip to Ireland</strong></font></a></p>
<p align=center><img src="GREEN.gif"
align=bottom width=600 height=10></p>
<p align=left><a href="111pr.htm">
<img src="SHAMROCK.gif" align=bottom width=20 height=22>
<font size=3><strong>11/1/96 - Shamrock Announces Merger
With VaporWare Creating Massive Co.</strong></font></a></p>
<p align=left><a href="1026pr.htm">
<img src="SHAMROCK.gif" align=bottom width=20 height=22>
<font size=3><strong>10/26/96 - Software Group Awards Shamrock
First Prize for IrishEyes Browser</strong></font></a></p>

</body>

</html>
```

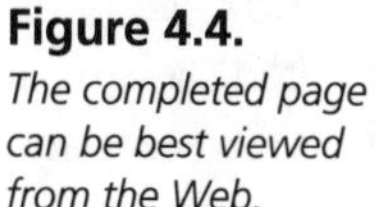

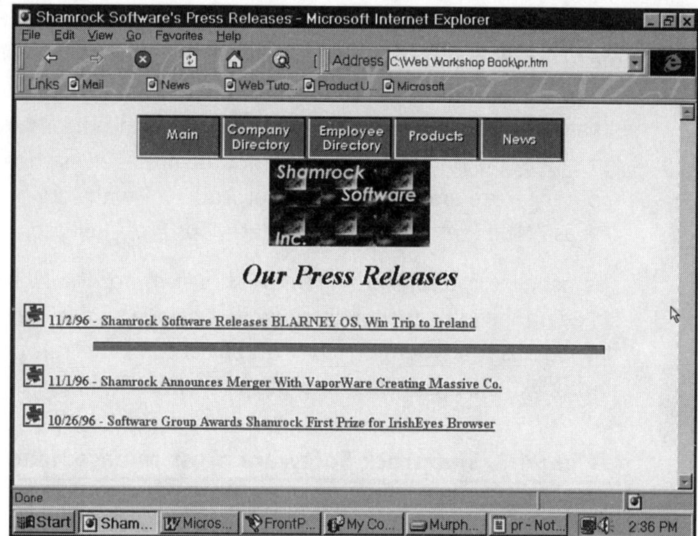


**Figure 4.4.**
*The completed page can be best viewed from the Web.*

# Designing and Creating a Press Release Format

You have press releases on your Web site for a reason—to get your company's message across to a wide audience. You could make each press release page a simple text document, doing nothing more than importing the text from your word processor. You wouldn't be alone—many companies do just that. I don't know if they do it because they think it looks cool in the typewriteresque Courier font or if they just haven't gotten around to reading this book yet. The bottom line, though, is that it doesn't make the page very impressive.

I don't know about you, but if it were up to me, when journalists or casual Web surfers select one of the headings I so carefully and cleverly wrote and laid out on my main press release archive page, I'd want them to land on a press release page that made an impression. This can happen if you spend a little time creating the page format in which your press releases will appear. The process is a simple step that does not take a lot of time or need advanced knowledge of HTML. There are, however, a few small—but important—wrinkles.

**NOTE:** The style of your actual press release page should be the same as your main press release archive page. Using the style sheets discussed in Chapter 2 can help ensure harmony among your pages. Remember, stay away from background graphics or colors that will hinder the reading of any of the text, and maintain the same link colors used on the main page.

Even if you have only a handful of press releases on your Web site, adding navigational tools will not only help users get around but will save you time in the long run. If you don't put them in now, you will only have to do so later as the number of press releases grows.

Paint Shop Pro is an excellent graphics utility that is included on the accompanying CD-ROM and can help you create navigational buttons for your press releases.

Press releases require a type of additional navigation system above and beyond the menu bar. By creating links to the previous or later press releases, you can allow users to browse through them without having to constantly return to the main archive page. It's easy enough to create a few three-dimensional buttons and place them on the top-left side of the page, just to the left of the press release headline. If you want a little more style, use graphics images that work well with your pages and add such simple text as "Next Press Release" and "Previous Press Release."

The headline for your press release should mirror the header tagline to which you linked on the main press release archive page. Use the <H2> tag and bold the text so that it grabs your attention. Use a graphical horizontal rule to set off the headline from the body of the press release. At this point, the HTML code should look like Listing 4.2.

**Listing 4.2. Shamrock Software press release header.**

```
<html>

<head>
<title>Shamrock Software Announces BLARNEY</title>
</head>

<body link="#008040">
<p align=center><a href="main.htm">
<img src="button1.gif" alt="Main Page"
align=bottom border=0 width=100 height=50></a>
<a href="company.htm"><img src=" button2.gif"
alt="Company Directory" align=bottom border=0 width=100
height=50 A> </a><a href="employees.htm">
<img src=" /button3.gif" alt="Employee Directory"
align=bottom border=0 width=100 height=50></a>
<a href="products.htm"><img src="button4.gif"
alt="Products" align=bottom border=0 width=100
height=50></a>
<a href="news.htm"><img src=" button5.gif"
alt="News" align=bottom border=0
width=100 height=50></a><br>
<img src=" SHAMLOW.gif" align=bottom
width=187 height=98></p>
<p align=left><img src="/NEXT.gif" align=bottom
width=140 height=40> <img src="PREVIOUS.gif"
align=bottom width=150 height=40></p>
<p align=left><font size=4><strong>11/2/96 - Shamrock Software
Releases BLARNEY OS, Win Trip to Ireland</strong></font></p>
<p align=left><font size=4><strong>
<imgsrc="GREEN.gif" align=bottom width=600
height=10></strong></font></p>

</html>
</BODY>
```

As you can see in Figure 4.5, the rest of the top of the press release page is standardized with the menu bar and the company logo. These basic elements present a simple and easy-to-read format.

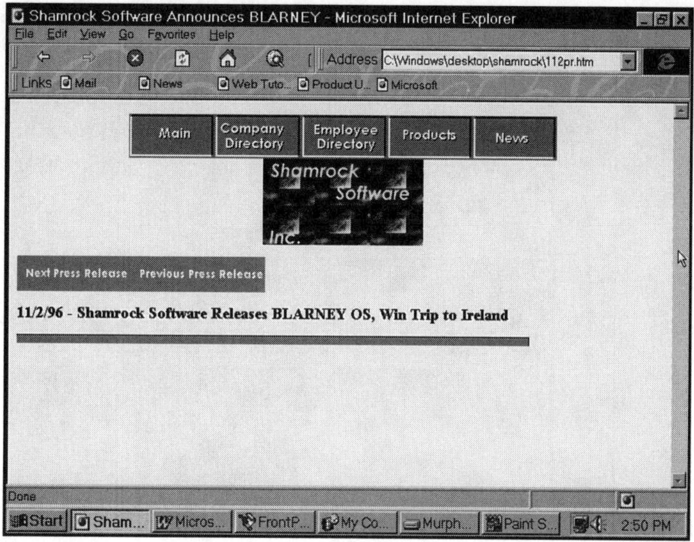


**Figure 4.5.**
*The heading of your press release is just the first step in making it a valuable tool and resource.*

# Adding Links in Press Releases

For your actual press releases to be truly useful and fully utilize the medium they're in, provide as many links as possible. By their very nature, press releases are supposed to be summaries of information. Providing links will encourage customers and writers to further explore your new product, joint venture, or whatever you want to focus on.

Actually, as you put together the press releases for your Web site, you'll find that they almost write links in themselves. Think about the press releases you've seen. How many have had a notation at the end about whom to contact for further information, along with phone and fax numbers and e-mail addresses? Don't you agree that a notation like that begs for a `mailto:` hyperlink? What kind of hyperlink? Simple—one that enables users to click the person's name and drop him or her a message.

The key is not necessarily to write your press releases with an eye toward hyperlinking, but simply to read them with that in the front of your mind.

When you finish putting in all the links identified in this task, you should have a press release archive that will enable both new users and *The New York Times* to easily access your new product announcements, business ventures, and roll-outs, complete with links to supporting information that provides background and perspective on the text.

When creating links, keep these suggestions in mind:

- ❑ Link the name of any product you announce in the release to the specific page on your Web site dedicated to the product.
- ❑ Use a `mailto:` or `<A HREF>` tag wherever people's names appear in the release to hyperlink their mail address or Web page.
- ❑ Consider linking to any business partners mentioned in the release.

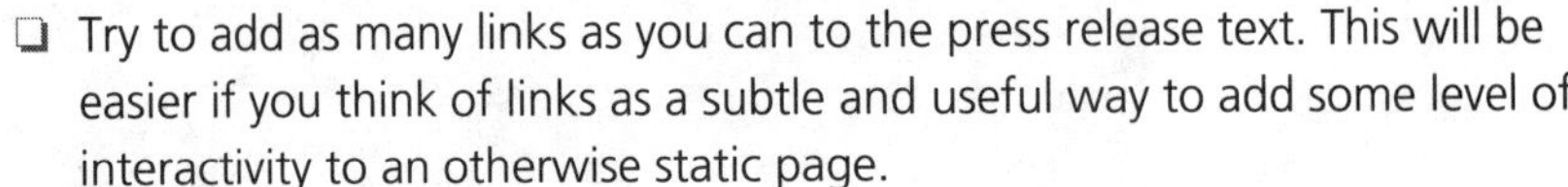

Adding links can create a depth to your press releases that is impossible to achieve on the printed page.

- ❑ Try to add as many links as you can to the press release text. This will be easier if you think of links as a subtle and useful way to add some level of interactivity to an otherwise static page.
- ❑ Look at the basic sample press release Web page in Figure 4.6. It now has several hyperlinks that can be selected, and its HTML code now contains many more `<A HREF>` tags.

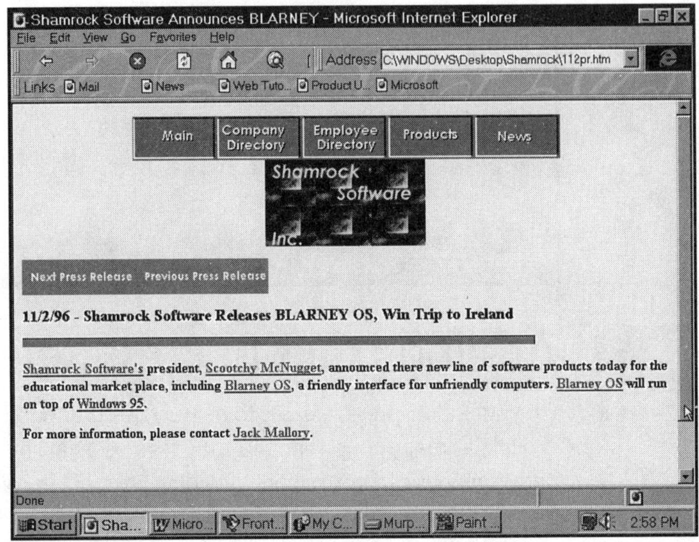


**Figure 4.6.**
*Hyperlinks are a way to add more information to a press release without adding additional copy.*

- ❑ At the bottom of the press release, right below the name of the public relations contact person, add a link to additional resource materials for journalists to use in their stories. Link to a simple Web page that provides additional links to the types of source materials a journalist would like to have in creating a story, including
  - ❑ High-resolution graphic files containing screen shots or photographs related to the release
  - ❑ Quotes or additional statements by company employees
  - ❑ Quotes from customers, analysts, or the public regarding the subject of the press release
  - ❑ Sound, video, or other multimedia files related to the release

Writers often have to justify to their editors why they should do a particular story. Providing additional resources will not only help them sell your story to the editor, but get the facts right as well.

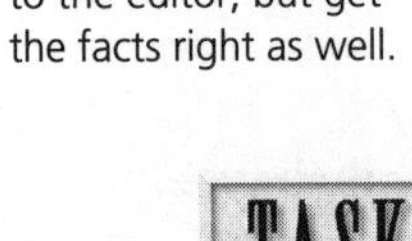

# Creating a Reference Page from Links

Do you want to create a basic Web page guaranteed to attract visitors to your site and keep them coming back? Then create a page of references and links to information that deals with a particular topic or topic area related to your business. This is the simplest way to make your Web site a useful tool for your customers beyond providing information about your own company and products and increase the number of hits on your pages. By finding an information niche of interest to your customers, you can quickly establish your Web page as an authoritative guide on that subject.

Creating the page is not difficult when you divide the procedures into a series of tasks and use one company's efforts as an example. In this case, the company is Old Dog Used Records, a fictional business that sells and trades used CDs, records, and tapes. Its goal was to create a very basic page containing in an organized fashion links to a variety of other sources on a topic.

## Finding the Links

Before you even begin to create your links, prepare by doing the following:

1. Determine your criteria or objectives.

   Before Old Dog began looking for links or actually creating the page of links, it defined these criteria. The page had to

   - Appeal directly to its customer base, people who buy and trade used music in any format
   - Target one particular niche—in this case, information on dealing with 8-track tapes. This information would appeal to Old Dog's customers, could be of interest to a lot of users, and be light-hearted enough to fit well within the persona Old Dog wanted to present through its Web pages

Usenet groups can be a valuable link by themselves and can also give you pointers to additional resources.

You don't want to forget any links you might find, so make a list. To do this quickly and easily, open up Notepad in Windows and copy and paste the URL for each link from the address line in whatever browser you might be using.

2. Scour the Net so that you can create a definitive set of links on the topic(s) you have chosen. Start with the search engines on the Web, such as AltaVista (`http://altavista.digital.com`) or InfoSeek (`http://www.infoseek.com`). Then search through a list of Usenet newsgroups for groups that might relate to your topic(s). Take your time and have fun surfing and compiling your list of links!

   When Old Dog did a search on AltaVista using the term "6-track," Old Dog found that the term was used in approximately 4,000 Web pages. A portion of the list appears in Figure 4.7. As you scroll through, you should have little or no difficulty identifying the most useful sites for the Old Dog page. At the same time you compile your list of Web pages dealing with 8-tracks, jot down quick notes or very brief descriptions that will help you when you actually put together your page and your visitors when they view it.
3. Compile a list of links that you feel will be good resources on your topic.

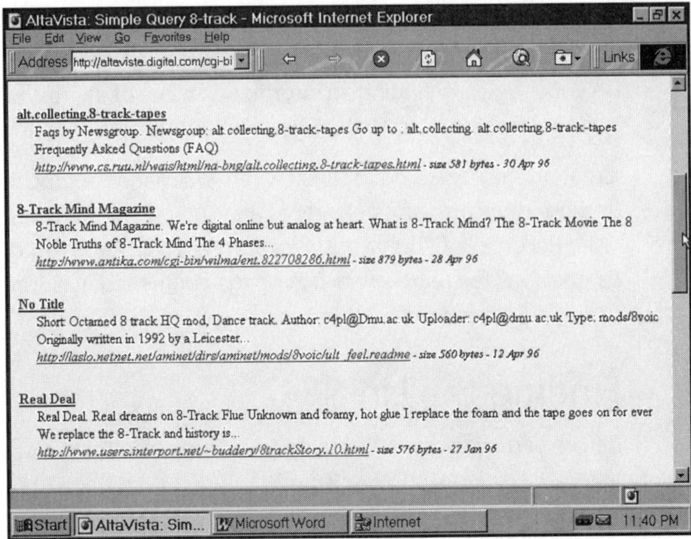


**Figure 4.7.**
*Web search engines can be a valuable research tool for creating original pages to draw users.*

## Creating the List of Links

The format or formats you use to assemble your list of information into a Web page depends on how fancy you want to get with your HTML coding. For bulleted lists, HTML provides native support through the <UL> tag.

For its page, Old Dog Used Records decided on a straightforward approach—a list format with a few categories. The list is fairly simple and uses the basic bulleted layout. Because a list is a fairly popular form on the Web, most Web editors provide a simple way to create a formatted list like the one on which Old Dog decided.

To generate a list using HotDog, follow these steps:

1. Go to Insert I List and select from the list of presentation options.
2. For a more customized presentation, specify the small graphic image you want to replace the bullet on your list.

You must have a <UL> tag—which stands for Unordered List as opposed to <OL>, which stands for Ordered (Numbered) List—at the beginning and end of the list. It tells the browser to present the information in bulleted list format. HotDog automatically generates these tags and should give you this HTML code:

```
<UL TYPE=circle>
<LH></LH>
<LI>
</UL>
```

The <LH> tag, which stands for List Header, enables you to specify text that will serve as the header for the list. Use this tag to break your bulleted list into several separate categories. Next, manually place an <LI> tag, which stands for List Item, in front of each item that you want presented separately on the bulleted list.

About twenty 8-track sites are going to be referenced on Old Dog's page, The KHList header for the page is The Vault: Your 8-Track Resource. To reference each 8-track site, place the list into HotDog and insert the necessary <LI> tags in front of each item. At this point, the HTML code for the Old Dog list should look like Listing 4.3.

**Listing 4.3. Old Dog's 8-track sites.**

```
<UL TYPE=circle>
<LH>The Vault:  Your 8-Track Resource</LH>
<LI>8-Track Heaven
<LI>8-Trackers Unite!
<LI>Matt's 8-Track Collection
<LI>My 8-Track Heart
<LI>Trackin' After Midnight
<LI>An 8-Track Newsgroup
<LI>8-Track Attack
<LI>70's 8-Track Gold
<LI>8-Track Traders
<LI>Old Technology and Old Music
</UL>
```

## Creating the Links

If you want users to be able to select a Web site from your reference page list and navigate to it quickly, having the list together and coded is not enough. You must code in the corresponding links as well. To accomplish this using HotDog, follow these steps:

1. Highlight the entire text of an item on the list.
2. Select the External Hypertext button from the toolbar.
3. Insert the resource's URL. HotDog will generate the <A HREF> tag for each item. For example:

   ```
   <LI><A HREF="http://www.8track.com">8-Track Heaven</A>
   ```

4. Generate the <A HREF> tag for each item in your list of references to make each a hyperlink in your Web page.

Make sure you verify the correct service with each link. For example, Usenet newsgroups must start with the `news:` reference.

# Inserting an Image

To add identity and style to your reference page, customize it with a graphic; that's what Old Dog Records did. The Old Dog page sports a graphic of an 8-track that it has customized for this page, using a scanned image of an 8-track (yes, they were able to find one) and the text tools of Paint Shop Pro on the accompanying CD-ROM. The graphic is pretty large and would look nice on the left side of the page with the hyperlinks on the right.

Chapter 1 fills you in on how to select graphics tools like Paint Shop Pro for your Web construction.

Using the following steps, you can accomplish what Old Dog did:

1. Go to HotDog's Insert | Image (Advanced) command, as shown in Figure 4.8.
2. Move the cursor to just after the `<BODY>` tag.
3. Select the image file, which in the case of Old Dog, is `8track.gif`.
4. Fill in the Alternate Text description. For Old Dog, this is "Old Dog Used Records Presents The Vault."
5. Select Left from the Alignment drop-down menu to get the 8-track image to appear on the left with the links on the right.

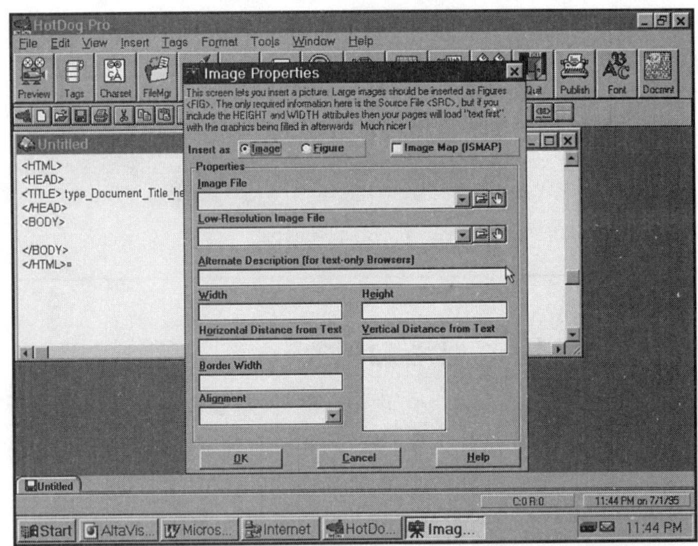


**Figure 4.8.**
*HotDog's Insert | Image menu provides advanced options for placement of the image on the page.*

TASK

# Finishing the Reference Page

To finish the reference page, put a link at the bottom of the page back to the main Web page and insert a `mailto:` link welcoming people's comments and additions.

Print Shop Pro, which is on the accompanying CD-ROM, is a powerful tool that makes working with images a lot easier.

Figure 4.9 shows the finished Old Dog reference page. The finished HTML code for the page follows in Listing 4.4.

You can often save yourself a lot of trouble with reference pages allowing your users to become your best resource for maintaining a comprehensive set of links.

**Listing 4.4. The 8-track reference list.**

```
<HTML>
<HEAD>
<TITLE>Old Dog Used Records' The Vault</TITLE>
</HEAD>
<BODY>
<IMG SRC="8trk.gif" ALT="Old Dog Used Records' The Vault"
WIDTH=329 HEIGHT=451 ALIGN=left>
<UL TYPE=circle>
```

```
<LH><STRONG><FONT  SIZE=+1>The Vault:
Your 8-Track Resource</FONT></STRONG></LH><BR><HR SIZE=4>
<LI><A HREF="http://www.8track.com">8-Track Heaven</A>
<LI><A HREF="http://www.8track.com">8-Trackers Unite! </A>
<LI><A HREF="http://www.8track.com">Matt's 8-Track Collection</A>
<LI><A HREF="http://www.8track.com">My 8-Track Heart</A>
<LI><A HREF="http://www.8track.com">Trackin' After Midnight</A>
<LI><A HREF="http://www.8track.com">An 8-Track Newsgroup</A>
<LI><A HREF="http://www.8track.com">8-Track Attack</A>
<LI><A HREF="http://www.8track.com">70's 8-Track Gold</A>
<LI><A HREF="http://www.8track.com">8-Track Traders</A>
<LI><A HREF="http://www.8track.com">Old Technology and Old Music</A>
<LI><A HREF="http://www.olddog.com">Old Dog's Home Page</A>

</UL>

</BODY>
</HTML>
```

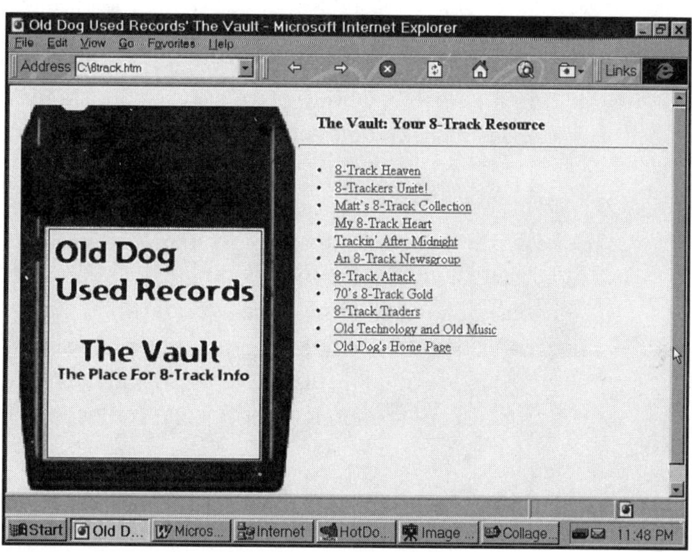


**Figure 4.9.**
*Old Dog's list of links is an example of how easy it can be to create a page with an original flavor that will draw your customers and potential customers.*

TASK

# Creating an Original Content Page

Rule number 1 for successful original content pages: Update the pages and the information in them on a regular basis. Stale Web pages are about as interesting as stale doughnuts are tasty. Like doughnuts, Web pages are best when served up fresh daily.

Original content pages are a lot like the reference page you just created. The difference is that with these pages you replace simple links with original, changing, fresh content. The goal is to add more value to your Web pages—for you and for your customers.

Obviously, the form of an original content page is not written in stone. Not only can the content be original, but the design and layout can be, too.

The company you'll use as an example for the task at hand—creating original content pages—is Knowall Cuisine Culinary Institute. Before you can create Knowall's pages, you need to know that

Before you create the pages, think about what interests you, what interests your existing and potential customers or clients, and what you can create that won't take more time than it does to run your business or cost more than you make in a year.

- Knowall's online Web site will contain links to information on the courses the school offers and to registration for classes.
- Knowall's target audience is both professionals and people with a desire to learn how to cook as a hobby.
- Knowall determined that a "Recipe of the Day" page would attract potential customers by giving users a different recipe each day, complete with preparation and cooking instructions. Over time, the site could become a repository for all of the recipes. Users would return to the page not only to see what the new recipe was, but also to look through the recipe archives for something tasty.

## Creating the Content

Do not think about designing your page until you have done two things:

- Created the content that will be included on the page
- Decided when and how you're going to update the page so that the information is current enough to keep visitors coming back

**NOTE:** Do not underestimate the tasks involved with creating the content for a Web page of this nature. No matter what tips I might give you on how to design a page and present the information, if the content isn't there the page will languish in obscurity. Great content can always draw people—even with poor page design. This, however, should not change your goal, which should be to be sure you have both great content and great design.

When those issues have been addressed, assemble your content—documents, pictures, audio, whatever. For Knowall, this means pulling together an extensive file of recipes unique to the school and often used in its classes and converting them to simple ASCII text files. Knowall also took pictures of each prepared recipe so it could add a tantalizing graphic to the "Recipe of the Day" page. This accomplished, the "Recipe of the Day" had all the ingredients it needed to be prepared and served.

## Designing the Page

To design the page, grab some scratch paper and doodle to come up with a layout you think would work. Take into account the number of different elements you are going to use on the page and how they relate to one another. Taking a design from paper and implementing it to HTML code is much simpler than trying to do it all at once.

The Recipe of the Day page calls for four core elements to be laid out on the page—a photograph of the prepared dish, the ingredients, the preparation instructions, and a shopping list that can be printed out to take to the grocery store. Knowall decided that the design for the page should try to at least mimic the traditional three-inch by five-inch recipe card, complete with a photo to one side. The shopping list then would be a hyperlink to another text-only page that could be printed out quickly without any graphics.

For detailed information on how the HTML <TABLE> tag operates, check out Laura Lemay's *More Web Publishing with HTML in a Week* from Sams.net Publishing.

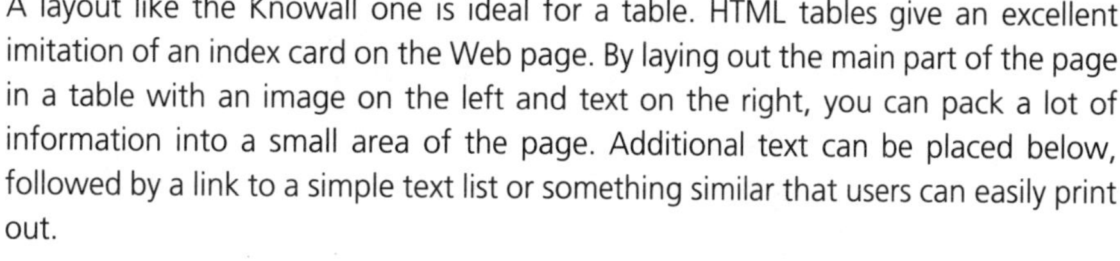

A layout like the Knowall one is ideal for a table. HTML tables give an excellent imitation of an index card on the Web page. By laying out the main part of the page in a table with an image on the left and text on the right, you can pack a lot of information into a small area of the page. Additional text can be placed below, followed by a link to a simple text list or something similar that users can easily print out.

Use a Web editor like HotDog, which is included on the accompanying CD-ROM, to create your basic table structure and then to manually manipulate the code for more advanced results. You will save a lot of time. Look at the Knowall page in Figure 4.10. Its layout was created using a Web editor. Note the nested table; the ingredients are a table in themselves, which is then placed in the right side of a two-column table that contains the meatloaf graphic on the left.

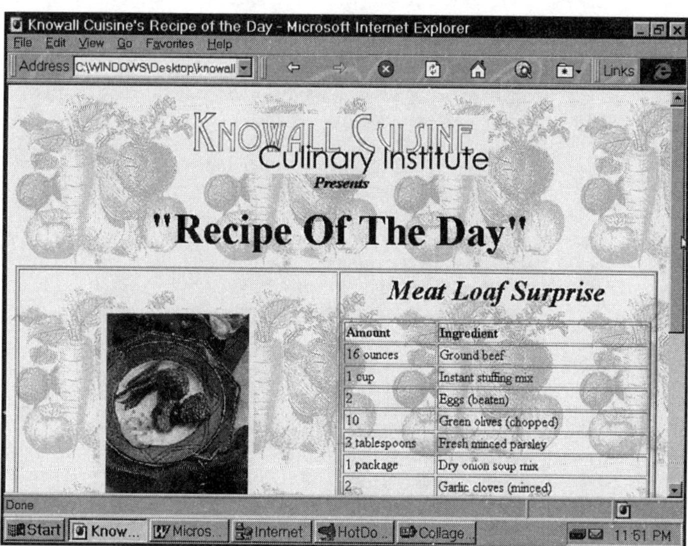


**Figure 4.10.**
*The Recipe of the Day was much simpler to create with the use of HotDog.*

**NOTE:** A working knowledge of HTML and the HotDog editor enables you to create this mildly complex code in less than an hour. I can't guess how long creating the Knowall page would take without a tool like HotDog, even with solid experience with HTML coding. You shouldn't have to reinvent the wheel each time you want to design a page. HotDog and other Web editors save you that trouble.

Evidence that Knowall's Recipe of the Day page came out well is shown in Figures 4.10 and 4.11. The HTML code used to generate the page appears in Listing 4.5.

### Listing 4.5. The Knowall Recipe of the Day Page.

```
<html>

<head>
<title>Knowall Cuisine's Recipe of the Day</title>
</head>

<body background="Backgd03.jpg">
<p align=center><font size=4><strong><br>
<img src="knowall.gif" align=bottom width=344 height=68><br>
</strong><em><strong>Presents</strong></em></font></p>
<p align=center><font size=7>
<strong>&quot;Recipe Of The Day&quot;</strong></font></p>
<table border=2 width=100%>
<tr><td align=center
valign=bottom width=50%><img src="Meatloaf.jpg"
align=middle width=180 height=226><p><em><strong>Don't
That Look Yummy</strong></em></p>
</td><td width=50%><p align=center><font size=6>
<em><strong>Meat Loaf Surprise</strong></em></font></p>
<table border=2 width=100%>
<tr><td width=30%><strong>Amount</strong></td>
<td width=60%><strong>Ingredient</strong></td></tr>
<tr><td width=30%>16 ounces</td>
<td width=60%>Ground beef</td></tr>
<tr><td width=30%>1 cup</td>
<td width=60%>Instant stuffing mix</td></tr>
<tr><td width=30%>2</td>
<td width=60%>Eggs (beaten)</td></tr>
<tr><td width=30%>10</td>
<td width=60%>Green olives (chopped)</td></tr>
<tr><td width=30%>3 tablespoons</td>
<td width=60%>Fresh minced parsley</td></tr>
<tr><td width=30%>1 package</td>
<td width=60%>Dry onion soup mix</td></tr>
<tr><td width=30%>2</td>
<td width=60%>Garlic cloves (minced)</td></tr>
```

```
<tr><td width=30%>1/2 cup</td>
<td width=60%>Dry red wine</td></tr>
</table>
</td></tr>
</table>
<p><font size=4><strong>Preparation Tips:</strong></font></p>
<p><font color="#FF0000">Preheat oven to 350 degrees.
Take all the delictable ingredients and mix them together
in a large ceramic bowl.
Lather up a 8 x 5 pan with Crisco or butter. Place pan in the oven
and bake for approximately 1 hour. Serves four
hungry, desperate sailors.</font></p>
<p><a href="http://list.htm">Click here
for an easy to print out shopping list.</a></p>
<p align=center><img src="hruler03.gif" align=bottom width=572 height=54></p>
<p align=center><a href="http://knowall.htm"><font size=5>
➥Back to Knowall Cuisine's Home Page</font></a></p>
</body>

</html>
```

Tables are one of the most powerful advances in the HTML language. HotDog, FrontPage, and Netscape Gold all enable you to create tables without the need to know all the specific variables for the <TABLE> tag.

Adding small graphic elements can do a lot to enhance your original content page. Just be careful not to overdo it. When you are deciding what graphics to add, keep in mind that most users will be accessing your pages at a baud rate (speed) of 28.8 or below, so keep the graphics few or keep them small.

## Keep to the Theme

Stick to your theme in your original content page design. For Knowall's Recipe of the Day page, for example, this meant food. That's why the background image and the horizontal rule at the bottom of the page are a grouping of vegetables.

## Put Your Name on It, Not All Over It

Place your logo at the top of the page with a link back to your main Web page at the bottom, and include your company name in the <TITLE> tag. But stop there. Keeping the user reminded of who is presenting information to them is important, but don't go over the top with references to your company. Try to create a site that advertises your business or product almost without mentioning its name.

Look at Figure 4.11. The Netscape title bar reads Knowall Cuisine's Recipe of the Day, and there's a large hyperlink at the bottom of the page back to Knowall's main page. This is a great example of how to get across your point—and your name—subtly.

**Figure 4.11.**
*This is one way to get your name across without getting it in the way of the content.*

# Creating Pages That Will Get You Bookmarked

Deciding what makes a great Web page is like deciding what makes a great book or movie. There are no universal rules that you can follow to make everyone love your pages, but there are guidelines that can help increase your odds of success. Some of the guidelines are driven by common sense, and others are driven by an understanding of the Web and how it works. All should help increase the quality of your Web pages.

**NOTE:** At the turn of the century, the head of the United States Patent Office suggested closing down the department because everything that could be invented already had been. Although sometimes it seems like every conceivable Web page has already been created, it hasn't. Originality will always set your pages apart from the pack.

Keeping these tips in mind when designing and creating your Web pages can increase the chances of your site getting bookmarked:

- Make the content original. Before you implement any idea, check with Web index and search services like Yahoo! (`http://www.yahoo.com`) or Infoseek (`http://www.infoseek.com`) to see if there are other pages similar in nature to the ones you want to create. Check out any similar pages you can find to see if they are truly up to par with what you had in mind. Just because a topic has Web pages does not mean that the pages are informative or that they fill the need for content in a given area.

People might like reruns on television, but they don't like them on the Web. Many Web users are accustomed to sites that are updated periodically throughout the day.

- Keep the content fresh. If you can't update daily, do it biweekly or weekly. If you want to keep people coming back, you need to give them a reason to, and maintaining changing content is the only way. Come up with a schedule, and stick to it religiously. If people know that every day at 9:00 a.m. the content will be updated, they'll start planning their visits to get the updated information.
- Stay with what you know. Don't try to make these content pages something that you or your business are not. Stick to information that you know well and that ties in well to your overall business plan. If you try to stray into another area because you think that is what people want, your pages are likely to pale in comparison to those of someone who has a true passion and knowledge in that area.

You know your customers and your business better than anyone. Design original content pages that interest you. An infusion of passion will do more for your Web page than a server full of Java applets, Shockwave movies, or ActiveX controls.

- Make your page invaluable. Create a Web page that users need more than you need them and you will have found a way onto the drop-down menus of browsers across the land. Knowall's goal, for example, is to get users to need its recipes to make dinner every night. When users visit the Web page daily, maybe they'll take that next step and sign up for a cooking class at the Institute. Look at it this way: Filling a need for information isn't what's important—to create a need for that information is. If you can't find a niche, create one by thinking about new ways to exploit the Web to bring information or value to your customers.

# Workshop Wrap-Up

No matter what business you're in or what product you make, there is an original Web page out there that will bring customers to your pages to do more than just look at your products or your company history. Create that page and implement it as soon as possible—before your competitor does.

If you have never written a press release, start writing them now and archiving them on your Web site. They're a great vehicle for acquainting a lot of people with your company and its product or service. Designing, creating, and implementing press release pages and the different kinds of links they can engender is only as complicated or tedious as you choose to make it. As you now know, you don't have to be an HTML guru to do it.

The advice you received about great content pages—keep to the theme and put your name on, not all over—can be applied to just about any page on your Web site. Combine these with the "guidelines" for creating a page likely to get bookmarked—make it original and invaluable and, above all, keep it fresh—and your efforts are sure to pay off.

## Next Steps

You're more than halfway through the how-to of basic business pages for the Web. There are just a few more of the basic Web site building blocks to add to your knowledge bank, and you'll be ready for even more interesting forays. Now...

- ❑ To find out how to sell your product and services on the Web, check out Chapter 6, "Online Catalogs and More: Presenting Your Products and Services."
- ❑ To see a real-world example of news, content, and reference pages in action, turn to Chapter 7, "Real-Life Examples: Putting the Basics Together."
- ❑ To gain know-how on getting information from users, see Chapter 8, "Gathering Information: Web-Based Surveys and Questionnaires."

## Q&A

**Q: I have just a small business, and we've never issued a press release in our history. Do I really need to set up an archive for nothing?**

**A:** The Web is the great equalizer in terms of respect given to companies of varying size. If you've never used press releases, maybe now is the time to start. Press releases will give your business or company a level of credibility and an appearance of professionalism that can let you hide endearing mom-and-pop qualities that initially might prevent wider acceptance.

**Q: Do I really need these reference links and original content pages? I just want to sell widgets.**

**A:** If a widget is sold on the Web and nobody pulls up the page, is the widget really there? If you want to sell your products and services to the people, you'll need the people to come and view your pages. Users have lots of choices (almost too many choices) on the Web, and reference or original content pages are worth your creation time to help draw new users and keep others coming back.

CHAPTER

FIVE

# Employee Directories and Biographies

## In this chapter, you

- ❑ Create an employee directory layout
- ❑ Create an alphabetical employee index
- ❑ Create a default employee directory page
- ❑ Design and create individual employee pages
- ❑ Make pages for frameless browsers (and users)

## Tasks in this chapter:

- ❑ Creating a Frame Layout
- ❑ Creating the Alphabetical Employee Listing
- ❑ Making Provisions for Frameless Browsers (and Users)

It takes hardworking and creative people to build great businesses. So depending on what business you're in, the people who work for you can be more than your best asset—they just might be the key "product" you'll be trying to sell through your Web pages. Every online business, including yours, can benefit by publicizing the people who make it what it is—the people behind the pages.

Making information about your employees available on your Web pages can be an effective tool for reaching potential customers and for putting a human face on the Web. Many customers and potential customers don't want to address their inquiries to an anonymous someone. They want to send their e-mail to a real person with a name, not to `Webmaster@acme.com`. Employee-focused Web pages are the solution for you and for them.

This chapter introduces you to basic types of employee information pages that in all probability will suit your commercial Web page endeavor. You'll learn techniques for presenting background and contact information for all the members of your organization in a compelling and useful form. Perhaps you have a consulting business or a law firm that you want to place on the Web. With businesses like these, people might well be your page's primary emphasis. This chapter shows you how to effectively present those people in a well-organized and easy-to-navigate Web page. Those of you whose business doesn't require that people be the Web page's primary emphasis will benefit, too, by discovering how presenting members of your organization can make a more interesting, informative Web site.

This chapter also shows you how to add some fun and creativity to your Web pages by allowing employees to express themselves and craft their own Web pages. Their individuality shows through, and the pages provide a human link to Web surfers and potential customers. One of the reasons the Web initially became so popular was that it enabled everyone to publish instantly to a worldwide audience. You can harness the excitement and innovation of this concept simply by allowing (better yet, encouraging) employee-designed Web pages.

## Creating an Employee Directory

Almost everyone knows how to use a telephone directory. They've done it forever, so it's easy. It stands to reason, then, that if you include an employee directory as part of your Web pages, you are giving customers and potential customers a great way to learn about the members of your organization. Let's face it: It's a familiar and easy-to-use interface. Access to individualized contact information for each employee saves you time and resources. At the very least, customers have a fast and easy way to get in direct contact on the first try with a person who can give them the information they need.

Your employee directory is used in conjunction with the company directory you created in the previous chapter, "Creating News, Reference, and Content Pages," and gives you the necessary links for each employee that is a part of each division's page.

Creating an employee directory is an ideal project for use with HTML's frames innovation. You can create a frame layout on your employee directory page that enables users to navigate between different employee pages (and the rest of your Web site) more efficiently than using a standard Web page.

When you create the company directory in Chapter 4, "Creating News, Reference, and Content Pages," you use a business called Two Cents Consulting as an example. You can use the same business as the example here to create an employee directory.

**NOTE:** Frames have become somewhat controversial as an HTML standard on the Net, and some users might not care for your pages that use frames. As a result, you'll see at the end of this example how to quickly make a nonframe option that users can select in order to view your employee directory.

# Creating a Frame Layout

The first thing you have to do to create an employee directory is to create the HTML code that will specify how the different frames are presented on the Web page. Follow these steps:

1. Sketch out—or have a mental picture—of what the frame setup should be. For Two Cents, the layout will be somewhat simple—a frame on the right to hold the employee page and a skinnier frame on the left to hold an alphabetical listing of employees.

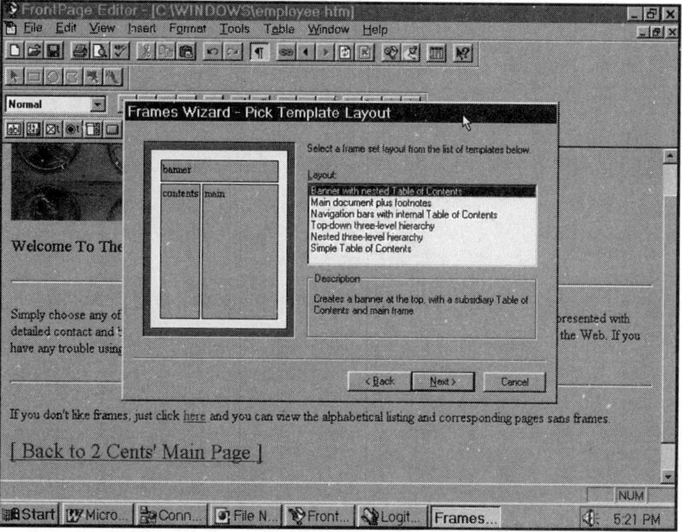


**Figure 5.1.**
*Microsoft's FrontPage provides advanced tools for creating frame page layouts.*

Many advanced HTML editors, such as Microsoft's FrontPage, contain advanced frame design and creation features that make implementing and working with frames easier. Figure 5.1 shows FrontPage's Frames Wizard.

2. Create the frameset document that tells the browser how to place the various directory elements on a single page. For Two Cents, use the `<FRAMESET>` and `<FRAME SRC>` tags to put together the document.

   To accommodate employees who have really long names, have the frame on the left side of the directory (which contains the alphabetical employee listing) take up about one-fourth of the screen. That leaves the remaining three-fourths of the browser window to present each employee's picture, contact information, and any other information you think customers will need or want to know.

Appendix B, "HTML 3.2 Reference," contains a detailed HTML reference guide that can help refresh your memory on these and other HTML tags.

Use this HTML code to implement these requirements:

```
<HTML>
<HEAD>
<TITLE>Alphabetical Employee Listing</TITLE>
</HEAD>
<BODY>
Two Cents<br>
Employee Listing
<P><IMG SRC="small2.gif">
<P><B> A ¦ B ¦ C ¦ D ¦ E ¦ F ¦ G ¦ H ¦<br>
I ¦ J ¦ K ¦ L ¦ M ¦ N ¦ O ¦ P ¦<br>
Q ¦ R ¦ S ¦ T ¦ U ¦ V ¦ W ¦ XYZ ¦</B>
</BODY>
</HTML>
```

This code gives you the following information, which you'll need to remember when you take the next step in creating the employee directory:

- ❑ Save the alphabetical listing Web page as `listing.htm` and place it in the same directory as your frameset document.
- ❑ Save the default Web page that fills the employee information window as `employee.htm`. Place it in the same directory as your frameset document.
- ❑ Remember to use the target name "employees" when you code the links for each employee name in the `listing.htm` Web document.

Later in this chapter, in the task titled "Making Provisions for Frameless Browsers (and Users)," you'll find out how to add the `<NOFRAME>` tag to this code to provide for frameless browsers.

You'll find out how to use the target name to have each employee's information appear in the right-hand frame when you work through the next step in this example.

3. Save the employee directory frameset document with an appropriate name, such as `directory.htm`. This simple document is actually the Web page to which you'll link on your site as your employee directory. Don't stop here, though. If you don't complete the next few tasks, it's going to be a pretty empty directory.

TASK

# Creating the Alphabetical Employee Listing

Now that you have your frames, you're ready to create the first Web page that fills one of them. The first document you should create is the alphabetical employee listing that will appear in the left frame. Save this document as `listing.htm`.

You'll want to be sure to give users a point of reference, no matter what is filling the frame on the right side of the document. The best way to do this is to start the employee listing document with a simple heading and a small logo graphic that indicates that it's the company's employee directory.

**NOTE:** The alphabetical listing will be the most static and permanent part of your employee directory. As users select an employee's name, the frame on the right is filled with information relevant to that particular employee.

Documents within frames can contain the same types of formatting as any HTML document, including background colors, images, and tables.

Depending on the size of your organization, you also might want to have the letters of the alphabet at the top of the listing page, usually on two or three lines. You can then make internal links from each letter to the appropriate area of the employee listing.

Think of these letters, which will appear as part of the left side of the employee directory page, as the ones that swim around in a bowl of alphabet soup. When you want to learn something about an employee named Jack Murphy, for example, you dip your spoon in the soup and pull out the letter M. Almost immediately a limited subset of employees, all with last names beginning with M, will appear. All you have to do now is scroll through the list to find the name you want.

Creating the alphabetical internal-linking index is extremely easy. Follow these steps:

1. Type in each letter of the alphabet, separating each with the pipestem character (¦) to make it easier for users to avoid inadvertently clicking on the wrong letter. Placing the letters on three different lines should work well with the document width you'll be dealing with here—25 percent of the browser window. Also, you can collapse together the letters X, Y, and Z because, in this example, Two Cents has only one employee with a last name starting with any of those letters.

If you would like to add some distinctive style to the directory, try using individual graphic images of the letters of the alphabet.

2. Create an alphabet header by using this basic HTML code:

```
<HTML>
<HEAD>
<TITLE>Alphabetical Employee Listing</TITLE>
</HEAD>
Two Cents<br>
Employee Listing
<P><IMG SRC="small2.gif">
<P><B> A ¦ B ¦ C ¦ D ¦ E ¦ F ¦ G ¦ H ¦<br>
I ¦ J ¦ K ¦ L ¦ M ¦ N ¦ O ¦ P ¦<br>
Q ¦ R ¦ S ¦ T ¦ U ¦ V ¦ W ¦ XYZ ¦</B>
</BODY>
</HTML>
```

**NOTE:** Remember that only the <TITLE> tag of the frameset document will appear in the title bar of a user's Web browser. The <TITLE> tags in any of the individual frames will be ignored when they are accessed as part of the "framed" Web page.

Applying the boldface tag (<B>) to the alphabet index will make the letters stand out a bit more, as shown in Figure 5.2.

3. Create the internal letter links to the portion of the listing that will be jumped to when a user selects the letter by applying a basic link tag to an anchor that appears later in the index. Keep it simple by naming each anchor and letter the same. The following is the excerpted HTML code for the first line of the alphabet after applying the necessary internal anchor references:

```
<B>
<A HREF="#A">A</A> ¦
<A HREF="#B">B</A> ¦
<A HREF="#C">C</A> ¦
<A HREF="#D">D</A> ¦
<A HREF="#E">E</A> ¦
<A HREF="#F">F</A> ¦
<A HREF="#G">G</A> ¦
<A HREF="#H">H</A> ¦
<br>
```

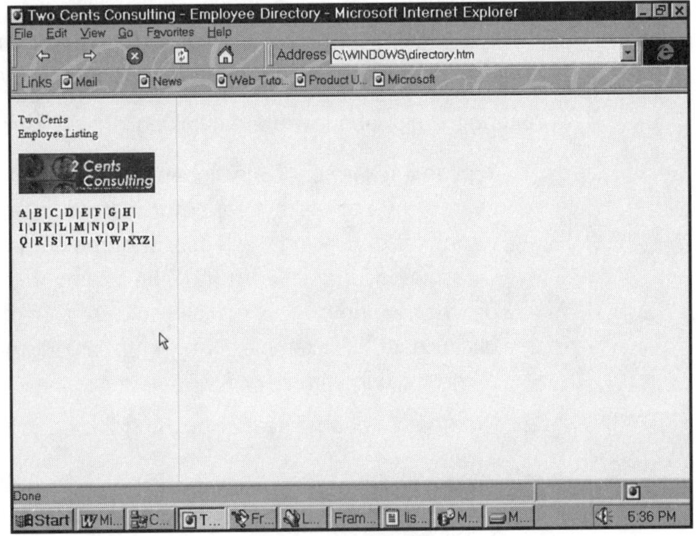


**Figure 5.2.**
*The first step in creating the alphabetical listing index frame.*

You'll create the anchor names for each letter of the listing in the next step of this example.

4. Repeat this code to create a link to the letter anchor for each letter in the initial alphabet index header.
5. Insert a horizontal rule with a setting of `<hr size=4>` after the alphabet index to provide a clean break from the employee name index that follows.
6. Enter the letter anchors for the rest of the document. You'll place the links to each employee Web page under these anchors. The anchors also will serve as headers for each portion of the employee listing. Keep this in mind when formatting.

   To create an anchor name, use the name attribute of the <A> links tag. Place the <A NAME> tag around the formatted letter header for each letter of the alphabet. Looking at this excerpt of the HTML code should help you better understand this:

Remember that this HTML code is still a work in progress. The final version will contain much more information after you enter employee names and links.

```
<a name="A"><h2>A</h2></a>
<a name="B"><h2>B</h2></a>
<a name="C"><h2>C</h2></a>
<a name="D"><h2>D</h2></a>
<a name="E"><h2>E</h2></a>
<a name="F"><h2>F</h2></a>
<a name="G"><h2>G</h2></a>
<a name="H"><h2>H</h2></a>
```

Once again, the anchor name for each letter is the same as the letter itself. As you can see in Figure 5.3, applying the <H2> format gives each letter more emphasis and makes it stand out as the subdivider for the employee listings. Of course, you don't have to apply that format. You can apply whatever HTML formatting you like to individual letters.

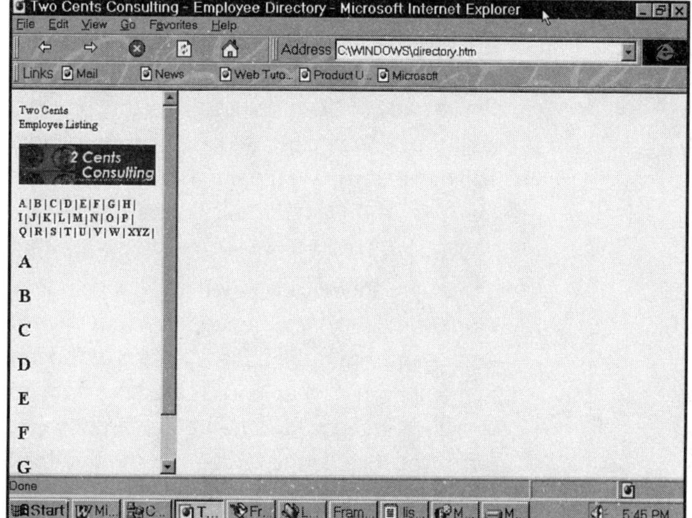


**Figure 5.3.**
*The large alphabetical subheads here act as anchors and are linked to the index listing.*

**TIP:** The Two Cents example uses the default color for the employees' hyperlinks. You can always specify the color of the links in any of your Web pages by applying the `LINK="#??????"` property to the <BODY> tag at the top of the page.

7. Enter the names of your employees and place them in the HTML code under the corresponding letter. This is the easiest part of preparing the employee directory, but it probably is the most time consuming as well. This is an excerpt of what the Two Cents' `listing.htm` HTML code looks like after completing this initial task:

```
<a name="A"><h2>A</h2></a>
Anderson, Bill<br>
Allen, Joe<br>
Armstrong, Neil<br>
<a name="B"><h2>B</h2></a>
Brimmer, Bob<br>
<a name="C"><h2>C</h2></a>
Carry, Harry<br>
<a name="D"><h2>D</h2></a>
DeVito, Pete<br>
<a name="E"><h2>E</h2></a>
Everly, Eunice<br>
<a name="F"><h2>F</h2></a>
Fete, John<br>
<a name="G"><h2>G</h2></a>
Gilligan, Buddy<br>
<a name="H"><h2>H</h2></a>
Homer, Doh
```

Don't forget to add the `<BR>` tag after each employee name.

8. Create a link from each employee name to the corresponding Web page. This is the final step in creating the `listing.htm` document that makes up the left side of the employee directory page. Code the link so that the employee's Web page is loaded into the frame on the right side of the page. The name of the Web page that Two Cents is creating for each employee is made up of the employee's last name plus the `.htm` extension. The Web page that's linked to Bill Anderson, for example, is `anderson.htm`.

   There's an added trick to what you'll be doing here. With a frame-based employee directory, you need to add a target name to the link tag for each employee so that the page is loaded in the frame on the right-hand side. Remember that when you created the frameset document for the employee directory, you gave this frame the target name `"employees"`. Therefore, when you include the target name within the link tag for each employee, you make it possible for a user to switch from one employee to another in the alphabetical listing and have only the frame on the right side change.

   As you can see here in the final stages of the excerpted HTML code for the `listing.htm` document, each employee name is linked to the corresponding Web page and will open in the frame:

```
<a name="A"><h2>A</h2></a>
<a href="anderson.htm" target="employees">Anderson, Bill</A><br>
<a href="allen.htm" target="employees">Allen, Joe</a><br>
<a href="armstrong.htm" target="employees">Armstrong, Neil</a>

<a name="B"><h2>B</h2></a>
<a href="brimmer.htm" target="employees">Brimmer, Bob</A>

<a name="C"><h2>C</h2></a>
<a href="carry.htm" target="employees">Carry, Harry</A>

<a name="D"><h2>D</h2></a>
<a href="devito.htm" target="employees">DeVito, Pete</A>
```

```
<a name="E"><h2>E</h2></a>
<a href="everly.htm" target="employees">Everly, Eunice</A>

<a name="F"><h2>F</h2></a>
<a href="fete.htm" target="employees">Fete, John</A>

<a name="G"><h2>G</h2></a>
<a href="gilligan.htm" target="employees">Gilligan, Buddy</A>

<a name="H"><h2>H</h2></a>
<a href="homer.htm" target="employees">Homer, Doh</A>
```

9. Save the HTML document as `listing.htm` and place it in the same directory as the frameset document, `directory.htm`. You're finished—at least with this portion of the project! If you want to make sure of where in the example you should be at this point, look at Figure 5.4.

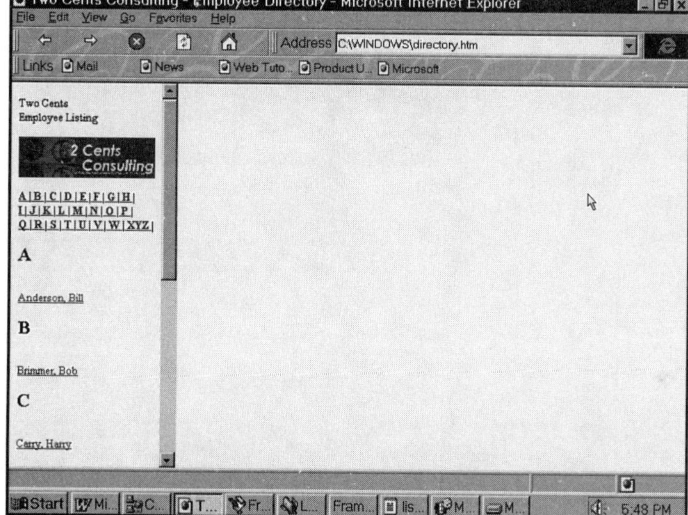


**Figure 5.4.**
*The completed listing is just a part of the framed directory.*

# Creating a Default Employee Directory Page

When you created the frameset document `directory.htm`, you entered two names: the target name `"employees"` and the document name `employees.htm` for the right frame. The primary function of the right frame is to display the employee Web pages that you just finished linking to each employee name. Now you need to create a default `employees.htm` Web page that will be loaded into this frame the first time the directory is brought up, before a user selects a specific employee name.

In the next section, you'll see an example of a typical employee Web page that can be used for an employee directory.

This default page acts as the placeholder for the main frame on your employee directory and should provide basic information about

- The employee directory
- The business or company
- The directions for using the directory with a frame-impaired browser

Many Web surfers consider a frame-impaired browser to be a blessing.

Figure 5.5 shows how the Two Cents employee directory default page looks. As you can see, it's a basic HTML page with the company's logo and basic instructions for using the employee directory. To make it easy to navigate to other pages, it also contains the menu bar for the Two Cents Web site.

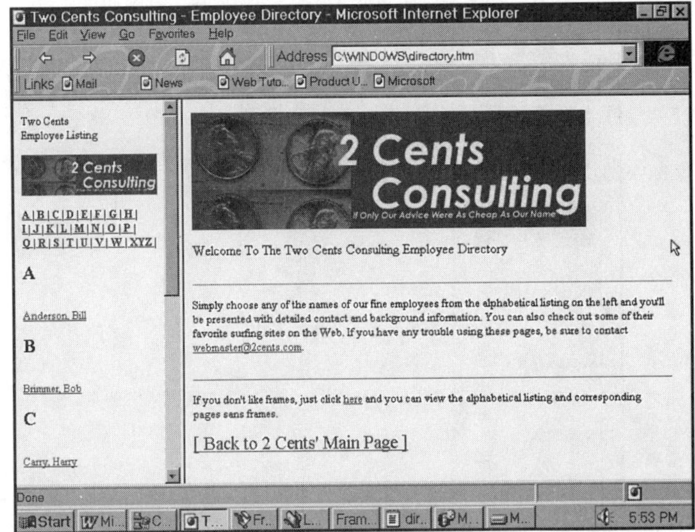


**Figure 5.5.**
*The default page fills the frame that will hold employee pages when the names on the left are selected.*

The implementation of this page is very straightforward, with only one twist—there is a link to a nonframes version of the directory for users who don't like frames. As the following HTML code indicates, the link is a direct one to `listing.htm`, which operates as a normal Web page, ignoring frame target properties when loaded by itself into a browser:

```
<html>
<head><title> Two Cents Employee Directory</title></head>

<body>
<p><img src="2cents.jpg" align=bottomwidth=461
 height=133></p>
<p>
<p><font size=4>Welcome to the Two Cents Consulting Employee
Directory<font></p>
<hr>
```

```
<p>Simply choose any of the names of our fine employees from
the alphabetical listing on the left and you'll be presented
with detailed contact and background information. You can also
check out some of their favorite surfing sites on the Web. If
you
have any trouble using these pages, be sure to contact
<a href="mailto:Webmaster@2cents.com">Webmaster@2cents.com</a>.
</p>
<hr>
<p>If you don't like frames, just click <a
href="listing.htm">here</a> and you can view the alphabetical
listing and corresponding pages sans frames.</p>
<p><a href="http://ww.2cents.com"><font size=5>[ Back to 2
Cents' Main Page ]</font></a></p>
</body>
</html>
```

For more information on designing and implementing a menu bar for use throughout your Web site, refer to Chapter 3, "Corporate Presence Pages."

**CAUTION:** Be careful when you design and code the default Web page that acts as the frame placeholder for your employee directory. When you plan and lay out all the elements that appear on the page, keep in mind that you will have certain constraints simply because the page will be loaded in a frame.

# About Individual Web Pages

Check out Chapter 1, "Selecting and Using Tools for Page Creation." It takes you through the process of setting up and customizing Web page templates using the HTML editor HotDog.

A scanner is a useful tool for designing all your Web pages, particularly the employee ones. Scanning in an employee's photo personalizes the user's experience by putting a face on the technology.

Until now, we've focused on putting together the navigational features that ultimately will make it easy to access the primary purpose of and information in your employee directory—the individual employee Web pages. The key is to initially come up with a standard layout template and then replicate the page for each employee by entering individualized information.

Obviously, the actual design of the employee Web pages for your organization should allow for creative design and expression on your part and on the part of your business. Nevertheless, to give the pages the functionality and usefulness that users expect, you'll have to include some basic elements.

- **Contact information.** Specific contact information is the single most important item of information you can place on an employee Web page. This includes a `mailto:` link that enables e-mail to be sent directly from an employee Web page to an employee address. To increase the value of the directory to your customers and reduce business costs by decreasing the time employees spend providing information to call-in customers, add such information as direct dial and fax numbers.

**CAUTION:** Update your employees' pages frequently to prevent the information from becoming outdated and useless. Giving users incorrect contact information is worse than giving them none at all.

- **Organization and department information.** The position of the employee and his or her department or organization within the company also needs to be part of each employee Web page. Linking each employee page to a department or division page is not quite enough. Provide a link from the employee page to the top-level directory for each department as well.

Don't forget the earlier discussion about setting up a company directory that you can link to each employee page.

**NOTE:** The goal of any directory is to provide useful information in an accessible format. By providing reciprocal links among various pages and directories on your Web site, you make all your information accessible—no matter what a user's search style or mind-set might be.

- **Employee background information.** The point of the employee directory should be, directly or indirectly, to sell your people. To accomplish this goal, you need to have functional, directed information on each employee page. Start by placing educational and professional background information in a standard format and layout on each employee page.

**TIP:** A resumé is an excellent resource for compiling background information on an employee. After all, the reason the person was hired in the first place probably was due in some part to the credentials and background observed on his or her resumé. A quick scan of the resumé and use of an optical character recognition (OCR) program can input the resumé into Web-usable format in no time.

  Always provide links to other materials by or about an employee that is located somewhere else on your site or the Web. Some employees, for example, might have contributed to an industry newsletter or some other online publication. The more information and links you can provide, the more users will turn to your directory as a jumping-off point for learning about the members of your team.

- **Some fun stuff.** A little levity never hurt any Web page. It doesn't have to be anything complex or deep. It could be as simple as an employee's own list of favorite links on the employee page of the directory. Try to provide some gimmick that will make your employees' pages stand out—even if it's just a little—from the multitude of pages on the crowded Web. The object is to make the pages memorable.

**CAUTION:** Although censorship is a touchy subject, you should be extremely cautious if you allow employees to place a list of links on their pages in the employee directory. If, for example, your company's main business is selling religious statues, you definitely don't want Bob in the mailroom having links to `www.penthousemag.com`.

## A Sample Employee Directory Page

Using the files on the accompanying CD-ROM with very basic HTML tags and the design tips mentioned in this chapter, you can put together a sample employee page with a simple layout like the one in Figure 5.6. Keep in mind that this page will be loaded into a frame as part of your employee directory. I like to align flush left information that will be loaded into a frame because it allows as much room as possible for presenting the information.

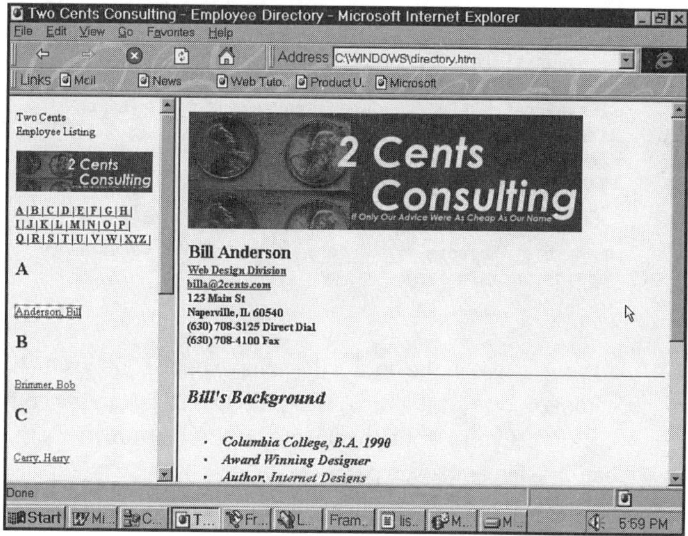


**Figure 5.6.**
*The employee's page is loaded into the frame with information and additional links to other sites and pages.*

Although the HTML code for this sample employee page is very basic, it presents the requisite elements and links to get the job accomplished.

```
<html>
<head><title>Anderson, Bill</title></head>

<body>
<p align=left><img src="2cents.jpg" align=bottom width=461
height=133></p>
<p align=left><font size=5><strong>Bill Anderson<br>
</strong></font><a href="design.htm"><font size=3><strong>Web
Design Division<br>
</strong></font></a><a href="mailto:billa@2cents.com"><font
size=3><strong>billa@2cents.com<br>
</strong></font></a><font size=3><strong>123 Main St<br>
Naperville, IL 60540<br>
(630) 708-3125 Direct Dial<br>
(630) 708-4100 Fax</strong></font></p>
<hr>
<p><font size=5><em><strong>Bill's Background
</strong></em></font></p>
<ul>
<li><font size=4><em><strong>Columbia College, B.A.
1990</strong></em></font></li>
<li><font size=4><em><strong>Award Winning
Designer</strong></em></font></li>
<li><font size=4><em><strong>Author, <
/strong></em></font><a
href="designs.htm"><font size=4><em><strong>Internet
Designs</strong></em></font></a></li>
</ul>
<hr>
<p><font size=5><em><strong>Bill's
Links</strong></em></font></p>
<ul>
<li><a href="http://www.cnn.com"><font
size=4><em>CNN</em></font></a></li>
<li><a href="http://espnnet.sportszone.com"><font
size=4><em>ESPN</em></font></a></li>
<li><a href="http://www.microsoft.com"><font
size=4><em>Microsoft</em></font></a></li>
</ul>
<hr>
<p><a href="2cents.htm"><font size=6>[To 2 Cents' Main
Page]</font></a></p>
</body>
</html>
```

Employee pages usually present an excellent opportunity for using bulleted lists with the <LI> tag.

To learn how to create a menu bar, turn to Chapter 3, "Corporate Presence Pages."

As you can see in the figure, the sample page contains such standard elements as the company logo (at the top of the page) and a link to the company's main page (at the bottom). If you want easy navigation throughout your site, consider placing a menu bar on each employee page.

After you place a page on your site for each member of your group, the employee directory will be ready to go. Make sure that the filename under which you save each employee's page matches the link you created previously in the alphabetical listing index. If the names don't match, you'll have a broken link, and users will receive errors when they use the directory.

# Making Provisions for Frameless Browsers (and Users)

Not everyone has a browser that supports frames. It is up to you to make certain when you construct your employee directory that these users can view your content. Even though the step to accomplish this is amazingly simple, you'd be surprised how often it is ignored and how annoyed users get with Web developers who don't take the time to do it.

All you have to do is use the `</NOFRAME>` tag. It enables you to specify alternative content for users who access your frame documents with a frameless browser. Here's the HTML code of the frameset document we created in this chapter:

```
<HTML>
<HEAD><TITLE>Two Cents Consulting - Employee
Directory</TITLE><HEAD>
<FRAMESET COLS="25%,75%">
<FRAME SRC="listing.htm">
<FRAME SRC="employees.htm" NAME="employees">
</FRAMESET></HTML>
```

You can help users without frames by adding a link directly to the `listing.htm` document that contains the alphabetical listing of employees. You will need to add the `</NOFRAME>` tag with the `<BODY>` tag within it so that other browsers will recognize the HTML code. Browser-supporting frames will ignore this portion of your code. The previous code might look like this after you insert these items:

```
<HTML>
<HEAD><TITLE>Two Cents Consulting - Employee
Directory</TITLE><HEAD>
<FRAMESET COLS="25%,75%">
<FRAME SRC="listing.htm">
<FRAME SRC="employees.htm" NAME="employees">
</FRAMESET>

<NOFRAMES>
<BODY>
This page was designed with frames.  However, if you select
<A HREF="listing.htm">here</A> you will be taken to an
alphabetical listing of our employees.  Thank you for your
patience.
</BODY>
</NOFRAMES>
</HTML>
```

The alternative for nonframe browsers doesn't have to be elaborate, nor does it require the designing of additional pages. After all, it's the thought that counts.

All you have to do is save the HTML code, and your employee directory will be as accessible as it can be. When users with nonframe browsers click on the link, they will be presented with the alphabetical listing that is shown in Figure 5.7. Now on to bigger and better things and more and more advanced commercial Web pages to spruce up your site.

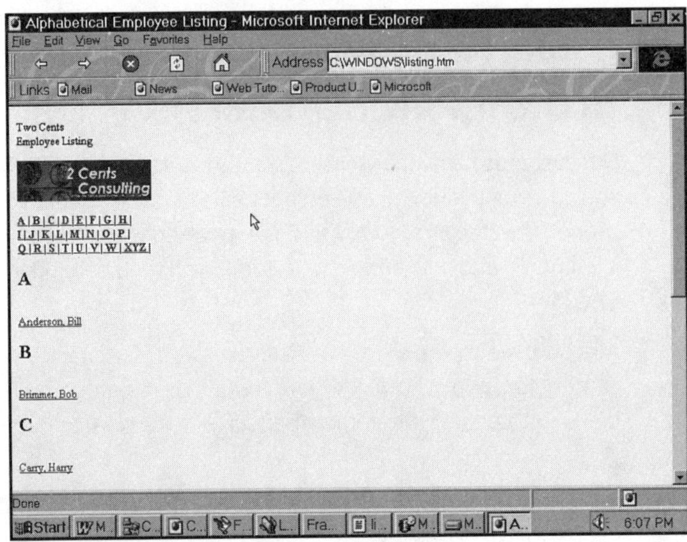

**Figure 5.7.**
*The alphabetical listing comes up when users with nonframe browsers click a link.*

# Workshop Wrap-Up

Creating an employee directory complete with alphabetical listing, employee profiles, and links to employee and company Web pages is not as difficult as one might think. It's simply a matter of "learning the basics" and "practice makes perfect." If you still feel squeamish about such things as HTML and codes, remember that there's help out there in the form of good HTML editors.

Given the increasing interest in the Net in general and the Web in particular, a Web site is a great place to market your company. In most cases, your employees are the company. Using a directory to introduce them to customers and to potential customers and encouraging them to lend their individuality to your company's presence on the Web in the form of employee Web pages is simply good business.

## Next Steps

Now...

- ❏ To find out how to sell your products in addition to your people, turn to Chapter 6, "Online Catalogs and More: Presenting Your Products and Services."
- ❏ To create a company directory that you can link to your employee pages, see Chapter 4, "Creating News, Reference, and Content Pages."
- ❏ To see a real-world example of employee directories in action, turn to Chapter 7, "Real-Life Examples: Putting the Basics Together."

## Q&A

**Q: Our business isn't that big—we have only about nine employees. Should we even bother with a directory on our Web pages?**

**A:** Absolutely. No matter how big or small your company, customers need to be able to get in touch with and find information about the people with whom they do business. In fact, these types of Web page employee directories are even more vital to smaller businesses than to larger ones because small companies might not enjoy the instant name recognition their competitors do. Employee directories enable you to reveal what's behind your business.

**Q: How much information about my employees should I really be placing on these pages? Is their position and e-mail address sufficient?**

**A:** The more information, the better. You need to differentiate yourself from every other Web site out there; therefore, don't skimp on the information you provide, even though it might take longer to make the pages. Try to add original content from your employees. In addition to putting together lists of their favorite links, perhaps they could write up small personal statements about the company. Remember, these pages can provide a connection from customers and potential customers to your employees—and then to your business.

CHAPTER

SIX

# Online Catalogs: Presenting Your Products and Services

## In this chapter, you

- ❑ Learn Web catalog design and navigation
- ❑ Create a product/price list catalog
- ❑ Create individual product pages
- ❑ Use advanced table formatting to add style and images to your catalog

## Tasks in this chapter:

- ❑ Creating a Basic Layout Using Tables
- ❑ Adding and Formatting Product and Price Information
- ❑ Hyperlinking Product Names to Product Pages
- ❑ Adding Table and Background Formatting
- ❑ Adding Information in Nested Tables
- ❑ Adding Product Images

Why do you want to set up a commercial Web page? Most likely to generate sales of your products and services. The elements discussed in earlier chapters will help you do that—but not directly. This chapter gives you the vehicle you need—online catalogs—to make that direct contact you desire.

**NOTE:** Don't be afraid to take the direct approach and develop an online catalog. Once upon a time, the Internet community would have frowned upon such crass (and hopefully profitable) commercialization, but no more. These days, the Web is seen as an excellent medium to help you sell your products and help consuming surfers find and buy products quickly and conveniently.

If you think a lot of different design options are available to sell your product or service through a paper catalog or brochure, wait until you see what's available in Web design for an online catalog. In this chapter, you see just some of what is at hand to create an online catalog that will generate first-time and repeat sales and customers. Don't let the fact that your business might be different from the ones used as examples throw you. Consider working through designing example pages a jumping-off spot for creating an online catalog, and then expand on the concept to customize it for your own Web site.

# What You Need to Know Up-Front: Catalog Design Tips

Chapter 13, "Advanced Catalogs," is the place to go for more complicated and advanced HTML techniques that will enable you to deliver customized catalogs and product presentations on the Web.

By now, you're probably sick of hearing that navigation is the key to everything. But it is, particularly when it comes to a vital sales tool like a catalog. No one said that combining the best of traditional catalog design with the Web medium would always be easy, but if you stick to basic overall structure and navigational plans, you should be able to get through the design phase unscathed.

## Creating "Layers" of Pages for a Web Catalog

To deliver information about your products and services to your customers most effectively on the Web, you must *layer* your information. This means placing it in pages of differing levels of detail that will enable users to drill down to the information level that best fits their needs.

Confused already? Think of it this way. You create a product/price list (layer 1) that enables users to select a product page for each item (layer 2) that will then bring up a page with more detailed information (layer 3). If that isn't enough layers for you, you can take it further, moving outward and creating a page with links to various product/price lists categorized by product line or company business area. Each layer of information enables a user to navigate among the depth of information he or she can use.

## Offline and Online Are Not the Same

Refer back to Chapter 3, "Corporate Presence Pages," and Chapter 4, "Creating News, Reference, and Content Pages," for discussions about navigational tools that might help you build your catalog.

You probably already have an offline (meaning "normal") catalog for your business. Don't confuse its design and layout with that of an online catalog—you're talking apples and oranges. The offline catalog is a good tool for providing images and data, but to use it on a Web page, you'll have to change the functional layout dramatically.

Approach online catalog design by surfing the Web and looking at Web catalog efforts, especially those of competitors. Some of the catalogs might be too complicated for your use, but even these might have certain elements you could borrow and incorporate into your design. At this stage of design, you'll have no better tool than your browser's View Source command.

# A Product/Price List

The View Source command shows you tricks Webmasters use for their page designs.

The product/price list like the one displayed in Figure 6.1 is one of the most popular (and simple) catalog styles on the Web. Actually, it's just a simple listing of products with some corresponding information—most important, price. A lot of people—and you can be one of them—take this simple page and make it much more visually impressive and useful to their customers.

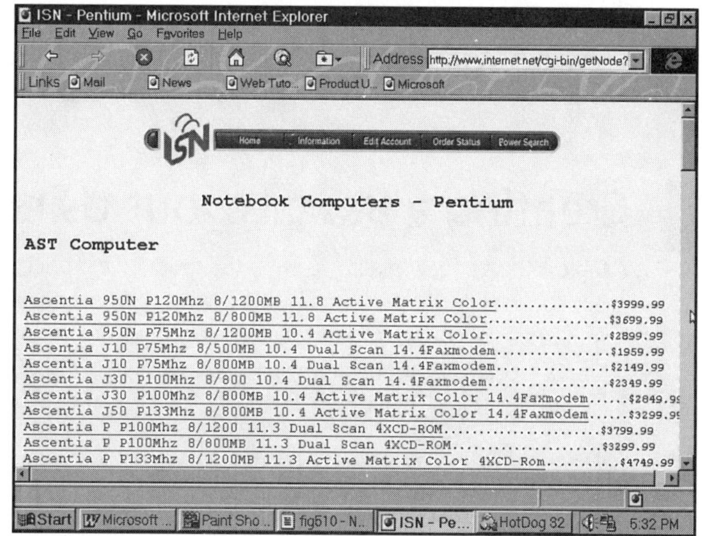


**Figure 6.1.**
*The product/price list is a common catalog type you'll find on the Web.*

If you haven't read Chapter 4 and are curious about Old Dog Used Records and its pages, check out the "Creating a Reference Page from Links" and "Creating an Original Content Page" tasks in that chapter.

You can learn the process of creating a product/price list by example, in this case a "build-it-how-you-want-it" example, or by actually building your own. Building the online catalog is cumulative. With each step, you add a little bit more to the design until, in the end, you find you have a rich Web-based catalog. The example product/price list we'll keep referring to is for Old Dog Used Records, the same company dealt with in Chapter 4.

**CAUTION:** Gone are the days when many browsers didn't support Web page tables. Tables and the related tags are now part of the most recently adopted version of HTML, and virtually every graphical browser supports them. If, however, you are extremely paranoid about compatibility issues, create a link to an ASCII document that provides the product/price list in a format viewable on any computer.

All the files used in this example, as well as in all the other examples in this book, are available on the accompanying CD-ROM and on the book's Web site at `http://www.murphnet.com`.

Turn to Appendix B, "HTML 3.2 Reference," for further background on HTML tags.

**NOTE:** Tables are an ideal tool to use to design a wide variety of catalog styles on your Web pages. There is probably no single HTML element you should know better than tables. You'll see tables used throughout this book to give you greater control over how your Web pages look to your customers.

**TIP:** The book's Web site contains links to many sites that implement the product/price list, as well as other styles of online catalogs that can help you get your creative juices flowing when you start to design your catalog.

TASK

## Creating a Basic Layout Using Tables

A table is the perfect "place" to enter the product and price information for an online product/price list. The table you create can be as simple or as complicated as you think it should be for your customers. For Old Dog, you'll create a three-column, ten-row table. One column is for the item number, another for the album title and artist(s), and the other for the product price.

Including the item number in the product/price list gives users an easy reference when they use the list to order a specific item or items.

**TIP:** Don't go overboard on the number of columns in your product/price list table. Using more than four or five columns can create problems for users with smaller screens or lower resolution and might not present your information as cleanly as you want. As you go along in this chapter, you'll be creating individual product pages that will link with the product/price list. As a result, you want to include only the most important information in your product/price list.

**NOTE:** Although you'll be creating the table for the Old Dog product/price list manually (making it harder than it has to be), feel free to use the Hot Dog editor included on the accompanying CD-ROM when you're actually creating your own list. Hot Dog, like many HTML editors, contains a table-building feature that makes the process much easier and faster.

Later in this chapter, in the "Adding Information in Nested Tables" task, you'll add additional columns for more advanced layout elements.

## Determine Table Proportions

Before you can create the Old Dog product/price list shown in various stages later in the chapter (in Figures 6.3 through 6.10), you have to think about how much of the screen each column in the table is going to take up. The price and item number columns can probably be pretty small in comparison to the album title and artist column; just make sure you don't put the squeeze on the smaller columns. You want your table to have a proper appearance and balance.

Experiment with different table proportions until you strike the balance that's right for your list.

The basic HTML code for the table follows. Each line of the code represents an individual row, as indicated by the <TR> and </TR> tags at the beginning and end of the line. The <TD> and </TD> tags within each row represent the individual cells that make up the row.

```
<TABLE>

<TR><TD></TD><TD></TD><TD></TD></TR>
<TR><TD></TD><TD></TD><TD></TD></TR>
<TR><TD></TD><TD></TD><TD></TD></TR>
<TR><TD></TD><TD></TD><TD></TD></TR>
<TR><TD></TD><TD></TD><TD></TD></TR>
<TR><TD></TD><TD></TD><TD></TD></TR>
<TR><TD></TD><TD></TD><TD></TD></TR>
<TR><TD></TD><TD></TD><TD></TD></TR>
<TR><TD></TD><TD></TD><TD></TD></TR>
<TR><TD></TD><TD></TD><TD></TD></TR>

</TABLE>
```

**TIP:** The <TR> tag is easy to remember because it stands for Table Row. The <TD> tag is a little less intuitive; it stands for Table Data Cell. I think of the <TD> tag as Table Division, which makes it easier to remember. For some people, creating a table without the assistance of a WYSIWYG (What-You-See-Is-What-You-Get) HTML editor makes it hard to visualize the table. If you're one of those people, laying out the initial HTML for a table, with each table row on a separate line, will help.

Even if you already know HTML, which I assume you do, you might want to check out *Teach Yourself Web Publishing with HTML* on the accompanying CD-ROM.

To define the proportions of the table, you have to add additional tag properties. If you don't add those properties, the size of each cell (or table division) will default to whatever size is needed to hold the text placed in the cell.

**NOTE:** Although you can add height and width properties to the size of your entire table, you probably should wait until you have completed the sizing of each individual cell within the table. Then, as a last step, enter the sum of these sizes for the entire table.

For maximum control, add width and height properties to each cell:

1. Use the <TD> tag to enter in specific values for the height and width properties.
2. Enter the number as pixels or percentages. Entering the number of pixels renders the table the same size without regard to the resolution of a user's screen or the size of the browser window in which the table is being viewed. If the table is larger than the browser window, the user has to scroll to see the rest of the information.

   When you enter the number as a percentage, the table applies your proportions and squeezes all the table information into whatever browser window or screen resolution is being used to view the table.

If you want to be certain how your product/price list catalog appears on a browser, play it safe and specify height and width values in pixels.

**NOTE:** When you enter values for height and width properties, you'll need to remember the most common resolution sizes in terms of pixels. The lowest common denominator is 640 pixels wide by 480 pixels high. Go beyond this range, and on most browsers the user will probably have to scroll to see the entire table. A resolution of 800 pixels wide by 600 pixels high is also very popular. Use it as a maximum for any browser window in which your table will be viewed.

**TIP:** Leave a cushion of about 20 percent in terms of pixels for whatever resolution you design. For example, if the 640×480 resolution is your target, the sum of your width properties shouldn't be greater than about 520. The extra pixels leave room for some blank space and minor variances in browser window sizes. Don't be as concerned with the height property; people generally need to scroll down to view anything but the shortest of tables. And, as you know, on a Web page, scrolling down is much more natural and expected than scrolling sideways.

Follow these steps to design the sample table:

1. Use the 640-pixel width as the starting point and limit your design to a sum of 520 pixels. Remember that you're designing a table for people who still think that 8-tracks are modern technology.
2. For width proportions, start with the item number and price of equal size (each about 15 percent of the table) and the album title and artist significantly larger (the remaining 70 percent of the table).
3. Place the item number in the first column and the price in the last column to have a more symmetrical appearance.
4. To correspond to the determined proportions, set the width of the item and price columns to 75 pixels and the middle column to 470 pixels.
5. Apply a basic height property of 50 pixels to each cell.
6. Drop in a single-letter placeholder so that you can see the table layout, shown in Figure 6.2. If you decide to use overly large text in any of the cells, you'll have to adjust the height property number upward.

Don't get out your calculator. I know these numbers aren't exactly right, but they'll be easier to work with than the real ones, and the "rules" here are merely working guidelines.

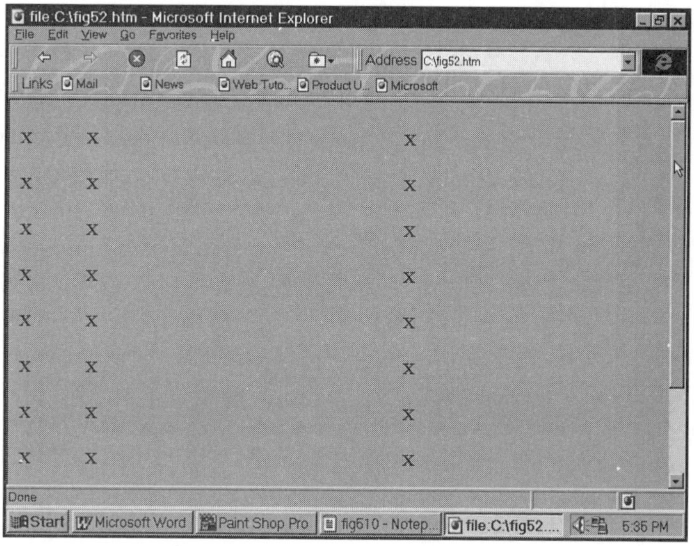

**Figure 6.2.**
*The table cell placeholders give you an initial look at your table layout and proportions.*

In basic HTML code, the basic table proportions and layout for each row would look like this:

```
<TR><TD WIDTH=75 HEIGHT=50>X</TD><TD WIDTH=370
HEIGHT=50>X</TD><TD WIDTH=75 HEIGHT=50>X</TD></TR
```

The <TR> and </TR> tags, of course, indicate the beginning and end of a row. The basic height, 50 pixels, for each cell is indicated by `HEIGHT=50`. The varying widths, also in pixels, of the different cells are indicated by `WIDTH=75` and `WIDTH=370`. This code must be repeated for each row of the table.

```
</TABLE>
```

**TIP:** As the HTML code for your table grows, it's impossible to keep each row on its own line. At this point, just make sure that each new row starts on a separate line so that the code is a little less confusing.

# Adding and Formatting Product and Price Information

Do as you learned in Chapter 1, and save the basic table layout as a template to use later on additional pages.

The table is set, so let's put some meat on it; in other words, let's place the necessary product and price information in the appropriate cells and format the text to suit the catalog style.

## To Add the Product and Price Information

For the example, enter the following information between the corresponding `<TD>` and `</TD>` tags for each cell in each of the three columns:

- First column: `Item Numbers`
- Second column: `Album Title and Artist`
- Third column: `Price`

Look at Figure 6.3 to see how the list looks so far. The following is an excerpt of the HTML code used; the information has been entered for only one of the rows:

```
<TR><TD WIDTH=75 HEIGHT=50> 14358 </TD>
<TD WIDTH=370 HEIGHT=50> Abba, You Can Dance, You Can Cry </TD>
<TD WIDTH=75 HEIGHT=50> $5.95 </TD></TR>
```

**TIP:** When you fill in the text for each table division, be sure to leave a space between the text and the beginning and ending tags. This will make it much easier for you to edit the code and spot problems or typos.

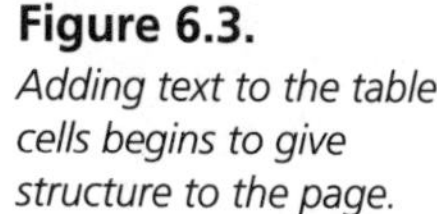

**Figure 6.3.**
*Adding text to the table cells begins to give structure to the page.*

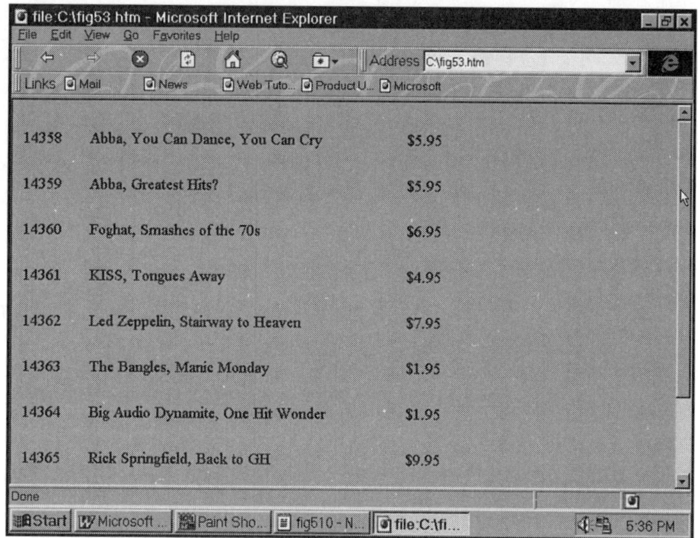

file:C:\fig53.htm - Microsoft Internet Explorer
File Edit View Go Favorites Help
Address C:\fig53.htm
Links Mail News Web Tuto... Product U... Microsoft
14358 Abba, You Can Dance, You Can Cry $5.95
14359 Abba, Greatest Hits? $5.95
14360 Foghat, Smashes of the 70s $6.95
14361 KISS, Tongues Away $4.95
14362 Led Zeppelin, Stairway to Heaven $7.95
14363 The Bangles, Manic Monday $1.95
14364 Big Audio Dynamite, One Hit Wonder $1.95
14365 Rick Springfield, Back to GH $9.95
Done
Start Microsoft ... Paint Sho... fig510 - N... file:C:\fi...
5:36 PM


## Formatting Table Text

Apply the same type of formatting to text within a table cell as you would to text placed anywhere else on a Web page, including font sizes, styles, and emphasis.

Creative, but careful, use of text formatting can add a lot to a product/price list catalog and make it stand out from the crowd.

With the introduction of the `<FONT FACE>` tag, a particularly useful and recent HTML innovation, you can set which typeface a user's browser will utilize to view each text element. This means that you're not stuck with the default typeface set by the browser for its program unless, of course, the user's browser does not yet support the `<FONT FACE>` tag.

**TIP:** The `<FONT FACE>` tag enables you to specify different typeface options so that if one is not available the browser will try the other one. If, for example, you put in "Helvetica, Arial," the browser will display Helvetica first and, if that's not available, the browser will try Arial. Because PCs and Macs often use different names for the same typeface, using this option can help you reach more users with the appropriate typeface.

**CAUTION:** Although the two most popular browsers, Microsoft's Internet Explorer and Netscape Navigator, currently support the `<FONT FACE>` tag, it is still a relatively recent development. Users who have browsers that don't support the `<FONT FACE>` tag won't be affected in an adverse way. They will be able to view the text using their default settings instead of the typeface you specified in your Web page.

When formatting the example, be sure to take into consideration the following directives:

- Use the Helvetica typeface. (That's what the owner of Old Dog Used Records likes best.)
- Add the bold tag `<B>` to each cell to make the text stand out a little more in the table.
- Don't specify a text color right now because your next task will be to hyperlink the text in this list.

Want more information on setting up text colors, background images, and other elements for your Web pages' theme? See Chapter 2, "Developing a Plan for Design and Site Management."

Figure 6.4 lets you see how the product/price list catalog looks at this point in development. When you look at the following HTML code, which was used to create the list in the figure, you'll understand why many people consider tables to be one of the more complex and difficult HTML elements to work with:

```
<FONT FACE="HELVETICA, ARIAL"><TR>
<TD WIDTH=75 HEIGHT=50><B> 14358 </B></TD>
<TD WIDTH=370 HEIGHT=50><B> Abba,
You Can Dance, You Can Cry </B></TD>
<TD WIDTH=75 HEIGHT=50><B> $5.95 </B></TD></TR>
```

**Figure 6.4.**
*Applying specific typefaces to data within each cell is an easy task.*

**NOTE:** To avoid repetitive coding you can place some text-formatting tags around as much of the table as you want. If you are using Microsoft Internet Explorer 3.0, for example, and set the `<FONT FACE>` tag at the very beginning, all the text on the page that comes after the tag will appear in that format until you put in another tag to alter it. The key here, though, is the term "some." For example, placing a `<B>` tag at the beginning of the table and a `</B>` tag at the end won't make everything between the two tags appear in boldface. Unfortunately, the tag has to be placed in front of the text in each cell.

# Hyperlinking Product Names to Product Pages

The greatest benefit of using the product/price list style of catalog is that it enables you to present the most important information about your for-sale items in as compact a format as possible. Unfortunately, that benefit is also a major detriment because the product/price style of a catalog probably doesn't have the depth of product detail and information you or many users want.

Remember the earlier section, "Creating 'Layers' of Pages for a Web Catalog"? Well, this is a good example of that layering.

You can, however, overcome the problem by adding a link tag so that a user can select a table item, click it, and be transported to a different Web page. When you add these hyperlinks, you are adding depth to the catalog without upsetting the benefits of the simple layout.

## Creating Product Pages

Before you add hyperlinks, you must create the pages to which the links will lead.

Product pages should

- Contain as much detail about the product as you have available to use
- Be creative and include such product-related items as photos, data sheets, customer testimonials, and media reviews
- Include your site's navigational menu bar and a prominent link back to the product/price list catalog

Refer to Chapter 3 for more information about designing and creating a menu bar.

For Old Dog Used Records, a separate product page for each album must be created. Each product page must include the following:

- The album cover or picture of the band (if available)
- A complete list of the songs on the album
- The record company

- ❑ The formats available (CD, tape, record, 8-track)
- ❑ The number of items in stock

It should go without saying (but I will say it anyway) that, for your business and products, you'll have to make a product-by-product decision about what's best to include. Remember—the more useful information, the better.

**CAUTION:** On a product's individual page, avoid placing any links other than the menu bar and the link back to the catalog. In this example, adding links to the band or record company's Web page might seem like a great thing to do, but don't do it! The person looking at your individual product page probably is about ready to buy. Adding extraneous links at this point could take that potential buyer down a path of no return, and you won't be able to close the sale.

Figure 6.5 shows a portion of an individual product page for Old Dog. Creating the entire page is an easy task, using this basic HTML code:

You can always use a more advanced design for these pages. For more advanced catalog design techniques, see Chapter 13, "Advanced Catalogs."

```
<HTML>
<HEAD>
<TITLE> Old Dog Used Records - ABBA </TITLE>
</HEAD>
<BODY>
<IMG SRC="abbacov.gif" ALT="ABBA - You Can Dance, You Can Cry">
<HR SIZE=4>
<H1>ABBA:  You Can Dance, You Can Cry</H1>
<H2> Arista Records </H2>
<B>Tracks:<br>
You Can Dance, You Can Cry<br>
Oh, Baby<br>
Baby Oh<br>
Dance Dance Cry<br>
Cry Cry Dance<br>
Dance Cry Dance<br>
<HR SIZE=4>
Available on:  CD ¦ Tape ¦ Record ¦ 8-Track<br>
5 In Stock</B>
</BODY>
</HTML>
```

**TIP:** You'll probably need to create a large number of product pages that are nearly identical in design and layout. Clearly, a template will help you tremendously in accomplishing this task. For insights on creating and using templates, see Chapter 1.

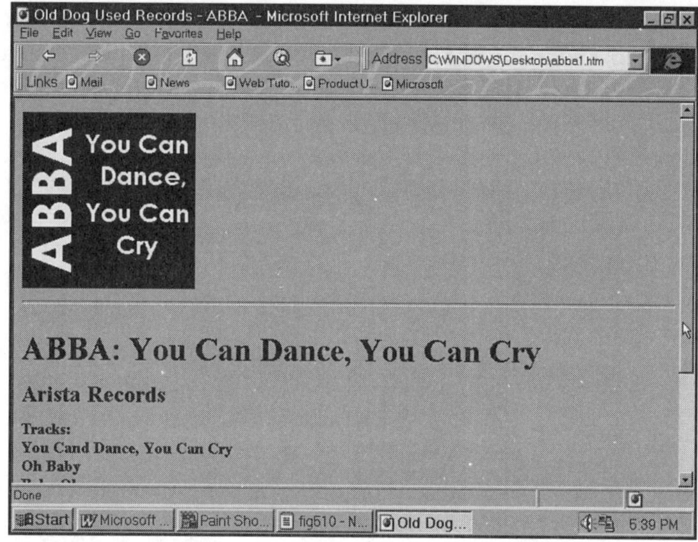


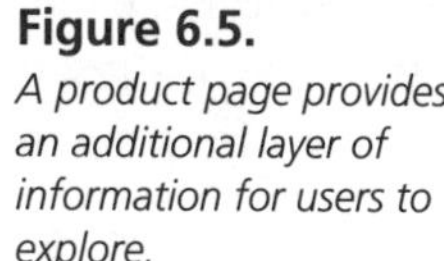

**Figure 6.5.**
*A product page provides an additional layer of information for users to explore.*

Make sure you save each product page under a logical name that you won't forget or be confused by it later. For Old Dog, saving the Abba album product page as `abba1.html` seems pretty logical. The reason for the `1`, of course, is that there's sure to be more than one Abba album (or 8-track) in the inventory.

## Linking Up the Product Pages

For each product, create a link for each item within each cell (for Old Dog, this means item number, title, and price) so that a user can click on any item and be taken to the product's individual page.

**NOTE:** Unfortunately, you can't just place an `<A HREF>` tag at the beginning of the row and an `</A>` tag at the end to create a link for the text contained in all the cells of that row. Although the links will be identical, you'll need to create separate ones for each cell in the row.

**TIP:** Place the `<A HREF>` tag just before the starting `<TD>` tag for each cell. That way, even if later you need to edit the text in a particular cell, you can be sure that it will be linked to the product page.

To create a basic working product/price list catalog like the one shown in Figure 6.6, place the appropriate link tags for each table cell throughout the document. The result will be a page that provides both summary top-level information in list form and a quick and easy method for accessing more detailed data.

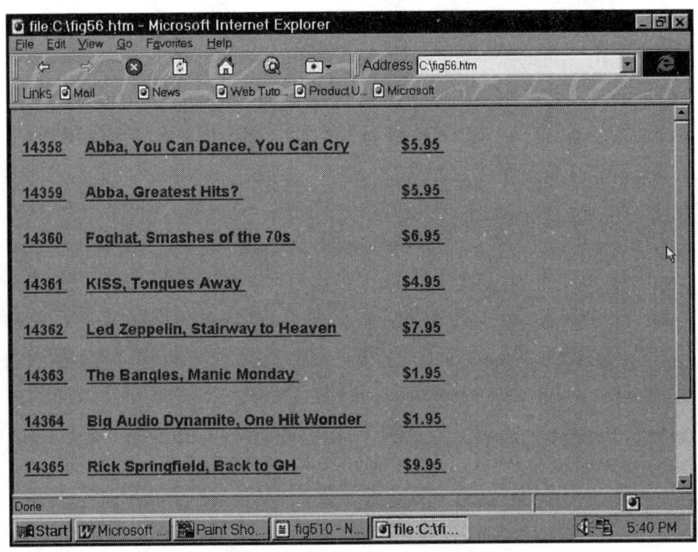


**Figure 6.6.**
*Adding links to the price/product list makes the catalog more useful.*

The color of the links in your product/price list is determined by the `LINK` property within the `<BODY>` tag at the beginning of your document. Unfortunately, you can't change the color of individual links in your pages now.

Don't be put off by the HTML code. It might not look easy, but it really is. Remember the excerpt you looked at earlier in the chapter when you were formatting table text? Well, this is the same excerpt, except that now it has links to the appropriate product page:

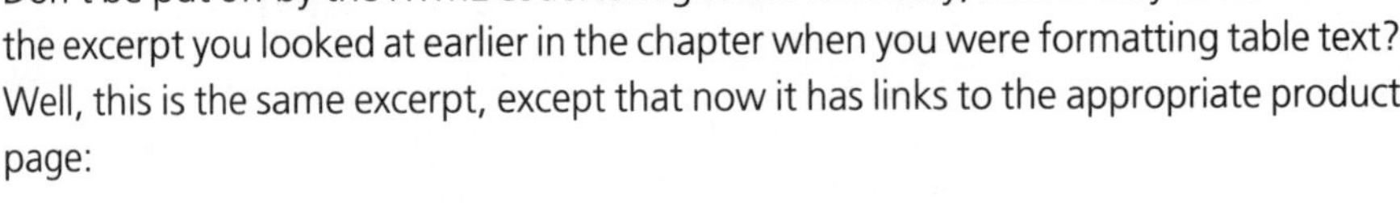

```
<FONT FACE="HELVETICA, ARIAL"><TR>
<TD WIDTH=75 HEIGHT=50> <B><A HREF="abba1.htm">14358</B> </TD>
<TD WIDTH=370 HEIGHT=50> <B><A HREF="abba1.htm">Abba,
You Can Dance, You Can Cry</A></B></TD>
<TD WIDTH=75 HEIGHT=50> <B><A HREF="abba1.htm"> $5.95 </TD></TR></FONT>
```

# Adding Table and Background Formatting

The product/price list catalog you have created so far is a usable catalog. If you want to make it more stylistic and attractive, apply properties to the <TABLE> tag that will format the table's appearance.

Refer to Chapter 2, "Developing a Plan for Design and Site Management," for tips on developing a color scheme for your pages and on using style sheets.

## Adding a Border

A border can add a nice three-dimensional effect to your product/price list. If you don't use the <TABLE> tag BORDER attribute to draw a border, the default will present the table without it.

The attribute lets you specify the size of the border in pixels. I suggest adding a value of 4. You can also specify within the <TABLE> tag a color for the border.

For the latest developments on the <TABLE> tag and other HTML elements, go to http://www.w3c.org, home of the official standards body for HTML.

If you compare Figure 6.6 and Figure 6.7, you'll see the radical change in appearance adding the simple BORDER=4 to the <TABLE> tag can make. As the following excerpt from the beginning of the HTML code that creates this page shows, none of the core HTML code for the catalog had to be altered to add this effect:

```
<TABLE BORDER=4><FONT FACE="HELVETICA, ARIAL"><B><TR><A HREF="abba1.htm">
<TD WIDTH=75 HEIGHT=50> 14358 </TD></A><A HREF="abba1.htm">
<TD WIDTH=370 HEIGHT=50> Abba, You Can Dance, You Can Cry</TD>
</A><A HREF="abba1.htm">
<TD WIDTH=75 HEIGHT=50> $5.95 </TD></A></TR></B>
<TABLE BORDER=4>

<FONT FACE="HELVETICA, ARIAL"><TR>
<TD WIDTH=75 HEIGHT=50> <B><A HREF="abba1.htm">14358</A></B> </TD>
<TD WIDTH=370 HEIGHT=50> <B><A HREF="abba1.htm">Abba, You Can Dance,
You Can Cry</A></B> </TD>
<TD WIDTH=75 HEIGHT=50> <B><A
HREF="abba1.htm">$5.95</A></B> </TD></TR></FONT>
```

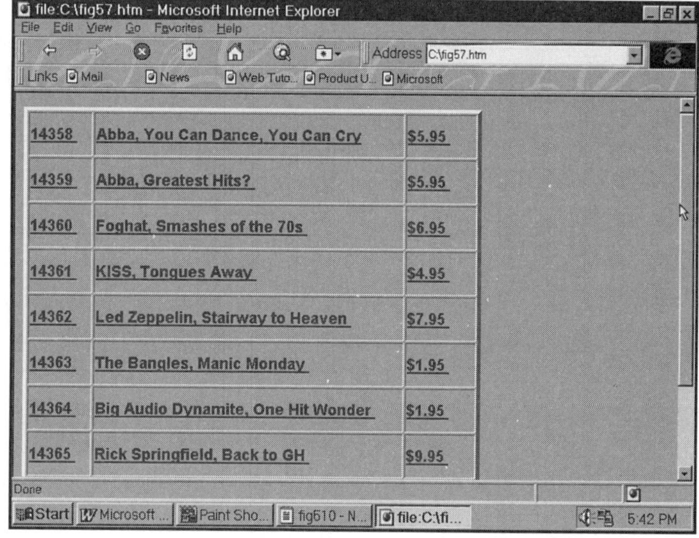


**Figure 6.7.**
*Adding table formatting can substantially alter the appearance of your page.*

When you create borders for your own catalog, experiment with sizes until you find what works best. Experimenting does not have to take a lot of time and won't create problems with the rest of your code.

## Adding to Background Colors

For the Old Dog example, set the table cell background colors to white by entering the color name "white" for the BGCOLOR attribute with each <TR> tag. You can see the results in Figure 6.8. The HTML code used in the figure is as follows:

```
<TABLE BORDER=4>
<FONT FACE="HELVETICA, ARIAL"><B><TR BGCOLOR="white">
<TD WIDTH=75 HEIGHT=50> <B><A HREF="abba1.htm">14358</A></B> </TD>
<TD WIDTH=370 HEIGHT=50> <B><A HREF="abba1.htm">Abba, You Can
Dance, You Can Cry</A></B> </TD>
TD WIDTH=75
HEIGHT=50> <B><A HREF="abba1.htm">$5.95 </A></B> </TD></TR></FONT>
```

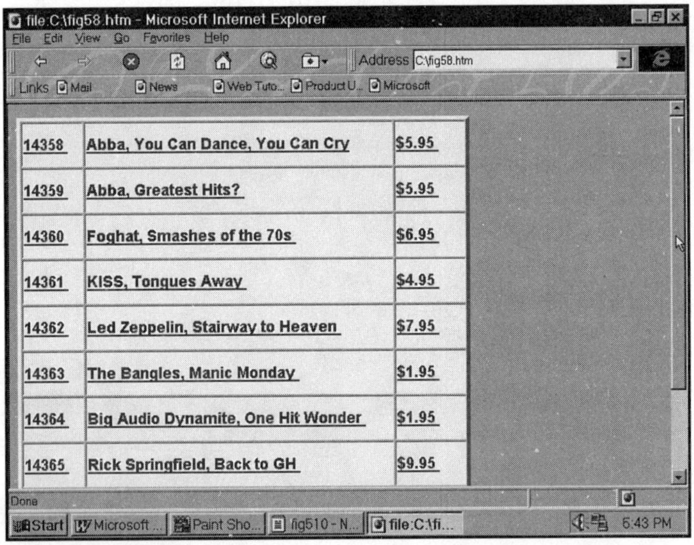

file:C:\fig58.htm - Microsoft Internet Explorer
File Edit View Go Favorites Help
Address C:\fig58.htm
Links Mail News Web Tuto... Product U... Microsoft
14358 Abba, You Can Dance, You Can Cry $5.95
14359 Abba, Greatest Hits? $5.95
14360 Foghat, Smashes of the 70s $6.95
14361 KISS, Tongues Away $4.95
14362 Led Zeppelin, Stairway to Heaven $7.95
14363 The Bangles, Manic Monday $1.95
14364 Big Audio Dynamite, One Hit Wonder $1.95
14365 Rick Springfield, Back to GH $9.95
Done
Start Microsoft ... Paint Sho... fig510 - N... file:C:\fi...
5:43 PM


**Figure 6.8.** *Using background colors for cells is yet another way to customize your catalog.*

Microsoft introduced the ability to add background colors for individual table cells with the second release of its Internet Explorer browser. In its latest browser, it expanded on the concept by enabling you to also specify a graphic image. Netscape has followed suit and provided support for these innovations, which now are in wide use on the Web. For the latest on what each browser supports, check out `http://www.microsoft.com/ie/` or `http://home.netscape.com`.

**CAUTION:** Set the BGCOLOR attribute for each row of the product/price list catalog. The attribute will not apply globally to all the cells in the table, only to cells in that row—and then only if individual cells don't have different colors specified with the <TD> tag.

## Adding Table Headings

Using the table heading tag <TH> enables you to insert rows that span the multiple columns using the COLSPAN attribute. Use the tag to add a table heading row at the top of your catalog, as a divider throughout sections of the price/product list, or both.

To refresh your memory on developing a color scheme for your Web pages, look again at Chapter 2.

If you want columns that act as table headings and span rows, use the **ROWSPAN** attribute.

To create the table headings for the Old Dog example, take these steps:

1. Insert a new row to divide each section according to the music type contained in that portion of the list.
2. Use a single `<TH>` tag and set the `COLSPAN` attribute to `3`.

**CAUTION:** Be careful about setting up your table headings too soon in your development. Later in this example, when you add columns to this table to accommodate additional information, you'll have to go back and increase the `COLSPAN` attribute in each table heading.

3. Set the font color apart from the rest of the table. Use a reverse color effect of white on black to accent the divisions within the list. Table headings are automatically centered for you in the header cell.

Figure 6.9 shows you Old Dog's list after the heading cells have been added. The HTML code for the figure and for the excerpt you've been working with should be the same.

```
<TABLE BORDER=4>
<FONT FACE="HELVETICA, ARIAL"><TR BGCOLOR="black"><TH COLSPAN="3">
<FONT COLOR="white"> Aussie Soft Rock </TH></TR>

<TR BGCOLOR="white">
<TD WIDTH=75 HEIGHT=50> <B><A HREF="abba1.htm">14358</A></B> </TD>
<TD WIDTH=370 HEIGHT=50> <B><A HREF="abba1.htm"><Abba, You Can Dance,
You Can Cry</A></B> </TD>
<TD WIDTH=75 HEIGHT=50> <B><A HREF="abba1.htm"><$5.95</A></B> </TR></FONT>
```

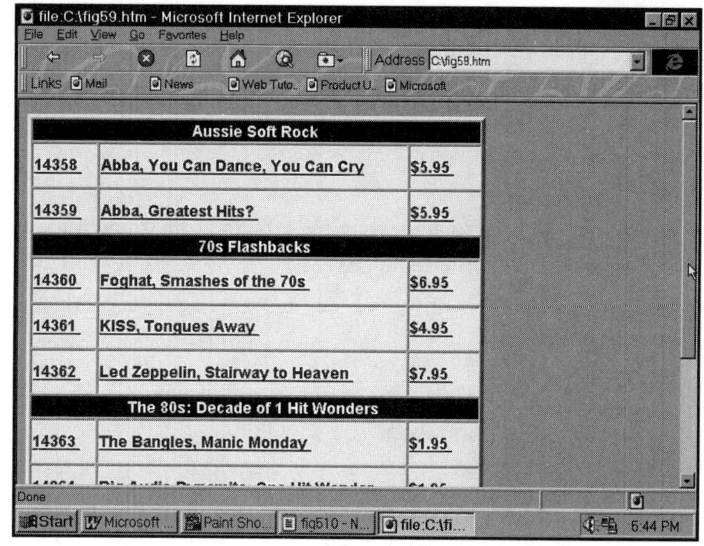


**Figure 6.9.**
*Table headings can help supply structure and organization.*

**TIP:** Keep your table headings apart from your other table code by inserting a blank line. Remember that blank lines (or spaces) in HTML code are not recognized by the browser and can be used to keep your code in a manageable form.

## Give the Text Some Space

Add a little space around the text within each cell so that the information doesn't appear to be touching the cell edges. The `<TABLE>` tag allows for a `CELLPADDING` attribute that lets you specify a number of blank pixels to insert between the text and the edges of the cell.

You can specify any number of pixels for your cell padding. If, for the Old Dog example, you use the common setting of `6` to avoid a cramped look, the `<TABLE>` tag portion of the code should look like this:

```
<TABLE BORDER=4 CELLPADDING=6>
```

# Adding Information in Nested Tables

One of the great design advantages of tables is that you can place a table within a table to achieve a more advanced and precise layout design. These tables within tables are known as *nested tables*.

Old Dog, for example, wants to add a column that specifies in which of the four formats—CDs, tapes, records, 8-tracks—each product is available. This can be achieved by creating a nested table of two rows and two columns. Because single-letter or single-digit abbreviations—C, T, R, 8—can be used, along with a small legend at the bottom, all the information fits into a relatively small cell.

**NOTE:** Remember that any HTML element, including another table, can be placed within a table cell.

Follow these steps to create the nested table in the example:

1. Create another row equal in size to the one containing the item number and price information. You should have a little bit of breathing room from the cushion you left when you created the original table.
2. Create a very basic two-by-two table, putting one of the abbreviations for each of the items available in a separate cell. Use this HTML code:

```
<TABLE>

<TR><TD> C </TD><TD> T </TD></TR>
<TR><TD> R </TD><TD> 8 </TD></TR>

</TABLE>
```

3. Drop the HTML code between the `<TD>` and `</TD>` tags of the new table cell you just created.

Figure 6.10 shows the finished product. The HTML code from the excerpt should look like this:

```
<TABLE BORDER=4 CELLPADDING=6>

<FONT FACE="HELVETICA, ARIAL"><TR BGCOLOR="black">
<TH COLSPAN=4><FONT COLOR="white"> ABBA </TH></TR>

<TR BGCOLOR="white">
<TD WIDTH=75 HEIGHT=50> <B><A HREF="abba1.htm">14358</A></B> </TD>
<TD WIDTH=370 HEIGHT=50> <B><A HREF="abba1.htm">Abba, You Can Dance,
You Can Cry</A></B> </TD>
<TD WIDTH=75 HEIGHT=50> <B><A HREF="abba1.htm">$5.95</A></B> </TD>
<TD WIDTH=75 HEIGHT=50>
<TABLE>
<TR><TD> C </TD><TD> T </TD></TR>
<TR><TD> R </TD><TD> 8 </TD></TR>
</TABLE>
</TD></TR></FONT>
```

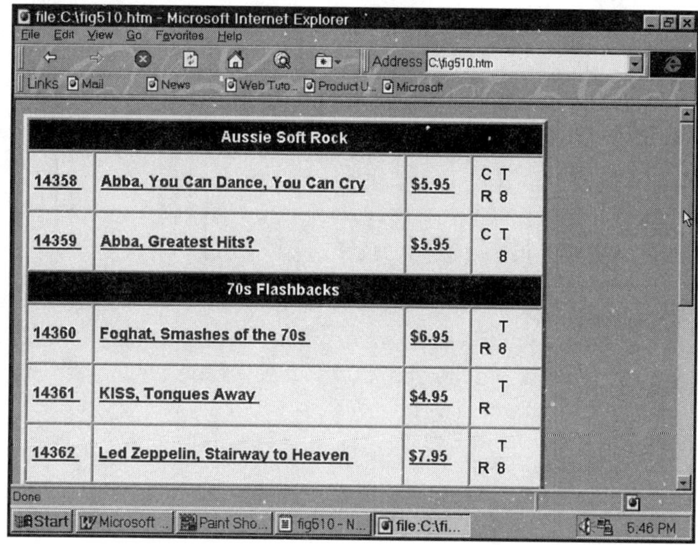


**Figure 6.10.**
*Using nested tables can increase the information provided in your catalog.*

Don't forget to change the **COLSPAN** attribute of your headers to **4** from **3**.

# Adding Product Images

To really stylize your pages, within the table cells add small product images that are hyperlinked to the individual product pages.

The Old Dog table already is pushing the maximum width of the screen, so any graphic images you use will have to be a replacement for something already in a cell. Assume that the most disposable item currently in the table is the product number information and replace it with a small graphic image of each album cover by dropping in the appropriate `<IMG SRC>` tag.

The HTML code would look like this:

```
<TR BGCOLOR="white">
<TD WIDTH=75
HEIGHT=50> <A HREF abba1.htm><IMG SRC="abbacov1.gif"></A> </TD>
<TD WIDTH=370 HEIGHT=50> <B><A HREF abba1.htm>Abba, You Can Dance,
You Can Cry</A></B> </TD>
<TD WIDTH=75 HEIGHT=50> <B><A HREF abba1.htm>$5.95</A></B> </TD>
<TD WIDTH=75 HEIGHT=50>
<TABLE>
<TR><TD> C </TD><TD> T </TD></TR>
<TR><TD> R </TD><TD> 8 </TD></TR>
</TABLE>
</TD></TR></FONT>
```

**CAUTION:** Make sure that the graphic you want to add is small enough to fit in the cell size you set in your table. You can always use Paint Shop Pro, included on the accompanying CD-ROM, to shrink an image down to the correct size.

# Workshop Wrap-Up

There's nothing mysterious or genius-level creative about developing an online catalog. As long as you remember that online and "normal" catalogs are not created equal and that the one you produce for the Web must have that "layered" look and feel for maximum effectiveness, you really can't go wrong.

Start with the easiest catalog layout and design, the product/price list. After reading this chapter, you know that the key to development and creation of this all-important Web catalog effort is the HTML table. Master that concept—which really isn't as difficult to do as some of your colleagues and competitors might want you to think—and you can create a product/price list interesting and innovative enough to draw customers, potential and otherwise, and generate sales. From there, going on to bigger, better, and even more innovative things is just a matter of seeing a need and finding the time to do so.

## Next Steps

The catalog style you produced in this chapter is very basic. Many of you will want to have a more comprehensive broader-based catalog. Now...

- ❑ To see some actual examples of completed catalogs, look at Chapter 7, "Real-Life Examples: Putting the Basics Together."
- ❑ To find out ways to gather information about your customers that will help you make decisions about what to include in your catalog, check out Chapter 8, "Gathering Information: Web-Based Surveys and Questionnaires."
- ❑ To get additional information about developing more advanced catalogs, turn to Chapter 13, "Advanced Catalogs."

## Q&A

**Q: This product/price list catalog looks pretty useful for some businesses, but mine is a service-based consulting business. What should I do?**

**A:** You can use the same basic table format, but instead of linking to specific products, link to specific employees with a specialty in a particular area you service. You could easily use the employee directory you created in Chapter 5, "Employee Directories and Biographies," as a valuable resource for a service industry catalog.

**Q: I've read a lot lately about being able to deliver customized versions of online catalogs to customers. Can this be done today?**

**A:** Yes. Using something known as cookies, you can set up different catalog types that will be available to Web users depending on their previous selections from your pages. This topic is covered in greater detail in Chapter 13, "Advanced Catalogs."

SEVEN

# Real-Life Examples: Putting the Basics Together

Examples in this chapter:

- Example 1: Arachnid WorldWide
- Example 2: Autometric, Inc.
- Example 3: ProMetrics, Inc.
- Example 4: Computer Parts & Pieces

The best way to learn about creating great commercial Web pages is by getting on the Net and seeing what other people are doing. It's often much easier to learn by example rather than instruction. The intent of this chapter (and the other Real-Life chapters) is to supplement the instruction with actual Web pages that use at least some of the techniques you've learned.

For more real-life examples, check out Chapter 12, "Real-Life Examples: Advancing Your Site," Chapter 19, "Real-Life Examples: Doing Business on the Web," and Chapter 22, "Real-Life Examples: Touting and Managing Your Site."

In this chapter, you'll see Web pages that are included on the accompanying CD-ROM (and available online) that utilize techniques you read about in Part II, "Basic Business Pages—Web Site Building Blocks" (Chapters 3 through 7). All the HTML code and necessary files are on the CD-ROM. For each sample page, you'll see what basic techniques were used and, if appropriate, what techniques could be used to make the page even better.

# Example 1: Arachnid WorldWide

**Document title:** Arachnid WorldWide (Figures 7.1, 7.2, 7.3, and 7.4)

**Document URL:** `http://homepage.interaccess.com/~arachnid`

## Basic Welcome Page and Menu Bar

**Files:** `index.html`, `imgmap1.gif`, `rpt1ico.gif`, `nw1ico.gif`, `tek1ico.gif`, `loop1ico.gif`, `tau1ico.gif`, `peop1ico.gif`, `img1ico.gif`, `hbar2.gif`.

**Description:** A basic company welcome page that implements a site-wide menu bar and directs users to various areas of the company's Web site. Arachnid WorldWide is a computer software company. The page's look, colors, and style are maintained throughout all the pages on Arachnid's site.

### Basic Welcome Page

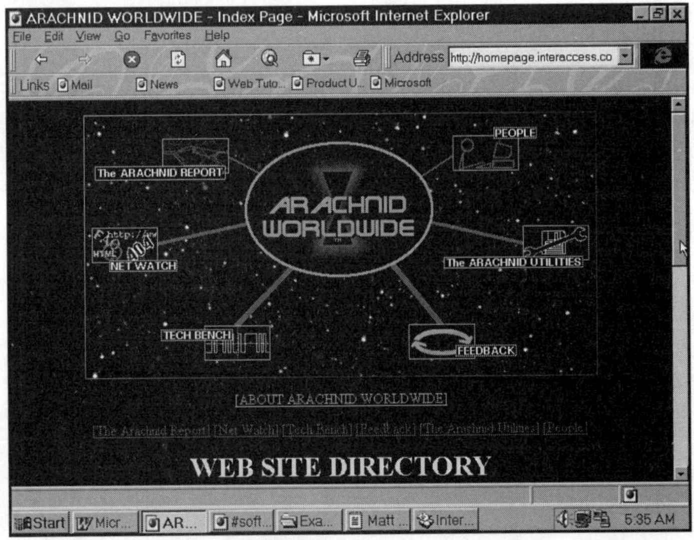


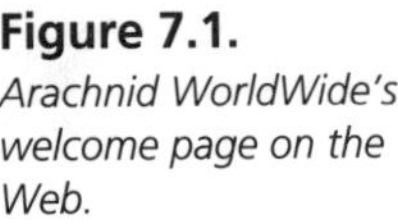

**Figure 7.1.**
*Arachnid WorldWide's welcome page on the Web.*

**Techniques and designs applied:**

**Theme and color scheme**. The page implements the company's Web site theme, emphasizing technology, computers, and the Internet. A color scheme is used to specify background and link colors to supplement this theme. (See Chapter 2, "Developing a Plan for Design and Site Management.")

**Small, progressive graphic images**. The page uses graphic images that have reduced color resolution. It also uses progressive rendering formats for faster loading. (See Chapter 3, "Corporate Presence Pages.")

**Basic welcome page design**. The page provides quick links to the most important pages on Arachnid's site as well as an easy link for contacting the creators. (See Chapter 3.)

## The Menu Bar

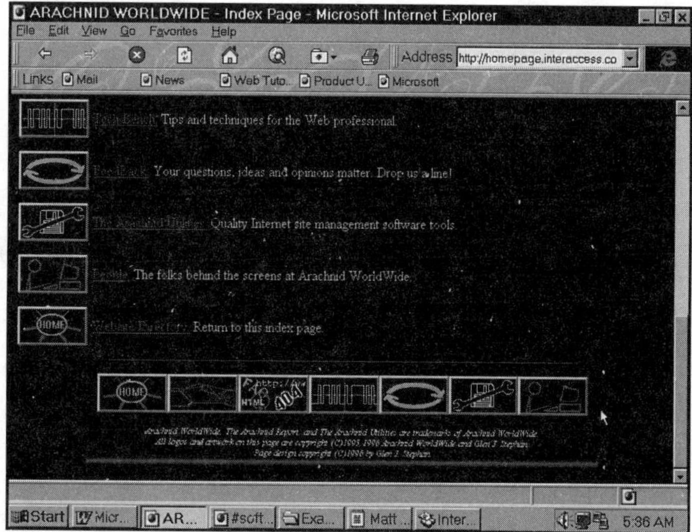


**Figure 7.2.**
*The Arachnid WorldWide menu bar is at the bottom of each page on the site.*

**Design applied:**

**Menu bar**. The page uses a menu bar that links to the most important pages throughout Arachnid's Web. The menu bar is implemented on every page of the Arachnid site as a constant navigational tool for users. (See Chapter 3.)

## Constructive Criticism

The menu bar's graphics are not necessarily intuitive and could benefit from either text within the images or just below them. Also, there is no "What's New" link to provide frequent visitors with the latest changes or developments to the site.

## Reference and Original Content Pages

**Files:** `nw1.html`, `head2nw.gif`, `adtag1.gif`, `rpt1ico.gif`, `nw1ico.gif`, `tek1ico.gif`, `loop1ico.gif`, `tau1ico.gif`, `peop1ico.gif`, `img1ico.gif`, `hbar2.gif`.

**Description:** The Arachnid Web site contains both a reference page and some original content pages. The focus of these pages is computer and Internet technology, attempting to draw Arachnid's natural customer base—computer users.

### Reference Links Page

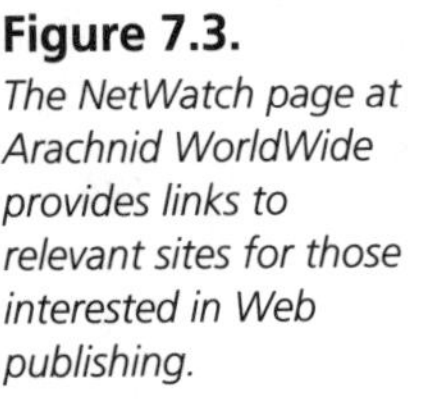

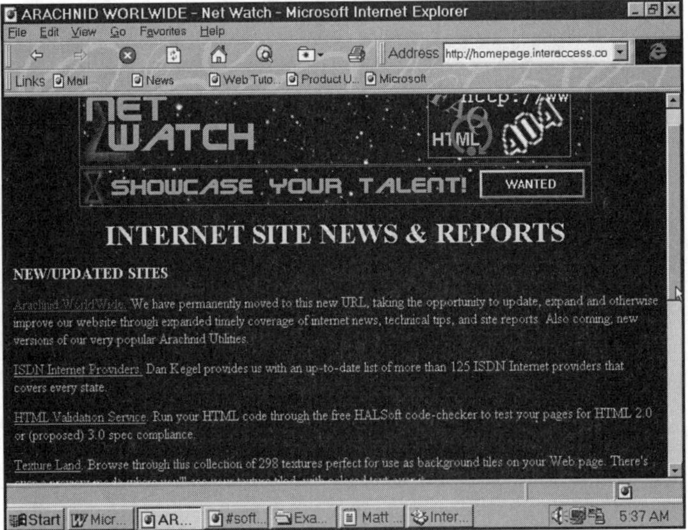


**Figure 7.3.**
*The NetWatch page at Arachnid WorldWide provides links to relevant sites for those interested in Web publishing.*

**Design applied:**

> **Reference page from links**. The page provides a set of reference links to other Web pages dealing with technologies or information that would be of use to burgeoning Web developers like yourself. (See Chapter 4, "Creating News, Reference, and Content Pages.")

## Original Content Page

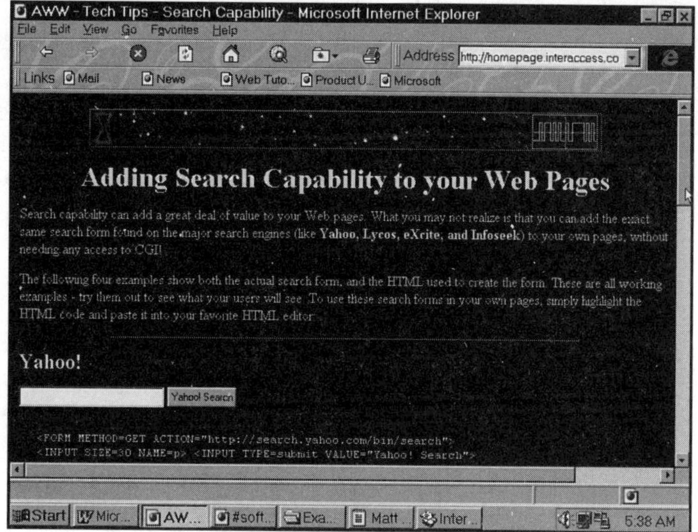


**Figure 7.4.**
*An original content page at Arachnid shows users how to add a little Yahoo! to their life (and pages).*

**Files:** `addsrch1.html`, `head1tek.gif`, `adtag1.gif`, `rpt1ico.gif`, `nw1ico.gif`, `tek1ico.gif`, `loop1ico.gif`, `tau1ico.gif`, `peop1ico.gif`, `img1ico.gif`, `hbar2.gif`

**Design applied:**

> **Making an original content page**. This is just one of several original content pages available on Arachnid's site. This page provides easy step-by-step instructions along with pre-made HTML code for adding powerful search engines such as Yahoo! or InfoSeek to any user's Web page. This is a useful service aimed directly at Arachnid's most likely visitors and customers. (See Chapter 4.)

## Constructive Criticism

Arachnid's reference links could stand to be a little more extensive and more frequently updated to be more valuable to visitors. The original content page, showing how to add search engines to Web pages, could provide even more search engines to choose from (although it covers all the biggies).

# Example 2: Autometric, Inc.

**Document title:** Autometric's Press Release Archive (Figures 7.5 and 7.6)

**Document URL:** `http://www.autometric.com/AUTO/html/press_archive.html`

## Press Release Archive

**Files:** `press_archive.html`, `press_archive_banner.gif`, `home_page_button.gif`, `toc_button.gif`, `search_button.gif`.

**Description:** Autometric's press release archive is a single Web page that acts as the repository for all of the company's press releases, going more than a year into the past. As its Web page says, Autometric "is a leading supplier of commercial off-the-shelf software for high performance, dynamic graphic 3D simulation, modeling and visualization for the commercial, government, and military markets."

**Techniques and designs applied:**

**The top of the archive page**. (See Figure 7.5.)

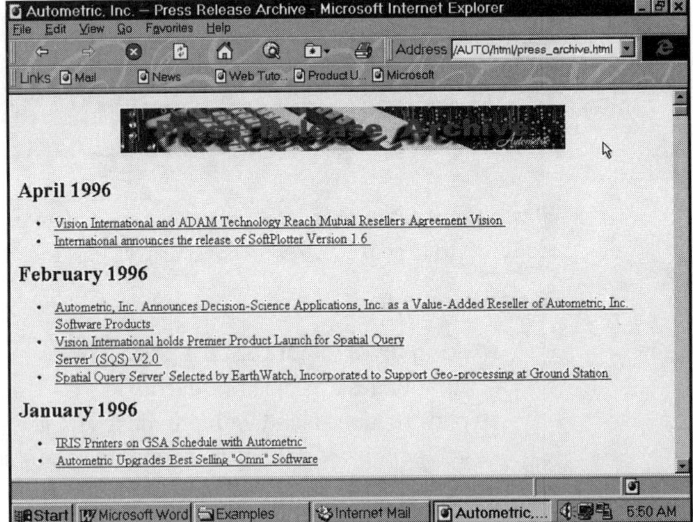


**Figure 7.5.**
*The top of Autometric's Press Release Archive.*

**Lots of information in a little link**. The Autometric press release archive contains release titles that pack a punch and identify immediately what the release is all about. (See Chapter 4.)

**An orderly listing**. Autometric lays out its release in reverse chronological order with the newest release right at the top of the page. Month and year dividers quickly put each release in its proper time frame for users. (See Chapter 4.)

**The Web press releases**. (See Figure 7.6.)

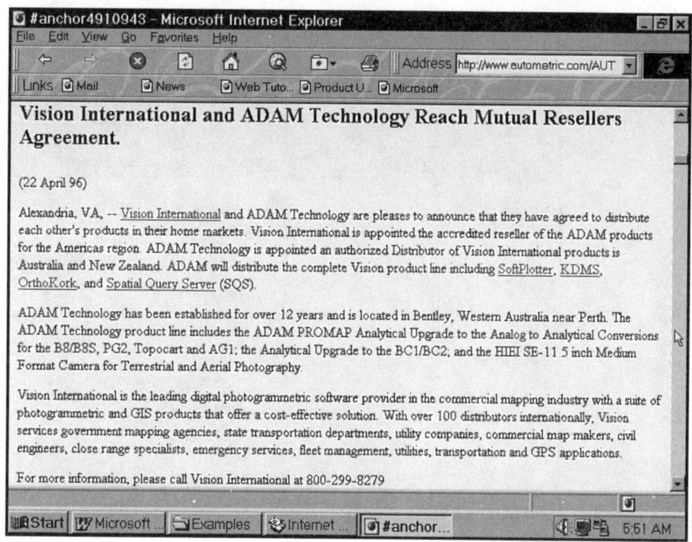

**Vision International and ADAM Technology Reach Mutual Resellers Agreement.**

(22 April 96)

Alexandria, VA, -- Vision International and ADAM Technology are pleases to announce that they have agreed to distribute each other's products in their home markets. Vision International is appointed the accredited reseller of the ADAM products for the Americas region. ADAM Technology is appointed an authorized Distributor of Vision International products is Australia and New Zealand. ADAM will distribute the complete Vision product line including SoftPlotter, KDMS, OrthoKork, and Spatial Query Server (SQS).

ADAM Technology has been established for over 12 years and is located in Bentley, Western Australia near Perth. The ADAM Technology product line includes the ADAM PROMAP Analytical Upgrade to the Analog to Analytical Conversions for the B8/B8S, PG2, Topocart and AG1; the Analytical Upgrade to the BC1/BC2; and the HIEI SE-11 5 inch Medium Format Camera for Terrestrial and Aerial Photography.

Vision International is the leading digital photogrammetric software provider in the commercial mapping industry with a suite of photogrammetric and GIS products that offer a cost-effective solution. With over 100 distributors internationally, Vision services government mapping agencies, state transportation departments, utility companies, commercial map makers, civil engineers, close range specialists, emergency services, fleet management, utilities, transportation and GPS applications.

For more information, please call Vision International at 800-299-8279

**Figure 7.6.** *A Web-based press release from Autometric.*

**Making the links live**. Selecting a release heading takes you to the press release further down the archive page. (See Chapter 4.)

**Creating the Web press release**. Autometric's press release contains hyperlinks to other companies and contact personnel at Autometric regarding the particular release. (See Chapter 4.)

## Constructive Criticism

Autometric's press release archive is large enough that it would merit establishing a basic archive page with subpages for each release instead of the all-in-one approach currently used. Fortunately, the document uses very few graphics, so download speed is not outrageous. The archive would also benefit from the addition of some navigational tools to move between releases.

# Example 3: ProMetrics, Inc.

**Document title:** ProMetrics - Employee Directory (Figures 7.7, 7.8, and 7.9)

**Document URL:** `http://www.prometrics.com/EMPLOYEE/EEDIR.html`

# Employee Directory Index and Default Page

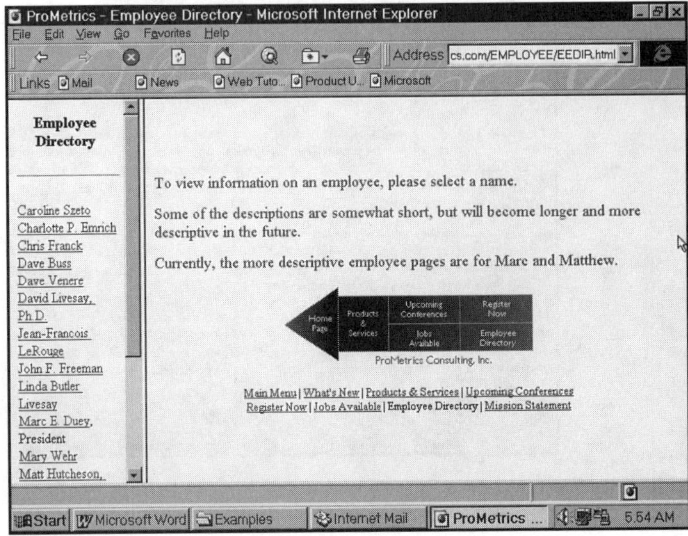


**Figure 7.7.**
*ProMetrics's main employee directory page, utilizing frames.*

**Files:** `EEDIR.html`, `EEDIRL.html`, `EEDIRR.html`, `DIRECT.GIF`

**Description:** ProMetrics's employee directory implements a dual-frame layout with an employee index in the left-hand frame and a default page with instructions and a site map in the right-hand frame. ProMetrics is a relatively small company that is involved in consulting in the health care industry.

**Techniques and designs applied:**

**Employee directory frameset**. The page uses a simple frameset layout. (See Chapter 5, "Employee Directories and Biographies.")

**Employee listing index**. The frame on the left contains the employee index with each name hyperlinked to the employee's directory page. (See Chapter 5.)

**Targeted links**. The employee's links contain frame target references so that the directory pages will open in the right-hand frame, replacing the default page. (See Chapter 5.)

**Employee directory frame holder**. The frame on the right contains the default page that holds the place for the employee pages and gives instructions on how to use ProMetrics's directory. (See Chapter 5.)

## Constructive Criticism

The employee index could be placed in alphabetical order and provide subdivisions by letter. Also, the default page could use a little zip by adding the company's logo and a quick `mailto:` link to the site's Webmaster.

## Basic Employee Page

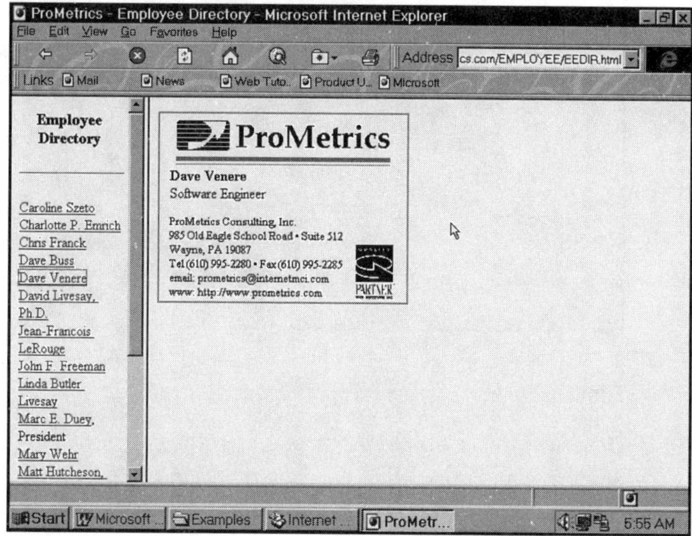


**Figure 7.8.**
*A basic employee page from the ProMetrics directory.*

**Files:** `Davev.html`, `PROGRAY.GIF`, `sasbig.gif`

**Description:** A basic employee page that is contained within the ProMetrics employee directory.

**Techniques and designs applied:**

> **Contact information**. The page contains all of the information necessary to contact the employee, including company address, phone, fax, and e-mail. (See Chapter 5.)
>
> **Organization and department information**. The page acts as a virtual business card and provides the employee's job title within the company. (See Chapter 5.)

## Constructive Criticism

The employee pages lack hyperlinks that could be useful for users to send e-mail to employees and to get back to the main default directory page or to other pages on the ProMetrics site.

## A Creative Employee Page

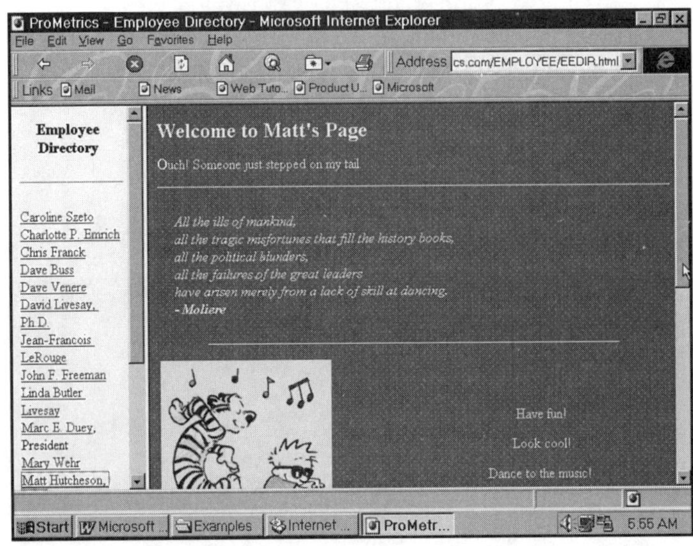


**Figure 7.9.**
*The work of a ProMetrics's employee who decided to use a little creativity in crafting his own directory page.*

**Files:** `Matt.html`, `bluedot.gif`, `candh.gif`, `mail.gif`

**Description:** An employee page within the directory. This page was created by the employee and is linked to his directory listing.

**Techniques and designs applied:**

> **Contact information**. The page contains a hyperlink directly to the employee's e-mail address. (See Chapter 5.)
>
> **Some fun stuff**. The employee's page contains a variety of elements, including the employee's favorite poem as well as links to his business card, diploma, and resume. The page also has a style unique to the employee. (See Chapter 5.)

### Constructive Criticism

The page could have more links to other places on the ProMetrics site and back to the default employee directory page.

# Example 4: Computer Parts & Pieces

**Document title:** Computer Parts & Pieces Current Price List Catalog (Figures 7.10, 7.11, and 7.12)

**Document URL:** `http://www.parts-n-pcs.com/cppprice.htm`

# Main Catalog Index Page

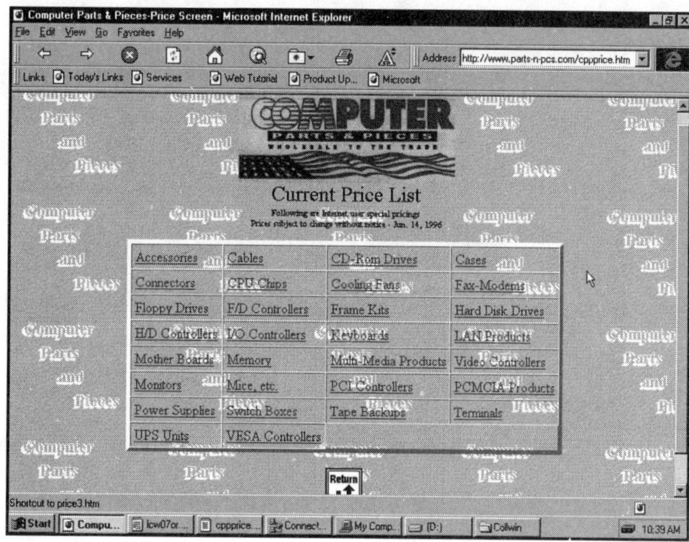


**Figure 7.10.**
*The main catalog index page.*

**Files:** `cppprice.htm`, `cppback.gif`, `cpp1st.jpg`, `return.gif`

**Description:** The page main catalog index page lists in a table a variety of product/price list pages for various computer product categories.

**Techniques and designs applied:**

> **Creating "layers" of pages for a Web catalog**. The catalog is broken down into a variety of subpages (or *layers*) containing price/product lists for each category. The main page simply provides an organized set of links to the lower, more specific, layers of the catalog. (See Chapter 6, "Online Catalogs and More: Presenting Your Products and Services.")
>
> **Setting the table**. The main catalog index uses a table for better layout and organization. (See Chapter 6.)

# Product/Price List Page

**Files:** `price3.htm`, `return.gif`

**Description:** The CD-ROM price/product list page of Computer Parts & Pieces maintains the same style and layout present on all the individual price list pages in the catalog.

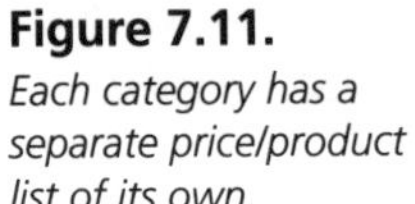

**Figure 7.11.**
*Each category has a separate price/product list of its own.*

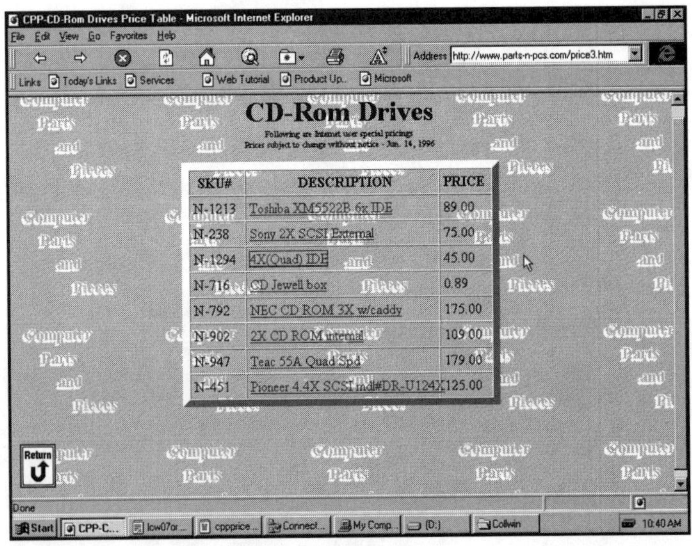


**Techniques and designs applied:**

**Prices and product numbers**. The list contains the important information necessary for shopping—the item name, product number, and (most important) the price. (See Chapter 6.)

**Links to product pages**. Each product name is linked to an individual page with more detailed information regarding each product in the catalog. (See Chapter 6.)

**Navigational tools**. The page contains a navigational return button to take the user back to the main catalog index page to continue shopping. (See Chapter 6.)

# Individual Product Page

**Files:** `N-1294.htm`, `return.gif`

**Description:** Each product in the Computer Parts & Pieces catalog has a separate page with more detailed information regarding the product, such as what is included with the purchase. This product page is linked to the product/price list page.

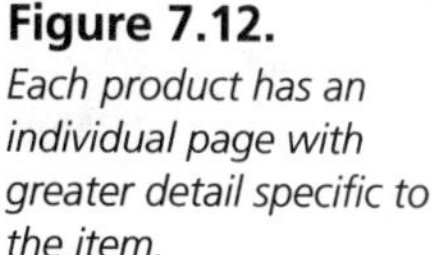

**Figure 7.12.**
*Each product has an individual page with greater detail specific to the item.*

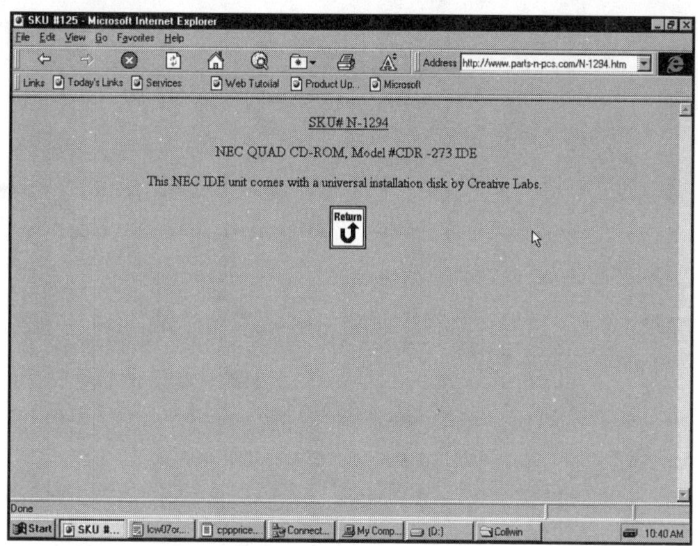


**Techniques and designs applied:**

**Product information**. The page contains some more detailed information about the product in the catalog, specifying the model number and SKU number to help the user order the product. It also specifies what software is included with the product. (See Chapter 6.)

**Navigational tools**. The page contains a navigational return button to take you back one step to the price/product list from which you selected this item. (See Chapter 6.)

## Constructive Criticism

Computer Parts & Pieces uses a background image on the main catalog and price/product list pages that make some of the items a little more difficult to read. The tables on the product/price list could benefit from some additional formatting, such as increased cell padding and background colors. Also, the product pages could be improved with some additional product information and perhaps a graphic of each product.

# Workshop Wrap-Up

Now that you've seen how other people are using some of the commercial Web page basics, you can begin using their examples as a jumping off point for creating your own pages. Also, you should spend as much time as possible looking at your competitor's pages and companies in similar businesses to get a flavor for what is already out there and to identify what might be lacking in those pages. You can then seize the opportunity to provide a high quality page that fills a void or niche in the Web marketplace.

## Next Steps

Now...

- In the next section, you'll see how to use more advanced design and coding elements to create your commercial Web pages. Chapter 8, "Gathering Information: Web-Based Surveys and Questionnaires," starts out by showing you how to use HTML forms to gather customer information and feedback.
- If you want to see more real-life examples, turn to Chapters 13, "Advanced Catalogs," 19, "Real-Life Examples: Doing Business on the Web," and 22, "Real-Life Examples: Touting and Managing Your Site." These chapters contain more real-world examples for their sections of the book.

## Q&A

**Q: Some of the links on the real-life sample pages on the CD-ROM don't seem to work. What's wrong?**

**A:** The sample pages included are only those pages of the company's site that directly relate to what you've read about in the previous chapters. We have not re-created on the CD-ROM the entire Web site of each company, so some links might not be operational locally. However, you can always use the URL provided, or get to the pages through links at `http://www.murphnet.com`, to see the entire site in a fully functional form.

PART

# III Taking Your Pages (and Your Business) Beyond the Basics


**Chapter 8** Gathering Information: Web-Based Surveys and Questionnaires

**9** Customer Support Pages: Boards and Beyond

**10** Advanced Information Pages: Tying Data to the Web

**11** Searching Your Site

**12** Real-Life Examples: Advancing Your Site

C H A P T E R

EIGHT

# Gathering Information: Web-Based Surveys and Questionnaires

The Web can be a powerful tool for collecting information that will help you better understand and serve your customers. If it were nothing more than a glorified brochure, you'd have a hard time finding out exactly what people did or did not like about your pages or your products. (After all, how many times have you filled out one of those customer comment cards at Denny's?) But that's not the case. The Web fosters and encourages interaction between users and your Web pages and, ultimately, with you.

## In this chapter, you

- ❑ Determine the approach to take to implement forms
- ❑ Create separate pages for forms
- ❑ Learn basic design tips for forms
- ❑ Learn the value of Web surveys
- ❑ Format and manage forms results

## Tasks in this chapter:

- ❑ Setting Up a Separate Page for Each Form
- ❑ Getting the Information You Need Using Forms
- ❑ Designing the Form
- ❑ Formatting and Managing Form Results

One of the most popular ways to accomplish this interaction is by using HTML forms. This chapter gives you the design tips and know-how to create useful and usable HTML forms. It also introduces you to various methods available for handling the information submitted on your forms. Equally important, you'll have a chance to get acquainted with free software included on the accompanying CD-ROM that can help you create a database of form responses and print reports.

# About HTML Forms

Properly used, HTML forms can deliver targeted, useful information to your desktop directly from your Web pages. Creatively used, they can get you more information about your customers and the future of your business than three high-priced consultants and a copy of the 1990 census on CD-ROM combined.

In essence, forms are a deceptively simple way in which users can find out more about your products or services, and you can learn more about your customers. Users can send you feedback and take part in online interactive surveys and contests that will keep them—and the friends to whom they recommend your site —coming back to your pages again and again.

**TIP:** If you need a primer or refresher course on the HTML basics relating to forms, browse Laura Lemay's *Teach Yourself Web Publishing with HTML*, included on the accompanying CD-ROM or, in this book, check out Appendix B, "HTML 3.2 Reference."

# Selecting an Approach To Implement Your Forms

Most commercial Web sites contain a form similar to the one in Figure 8.1. Customers use the form to submit such basic information as their name, address, and e-mail address. Or, as in the case of the form in the figure, to state preferences and capabilities. Forms like these are one way a business has of getting names to put on a mailing list for its products, services, or special offers. This kind of form serves as a good first step in implementing the use of interactive HTML forms on your pages.

Originally, if you wanted to implement this or any other HTML form on your Web pages, you had to use a CGI script customized for the form coded on your page and adapted for use on your particular server platform. That no longer is the case. Now you can choose between two approaches: `mailto:` or CGI scripting. In many cases, the main difference between using one as opposed to the other is simply the difference in what you type in the `ACTION=""` parameter.

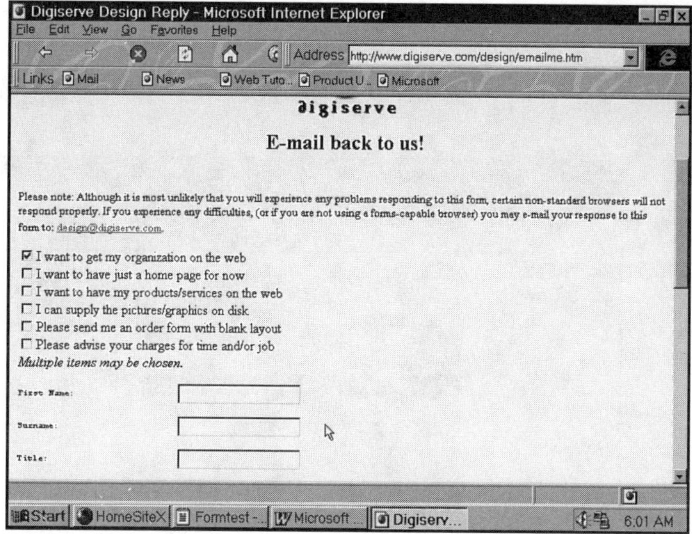


**Figure 8.1.**
*Forms are an excellent method for getting feedback from and data about customers.*

## Using `Mailto:`

The `mailto:` action is used as the default form process in the examples for this chapter.

The `mailto:` function is supported by browsers as an action within the `<FORM>` tag created at the beginning of any form. However, you need to remember that `mailto:`

- Requires the use of an external program to format e-mail messages when they are received because the browser sends the results in URL-encoded format, rendering the data if not unreadable, unusable
- Invokes no server process—it's entirely client-side
- Might offer no confirmation on the user's end that a form is submitted, so include a small JavaScript function (the code for which appears following), which is called up after a user presses Submit. It pulls the name submitted on the form and enters it into a dialog box, thanking and notifying the user that the information has been received. Figure 8.2 shows you a typical dialog box.

Make sure that in your HTML form code you include the `<SCRIPT>` tag and `onClick="test Results(this.form)"` with the Submit button.

```
<HTML>
<HEAD>
<TITLE>Introduction to Javascript </TITLE>
<SCRIPT LANGUAGE="JavaScript">
function testResults (form) {
var TestVar = form.name.value;
alert ("Thanks for the info" + TestVar + ", please continue surfing."); }
</SCRIPT>
</HEAD>
</BODY>
<FORM NAME="myform" ACTION="" METHOD="GET">Enter
something in the box: <BR>
<INPUT TYPE="text" NAME="name" VALUE=""><P>
```

```
<INPUT TYPE="submit" NAME="submit" Value="Submit"
onClick="testResults(this.form)">
</FORM>
</BODY>
</HTML>
```

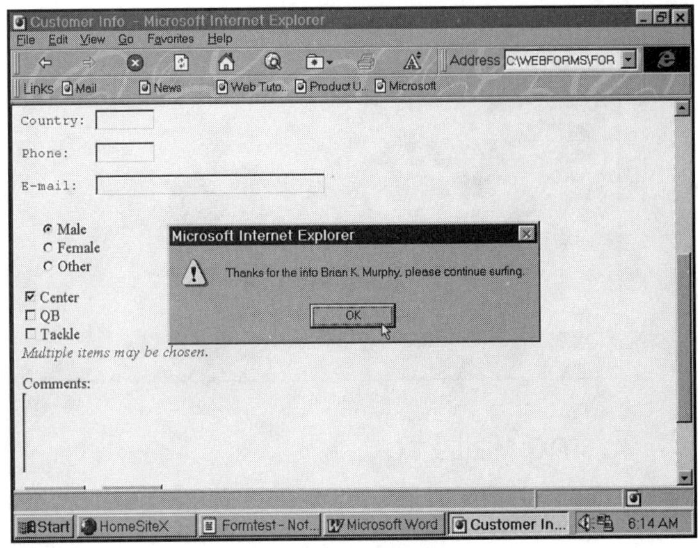


**Figure 8.2.**
*The JavaScript pulls up a dialog box informing the user that his or her form has been submitted.*

## Using CGI Scripting

On the accompanying CD-ROM are two excellent freeware programs that enable you to take e-mail received via the `mailto:` action, format it, and use it in a simple but powerful and useful database of results.

CGI scripts will, in essence, accomplish the same goals as `mailto:`. Additionally, most CGI scripts provide a variable where you can set a particular URL to be automatically loaded when a form is successfully submitted.

Keep in mind, however, that using CGI scripts can involve the following:

- Complicated setup
- Additional server costs
- Additional load on the server

# Setting Up a Separate Page for Each Form

Virtually every forms-capable browser today can take the data from the form and forward it to you via e-mail.

Although any form you use on your Web site should fit in with your other pages and overall site, each form should have its own separate page. Web users are a paranoid bunch when it comes to personal privacy—and rightly so if you've ever taken a look at your credit report. It stands to reason, then, that you will have more success if you try to solicit the information you need or want in a noninvasive way that appears—and is—separate from your other pages.

Figure 8.3 shows an example of a form on its own separate page. The benefits to structuring your Web site so that you have a separate page like this one include the following:

- Users can initiate the form process.
- You can individually format each form using standard page elements or cascading style sheets.
- Users can access different forms easily from different or multiple pages on your site.
- You can change form layout and formatting quickly without altering the design of other pages.

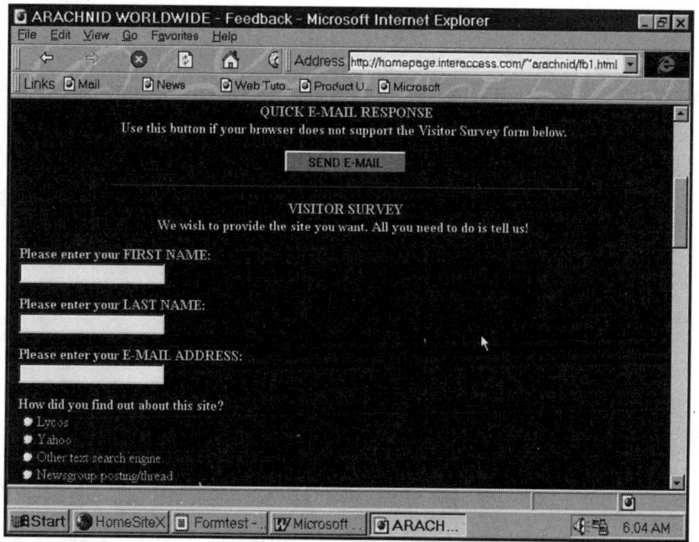


**Figure 8.3.**
*Setting up a separate page for each form makes forms less intrusive and more manageable.*

Refer to the "About Style Sheets" section in Chapter 2, "Developing a Plan for Design and Site Management," for additional information on cascading style sheets.

**TIP:** Not all users who visit your site will fill out your forms. It would probably be a help to know how many didn't and why. Creating a separate Web page for each form will help you get that feedback. By looking at the number of hits your server takes on a particular form page and comparing that with the number of filled-in responses you receive, you can analyze whether the form is really performing as planned. If you fall below a 50 percent ratio, consider making fundamental changes to your form layout and design.

When creating a form page, you need to keep in mind certain points. These points are incorporated into the following steps:

See Chapter 2, "Developing a Plan for Design and Site Management," and Chapter 3, "Corporate Presence Pages," for additional tips on developing standard elements for your Web pages.

- Include all the standard elements that you put on your other pages, such as a menu bar.
- Use color and style elements that are consistent with your other pages.
- Keep it simple—one question about how to use the form is one too many.
- Enter the title of the form in the <TITLE> tag.
- Place a link that will draw in users, using phrases like the one used in Figure 8.4—"Your questions, ideas, and opinions matter. Drop us a line!" If you don't like that one, create one of your own or use one of these: "Help Us Help You," "Give Us A Piece Of Your Mind," "Who Are You?," or "Don't Click Here."

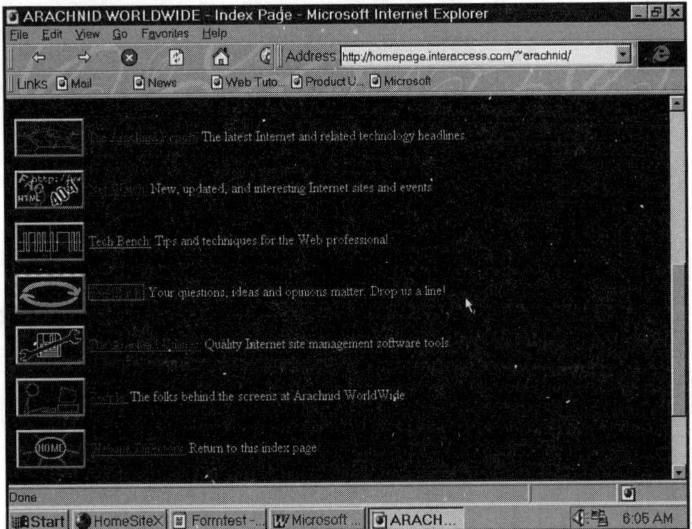


**Figure 8.4.**
*Your form links should give users a specific reason to click.*

**NOTE:** A good tactic to employ to get users to fill out a form is to insert some humor. Be creative, and make the links to the form humorous. You're asking Joe and Jennie Surfer to take at least a few minutes out of their precious surfing time to go through the somewhat tedious task of filling out a form, so you'll need a link that will catch their eye or make them smile. The old saying, "A little humor goes a long way," still rings true even in the '90s.

**TIP:** Use a graphic image file as a link to your form. It's a great way to generate traffic to your form's pages.

# Getting the Information You Need Using Forms

Up-front planning will save you time during the actual HTML coding process. It also will improve the overall look and effectiveness of your Web-based customer information forms. As the steps that follow indicate, planning is integral to creating any kind of form:

1. Decide exactly what questions you're going to ask so that you get as much useful information as possible without annoying or harassing Web visitors willing to fill out the form.
2. Be sure to ask for name, e-mail address, areas of interest, and comments or feedback. Request addresses only if you are going to have a mailing that a user needs or wants to receive.

   For the Old Dog example in Figure 8.5, use the following excerpt of the HTML code to "title" the page and put in some of the elements.

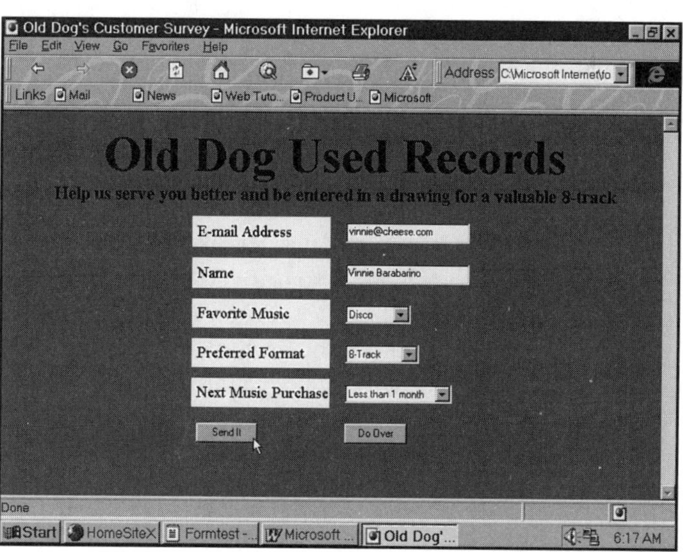


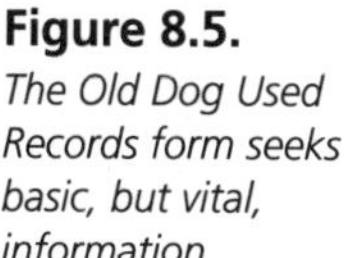

**Figure 8.5.**
*The Old Dog Used Records form seeks basic, but vital, information.*

The entire HTML code used to create the Old Dog Used Records form is available on the accompanying CD-ROM.

```
<HTML>
<HEAD><TITLE>Old Dog's Customer Survey</TITLE>
<SCRIPT LANGUAGE="JavaScript">
function testResults (form)
{
var TestVar = form.name.value;
alert ("Thanks for the info " + TestVar + ",
please continue surfing."); alert}

</SCRIPT>
</HEAD>
<BODY BGCOLOR="#008080">

<center><FONT SIZE=+5><B>Old Dog Used Records</FONT><br>
<FONT SIZE=+1>Help us serve you better and be entered
in a drawing for a valuable 8-track</FONT></B><br>

<FORM ACTION="mailto:bowwow@olddog.com" METHOD="POST">
<TABLE CELLPADDING=6 CELLSPACING=12 WIDTH=0 BORDER=0>
<TR>
<TD BGCOLOR="white"> E-mail Address
</TD>
<TD><INPUT TYPE="TEXT" NAME="e-mail" VALUE="" SIZE=25 MAXLENGTH=0></TD>
</TR>
```

3. Do not include telephone numbers, race, or religion.
4. Offer discounts or coupons to users who fill out your forms.
5. Explain yourself with a simple statement, such as "Help us develop products you want." Telling users why you want the information gives them a better sense of purpose.
6. Always follow up with a nonform thank-you for each customer who submits a form. After all, if a customer can take two minutes to help you, you can take two minutes to thank him or her.

**CAUTION:** You have to walk a fine line when you create your forms. Get as much information as possible without crossing that line. Time is an important commodity, so make sure that it takes no longer than two minutes to completely fill out and submit a basic customer information form. Before you put your form on the Web, try it yourself. If it takes longer than two minutes to fill out, start cutting out questions.

Think about and conceptualize the data you want in terms of form elements you can use. They will help you develop questions that fit into a format users can answer most easily. After all, everyone prefers a multiple choice test to an essay exam.

7. Determine which form elements to use; think of the best and easiest way to enable your users to send you information about themselves. As you can see, you can select from a variety of elements (and HTML tags like the ones in parentheses below):
   - Text (TEXT)—Use for items that take up a single line; for example, names and e-mail addresses.

- Drop-down menus (SELECT)—Use for presenting multiple choices that call for the selection of only one option, such as user's favorite type of music. The following excerpt of HTML code generates one of the drop-down menus in Figure 8.5:

```
<TR
<TD BGCOLOR="white"> Name </TD>
<TD> <INPUT TYPE="TEXT" NAME="Name" VALUE="" SIZE=25 MAXLENGTH=0></
TD>
</TR>

<TR>
<TD BGCOLOR="white"> Favorite Music </TD>
<TD> <SELECT NAME="Music">
<OPTION>Pop
<OPTION>Rock
<OPTION>Disco
<OPTION>Classical
<OPTION>Country
<OPTION>Western
</SELECT>
</TD>
</TR>
<TR>

<TD BGCOLOR="white"> Preferred Format </TD>
<TD> <SELECT NAME="format">
<OPTION>CD
<OPTION>8-Track
<OPTION>Tape
<OPTION>LP
<OPTION>Reel-to-Reel
</SELECT>
</TD>
</TR>

<TR>
<TD BGCOLOR="white"> Next Music Purchase</TD>
<TD> <SELECT NAME="purchase">
<OPTION>Less than 1 month
<OPTION>1-2 months
<OPTION>3-6 months
<OPTION>6-12 months
<OPTION>Never will buy again
</SELECT>
</TD>
</TR>
```

- Radio buttons (RADIO)—Use when only one of two or three options presented applies; for example, Sex— male or female
- Checkboxes (CHECKBOX)—Use when you are presenting many options with no limit on the number a user can choose. For example, services, areas, or products in which a user might be interested
- Text area (TEXT AREA)—Use for multiple lines of text input; for example, comments or suggestions

**TIP:** HomeSiteX, shown in Figure 8.6, contains useful tools for creating all of these form elements.

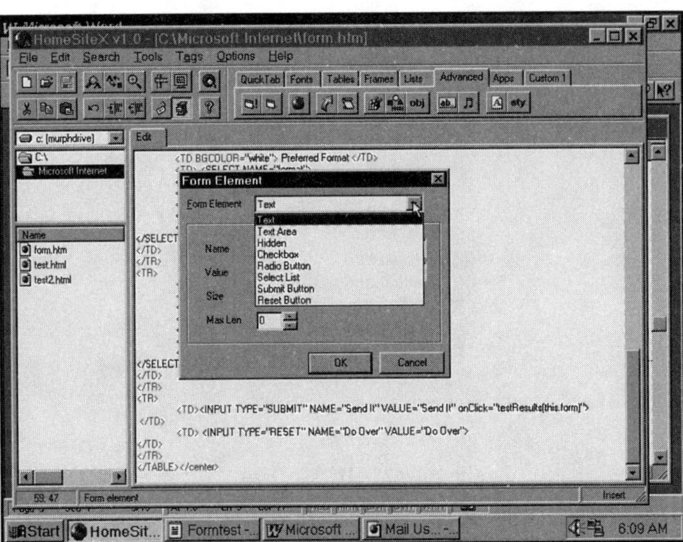


**Figure 8.6.**
*HomeSiteX contains powerful tools for creating form elements.*

Think about and conceptualize the data you want in terms of form elements you can use. They will help you develop questions that fit into a format users can answer most easily. After all, everyone prefers a multiple choice test to an essay exam.

**TIP:** When you design your forms, do as much as possible for your users. For example, if you need someone's address on the form, instead of having a text element for "State," have a drop-down menu with a listing of all 50 states. The easier you make it for the user, the greater the number of completed forms you'll get back.

Don't be surprised if a user starts to fill out your form, answers the first question, skips over the rest, and presses Submit. Front-loading the important questions can help. At the very least, it should minimize the impact of the impatient surfing public.

8. Lay out the form elements in ranked order—the most important at the top, the least important at the bottom—according to the value you place on the corresponding data. For example, if you think an e-mail address is more important to know than the person's name, put the e-mail address above the user's name.

# Designing the Form

It's important to put together your form in an aesthetically pleasing and easy-to-use format. You can do that if you keep in mind these basic design tips:

- ❑ Write the <FORM ACTION> tag first. For the examples, use the "mailto:*yourname@yourserver*.com" action and the POST method, using this basic <FORM> tag:

```
<FORM ACTION="mailto:yourname@yourserver.com" method="POST">
```

**CAUTION:** If you use a CGI script for your forms, be sure to enter the script name and fill in any and all necessary hidden value tags, including your e-mail address and subject line. You need to do this for your data to be in the location and in the format you want.

**TIP:** If you have the capability, set up an e-mail alias for each different form on your site. Having an e-mail address info@yourserver.com for your customer information form makes working with the results as they come in easier.

Later in this chapter, in the "Working with Form Results" task, you'll discover software that enables you to use the responses you get when you use the mailto: form action.

- ❑ The table is the most useful form element. For the example—the Old Dog Used Records form in Figure 8.5—set up a two-column table, enter the name for each form element in the column on the left, and place the actual form element in the column on the right. This makes aligning the starting point of the form spaces easier.

**TIP:** Tables can give you a greater degree of control over the vertical spacing between each form element than is possible with the <br> tag, for example. Use the CELLPADDING attribute to place as much, or as little, space as you like between the lines of your forms.

- ❑ With a form that uses only text elements and drop-down menus, use a background image or color for your page and a white background for the table cells that contain the form element descriptions to achieve an added three-dimensional quality like the one in the Old Dog form in Figure 6.5.

**CAUTION:** Think carefully before you add images or multimedia files. Keeping a form relatively simple is the best way to ensure that your users don't get too distracted, quickly enter their information, and press Submit.

# The Value of Web Surveys

Taking your forms beyond the basic customer information model and using them to directly and indirectly accumulate a good deal of data on your customers is well worth the effort. It's not very difficult either, because the design elements remain the same. It's just a matter of coming up with questions that are more detailed or that are focused in one particular area.

There are many form-based surveys from which you can choose to generate additional information from your users.

- Preference surveys—surveys that explore what users like or don't like in products in your business area
- Test surveys—surveys that present users with true/false or multiple choice questions about your products or services and your business
- Topical surveys—surveys that enable users to express their opinions about specified popular issues of the day
- Contest surveys—surveys that incorporate questions about your products into a contest for such prizes as products, services, or discounts

Regardless of which kind of survey you decide on, if you want people to use it, take a light approach. Focus on the information you need to make your business and your pages a success—but in a way that is fun and as light-hearted as possible.

# Formatting and Managing Form Results

All the effort you expended creating your forms will be wasted if you cannot use the data actually submitted. As you have learned, when you use the `mailto:` form action, the browser will e-mail the form results to you in a basically unusable URL-encoded format.

## Formatting Your Results

When you receive your form results as attachments to e-mails from your users, follow these steps:

1. Open the attachments using the mailto: Formatter.
2. Click Convert File.
3. Determine to which configuration you want the program to convert the file by selecting the corresponding options as shown in Figure 8.7.

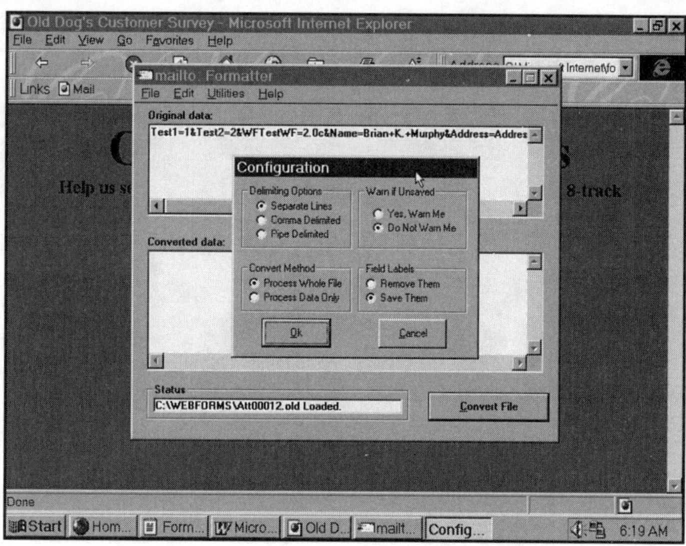

**Figure 8.7.**
*The mailto: Formatter program gives you the power to convert your responses to a variety of different data formats.*

The mailto: Formatter program strips away all the encoding information and converts the file to one of a variety of different database file formats.

4. Click Save As or Append To to save the results of the conversion.
5. Print the results in an easy-to-read format that breaks down the form results by category, or load the data into the companion database program, the mailto: Manager program.

## Managing Your Results

Use the mailto: Manager program to import the formatted results into a database through which you can more easily manage the information you collect. Use the program's report function, displayed in Figure 8.8, to search and display results according to specified fields.

The mailto: Manager can be launched directly from the mailto: Formatter program. If you use a spreadsheet program, such as Excel, to work with the formatted results of the form data, use the Configure command in mailto: Formatter to specify the comma-delimited format.

**CAUTION:** If you plan to add users' names to a mass mailing list, be sure to place a small notification somewhere on the page so they know that when they fill out the form. Virtually no one appreciates uninvited e-mail.

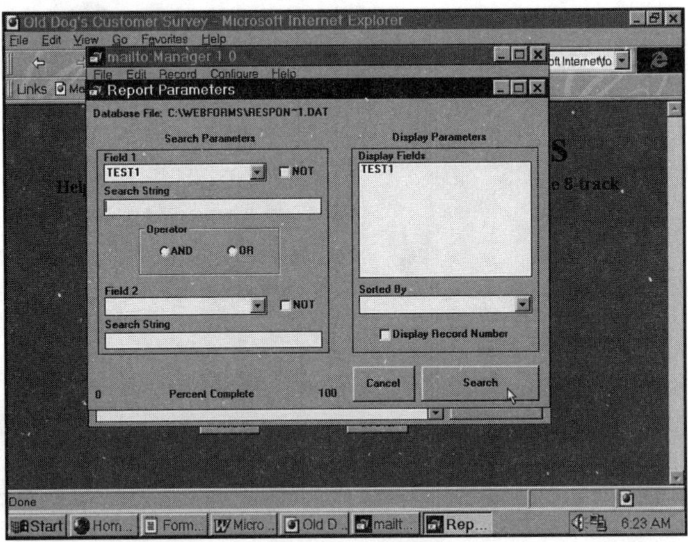


**Figure 8.8.**
*The mailto: Manager report function searches your form results and generates printed reports.*

# Workshop Wrap-Up

Customer information forms and surveys fulfill a very important function regardless of whether yours is a service organization or a for-profit business. They are a vehicle you can use to generate direct communication with and feedback from potential or existing customers or clients.

Powerful e-mail list manager software is available that can enable you to create and maintain a list of customers from your form data. Look on the Web at `http://www.cwsapps.com` or `http://www.tucows.com` for some options. You can use lists like these for many different purposes, including sending customized newsletters or periodic messages about new developments at your Web site or new services or products.

Just remember to plan up-front and to keep your forms separate and simple. How you tally and use the resulting data is strictly up to you. However, that will be a moot point if no one fills out the form because it takes too long to fill out, isn't targeted or creative enough to catch a surfer's eye and hold his or her attention, or is out of sync with the rest of the pages on your Web site.

## Next Steps

At this point, you should have a pretty clear idea of how to create and implement your forms. Now...

- ❑ To gain insights into how to use your Web pages to help you help your customers, look at Chapter 9, "Customer Support Pages: Boards and Beyond."
- ❑ To see some real-life examples of forms, turn to Chapter 12, "Real-Life Examples: Advancing Your Site."
- ❑ To find out more about data and the Web, check out Chapter 10, "Advanced Information Pages: Tying Data to the Web."

## Q&A

**Q: I'd like the most hassle-free way for creating forms for my Web pages without needing to customize any CGI scripts or use any `mailto:` formatting programs. What are my options?**

**A:** Well, even though that's asking for a lot, there actually is a simple solution. Remote Software (`http://www.remote.com`) provides what you want in its Free Mail and Form Mail services, which enable you to use advanced forms on your pages but utilize preset CGI scripts that run on Remote's servers and generate formatted e-mail responses. The Free Mail service (which is free) only allows a very limited number of form fields. The Form Mail service, which is inexpensive, is more robust. Both are quick and inexpensive solutions if you need a quick fix.

**Q: Are there any special server requirements for using forms?**

**A:** Yes and No.

No, if you use the `mailto:` form action. The work is done on the user's computer (the client side). The only additional interaction with the server is to forward the mail to your mailbox.

Yes, if you use CGI scripts. They require that you have permission either to access your server's `cgi-bin` directory or to place CGI scripts directly into your Web directory. Your systems administrator can tell you what scripts you can use for forms processing.

CHAPTER

NINE

# Customer Support Pages: Boards and Beyond

## In this chapter, you

- ❑ Create a FAQ list and answer database
- ❑ Set up a customer support Web bulletin board
- ❑ Use multimedia to answer questions
- ❑ Set up a Web phone to provide support

## Tasks in this chapter:

- ❑ Creating Product FAQs
- ❑ Setting Up a Customer Support Web Bulletin Board
- ❑ Setting Up a Web Phone to Provide Support

The Web has been touted time and time again as a new medium for doing commerce and generating sales. However, currently the best use of the Web is probably to communicate with and provide support for your current customers. Many users come online not looking to buy, but rather looking for help. Your Web site should contain as much support for your products and customers as you can afford. This investment is guaranteed to reap dividends in the way of satisfied customers.

Chapter 5, "Employee Directories and Biographies," and Chapter 13, "Advanced Catalogs," show you how to design catalogs that sell to users and make them your customers in the first place.

A bevy of options is available to you to offer support to your customers through your commercial Web pages. On one end of the spectrum you have simple text-based lists of answers to frequently asked questions (FAQs), and on the other end you have advanced Web-based multimedia and interaction using bulletin boards and Internet phones. You'll need to determine what mix of pages and technologies is best for your business. In this chapter, you'll be presented with the information necessary to use each of these.

If you've used the Web for any period of time, you have no doubt paid a visit to the Web pages of Microsoft, Netscape, or some other company in order to find an answer to a question or to get the solution to a problem. You might very well have been disappointed because you were not able to find the information you wanted. When designing customer support pages, you need to put yourself as much as possible in your customers' shoes (or browsers) in order to anticipate every potential means by which you can endear them to both your products and business by simply giving them something you already have—information.

This chapter walks you through some of the various support options available for integration with your Web pages.

# Create a FAQ List and Answer Database

You probably have come across FAQs (frequently asked questions) while using the Web or a Usenet newsgroup. The FAQ format is useful in the context of providing customer support for your business and products. A more advanced version of a FAQ list—an answer database—expands on this concept by attempting to provide answers to all possible questions and not just those that are frequently asked.

## Creating Product FAQs

You should always approach the implementation of FAQs on your Web site in the same way you tackled the problem of designing and creating a product catalog. Just as every product should have its own page of detailed product information, each product should also have a separate FAQ page that users can easily pull up to review the most often sought-after information concerning customer questions and problems.

Chapter 6, "Online Catalogs and More: Presenting Your Products and Services," explains the concept of providing information through layers of pages in the catalog concept.

Many times it works best to design a Web page from the top of the information down by first creating your home page and then adding the links and subpages. The opposite tactic is necessary when you develop a set of FAQs for use on your pages.

**TIP:** FAQs are useful in a variety of ways on your Web pages. You should establish a separate set of pages that comprise an archive of FAQs on your various products or services. However, you can then also tie in the links to the various product-specific FAQs on any related page, such as the product's catalog page or even a press release.

The following are the steps you should go through to establish a set of product or service FAQs for use on your commercial Web pages:

1. Identify the questions (and answers) to include for each product.
2. Create a separate FAQ page using these questions and answers for each product or service.
3. Create an index page of all your FAQs.
4. Insert links to the FAQ index and to individual FAQs where appropriate.
5. Create a search option for FAQs.

The FAQ index page is an excellent candidate for inclusion as part of your main menu bar, as discussed in Chapter 3, "Corporate Presence Pages."

The design and creation of customer support FAQs will probably involve more offline work than any other pages you'll create for your commercial Web site. Significant preparation time is required in determining what questions to include and the detail of the answers you're going to provide. The value of your customer support pages is only as good as the information provided.

**CAUTION:** There's an old cliché that goes "Don't let the perfect be the enemy of the good." Depending on the number of products or services you have, creating all the necessary FAQs can take a good deal of time. Try to start with your most popular (or most troublesome) products and add those FAQs to your Web pages as soon as possible. Over time, you can add additional items as well as tweak the first ones.

## Creating the Individual FAQ Pages

I'll jump past the first step, which is actually identifying what questions are the most frequently asked, and assume that you probably know the best way for determining the most frequently asked questions and the appropriate answers. I'll just note that you should avoid being overly technical or obtuse in developing the answers. The key is not just to provide information and correct answers, but to provide useful information and understandable answers.

The basic layout for each product's FAQ page is a relatively simple HTML designing and coding project. The focus of the FAQ is the questions and answers. Make sure you avoid any design elements that will take away from the readability of these items.

**TIP:** Avoid using background images on your FAQ pages. Use a basic background color such as gray or white to give the page maximum clarity. This will also give the FAQ page a better appearance if your customers print it out for later reference.

## The Basic FAQ Layout

At the top of each individual FAQ page should be the name of the product or service that the page addresses, as well as the date the FAQ was last updated (see Figure 9.1). You can also add information such as model and product numbers, if applicable. Including a small photo or graphic of the product or service is also a nice touch.

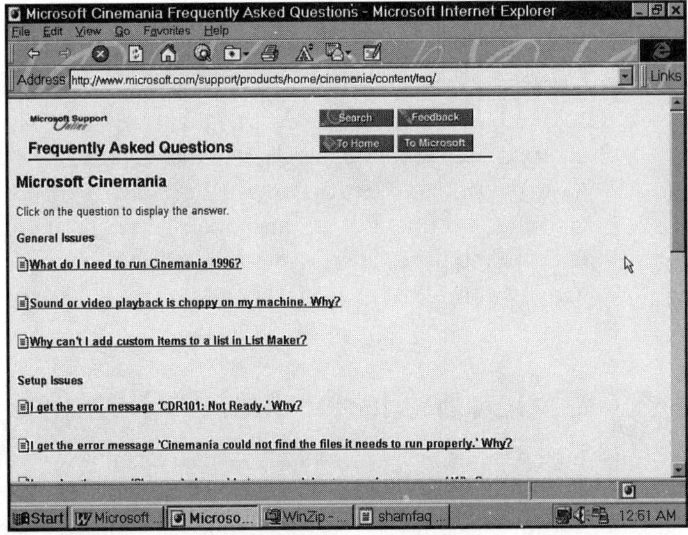


**Figure 9.1.**
*The top of a sample product FAQ page.*

Refer to Chapter 2, "Developing a Plan for Design and Site Management," for information about creating a theme and color scheme for your Web site that you can use when creating your FAQ pages.

The layout of your FAQ page should put the questions that are answered at the very top of the page. Place the questions in a list format using the <UL> tag and then create internal hyperlinks to later portions of the page where you'll place the questions along with the full answers. Figure 9.2 shows the top of a typical FAQ page implementing these elements. Here's an excerpt of the simple HTML code that demonstrates how to link the questions at the top of the page:

```
<HEAD>
<TITLE>Shamrock Software's Emerald OS FAQ</TITLE>
</HEAD>

<BODY BGCOLOR=#FFFFFF VLINK=#000080 TOPMARGIN=0 LEFTMARGIN=0>
<br>
<br>
<br>
<br>
<br>
<CENTER><IMG SRC="shamrock.gif" BORDER=0 ALT="Shamrock Software, Inc."><br>

<P><FONT FACE=ARIAL SIZE=3><B> Frequently Asked Questions <BR>
 Emerald OS From Shamrock</B></FONT><BR>
<P><FONT FACE=ARIAL SIZE=1> FAQ Last Updated March 17, 1996</CENTER>
<FONT FACE=ARIAL SIZE=2>
<P><A NAME="Top">
<UL>
<LI><A HREF="#1">How do I delete Emerald from my hard drive?</A>
<LI><A HREF="#2">Can I get my money back?</A>
<LI><A HREF="#3">Who is responsible for this program?</A>
<LI><A HREF="#4">When I start up Emerald, it just blinks 12:00,
➥what should I do?</A>
<LI><A HREF="#5">Emerald, what's up with that?</A>
<LI><A HREF="#6">Is there a user group I could turn to for support?</A>
<LI><A HREF="#7">Is there going to be an Emerald97?</A>
</UL>
```

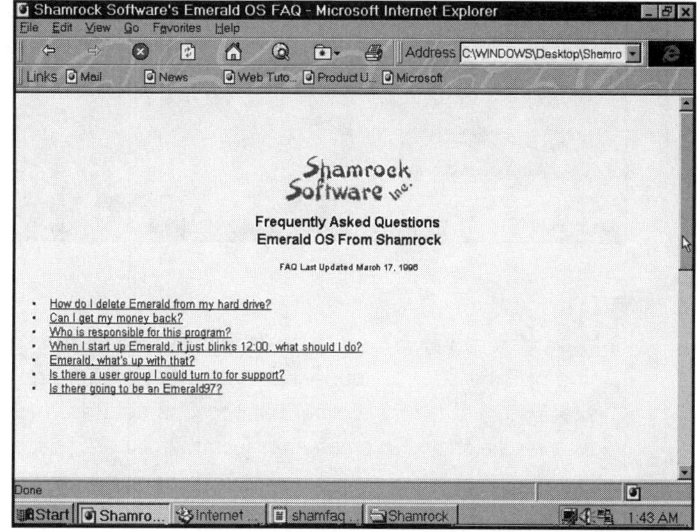


**Figure 9.2.**
*The top of the FAQ should contain a bulleted list of hyperlinked questions.*

## Formatting the Questions and Answers

The next step in designing each product's FAQ page is to enter and format the actual questions and answers. Obviously, the questions will appear on the FAQ page twice—once at the top of the page, as demonstrated in Figure 9.2, and then later in the body of the page. You'll need to make sure that you enter the appropriate anchor information for the questions to make the internal links operational, which appear as `<HREF="#1">` tags in the code snippet. This means that you will need to create a working relationship between the questions and the answers that appear later in the document.

Formatting the questions and answers provides little room (although still some) for creativity. The questions should be in bold followed by the answer in regular text. The one area in which you can put your own touch on the page is by specifying a font style using the `<FONT FACE>` tag, as shown in Figure 9.3. Both Netscape's Navigator and Microsoft's Internet Explorer now support this option. After you've applied the formatting to the text, you should add one more element at the end of each answer—an internal link.

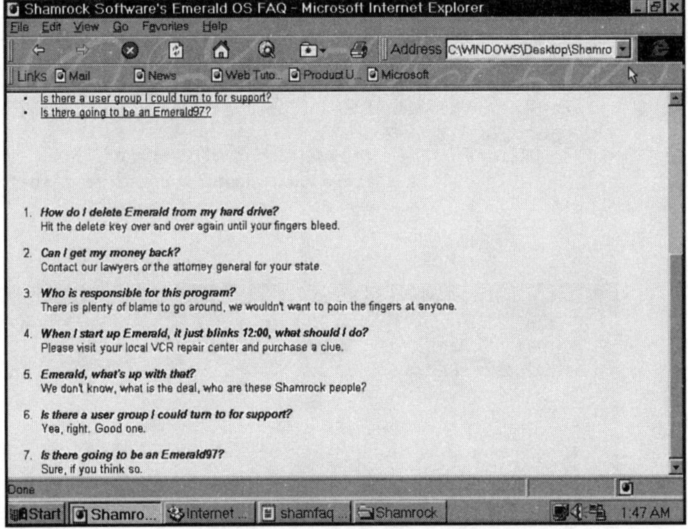


**Figure 9.3.**
*You can specify a font style to add a little pizzazz to your FAQ pages.*

Consider setting up a Web page template for creating FAQ pages. This is discussed in Chapter 1, "Selecting and Using Tools for Page Creation."

**TIP:** You can always use a cascading style sheet to apply advanced formatting options, such as specifying font styles, to pages throughout your Web site. You might want to refer back to Chapter 2 for more information on how to use style sheets to create your commercial Web pages.

## The Importance of Internal Links

On your FAQ pages, you should think of internal links as always being a two-way street. You just saw the importance of placing the questions at the top of the page and hyperlinking them to the question and answer combination later in the page.

**TIP:** A nice touch here is to use a linked graphic on which users can click to take them back to the top of the page (see Figure 9.4). A little variety here will break up the pace of your otherwise all-text FAQs.

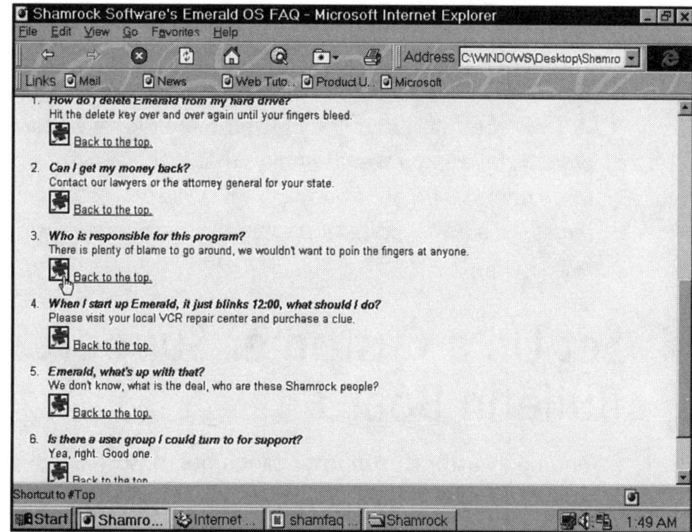


**Figure 9.4.**
*The small shamrock graphic is an internal link to the top of the page.*

You should also place an internal link at the end of each answer that points to an anchor at the top of the page. As users select questions and jump down to the answer, you can be sure that they'll want to return to the list of questions for further problem solving. Once again, this simply provides a navigational tool for users to make better use of your pages.

# Answer Databases

Another, more detailed, resource you can create for your customers is an answer database that provides information on a broad range of topics, broken down by keyword or phrase. You can think of this as being similar to the Windows help system, where you can search for answers to problems by looking at an index of keywords and phrases.

**NOTE:** Even Microsoft has firmly acknowledged the value of HTML in providing customer support. The company recently announced that all of its products' help files will be converted into HTML format in the very near future.

The main difference between FAQs and answer databases is that the FAQs address only the most popular questions and provide a detailed answer to those specific questions. An answer database is aimed at delivering as much information about a specific product as possible so that a user will be able to find the solution to any question or problem he or she might have by looking at the information associated with the various keywords and phrases.

**TIP:** A good way to quickly increase the power of your answer database pages is by using a search engine that is specific to this subset of pages. For more information about how to set up such a search engine on your Web pages, be sure to look at Chapter 11, "Searching Your Site."

# Set Up a Customer Support Web Bulletin Board

Setting up a customer support bulletin board, such as the one shown in Figure 9.5, is probably one of the best Web investments you can make in a commercial setting. A customer support bulletin board gives your customers a sense of empowerment because they have somewhere specific to go and get answers to any questions they might have. The limits of both FAQs and answer databases are removed in this format.

## Usenet Without the Flames

The best way to think about a customer support bulletin board is as a Web-based private Usenet newsgroup dedicated to your company or to each of your products or services. Users are able to post comments or questions, and you can respond with answers. Your answers not only help the specific customer, but also every customer who comes along and reads the board.

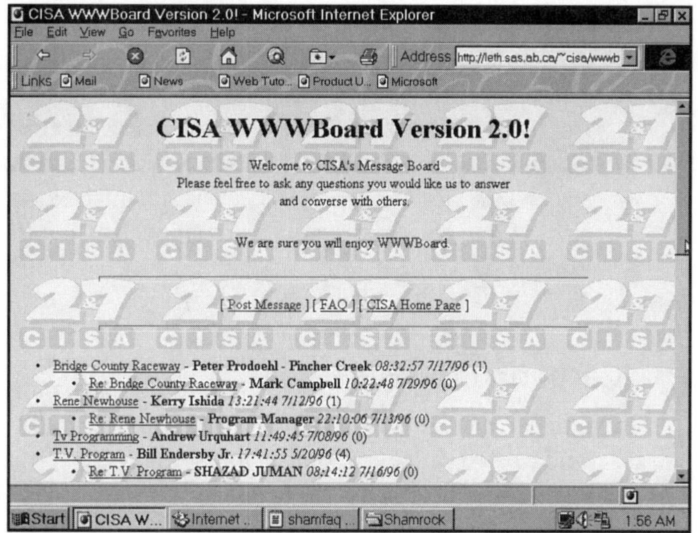


**Figure 9.5.**
*A customer support bulletin board implemented on a Web page.*

Not every company is like Microsoft and can afford to set up its own NNTP news server and provide 271 (yes, 271) separate newsgroups for its products.

The biggest key to success for your customer support bulletin boards is to make certain that they don't languish in obscurity and that you assign an employee to each board to closely monitor the postings and provide answers and feedback to customers quickly and consistently. The goal should be to provide answers to customer postings within hours, not days. Also, your employees will build up credibility with customers who frequent the products' boards.

## Setting Up the Boards: A Script for Success

The key to setting up Web-based bulletin boards is to get your hands on a good CGI script for implementing the bulletin board system. You could pay a developer to create a custom script for you, or you could troll the Internet to see what other people are using and then try to locate those scripts. Or you can simply look on the accompanying CD-ROM and use the best of the bunch—WWWBoard, a freeware CGI script created by Matt Wright and also available online at his CGI/Perl script archive at

```
http://www.worldwidemart.com/scripts
```

**NOTE:** WWWBoard is intended for use with UNIX-based Web servers.

**NOTE:** The only real viable alternative to using CGI scripts to implement a Web bulletin board is to use the Web bots included with Microsoft's FrontPage HTML editor. FrontPage has wizards that can enable users to automatically set up a product support bulletin board without the need for any knowledge of CGI, or HTML, for that matter. However, you'll need to have a Web server that supports the proprietary (but free) FrontPage extensions.

## Gathering the Files

Setting up WWWBoard is relatively simple and painless, but can be confusing if you haven't worked with CGI scripts on many occasions. You should first have a general overview of the files that will be necessary for implementing each discussion board you want to include on your Web site. Here are the files necessary for running a WWWBoard and a brief description of each:

| *Filename* | *Description* |
|---|---|
| `wwwboard.pl` | The CGI script that actually drives (or executes) the bulletin board. |
| `wwwboard.html` | A sample Web page that implements the WWWBoard, complete with necessary forms (see Figure 9.6). |
| `data.txt` | A necessary file for the server to write in order to store the filename number (meaning messages). |
| `wwwadmin.pl` | A CGI administration tool that enables you to maintain each board by deleting old (or rude) posts. |
| `faq.html` | A ready-to-go FAQ page, shown in Figure 9.7, that is linked to the WWWBoard to answer users' questions about the board (so they can focus on your products) |

## Customizing the Files

You'll need to edit some of the files that make up the WWWBoard. Fortunately, you don't need to be proficient in programming or writing CGI scripts in order to make the necessary adjustments to get WWWBoard working for you and your organization.

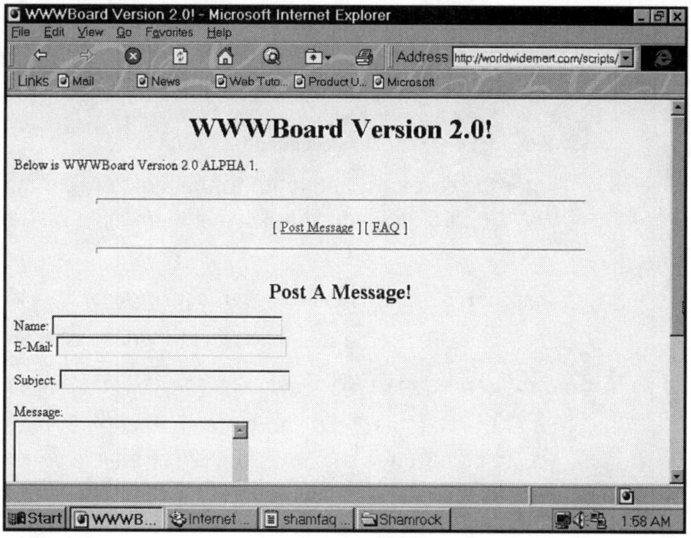

**Figure 9.6.**
*The standard* `wwwboard.html` *Web page.*

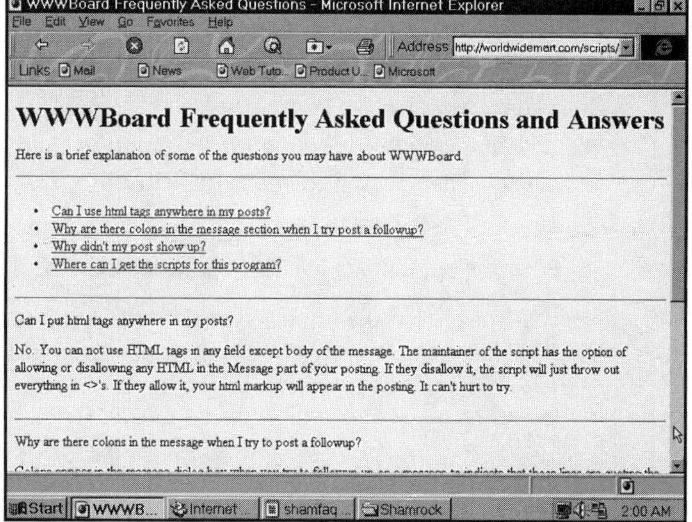


**Figure 9.7.**
*The* `faq.html` *Web page that helps users work with WWWBoard.*

**TIP:** WWWBoard comes with an excellent `readme` file containing detailed installation instructions and a full explanation of the script and all the potential adjustments you can make in customizing it to your uses.

You'll need to set only a few different variables within the `wwwboard.pl` script in order to get the WWWBoard up and running. Here's a quick rundown of the variables you'll need to set and what information you'll need for each:

1. `$basedir = "/path/wwwboard"`

   Enter the correct system path to the directory containing all your WWWBoard files (you should have them all in their own directory on your server).

2. `$baseurl = "http://www.server.com/wwwboard"`

   Enter the URL to the `wwwboard` directory discussed previously.

3. `$cgi_url = "http://www.server.com/cgi-bin/wwwboard.pl"`

   Enter the URL that points to the actual script. Some servers might require you to place it in a `cgi-bin` directory or enable you to have the file in your own directory.

4. `$msgfile = "wwwboard.html"`

   The name of the Web page that will operate as the bulletin board on your site. Make sure you have this in your `wwwboard` directory. You can rename the file to whatever you like (for example, `product_name.html`).

5. `$date_command = "/bin/date"`

   Enter the path to your server's date command so that WWWBoard can identify when posts were made to the board.

6. `$title = "Your Title Here"`

   Enter the appropriate title for your bulletin board.

Next, you'll need to make some very minor edits to `wwwboard.html`. (Although you should feel free to make more and customize it to your heart's delight.) Here are the options you'll need to set:

1. `<TITLE>`

   By default, the `<TITLE>` tag and the top of the document (the `<H1>` tag) contain `WWWBoard Version 2.0!`. Enter the title information for your support board.

2. `ACTION`

   The action portion of the `<FORM>` tag needs to be customized to point to the full URL of the `wwwboard.pl` file (such as `action="http://www.server.com/cgi-bin/wwwboard.pl"`).

### Placing the Files

As discussed previously, you should create a separate directory on your Web server for the WWWBoard files. Within that directory you'll also need to create a subdirectory called `messages` so that WWWBoard knows where to store (and retrieve) messages posted to your board.

**CAUTION:** You'll need to set the server rights for several of the files so that they operate properly. You'll need to apply `chmod 755` to `wwwboard.pl`; `chmod 777` to `wwwboard.html`, `data.txt`, and the messages directory; and `chmod 744` to `faq.html`.

**TIP:** You can easily set up numerous Web bulletin boards on the same server using WWWBoard. Just create a separate directory for each board and copy all the necessary WWWBoard files into that directory and make the appropriate URL reference adjustments for each board in all the requisite files discussed previously.

After you've completed these task, you're ready to get up and rolling with a Web-based customer support bulletin board. Setting it up is the easy part—maintaining it and the information on it might pose a little bit more of a challenge, but should pay big rewards in customer satisfaction.

## Use Multimedia to Answer Questions

One of the most effective ways to use multimedia on your Web pages is to present video or audio assistance in solving a customer's problems or answering his or her questions. Multimedia can be particularly effective when used in conjunction with the FAQs or answer databases.

**CAUTION:** When you create or use multimedia files for customer support purposes, be sure to use the most efficient format available. Most users (and thus customers) access the Internet through a dial-up modem with a speed of 28.8 Kbps or less. Using formats that yield smaller file sizes, such as MPEG for video or AU for audio, will help reduce any download time. You should also try to use real-time formats (such as RealAudio or VDOLive) whenever possible.

**TIP:** Macromedia recently released an upgrade to its extremely popular Shockwave plug-in that includes support for streaming (meaning real-time) audio. The huge benefit to using the Shockwave audio format over competitors is that the sound quality is absolutely amazing, and you don't need special server software in order to offer the files on your pages. For more information, check out

`http://www.macromedia.com`

## Choose and Use Only Popular Formats

If you're going to supplement your pages with a how-to video or audio instruction, make certain that you stick with only the tried-and-true (and widely available) formats on the market. For audio files this means staying with au, wav, RealAudio, or Shockwave. For video files stick with AVI, MPEG, QuickTime, or VDO.

If new formats become available (and it seems as if they do every day), make sure you hold off until the format has reached critical mass on the Net. The preceding formats are far and away the standards for multimedia and will enable most users to access your files.

# Setting Up a Web Phone to Provide Support

At this point, you've probably heard and read a lot about the advent of so-called Internet or Web phones that enable Internet users to make long-distance (and even international) phone calls without incurring any costs other than those involved with securing Internet access from their local Internet Service Provider.

Originally, this technology was limited to use by those on technology's bleeding edge. However, now Web phones are widely available from such companies as Microsoft and Intel, and millions of users have the capability on their desktop to make phone calls over the Internet using one of many available software products.

**NOTE:** Web phone technology is still somewhat of an evolving standard. You'll need to keep up-to-date on the latest developments if you decide to use this technology as part of your Web-based customer support plan. For an excellent resource, check with `http://www.pulver.com`. For the latest product developments, look at `http://www.cwsapps.com` or `http://www.tucows.com`.

These Web phones also offer a benefit to you in the form of lower telecommunications charges. Just as users can make free long-distance calls, you can provide what is in essence an international toll-free support number without the need to incur the often substantial costs involved with setting up (and operating) such a number.

**TIP:** Using Web phones can also endear your company to its most Net-addicted customers. Many users access the Web from home, where they might have only one line. By providing a Web phone solution for getting in contact with your company, they can continue their surfing session without the need to disconnect and use Ma Bell.

## Selecting a Web Phone to Support (For Support)

The biggest and most important step in establishing a Web phone for support through your pages is deciding on the product to use on your end. Of course, this starts by figuring out what most of your customers will be using on their end. The number and variety of Web phones is a little mind-boggling: Internet Phone, Web Phone, DigiPhone, CoolTalk, and NetMeeting, just to name a few.

The two biggies on the block in this game are CoolTalk and NetMeeting. CoolTalk comes as part of Netscape's latest browser offering. NetMeeting, shown in Figure 9.8, is Microsoft's entry into the Web-based phone and conferencing arena. At the moment, you're probably better off going with Microsoft's NetMeeting. NetMeeting uses international standards that enable you to use the product with many different programs from other vendors—a vital consideration in the fractured Web phone market.

**NOTE:** Netscape has also announced that the next version of its CoolTalk software will support the international standards in the same way NetMeeting does. Intel has also recently shipped a Web phone that complies with these standards. As these developments continue, which particular software product you choose will matter less and less.

## Setting Up the Web Phone on Your Web Page

When you have your Web phone installed and running (which could be the subject of an entire book itself), you'll need to place necessary links or information on your

Web pages so that users are able to contact you via the Web phone. Assuming you'll be using Microsoft's NetMeeting, you should implement two different methods on your pages.

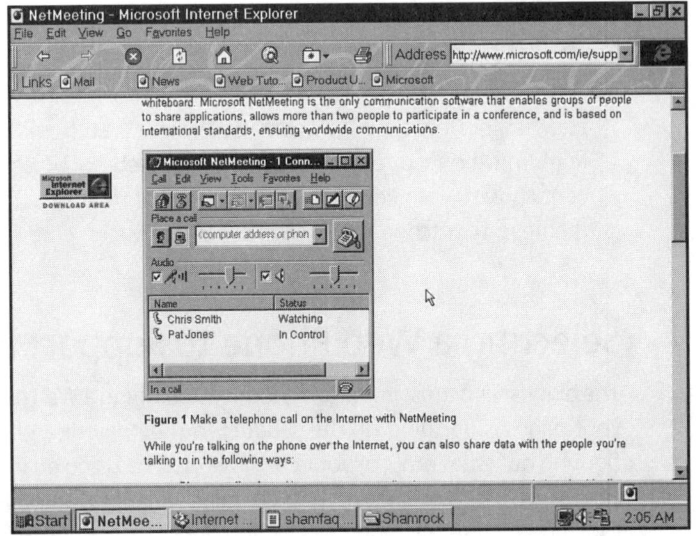


**Figure 9.8.**
*Microsoft's NetMeeting is an excellent (and free) Web phone with many additional collaboration features.*

**TIP:** Microsoft has announced that the first official release of NetMeeting will be available for free downloading from its Web site at

`http://www.microsoft.com`

## Creating a Link

You can embed a link into your Web page that will launch a user's NetMeeting client and provide him or her with immediate access to your Web phone. When you place this link on your page, be sure to inform users that they'll need NetMeeting for the link to work and direct them to where they can download the product, if necessary.

A link is the Web phone version of speed dial.

To create the necessary link on your page, use the following HTML code and syntax:

```
<A HREF="uls://uls.microsoft.com/your_e-mail@server.com">
➥Call Us With NetMeeting</A>
```

**CAUTION:** Using this link format will require that both you and the caller be connected to the same ULS (Universal Locator Service) server. However, most users will be using the default `uls.microsoft.com` server, and you should as well for maximum interoperability.

### Providing Alternative Contact Information

You should also provide some text information that will enable users of other Web phone products to contact you if their clients comply with the international standards used by NetMeeting. The key information for this is the IP address that the NetMeeting client uses to operate on the Net. Providing the necessary IP address is very similar to giving out your actual phone number, which people can use to place a call to you. Although it is not as easy as a link, it will do the trick.

**CAUTION:** The Web phone is still a relatively new technology (as is the Web itself), and no standard has yet emerged as the standard linking format for the medium, particularly between different clients. Providing your IP address is the safest way to ensure that users can get in touch with you, even as the technology matures.

## Workshop Wrap-Up

Providing customer support is one of the most effective uses you can make of the Web today. Although many consumers might be a little careful about buying products over the Net, very few are reluctant to ask questions and seek answers through this medium.

FAQs, bulletin boards, and Web phones are just a few of the options that are available to you in reaching out to and helping your customers (and potential customers). Also, the simple use of e-mail to answer customer questions directly and quickly should not be forgotten. All of these should combine to create a Web presence that will truly be a resource for information about your company and products.

## Next Steps

Now...

- To see how to add a search engine to your Web pages, turn to Chapter 11, "Searching Your Site."
- Find out how to sell products you'll need to support in Chapter 13, "Advanced Catalogs."

## Q&A

**Q: I've seen a lot of customer support options. Which one should I choose?**

**A:** This is not an either/or proposition. A great customer support Web will combine all of the best of these elements—a FAQ page relying on multimedia, tied into an interactive bulletin board, for example. Don't limit yourself to any single idea or concept, but rather think of ways you can integrate as much customer support as possible into your commercial Web pages.

**Q: I'd like to include multimedia-like video and audio to show my customers short "how-to's," but isn't that kind of stuff extremely expensive to make?**

**A:** Audio and video capture and manipulation hardware and software have come down dramatically in price in the last few years. What once cost several thousand dollars is now a few hundred dollars (and getting cheaper every day). You should pay careful attention to the release of Intel's new Pentium chips with multimedia extensions (MMX), which will open a lot of possibilities for creating these types of projects cheaply and easily.

CHAPTER TEN

# Advanced Information Pages: Tying Data to the Web

By now, you are probably well on your way to having your business online. In fact, if you have followed the previous chapters, you should have a serious site in mind or already developed. Your site, whether in mind or online, might have interactive forms, an online catalog, and well-laid pages of meaningful, interesting, and easy-to-locate content. What else would you want for your site? Possibly all of the information on your business, products, and services that you want to make available to the public?

You might know of or remember general stores in which some merchandise was laid out for customer inspection, and for other items you had to ask the proprietor. Is your site like this, providing an overview of your business and providing detailed information on select items? Do customers and other visitors have to e-mail you for information that is not available from your site? There's a good chance that many will not bother to send a request, but go somewhere else for information.

## In this chapter, you

- Build a database with Internet Assistant for Microsoft Access
- Use mSQL, a shareware database
- Use SQL
- Write a simple CGI spreadsheet
- Create static spreadsheets

## Tasks in this chapter:

- Building a Database with Internet Assistant for Microsoft Access
- Using mSQL, a Shareware Database
- Writing a Simple CGI Spreadsheet
- Creating Static Spreadsheets

Would you rather your site be like a large super-store, where everything is readily available to the customer? Sure, your site will be quite large and complex, and creating all those Web pages will be a chore. But what if you could provide the content without generating all those extra pages? In this way, you could

- Provide information on all the products and services you provide.
- Give visitors the ability to quickly locate a particular item out of the many you offer.
- Post quarterly and annual financial reports and balance sheets.
- Display a spreadsheet showing the advantages of your business's products and services.
- Show sales and marketing trends.
- Give customers and investors all the information they need to know that your business is the one for them.

You can provide all these features and more without writing numerous Web pages. By using databases, spreadsheets, and applications that provide an interface to the Web, you can make readily available all the information you want to be public without creating an enormous amount of work writing Web pages.

In this chapter, you learn how to put your information online with

- Product databases, which covers how to create static Web pages from database information, using online databases, and setting up an interactive Web-database interface.
- Financial spreadsheets, which covers setting up static Web pages for putting spreadsheet information online and using an interactive Web spreadsheet program.
- Investor relations pages, which covers putting information online for investors, suppliers, creditors, and other parties with a financial interest in your business.

Most of this chapter focuses on databases. Financial spreadsheets and investor relations pages are not less important, but databases are more likely to be used in a site and typically have more application.

Sams Publishing offers several books on database programming and use. Be sure to check your favorite bookstore or visit `http://www.mcp.com/` for more information on the books offered and to find a bookstore near you.

## Product Databases

A database is much like a Rolodex file: You simply search through the index to locate the appropriate card (record). Each record will likely have several pieces of information (fields), such as a name, an address, and a phone number. With a computer database, the process is not only easier, but you can perform more detailed searches. Not only can you look for records by an index field (such as a name), but you can search records by any of the fields. You can find records based on address, city, phone extension or area code, or any other data you might have. Furthermore, computer databases can be, for most individuals and organizations, more organized, reliable, and easier to use than hard copy records and files.

**NOTE:** I should probably refer to many of the modern database applications as database management systems or DBMSs. In this chapter, however, because we could be dealing with just one simple flat text database or a large relational database management system, I simply use the term *database* or *database application*.

You likely use and are already familiar with databases for your business. Many businesses employ databases to maintain records of sales, expenses, payroll, inventory, and customers. By being online, you can open some of your databases for customers and other interested parties to use. Obviously, you would not want to grant access to confidential or private records, but you might want to put a database of records of your product line online.

With a product database, your customers could search for and easily locate information on specific goods or services. The database could contain several fields of specific information on the products, name, description, price, weight, size, color, and any other fields appropriate to your product line. An example for a fictitious used motorcycle dealer, Hawg's Harleys, is shown in Table 10.1.

**Table 10.1. Example of a simple product database.**

| *Year* | *Model* | *Name* | *Color* | *Mileage* | *Price* |
|---|---|---|---|---|---|
| 1991 | FXRS | Low Rider | Red | 28500 | $12000.00 |
| 1993 | FLHS | Electra Glide Sport | Blue | 30200 | $15000.00 |
| 1992 | FXSTC | Softtail Custom | Black | 48000 | $14500.00 |
| 1990 | XLH | Sportster | Green | 12600 | $5000.00 |
| 1992 | FXDC | Dyna Glide Custom | Silver | 22300 | $13000.00 |
| 1990 | FLHTC | Electra Glide Classical | Black | 18400 | $10000.00 |
| 1991 | FLSTC | Heritage Softtail Classic | Blue | 12300 | $14000.00 |
| 1990 | FXR | Super Glide | Red | 22500 | $12000.00 |

Customers could search the database on any combination of the fields to locate the specific bike for which they are looking. For example, if a customer were seeking an

FXSTC with fewer than 50,000 miles made after 1990, the following record would be returned:

```
1992 FXSTC  Softtail Custom             Black    48000    $14500.00
```

The information does not necessarily have to be displayed as a one-line record. The database interface would likely format the records returned with a presentable HTML format. Figure 10.1 shows a report that the customer might receive.

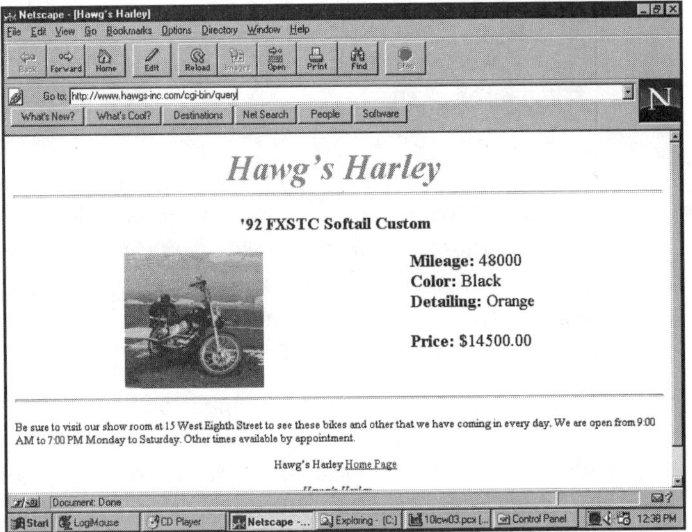


**Figure 10.1.**
*A sample report sent in response to a customer's query.*

**NOTE:** You can set up many database systems to provide customized reports. Your Web-database interface will be doing the same, providing a customized report on specific data in the database, except the report will be online.

A variety of database and server interfaces are available for making product information records available online:

- Static pages created with HTML tables can display database records and reports but do not allow for queries or other user input.
- Shareware database programs are available for putting information on the Web and taking in information from users.
- You can often access databases conforming to the ODBC specification by the Web server through special drivers and other interfaces.
- Custom CGI scripts and programs (such as Visual Basic routines).
- Custom programs using Web and database server APIs.

Application Programming Interface (API) is a set of shared libraries and specific functions for developing programs to interact with a specific application.

**NOTE:** Typically, you must have a certain level of expertise to develop custom scripts and programs. Also, the custom scripts and programs are usually set up for a specific use with a specific application or server. The other types of interfaces are more open and do not require a high level of programming expertise. You learn these other types later in this chapter, in the sections, "Using mSql" and "Creating Web-Database Applications."

## Static Database Pages

Although a static Web page might not be categorized strictly as a Web-database interface, it is a means to present database information on the Web. For a short line of products, the static page might be better than a dynamic interface. A static page is a tabular display of the complete database or a portion of the database. HTML editors and special applications (such as Microsoft's Internet Assistant for Access) can create a tabular display of your database.

A static page of database information can be preferable to an interactive Web-database interface when you are using a small database that does not change frequently. Customers can usually scan a short static page more quickly than they can enter a query and receive the response. Also, the customers will likely need to use fewer keystrokes to locate the information on a short static than they would have to use for locating information with a query form.

From your point of view (that of a Web developer), a static page will be easier to set up than an interactive interface. However, if the database information changes, you will need to update the static page to reflect the changes. If the changes are frequent (even weekly or possibly monthly) your efforts would probably be more effective by setting up an interactive interface than by setting and maintaining a static page.

**NOTE:** Although customers won't be able to query your database, a static page can be better than a dynamic page for small databases. For a limited set of records, a dynamic interface will not be beneficial to the customer or to you.

Please refer to Chapter 1, "Selecting and Using Tools for Page Creation," for information on setting up a Web page.

### HTML or Text Editors

With your favorite HTML editor (mine is Notepad), you can generate code similar to the following, which produces the table display shown in Figure 10.2.

```
<CENTER>
<TABLE WIDTH="80%" ALIGN=CENTER>
<CAPTION><FONT SIZE="+2"><B>Hawg's Harley Line Up</B></FONT> <BR></CAPTION>
<TR><TH WIDTH=50>  </TH><TH ALIGN=LEFT>Year </TH><TH ALIGN=LEFT> Model </TH>
 <TH ALIGN=LEFT> Price<BR></TH></TR>
<TR><TD> </TD><TD> 1991  </TD><TD> FXRS </TD><TD> $12000.00<BR><TD></TR>
<TR><TD> </TD><TD> 1993  </TD><TD> FLHS </TD><TD>  $15000.00<BR><TD></TR>
<TR><TD> </TD><TD> 1992 </TD><TD> FXSTC </TD><TD> $14500.00<BR><TD></TR>
<TR><TD> </TD><TD> 1990  </TD><TD> XLH </TD><TD> $5000.00<BR><TD></TR>
<TR><TD> </TD><TD> 1992  </TD><TD> FXDC </TD><TD> $13000.00<BR><TD></TR>
<TR><TD> </TD><TD> 1990  </TD><TD> FLHTC </TD><TD> $10000.00<BR><TD></TR>
<TR><TD> </TD><TD> 1991  </TD><TD> FLSTC </TD><TD> $14000.00<BR><TD></TR>
<TR><TD> </TD><TD> 1990  </TD><TD> FXR </TD><TD> $12000.00<BR><TD></TR>
</TABLE>
</CENTER>
```

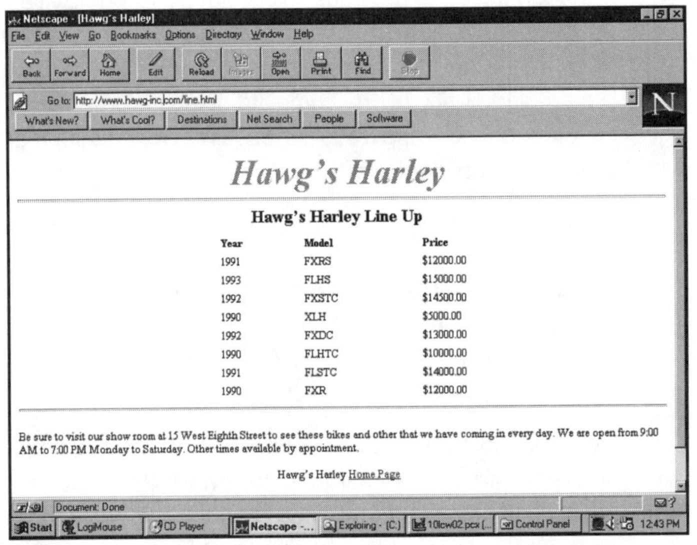


**Figure 10.2.**
*A database table created with HTML table tags.*

You might want to refer to Chapter 6, "Online Catalogs and More: Presenting Your Products and Services," for examples of creating stylized table presentations.

**TIP:** Putting spaces around the entry in each table cell creates a reasonable display for customers who don't have a table-capable browser. Also, a `<BR>` or `<P>` at the end of the entry of the last cell in each row will keep the rows from running together.

**TIP:** Put fields of primary interest on the left side of the page. A field of primary interest is one that the customer would use to search the database table, such as the name of the product. For the Hawg's Harleys example, the customers will likely use the year and model fields to search the database table. Although the price can be very important to the customers, they will more than likely search for a specific model and year.

The alternative to using an HTML table is to use preformat tags. Simply lay out your data records using a monospaced font and enclose the text with the <PRE> and </PRE> tags.

The following code produces the display shown in Figure 10.3:

```
<PRE>
                        Hawg's Harley Line Up
Year Model  Name                             Color      Mileage    Price
1991 FXRS   Low Rider                        Red        28500    $12000.00
1993 FLHS   Electra Glide Sport              Blue       30200    $15000.00
1992 FXSTC  Softtail Custom                  Black      48000    $14500.00
1990 XLH    Sportster                        Green      12600    $ 5000.00
1992 FXDC   Dyna Glide Custom                Silver     22300    $13000.00
1990 FLHTC  Electra Glide Classical          Black      18400    $10000.00
1991 FLSTC  Heritage Softtail Classic        Blue       12300    $14000.00
1990 FXR    Super Glide                      Red        22500    $12000.00
</PRE>
```

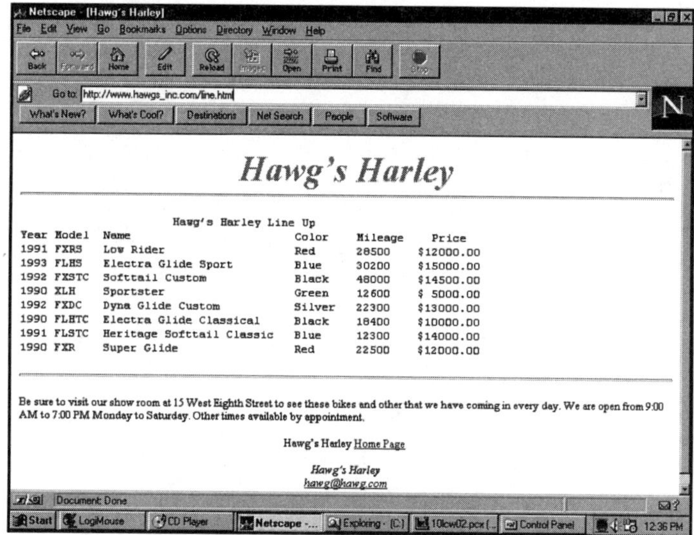


**Figure 10.3.**
*A database table created with preformat tags.*

**TIP:** For clarity, I have omitted a lot of content from the example. For your own page, you will want to make the page conform to the standard layout for your site. Include home page and other links, any specific header and footer information you use on other pages, and other appropriate content.

**CAUTION:** With the preformat tags, the text can easily run off the edge of the browser window, particularly if the customer is using a narrow browser window. If possible, try to keep preformatted text to a line length of 60 characters or fewer. If it is not possible to limit line length, try to keep the fields of primary interest to the customer on the left side of the window.

Tables can also run off the edge of the window to a lesser extent than preformat tags. The content of the table cells wrap inside the cells unless the NOWRAP attribute is used, thus often enabling the table to fit the browser window. Still, it is good practice to keep the fields of primary interest on the left side of the table.

TASK

## Building a Database with Internet Assistant for Microsoft Access

Internet Assistant for Access is included on this book's CD-ROM and is freely available from the Microsoft site, `www.microsoft.com`, and is fairly easy to set up and use.

If you already have a database table, you can use a converter to create an HTML table of the data. One popular converter program is Microsoft's Internet Assistant for Access. Internet Assistant is an add-in for Microsoft's Access database. To install Internet Assistant for Access, follow these steps:

1. Download the executable setup file.
2. Run the file to set up and install Internet Assistant.
3. Internet Assistant is now available as an add-in to Access.

To use Internet Assistant, follow these steps:

1. Open your database.
2. Select the tables, reports, queries, or forms for which you want to generate Web pages.
3. Select a template or select the no-template option.
4. Select the directory in which to store the Web pages.
5. Click Finish, and Internet Assistant creates your Web pages.

Microsoft has several useful tools for Web development, including various versions of Internet Assistant for different applications. Be sure to check `http://www.microsoft.com/` for the latest software.

The files created are given the name of the database object from which they were made, with the `.htm` extension.

**TIP:** Using a template instead of having Internet Assistant create an entire new page will decrease your workload. With a template, you won't have to fill in common features including header and footer information, menu bars, or common links that you use on all your site's pages. Even when you make only one database page, if you don't use a template, you will have to overwrite the file with any updates and reenter the content.

If you want to use a template to standardize your database pages, you can select one that Microsoft provides or one that you created. To make your own template, follow these steps:

1. Create a Web page exactly as you want the database page to look, but without the database content. Be sure to include body tag attributes, links, headers, address sections, and everything else that is standard on all your site's pages.
2. Insert the placeholders for the database content. Internet Assistant uses two placeholders, as follows:

   - <!ACCESSTEMPLATE_TITLE> is replaced by the name of the database object (table, report, and so on) as the title of the page. If you do not use this placeholder, the page's title will be the page's filename.
   - <!ACCESSTEMPLATE_BODY> is replaced by the content of the database object. If you do not specify this placeholder, the contents of the database object will replace the entire body section of the template.

Did you know that there are only two HTML tags that are required in every HTML document by specification? They are <TITLE> and </TITLE>. All other tags are optional or depend on page content. Every HTML document by specification must have a title.

Refer to Chapter 2, "Developing a Plan for Design and Site Management," for information on creating specific styles or themes for your site.

Use the following as a template for our Hawg's Harleys example.

```
<HTML>
<TITLE>Hawg's Harley - <!ACCESSTEMPLATE_TITLE></TITLE>
<BODY BACKGROUND="image.gif"
    TEXT="#009900" LINK="#0000FF" VLINK="#FF00FF" ALINK="#FF0000">
<H1 ALIGN=CENTER>Hawg's Harley</H1>
<H2 ALIGN=CENTER>Our Line of Previously Owned Motorcycles</H2>
<!ACCESSTEMPLATE_BODY>
<P>
Be sure to visit our show room at 15 West Eighth Street to see these bikes
and other that we have coming in every day.  We are open from 9:00 AM to
7:00 PM Monday to Saturday.  Other times available by appointment.
<P ALIGN=CENTER>
Hawg's Harley <A HREF="/index.html">Home Page</A>
<ADDRESS>
<P ALIGN=CENTER>
Hawg's Harley<BR>
<A HREF="mailto:hawg@hawg.com">hawg@hawg.com</A><BR>
</ADDRESS>
</BODY>
</HTML>
```

The template with our example database creates the Web page shown in Figure 10.4.

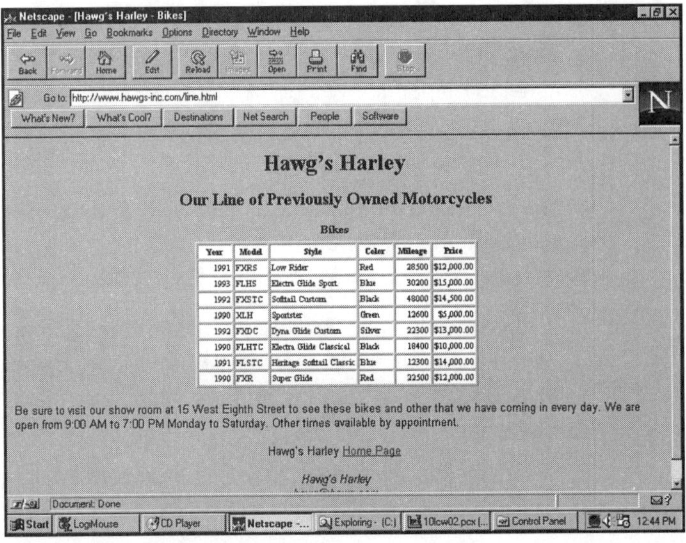


**Figure 10.4.** *The Web page generated by the sample template and database.*

# Using mSQL, a Shareware Database

mSQL shareware is available for evaluation on this book's CD-ROM and from `http://hughes.com.au/`. To use the software commercially requires registration and a small fee. The `au` domain is Australia.

**NOTE:** Mini SQL (mSQL) is copyright Hughes Technologies of Australia and is included with their permission. mSQL is not free software; any commercial use of the software requires the purchase of a commercial use license. More information on mSQL can be found on the Hughes Technologies Web site at `http://www.Hughes.com.au/`.

Several shareware databases are available to download off the Internet. mSQL, one such database in which you might be interested (included on this book's CD-ROM), is a small database program that uses a subset of the SQL standard. Numerous tools and other applications supporting mSQL have been written and are available at `http://hughes.com.au/`, including applications for Windows machines.

**TIP:** If you use mSQL and related applications, please be sure to register the software and pay the nominal fee. Because mSQL is shareware, the registration fee is the only means to support this product and further development.

Several mechanisms exist for connecting a Web server to mSQL:

- The standard mSQL distribution comes with an API library for C programs. A programmer can set up a CGI routine to interface with the database engine for queries and other actions.
- W3-mSQL is an application that serves as an interface between mSQL and the Web server. Users unfamiliar with programming and CGI scripts will find W3-mSQL a great benefit.
- Other tools and interfaces of various programming and scripting languages are available at `http://hughes.com.au/`, including Perl, Tcl, and Python applications.

W3-mSQL is one of many useful mSQL applications available at `http://hughes.com.au/`.

## Installing mSQL on Your Server

**NOTE:** mSQL was developed for UNIX-type platforms; because many sites use a UNIX server, the following routine is given for setting up mSQL on a UNIX-type platform. Even if you are not personally using a UNIX machine, you can use mSQL on a UNIX server to put your data online. See `http://hughes.com.au/` for applications for using mSQL with other platforms.

Installing mSQL is fairly easy and straightforward. Although you should follow the instructions provided with the version you downloaded, the basic routine is as follows:

**NOTE:** Although the setup and installation is easy and straightforward, your system administrator might have to install mSQL for you.

1. Download, uncompress, and unarchive the mSQL files.
2. Enter `make target`. The make file will create a target directory and subdirectory for the necessary object files on your system and install the setup routine.
3. `cd` (change directory) to the target's directory and subdirectory for your particular system.
4. Run `setup` to run the mSQL configuration scripts for your system.
5. Run `make install`. You will be prompted for a directory in which mSQL is to be installed.

mSQL is now installed and ready for operation on your server.

Please refer to the section, "Using SQL," for more information on SQL statements.

## W3-mSQL

W3-mSQL is an easy-to-use interface between the Web site and an mSQL database. No CGI programming is required. The mSQL commands are embedded in an HTML document, which is parsed by W3-mSQL before being sent to the user. W3-mSQL is installed in your CGI directory (usually `cgi-bin`). The pages with the embedded mSQL commands are passed through W3-mSQL by calling the pages referring to them with

```
/CGI-bin/w3-msql/path/filename
```

where *`path/filename`* is a page with the embedded command. W3-mSQL will generate mSQL queries on the fly and incorporate the results in the Web page.

A sample of the embedded commands follow:

> `<! msql connect host>`. If you are connecting to a database on your own server, *`host`* is optional. Otherwise, the domain name of the server being accessed will replace *`host`*.

**NOTE:** With W3-mSQL, you can connect to only one server at a time. Other applications may support simultaneous connections to multiple servers.

> `<! msql close>`. Closes the current database connection. After closing the connection, you can connect to another or the same database with the `connect` command.
>
> `<! msql database name>`. Opens the named database. You can access multiple databases on the same server by using a database command for each.
>
> `<! msql query "query string" QueryHandle>`. *`Query string`* is the SQL statement to be processed. *`QueryHandle`* is the handle used to refer to the results for the query elsewhere on the page (basically, a variable name to refer to the results). *`QueryHandle`* can contain several records. The records in the *`QueryHandle`* can be processed one at a time. The first record from the query is the "current record," which will be the one processed by single record operations. The current record can be changed through the `fetch` and `seek` commands, described later in this section.

**NOTE:** A query does not necessarily imply a request for information. A query is a database operation that can include information requests or other actions such as inserting a new record, modifying data, and deleting records.

<! msql free *QueryHandle*>. Releases the *QueryHandle* from any data it might contain.

Before proceeding with the other commands, you should learn how W3-mSQL handles variables.

In many programming languages, such as C, numbering and counting schemes start with 0, not 1.

You can use W3-mSQL variables to specify and conditionally test values in the current record, environment variables, and the values in a URL query string (HTML form input).

Values in the current record are accessed by the name for the *QueryHandle* and the field (column) number. Field numbers start at 0, so the fifth field is numbered 4. In the following example, `a1` is the *QueryHandle*, and `bikes` is the name of the database with the fields `year`, `model`, and `price` in it:

```
<! msql query "select year, model, price from bikes" a1>
```

**NOTE:** The database fields might not necessarily be in the same order shown in the preceding statement, and `bikes` could contain other fields. However, only the fields in the preceding example string will be stored in `a1`, and in the order shown. The numbering of the fields is `0` for the year field, `1` for the model field, and `2` for the price field.

Field values of the current record are identified by the "at" symbol, `@`, the *QueryHandle* name, a period, and the field number. Therefore, for the preceding example, the model in the current record would be `@a1.1`.

W3-mSQL stores values from an URL query, which can be accessed and used in the embedded commands. For example, the input from an HTML form (using `METHOD=GET`) might be

```
/CGI-bin/w3-msql/mypath/myfile.html?year=1992&model=FXSTC
```

The URL query string values are specified in W3-mSQL by the dollar sign, `$`, followed by the name of the values. For this example, the query string variables are `$year` and `$make` with respective values of `1992` and `FXSTC`.

Environment variables, such as `PATH` and `HOST`, are accessed the same way as query string variables—a dollar symbol followed by the variables name. For example, the host name of your server could be accessed by `$HOST`.

**NOTE:** Query string variables are accessed first, then environment variables. Therefore, if a query string variable has the same name as an environment variable, the query string variable would be used. For example, if your form has a field named PATH, W3-mSQL will use the value submitted by the form, not the environment variable PATH.

Now that you have learned variables, you can get back on track with the embedded W3-mSQL commands.

Complete documentation for mSQL and W3-mSQL is included with the distribution of these applications, available at `http://hughes.com.au/`.

<! msql print "*string*">. Much like the print command in Perl, this command prints out the contents and variable values in the specified *string*. Text, HTML tags, W3-mSQL variables, and the escape sequence for a newline (\n) can be included in the string. From the previous examples of a form the URL query string was

```
/CGI-bin/w3-msql/mypath/myfile.html?age=1992&type=FXSTC
```

We could use an embedded W3-mSQL command as follows:

```
<! msql query "select year, model, price from bikes
➥     where year > $age and model = $type" a1>
```

You can send the fields of the current record in a1 to the customer by typing in the following code:

```
<! msql print "You entered $age and $type<BR>">
<! msql print "a result was @a1.0 @a1.1">
```

The section, "Using SQL," a little later in this chapter gives an overview of the basic SQL statements that will be useful for most Web sites.

<! msql print_rows *QueryHandle* "string">. Prints all the rows contained in the *QueryHandle*. For the current example that we have been using, an embedded print rows command is used as shown in the following:

```
<! msql query "select year, model, price from bikes
➥     where year > $age and model = $type" a1>
<TABLE><TR><TH> Year </TH><TH> Model <BR></TH></TR>
<! msql print_rows "<TR><TD> @a1.0 </TD><TD> @a1.1 <BR></TD></TR>">
</TABLE>
```

The preceding code generates a pretty nice table of the query results, with each record in a separate table row. You can also create lists and menus in a similar manner.

<! msql fetch *QueryHandle*>. Makes the next record in the query handle the current record.

<! msql seek *QueryHandle Position*>. Positions the record number (starting at 0 for the first record) of the record you want to make the current record. For example, to make the eighth record current, you would use <! msql seek a1 7>.

The final commands are the conditional ones that, as with many programming languages, give real power and utility to the application.

```
<! msql if (statement)>
<! msql else>
<! msql fi>
```

All the text, HTML tags, and other mSQL commands between the `if` and `else` commands (or the `fi` when `else` is omitted) are read only if the *`statement`* evaluates to `true`. The page content between the `else` (when used) and `fi` is read only when the *`statement`* is false.

The *`statement`* in the `if` command is any logical expression, such as `a == 2`. You can use the following operators:

- == equal to (note the double equal sign)
- != not equal to
- > greater than
- < less than
- >= greater than or equal to
- <= less than or equal to

You can also connect statements with the following:

- && and
- || or

For example, to evaluate a condition where `a` is not equal to `2` and `b` is less than `4` or `c` is equal to `5`, you would write

```
if( ( (a!=2)&&(b<4) ) || (c==5) )
```

Note that the parentheses control the order of evaluation.

**CAUTION:** Be careful not to use a single equal sign in your logic statements. In many programming languages, a single equal sign is an assignment operator, and a double equal sign is used for logic statements.

The variable can be strings or numbers, although string variables use only the == and != operators; for example, `a == "dog"` or `b != "cat"`. For the Hawg's Harleys example, where the URL query string and the embedded query command are

```
/CGI-bin/w3-msql/mypath/myfile.html?age=1992&type=FXSTC
```

and

```
<! msql query "select year, model, price from bikes" a1>
```

an `if` statement could be written as the following:

```
if( (a1.1 == $type) && (a1.0 >= $age) )
```

In fact, you can use the conditional statement to control the output to the customer. An example of a portion of a page to handle a customer's query follows:

```
<! msql query "select year, model, price from bikes" a1>
<! msql if( (a1.1 == $type) && (a1.0 >= $age) )>
<! msql print "a1.0 a1.1 a1.2>
<! msql fi>
```

You can use the code in Listing 10.1 as a W3-mSQL template for the Hawg's Harleys example.

### Listing 10.1. Example W3-mSQL template.

```
<HTML>
<TITLE>Hawg's Harley - Product Query Results</TITLE>
<BODY BACKGROUND="image.gif"
    TEXT="#009900" LINK="#0000FF" VLINK="#FF00FF" ALINK="#FF0000">
<H1 ALIGN=CENTER>Hawg's Harley</H1>
<H2 ALIGN=CENTER>Our Line of Previously Owned Motorcycles</H2>
<! msql print "Your request for a %age% %type% has found;">
<! msql query "select year, model, price from bikes
➥     where year > $year and model = $model" a1>
<P><CENTER><TABLE ALIGN=CENTER WIDTH="80%">
<TR><TH> Year </TH><TH> Model <BR></TH><TH> Price <BR></TH></TR>
<! msql print_rows "<TR><TD> @a1.0 </TD><TD> @a1.1 </TD>
<TD> @a1.2 <BR></TD></TR>">
</TABLE>
<P>
Be sure to visit our show room at 15 West Eighth Street to see these bikes
and other that we have coming in every day.  We are open from 9:00 AM to
7:00 PM Monday to Saturday.  Other times available by appointment.
<P ALIGN=CENTER>
Hawg's Harley <A HREF="/index.html">Home Page</A>
<ADDRESS>
<P ALIGN=CENTER>
Hawg's Harley<BR>
<A HREF="mailto:hawg@hawg.com">hawg@hawg.com</A><BR>
</ADDRESS>
</BODY>
</HTML>
```

With an URL and query string of the following, our template will produce the Web page shown in Figure 10.5.

```
/CGI-bin/w3-msql/mypath/myfile.html?age=1992&type=FXSTC
```

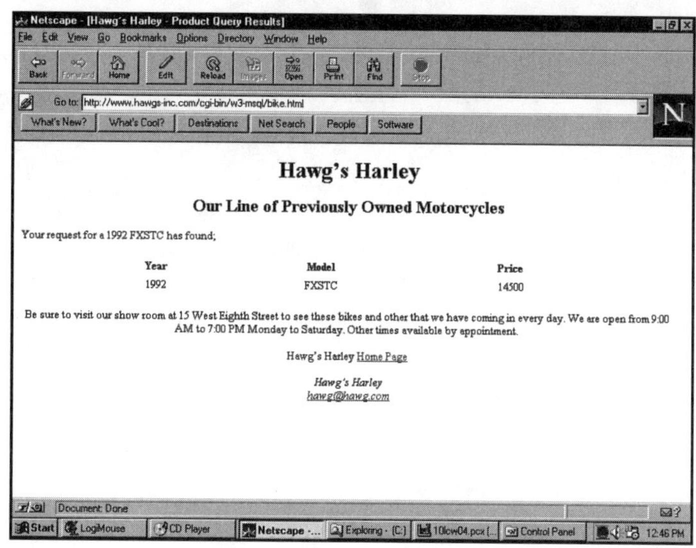


**Figure 10.5.** *The Web page generated by the example W3-mSQL template and mSQL database.*

# OBDC Databases

ODBC, Open Database Connectivity, is an standard for database applications to permit access from other applications through an ODBC driver (interface).

Several servers employ various techniques to access databases and to perform database operations. A few examples of these are Netscape's Livewire and Microsoft IIS's Inter Database Connector. Other techniques such as using CGI and server APIs are also used, but typically require programming expertise to implement.

SQL statements access most database back ends through ODBC drivers. With Livewire, IIS, and others, the statements are embedded in HTML files (as with W3-mSQL) or as simple scripts in text files. When the files are accessed by the server they process, the statements are executed and the results are sent to the user.

TASK

# Using SQL

For a good source of information and to learn SQL, read *Teach Yourself SQL in 14 Days* from Sams Publishing by Jeff Perkins and Bryan Morgan.

SQL (pronounced *sequel*), or Structured Query Language, is a specification for instructions to a database driver. SQL is not a language to directly access the database and perform the necessary operations, but rather a set of commands to the application that performs the database operations. SQL can be likened to an army officer who instructs a sergeant to perform a certain task. The sergeant directs the troops to accomplish the task and reports back to the officer with the results (task complete).

Several of the more commonly used SQL keywords follow:

- `SELECT` specifies which columns (fields) are to be returned from records matching a query. The fields will be returned in the order they are specified with `SELECT`, regardless of their order in the database. With more than one field specified, the field names are listed separated by commas; for example, `SELECT` *`field1,field2,field3`*.

- `FROM` specifies which database table is to be accessed.
- `WHERE` specifies a condition to be evaluated before the statement is performed on a row (record). Multiple conditions are joined with an `AND` or an `OR` to specify the logical relationship of the conditions. For both conditions to be true, you would enter `WHERE` *`condition1`* `AND` *`condition2`*. For either or both conditions to be true, enter `WHERE` *`condition1`* `OR` *`condition2`*.
- `INSERT INTO` adds a new record to the database table.
- `VALUES`, used with `INSERT`, specifies the field values to be added.
- `UPDATE` specifies a table in which records are to be modified (updated).
- `SET`, with `UPDATE`, modifies the specified field.
- ; ends each SQL statement; for example:

```
SELECT year,model
FROM bikes
WHERE year>=1992;
```

**NOTE:** Case usually does not matter—upper-, lower-, or mixed case is permitted in the SQL statement. This is not universal with all database programs, however. You might need to check your particular documentation for more details.

**TIP:** Using uppercase for the SQL keywords and putting each keyword on its own line can help you view the various parts of the statement for typos and other problems. Also, this format helps you read the different parts of the statement easily when you modify the statement.

The sample database table named bikes, shown in Table 10.2, is used in the following discussion of the SQL statements.

**Table 10.2. Example of a simple product database.**

| *Year* | *Model* | *Name* | *Color* | *Mileage* | *Price* |
|---|---|---|---|---|---|
| 1991 | FXRS | Low Rider | Red | 28500 | $12000.00 |
| 1993 | FLHS | Electra Glide Sport | Blue | 30200 | $15000.00 |
| 1992 | FXSTC | Softtail Custom | Black | 48000 | $14500.00 |

| *Year* | *Model* | *Name* | *Color* | *Mileage* | *Price* |
|---|---|---|---|---|---|
| 1990 | XLH | Sportster | Green | 12600 | $5000.00 |
| 1992 | FXDC | Dyna Glide Custom | Silver | 22300 | $13000.00 |
| 1990 | FLHTC | Electra Glide Classical | Black | 18400 | $10000.00 |
| 1991 | FLSTC | Heritage Softtail Classic | Blue | 12300 | $14000.00 |
| 1990 | FXR | Super Glide | Red | 22500 | $12000.00 |

## SELECT

To query the example database `bikes` for the year and model of any black motorcycle, you would write

```
SELECT Year, Model
FROM bikes
WHERE color = 'Black';
```

The following would be returned:

```
1990 FLHTC
```

If you wrote

```
SELECT Year, Model
FROM bikes
WHERE color = 'Black' AND year >= 1992;
```

the results would be

```
1992 FXSTC
```

## INSERT

Suppose you allowed people to add listings for bikes they wanted you to sell for them, where the appropriate entry corresponding to the field name in the line above it would replace each value in the VALUES line:

```
INSERT INTO bikes
(Year, Model, Name, Color, Mileage, Price)
VALUES (value, value, value, value, value, value);
```

Of course, you probably would not have others updating your product line, but the preceding example demonstrates how you can add customer information to a database of orders, requests, or other form input.

## UPDATE

If you need to update or correct a record in your database, you would use UPDATE. For example, if you found that the color listed for the Super Glide was incorrect, you would use UPDATE as in the following example:

```
UPDATE bikes
SET Color = 'Blue'
Where Model = 'FXR';
```

If you decided to knock ten percent off all prices, you would use `UPDATE` as in the following example:

```
UPDATE bikes
SET Price = Price * 0.9;
```

You can use mathematical expression such as +, -, *, and / to evaluate and set numerical field values.

## Creating Web-Database Applications

Now that you have an overview of SQL, let's proceed with how to get your database online. The typical Web server interface needs to connect to the database, perform the SQL statements, send the results to the user, and close the connection.

The actual method, format, and type of files you need to access your database depend on your specific server and the interface it uses. You learn the Microsoft IIS Internet Database Connector (IDC) briefly, not to demonstrate its particular techniques but to demonstrate the use of Web-database interfaces in general. IISIDC is somewhat simpler to use than (though similar to) many other interface servers, so discussion of IDC provides a good way to learn about database interfaces.

IDC uses two sets of files: `idc` files with the file extension `.idc` and response templates with the file extension `.htx`. The `idc` files, like CGI scripts, contain the SQL statements for your application. The `htx` files are HTML templates with embedded variables and statements that are processed and sent in response to the user.

In the `.idc` file, you specify

- `Datasource:` *`name`*. The name given to the ODBC driver for your database. This should have been specified when your system administrator installed the database.
- `Username:` *`logon`*. This name is an appropriate user name for your database.
- `Template:` *`yourfile`*`.htx`. This name is the response page for this query.
- `SQLStatement:` *`statement`*. This is the SQL statement to be executed.

The `htx` file contains embedded variables from the submitted form and from the results of the `idc` file.

When a customer or other user submits a query form with an `ACTION="/CGI/`*`yourfile.idc`*`"`, IDC executes the SQL statements in the specified `idc` file, then loads and processes the appropriate `htx` file, sending the results to the user.

For the Hawg's Harleys example we have been using in this chapter, you provide the customer with a form such as the following:

```
<FORM METHOD=GET ACTION="/CGI/seek.idc">
The customer would enter the year and model of bike
➥for which he or she is looking.
Please enter Year and Model of the bike you are seeking<BR>
<INPUT NAME=Age> Year<BR>
<INPUT NAME=Type> Model<BR>
<INPUT TYPE=SUBMIT VALUE="Send">
```

The `idc` file, `seek.idc`, (which processes the form input) is as follows:

```
Datasource: Web SQL
Username: hawgs
Template: results.htx

The SQLStatement:
+ SELECT year, model, price
+ From bikes
+ WHERE year >= %Age% AND model = %Type%;
```

**NOTE:** IDC variables are represented by a percent sign, %, followed by the variable's name and closing with another percent sign. For example, the type field from the form is identified by `%type%`.

The response template, `results.htx`, could look like Listing 10.2.

### Listing 10.2. An example `htx` file.

```
<HTML>
<HEAD>
<TITLE>Hawg's Harley - Query Results</TITLE>
</HEAD>
<BODY>
<H1 ALIGN=CENTER>

Thank for your request, of a %idc.age% %idc.type% currently we have

<TABLE>
<TR><TH>year </TH><TH>model </TH><TH> </TH><TH> price<BR></TH></TR>

<%begindetail%>
<TR><TD>year </TD><TD>model </TD><TD> </TD><TD> price<BR></TD></TR>
<%enddetail%>

</TABLE>

<%if CurrentRecord EQ 0%>
Sorry we don't have your bike. Please check back
we're getting more bikes every day
<%endif%>
```

*continues*

**Listing 10.2. continued**

```
Return to <A HREF="/index.html">Hawg's Home Page</A>

<ADDRESS>
<P ALIGN=CENTER>
Hawg's Harley
<A HREF="mailto:hawg@hawg.com">hawg@hawg.com</A>
</BODY>
</HTML>
```

Refer to Chapter 2, "Developing a Plan for Design and Site Management," for tips on creating a specific style and theme for your site.

I have left out much of the HTML code for easier reading, although you would want to include all page formatting, styling content, and footer information to fit the standard of your site.

IDC uses `<%begindetail%>` `<%enddetail%>` to mark a portion for the page where the results of the query will be posted. This portion of the page will be repeated for each record returned and is bypassed if no records are returned.

With `<%if condition%>` `<%endif%>`, IDC marks a section of the page that will be processed only if the condition is true. `CurrentRecord EQ 0` checks whether the pointer for the stack of query results is at the first record (record number 0). If any records were returned, `<%begindetail%>` would have advanced the pointer from the first record, making the `if` statement false. Placing this `if` statement after the `begindetail` section is a good way to check whether the query was successful.

# Financial Spreadsheets

Spreadsheets have been used extensively in the business world for years. Several spreadsheet applications have come about with the advent of large-scale computer use in business. Lotus 1-2-3 and Microsoft Excel are two of the most popular spreadsheet applications, with Excel probably more commom. Large spreadsheet applications are not widely used on the Web today, however.

**NOTE:** A large spreadsheet with hundreds or perhaps thousands of calculations could put a serious load on a server. If requests for the spreadsheet were frequent enough, the server performance could be severely diminished.

You can use a spreadsheet to perform the following tasks:

- Show how your products and services provide cost savings.
- Chart how your business is meeting market needs (sales, demand, production, and so on).

- Provide performance measurements (production up, costs going down, total assets increasing, and so on).
- Publish financial reports.
- Make available quarterly and yearly balance sheets on your business's finances.
- Provide a way for customers to make calculations (such as an air conditioning BTU calculation, in which the customers enter individual room measurements, temperatures, wall thickness, and so on).
- Allow customers to determine the cost of an order, including shipping and taxes.

These are just some ideas of what you could do by putting a spreadsheet online. Of course, you probably will have better ideas of what to put online for your business. You can put any spreadsheet information, though not confidential or private information, online. You can present spreadsheet information to customers, investors, and other users in several ways:

- A CGI spreadsheet program. Use the simple program included on this book's CD-ROM or a custom-built or commercial application.
- A Web page using an HTML table or preformat tags.

**TIP:** Use an HTML table to display your spreadsheet data if possible (if no user input or interaction is required). A spreadsheet with a large number of calculations can put high load on the server. If user input is required and an interactive page has to be used, try to keep the number of calculations to a minimum.

## Writing a Simple CGI Spreadsheet

Included on this book's CD-ROM is a simple C CGI spreadsheet program, `ssheet`. You can use this program to present to visitors to your site a spreadsheet in which they can enter values, submit the input, and receive an updated spreadsheet. When the program is called, it takes the following steps:

1. Accesses a configuration file to set itself up for your particular application.
2. Returns a default spreadsheet to the user.
3. Receives the spreadsheet from the user with any changes made.
4. Recalculates the spreadsheet.

5. Returns the updated spreadsheet to the user.
6. Enables the user to continue to make changes and submit the spreadsheet for further recalculations.

The `ssheet` program uses HTML form input elements to create the spreadsheet display. A sample spreadsheet is shown in Figure 10.6.

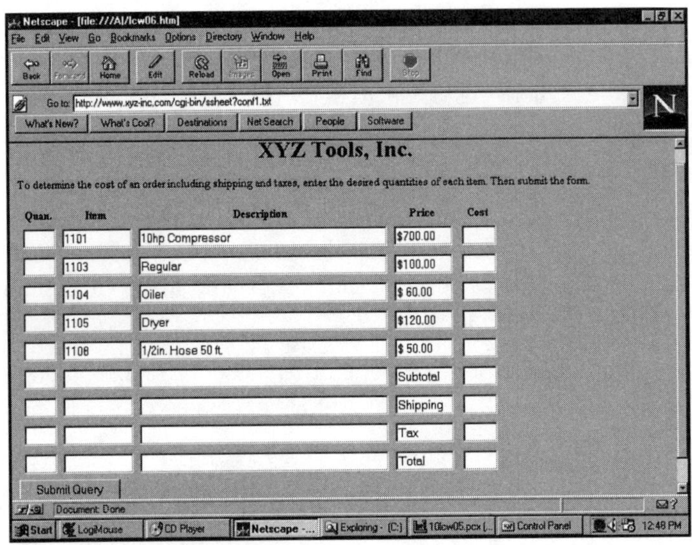


**Figure 10.6.**
*A spreadsheet from the* `ssheet` *program.*

To set up the spreadsheet program, follow these steps:

1. Load the spreadsheet file in a directory that allows CGI applications.
2. Add a file extension if needed (that is, `.CGI`, `.exe`, and so on).
3. Create the configuration file, a plain text file in which the following directives are used:
   - `file:` ***`path/filename`***. An optional template used to customize the display of the spreadsheet, give instruction to the user, and provide links to your home page and other locations.
   - `columns:` ***`letter`***. A letter specifying the last column in the spreadsheet. Can be upper- or lowercase. Only one letter can be used, so the spreadsheet is limited to 26 columns. This is a required directive.
   - `rows:` ***`number`***. The number of rows in your spreadsheet. This is a required directive.
   - `header:` ***`list`***. A comma-delimited list of the headers to be displayed for each column. The headers are applied in the order in which they are listed. To skip a column, simply use a space for the particular column in

Depending on your particular server, its configuration, and where the CGI program is loaded, you might need a special filename extension. Your system administrator should be able to inform you of what you need.

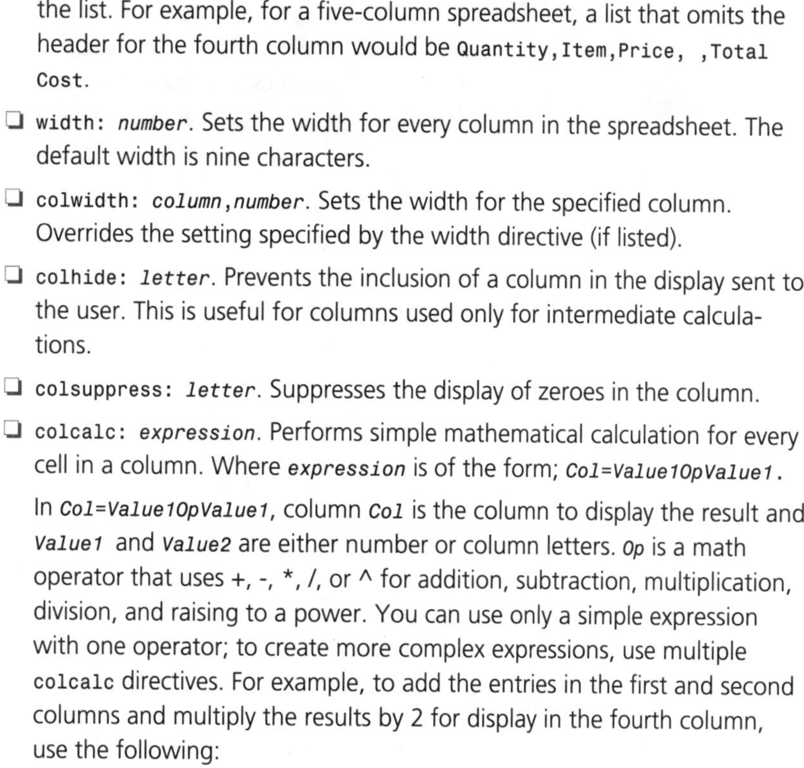

the list. For example, for a five-column spreadsheet, a list that omits the header for the fourth column would be `Quantity,Item,Price, ,Total Cost`.

- `width:` *`number`*. Sets the width for every column in the spreadsheet. The default width is nine characters.
- `colwidth:` *`column,number`*. Sets the width for the specified column. Overrides the setting specified by the width directive (if listed).
- `colhide:` *`letter`*. Prevents the inclusion of a column in the display sent to the user. This is useful for columns used only for intermediate calculations.
- `colsuppress:` *`letter`*. Suppresses the display of zeroes in the column.
- `colcalc:` *`expression`*. Performs simple mathematical calculation for every cell in a column. Where *`expression`* is of the form; *`Col=Value1OpValue1`*.

  In *`Col=Value1OpValue1`*, column *`Col`* is the column to display the result and *`Value1`* and *`Value2`* are either number or column letters. *`Op`* is a math operator that uses +, -, *, /, or ^ for addition, subtraction, multiplication, division, and raising to a power. You can use only a simple expression with one operator; to create more complex expressions, use multiple `colcalc` directives. For example, to add the entries in the first and second columns and multiply the results by 2 for display in the fourth column, use the following:

```
colcalc: C=A+B
colcalc: D=2*C
```

**NOTE:** Calculations are performed in the order in which the `colcalc` directives are listed.

- `coleval:` *statement*. Evaluates the logic *`statement`* and returns `1` or `0` if the *`statement`* is `true` or `false`. The statement is a simple logic expression of the form *`Col=Value1OpValue2`*, where *`Col`* is the column to contain the results and *`Value1`* and *`Value2`* are numbers, strings (must be in quotes, for example `"abc"`), or column letters. *`Op`* is a logical operator that can use `==`, `!=`, `>`, `<`, `<=`, or `>=` for equal to, not equal to, greater than, less than, less than/equal to, and greater than/equal to. For example, to display the addition of two columns only if the first column has a value greater than 0, use the following code:

```
colsuppress: E
colcalc: C=A+B
coleval: D=A>0
colcalc: E=D*C
```

- `colsum:` *`cell,column`*. Sums all the values in the designated column above the row containing the cell. The result is entered in the specified cell, which is specified by its column and row. For example, the third cell in the fourth row is C4. To sum all the cells in the third column from the first through third rows, you would enter

  ```
  colsum: C4,C
  ```

- `cellcalc:` *`expression`*. Performs the mathematical expression only in the designated cell. The *`expression`* is in the form *`Cell=Value1OpValue2`*. *`Cell`* is the column row address; for example, the third cell in the fourth row is C4. *`Value1`* and *`Value2`* are either numbers or cell addresses. *`Op`* is exactly the same as it was described for the `colcalc` directive.
- `cellsuppress:` *`cell`*. Suppresses the display of `0` in the specified cell.
- `value:` *`cell,value`*. Places the specified value in the cell. The value can be a number or a string. String values should be in quotation marks (`"abc"`).
- `colvalue:` *`column,value`*. Places the specified value in every cell of the column. The value can be a number or a string. String values should be in quotation marks (`"abc"`).

**NOTE:** It is important to remember that all calculations and evaluations are performed in the order listed in the configuration file. For example, a cell that contains a column sum is overwritten by `colcalc` for its column, thus the `colsum` directive should be listed after the `colcalc` directive.

Refer to Chapter 2 for ideas on creating a theme for your entire site.

4. Create the template page if one is to be used.
   - Create the template with the content and layout that you want.
   - Use the tag `{spreadsheet}` on your page where you want `ssheet` to position the spreadsheet.
5. Make a link to `ssheet` specifying the configuration file as a query string. For example, try `<A HREF="/CGI-bin/ssheet?myConFig.txt">Spreadsheet</A>`.

An example `ssheet` configuration file is included on the CD-ROM.

**TIP:** Although `ssheet` can simply send its output to the user, it is best to use a template. With the template, `ssheet`'s output page will match the style of your site, provide additional information to the user, and provide links to your home page and other areas of your site.

# Creating Static Spreadsheets

Often with spreadsheets, the display of the information is important, not the interaction with the user. In these cases, a static page displaying the spreadsheet for viewing is all that you need. As described in the section, "Static Database Pages," in this chapter, you can create the static pages with HTML table tags or with preformat tags.

An alternative is simply to send the user the spreadsheet file, though you must be sure that your server identifies the right MIME type for your file or uses a generic type of application/octet-stream. Many spreadsheet applications can use files from another application. For example, if you use Excel and a user has Lotus 1-2-3, the user could still load and view your file in Lotus.

You can obtain Internet Assistant for Excel from the Microsoft Web site at `http://www.microsoft.com/`.

Applications that create Web pages directly from spreadsheet files are also available. Microsoft Internet Assistant for Excel is one such freely available application.

## Creating an HTML Page from an Excel Spreadsheet

The procedure for installing Internet Assistant for Excel is fairly easy and straightforward.

1. After you have downloaded the file, place it in the Excel Library directory (usually the following):

   `C:\Excel\Library or C:\MSOffice\Excel\Library)`

2. From the Tools menu in Excel, select Add-Ins.
3. Select Internet Assistant Wizard.

To use Internet Assistant, follow these steps:

1. Select Internet Assistant Wizard from the Tool menu.
2. Select the spreadsheet cells you want to include and select Next.
3. Select whether to create a new HTML document or to use an existing document.
   - ❑ If you choose to use an existing document as a template, it must have the string `##Table##` in it so the Wizard knows where to insert the spreadsheet table.
   - ❑ If you choose to use a new document, you will be prompted for title, header, and footer information.

4. Select Next. Then select whether to incorporate the special formatting (background colors, font size, and so on) of your spreadsheet or just place the data without formatting in the Web page. Select Next.
5. Enter the path/filename for the document and select Finish.

**TIP:** Using an existing document as your template will help standardize the spreadsheet page with the rest of your site. Be sure the template has the string `##Table##` to locate the appropriate spot for the spreadsheet table. Using the template can greatly decrease the amount of work needed to create several standardized pages or to update a document with new data (the Wizard will simply overwrite the existing file).

Microsoft has several free Web development tools that you can download at its site, `http://www.microsoft.com/`.

Internet Assistant now has created an HTML document from your spreadsheet. Figure 10.7 shows an example of a page generated by Internet Assistant.

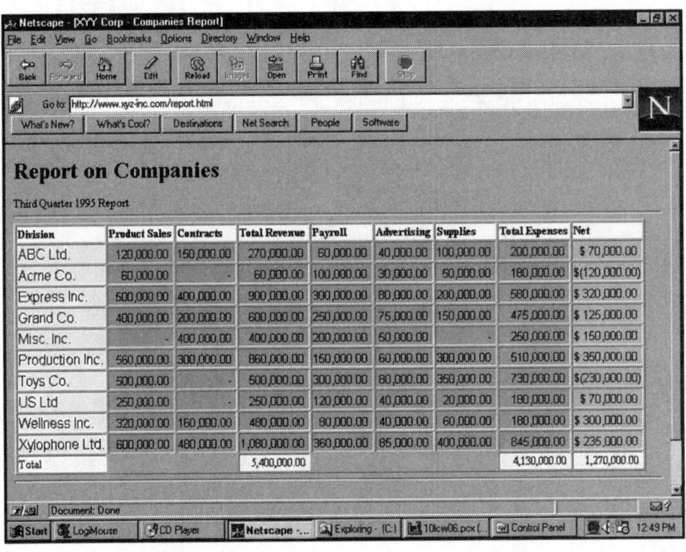


**Report on Companies**

Third Quarter 1995 Report

| Division | Product Sales | Contracts | Total Revenue | Payroll | Advertising | Supplies | Total Expenses | Net |
|---|---|---|---|---|---|---|---|---|
| ABC Ltd. | 120,000.00 | 150,000.00 | 270,000.00 | 60,000.00 | 40,000.00 | 100,000.00 | 200,000.00 | $ 70,000.00 |
| Acme Co. | 60,000.00 | - | 60,000.00 | 100,000.00 | 30,000.00 | 50,000.00 | 180,000.00 | $(120,000.00) |
| Express Inc. | 500,000.00 | 400,000.00 | 900,000.00 | 300,000.00 | 80,000.00 | 200,000.00 | 580,000.00 | $ 320,000.00 |
| Grand Co. | 400,000.00 | 200,000.00 | 600,000.00 | 250,000.00 | 75,000.00 | 150,000.00 | 475,000.00 | $ 125,000.00 |
| Misc. Inc. | - | 400,000.00 | 400,000.00 | 200,000.00 | 50,000.00 | - | 250,000.00 | $ 150,000.00 |
| Production Inc. | 560,000.00 | 300,000.00 | 860,000.00 | 150,000.00 | 60,000.00 | 300,000.00 | 510,000.00 | $ 350,000.00 |
| Toys Co. | 500,000.00 | - | 500,000.00 | 300,000.00 | 80,000.00 | 350,000.00 | 730,000.00 | $(230,000.00) |
| US Ltd | 250,000.00 | - | 250,000.00 | 120,000.00 | 40,000.00 | 20,000.00 | 180,000.00 | $ 70,000.00 |
| Wellness Inc. | 320,000.00 | 160,000.00 | 480,000.00 | 80,000.00 | 40,000.00 | 60,000.00 | 180,000.00 | $ 300,000.00 |
| Xylophone Ltd. | 600,000.00 | 480,000.00 | 1,080,000.00 | 360,000.00 | 85,000.00 | 400,000.00 | 845,000.00 | $ 235,000.00 |
| Total | | | 5,400,000.00 | | | | 4,130,000.00 | 1,270,000.00 |

**Figure 10.7.**
*A Web page generated by Microsoft's Internet Assistant for Excel.*

# Investor Relations Pages

You might want to check out the National Investor Relations Institute site at `http://www.niri.org/`.

You have learned how to put your databases and spreadsheets online and make them available. An important area not to overlook is investor relations. Whether you are a small business or a large corporation, investor relations are important to you.

Investor relations do not involve just stock holders, but also a whole range of individuals and organizations with a financial interest in your business. These can include the following:

- Banks and other institutions from which you seek a loan. Your business's finances not only affect the decision to grant a loan, but also affect the rate and term of the loan.
- Suppliers who might extend a line of credit to your business.
- Customers who might depend on your business for supplies and other products.
- Other businesses that might seek to enter a partnership with you.
- Organizations and individuals who you might want to acquire your business.

Investor relations refer basically to providing the information dealing with the financial health and future of your business.

Read Chapter 3, "Corporate Presence Pages," for more ideas on putting business information online.

You might want to include several items in your investor relations pages:

- Press releases
- Customer references and testimonials
- An overview of your company
- Your business plan
- Your budget
- A balance sheet for the quarter and year showing assets and liabilities

The balance sheet is simply a basic spreadsheet that groups together assets, liabilities, expenses, and revenues. The sums of the individual groups as well as overall balance are shown. Commonly, the figures for the current quarter are compared to past quarters, particularly the same quarter in the past year. Also, the yearly balance sheet can contain figures from previous years for comparison.

# Workshop Wrap-Up

In this chapter, you learned

- How to get your database information online and available to customers. You learned several techniques, including using a static page of information, using a shareware database (mSQL), with a Web interface (W3-mSQL), and server Web-database interfaces.
- How to get your spreadsheets online. You learned a rather simple CGI spreadsheet and how to generate static Web pages from a spreadsheet file.
- The importance of investor relations and items of interest to investors that you can put on Web pages.

## Next Steps

Now...

- ❑ Chapter 13, "Advanced Catalogs." Use databases to generate online catalog and product description pages on the fly.
- ❑ Chapter 14, "Web Shopping Carts." Learn how to allow customers to select items from different pages (and different catalogs) without having to place a separate order for each selected item.
- ❑ Chapter 18, "Order and Shipment Tracking on the Web." Use databases to collect customer and order information. Also use databases to track orders, maintain inventory, and analyze sales data.

## Q&A

**Q: Does every site marketing products on the Web need to use a product database for their customers?**

**A:** The right approach is to make your product information readily available to customers. A database is one way to accomplish this. A site with a limited line of goods probably is better off with a list or a table of product information. A large line of products can be difficult for customers to search through, however, so a database can be beneficial.

**Q: Can anyone on the Internet access a company's databases through the company's Web server?**

**A:** Security is also a main concern. Locating the databases so the interface you create and control, not the Web server by itself, can access the databases helps limit access to the databases. Also, if your database application allows for limiting access to certain hosts, then this will provide additional security.

**Q: Why aren't there many spreadsheet applications on the Web?**

**A:** Actually, there are several of them. Online shopping carts and order forms that tally your purchases and calculate the charge are simple spreadsheets. A large spreadsheet can consume much of a server's resources if it is accessed frequently, however.

**Q: Why did you include the investor relations section?**

**A:** Investor relations have been an important part of doing business, though they are often overlooked. With the database and spreadsheet applications that you learn in this chapter, a business's investor relations information can be made readily available.

CHAPTER ELEVEN

# Searching Your Site

## In this chapter, you

- Set up a site table of contents
- Install a site search engine
- Learn design tips for site searching and navigation

## Tasks in this chapter:

- Creating a Table of Contents
- Using an Indexing Program
- Making a Site Map
- Setting Up a Search Engine for Your Site
- Setting Up an Advanced Search Engine

Glad you made it here to Chapter 11. It was probably not difficult to get to this point in the book. Unless you were either reading the book from beginning to end or were just browsing through, it is most likely the table of contents or the index that directed you to this page. If you were looking for this specific subject, the table of contents made it easy for you to find this section of the book quickly. Perhaps you picked up this book and just looked through the table of contents to see what information the book contains and came to this page because the description interested you.

The easy navigation and use of the site is the goal. A table of contents and site index are means to this goal.

A Web site, like a book, needs a means for visitors to easily see what content the site has and to quickly go to the content that interests them. Imagine if this book didn't have a table of contents or an index. It would be very difficult to locate specific chapters and subjects. Setting up a table of contents or an index for your site will make your site more accessible and user-friendly. (See Figure 11.1.)

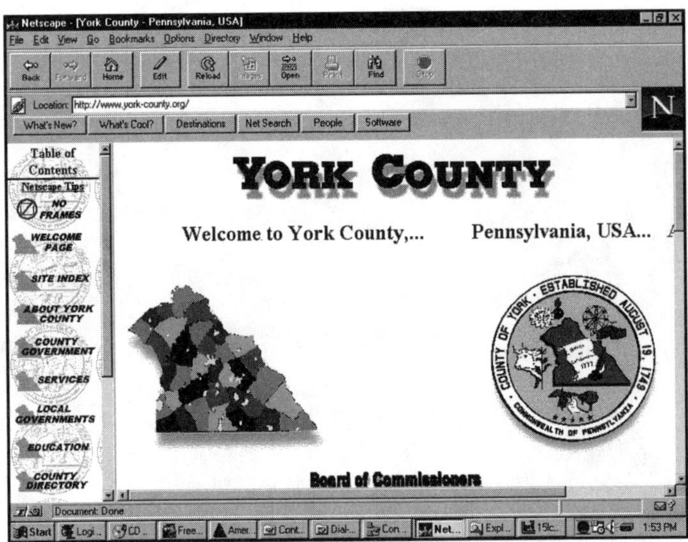


**Figure 11.1.**
*An example of a site's home page with a table of contents.*

An example of a site search engine can be found at `http://www.lifetimetv.com/search/lifetime.html`.

On large and complex sites with many documents, a site search engine can be a big help to visitors. Like their big brothers on the Web (such as `www.lycos.com` and `altavista.digital.com`), the site search engines locate documents based on visitor input. Using keywords that the user inputs to describe the sought-after content, the site search engine returns a listing of the site pages that match the keyword description. And several search engines can even rate the pages, indicating how closely each found page matches the user's keyword description.

# Creating a Site Index and Table of Contents

Remember, your Web site is a place of business, the same as your office, store, or shop.

As previously mentioned, tables of contents and indexes are a great benefit to users in many sites and are a necessity in large, complex sites. Just as you wouldn't want customers to wander about your place of business without offering them assistance, you wouldn't want visitors to do the same at your Web site . Have you ever had the experience of not finding what you want at a store and not receiving any help? If you have, then you'll know how frustrating it could be for a customer at your site.

## Site Indexes

A *site index* and a table of contents are very similar, and at times the two terms are used interchangeably. A table of contents is more of an outline of the site, following the site's structure and providing links to key sections.

A site index is more information-oriented than structure-oriented. The index typically groups the portions of the site into areas of interest for the visitor. Furthermore, the site index typically lists the entire site, providing access to any point within the site.

**NOTE:** A site index can be set up as an alphabetical listing of the site's pages, although this is not usually the case. Typically, this might be done for a large site, where visitors know what they are looking for and need a link to get them to the right page. For a good example of an alphabetical site index, go to

`http://sunsite.unc.edu/alpha-index/`

Because the site's layout or structure is usually set up to reflect content, the index and table of contents are pretty similar.

See `http://www.york-county.org/toc.htm` for an example of a site index.

To create a site index, you use the techniques for creating a table of contents. Basically, you create a full table of contents for the entire site, adding short descriptive phrases to the links.

# Creating a Table of Contents

The table of contents serves two important functions for your site:

- It gives visitors an overview of the site and its content. Even if users come across your site while Web surfing, something in the table of contents might interest them, and they will look further into your site. When I am looking for a book to buy, I browse the table of contents to see if the book has what I want in it.
- It lists the main sections and subsections of your site. Visitors can quickly locate the subject area in which they are interested and navigate to that portion of the site.

The following guidelines can help you set up the table of contents:

- List the main sections that reflect the structure of your site.
- If you are including subsections in the table, group them under the appropriate main section.

Be sure to make the section in the table of contents easy to see and identify.

- ❑ Use different font sizes, indentation, or other means to make the main section listings easily distinguishable from the subsections.

**TIP:** Colored balls, stars, or other small images are helpful for making the sections and entries in the table of contents easy to see and distinguish.

- ❑ Each entry for the section (and the subsection if included) should be linked to the first page of the section or subsection.

**NOTE:** The main section headers need not be links if the subsections are included in the table and if the site does not have a main page for the section. (See `http://www.w3.org/`.) Still, there needs to be a header for the section to aid the visitor in locating the right subsection.

- ❑ Separate the main sections of the table of contents using paragraphs, HTML tables, or some other means.

**NOTE:** Not every table of contents needs to list subsections. Small sites might not even have subsections, and large sites might have too many levels of subsections to be listed on a single table. For very large sites, the different subsections can have their own table of contents on separate pages. Remember that what's important is giving the user a quick-and-easy way to locate information on your site.

As with any job, creating a site table of contents is easier if you have the right tools. Even without an HTML editor, creating a table is not hard.

## Text Editors

You can easily put together a table of contents for the site by using a text editor such as Notepad. A text editor handles creating a table of contents nicely; you copy and paste the code for one of the lines in the table several times and then simply add the URLs and the descriptions.

```
<LI><A HREF="foreign.html">Foreign Cars</A></LI>
<LI><A HREF="us86_96.html">Domestic 1986-1996</A></LI>
<LI><A HREF="us70_85.html">Domestic 1970-1985</A></LI>
<LI><A HREF=""></A></LI>
<LI><A HREF=""></A></LI>
<LI><A HREF=""></A></LI>
```

The extra lines are simply deleted (cut) from the preceding code.

## HTML Editors

Of course, you can use your favorite HTML editor to build such a list. Create a list of the descriptions, and then select each description, add the link properties for each, and, violà, you have your table of contents.

# Using an Indexing Program

Refer to Chapter 1, "Selecting and Using Tools for Page Creation," for more information on HTML editors.

A Win32 program (Windows 95 and Windows NT), `indexer.exe`, creates a list of links to every HTML page in a directory (including the files in any subdirectories). The `indexer.exe` program searches the directory and subdirectories for Web page files (files with an `.htm` or `.html` extension) and stores the path and filenames of the Web pages in a temporary file. Then, `indexer.exe` reads the pages one at a time from the temporary file and does the following:

- ❑ Opens the Web page's file
- ❑ Extracts the page's title
- ❑ Closes the Web page's file
- ❑ Creates a link to the Web page

The links are written to a file named `tmp_toc.htm` and are comprised of the relative URLs of the pages (relative to the directory containing `indexer.exe`), and they have the pages' titles as link descriptions, as shown in Figure 11.2.

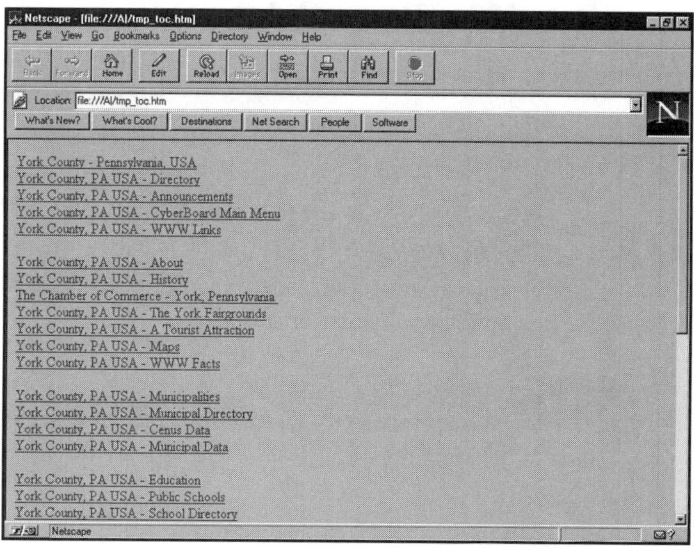


**Figure 11.2.**
*A list of links generated by* `indexer.exe`.

**NOTE:** If a page does not have a title (by standards every HTML page is suppose to have a title), the relative URL is used for the link's description.

The list of page links is broken into paragraphs, and one paragraph for each subdirectory has HTML files. The coding of the list generated by `indexer.exe` is shown in Figure 11.3.

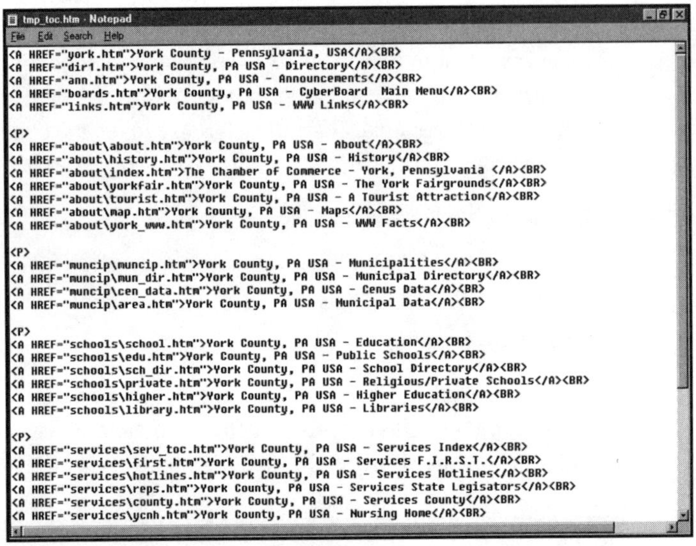

**Figure 11.3.**
*The text and HTML code generated by* `indexer.exe`.

tmp_toc.htm - Notepad

File Edit Search Help

```
<A HREF="york.htm">York County - Pennsylvania, USA</A><BR>
<A HREF="dir1.htm">York County, PA USA - Directory</A><BR>
<A HREF="ann.htm">York County, PA USA - Announcements</A><BR>
<A HREF="boards.htm">York County, PA USA - CyberBoard  Main Menu</A><BR>
<A HREF="links.htm">York County, PA USA - WWW Links</A><BR>

<P>
<A HREF="about\about.htm">York County, PA USA - About</A><BR>
<A HREF="about\history.htm">York County, PA USA - History</A><BR>
<A HREF="about\index.htm">The Chamber of Commerce - York, Pennsylvania </A><BR>
<A HREF="about\yorkfair.htm">York County, PA USA - The York Fairgrounds</A><BR>
<A HREF="about\tourist.htm">York County, PA USA - A Tourist Attraction</A><BR>
<A HREF="about\map.htm">York County, PA USA - Maps</A><BR>
<A HREF="about\york_www.htm">York County, PA USA - WWW Facts</A><BR>

<P>
<A HREF="muncip\muncip.htm">York County, PA USA - Municipalities</A><BR>
<A HREF="muncip\mun_dir.htm">York County, PA USA - Municipal Directory</A><BR>
<A HREF="muncip\cen_data.htm">York County, PA USA - Cenus Data</A><BR>
<A HREF="muncip\area.htm">York County, PA USA - Municipal Data</A><BR>

<P>
<A HREF="schools\school.htm">York County, PA USA - Education</A><BR>
<A HREF="schools\edu.htm">York County, PA USA - Public Schools</A><BR>
<A HREF="schools\sch_dir.htm">York County, PA USA - School Directory</A><BR>
<A HREF="schools\private.htm">York County, PA USA - Religious/Private Schools</A><BR>
<A HREF="schools\higher.htm">York County, PA USA - Higher Education</A><BR>
<A HREF="schools\library.htm">York County, PA USA - Libraries</A><BR>

<P>
<A HREF="services\serv_toc.htm">York County, PA USA - Services Index</A><BR>
<A HREF="services\first.htm">York County, PA USA - Services F.I.R.S.T.</A><BR>
<A HREF="services\hotlines.htm">York County, PA USA - Services Hotlines</A><BR>
<A HREF="services\reps.htm">York County, PA USA - Services State Legisators</A><BR>
<A HREF="services\county.htm">York County, PA USA - Services County</A><BR>
<A HREF="services\ycnh.htm">York County, PA USA - Nursing Home</A><BR>
```

When `indexer.exe` is finished generating the list of links in the `tmp_toc.htm` file, the temporary file of the path or filenames is deleted and `indexer.exe` closes. To use `indexer.exe`, follow these steps:

1. Copy `indexer.exe` to the main directory of your site or the directory from which you want to start making the index.
2. Run `indexer.exe` (double-click it in Windows Explorer, or open it from the Run option on the Start menu).

**NOTE:** It might take `indexer.exe` a few minutes to read through all the files and to generate the link list.

Refer to Chapter 1 for information on creating templates and using HTML editors.

3. Delete unwanted links from the list.
4. Either add a header and footer section to `tmp_toc.htm` or cut and paste the link list into an existing Web page or template.
5. If needed, use a text or HTML editor to add headers to each section in the link list, as shown in Figure 11.4.

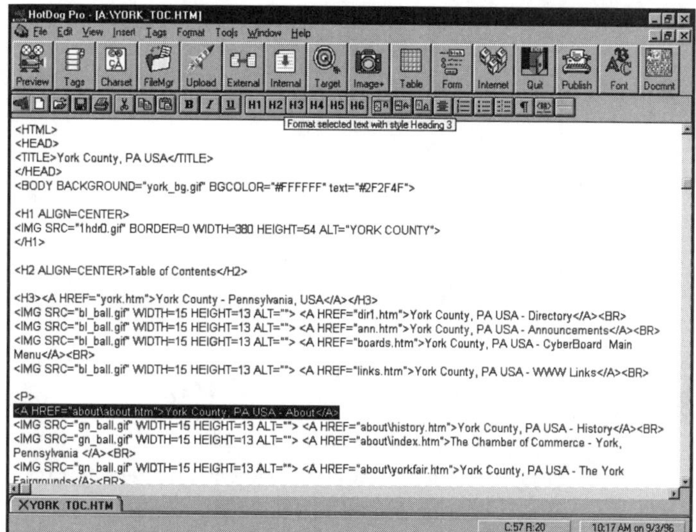


**Figure 11.4.**
*Editing the list created by* `indexer.exe`.

6. You can stylize the list by using ordered or unordered lists or by adding an icon to the links.

**NOTE:** You might want to rename `tmp_toc.htm`. Although you can use the `tmp_toc.htm` file as is, you might want to rename the file to a name more suitable for your site.

A final version of a table of contents created by `indexer.exe` and edited to add style features is shown in Figure 11.5.

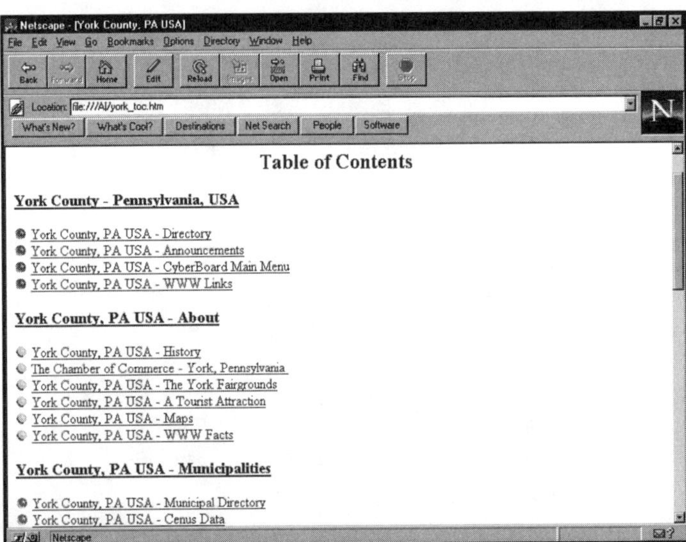


**Figure 11.5.**
*The final version of the table of contents.*

# Making a Site Map

You can create a somewhat graphical table of contents using a site map. A *site map* lays out the links to the site's files in an image map or a table, as shown in Figure 11.6. The links are grouped by directory or by links to each other. For the directory grouping, the files that comprise each subsection of the site need to be in their own subdirectories.

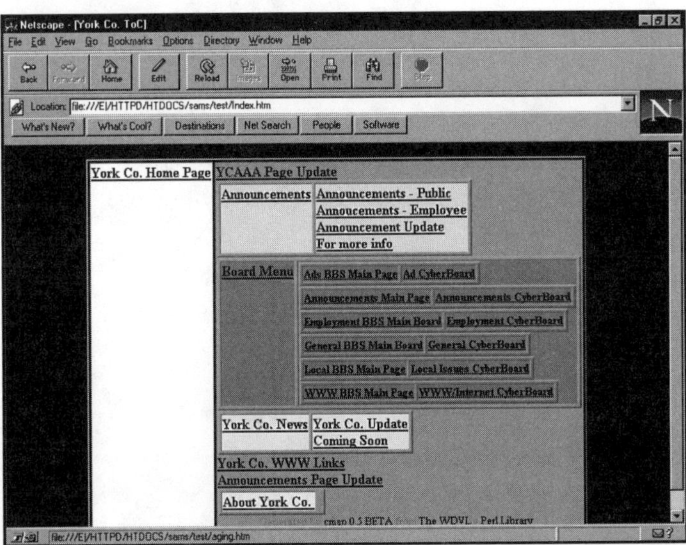


**Figure 11.6.**
*A site map is an alternative to a table of contents.*

An image map editor, Map This, is discussed in Chapter 1.

Creating a site map is a fairly straightforward process, especially if you are using an image map. However, using an HTML table can be somewhat involved. The individual table cells of an HTML table contain a page or a subsection of the site. The sizing and placement of the cells indicates the site's structure. Fortunately, software tools exist to help you develop site maps using HTML tables. A freeware application, `cmap`, is one such tool.

See `http://www.stars.com/Navigation/ToC/` for a look at an actual site map.

As a Web developer, you'll be interested in the other resources at `http://www.stars/com/`, the Web Developer's Virtual Library.

You can find information on Perl and the code for various platforms at `http://www.perl.com/perl/`.

## cmap

Many sites are set up by subdirectories, with each subdirectory related to a particular area or subject—this aids site setup, management, and maintenance. The Web Developer's Virtual Library site (`http://www.stars.com/`) is laid out in this manner and uses a site map (see `http://www.stars.com/Navigation/ToC/`). The script used to generate the site map is called `cmap` and is available, along with the necessary subroutine file `ht_subs.pl`, for download at `http://www.stars.com/Software/Perl/`.

`cmap` is a Perl script that can be run on any computer that has Perl interpreter software.

**NOTE:** The Perl interpreter (simply called perl) is available on most WWW servers. Perl is one of the most, if not the most, widely used languages for creating CGI scripts.

Follow these steps to use `cmap`:

1. Generate a directory/file list of all the subdirectories and files you want to include in the site map. In the directory that the map is to start, enter the following at the command prompt:

   ```
   find ./ -name "*.htm" -print > list.txt (for Unix)
   ```

   ```
   dir .\*.htm /S/B > list.txt (a DOS window for Windows)
   ```

2. Verify that the first line of the script, `#!/usr/bin/perl`, reflects the correct path/filename for perl (the Perl interpreter). Check with your system administrator if you are not sure.
3. If your site does not a have default file in each of your subdirectories, copy the main file in each subdirectory to the default file.

Having a file with the default name in each directory and subdirectory on your server can stop people from looking at and accessing files and subdirectories you might want to keep hidden.

**TIP:** Having the main file in each directory/subdirectory named as the default file helps users who are looking for your home page or the main file but do not have the filename. They can enter `http://yoursite.com/yourdirectory/` and receive the default file.

The default file is set by server configuration; it is typically `index.html`, `home.html`, or `default.html` (`.html` can be replaced by `.htm`). Your system administrator can give you the name of the default file.

**NOTE:** `cmap` uses the default file in each subdirectory to properly indent the subdirectory.

4. Set the following variables in the script:
   - `$sub` The path to the Perl subroutine file `ht_subs.pl`. Just include the directory path, not the filename. On UNIX, you might use `$sub = '/usr/lib/perl';`.
   - `$v{'Title'}` The title you want to have for the site map page. The default, `$v{'Title'} = 'Site Content Map';`, will probably be significant.
   - `$index` The name of the default file to use on your server. Usually, it is `index`, `default`, or `home`. Do not include the extension (for example, `$index = 'home';`).
   - `$html` The extension used for HTML files on your server. Use either `htm` or `html` (for example, `$html = 'htm';`).
   - `$max` The number of directory levels you want the map to have. `$max = 3;` has the main directory and two levels of subdirectories.

**CAUTION:** An overly detailed site map can be difficult to read. Use it to show your site's basic structure, but not necessarily every page. Limit the amount of detail by limiting the directory levels to be mapped.

   - `$banner` This is part of the `ht_sub` routines. It installs an advertising banner on the page. You can leave this variable alone because you'll be removing the line that uses it.
   - `$border` HTML tables are used to create the layout of the site map. `$border` sets the width of the table borders that outline the map. The default value, `$border = 2;`, should be sufficient.
   - Assign a new variable, `$mpfile`. Just below the line that begins with `$border`, add `$mpfile = 'site_map';`. This variable is used to create the map file; otherwise, the default filename will be used.
5. Just below the variable list, change `$index` to `$mpfile` in the line that reads `open ( OUT, ">$index.$html")¦¦die$!;`
6. Locate the line `&Head ($banner);`. Either delete this line or comment it out. This line inserts a specialized header for your file that won't be suitable for your page. To comment out a line, insert `#` at the beginning of the line.
7. Edit the script's stop list, which contains files and subdirectories that are not to be shown on the map.

8. At the end of the file (just before `EOT`), add a line with the HTML tags </TR></TABLE>.
9. Delete or comment out the line with `&foot ;`—it adds a specialized footer to the page that would not be right for your site.
10. Save the script file.
11. Run `cmap` using the `list.txt` file for input. From the command prompt `cmap < list.txt`, `cmap` creates the site map as an HTML file with the default filename in the main directory.
12. Edit the map file. You might want to remove or add files to the map.

**TIP:** You might want to apply a color scheme to the map using the `bgcolor` attributes in the table cell tags.

**NOTE:** Retain the credits and links back to the WDVL. They have provided this script at no cost to you.

See Chapter 2, "Developing a Plan for Design and Site Management," for information on making a site theme.

13. You might want to copy the map into a specific file or add more content to the map file.

**NOTE:** The `cmap` script, as set up in this list and shown in Figure 11.7, does not include any HTML head information.

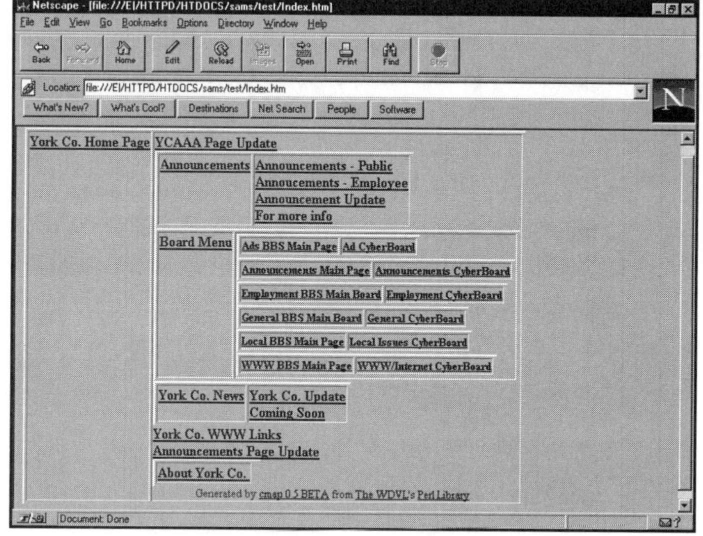


**Figure 11.7.**
*`cmap` creates a site map page that can be made into a Web page or copied into another.*

# Setting Up a Search Engine for Your Site

Imagine walking into a large office for an appointment with John Smith and James Jones. There's an office directory in the main lobby, but it lists only the different departments and key personnel. You go to the receptionist, describe who you are looking for, and are immediately directed to the right office for your meeting.

A list of free and commercially available search engines can be found at `http://www.boutell.com/faq/search.htm`.

Your site is a place of business for you. A rather large site can be likened to the large office. Wouldn't it be great to have a receptionist for your site to direct visitors to the various parts of your site?

Large sites with numerous pages can help visitors find content by offering a site search engine. Instead of searching through a large site index, visitors can describe what they are seeking and be directed to the appropriate page.

An actual site search engine can be used for searching the site at `http://www.ee.fit.edu/users/lpinto/`.

## A Simple Search Script

A freely distributed search engine is available from Matt's Script Archive. Three files are associated with Matt's search script: `readme`, `search.htm`, and `search.pl`.

You can see a CGI search engine at `http://divrse.com/vmf/`.

The `readme` file is in ASCII text and provides installation and setup instructions. Installation and setup are fairly simple tasks that can be accomplished by a novice. In fact, no familiarity with Perl or other programming languages is needed. Simply make the necessary changes to the Perl and HTML files as mentioned in the `readme` file (and in the following paragraphs) and load the files into the appropriate directories on the server. An overview of the script and Matthew Wright's copyright notice (giving permission to use the script) are also on the `readme` file.

Matt's Script Archive contains many useful scripts for Web development. A collection of Matt's scripts are on this book's accompanying CD-ROM. Also, these scripts can be obtained from `http://www.worldwidemart.com/scripts/`.

**NOTE:** Always leave an author's copyright notice in any script, even if you modify the script. Besides the possible legal ramifications, it is only right to give credit to the author, especially when he or she does not charge for the time and effort spent creating the script.

The `search.html` file is an example of the form used by the site's visitors to enter and submit search queries. You can use the file in your site by changing the `action` attribute of the form element's tag to the `search.pl` script on your server.

Even if you do not have a Perl interpreter on your own computer, you can still setup and install Perl scripts on your server.

```
<FORM METHOD=POST ACTION="http://your.server.com/path_to_search.pl">
```

However, you'll likely want to place the search form on one of your own pages. The form code should be as follows:

```
<FORM METHOD=POST ACTION="http://your.server.com/path_to_search.pl">
Text to Search For:
<input type=text name="terms" size=40><br>
```

```
Boolean: <select name="boolean">
<option>AND
<option>OR
</select>

Case <select name="case">
<option>Insensitive
<option>Sensitive
</select><br>

<input type=submit value="Search!">
<input type=reset><br>
</form>
```

If you are not familiar with HTML tags, an editor such as Hot Dog can easily create the necessary form on your page. (See Chapter 1.)

**NOTE:** The order, the names, and the values of the form elements should not be changed; otherwise, the script might not function properly.

**CAUTION:** Be sure to capitalize the names and choices as shown in the previous code example, and also in `search.html`.

**TIP:** You can use additional HTML tags to create a more suitable layout for the form, such as an HTML table similar to the one Matt uses in `search.html`.

Information on Perl and the code for various platforms can found at `http://www.perl.com/perl/`.

**NOTE:** The Perl interpreter (simply called perl) is available on most WWW servers. Perl is one of the most, if not the most, widely used languages for creating CGI scripts.

The file `search.pl` contains the script that is compiled and executed at runtime by the server's Perl interpreter. The script is straight ASCII text and can be changed in a text editor (such as Notepad) or a word processor that can save the file as text (most will). The lines beginning with # are comments and are included to provide information to you about the script. The comments are not compiled into the runtime code and are not seen by visitors using the script.

The first line, `#!/usr/bin/perl`, instructs the server to call the Perl interpreter (the filename of the interpreter is `perl`). This line needs the exact path/filename to `perl`. Although the path/filename `/usr/bin/perl` is the common location for `perl` on many servers, you'll need to confirm this with your system administrator. If necessary, change the path/filename in the line to reflect `perl`'s location on your server.

Other than checking the location of the Perl interpreter, the only other thing you need to do to use the script is to set the following variables (as shown in `search.pl`):

```
##############################################################
# Define Variables                                           #

$basedir = '/mnt/web/guide/worldwidemart/scripts/';
$baseurl = 'http://worldwidemart.com/scripts/';
@files = ('*.shtml','demos/links/*.html','demos/guest/*.html');
$title = "Matt's Script Archive";
$title_url = 'http://worldwidemart.com/scripts/';
$search_url = 'http://worldwidemart.com/scripts/demos/search/search.html';

# Done                                                       #
##############################################################
```

`$basedir` is the directory from which you want to start your search. The script searches all files in this directory, unless limited by the values entered for `@files` (about which you learn in a few paragraphs). Subdirectories of this directory can be added to `@files` to have them included in the search. For example, if your WWW files are located in `/account/business/yoursite/wwwdocs/`, enter the following path for `$basedir`:

```
$basedir = ' /account/business/yoursite/wwwdocs/';
```

`$baseurl` is the URL for your base directory. For this example, if `wwwdocs` is your site's root directory, the path to it might be `http://www.yoursite.com/`:

```
$baseurl = ' http://www.yoursite.com/';
```

If the search script matches a file, it will append the file to `$baseurl` to create a link to the file. For example, if the file `myfirm.htm` in the base directory is a match, then the script appends the filename to the base URL to create an absolute URL of `http://www.yoursite.com/yourfirm.htm` for a link to this file. Similarly, for matching files in subdirectories, the subdirectory and the filenames are appended to the base URL to create absolute URLs to the files.

`@files` is an array in which you enter the files and subdirectories you want to be included in searches. A wildcard (*) can be used to specify files: `*.htm` will search for any file with an `.htm` extension in the directory. If no file is specified, then all ASCII text files in the directory are searched.

Subdirectories can be added. If you have a subdirectory named `parts` in which you want only the html files searched, you would add `'parts/*.htm'` (or if the extension is `.html`, then `'parts/*.html'`). For a subdirectory in which you want to have all files searched, you would add `'products/'`, not specifying any file type. Here is an example:

```
@file = ('parts/*.htm','products/','manuals/*.txt');
```

All text files (`.txt`, `.htm`, `.html`, and so on) in the base directory and the `products` subdirectory are searched because no file type is specified. (To specify a file type for the base directory, you would enter `'*.txt'`, `'*.htm'`, and so on.) Only files with the extension `.htm` in the `parts` subdirectory and files with the extension `.txt` in the `manuals` subdirectory are searched. Files in subdirectories other than `products`, `parts`, and `manuals` are not searched because the other subdirectories are not listed.

**NOTE:** Each entry in the `@file` array is a text string and must be enclosed in quotes. Also, the entries are separate elements of the array and must be separated by commas.

`$title` is the title, or a short description, of a link that returns visitors to the rest of your site. The script makes a link to another page that you specify on the results page to create for each search. Therefore, visitors can easily return to your pages after performing a search.

`$title` is the title, or a short description, of the page for the link. This can be your home page or another page in your site:

```
$title = 'Your Company's Home Page';
```

`$title_url` is the absolute URL address to the page described by `$title` and is used for the link to that page:

```
$title_url = 'http://www.yourcompany.com/'
```

`$search_url` is the URL address to your `search.htm` page. This provides a link on the results page back to the search form for visitors to make additional searches if needed:

```
$search_url = 'http://www.yourcompany.com/search.htm'
```

Save the file when you are finished editing it. Upload it to the CGI directory for your site.

**CAUTION:** Be sure that your server allows executable scripts in the directory in which the `search.pl` file is placed. Check with your system administrator if you are not sure.

Many servers, such those with a UNIX operating system, need to have a file permission set to execute a file (executable bit or flag). Be sure to set the file permission or check with your system administrator.

After you have the search form file and the `search.pl` file uploaded to your server, they are ready to be used. Results from a search with Matt's script is shown in Figure 11.8.

**TIP:** Be sure to put a link to your search form from your home page or other prominent part of your site so that visitors will know that it's available and can easily get to it.

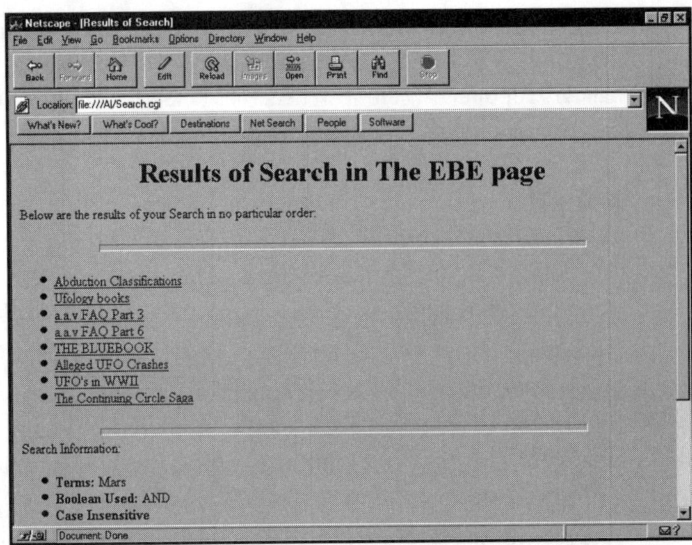


**Figure 11.8.**
*A search result from Matt's search script.*

# Setting Up an Advanced Search Engine

Other search engines, both free and commercial, can quickly search a site by creating a site index file. The engine actually searches the index file instead of the site. The index file is basically a list or database with each indexed Web page having a separate record. The index file contains page information such as title, URL or location, and possibly a short description of the content. Also, the record contains a list of most of the words in the page. (Short one- or two-letter words and common words such as "the" and "and" are usually omitted.) Each word is listed once in the index regardless of the number of times it appears in the actual file. Thus, the index will be smaller than the combined size of all the site's files.

Different engines include various types of other information, such as the number of times a word appears in a page or even the positions the word occupies (for example, third word or two-hundredth word). This other information allows for more efficient and more detailed searching; however, the index file size can get rather large.

A more advanced site search engine can be seen at `http://www.sportsline.com/u/ATsearch/`.

Searches are made more efficient and quicker by using an index file (because the index file is smaller than the site, only one file has to be opened, and the index file is set up especially for searching). On a small site, the index file might not be very beneficial; however, large sites with hundreds or thousands of files will get a remarkable increase in search performance.

Typically, an index file will be between 15 to 40 percent of the combined size of all the file indexed.

Because the search engine will be searching the index file instead of the actual site, the index file has to be updated whenever changes are made to the site. With some sites, the index file is updated nightly at off-peak hours. Others sites might update the index file only when significant site changes are made.

**TIP:** If a site is continuously being updated and changed, then the index file should be updated nightly.

The free version of EWS has a $995 yearly maintenance contract, if desired. It is not necessary to purchase the maintenance contract to run EWS, but if you want to have technical support for EWS, you will have to purchase the contract.

Excite for Web Servers (EWS) is a search engine available in both free and commercial versions.

EWS is available from the Excite site at this address:

`http://www.excite.com/navigate/download.cgi`

Only versions for UNIX servers are available at this time. The procedure for setting up EWS is fairly straightforward, although it has to be installed from the root (system administrator's) account. EWS installation and setup is form driven; the installation will guide you through the process. (See Figure 11.9.)

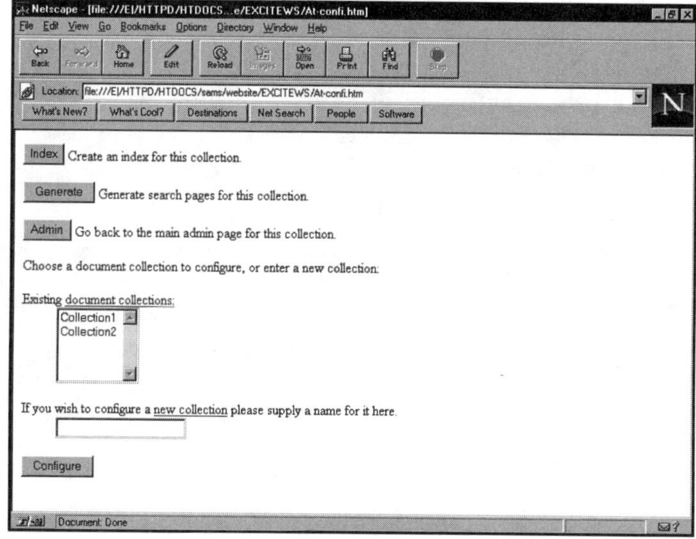


**Figure 11.9.**
*A sample form from EWS installation and administration scripts.*

Here is an overview of the process:

1. Download EWS from `http://www.excite.com/navigate/download.cgi`. The files are archived in a `tar` file.
2. Unarchive the downloaded file. You'll have a `readme` file, an install file (`install-Architext`), and a compressed archived file. Do not uncompress the file because the installation script does this automatically.
3. Run the shell script `install-Architext` in the same directory as the compressed archived file `'Architext.tar.Z'`.
4. Set up daily (or nightly) site indexing, if desired.

During installation, you'll get to do the following:

- Set up file collections. These are groups of files for which you can set specific search rules.
- Index the site. This might require some time. Figure approximately half an hour per 100MB of files.
- Set up the search form. The installation script provides a form in which you select the search form you want and the various search options. The script then generates it.

**NOTE:** An advanced search engine, such as EWS, might in fact be easier to set up than a simpler search engine. This is because installation scripts handle most of the details of installing the search engine and making it functional.

**TIP:** Whichever search engine you install, be sure to test it yourself to make sure that it is functioning the way you want it to. Figure 11.10 shows the results of an EWS search engine.

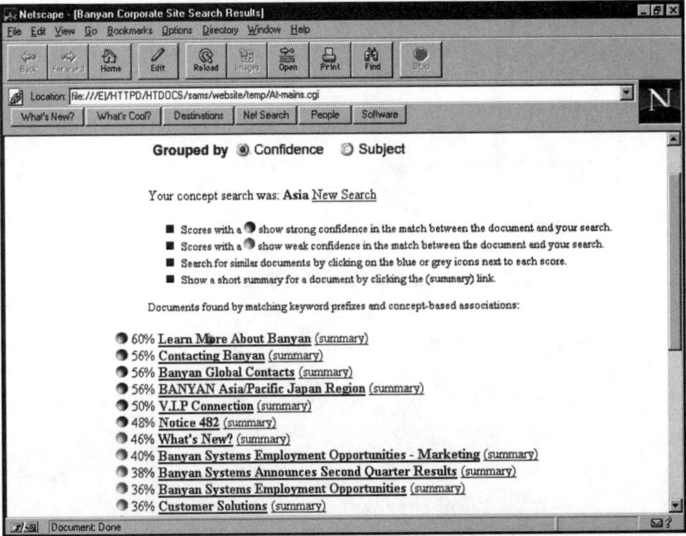


**Figure 11.10.**
*Results from an EWS search engine.*

# Site Searching and Navigation: Some Design Tips

Any customers who walk into your place of business should be greeted and given whatever assistance they need. Your site is a place of business for you. Customers come in, look around, find out what you have to offer, and hopefully conduct some sort of transaction with you. Your home or welcome page greets most customers visiting your site. It is here that you should assist in giving customers the information and other content they need.

For a small site, a table of contents can be placed on the home page so that customers can get right to the page that interests them. A larger site, however, will obviously need a larger table of contents. As the table gets bigger, it will fill up more of the home page.

## Multiple Tables of Contents

To limit the size of the table on the home page, an abbreviated table that lists only the main sections of the site and possibly the main subsections can be placed in the home page. The links from the home page can take the customer into the site to a page that has more detailed tables for particular subsections.

Sectioning the table and putting detailed information in separate subtables greatly aids the visitor in locating the right content.

Take a look at the Netscape site at `http://home.netscape.com/`. Netscape has a sectional table of contents at the bottom of its page that frequently takes the visitor to a page having another index or table for that particular part of the site.

## Separate Table of Contents Page

Some sites offer a table of contents as a separate page. The table can be larger when it's on its own page. However, it still should be sectionalized, with the main header in a large font so that the visitor can easily locate the desired content. Even with the separate table of contents page, a brief navigation menu with links to the major parts of the site and the table of contents should be on the home page.

See Chapter 2 for information on navigation and menu bars.

## Navigation from Any Page

Because a visitor can enter a site on any page, each page should at least have a menu bar that provides links back to the home page and other major pages.

The WWW consortium's site, `http://www.w3.org/`, uses an HTML table to place a site index at the side of the home page.

## Tables and Frames

More sites are using tables and frames to offset the tables of contents from the rest of the page. (See Figure 11.11.) This makes it readily visible and accessible to visitors, but not distracting to the rest of the page.

**Figure 11.11.**
*A site using frames to provide a fixed table of contents. This site also offers a "no frame" version.*

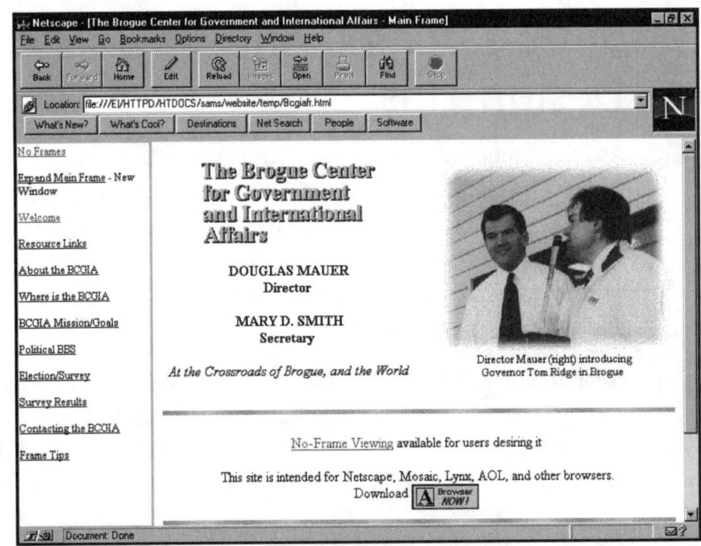


Frames also allow for a fixed table of contents, regardless of where in the site a visitor may go.

To have table content display on nontable browsers, add spaces around table cell content. Use `<BR>` or `<P>` as the last cell of each row.

If you are JavaScript savvy, take at look at `http://edbo.com/frames/` for setting up "frame" and "no frame" versions of the same site.

**CAUTION:** There are still several browsers that do not support tables or frames. Be sure that your site can provide support for these browsers.

**NOTE:** Many people with frame-capable browsers do not want to view a site in frames for various reasons. If you use frames for your site, be sure to provide a "no frame" version for people who do not want to or cannot use frames.

## Site Search Engine

If you decide to use a site search engine, it needs to be readily accessible to the visitor. It doesn't necessarily have to be on the home page or with the table of contents. However, putting a link to the search form from the home page and the table of contents will

- Let the visitor know that your site has this feature
- Give the visitor quick access to the search engine

**TIP:** Including a link to the search form on each page of your site is a pretty good idea. No matter where visitors might enter or go in your site, they will always have direct access to the search engine. A good spot is the navigation menu or bar, if used, on the bottom of each page.

# Workshop Wrap-Up

How you help customers navigate and use your site is very important to having a successful presence on the Internet. Be sure that the table of contents, index, or search engine that you set up function in a logical, easy-to-use manner. Remember, your customers are not going to be familiar with how you intend the site navigation to function. Make sure that everything is clear and easy to use.

In this chapter you learned the following topics:

- ❑ Setting up a table of contents and site index to give visitors a quick overview of the site and ready navigation into the site
- ❑ Installing a search engine so that visitors can locate and get to specific content in your site
- ❑ Design tips for creating easy, user-friendly navigation for your site

## Next Steps

Now...

- ❑ Chapter 12, "Real-Life Examples: Advancing Your Site."
- ❑ Part IV, "Creating Commerce in Cyberspace: Online Ordering and Advertising Techniques."

## Q&A

**Q: Should I use a smaller table of contents on my home page and provide more detailed tables in the different sections of my site?**

**A:** A lot depends on your site. Obviously, a site with a few pages would use only one simple table of contents. As the size of the site gets bigger, more listings have to be made in the table of contents. Eventually a point will be reached where a rather large table of contents will be difficult to use. At this point, it will be best to use a main table to direct visitors to the subtables that have more detailed listings.

**Q: Should every site have a table of contents on the home page?**

**A:** No, it is not necessary to have it right on the home page. However, it should be directly accessible from the home page as well as other pages in your site.

**Q: Does every site need to have a table of contents or a site index?**

**A:** No, but every site needs a means for visitors to access the rest of the site. A site having only a few pages can simply use a menu bar or links in the content of the home page.

**Q: How can a Perl search script be set up on Windows or a Mac, before upload to the Web server?**

**A:** The script is a straight ASCII text file, which can be edited and set up on almost any computer. All that is needed is a text editor or a word processor that can save the file as text. Besides, if needed, a Perl interpreter can be installed on both Windows and Mac machines.

**Q: Should every site have a search engine?**

**A:** No, what every site needs is a quick-and-easy way for visitors to find content and to navigate the site. The search engine and the table of contents are ways to provide this. Visitors to a small site are not going to benefit from a search engine that looks through only a few pages. In fact, a search engine on a small site could be more of a distraction than an aid to the visitor.

TWELVE

# Real-Life Examples: Advancing Your Site

## Examples in this chapter:

- Example 1: Customer Forms and Surveys
- Example 2: Customer Support Elements
- Example 3: Tying Data to the Web
- Example 4: Searches and Tables of Contents

When you start getting into more advanced sites and pages, the importance of learning by example becomes even more critical. Trying to debug a CGI script implementation is extremely difficult when you don't have an online working model to use for comparison purposes. This chapter shows you how some of the most important elements and features in the previous chapters of this section (Chapters 8 through 11) are being used as actual commercial Web pages all over the Net.

Unfortunately, because these pages employ advanced interactive elements, it's not possible to re-create them on the CD-ROM as you saw in Chapter 7, "Real-Life Examples: Putting the Basics Together." However, you can always get to the pages by typing in the corresponding URL or using the links on the CD-ROM and the Web site at `http://www.murphnet.com`.

For more real-life examples, check out Chapters 7, 19, and 22.

For each of the example pages in this chapter, you see what advanced elements, techniques, and scripts are implemented and, if appropriate, what could be done to make the page even better.

# Example 1: Customer Forms and Surveys

Gathering customer data is among the most useful and important benefits of getting on the Web and creating commercial Web pages. As more and more people come online, this aspect of page design will become even more critical. Doing it well, however, is a tricky proposition. The following examples demonstrate how to use forms and surveys to get the information you want from the customers you want without turning them off or away.

## Business on the Move

**Document title:** Competition Entry Form (Figures 12.1, 12.2, and 12.3)

**Document URL:** `http://www.21store.com/botm/comptemp.htm`

**Description:** A form designed to gather potential customer information in the format of a contest entry for a product that the company sells. In this example, Business on the Move sells portable electronic products through its Web presence and elsewhere. The company is giving away one of its products, a Sharp PDA, and entrants must fill out a short questionnaire and form to enter. The form uses a CGI script from Selena Sol to process and mail the results.

**Techniques and Designs applied:**

**A Clickable Link.** (See Chapter 8, "Gathering Information: Web-Based Surveys and Questionnaires.") A customer data form isn't really very valuable if no one fills it out. Business on the Move has a link to the contest entry form, shown in Figure 12.1. As you can see, it would be hard to resist selecting the link.

**Survey Questions.** (See Chapter 8.) The form starts with a brief survey for customers, shown in Figure 12.2, regarding the type of features users find most important in a PDA, the product being given away in the contest. This is an excellent example of how to use short and subtle questions to gather valuable customer data.

**Ease of Use.** (See Chapter 8.) The survey portion of the form provides easy-to-use drop-down selection menus to help users answer the questions in as easy a format as possible.

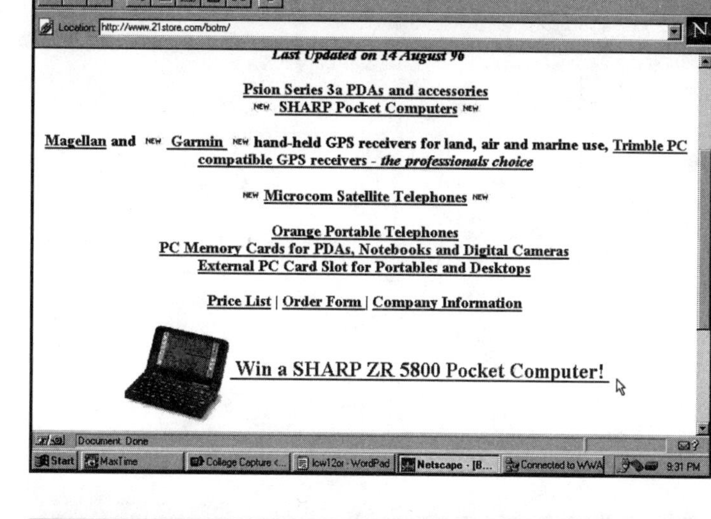


**Figure 12.1.**
*The Business on the Move page encourages users to fill out a form by providing a contest-oriented link.*

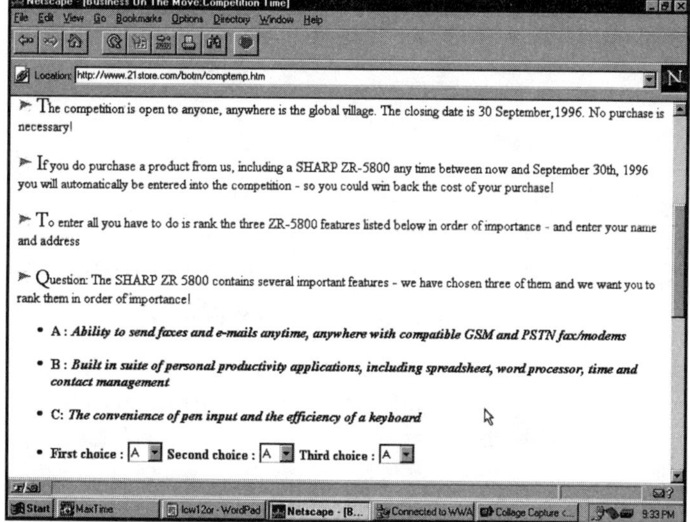


**Figure 12.2.**
*The survey portion of the firm is subtle, but informative for the business.*

**Basic Customer Information.** (See Chapter 8.) The form gathers only the necessary information for this particular use, which is to get basic contact data, as shown in Figure 12.3. Obviously, users should be willing to give their address in this context unless they don't want to receive the prize.

**CGI Form Script.** (See Chapter 8.) The contest form uses a CGI script for form submissions available from Selena Sol's Script Archive at `http://www.eff.org/~erict/Scripts`. However, the same form could easily have been accomplished using the `mailto:` action if necessary.

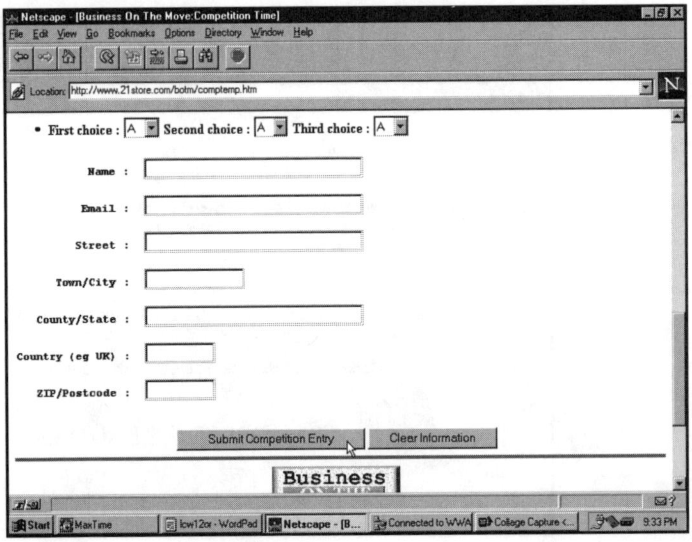

**Figure 12.3.**
*The contest entry forms gather the necessary customer information without being too intrusive.*

## Rolling Hills Golf, Inc.

**Document title:** Guest Book (Figure 12.4)

**Document URL:** `http://www.jadebbs.com/jlanderson/guestbk.htm`

**Description:** A simple form designed to gather basic customer information and to allow a simple way for users to join a company mailing list. Rolling Hills Golf sells golf books and tapes to a different kind of hacker. The form uses HTML enhancements to make the process of filling out the form more engaging.

**Techniques and Designs Applied:**

**Advanced HTML Formatting.** (See Chapter 8.) The form effectively uses HTML advancements to enhance the Web surfer's experience. At the bottom of the screen, as shown in Figure 12.4, you can see some scrolling text that is generated by a JavaScript applet. Also, the background image over which the form is superimposed helps give a three-dimensional feel to the form while also acting as a subtle reinforcement of the company's name.

**`mailto:` Action.** (See Chapter 8.) The Rolling Hills form also is an excellent example of what can be done using the `mailto:` action in your form tag. You can see that there is no difference to the naked eye between a form using the `mailto:` action and one using a CGI script, as shown in the previous example.

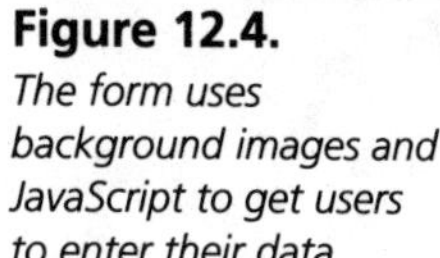

**Figure 12.4.**
*The form uses background images and JavaScript to get users to enter their data.*

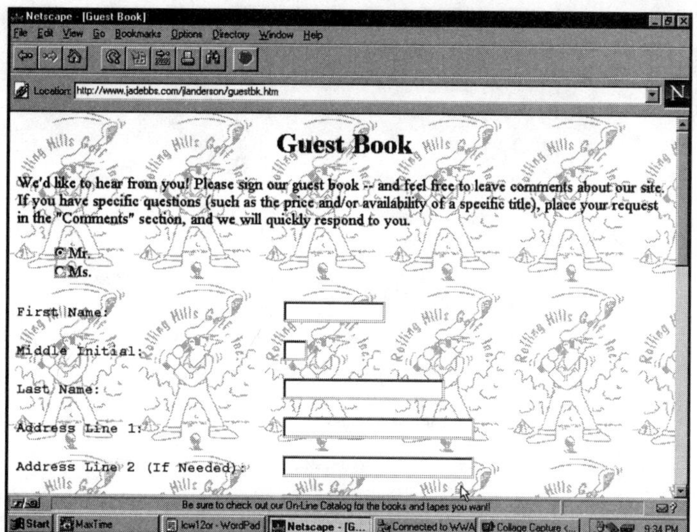


# Example 2: Customer Support Elements

Once you get some customers with your commercial Web pages, you'll want to keep them. Supporting and servicing your customers should be a major focus of at least some portion of your Web site. The following examples demonstrate the wide variety of options that are available for providing information about your products and services and answering questions your customers might have.

## Microsoft Gaming Zone FAQ

**Document title:** Microsoft Gaming Zone FAQ (Figures 12.5 and 12.6)

**Document URL:** `http://www.microsoft.com/support/products/home/games/content/zone/faqs/`

**Description:** Just one of the many FAQs that Microsoft makes available for all of its products from its Web site. The FAQ answers the important questions regarding the company's new Internet gaming service, the Internet Gaming Zone. The FAQ follows a standard format used by Microsoft for most of its products.

**Techniques and designs applied:**

> **Simple Formatting.** (See Chapter 9, "Customer Support Pages: Boards and Beyond.") The Gaming Zone FAQ uses a clean interface devoid of background images and confusing HTML layout to crisply present the necessary information, as shown in Figure 12.5.

**Figure 12.5.**
*The Gaming Zone FAQ is easy to read, easy to follow, and easy to use.*

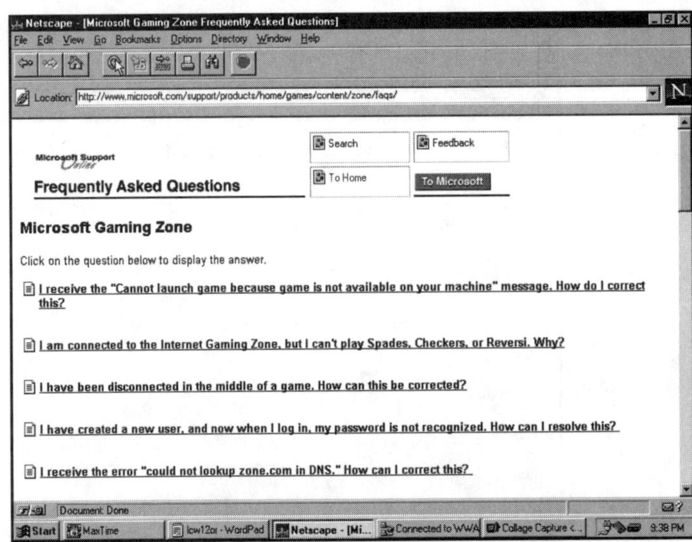


**Linking Up.** (See Chapter 9.) The links on the Microsoft pages utilize font and font color tags to present the FAQ index in a stylized manner. The questions are presented as links so that the answer is only a click away.

**Individual FAQ Pages.** (See Chapter 9.) The Gaming Zone FAQ is an excellent example of how to create individual pages with the answer to each FAQ. As you can see from Figure 12.6, the question's link brings you to a page where you can get your answer, complete with any additional links you might need to follow to solve your problem.

**Figure 12.6.**
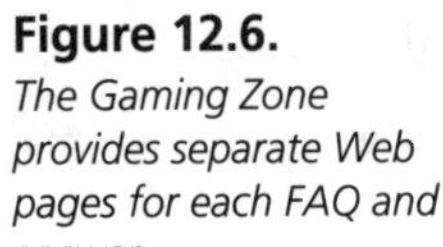
*The Gaming Zone provides separate Web pages for each FAQ and answer.*

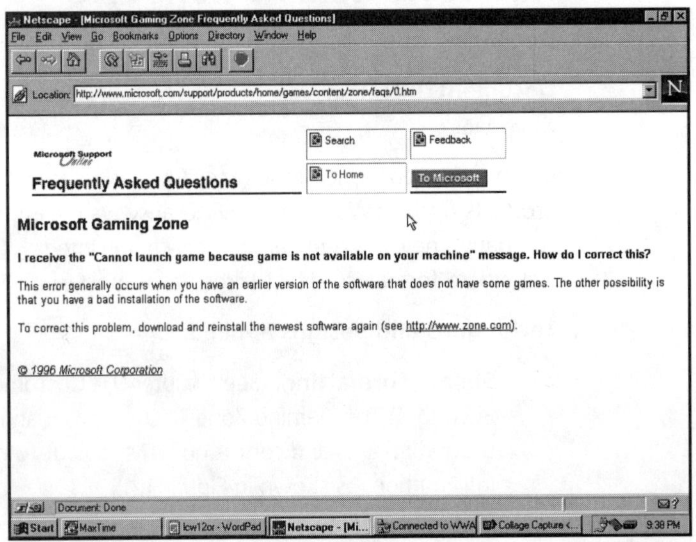

# Medtronic's FAQ and Answer Database

**Document title:** Frequently Asked Questions About Medtronic Products (Figures 12.7 and 12.8)

**Document URL:** `http://www.medtronic.com/public/technical/faq/`

**Description:** Although the Medtronics page is titled a FAQ, it is really designed as more of an answer database. The information is presented product by product and not question by question. Each link leads to more detailed general information about each of the products.

**Techniques and designs applied:**

**Simple Formatting.** (See Chapter 9.) The Medtronic index page, as shown in Figure 12.7, again uses only basic HTML formatting to deliver the necessary information. Simplicity is extremely important on your FAQ and Answer Database pages.

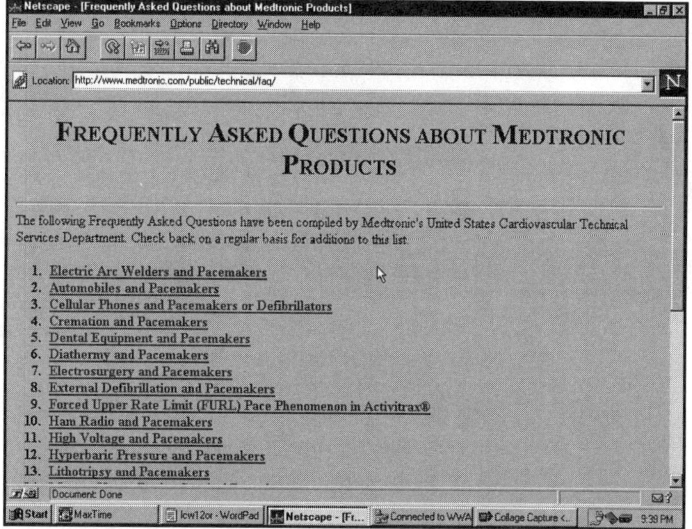


**Figure 12.7.**
*The Medtronic page provides information on a product, rather than question, basis.*

**Detailed Information.** Each link from the index page leads to a much more detailed page, as shown in Figure 12.8. You can see that each of these individual pages provides a great deal of general information relevant to each product or product category that the company carries.

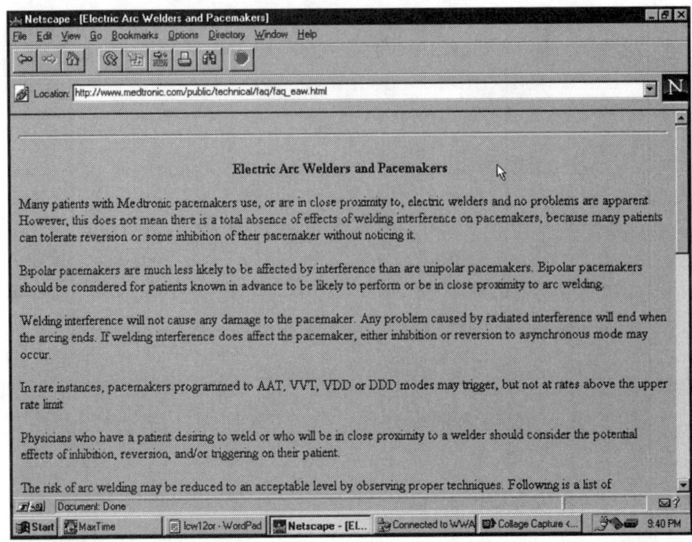


**Figure 12.8.**
*Providing general product information will answer many user's questions, even those not frequently asked.*

## Mutual Funds Interactive

**Document title:** Mutual Funds Interactive Moderated Newsgroup (Figures 12.9 and 12.10)

**Document URL:** `http://www.brill.com/wwwboard/`

**Description:** The Mutual Funds Interactive Moderated Newsgroup is a Web-based bulletin board system for discussing the buying and selling of mutual funds. The system uses the WWWBoard CGI script, available from `http://worldwidemart.com/scripts/`.

**Techniques and Designs Applied:**

**Usenet Without Flames.** (See Chapter 9.) This newsgroup is not a traditional newsgroup in that it's not carried by Usenet; it is only on the Mutual Funds Interactive page. Discussion groups implemented on a Web page in this manner are much more manageable and controllable.

**WWWBoard CGI Script.** (See Chapter 9.) The page uses the WWWBoard CGI script from Matt Wright at `http://worldwidemart.com/scripts/`. The initial page, shown in Figure 12.9, displays a subject-by-subject listing complete with the poster's name and the date of the posting.

**FAQ Link.** (See Chapter 9.) Another important feature of this newsgroup is that WWWBoard provides the ready-to-use FAQ that is linked on the main message page. Users can use the FAQ to get up to speed on the system without your needing to spend additional time generating this type of document.

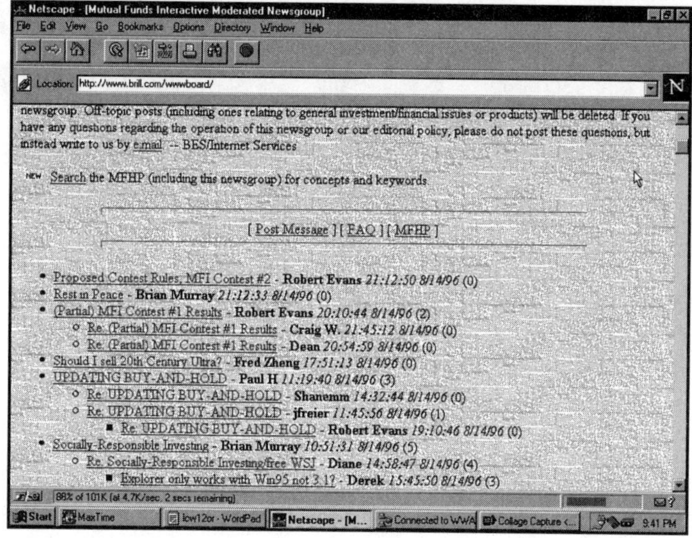


**Figure 12.9.**
*The WWWBoard script generates a constantly updated index of messages on a Web page.*

**WWWBoard Messages.** (See Chapter 9.) The WWWBoard script takes a user's posting and generates an HTML page, as shown in Figure 12.10. The title of the posting appears in large text at the top of the page and the poster's name appears as a `mailto:` link for easy response.

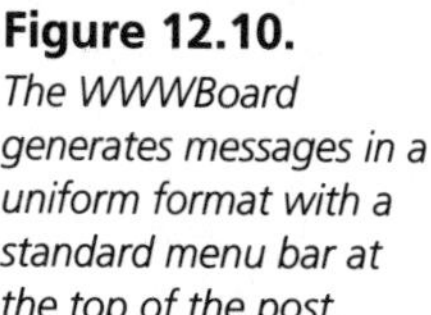

**Figure 12.10.**
*The WWWBoard generates messages in a uniform format with a standard menu bar at the top of the post.*

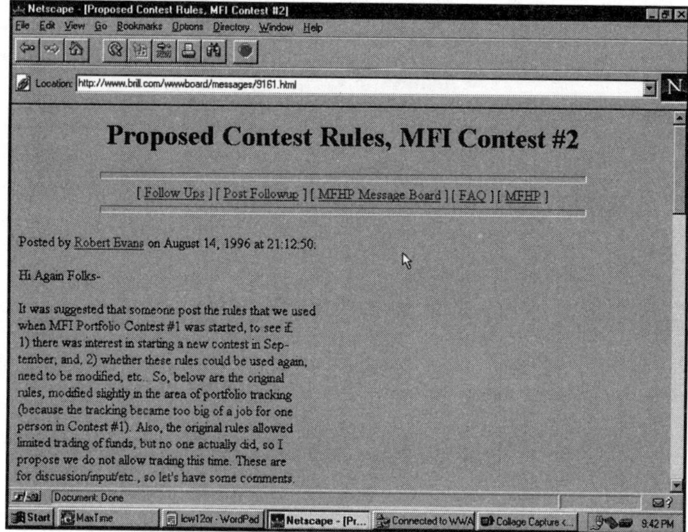

# Example 3: Tying Data to the Web

Probably no single topic covered in this book has as broad a potential for application and development as this one. The potential for new and creative ways to integrate a broad variety of data types into your Web pages is enormous. Of course, some companies are already seizing the Web and using advanced techniques to create powerful and informative sites.

## The Internet Shopping Network

**Document title:** The Internet Shopping Network's Power Search

**Document URL:** `http://www.isn.com`

**Description:** The Internet Shopping Network demonstrates one of the most advanced uses of exploiting the interplay between data and the Web. The site uses complex databases for order placement and tracking along with product selection. The Power Search facility is just one example of how they successfully took data and put a useful and pretty face on it for the Web.

**Techniques and designs applied:**

**Product Databases.** (See Chapter 10, "Advanced Information Pages: Tying Data to the Web.") The Power Search page at the Internet Shopping Network provides an interface to the company's huge product database. The database, while extraordinarily complex, is masked under a simple search interface on a Web page.

**Combination Field Searches.** (See Chapter 10.) The real thing that puts the power in ISN's Power Search is the capability to search the product database by specifying settings for different fields, including product category or product manufacturer. A combination of different field settings enables users to search the database and find what they're looking for without sifting through too much noise.

# Example 4: Searches and Tables of Contents

To use your site and view your pages, Web surfers are going to need to know how to find their way around. You wouldn't go on a family vacation without a map, would you? Helping users navigate your pages can't be emphasized enough, and the following examples show just how useful and beneficial these elements can be on your pages.

# The Faxon Company

**Document title:** The Faxon Company World Wide Web Server: Table of Contents (Figure 12.11)

**Document URL:** `http://www.faxon.com/WWWTOC.html`

**Description:** The Faxon Company is in the business of selling periodical and journal subscriptions, mainly to libraries. The table of contents page is an excellent example of how to use this concept to give users a complete overview of how your pages are structured throughout your site. Faxon's ToC is an excellent navigational tool.

**Techniques and designs applied:**

> **Bullets.** (See Chapter 11, "Searching Your Site.") As you can see from Figure 12.11, the Faxon ToC uses bullets and blocks to add to the organizational appearance of the index. Following the bullets helps you follow the layout of the site.

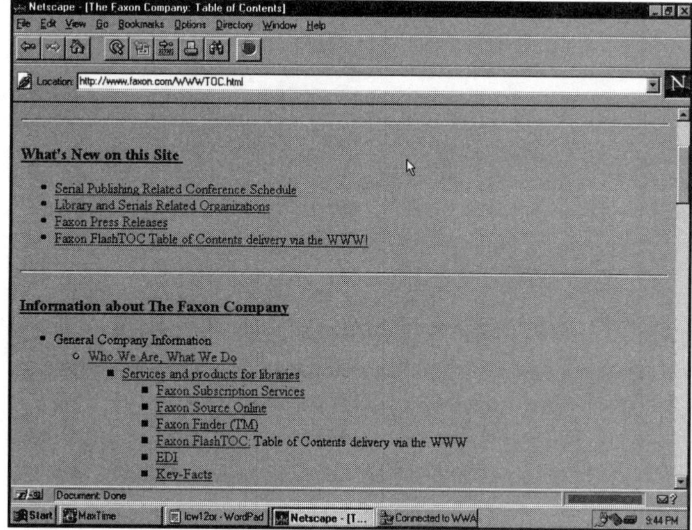


**Figure 12.11.**
*The Table of Contents page should provide almost a visual picture of how the Web site flows.*

> **Indentation of Sections/Subsections.** (See Chapter 11.) The Faxon page does an excellent job of laying out the contents under appropriate sections and subsections. You can see that the main sections appear in larger and bold text and subsections are indented farther on the page.

## VMF Sales

**Document title:** VMF Sales Merchandise Cyber-Catalog (Figure 12.12)

**Document URL:** `http://www.divrse.com/vmf/`

**Description:** VMF offers for sale a wide variety of products through its site on the Web. In order to facilitate shopping on its pages, the company integrated a site-wide search engine. In this case, it chose Matt Wright's Simple Search CGI script to get the job done.

**Techniques and designs applied:**

**Simple Search.** (See Chapter 11.) The VMF search form, shown in Figure 12.12, is driven by the Simple Search engine from Matt Wright. The script is available on the CD-ROM and online at `http://worldwidemart.com/scripts/`.

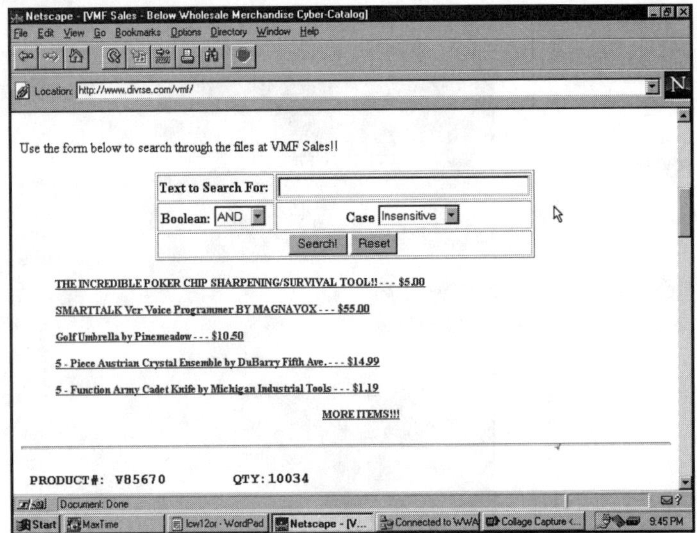


**Figure 12.12.**
*The Simple Search form is simple in form but not in function.*

**Form Placement.** (See Chapter 11.) The search form is useful only if users have easy access to it on your page. VMF provides a prominent placement for its search form to make it easy and effective to use.

## Attachmate SupportWeb!

**Document title:** Search the Knowledgebase (Figure 12.13)

**Document URL:** `http://supportWeb.attachmate.com/kb/kbmenu.html`

**Description:** Attachmate's Web site is an excellent example of how you can use a site search engine to further the types of customer support options you looked at in Chapter 8. The Attachmate site uses the Excite for Web Servers engine that is freely available from `http://www.excite.com`.

**Techniques and designs applied:**

> **Excite for Web Servers.** (See Chapter 11.) As you can readily see from Figure 12.13, the Attachmate page relies on the CGI search engine from Excite (`http://www.excite.com`) to provide search capabilities for its site.

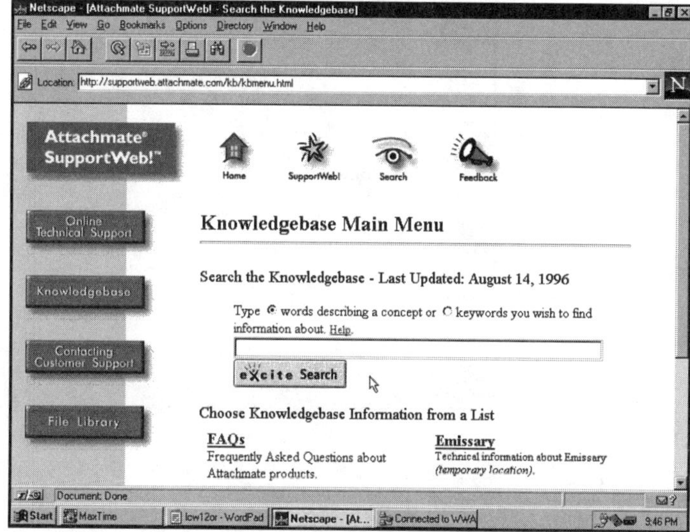


**Figure 12.13.**
*Attachmate uses Excite's Web Server search engine to assist in delivering customer support.*

> **Selectable Query Format.** (See Chapter 11.) The Excite search engine enables users to choose varying types of search queries, depending on whether they want to search by concept or by keyword.

## Enteract

**Document title:** Enteract Search Form (Figures 12.14 and 12.15)

**Document URL:** `http://www.enteract.com/net.html`

**Description:** Each page on Enteract's Web site contains a simple search form that utilizes the WebGlimpse search engine. The placement of the search form on every page on the site is a simple task that puts a useful tool only a click away to users, no matter where they are on the site.

**Techniques and designs applied:**

**Form Placement.** (See Chapter 11.) Enteract places the search form, shown in Figure 12.14, on every page on the site. The compact and simple design of the form means that it is both unobtrusive and efficient when it comes to adding additional download time to a page.

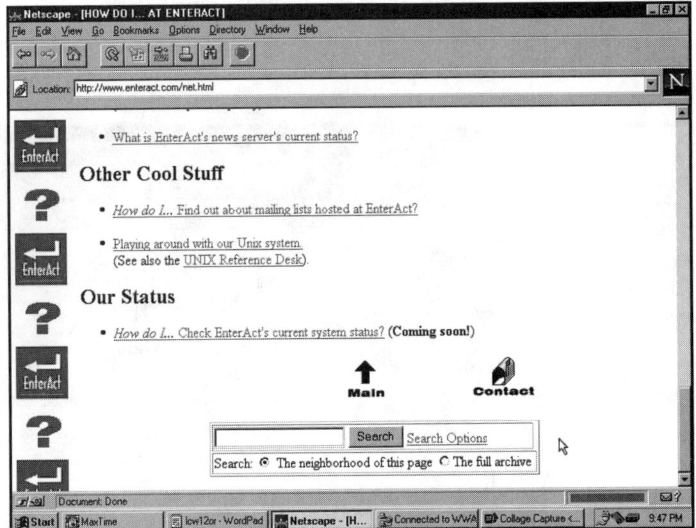


**Figure 12.14.**
*Enteract's site uses the WebGlimpse engine to enable users to search from every page on its site.*

**CGI Search Scripts.** (See Chapter 11.) The Enteract site uses the WebGlimpse CGI script, available from `http://glimpse.cs.arizona.edu/Webglimpse`. You'll probably find no better choice in the search engine department. As you can see, WebGlimpse enables you to search either broadly or narrowly from a page on a site.

**Customizable Queries.** (See Chapter 11.) The WebGlimpse engine enables users to perform a highly customized search on Enteract's site by selecting the Search Options link from the main search form. Users are then presented with the much more detailed form shown in Figure 12.15.

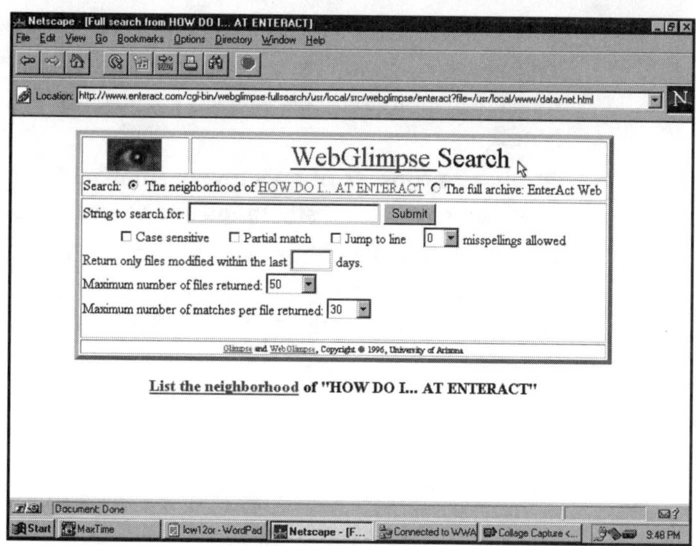


**Figure 12.15.**
*WebGlimpse presents a bevy of options to customize your search.*

# Workshop Wrap-Up

After looking at so many examples, you're probably itching to start putting together your commercial pages right now. Using these examples as a model for creating your own pages will serve you (and your customers) well. The topics covered by these examples cover the fundamental advanced aspects of any top-quality professional Web site. Learning from the best of what's already out there should enable you to create pages that support customers and your business well into the future.

## Next Steps

In the next section, you see how to take your site to the next level and begin using online commerce techniques to turn your Web site into a cash generator. Chapter 13, "Advanced Catalogs," starts out by showing you how to create advanced catalogs to present your products.

If you want to see more real-life examples, turn to either Chapter 7, 19, "Real-Life Examples: Doing Business on the Web," or 22, "Real-Life Examples: Touting and Managing Your Site," all of which contain more real examples for each section of the book.

# Q&A

**Q: Why aren't these pages on the CD-ROM?**

**A:** Most of these pages use CGI scripts for some of their functionality. In order to operate properly, CGI scripts must be run from a Web server that can run them, and this usually requires a Perl interpreter. You should bear this in mind when you are viewing these sites on the Web. Check with your system administrator to be sure you are able to use CGI scripts on your pages.

**Q: Our site consists of only a very small number of pages; do we need to worry about site maps and search engines at this point?**

**A:** Absolutely, just because your site is small doesn't mean you shouldn't give users the best navigational tools for getting around and using your pages. Of course, if your site is small, this task will take even less time and should be easier to implement.

PART

IV

# Creating Commerce in Cyberspace: Online Ordering and Advertising Techniques

**Chapter 13** Advanced Catalogs

**14** Web Shopping Carts

**15** Web Cash Registers: Taking and Making Money on the Net

**16** Providing Content for a Price on the Web

**17** Setting Up Advertising-Supported Web Sites

**18** Order and Shipment Tracking on the Web

**19** Real-Life Examples: Doing Business on the Web

# CHAPTER THIRTEEN

# Advanced Catalogs

## In this chapter, you

- ❑ Learn to provide different catalogs for different customers and offer specific customers specialized catalogs designed for their particular interests
- ❑ Create customized product presentations and specialized pages to enhance the appeal of each product
- ❑ Use multimedia and interactive catalogs to make your site more useful and attractive to customers and other visitors

## Tasks in this chapter:

- ❑ Creating Catalogs on the Fly
- ❑ Working with Text-Only Catalogs
- ❑ Customizing Product Presentations

In Chapter 6, "Online Catalogs and More: Presenting Your Products and Services," you learn how to set up an online catalog. Although you will do well to follow what you learn there, you can advance the catalog presentation with several additional techniques. These techniques not only enhance the visual appeal, but satisfy customer preferences and interests.

You can offer catalog pages for only those items in which a customer indicates an interest. You can change the presentation of each product to a format that is unique and likely to interest that customer in making a sale. To further enhance your catalog, you can include animation, sound, video, and other multimedia on your catalog pages. By making it easier for customers to locate specific items, place an order, and otherwise interact with your site, you can increase the likelihood of customers returning and also of attracting new customers.

# Different Catalogs for Different Customers

See a site that uses different catalogs at `http://www.llbean.com/products/`.

Imagine walking into a department store and finding that the merchandise, instead of being organized into separate sections (departments), is randomly placed. Sporting goods, shoes, clothing, appliances, furniture, hardware, jewelry, and toys are all together. If you had a day to kill, trying to locate the items you want might be an interesting adventure, but like most people, you have better things to do and would more than likely go shop at a better organized store.

Your online catalog is not just like a real store, it is a real store. Customers will come to your catalog to browse and shop, look at the items that interest them, and make a purchase. Although this has been mentioned several times throughout this book, it bears re-emphasis: Navigation is the key to your site. Customers must be able to easily locate what they are looking for and get to it quickly. Even the customer who just comes in to browse will need an organized layout to follow.

Although Sears does not have catalogs anymore, it is online at `http://www.sears.com/`.

This brings us to the point of this section, presenting different catalogs for different customers. When Sears—back when it was Sears-Roebuck—had catalogs, it had a general catalog that covered most of its lines of merchandise. It was a huge book, about the size of the New York City phone book. But Sears also had smaller, specialized catalogs that covered only a particular type of product, such as hardware, lawn and garden, appliances, and so on. Customers with a certain interest could get a small, specialized catalog that suited their needs rather than the large "everything under the sun" general catalog.

How do you go about giving different customers different catalogs? The easiest and perhaps simplest method is to sectionalize your catalog or create separate individual catalogs, and then provide a menu with links customers can select for the catalog they want to view.

**NOTE:** Be sure to provide a link back to your menu. Customers might be interested in more than one catalog, and the link will provide easy navigation to the menu and the other sections/catalogs.

Another approach is to generate the catalog on the fly. A database containing information on your merchandise could be accessed by a catalog program to extract information only on the particular products that interest the customer.

The one area you don't want to forget is providing content for customers who have browsers without all the features you have used to design your site. These customers can include people with low bandwidth connections, the sightless, and people with a text-only browser (there are still some left). You wouldn't want to lock these customers out of your catalog, so providing a text-only version of your catalog would be beneficial.

## Separate Catalog Pages

Chapter 6, "Online Catalogs and More: Presenting Your Products and Services," describes how to set up individual catalog pages.

Creating a sectionalized catalog or separate catalogs for different products isn't much more difficult than setting up just one catalog. Using the methods you learn in Chapter 6, you can create separate catalog product list pages, except now, pay particular attention to which items are included on which page. You will need to

- ❑ Determine the different categories into which you can split your product line.
- ❑ Set up a catalog (product list), as described in Chapter 6, for each of the categories you decide to use.

**TIP:** If you have products that might fit into more than one category, include them in each appropriate catalog. For example, in the Old Dog Used Records site, you might have Linda Ronstadt in both the country and rock catalogs. Although some cross-listing will be good for certain hard to categorize items, too much will defeat the purpose of separate catalogs.

- ❑ Make a main catalog menu or index with a description and link for each of the catalogs you have.
- ❑ Be sure to include return links on each catalog page to the main menu and your home page.
- ❑ Create your product description pages as described in Chapter 6, but now include links back to the appropriate catalog(s).

**TIP:** You don't have to divide all the catalogs only along the lines of product type. With Old Dog Used Records, besides catalogs for rock, country, ska, folk, and so on, you might include catalogs that have music that can belong in any of the type categories. For Old Dog Used Records, these catalogs could include categories like 1960s, instrumentals, and female singers.

Although a catalog for 1970s Swedish bands with a name formed by the members' initials is probably stretching the categories, you can create several different catalogs catering to the various tastes and interests of your customers. (By the way, a 1970s Swedish band whose name is formed from the band members' initials was ABBA.)

# Creating Catalogs on the Fly

Generating your catalog on the fly with a database and a CGI program or your Web-database interface can have several advantages:

- You can have a template for your catalog pages instead of having several separate pages.
- You can maintain and update your product line and data easily with your database program.
- You can define categories of products that will be useful for creating different catalogs for different customers.

## Set Up the Database

The first item for making your on-the-fly catalogs is to set up the database of your product line. The basic procedure follows:

Refer to Chapter 10, "Advanced Information Pages: Tying Data to the Web," for information on using databases online.

1. Create your database of products.
2. Create a field for the category (catalog) in which an item belongs.
3. Create the template for your catalog (product list) pages.
4. Create the template for your product description pages, if you will be generating these on the fly, too.

**TIP:** You will probably want fields (columns) in your database for product number or ID, product name, description, image file, and price, as well as the category. Other fields you might want to include are wholesale prices for volume buyers and, depending on if and how customer orders are processed, sales tax and shipping weight.

## Main Menu or Index

When customers first come to your site, they'll need to navigate to the catalog in which they are interested. Your main menu or index will describe your product lines and the catalogs you have to the customers. The customers then can select the catalog that interests them. Repeat customers can bookmark the catalog page, or you can record their preferences so that their catalog is served when they enter the site (see the section "Registering Customer Preferences").

**NOTE:** The method you provide for the customer to access the catalogs depends on your site's style and somewhat on the method you use to provide the separate catalogs. Most database interfaces can receive input via the GET and POST methods. Your particular interface, if you are using on-the-fly catalogs, might require you to use only POST, in which case you will need to use an HTML form for customers to select a catalog.

You can use an HTML form as your main menu. This does not mean that customers will have to fill in fields for their preferences; the menu can simply consist of buttons. The button the customer selects will send a unique `name=value` pair to your Web-database interface. The unique `name=value` pair will identify to the interface which catalog was selected.

You might want to look at `http://www.physics.gla.ac.uk/trysub.html` for some ideas on stylizing your submit buttons.

The HTML for your main menu might be similar to the following code:

```
<FORM METHOD="POST" ACTION="/CGI-bin/w3-msql/myCatalog">
<INPUT TYPE=SUBMIT NAME="category" VALUE="Rock"><BR>
<INPUT TYPE=SUBMIT NAME="category" VALUE="Classical"><BR>
<INPUT TYPE=SUBMIT NAME="category" VALUE="Blues"><BR>
<INPUT TYPE=SUBMIT NAME="category" VALUE="Country"><BR>
<INPUT TYPE=SUBMIT NAME="category" VALUE="Ska"><BR>
<INPUT TYPE=SUBMIT NAME="category" VALUE="Folk"><BR>
</FORM>
```

**NOTE:** If with your Web-database interface you can use both the POST and GET method, you can specify either method for your menu form. Otherwise, you will need to specify the appropriate method for your interface. W3-mSQL accepts either method.

If you want, you can also use links for your menu if your interface will accept the GET method. For example:

```
<UL>
<LI><A HREF="/CGI-bin/w3-msql/myCatalog?category=Rock">Rock</A>
<LI><A HREF="/CGI-bin/w3-msql/myCatalog?category=Classical">Classical</A>
<LI><A HREF="/CGI-bin/w3-msql/myCatalog?category=Blues">Blues</A>
<LI><A HREF="/CGI-bin/w3-msql/myCatalog?category=Country">Country</A>
<LI><A HREF="/CGI-bin/w3-msql/myCatalog?category=Ska">Ska</A>
<LI><A HREF="/CGI-bin/w3-msql/myCatalog?category=Folk">Folk</A>
</UL>
```

**TIP:** For clarity in the preceding examples, catalog descriptions and style enhancements have been omitted. You might want to add a brief description to each selection and perhaps enhance the presentation of the menu page with images, an HTML table, or other items.

Figure 13.1 shows an example of a catalog menu.

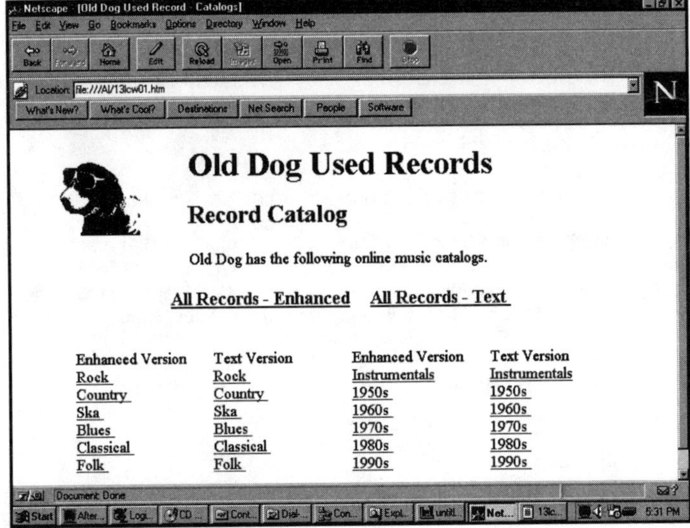


**Figure 13.1.**
*A sample catalog menu.*

## Catalog Templates

To create catalogs on the fly, you need to specify a template that your Web-database interface will use to create the catalog pages. The template you use depends on the Web-database interface you use. The basic procedure follows:

See Chapter 10 for information on SQL.

1. Lay out the HTML and text for the page.
2. Determine and insert the appropriate SQL (or other language) statement.
3. Insert the appropriate embedded response tags where you want the product list to start.
4. Insert embedded fieldname commands where appropriate on the template.

**NOTE:** For different interfaces, the procedure can be somewhat different. For example, with Microsoft's IDC, you would place the SQL statement on an `.idc` file to fill in the template with the response from the SQL query.

If our database "tunes" had the following fields:

```
Category,  Band, URL, Album
```

and we had a request for the type

```
http://www.olddog.com/CGI-bin/w3-msql/catalog.html?category=Rock
```

W3-mSQL is a Web-database interface described in Chapter 10.

where URL is the URL to the product description page for the record, a sample W3-mSQL template for our Old Dog Records might look like Listing 13.1.

**Listing 13.1. Sample W3-mSQL template for product description pages.**

```
<HTML>
<HEAD>
<! msql  connect>
<! msql database tunes>
<! msql query "select Band,URL,Album from tunes where category=$category" a1>
<TITLE>
<! msql print "Old Dog Used Records - $category">
</TITLE>
</HEAD>
<BODY>

<H1 ALIGN=CENTER>Old Dog Used Records</H1>
<H2 ALIGN=CENTER><! msql print "$category  Catalog"></H2>

<TABLE>
<! msql print_rows "<TR><TD>@a1.0<TD><A  HREF=@a1.1>@a1.2</A>">
</TABLE>

<! msql close>
<HR>
<CENTER>
<TABLE WIDTH="90%" ALIGN=CENTER>>
<TR><TD ALIGN=CENTER>
Return to the <A HREF="menu.html">Catalog Menu</A></TD>
<TD ALIGN=CENTER>
Return to Old Dog's <A HREF="menu.html">Home Page</A></TD>
</TR></TABLE></CENTER>
<ADDRESS>
<P ALIGN=CENTER>
Old Dog Used Records<BR>
<A HREF="mailto:info@olddog.com">olddog@olddog.com</A>
</ADDRESS>
</BODY>
</HTML>
```

Refer to Chapter 6 for ideas on stylizing product lists.

**NOTE:** I have omitted most of the styling techniques from Listing 13.1 for clarity. In actual use, you could include the techniques discussed in Chapters 2 and 5.

If you were using on-the-fly product description pages, you would have made the link in Listing 13.1 as

```
http://www.olddog.com/CGI-bin/w3-msql/catalog.html?category=Rock
<A HREF=/CGI-bin/w3-msql/product.html?item=@a1.1>
```

## Working with Text-Only Catalogs

For information on creating Web pages viewable by all visitors, see `http://www.w3.org/pub/WWW/Provider/Style/`.

A small percentage of your customers will likely be using Web browsers that are text-only, have image loading off, cannot handle tables, or do not support some of the advanced features included in your catalog. You certainly do not want to lose these customers' business, so how can you accommodate them? You can create a text-only version of your catalogs.

If you use separate catalog pages, creating text versions can be a lot of extra work. Some design tips for making the pages you already have for your regular catalogs readable to all browsers follow:

- Place a space in the beginning of each table cell, at the end of each cell, or both to keep the words from forming a continuous string on browsers that do not support tables.
- Place a `<BR>` or `<P>` at the end of the last cell or at the beginning of the first cell in each row to keep the rows separate on browsers that do not support tables.
- Be sure to use the `ALT` attribute for each image tag—either a blank (`ALT=" "`) or a descriptive phrase, if one is needed in lieu of the image. This will help customers who have image loading off or non-graphical browsers.
- Be sure to validate your page or template with an HTML validator to help catch any errors or typos in your code. For example, I'm always leaving off a closing quote.

If your HTML editor does not validate HTML code, you can find HTML validators at `http://www.w3.org/pub/WWW/Tools`.

**TIP:** It is always a good idea to validate your HTML pages with software especially designed for checking HTML code for errors that might not be seen with your browser.

If you are generating your catalog pages on the fly with a template, you can create a template for a text-only version. A text-only template for the previous example follows:

```
<! msql  connect>
<! msql database tunes>
```

```
<! msql query "select Band, URL, Album, Price
➥ from tunes where category=$category" a1>
<TITLE>
<! msql print "Old Dog Used Records - $category">
</TITLE>
</HEAD>
<BODY>

<H1 ALIGN=CENTER>Old Dog Used Records</H1>
<H2 ALIGN=CENTER><! msql print "$category  Catalog"></H2>

<! msql print_rows "<A  HREF=@a1.1><STRONG>@a1.0:</STRONG>
➥ @a1.2, @a1.3</A><BR>">

<! msql close>
<HR>
<CENTER>
Return to the <A HREF="menu.html">Catalog Menu</A><BR>
Return to Old Dog's <A HREF="menu.html">Home Page</A>
<ADDRESS>
<P ALIGN=CENTER>
Old Dog Used Records<BR>
<A HREF="mailto:info@olddog.com">olddog@olddog.com</A>
</ADDRESS>
</BODY>
</HTML>
```

Of course, we will use a different URL in our menu:

```
http://www.olddog.com/CGI-bin/w3-msql/text.html?category=Rock
```

A text version of the catalog is shown in Figure 13.2.

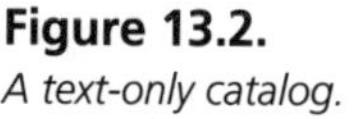

**Figure 13.2.**
*A text-only catalog.*

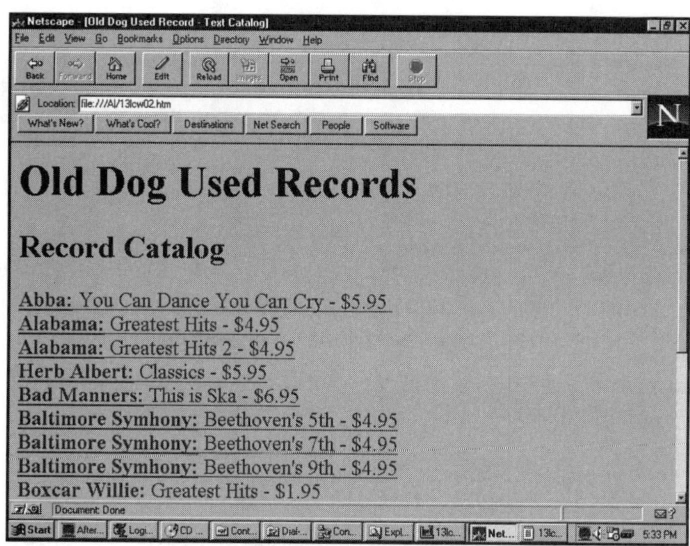

# Customizing Product Presentations

If you have different products, you want to create a special presentation for each product. The visual appeal of your product can help move a sale. You can spend a lot of time creating separate Web pages for every product you have, but if you do, you might not have time to enjoy the money your site will be making.

Old Dog Used Records will have wide range of page presentations to represent the mood and tune of the various records it carries. Ray Charles' "Rainy Night in Georgia" probably will have a dark somber mood to its page, the Starland Vocal Band's "Afternoon Delight" page should be upbeat and happy, Meatloaf's "Bat Out of Hell" probably would have a gothic atmosphere, and so on.

See Chapter 6 for information on setting up a product's description page.

You might want different features on each product page to create an individual customized page. Obviously, the text and the images on each product page will be different, but other features that you might want to change for each product include the following:

- Background color and image
- Text, link, and visited link color (if you want to bother with it)
- Font face
- Font size
- Page layout

**TIP:** We are departing somewhat from the site's theme to customize the product pages. You should try to keep the site's common menu bar or other links on each product, however. This gives the customers a familiar way to move about the site.

Designing and creating a separate page for each product would be very time consuming and probably not worth the effort (cost versus returns). You can create several basic page layouts that will cover most of your products, however, then it would be relatively easy to add a few individualizing characteristics to the pages for each product.

## Creating Separate Pages

If you are maintaining separate pages for each product, you probably made a template first, as described in Chapter 6, and then simply added the particulars for each page and saved it as a separate file.

To start customizing your product pages, you probably want to create several templates for different basic layouts. There might not be much in the layout to change, however—you might have an H1 header, possibly an image, and the product description. You probably won't want to change the head section and footer information (links and address section). For various templates, along with a space for the product description, you might want to include the following:

- A centered H1 header
- An uncentered H1 header
- An image as the H1 header
- An image with each of the preceding features
- A table for laying out an image and its description side by side

**NOTE:** The preceding list just provides ideas—you probably have a better idea of what various layouts would be best for your products. You will probably want to include the HTML for body tag attributes (background, text, link, and visited link colors), font face, and font size, the values of which you will fill out for each individual page.

**TIP:** You might want to look at the different layouts that other sites use for ideas on the various templates you might want to use.

Follow these steps after you choose the layouts:

1. Create the templates.
2. Pick a template for each product.
3. Add the content (title, header, description, and so on).
4. Add the URLs as needed for background and inline images.
5. Insert your choice of text, link, and vlink colors.
6. If needed, add the font face and size values.
7. Save the filled-in template as a separate file.

**TIP:** If you are anything like me, you will occasionally overwrite your template instead of saving it as a separate file. Remember to keep a backup copy of all your templates.

## On-the-Fly Product Pages

Just as in the previous section, "Creating Separate Pages," in order to start the customization process with on-the-fly pages, you need to create several different templates. To simplify matters, however, instead of having several files for templates, you can create different layouts in one file and use conditional statements to control which layout is used. Add a field in your product database to specify a particular layout for each product.

To generate the different layouts, follow these steps:

1. Take the original template and repeat its content several times (copy and paste).
2. Add conditional statements to select the layout for a particular product.
3. Add a field in your database to specify which layout you want for each product.

See the following listing for the Old Dog Used Records sample database.

```
Category,  Band, URL, Album, Layout

our template will be;

<HTML>
<HEAD>
<! msql  connect>
<! msql database tunes>
<! msql query "select Band,URL,Album,Layout from tunes where
➥ category=$category" a1>
<TITLE>
<! msql print "Old Dog Used Records - $category">
</TITLE>
</HEAD>
<BODY>

<! msql if (a1.3==1 >
<!-- Layout 1 would go here>
 <! msql fi>

<! msql if (a1.3==2 >
<!-- Layout 2 would go here>
<! msql fi>

<! msql if (a1.3==3 >
<!-- Layout 3 would go here>
<! msql fi>

<! msql if (a1.3==4 >

<!--... and so on for all the layouts we use -- >

<! msql fi>
```

```
<TABLE WIDTH="90%" ALIGN=CENTER>>
<TR><TD ALIGN=CENTER>
Return to the <A HREF="menu.html">Catalog Menu</A></TD>
<TD ALIGN=CENTER>
Return to Old Dog's <A HREF="menu.html">Home Page</A></TD>
</TR></TABLE></CENTER>
<ADDRESS>
<P ALIGN=CENTER>
Old Dog Used Records<BR>
<A HREF="mailto:info@olddog.com">olddog@olddog.com</A>
</ADDRESS>
</BODY>
</HTML>
```

Although this can make for a rather long file, remember that only the portions for a particular layout will be sent to the customer.

Also in your database, you want to add fields for the various page format items you want to customize. Some of these fields could be any of the following:

- Background image
- Bgcolor
- Text color
- Link color
- Vlink color
- Font face
- Font size
- Font color
- Image file

The Old Dog sample template is shown in the following listing:

```
<HTML>
<HEAD>
<! msql  connect>
<! msql database tunes>
<! msql query "select Band,URL,Album,Layout,Background,BGColor,Text,Link,
➥ Vlink from tunes where category=$category" a1>
<TITLE>
<! msql print "Old Dog Used Records - $category">
</TITLE>
</HEAD>
<BODY
   background=<! msql print "$a1.4">
   bgcolor=<! msql print "$a1.5">
   text=<! msql print "$a1.6">
   link=<! msql print "$a1.7">
   vlink=<! msql print "$a1.8">
>
<! -- the conditional layouts would go here -- >

<!-- end last layout -- >
<! -- begin common footer information -- >
```

```
<CENTER>
<TABLE WIDTH="90%" ALIGN=CENTER>>
<TR><TD ALIGN=CENTER>
Return to the <A HREF="menu.html">Catalog Menu</A></TD>
<TD ALIGN=CENTER>
Return to Old Dog's <A HREF="menu.html">Home Page</A></TD>
</TR></TABLE></CENTER>
<ADDRESS>
<P ALIGN=CENTER>
Old Dog Used Records<BR>
<A HREF="mailto:info@olddog.com">olddog@olddog.com</A>
</ADDRESS>
</BODY>
</HTML>
```

**NOTE:** I left the layout code and other code out of the last two examples for clarity. The code for layout and style control will, of course, be included in actual templates.

# Multimedia and Interactive Catalogs

One of the main reasons for the popularity of the World Wide Web is the Web's capability to provide for multimedia and interaction. Although a plain catalog will likely be sufficient in most cases, using multimedia and providing for customer interaction can greatly enhance the catalog. Multimedia is not just for entertainment, it can be used to present samples or demonstrations of your products and services. Customer interaction can make the catalog more effective for both you and your customers. Performing a keyword search for catalog items, customizing the catalog for personal preferences, and placing orders are some examples of customer interaction you may want to include in your catalog.

## Multimedia

Multimedia includes many different applications. The word itself means several different methods for presenting information. Today, practically every Web page contains text and images, both of which are types of media, but multimedia has come to mean more than just text and images. The following are considered to be multimedia:

Netscape offers or provides links to several multimedia plug-ins for its browsers at `http://home.netscape.com/`.

- Video: Motion picture files that can show directly on your page (inline) or in a separate video viewer. Typical formats are mpeg, avi, and quicktime. Video typically includes audio. Several applications offer streaming video, which enables users to view the video as it is downloading (though they should have a fast connection). Animated GIF images might also be considered a type of video.

- Audio: Sound files that the customer can play. Several audio formats are in use; wav, aiff, and au are common. Real Audio and other applications offer streaming audio, which enables the user to listen to a file as it is downloading.
- VRML: Virtual Reality Modeling Language (VRML) creates a navigable 3-D display (world). Users can view the 3-D display from different perspectives (views) as if they were actually moving through the display. VRML creates 3-D objects that are located spatially in the 3-D world rendered in the display. The 3-D objects can contain hyperlinks to other VRML files or HTML documents. A VRML page is shown in Figure 13.3.

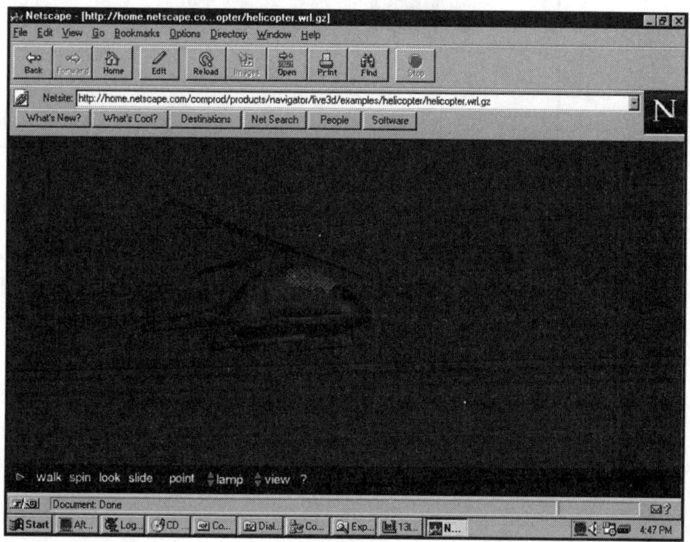


**Figure 13.3.**
*A VRML page.*

See examples of Java Applets at `http:\\www.sun.com\`.

- Java applets: Small applications (programs) that can be embedded in a Web page. Java applets can incorporate text, audio, image, and video objects.

See examples and information on Shockwave at `http://www.macromedia.com/`.

There are several applications available that use one or more types of multimedia for inclusion in Web pages. An interactive multimedia application that uses audio and video and has become somewhat popular is Shockwave (see Figure 13.4).

Shockwave is an application that combines interactive video and audio. Macromedia freely distributes Shockwave plug-ins for Netscape and Microsoft browsers. Shockwave files are Macromedia Director, Freehand, or Authorware files that are compressed for use on the Web. The application used to convert the Macromedia files is free, although you need Director, Freehand, or Authorware to make the original files, and these applications cost several hundred dollars.

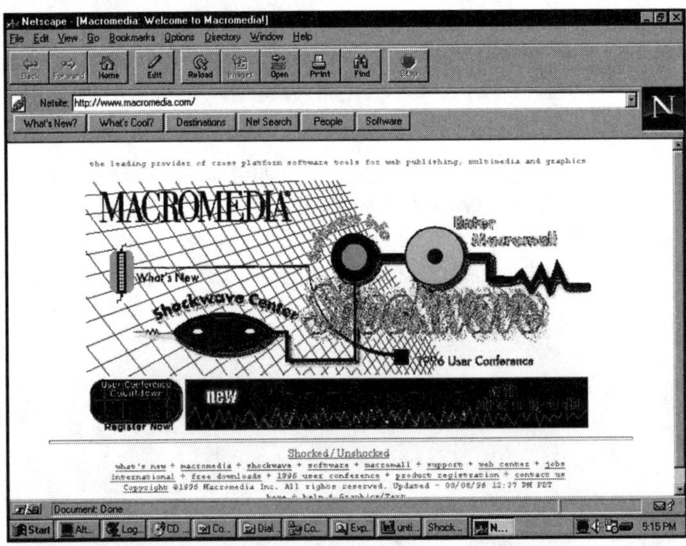


**Figure 13.4.**
*Shockwave is an interactive multimedia site.*

The problem with most multimedia items is large file size and lengthy download time (even with file compression). Video files are typically the largest, followed by audio files. Java applet files can be small enough not to appreciably affect download time, though download time can significantly increase when image and audio files are incorporated within the applet.

**NOTE:** Many of the multimedia applications can require costly software or a level of expertise that could take some time to develop. Other applications such as sound files can be created fairly easily and without cost. Also, many multimedia files can also be downloaded for free from various sites.

**TIP:** To find freely available multiple files, you can use search engines such as Lycos or AltaVista to find sites. For example, to locate wav files, use keywords such as `wav audio`. Another spot to look is the site of the companies that distribute the multimedia applications. For example, `www.macromedia.com` has links to sites using Shockwave.

**CAUTION:** If you download and use multimedia files in your site, be careful that you do not violate someone's copyright. Although many developers allow free use of the files they make, there might be certain provisions to the use of the files. Be safe. If permission isn't clearly given, ask (via e-mail) or do not use the file.

You might still want to incorporate some multimedia into your catalog. At Old Dog Used Records, we can offer samples of the various albums in stock. We can offer a Java music trivia game for customers to test and entertain themselves. The trivia might not seem to have direct bearing on sales, but it lures potential customers and helps keep old customers coming back. We might also offer short videos of various concerts and other music happenings.

Multimedia can enhance your site and make your catalog more interesting and pleasing to the customers. To use multimedia effectively, remember the following:

Microsoft offers multimedia applications for its browser. See `http://www.microsoft.com/ie/`.

- ❑ Determine what would be of interest to your customers and beneficial to your catalog (as with Old Dog Used Records, sound bites of various songs).
- ❑ Do not force the multimedia files on your customers. Although there are ways to load and play audio and video files automatically, please don't use them. Many people do not want to download the large files or do not want to hear the uninvited sound.
- ❑ Provide a link or other means for the customer to choose to view, listen to, or use the multimedia file. Those who want to use multimedia will appreciate that it's available.
- ❑ Do not rely on multimedia to get your message across to the customer. Many customers are not able to use (view, listen to, or use) the files. Others simply might not choose to download the files.
- ❑ For large files, try to indicate the file size near the link so that the customer will have an idea of how long the file will take to download. The following is an example (120K is the file size in bytes):

```
Listen to a <A HREF="demo.ra">demo</A> of this album (120K).
```

**TIP:** As we've mentioned before in this book, a good way to get ideas for your site is to look at other sites. The same goes for your catalog and multimedia—see what others are using with their catalogs.

## Interaction

One great thing about the Web is that users can interact with different sites. Although interaction can be as simple as selecting a link, some of the more interactive features about which you learn in this section follow:

- Searching the catalog
- Customizing the catalog
- Registering preferences with the site
- Ordering products

## Searching the Catalog

Although you have several catalogs for the customers to easily find what they are looking for, sometimes a customer might not find the particular item. The item might be in several different catalogs or might not seem to fit into any of the catalogs. Perhaps the customer is in a hurry and does not have the time to look for the product. A search feature for your catalog can be a great help.

Many browsers have a search or find feature, typically under the Edit menu.

The site searches discussed in Chapter 11 can get the customer to the right product description page or the right catalog (product list) page. To get to the right line on the catalog page, the customer might use the browser's search feature, which searches the Web page for a word or phrase, taking the user to a point on the page where the word is located. Some users might know that they have this feature, but consider adding a brief message on the page to inform other customers who don't know about this feature.

If your catalog pages are generated on the fly, a site search engine is not going to work. The catalog page files do not exist and thus cannot be searched. But you have something better—your database interface can search the database and return a results page with all the pertinent data and only the pertinent data on it. Creating a query form and the response template is described in Chapter 10, "Advanced Information Pages: Tying Data to the Web," though a brief overview of the process follows:

1. Create your query form.
2. Create your response template.

For information on Microsoft's IDC Web-database interface, see Chapter 10.

**NOTE:** Certain Web-database interfaces can require more than just a template. For example, Microsoft's IDC will need an idc file for database commands.

## Customizing the Catalog

You have learned how to provide different catalogs for different customers, so now let's see how to give these customers their own personalized catalog. Customers might want a certain layout for the product description pages; some information can be more important to them than other information. Some might prefer sound and other multimedia in the presentation while others prefer none. A customer may prefer particular types of items in several different categories used for making different catalogs.

For example, with Old Dog Used Records, a customer might be interested in 1960s music. This customer also might want to hear a sample of the music when selecting a description of the album. Another customer might be interested in records only by one band or artist. Because the product list won't be too long, this customer would like to have the record description included on the product list instead of having to go to a separate page for each description.

To accommodate these different customer preferences, I could suggest that you ask that they e-mail their preferences to you so you can make special pages for them, but you would probably think I'm crazy if I do, so I won't. However, if you are generating your catalogs on the fly, you can let the customers decide what and how they want to view the catalogs.

For customers to enter their preferences, you'll need a form for them to indicate what they want. The different form fields you provide for customers to enter preferences will depend a lot on your product line. At Old Dog Used Records, customers can choose one of the following options:

- ❑ Music Category (Rock, County, Blues, and so on)
- ❑ Name of band or artist
- ❑ Decade ('50s, '60s, '70s, and so on)
- ❑ Music style (groups, duets, female artist, male artist, instrumentals)

We also provide an opportunity for customers to select the certain fields they want displayed in the catalog.

- ❑ Show record description on catalog page
- ❑ Text only, no stylized pages, background images, or colors
- ❑ Play a sample of a record when loading a page

Because we will be adding extra fields in our database to hold values for these options, and we need the customer preferences to exactly match these values, all the option fields, with the exception of the Name of Band or Artist, will be predefined values using select boxes or radio buttons.

**NOTE:** The e-mail address field in the form is used to record the customer's preferences for future visits. This feature is discussed in the next section, "Registering Customer Preferences."

To generate the customized catalog in the template (omitting the standard features for clarity), see the following code:

```
<! msql connect>
<! msql database tunes>
<! msql if($option == 1>   <!-- extract data based on customer preferences -- >
<! msql query "select * from tunes where Category=$choice" a1>
<! msql fi>
<! msql if($option == 2>
<! msql query "select * from tunes where Band=$choice" a1>
<! msql fi>
<! msql if($option == 3>
<! msql query "select * from tunes where Decade=$choice" a1>
<! msql fi>
<! msql if($option == 4>
<! msql query "select * from tunes where Style=$choice" a1>
<! msql fi>
<! msql if($layout==1> <! -- catalog layout based upon customer preference -- >
<! msql print_rows "a1.1<BR>a1.2 a1.3 a1.4<P>">
<! msql fi>

<! -- Other layout options -- >

<! msql close>
</BODY>
</HTML>
```

**NOTE:** mSQL offers a limited range of SQL; other Web-database interfaces will likely support the SQL set. With other databases, you can create a more compact template by nesting or joining SQL statements.

You might want to obtain Sams Publishing's *Teach Yourself SQL in 14 Days* by Jeff Perkins and Bryan Morgan to learn more about SQL.

## Registering Customer Preference

In the previous section, "Customizing the Catalog," you created a customized catalog for the customer. In the form, you requested the customer's e-mail address. The address provides a unique identifier for the customer with which you store and later retrieve the customer preferences. You can use the following W3-mSQL commands to add the preferences data to a customer database:

```
<! msql database customers>
<! msql query "insert into customers (ID, option,choice, layout)
➥ Values ($email, $option, $choice, $layout)">
```

Later, when customers return to the site, they enter their e-mail addresses in a form on the main menu page to receive their customized catalog. The form is rather simple:

```
<FORM METHOD=GET ACTION="/CGI-bin/w3-msql/customer.html">
prompt will appear for the user, saying "For customers who have a personalized
catalog, please enter your e-mail address<BR>." The code follows:
<INPUT NAME=email> <INPUT TYPE=SUBMIT VALUE="Submit">
</FORM>
```

To process the customer's entry from the preceding form and to serve the customized catalog, we will use a template similar to the template in the previous section, "Customizing the Catalog," except that now we will open an additional database (named customers in the following code example) and use another SQL SELECT statement to extract customer preference information from this database (customers). The template will contain the following code:

```
<! msql connect>
<! msql database customers>
<! msql database tunes>
<! msql query "select * from tunes where ID=$email" a2>
<! msql if(@a2.1 == 1>   <!-- extract data based on customer preferences -- >
<! msql query "select * from tunes where Category=@a2.2" a1>
...
```

For information on using Netscape cookies, see `newsref/std/cookie_spec.html`.

**NOTE:** Another method that is becoming popular is using Netscape cookies to store a unique ID code on the customer's computer. When a customer returns to the catalog, he or she can retrieve this code automatically and use it to extract the information from your database.

Cookies are an innovation by Netscape that enable Web servers to store small amounts of information on a visitor's computer. The purpose of the cookie is to maintain information from one visit at a site to another visit at the same site. By storing a cookie on a visitor's computer, the server can identify the visitor when that visitor returns to the site.

The basic process is, the server uses a CGI script or JavaScript to store the cookie information on the visitor's computer. Then, whenever the visitor's browser requests another document from the same server, it will send the cookie information back to the server.

Cookies are not supported by all browsers, but most browsers in use (such as Netscape and Microsoft) support cookies.

## Ordering

Web shopping cart applications are described in Chapter 14, "Web Shopping Carts."

Perhaps the most important interaction between you and your customer is the customer's ability to place an order directly from your catalog. To make this possible on your catalog page, you can

- Enclose the entire product list in an HTML form.
- Use the form action as your order script.
- Add an input field at each product line:

  Have the field name equal the product code, number, or other unique identifier.

  The field value will be the quantity ordered by the customer.

**NOTE:** Depending on your order processing script, you may have to use hidden fields to specify each product code and have the input field names be a word, such as `quantity`. For example:

```
<INPUT TYPE="HIDDEN" NAME="ITEM" VALUE="11023">
<INPUT NAME="quantity">
```

- At the bottom of the product list, include fields for completing an order, such as name, address, payment information, and so on.

# Workshop Wrap-Up

This chapter covered a lot, including

- Setting up different catalogs for different customers, including generating specific catalogs on the fly from a database
- Creating customized product presentations so that each product can be displayed in the best way
- Using multimedia to enhance your pages and to make your catalog more attractive to customers
- Making your catalog interactive to provide product searches, personalized versions for customers, and to enable customers to order from your catalog

**NOTE:** Although you use the W3-mSQL Web-database interface in the examples of this chapter, you can use a different interface with statements similar to the statements in the examples.

## Next Steps

Now...

- ❑ Chapter 14, "Web Shopping Carts." The next logical step from a catalog is a shopping cart. With a shopping cart system, your customer not only can place orders, but can also select items from different pages and catalogs before placing the order.
- ❑ Chapter 15, "Web Cash Registers: Taking and Making Money on the Net." Now that you have set up a catalog, you will be ready to accept orders and take payment. Chapter 15 describes how to accept orders, provide different payment options, and provide for secure transactions.
- ❑ Chapter 18, "Order and Shipment Tracking on the Web." Once you are accepting orders, you will want use the order information to process orders, track orders, maintain inventories, and perform sales analysis.

## Q&A

**Q: If a catalog has only 20 items on it, is there any reason to provide more than one version of the catalog?**

**A:** For a small line of products, maintaining separate catalogs would not offer any advantages. Customers could quickly scan through the entire catalog to find the item they seek. A possibility would be to create a text version of the catalog, however, if the original catalog is highly stylized and some customers are not able to read it on their browsers.

**Q: Doesn't having customized product pages create a lot of extra work in maintaining the pages?**

**A:** Not really. You would have separate product pages even if they were not customized. Whether you use customized pages or not, you would still have to update the pages for any product changes.

**Q: How much would it cost to add multimedia to the catalog?**

**A:** A lot depends on the type of multimedia you want to use and how you obtain the multimedia files. You can download many files off the Internet for free or for a nominal charge. If you need to make your own files, you can usually make audio files with the hardware and software already included on most computers. Video files and other multimedia can cost several hundred dollars for the software and hardware (not including a video camera).

**Q: Is it possible to allow customers to order from several catalogs at the same time instead of submitting separate orders for each?**

**A:** Yes, it is. The next chapter, "Web Shopping Carts," discusses how to do this.

CHAPTER FOURTEEN

# Web Shopping Carts

## In this chapter, you

- ❑ Prepare files for a CGI-based shopping cart system
- ❑ Configure your server to work with the shopping cart system
- ❑ Customize HTML headers and footers for shopping cart pages
- ❑ Design forms for customers to make purchases from by using their Web-based shopping carts

## Tasks in this chapter:

- ❑ Preparing the Shopping Cart Files and Directory
- ❑ Creating an Online Store

In many ways, Web shopping carts are simply another, more advanced type of Web catalog—a more advanced and more functional type that will help you generate sales. The idea of making it easier for people to select and purchase products from catalogs will have many business people salivating, I'm sure.

Web shopping carts make it easier for users to shop while navigating through your site. Imagine if you went into a grocery store and had to pick up items one at a time and bring them to the cashier to check out and then had to repeat this process for each individual item you wanted to buy. Some Web sites still rely on technology that requires this kind of insanity for shopping on the Web. However, you won't, after you see how easy it is to create and install a Web shopping cart.

Another excellent potential use for shopping carts is developing a Web mall. A Web mall enables you to join with other merchants to offer all of your products across a variety of categories. Users can shop with ease by choosing products from each store as they go along, needing to check out only once at the very end.

Web malls, like their suburban brethren, normally provide a boost in traffic (or crowds), which provides more potential customers than a single page or store could on its own.

This chapter walks you through the installation, configuration, and setup of a complete Web-based shopping cart system. There are many shopping cart products available on the Web, and although you'll be using only one in this chapter, you'll get pointers to others that might suit your needs.

Creating a Web shopping cart can be a very complex and somewhat confusing task. As a result, this chapter takes you through the process step-by-step (and task-by-task) and distills the information you need to get up and running (and selling).

Appendix A contains full listings of URL references used in this book, broken down by category.

# Shopping Carts: How'd They Do That?

Before you jump head-first into creating a Web shopping cart, you might want to know exactly what they are and how they work. Without a little background, a difficult project becomes even more perplexing.

In this chapter you'll be working with the OopShop Shopping Cart System, available for free on the Web from `http://www.ids.net/~oops/cart/` and shown in Figure 14.1 for a variety of different Web servers. The OopShop shopping cart is a set of CGI scripts and HTML files that you can customize to implement a shopping cart system on your pages.

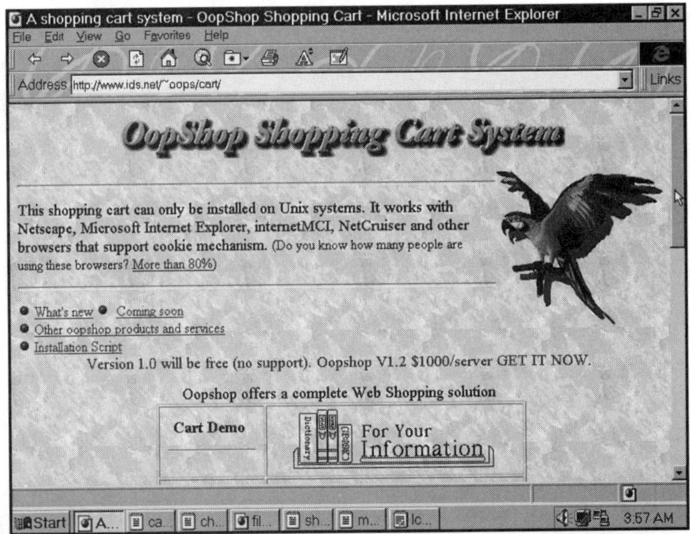


**Figure 14.1.**
*The OopShop Shopping Cart System has a Web page with all the files and information you need to get started.*

If you don't find a set of OopShop scripts for your server platform, contact the scripts' authors at `oops@ids.net` and they'll compile a set for you.

The OopShop scripts use "cookies" to read and write to a file on each user's computer. Cookies are a small file that resides on a user's computer. The server can read and write to this file, and this can be used for a variety of things, including tracking exactly where that user has visited on the site. As a result, the system enables Web surfers to go from page to page selecting different products and specifying different quantities. When a user is finished, the system culls together all the information regarding the products selected and presents the user with a total and enables him or her to check out (that is, to purchase the items). All of this is accomplished through the use of OopShop's custom CGI scripts.

**NOTE:** Because the shopping cart requires the use of CGI scripts, it is impossible to create on the CD-ROM the working example that is presented in this chapter. The shopping cart example is implemented on the Web site at `http://www.murphnet.com`, and you can also find examples (and even create your own) from OopShop's pages at `http://www.ids.net/~oops/cart/`.

Throughout this example you'll be working heavily with two of the more complicated HTML elements (in addition to the CGI scripts): tables and forms. Remember, you can always refer to the complete text of Laura Lemay's *Teach Yourself Web Publishing with HTML in 14 Days, Professional Reference Edition*, included on the accompanying CD-ROM. Appendix B also has a complete HTML 3.2 reference guide.

# Preparing the Shopping Cart Files and Directory

On this project you'll be working with your friends at Old Dog Records. They want to be able to give users the ability to choose ABBA 8-tracks from one page, Hootie and the Blowfish CDs from another, and to check out all at once.

You'll need to go through some preliminary steps to prepare the shopping cart files and your Web server for implementing this system. I'll assume at this point that you've retrieved the appropriate OopShop files for your system from the site mentioned in the previous note. Now, follow these steps:

1. Create a new directory at the root of your main Web page. Use a descriptive name like "cart" or "shopping" for the directory. For example, make a directory `http://www.olddog.com/cart/`.

2. Copy all the OopShop files into the newly created directory (`http://www.olddog.com/cart/`). There should be 14 files, as shown in Table 14.1. You'll see an explanation of each of the files and how to configure them later in this chapter.
3. The program also creates two additional files that need to have their modes adjusted on your server. Enter `chmod 666 c_counter.dat` and `chmod 622 order`. The `c_counter.dat` file keeps track of the number of orders, and the `order` file is where orders are actually saved on the server (thus, the need to set the mode so that only you can view its contents).
4. Set `chmod 644` for all your `*.html` files in the directory and `chmod 711` for all the `*.cgi` files.

**TIP:** OopShop has an installation script available (`install-oops`) that will do much of the preliminary work for configuring the shopping cart at the start. However, you should always work through installations like these manually the first time so you know exactly what is being done to the system by the script. (Also, the script might fail—after all, we're talking about software here.)

**Table 14.1. A list of the OopShop files.**

| *File* | *Purpose* | *Required/Optional* | *Edit* |
|---|---|---|---|
| `shop.cgi` | Main cart program | Required | N |
| `view_cartcgi` | Shows cart's contents to user | Required | N |
| `clear.cgi` | Empties user's cart at any time | Required | N |
| `checkout.cgi` | Saves orders | Required | N |
| `checkout.html` | Sample order form | Required | Y |
| `cart.conf` | Configuration file for OopShop | Required | Y |
| `head.html` | Text and/or gifs to display at the top of the shopping cart pages | Optional | Y |

| *File* | *Purpose* | *Required/Optional* | *Edit* |
|---|---|---|---|
| `foot.html` | Text and/or gifs to display at the bottom of the shopping cart page | Optional | Y |
| `shop1.html` | Sample store page | Required | Y |
| `background.jpg` | Graphic for page backgrounds | Optional | Y |
| `makestore.cgi` | Program to create new stores or departments | Optional | N |
| `makestore.html` | Form to create new stores or departments | Optional | N |
| `state_tax.db` | Database of tax rates of different states for the order form | Optional | Y |
| `ship_fee.db` | Database of shipping and handling fees for the order form | Optional | Y |
| `c_counter.dat` | The system to track the number of orders (created by OopShop) | Required | N |
| `order` | Stores customer order data (created by OopShop) | Required | N |

## Edit the `cart.conf` Configuration File

The next step in setting up your shopping cart system is to edit the `cart.conf` file that comes with the OopShop program. This is the configuration file for the OopShop Shopping Cart System and will require customization for your particular setup.

To customize the `cart.conf` file for use on your system, simply work through the following steps and enter the appropriate settings:

1. `cgi-bin=/~oops/cart/`

   Replace `/~oops/cart/` with the directory on your server where your cgi programs are stored. Sometimes you are required to place all scripts in a special `cgi-bin` directory.

2. `storefront=/~oops/cart/shop1.html`

   Replace `/~oops/cart/shop1.html` with the URL of the main Web page for your shopping cart system (usually the top page of your catalog or Web mall).

3. `document_root=/home/oops/www/cart/`

   Replace `/home/oops/www/cart/` with the location of the directory for your OopShop scripts and where `c_counter.dat`, `order`, and `checkout.html` will be stored. You must specify the absolute path to the directory, which might be different than its URL and can be discovered by entering `pwd` while in the directory.

4. `url_of_doc_root=/~oops/cart/`

   Replace `/~oops/cart/` with the URL for the root directory for which you entered the absolute path in step 3.

5. `head=/home/oops/www/cart/head.html`

   Replace `/home/oops/www/cart/head.html` with the location of the HTML file you want to appear at the top of each OopShop page.

6. `foot=/home/oops/www/cart/foot.html`

   Replace `/home/oops/www/cart/foot.html` with the location of the HTML file you want to appear at the bottom of each OopShop page.

7. The `cart.conf` file also contains settings for state tax rates (`tax_rate`), shipping fees (`ship_handle`), and electronic cash transactions (`ecash_cgi`). Some additional adjustments will need to be made here. For information on these settings, refer to Chapter 15, "Web Cash Registers: Taking and Making Money on the Net."

Talk to your system administrator to determine your absolute path if you're still uncertain or have problems.

In the next step of this task, you'll see how to customize the `head.html` file with your own text and graphics.

In the following steps, you'll also see how to customize the `foot.html` file with your own text and graphics.

Don't forget to save the file as `cart.conf` and place it in your main OopShop cart directory.

Next, you'll need to customize some additional files to make sure the shopping cart has a style all your (and your company's) own.

## Customizing the Shopping Cart Header (`head.html`)

The OopShop system will use its script to automatically generate particular Web pages for users as they shop on your site. For example, when users view the contents of their shopping cart (by selecting a link) or go to check out, the OopShop program's scripts create Web pages on-the-fly, entering the appropriate customized data for that user's shopping experience.

The `head.html` file (along with the `foot.html` and `background.jpeg` files, which we'll look at next) gives you a small, although important, level of control over how these pages look. You can simply edit the `head.html` file to include any HTML code or tags that you can incorporate in any Web page. OopShop then simply pulls this mini-Web page and integrates it at the top of the pages that the program generates.

The `head.html` file of most shopping carts should look fairly similar in what it contains. Here are a few simple steps you should go through to generate a sample `head.html` file for OopShop:

1. For the `head.html` file, you don't need to bother with preliminary tags such as `<TITLE>`, `<HTML>`, or `<BODY>`—just jump right into the meat of the code.
2. If you would like to set a background color for the page in lieu of using the `background.jpeg` file, you can enter a `<BODY BGCOLOR="FFFFFF">` tag.
3. Insert your company's graphic logo using the `<IMG SRC>` tag, and then hyperlink the image to your main Web page.
4. Insert the necessary HTML code for your Web site's menu bar just below the logo.
5. Create and enter a simple line of HTML code to implement a type of cart navigation menu that provides for shopping cart-specific options. Include options for Continue Shopping, View Shopping Cart Contents, Check Out, and Empty Cart. The last three will point to OopShop scripts and the first option should link back to the main starting page. Here's a sample of what this code could look like:

```
<A HREF="shop1.html">[ Continue Shopping ]</A><A HREF="view_cart.cgi">
➥[ View Shopping Cart Contents ]</A><A HREF="checkout.cgi">
➥[ Check Out ]</A><A HREF="clear.cgi">[ Empty Cart ]</A>
```

Chapter 3, "Corporate Presence Pages," gives you details on how to design and create a menu bar for your site.

**TIP:** Of course, you could be more creative and elaborate with the shopping cart navigational options. Feel free to apply font styles and colors and even use graphic images as buttons to give the selections more style.

Using these steps to create a simple `head.html` file for the folks at Old Dog Used Records results in the page header shown in Figure 14.2. You should always view the `head.html` file on its own with a browser to catch any coding errors.

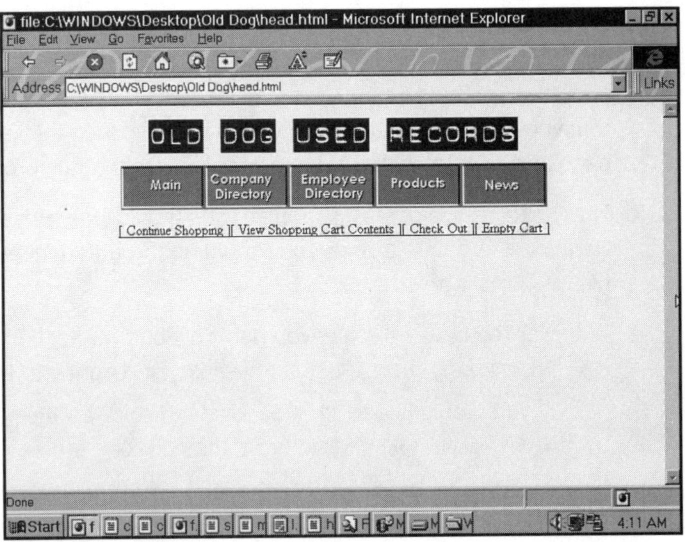


**Figure 14.2.**
*A sample* `head.html` *file using all the standard elements.*

## Customizing the Shopping Cart Footer (`foot.html`)

The `foot.html` document works exactly like `head.html`, only this time the `foot.html` code is placed at the very bottom of the shopping cart pages. Of course, most of the general items covered with `head.html` apply to this file as well. For example, you don't need to enter the `<TITLE>` or `<HTML>` tags. When you work with the `foot.html` file, follow these steps:

1. Enter a horizontal rule at the very beginning of the document to give it an easy-to-identify separator from the rest of the page.
2. Include the same shopping cart navigation menu that you created in step 5 with the `head.html` file. It's important to give users navigational flexibility no matter where they're located on your page.
3. Include a `mailto:` link to your e-mail address so that users can give you feedback or get questions answered.
4. Include any standard copyright or disclaimer text that you might make part of all your standard pages.

That was simple enough, wasn't it? Now, just save the file using the `foot.html` name, as shown in Figure 14.3. Then place it in the main OopShop Web server directory. Now that you have the basic files ready to go, let's start making some stores.

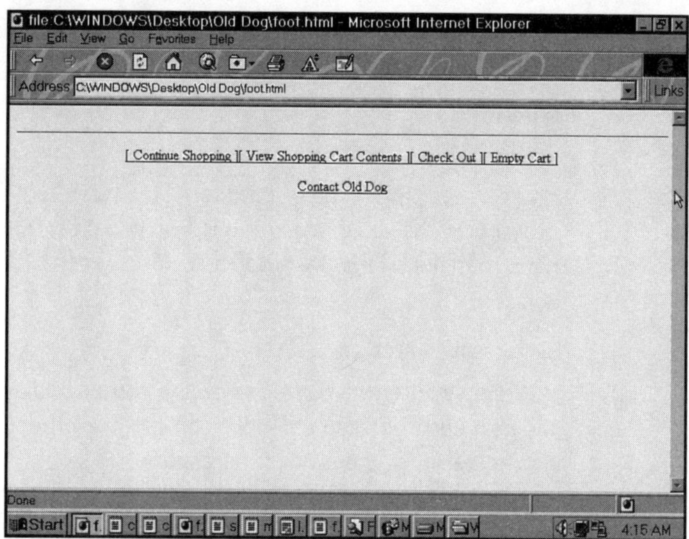


**Figure 14.3.**
*The* `foot.html` *page will be inserted at the bottom of every OopShop-generated page.*

# Creating an Online Store

The next step in implementing the OopShop shopping cart system is to actually create a store (or an entire online mall) where people can shop by placing items in their carts for purchase. OopShop also comes with the `makestore.html` and `makestore.cgi` combination that enable you to create a simple store in seconds.

## The Rule of Threes

The easiest way to remember how to create a store using OopShop is to use the rule of threes. In order for a customer to be able to shop for products on a page and add them to their cart, there has to be three entries for each product. You can think of a shamrock, or you can even use the silly acronym I created: Q-tiPS. The Q is for quantity, the P is for price, and the S is for the store name. These are the three entries each item must contain.

You make these three entries for each product as part of a form. Each store you operate must have at least one form on the Web page. Don't think of this as a typical form like the customer registration forms you looked at in Chapter 8, "Gathering Information: Web-Based Surveys and Questionnaires." Instead, it really just allows for user input—normally just in quantity—so that the shopping cart can identify purchases.

Here's a quick rundown of the three entries that must exist within the form for each of the products you want to set up to work with the shopping cart:

1. **Quantity**

   `NAME="quantity" VALUE=""`

   You can alter the name of this first entry, but it must be the same for each product on the same page (that is, you could use `"quant"`, but you would need to make sure every product used `"quant"`).

2. **Price**

   `NAME="9.99" VALUE="Product Description"`

   You simply enter the correct price and corresponding product description. In the next entry you can enter the name of the product. Therefore, use a more general term for the product description.

3. **Store**

   `NAME="Store Name" VALUE="Product Name"`

   Enter the store name and the product name. You might want to use a product number in lieu of its name for accounting or tracking purposes.

In the next step, you'll see why items 2 and 3 are normally hidden fields within your forms.

## Form-ulating Stores and Aisles

In many ways, you shouldn't think of this step as creating new pages, but rather as adding appropriate form tags to give shopping cart functionality to any of your pages—whether they are new or current pages. For this example, we'll be modifying the price/product list catalog that you created in Chapter 5, "Employee Directories and Biographies." You'll see how easy it is to convert a catalog from a static page to an interactive Web shopping cart.

The following is an excerpt from the Old Dog Used Records product/price list catalog that you created in Chapter 5. (See Figure 14.4.) You'll be modifying the code from this excerpt to see how easy it is to add OopShop's cart functionality.

```
<TR BGCOLOR="white"><TD WIDTH=75 HEIGHT=50><B>
<A HREF="abba1.htm"> 14358 </TD><TD WIDTH=370 HEIGHT=50><B>
<A HREF="abba1.htm"> Abba, You Can Dance, You Can Cry</TD>
➥<TD WIDTH=75 HEIGHT=50><B>
<A HREF="abba1.htm"> $5.95 </TD><TD WIDTH=75 HEIGHT=50>
<TABLE><TR><B><TD> C </TD><TD> T </TD></TR>
<TR><TD> R </TD><TD> 8 </TD></TR>
</TABLE></TD>
</TR></B>
```

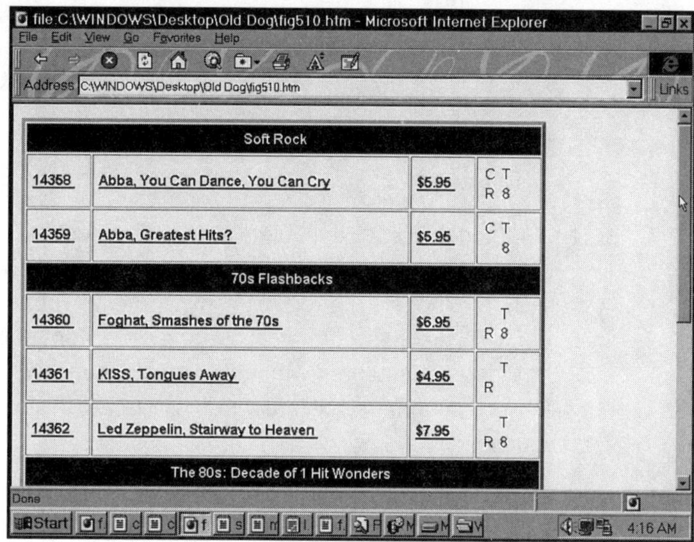


**Figure 14.4.**
*OopShop enables you to turn this static catalog into an interactive shopping cart.*

Now, let's get down to work. Here are the step-by-step procedures you should follow to modify this catalog with OopShop's scripts:

1. At the top of the page, just after the initial tags, insert a form method tag (using `POST`) that will call to the main OopShop script, `shop.cgi`. Here's an example:

   ```
   <FORM METHOD="POST" ACTION="http://www.server.com/cart/shop.cgi>
   ```

2. You'll replace the table cell containing the available formats with a text box for entering the quantity purchased. Clear those tables of all information.
3. Enter the first required entry (quantity) for the first product (Abba) in the just-cleared table cell. In addition to using the basic settings for name and value shown above, you'll need to specify the input type, which is text, and create a size for the input box. Here's an example:

   ```
   <INPUT TYPE="text" NAME="quantity" VALUE=""
   SIZE="3" MAXLENGTH="3">
   ```

Unless you plan on selling mass quantities of products, specifying a text box size and maximum length of 3 should work well for almost all products.

4. Enter the second required entry (price) within the same cell for this product. Of course, the price is already listed in the HTML code on the left side of the row for this item. As a result, you can make this entry a hidden input type. Normally, you'll want to make both the second and third entries (price and store) hidden entries. Users aren't able to change either of these and have no need to see them. Remember that you should enter a generalized product name at this point. Here's an example:

   ```
   <INPUT TYPE="hidden" NAME="5.95" VALUE="Abba">
   ```

5. Enter the third required entry (store name) immediately after the price entry. Once again, the input type will be hidden for this entry. You can also include a more specific product name or number. Here's an example:

```
<INPUT TYPE="hidden" NAME="Old Dog" VALUE="You Can Dance">
```

**TIP:** Although the third required entry is the store name, this is a little deceiving. You can actually use this property to create pages comprised of different product areas or departments and have virtual aisles within your store. Users can choose from each of the pages (or aisles) and during check-out they will be presented with a nice breakdown of what they bought and where they bought it (well, really just selected at this point, but I'm optimistic) on your site.

6. Repeat each of these steps for each of the items on the page. Remember that the only items that have to remain the same are `NAME="quantity"` and `NAME="Old Dog"`. You can fill in the appropriate price and product information for each item. Each album will then have a quantity input box, as shown in Figure 14.5.

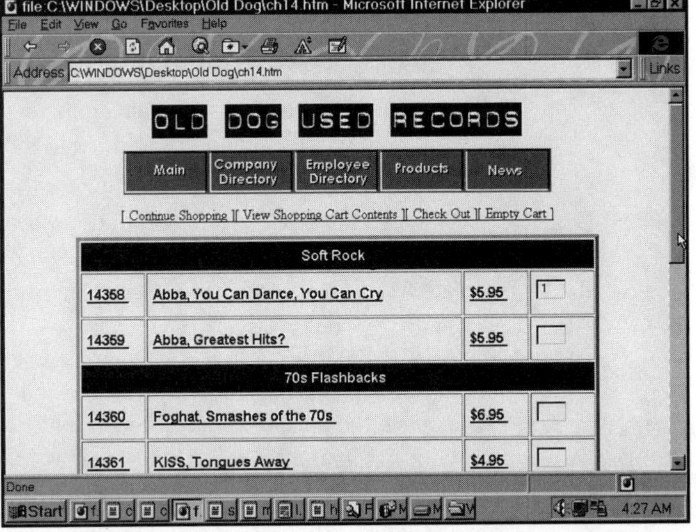


**Figure 14.5.**
*Each album now has a separate quantity input box.*

7. Create a submission button at the bottom of the page that adds the selected items to the shopping cart, as shown in Figure 14.6. You can use any name and value for the button that suits your tastes. Here's an example:

```
<INPUT TYPE="submit" NAME="Old Dog" Value="Place In Cart">
```

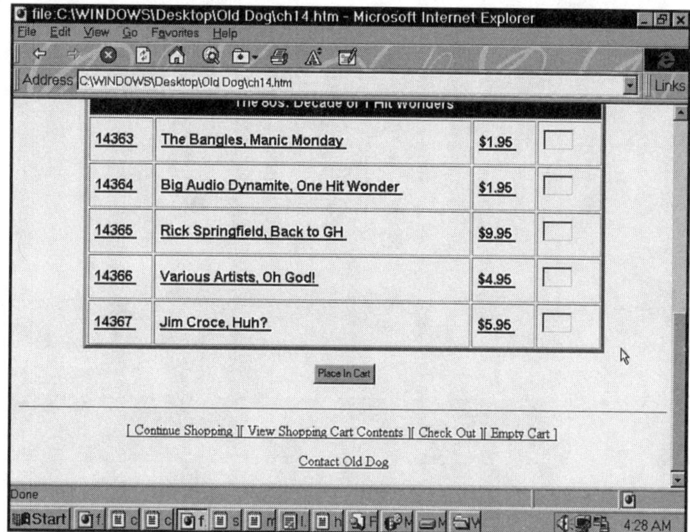


**Figure 14.6.**
*The submission button (Place In Cart) is a vital element in making OopShop work.*

8. Finally, cut and paste the code from `head.html` (see Figure 14.5) to the top of the document and then cut and paste the code from `foot.html` (see Figure 14.6) to the bottom of this document. OopShop accesses these files only when it is creating pages on-the-fly (as when it shows users the contents of their carts). This gives the pages more consistency.

At this point, your work is finished. In the next chapter we'll pick up with this example and I'll show you how users complete the transaction (that is, check out) by providing shipping and payment information. But as far as the shopping cart portion of the project is considered, you have done your work—now OopShop can do the rest.

# OopShop in Action

When a user enters a quantity and selects the Place In Cart button, he or she is presented with a screen like the one shown in Figure 14.7. If the customer continues to shop and just wants to see what is in the cart so far, he or she can select View Shopping Cart Contents, and OopShop presents the information as shown in Figure 14.8.

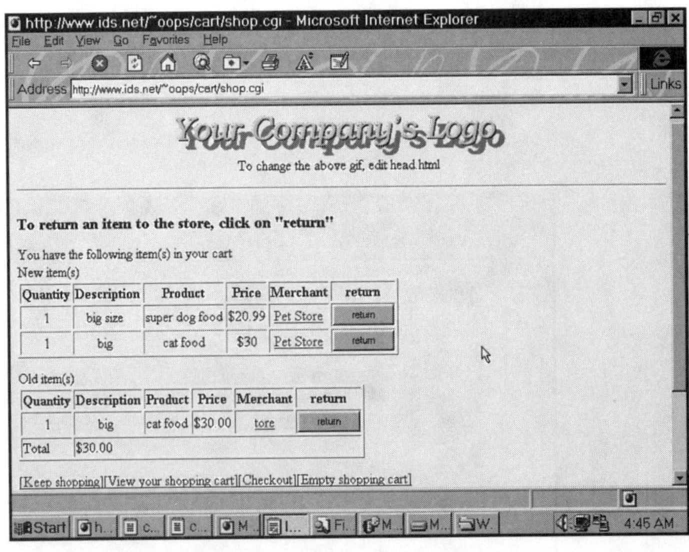


**Figure 14.7.**
*The confirmation screen that users receive after placing items in their cart.*

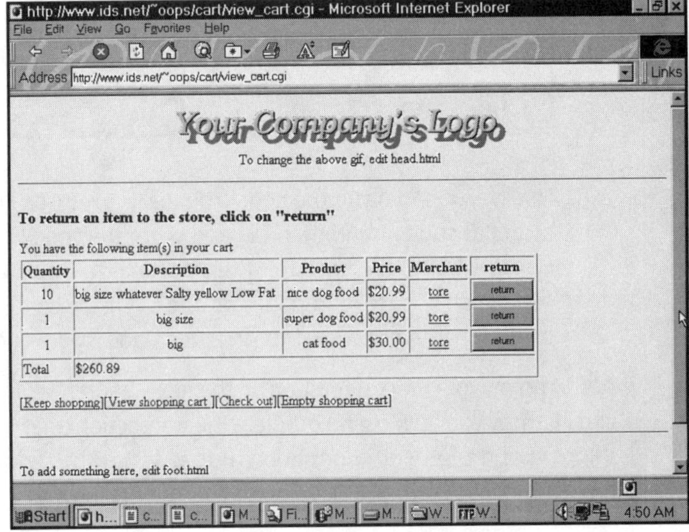


**Figure 14.8.**
*Users can check at any time while browsing to make sure their cart isn't too full (that is, over budget).*

Of course, some users might change their minds and want to put some items back on the shelves before checking out. A simple click of OopShop's Empty Shopping Cart selection will clear their carts, as confirmed in Figure 14.9.

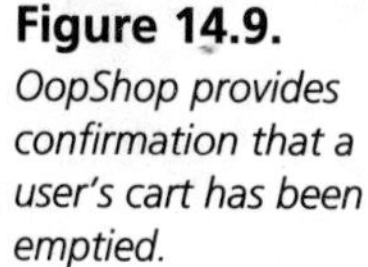

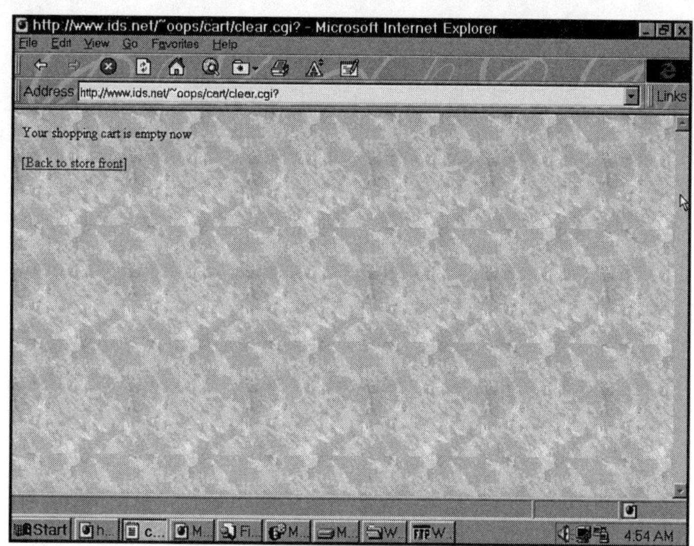


**Figure 14.9.**
*OopShop provides confirmation that a user's cart has been emptied.*

Again, you haven't reached the end of your journey with OopShop just yet. What lies ahead is one of the most exciting and enticing parts of the product—collecting the dough from your customers and closing the sale. Luckily, that chapter is next.

# Workshop Wrap-Up

OopShop is one of the many Web-based shopping carts that uses a technology called *cookies* to track user purchases on a Web site, allowing for unlimited browsing with a single checkout procedure.

You can effectively integrate OopShop's shopping cart mechanism into new or existing pages. Taking the time to properly configure and set up the CGI scripts is the most delicate part of the process. Once that has been done, coding the necessary HTML pages is a breeze.

Using OopShop, you can either set up a Web-based mall where several stores can join together to offer their products, or you can have separate departments or aisles on a single site. The power and flexibility that shopping carts offer to developers and users alike is a primary reason for the rising popularity of this technology.

## Next Steps

Now...

- ❑ If you want to see how to finish up with OopShop and close the sale, you should turn to Chapter 15, "Web Cash Registers: Taking and Making Money on the Net."

- ❏ To see some real-life shopping cart examples, turn to Chapter 19, "Real-Life Examples: Doing Business on the Web."
- ❏ If you're ready to start drawing cart customers to your pages, you might want to take a look at Chapter 20, "Marketing Your Web Pages."

# Q&A

**Q: OopShop seems pretty cool, but are there any alternatives for creating shopping carts?**

**A:** Absolutely. Unfortunately, it would take an entire book to fully explore the ins and outs of every Web shopping cart program out on the Net. Selena Sol's Script Archive has several different excellent Web-based shopping cart programs available from `http://www2.eff.org/~erict/Scripts/`. Also, a quick search of Yahoo! will always turn up the latest releases of similar products.

**Q: I've heard people are afraid of cookies. Will this turn off customers?**

**A:** It's true that some Web users are extremely sensitive about any program accessing their computer and saving and retrieving information, and this is precisely what cookies do. However, those users can always peruse your site without activating the cookies mechanism by never placing items in a cart. You should also always include a way to purchase products using traditional means for those customers who are Web weary when it comes to transactions.

C H A P T E R

FIFTEEN

# Web Cash Registers: Taking and Making Money on the Net

Now it's time to see how to receive payback for all your hard work. Through your site you can sell goods and services to your customers, and you can receive payment immediately online or allow customers to send payment offline.

## In this chapter, you

- Learn how to present payment options. You offer the customer a variety of payment options that facilitate the business transaction.
- Secure transactions to protect you and your customers.
- Take digital cash—allowing customers to pay with this new, safe, electronic form of money.
- Use online and offline ordering systems to provide the customer with the best means possible to do business with you.

## Tasks in this chapter:

- Securing Transactions on Your Site
- Preparing for Third-Party Transactions
- Providing Both Online and Offline Ordering

Secure transactions involve encrypting data sent between sever and browser.

Digital cash is electronic tokens (strings of digital information) that are encoded with information on the issuing bank, the denomination of the token, and other information for transaction processing and security.

You might want to check the electronic commerce references and resources at `www.commerce.net/jump/`.

# Presenting Payment Options

Various customers prefer different payment methods. Many prefer an immediate online way to pay. Others might prefer to send payment offline, especially if a secure transaction is not provided. Many will want to make a charge to their credit card, and others will want to use a check. Digital cash, such as "ecash," and third-party transactions are coming into use for online purchasing.

Here are some of the payment options you might want to offer:

- *Credit card*. Customers send account information online for you to charge payment to their credit card.
- *Check*. Customers send bank and account information for you to make a withdrawal on their accounts.
- *Phone*. Customers call you with the payment information.
- *Fax*. Customers fax the payment information to you.
- *Mail* (postal service). Customers mail a check or account information for you to make a charge against their accounts.
- *Digital cash*. Customers send you their payment electronically.
- *Third-party transactions*. You and the customer have arrangements made for an online financial company to charge the customer's account and to credit your account.
- *Invoice*. You accept the order and send the customer a bill for payment.

**NOTE:** Many of these options carry a charge for the service. Merchant accounts for credit cards, check cashing, digital cash, and third-party transactions have fixed costs and a percentage charge for transactions.

To offer your goods and services to the widest possible customer base, you need to accept as many payment options as is practical. For example, you could place the following selections on the order form:

```
<P><STRONG>Payment Option</STRONG><P>
<SELECT NAME="pay">
<OPTION SELECTED>Charge Credit Card
<OPTION>Charge Checking Account
<OPTION>Will send check
<OPTION>Will call with payment information
<OPTION>Send an invoice
<OPTION>ecash
</SELECT>
```

**NOTE:** Fields for entering credit card or checking account information should be added separately to the form so customers can use these options.

**TIP:** To help you determine what options you might want to offer at your site, see what is offered by sites similar to yours.

See `http://www.jan-lind.com/cpwindow.html` for information on accepting checks online or by phone.

The following procedure is a guide for offering payment options:

1. Determine which payment methods are practical. For example, if you are providing immediate download of software, a slow method such as a check might not be practical.
2. List which methods of payment you can accept (checks, credit cards, digital cash, and so on).
3. Obtain merchant accounts for other methods (digital cash, third-party transactions, and so on) that you want to offer.
4. Provide a select list (a drop-down menu) or a radio button list of the options on your order form.

**TIP:** Have the method you prefer, if any, as the default method (selected or checked in the initial form).

5. If your system permits, have the order-processing script return a form to the customer for entering information to pay with a credit card, checking account, and so on, if one of these options is selected.
6. If your shopping/ordering system does not allow for sending another form, then include the necessary credit card or checking account fields on the order form.

**CAUTION:** Be sure the order form is as secure as possible.

Figure 15.1 shows an example of an order form with payment options.

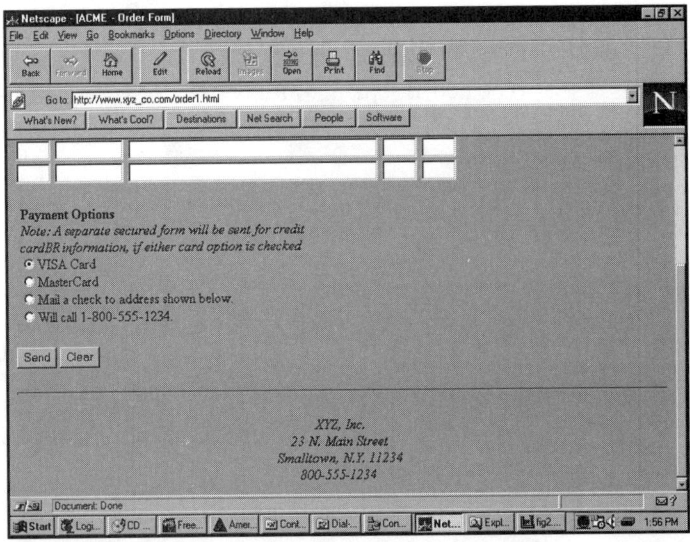


**Figure 15.1.**
*Providing payment options on an order form.*

## Securing Transactions on Your Site

Secure Socket Layers (SSL) is the protocol commonly used to secure transactions.

Financial transaction on the Internet face two major security risks:

- Misuse of account information by merchants or their staff. But because you and your staff are honest people, this risk is not a problem.
- Transaction data can be routed through any number of systems throughout the world before reaching its destination. At any of these points, a sniffer can be checking the data stream for number sequences common to credit cards.

**NOTE:** A *sniffer*, as used in the preceding paragraph, is a device that monitors streams of data and detects certain data sequences. The sniffer detects and records data sequences that could be credit card numbers and expiration dates.

Although the odds that one of your transactions will be picked up by sniffing are extremely small, several relatively simple methods can be used to protect both you and your customers.

- Use a secured server for transactions. This means the customer's browser must be able to handle secure transactions.
- Use a third-party server for transactions.

Information on the SSL protocol can be found at `http:/www.netscape.com/newsref/std/SSL.html`.

- Jumble the information to make it difficult to detect.
- Use common sense in creating the fields for sensitive information on your form.

## Common Sense Security

Internet security references can be found at `http://www.w3.org/Security/`.

Here are some basic common sense form design items:

- Do not name the fields with a word that reflects that field's content. For example, `<INPUT NAME="Card_num">` would be pretty obvious that the associated value is a card number.
- Use separate fields for portions of the card information. Data sniffers look for sequences of sixteen numbers and other data typical of credit cards. Split the card number field into four or more fields and split the expiration date into month and year fields. (Don't name them `card_mo` and `card_yr`.)
- If possible, have the sensitive information sent in a separate form. The card data cannot be used without the cardholder's name. Using separate forms will make it almost impossible for a sniffer to get all the information needed to misuse the account.
- Whenever possible, use a secured server for transactions.

A fast computer would take a year of continuous running to break the encryption for a single transaction.

**NOTE:** Using a secured server eliminates the need for the first three items in this list.

## Secured Server

Information on Netscape servers can be found at `http://home.netscape.com/comprod/server_central/`.

Several Web servers offer secured transactions by encrypting transmissions. The Netscape Commerce and Enterprise, the latest Microsoft IIS, and the Apache SSL are popular servers that provide security. The more popular browsers, such as those offered by Netscape and Microsoft, handle secure transactions.

**NOTE:** Both the server and browser must be able to handle secure transactions.

A secured server uses a special protocol called `https` instead of the more familiar `http`. Almost always, a machine having a secure server will have an unsecured server running simultaneously. The secured server uses a different port, so both servers can coexist on the same machine. Normal traffic uses the unsecured server, and any sensitive traffic is directed to the secure server.

For example, a "shopping cart" system that uses a link for the customer to proceed to the checkout can have the link be directed to a secured server. Therefore, if the system has the following link:

```
[<a href="http:/yourstore.com/checkout.cgi">Check out</a>]
```

it can be changed to this:

```
[<a href="http:/yourstore.com/checkout.cgi">Unsecured Check out</a>]
[<a href="https:/yourstore.com/checkout.cgi">Secured Check out</a>]
```

Information on the Microsoft IIS server can be found at `http://www.microsoft.com/infoserv/`.

Information on the Apache-SSL server can be found at `http://apachessl.c2.net/`.

**NOTE:** Not all browsers support secured transactions, which is why you also need to provide an unsecured link.

While the store uses the unsecured pages for customers to browse and shop, it switches to the secured server to transmit sensitive information.

- For normal, "unsensitive" material, use the unsecured server (for example, `http://`*`yourstore`*`.com/`*`cat_page1`*`.html`).
- For forms in which the customer can submit sensitive material, such as a credit card number, use the secured server (for example, `http://`*`yourstore`*`.com/`*`order`*`.html`).

The SSL protocol involves encrypting all data transmission between the server and the client (browser).

**TIP:** Use the secured server only for sensitive information; encryption and decoding data puts a higher load on the server's CPU.

**NOTE:** The Netscape browser places a thin blue line at the top of the browser window and shows a small, unbroken key at the bottom-left corner when in the secure mode (see Figure 15.2). The small key is shown broken for the unsecured mode. In the secure mode, the unbroken key has one tooth for medium security (commonly used) or two teeth for high security (this will become more commonly used in the future).

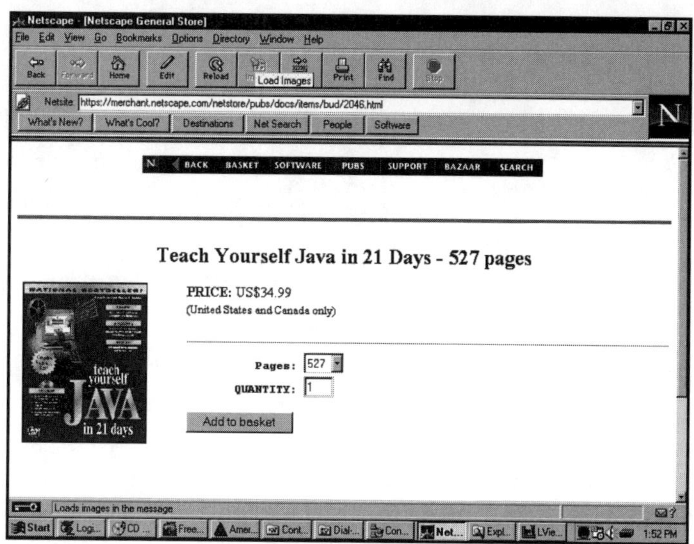


**Figure 15.2.**
*The Netscape Navigator browser in the secured mode. (Notice the unbroken key at the bottom-left corner of the screen).*

For customers who do not have a browser capable of handling secured transactions, provide a form through the unsecured server (for example, `http://`*`yourstore`*`.com/`*`order1`*`.html`).

**CAUTION:** You as the merchant can be liable of fraudulent credit card use for not providing adequate transaction security.

**NOTE:** Give the unsecured customers a different form that either does not enable them to enter sensitive data or at least jumbles the sensitive data.

## Preparing for Third-Party Transactions

`http://www.mrkmrk.com/ces.html` provides information on third-party transactions.

A third-party server can enable you to handle secure transactions, plus give you other benefits. Besides the obviously secured transaction, the third-party server can handle the credit card validation and processing for you and deposit the funds in your bank account. Of course, the third party will deduct transaction fees, which might or might not be a significant cost to you.

Here are the steps for the setup and use of a third-party server:

1. Set up your site on your own server.
2. Direct the links for the order form to the third-party server.
3. The customer submits his or her order information to the third-party server.
4. The third-party server processes the order and verifies the credit card information.
5. The third-party server lets the customer know if his or her order has been accepted or denied.
6. Often, the third-party server sends you and the customer an e-mail notice of the order.

The third party's server can actually provide real-time verification and processing of credit card transactions.

An obvious advantage of this system is that you do not have to handle the credit card information; in fact, you would not even need to see any of it. A disadvantage is the cost. There is normally a setup charge and a transaction fee (in addition to the fees from the credit card companies).

`http://www.versanet.com/ats/secure.htm` also provides information on third-party transactions.

## Jumbling the Data

Data sniffers check for sequences of numbers and words common to credit cards and bank account information. If you need to accept card or bank account information and cannot use a secure transaction, then jumble, hide, and scramble the data the best you can.

**CAUTION:** Jumbling or hiding the data does not secure the data. It only makes it difficult for another party to detect and extract the data.

Separating the card number field into sixteen fields for each digit and interspersing these fields with dummy data helps hide the actual data. Here's an example:

```
<INPUT TYPE="HIDDEN" NAME="a" VALUE="8">
<INPUT TYPE="HIDDEN" NAME="b" VALUE="4">
<INPUT NAME="c" SIZE=2>
<INPUT TYPE="HIDDEN" NAME="d" VALUE="3">
<INPUT NAME="e" SIZE=2>
<INPUT NAME="f" SIZE=2>
<INPUT TYPE="HIDDEN" NAME="g" VALUE=" ">
<INPUT TYPE="HIDDEN" NAME="h" VALUE="3">
<INPUT NAME="i" SIZE=2>
<INPUT TYPE="HIDDEN" NAME="j" VALUE="7">
...
```

The expiration date can be similarly handled:

```
<INPUT TYPE="RADIO" NAME="ak" VALUE="Frank">January
<INPUT TYPE="RADIO" NAME="ak" VALUE="Books">February
<INPUT TYPE="RADIO" NAME="ak" VALUE="10">March
<INPUT TYPE="RADIO" NAME="ak" VALUE="dog">April
....
<INPUT TYPE="HIDDEN" NAME="al" VALUE="blue">
<INPUT TYPE="HIDDEN" NAME="am" VALUE="127">
<SELECT NAME="an">
<OPTION VALUE="home">1996
<OPTION VALUE="apartment">1997
<OPTION VALUE="radio">1998
<OPTION VALUE="Ford">1999
<OPTION VALUE="baseball">2000
</SELECT>
<INPUT TYPE="HIDDEN" NAME="ao" VALUE="book">
<INPUT TYPE="HIDDEN" NAME="ap" VALUE="526">
...
```

**NOTE:** You'll obviously need to remember which fields contain the actual data and what any code words mean; otherwise, you, too, will have a difficult time extracting the information.

# Taking Digital Cash

Digicash's site is at `http://www.digicash.com/`.

Digital cash is basically encoded digital tokens that the consumer can withdraw from a participating bank. The consumer then can send the tokens over the Internet to pay for goods and services. Tokens contain digitized information about the issuing bank, the denomination of the token, and other codes for processing and security. Digicash's ecash system was one of the first such digital cash (token) systems made publicly available.

## Ecash

Other digital cash schemes and companies can be seen at `http://www.fv.com/` and `http://www.cybercash.com/`.

Ecash is a form of electronic money, or digital cash. Consumers establish an account with a financial institution (bank) that issues ecash tokens, withdraws the tokens from the bank, and stores the tokens on their computer. Whenever the consumers want to make a purchase from a merchant accepting ecash, they simply send the appropriate amount of tokens to the merchant. It's pretty similar to walking into a store, buying an item, and taking money from your wallet to pay the cashier.

## Ecash on Your Server

You can accept ecash without actually setting ecash up on your server. Customers can send payment to your account.

Ecash is available for several UNIX, Windows, and Mac servers. The basic procedure for setting up ecash on your server follows (various servers require some change to the basic procedure).

**NOTE:** This basic procedure only allows for selling access to files stored in the `ecash` directory on your server. In the following sections, I discuss ways to collect payment for other goods and services.

A list of ecash issuers can be found at `http://digicash.com/ecash/ecash-issuers.html`.

`http://www.commerce.net/jump/techno/digicash.html` is list of various digital cash providers, including digicash.

1. Register with an ecash issuer. Open a merchant account with that bank and obtain an account ID and password.
2. Download the ecash software for your server.
3. Make a directory for `ecash`.
4. Install the ecash software.
5. In the ecash directory, make a subdirectory `shop` that is accessible by the Web server.
6. Create subdirectories called `data` and `cgi` in the `shop` subdirectory.
7. Create a price list called `price_conf`. This file is a price list used by ecash to sell access to the files in the data directory and executable scripts in the `cgi` directory.
8. Create a `failed.htm` file in the `shop` subdirectory. If the ecash program is unable to collect payment, the `failed.htm` file will be served to the customer. The `failed.htm` file should direct the customer to retry by reloading the file, as well as provide an alternative means of payment.
9. Create links from the Web pages on which your customers will be placing orders. The links will be similar to the following:

```
Unix <A HREF="/cgi-bin/nph-charge.cgi?buy_file.htm">
Windows <A HREF="/cgi-bin/charge.exe?buy_file.htm">
```

## Ecash for Payment

`http://marktwain.com/` is a bank's site where you can establish an ecash account.

The previous section shows you how to set up an ecash account and how to sell files and information online. However, if you are selling goods and services that cannot be sent over the Internet, your consumers will need to send you their payments. The simplest method is to have on the order form a payment option for ecash and to include instructions for customers to send payment to your ecash account.

```
<STRONG>Payment Options</STRONG>
<INPUT TYPE=RADIO NAME=OPT VALUE=01>Charge My Visa<BR>
<INPUT TYPE=RADIO NAME=OPT VALUE=02>Charge My MasterCard<BR>
<INPUT TYPE=RADIO NAME=OPT VALUE=01>I am sending ecash per
➥<A HREF="ec_info.html">instructions</A><BR>
<INPUT TYPE=RADIO NAME=OPT VALUE=01>I am mailing a check<BR>
<INPUT TYPE=RADIO NAME=OPT VALUE=01>I'll call 1-800-555-2222<BR>
```

The file `ec_info.html`, referenced in the preceding code, is a Web page you create to instruct the customer to

- ❑ Continue with processing the order.
- ❑ Send payment to your ecash account.
- ❑ Enter the invoice number or other means of identification in the ecash transaction description (part of the ecash display).

You'll receive a payment receipt notification from your ecash bank (the financial institution with whom you established your ecash account) that shows the amount and description the customer entered. With this and the order information sent by the customer, you can process the customer's request.

**NOTE:** To receive payment sent in by the customer, you do not need to have ecash installed on your server. However, you still need to establish an ecash account and have the ecash account software install on any computer you use.

**TIP:** Include a link to the bank in which you have your digital cash account. Customers then can establish their own accounts and return to your site later to make digital cash purchases.

## Remote Ecash System

If you cannot set up ecash on your server and want to sell files and other information online, Digicash has the Ecash Remote Shop Server.

`http://www.eunet.fi/` is a European bank's site where you can establish an ecash account.

To set up your site to use the ecash remote shop server, follow these steps:

1. Register with an ecash issuer. Open a merchant account with that bank and obtain an account ID and password.
2. Make a directory accessible to your Web server, but restrict access to requests only from host `digicash.com`.

3. Create a `price_conf` file with
   - ❑ The first line containing your ecash account ID.
   - ❑ The next line containing the e-mail address to which Digicash should send transaction notification (make a blank line if you don't want notification).
   - ❑ The price list, formatted as *filename*[tab]*price*[tab]*description*[return].
4. Make a `failed.htm` file the same as you did in the section on setting up ecash on your server.

**NOTE:** Be sure to use absolute URLs for links, image files, and other addresses, because the files will be served from Digicash's server, not yours.

5. Set up your order links like this:

```
<A HREF="http://www.digicash.com/cgi-bin/shopgate2?
➥http://yourcompany.com/dir/file.htm">
buy this file</A>
```

**NOTE:** As with setting up ecash on your own server, the Ecash Remote Shopcash Server can sell only files and information that can be sent through the World Wide Web. For other goods and services, the customer has to send payment to your account.

TASK

# Providing Both Online and Offline Ordering

See Chapter 8, "Gathering Information: Web-Based Surveys and Questionnaires," for information on forms.

To offer the customer the best possible selection of payment and ordering options, you need to offer both online and offline methods. For online methods, you need to be able to process the form data.

## Online Ordering

Online ordering is perhaps the easiest, most efficient way for you and the consumer to transact business. To use online ordering, you need to provide the means for the customer to send order and payment information and for your server to process the information. The first part is easy—an HTML form is used for consumer input. The second part, processing the information, can be somewhat difficult.

Browsers send form data in a continuous stream of `name=value` pairs with spaces converted to plus symbols and most other non-alphanumeric characters converted to hexadecimal code (URL encoded). If the form data is stored directly to a file or sent to you via e-mail, you can read the data, but it won't be easy.

Information on form processing and URL encoding can be found at `http://hoohoo.ncsa.uiuc.edu/cgi/forms.html`.

For example, if a form had the field names and customer-entered values as in Table 15.1, you would get this:

```
name=James+Jones&address=1+First+Street+%232&city=sometown
```

**Table 15.1. Sample form name value pairs.**

| *Field Name* | *Entered Value* |
|---|---|
| `Name` | James Jones |
| `Address` | 1 First Street Apt #2 |
| `City` | Sometown |

Imagine trying to read a complete order form with product descriptions, quantities, prices, payment information, and so on, in it. Fortunately, there is software available, both free and commercial, that will process the form data for you.

## Matt's Formmail

Even if you do not have a Perl interpreter on your own computer, you can still set and install Perl scripts on your server.

Several of Matt's quite useful scripts are available at `http://www.worldwidemart.com/scripts/` and are included on this book's CD-ROM.

Formmail is a CGI script in Perl that is freely available online at Matt's Script Archive (`www.worldwidemart.com/scripts/`) and on this book's accompanying CD-ROM. Formmail is fairly easy to set up and use. Form results are sent to you via e-mail.

**NOTE:** The Perl interpreter (simply called perl) is available on most WWW servers. Perl is one of the most, if not the most, widely used languages for creating CGI scripts.

**NOTE:** Always leave an author's copyright notice in any script, even if you modify the script. Besides the possible legal ramifications, it is only right to give credit to the author, especially when he or she does not charge for the time and effort spent creating the script.

Here's how to set up formmail:

1. Three lines in the script `'formmail.pl'` need to be set up for your use:
   - The very first line, `#!/usr/bin/perl`, must be the path to the perl file on your server. Please check with your system administrator if you are not sure.
   - The variable `$mailprog = '/usr/lib/sendmail';` is the path to the sendmail program. Again, please check with your system administrator if you are not sure.
   - The array `@referers = ('www.worldwide.com','worldwidemart.com', '206.31.72.203');` contains the servers that can use this script. Without this array, anyone in the world could use your server to process his or her forms. The array should contain the domain names and/or the IP addresses of the servers from which the script should accept form data.

     Each entry in the `@referers` array is a text string and must be enclosed in quotes. Also, the entries are separate elements of the array and must be separated by commas.
2. Having made the necessary changes to the script, you simply upload it to your server and it is ready to go.

Only one copy of formmail needs to be installed on a server for all of the machine accounts to use it.

**NOTE:** The script needs to be in a directory that allows CGI scripts, and, depending on server configuration, might need to be renamed `formmail.cgi`. Your system administrator should be able to provide any needed assistance and information for installing a CGI script on your particular server, or might even offer to install it for you and the other users.

Information on Perl and the code for various platforms can be found at `http://www.perl.com/perl/`.

3. Any form to be processed by formmail must have a `recipient` field. Simply add `<INPUT TYPE="HIDDEN" NAME="recipient" value="you@yoursite.com">` to the form. This field is the e-mail address to which the processed data is sent.
4. Add the fields for the order form. Formmail processes all the fields and then e-mails the data to you in an easy-to-read format.
5. The action attribute for the form needs to be the formmail script (for example, `<FORM METHOD="POST" ACTION="/cgi-bin/formmail.pl">`).

**TIP:** You can customize the appearance of the response page sent to the customers through special form fields. Check the readme file associated with formmail.

## FrontPage

See Chapter 1, "Selecting and Using Tools for Page Creation," for information on FrontPage.

If your server supports Microsoft's FrontPage extensions, you can use the Save Results bot in FrontPage. The Save Results bot writes the form data in a file you specify and in the format you select.

Simply select the Save Results bot from the form handler field of the Form Properties box. Then, click the Settings button to specify the options you want to use.

**TIP:** If you are going to import the results into a database or spreadsheet, use one of the text database formats. If you are going to import the results into a word processor, choose the formatted text.

## Shopping Cart and Ordering Systems

Somewhat more sophisticated systems can add tally sales, include shipping costs, and charge tax. OopShop, described in Chapter 14, "Web Shopping Carts," is one shopping cart system that tallies and adds shipping charges and taxes.

When customers select a link to place an order, they are shown a form in which they can indicated the state in which they live and the preferred method of shipping, as shown in Figure 15.3. These fields are used to determine the appropriate charges for sales tax and shipping.

**NOTE:** You might have to verify customer input to ensure that appropriate tax location is specified.

When a customer submits an order, the processing script tallies the subtotal, determines shipping and tax charges, and then calculates the grand total. The customer is sent a confirmation notice showing the items ordered, the shipping information, and the costs. (See Figure 15.4.)

Netscape - [XYZ Inc. - Order Form]

Go to: http://www.xyz_co.com/order.html

Address:

City: State/Province:

Country: Zip/Postal code:

Billing Phone:

Email Address:

Credit cards: AMERICAN EXPRESS

State Tax: florida

Shipping method: Ups

Snail
Ups
Fedex

**Figure 15.3.**
*An OopShop shopping cart order form showing State Tax and Shipping Method selection boxes.*

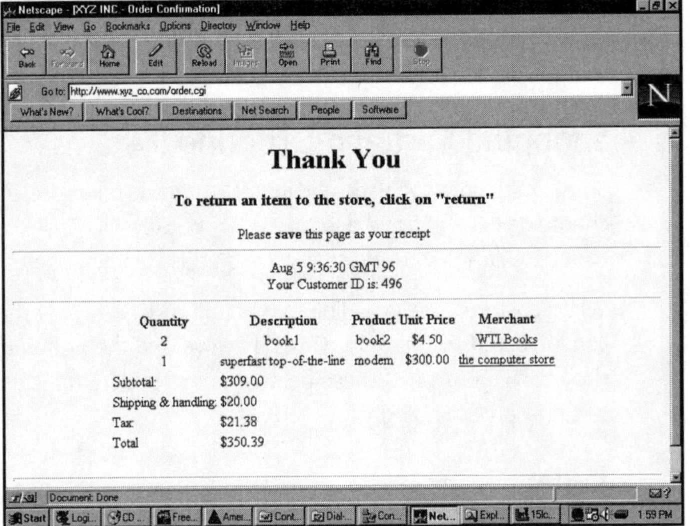

Netscape - [XYZ INC - Order Confirmation]

Go to: http://www.xyz_co.com/order.cgi

**Thank You**

**To return an item to the store, click on "return"**

Please **save** this page as your receipt

Aug 5 9:36:30 GMT 96
Your Customer ID is: 496

| Quantity | Description | Product | Unit Price | Merchant |
|---|---|---|---|---|
| 2 | book1 | book2 | $4.50 | WTI Books |
| 1 | superfast top-of-the-line | modem | $300.00 | the computer store |

| | |
|---|---|
| Subtotal: | $309.00 |
| Shipping & handling: | $20.00 |
| Tax | $21.38 |
| Total | $350.39 |

**Figure 15.4.**
*A customer's order confirmation notice.*

**NOTE:** Notice that the customer is assigned a unique number, which can be helpful in tracking the order.

The setup of the shopping cart system is discussed in Chapter 14. However, to have the system handle the order processing, you'll need to do the following:

1. Edit the file `state_tax.db` for the locations where you must collect sales tax:
    - ❑ Each line in the file is a name value pair of the location and the tax rate.
    - ❑ The tax rate is a decimal number, not a percent. Therefore, for a six percent tax, you need to enter a value of 0.06.
    - ❑ Enter each location and its tax rate on a new line.
    - ❑ Use the format `location=tax rate`.
    - ❑ The location you enter must be exactly the same as the location used in the form field `state_tax` of the `checkout.htm` file.
    - ❑ For example, if you need to collect a 6.5% tax for Florida and a 10% tax for California, you would enter the following:

      ```
      florida=0.065
      california=0.1
      ```
    - ❑ Delete any sample entries that might be in the file.
2. Edit the file `ship_fee.db` for the shipping methods for which you have to charge.
    - ❑ Each line in the file is a name value pair of the shipping method and the shipping charge.
    - ❑ Shipping fees can be a percent of the total cost, or they can be a flat fee.
    - ❑ Enter each shipping method and its tax charge on a new line.
    - ❑ Use the format *`method=charge`*.
    - ❑ The method you enter must be exactly the same as the method used in the form field `ship_fee` of the `checkout.htm` file.
    - ❑ To specify a percent of the total, put a percent sign (%) after the value. Otherwise, the value is treated as a flat fee for the particular shipping method.
    - ❑ For example, if you were to charge 10% of the total cost for shipping normal delivery, and a flat $30 for Next Day Air, you would enter

      ```
      normal=10%
      nextday=30
      ```

      where `normal` and `nextday` exactly match the options available in the field `ship_fee` of the file `checkout.htm`.
    - ❑ Delete any sample entries that might be in the file.

3. Edit the file `checkout.htm` per the following. (The Oopshop order script will process the fields you enter).
   - ❑ Have the `action` attribute of the form tag point to the URL of the checkout script.
   - ❑ Delete any fields that you do not want.
   - ❑ Add any fields you need.
   - ❑ Change the options in the State Tax select menu (drop-down menu) to the locations you specified in the `state_tax.db` file.
   - ❑ Change the options in the Shipping Method select menu (drop-down menu) to the methods you specified in the `state_tax.db` file.

**TIP:** Use the `value` attribute of the `option` tags in both the State Tax and Shipping Method select menus (drop-down menus) so you use labels different from the values (for example, `<OPTION VALUE="florida">Florida`).

4. Make sure that the "order" file can be written to by the Web server.

Now your shopping cart system is ready to start taking orders. Results are written to the order file, which records all the field values from the form.

## Other Online Ordering Services

Polyforms and Webforms are two popular form-processing (and form-generating) packages. See `http://polform.ora.com/` and `http://ww.q-d.com/wf.htm`.

Many service providers offer other form-processing software in addition to, or in lieu of, the FrontPage extensions. These can be scripts such as Matt's formmail script (discussed previously) or programs such as Polyforms and Webforms. The specifics of the software and how to use it is information your system administrator will be able to supply (if these programs are available on your server). Also, the software's developer or marketer will usually have a Web site from which you can obtain additional information.

**NOTE:** More sophisticated form routines that tie into the server's back-end programs and databases can be obtained and installed by the system administrator or a consultant. However, they do require a level of system and programming knowledge that might be beyond the expertise of many Webmasters or site administrators.

A listing of online shopping malls can be found at `http://yahoo.com/Business_and_Economy/Companies/Shopping_Centers/Online_Malls/`.

There are several shopping mall sites on the Web. By signing up with one of these sites, you'll likely be able to use their order processing facilities. Here are some of the benefits to using the shopping mall sites:

- Order processing.
- Payment processing.
- Many malls attract high traffic.

However, there is a downside:

- You might be limited to using only the payment options offered by the mall.
- Your site will likely have to be on the mall's server.
- The cost of being part of the mall can be high.

## Offline Ordering

Although customers can browse your site and possibly determine items they want to purchase, they might decide to order offline. The reasons for offline ordering are many. Here are a few:

- The customer can't use your online payment options (for example, the customer might not have a credit card).
- The customer might want to get input from a spouse or friend.
- The customer might have a personal preference for not using online transactions (the user might be concerned about sending personal and financial information over the Internet).
- The customer might need to look at a color scheme or check dimensions at home.
- The customer might need for the business transaction to go through a certain purchasing process.

Whatever the reasons, offering customers a way to place offline orders will only help ensure that you do not lose these sales.

### Order Form Download

Several sites offer pages of their goods and services for online browsing by the consumers. Customers are offered an option to download an order form that can be filled out and sent in by the customer via the postal service (snail mail), fax, or e-mail.

Although a form as an image can be attractive, it takes longer to download, and the consumer cannot easily load it into a word processor or text editor. Provide a text file, if possible.

If you need to send a form with a special layout, try providing it in several popular formats (MS Word, Postscript, and so on) as well as plain text. An HTML page could be used, but the customer will still need to print it out to complete it, and the layout of the form will probably be different on different browsers and computers.

**NOTE:** HTML forms cannot be printed from many browsers because the form fields will be omitted. To provide a printable HTML order form, you'll have to avoid using form elements (tags).

Be sure to place your mailing address, fax number, or e-mail address on the form. Also, include your Web address so the customer can refer back to your site.

**TIP:** If you are able to provide a compressed file of your site or product description pages, then be sure to provide several versions in the popular formats (pkzip, gzip, and so on). This way, customers can easily refer to your pages offline at their leisure. Be sure to use relative URLs in links and images.

## Phone Orders

Ordering by telephone makes good sense to many customers. Here are some reasons why:

- They are used to placing orders over the phone.
- They desire more information before ordering.
- Any of the reasons previously listed for ordering offline.
- Any number of reasons for not ordering immediately.
- You might not offer online ordering.

If customers are interested in your product, they will give you a call even if they have to pay for the call. However, providing an 800 or 888 toll-free number will help encourage your customers to call.

**TIP:** Besides being a means for placing an order, the phone number might get the customer to call for more information. Then, you or your sales force can assist the customer with any questions, and possibly gain an additional sale that you might not have made otherwise.

To provide for telephone orders,

1. Obtain a toll-free phone number.
2. List your toll-free number as well as your local number on your site (preferably at the bottom of every page).
3. If your office is not available 24 hours a day, have an answering machine or voice mail system inviting customers to do the following:
   - Leave an order.
   - Call back during your business hours. (Be sure to have the message give your business hours and the time zone.)
   - Leave a name and number so that you can call them back.

# Workshop Wrap-Up

In this chapter, you learned the following:

- How to offer customers various payment options. Providing a variety of online and offline payment schemes on the order, when practical, makes the transaction more attractive to the customer.
- Securing transactions to protect you and your customers. Many people are still leery of sending financial information online. Providing a secure means will help ease customer security concerns.
- Digital cash offers a secure, user-friendly way to directly transfer funds electronically.
- The various ways in which you can set up order taking. Several methods can be provided to let customers select the option they prefer the most.

## Next Steps

Now, you'll probably want to check related topics in these chapters:

- Chapter 16, "Providing Content for a Price on the Web"
- Chapter 18, "Order and Shipment Tracking on the Web"
- Chapter 19, Real-Life Examples: Doing Business on the Web"
- Section V, "Putting It All Together"

## Q&A

**Q: Should all payment options be given to customers?**

**A:** Only when practical. More than likely, a business cannot afford to provide all the payment options offered to customers. Merchant accounts for credit cards, check cashing, digital money, third-party transactions, and so on all require setup costs and monthly or yearly fees.

Even though it might be desirable to offer every possible payment scheme, you should choose the ones that will be cost effective for you, fit the needs of your sites, and still provide customers with a good set of options.

**Q: Running a site entirely on a secured server seems like a good idea. Why isn't this done?**

**A:** A secured site uses a special protocol—`https`—and encrypts data transmissions. Here are three reasons you should use the secured server for sensitive transactions only:

- Not all browsers support secure transmissions. They cannot use the special protocol `https` nor encrypt and decipher the transmission. Thus, a site will be effectively locking out customers with these browsers.
- The encryption and deciphering processes put a load on the server. Having the site entirely on the secured server will unnecessarily create a high server load.
- WWW search engines, such as Lycos and Altavista, will not be able to index the site. Thus, potential customers might not be able to locate your site.

**Q: Because digital cash is not yet widely used, why should a site be set up to receive it?**

**A:** Although at this time there might not be many people using digital cash, its use will become more widespread and common. By setting up the site to except this form of payment, you not only attract customers that currently have it, but encourage others to use this easy payment method (easy for both you and the customer). Offering this option with a link to the bank with which you have your account gives your customers the chance to set up their own accounts and return later to your site to make a digital cash purchase.

**Q: Can a site be strictly set up to use offline ordering?**

**A:** At times, offline ordering might be the only practical method for a site to accept orders. However, more and more customers are becoming accustomed to being online and appreciate the ease and quickness of online service. All sites that sell products and services should offer both online and offline ordering methods.

CHAPTER

SIXTEEN

# Providing Content for a Price on the Web

## In this chapter, you

- ❑ Learn how to develop subscription services
- ❑ Identify potential online money makers
- ❑ Customize a password authorization form
- ❑ Use ecash for pay-per-use services

## Tasks in this chapter:

- ❑ Identifying Premium Content
- ❑ Setting Up Registration Forms
- ❑ Gathering Payment Information for a Free Trial

Now that you've seen all the different options for getting users to send you payment over the Web, you should look at some different ways for getting them to want to do just that. Of course, you've already seen in Chapter 5, "Employee Directories and Biographies," and Chapter 13, "Advanced Catalogs," how to present your products and services in an online catalog. But now you can start thinking about ways to provide information for a price.

If you're considering starting up a new Web-based information service or simply want to augment your current business by offering customers access to specialized help or data, this chapter will help you see the ways to start turning your ideas (and your data) into a stream of income.

The keys to developing a successful Web site that charges users for content is a tricky undertaking that takes much more in the way of business planning than HTML coding. As a Web page developer, you probably realize by now how hard it is to get people to visit your pages when CNN, Time-Warner, ESPN, and Disney are spending millions of dollars to create online playgrounds. Of course, this will get even harder when you try to charge for access to information when so much information, news, and data is available for free on the Web.

The Web's popularity originally was in large part due to the unlimited "free" access to information, which contrasted with online service charging an hourly fee.

However, information is sold on the Web every day. As long as you go into it by correctly identifying what type of information to charge for and knowing how to market this information and draw users to it, you should be successful in establishing a premium content Web page. You'll also need to figure out the HTML mechanics for providing restricted access to your information.

**NOTE:** You can begin to charge for content on the Web only once you've established for users your ability to provide information in a useful and understandable manner. Not even the Wall Street Journal started out by charging users to access its online newspaper. Initially, it set up a comprehensive Web site and provided users unlimited free access. Then, and only then, could it prove that users could justify paying a premium for the content.

TASK

## Identifying Premium Content

Perhaps the key step in being able to provide content for a price on the Web is correctly identifying the content for which people will be willing to pay on your pages. You'll need to be extremely careful in making this decision. For example, if you make the shift to charging for virtually all the content on your pages, users might find this approach too aggressive (even the Wall Street Journal provides substantial free areas, as shown in Figure 16.1). If you charge for content and don't provide enough value or information in return, users will be disappointed and probably will not give you a second chance.

**TIP:** The most important word to keep in mind when developing a plan for what content to charge for is *niche*. You need to find a market niche in which you can provide content and information to a discrete group of users who will willingly pay for such a service. You shouldn't be thinking about this in terms of a broad market, because premium content on the Web is still not a universally accepted business model for most users.

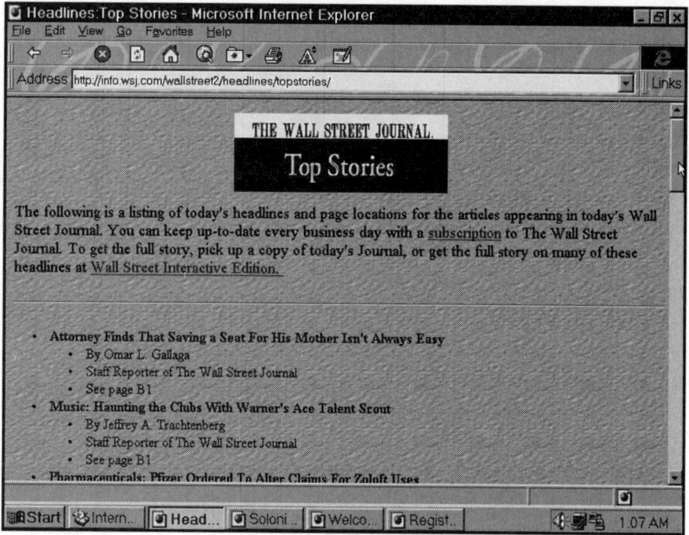


**Figure 16.1.**
*Free areas, such as the one from the Wall Street Journal, enable users to evaluate what you are offering.*

Let's face it; every person or business has a different idea about what kind of content they want to place on a Web page to start charging users to access. However, anyone with a little experience on the Web (or in business) can quickly identify the things people won't pay for. Here are a few rules of thumb for content that might not be best suited for premium Web pages:

- If it's available for free from somewhere else online, they're not going to pay you for it. (For example, sports scores and news headlines.)
- If it should be free, they're not going to pay for it. (For example, FAQs about your products.)
- If you provide it for free offline, they're not going to pay for it online. (For example, customer product sheets and updates.)
- If you wouldn't pay for it, don't expect others to, either.

Of course, there are exceptions to every rule, but you shouldn't start your planning with the intent of being the exception where others have failed.

You should also be aware that there are certain somewhat established categories that have demonstrated they warrant a premium from users. Working with this list will probably be more helpful in trying to determine what information or data you can generate independent revenue from on your Web pages. Among the proven prospects are the following:

- *Specialized online newsletters.* These newsletters provide news coverage of a distinct market from a unique perspective. A good example is Morph's Daily Spectrum at `http://www.morph.com`, a daily technology briefing for information executives. (See Figure 16.2.)

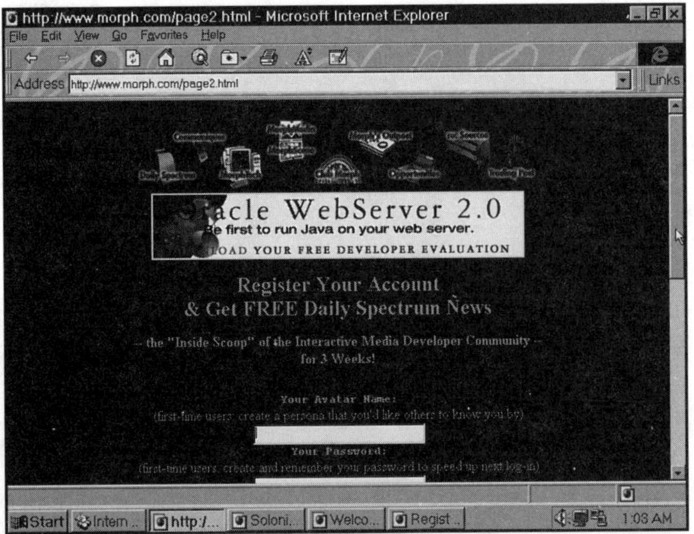


**Figure 16.2.**
*Morph's Daily Spectrum is a model of the type of online subscription service that works.*

- *Individualized and customized customer support or assistance.* Some examples are Web-based interactive chats and specialized workshops that provide advanced customer support.
- *Enhanced entertainment content.* Using advanced multimedia for online gaming, and interactive news and information.
- *Advanced specialized interactive applications.* An example is a Web-based financial analysis tool created using Java or ActiveX.
- *Online multimedia libraries/stores.* An example is digital stock photography.

**NOTE:** As you can see, every potential area for selling content online might not mesh with your business plan. Some of these items are aimed at developers looking to create entirely new Web-based content business, while others are more appropriate for traditional businesses that want to exploit the potential of the Web.

## Setting Up Registration Forms

The road to charging for content on the Web can be a long and winding one. I've already shown you how to identify and give away the content for which you want to eventually charge. I'm sure at this point you want to start taking credit card numbers and generating revenue. However, you'll still need to go through a transitional phase before going full-speed ahead on premium content.

**TIP:** Even if you never plan on charging for content on your Web pages, you might eventually decide to require users to register or acquire a user name and password to access some areas of your Web site. The information you glean from these registrations can be a very valuable asset to you and your company.

**NOTE:** Registrations are a common and widespread technique used on the Web. Users normally will not be turned away by having to fill out a basic (or even an extensive) registration form in order to get access to your content. You should use the registration phase as a test for determining whether or not your premium content pages will ultimately be successful. If you find that only one out of every five users is willing to go to the trouble of filling out a simple form, you might want to think long and hard about whether they'll go to the additional trouble, pain, and expense of actually paying to access those pages. If not, you might need to refocus your pages or business model, and perhaps rely more on advertising support. This is explained in Chapter 17, "Setting Up Advertising-Supported Web Sites."

## The Registration Form

In Chapter 8, "Gathering Information: Web-Based Surveys and Questionnaires," you create a form for gathering basic customer information on your Web pages. The registration form that you should implement as a precursor to charging for content should be much more detailed and involved so that you can minimize duplication when you actually begin charging for content, which should only require users to supplement their data by providing a suitable payment method.

Chapter 15, "Web Cash Registers: Taking and Making Money on the Net," provides an excellent point of reference for the types of registration forms you'll want to use on a Web-based subscription service.

Here is a list of some of the information you should include in a basic registration:

- Name
- Address (business and home)
- Phone and fax numbers
- E-mail address
- Business or profession
- Topical areas of interest
- Questions regarding willingness to pay
- User name (selected by user)
- Password (selected by user)

**TIP:** The direct approach is best when you are determining if and what users will pay for the premium content you intend to make available on your Web pages. The registration form is an appropriate place to quickly explore these issues with your potential customers and determine whether or not you should charge for certain content as well as the price you should apply.

In Chapter 8 you use the `mailto:` form action and several utilities to create the necessary online form. In Chapter 15 you work with Formmail to create online forms. You could also use either of these methods for registrations, but you'll probably be better off using a set of CGI scripts specifically designed for registration and authentication, such as Authentication 5.0, which is available on the accompanying CD-ROM as well as from `http://www2.eff.org/~erict/Scripts/`. (See Figure 16.3.)

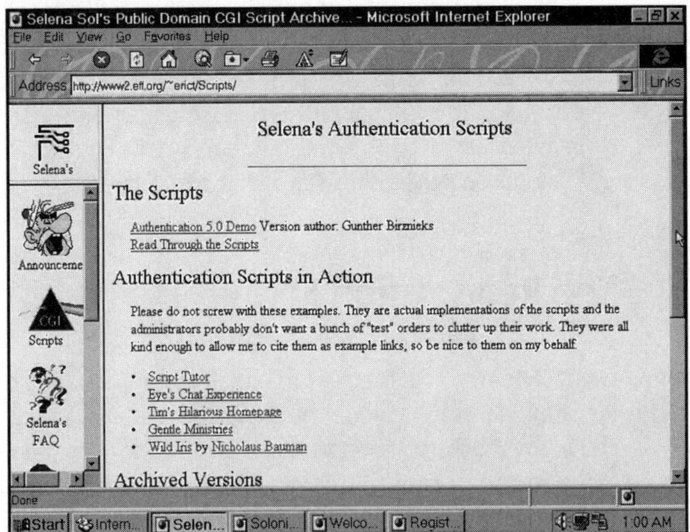


**Figure 16.3.**
*Authentication 5.0 is available, along with many other CGI scripts, from Selena Sol's Web site.*

## Preparing the Authentication Script

You'll need to edit the `html-auth.setup` file that accompanies the Authentication 5.0 scripts to specify the additional fields you would like to include in your registration setup. The file contains these additional field settings by default (user name and password selection are always included):

```
@auth_extra_fields = ("auth_first_name",
                      "auth_last_name",
                      "auth_email");

@auth_extra_desc = ("First Name",
                    "Last Name",
                    "Email");
```

The name given for `"auth_extra_fields"` is the same name you must specify when you enter the `<FORM>` tag in the HTML code for the registration page. Again, refer to Chapters 8 and 15 for more information about form design specifics. Also refer to Appendix B, "HTML 3.2 Reference."

**NOTE:** Authentication 5.0 is written in Perl. You must have a Perl interpreter installed on your Web server in order for it to operate correctly. Don't worry, most Web servers include this capability; however, you should check with your system administrator to be certain. Often, you might need to save the script in a particular directory with a file extension `*.cgi`.

For example, say you wanted to take the base Authentication script and form and add the type of additional fields we've talked about. The basic script comes with fields for user name and password in addition to the fields for first name, last name, and e-mail. Here are the fields you'll want to add for your registration form for this simplified example:

- Address
- City
- State
- Phone
- Profession
- Willingness to pay

The first step is to go back and edit the Perl script to add the additional fields. You'll need to come up with field name descriptions for each of these options, which you'll have to remember when you design the form in the next step.

**TIP:** It's very easy to edit CGI scripts written in Perl with absolutely no programming experience. Perl scripts often include detailed comments within the source code that explain each of the script's functions and how to go about customizing them for your use. You can edit Perl scripts and save them as simple text files without using a compiler or other programming tools.

You can add the additional fields in the portion of the Perl script that we looked at previously. Here's what it should look like with your additional registration fields:

```
@auth_extra_fields = ("auth_first_name",
                         "auth_last_name",
                         "auth_email",
                      "auth_address",
                      "auth_city",
                      "auth_state",
                      "auth_phone",
                      "auth_profession",
                      "auth_pay");

@auth_extra_desc = ("First Name",
                         "Last Name",
                         "Email",
                      "Address",
                      "City",
                      "State",
                      "Phone",
                      "Profession",
                      "Willing to Pay?");
```

All added fields must begin with the `auth` designation to work properly.

Now you'll need to create a Web page and form that uses all these fields. Doing this shouldn't be too difficult as long as you remember to use the field names you just added (from `@auth_extra_fields`). However, before creating the registration area, you'll need to create an initial page that asks for a user name and password, with selections for users to register for your service. Here's a small bit of HTML code that accomplishes this (it's also displayed in Figure 16.4):

```
<FORM METHOD=POST ACTION=html-auth.cgi>
<CENTER>
<TABLE>
<TR><TH>Username</TH>
<TD><INPUT TYPE=TEXT NAME=auth_user_name></td></tr>
<tr><th>Password</th>
<td><input type=password name=auth_password></td></tr>
</TABLE><p>
<input type=submit name=auth_logon_op
value="Logon To The System"><p>
<input type=submit name=auth_register_screen_op
value="Register For An Account"><p>
<hr>
</center>
</form>
```

After you've dropped this code into your page, the script will generate the registration page on-the-fly, making form entries for each of your extra fields and filling in the descriptions you provide, as shown in Figure 16.5. The script will also automatically enter and save the appropriate user name and password information in a file called `user.dat`.

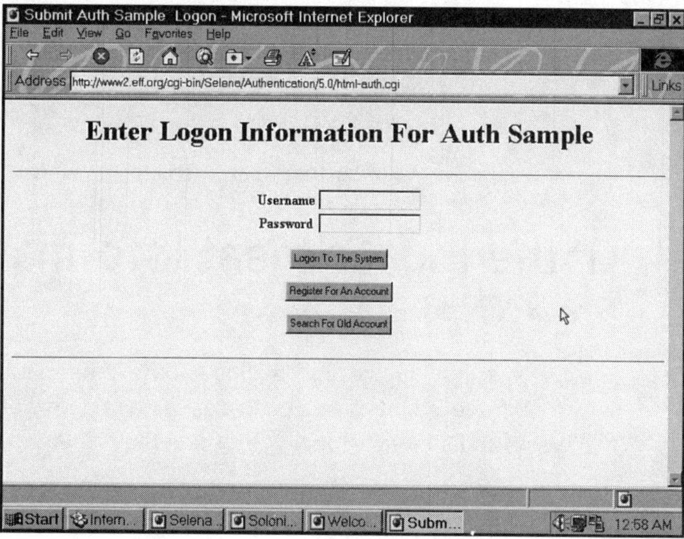


**Figure 16.4.**
*A basic Authentication login page.*

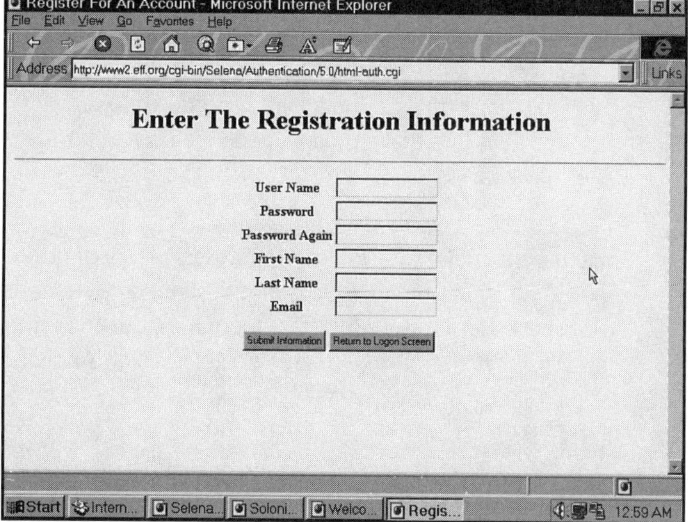


**Figure 16.5.**
*The registration page is created by the Authentication script.*

**NOTE:** A more robust form of password authentication is available using your Web server software in lieu of something like the Authentication script. A detailed explanation of how to set up several different Web servers for restricted password-protected access is included in Chapter 14 of Laura Lemay's *Teach Yourself Web Publishing with HTML in 14 Days, Professional Reference Edition*, included on the accompanying CD-ROM.

The Authentication script also allows for a wide variety of other options and settings (such as determining whether to generate a password and e-mail it to new users). If you'd like to get into more advanced uses of the script, then you should check out the site at

```
http://www.eff.org/erict/Scripts/authentication.html
```

## Gathering Payment Information for a Free Trial

The next step in the process of creating a subscription-based Web service is to begin setting up trial accounts where people are given a period of time, normally between two weeks and a month, to try out for free the content that you plan to sell.

**TIP:** How many AOL disks with offers of 15 free hours do you have sitting on your desk? Theoretically, you could use all those disks to have free access until the year 2000. However, AOL will limit your ability to sign up for a second trial account by allowing only one trial account per credit card submitted. You should be certain to implement procedures to prevent users from receiving more than one trial period. A good idea is to limit the trial to one per valid e-mail address.

You have to make sure you give your users plenty of notice when you first make the shift to a payment model. You might even want to extend the trial period for your users. For example, the Wall Street Journal announced in May its plan to start charging for its service, but gave users free access through August 31.

It often takes giving away free content to make money off content. Give a little content and get a customer in return.

**NOTE:** There is no time like the present to go back and take a quick look at Chapter 15, "Web Cash Registers: Taking and Making Money on the Net," for a refresher on the many online (and offline) payment options available for use on your Web page. If you want to offer content and services for a price online, you should employ as many means as possible for allowing people to pay, from a check in the mail to digital cash on the Web.

The following are a few steps you should go through to prepare for and accomplish the goal of moving all of your registered users to a trial account on your system:

1. Post a notice on your Web pages as far in advance as possible notifying users of your intention to start charging for some content. Give one to three months notice.

2. Contact all registered users via e-mail with a full explanation of what you plan to offer, what you plan to charge, and the trial subscription they are automatically eligible to receive.
3. Give users the information necessary to submit a credit card number (or digital cash) to be eligible for an account. Also, include offline methods (for example, a toll-free phone number) for users to give you this information.
4. Create additional incentives for early subscribers (charter members) and be sure to have a referral policy in place (and make sure users know about it).
5. Contact all registered users three to five days prior to their losing access to any of your content, whether it be when you initially start up or at the end of the trial period. Make the e-mail cautionary rather than salesman-like (for example, "After Tuesday you will be unable to access Acme's Premium Support Area. In order to maintain access to this valuable resource…").

Persistence pays, harassment doesn't. It's entirely appropriate to use a follow-up e-mail (or even two if you can identify a discrete set of users who frequent your pages), but don't be too pushy or else you might end up on a dreaded spamming blacklist. (See Chapter 20, "Marketing Your Web Pages.")

Establish new passwords for all the users of the new trial accounts. Again, refer to Chapter 14 of Laura Lemay's *Teach Yourself Web Publishing with HTML in 14 Days, Professional Reference Edition*, included on this book's CD-ROM. Be sure to remove any previously registered users who have not opted to register for the trial.

# After the Trial: Making Real Money

When the two-week or one-month trial period is up, you should send an e-mail to each user one or two days prior and let them know that their account will be charged if they continue to access your pages after a certain date. You should also give them the option of having the account turned off immediately. Hopefully, most won't opt for this.

Don't ever try to trick someone into becoming a subscriber or play the "gotcha" game. The bad word of mouth you can get as a result will outweigh the few dollars that this technique can generate.

One of the major keys to successfully selling content on the Web is to make sure you're still able to generate site traffic from the nonpaying, Web-surfing public through ad-supported areas or by having a limited amount of information in a free area. People love tasting cheese samples at the store, so consider this an online alternative to supermarket samplers.

# Pay Per View/Use/Download Services

The Web is similar to cable television in the revenue models it offers for selling content online. On cable, you have subscription premium services such as Home Box Office and The Movie Channel for which you're charged a flat monthly fee for all the programming that month. Then you have pay-per-view channels where you are charged a specific sum for watching a movie or special event just once. The same types of arrangements are prevalent on the Web. For example, ESPN's SportsZone offers unlimited access for a monthly fee while Individual's NewsPage charges you for each article you view or download.

**CAUTION:** Even in the cable industry, where the technology for ordering pay-per-view items is much more simple (and secure), subscription-based services are used by far more people (and more often) than pay-per-view products. You should expect the same experience online and reserve use of this model for truly special or value-added content or services.

There are a wide variety of ways in which you can create a pay-per-use or pay-per-view Web service. The real key to these types of pages is the payment methods. For the variety of options you can use, look at Chapter 15. The real candidates for these types of services are digital cash programs.

## A Sample Pay-Per-Use Site

A good example of a technology that is used to pay for content or services on an individual basis is ecash. Ecash is available online from the Mark Twain Bank (`http://www.marktwain.com`) and requires a program to be running (an electronic wallet) while a user visits your site in order for the transaction to be completed.

One page using ecash is the Solonian Journal at `http://www.solonian.org`. As you can see from Figure 16.6, Solonian sells some reprints of articles that the organization has published. It would be hard to imagine someone going to the trouble of providing credit card information to purchase an article for 16 cents, but ecash makes this purchase more feasible.

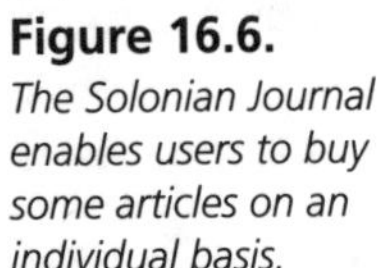

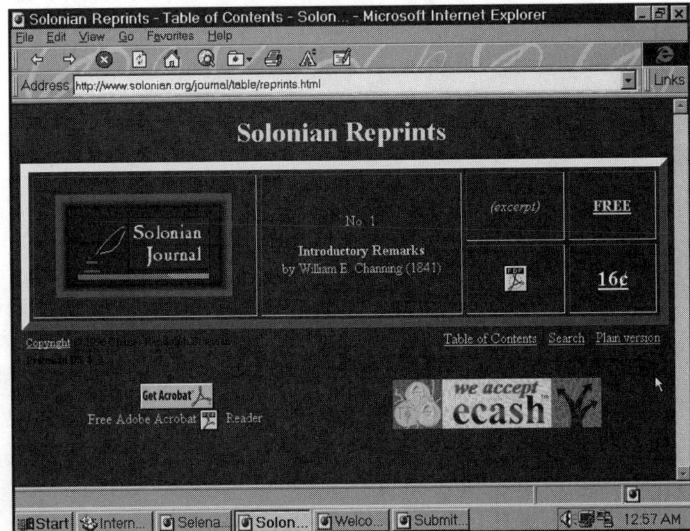


**Figure 16.6.**
*The Solonian Journal enables users to buy some articles on an individual basis.*

You can see from the figure that the purchase price of the article is a hyperlink. A quick look at the source code to that link shows you one basic way that ecash (as well as other systems) works on a Web page:

```
http://www.solonian.org/cgi-bin/nph-charge.eshop1/slrp001.pdf
```

Different ecash Web sites can use different CGI scripts in the HTML code, depending on the type of Web server software they are using.

The link simply points to a CGI script that processes the transaction by attempting to communicate with the ecash client on the user's end. If the user doesn't have ecash (or it's not running), he or she gets the message shown in Figure 16.7. Otherwise, the ecash program would have transferred 16 cents from the Web surfer's "wallet" to the Mark Twain Bank and then on to the merchant. Meanwhile, the user gets instant access to the content item.

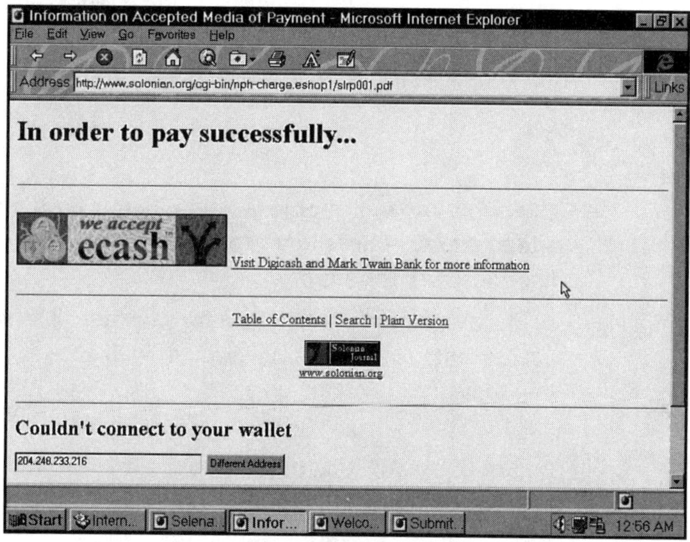


**Figure 16.7.**
*Users without digital wallets are shown where to go to sign up with ecash.*

One of the major benefits of digital cash systems such as ecash is that they allow for completely anonymous transactions, similar to green cash.

**TIP:** If you want to sell items using ecash, you'll need to become a registered merchant and set up the necessary CGI scripts on your Web server. For more information, check out the following site:

`http://www.digicash.com/ecash/mtbuildshop.html.`

# Workshop Wrap-Up

Now you've seen how to start making real money on the Web. Providing content for sale is not only a financial benefit to you and your company, but it can often work out well for users who would have to use alternative, less efficient means to acquire the information you provide.

The free ride on the Web cannot last forever because Web development costs continue to skyrocket (but are dramatically reduced by books like this, right?). Knowing how to go about implementing and running a subscription or pay-per-use Web site will position you for the opportunities that could be just around the corner.

## Next Steps

Now...

- ❑ If you're more concerned with selling products than content, you should look at Chapter 18, "Order and Shipment Tracking on the Web."
- ❑ For some real-life examples of pages that provide content for a price, turn to Chapter 19, "Real-Life Examples: Doing Business on the Web."
- ❑ If you're ready to start generating subscribers, turn to Chapter 20, "Marketing Your Web Pages."

## Q&A

**Q: I don't know if people would pay much on a monthly basis for my site alone. Are there any Web cooperatives for subscription services like there are for ads?**

**A:** The only type of cooperatives for subscription services to date all involve adult-oriented Web sites. However, as with everything on the Web, I'm sure that someone is working on a project to provide this type of service. A good place to check for developments like this is `http://www.Webreference.com`.

**Q: Are there any alternatives to digital cash for providing access to content on a pay-per-use or a pay-per-view basis? I'm thinking about selling some software through my pages.**

**A:** A good alternative for this type of scenario is to create a password-encrypted zip file using the WinZip utility included on this book's CD-ROM. You could then have people either phone in credit card information or provide this information online using the tools you worked with in Chapter 15. You then give them a password to unlock the file to start using it right away.

# CHAPTER SEVENTEEN

# Setting Up Advertising-Supported Web Sites

## In this chapter, you

- ❑ Learn Web advertising basics
- ❑ Create an animated ad
- ❑ Customize a billboard applet
- ❑ Join an advertising network

## Tasks in this chapter:

- ❑ Creating an Animated Banner Advertisement
- ❑ Inserting the Banner Advertisement in Your Page
- ❑ Creating Ads with the BillBoard Applet
- ❑ Using the Commonwealth Network

If you want to create commercial Web pages, you might just want to add some "commercials" to those pages in order to generate additional revenue streams from your site. More and more sites are coming online simply to provide unique content to users, and they're able to do so by supporting their efforts through the use of Web page advertisements. Whether you find Web advertising enticing or offensive, it's a reality of the modern Web that you'll need to know and need to know how to use.

**NOTE:** There are two popular business models used to generate income from Web sites: subscriptions and advertising. Advertising is the more popular of the two and is used on a large number and broad range of web sites. Many sites, such as ESPN's SportsZone, use a hybrid approach, providing some content for free with advertising support and then having additional premium subscription areas (although you'll still get ads there, as well). For information on a subscription-based model, turn to Chapter 16, "Providing Content for a Price on the Web."

This chapter explains to you the myriad of options that are available for offering Web page advertisements, for tracking how effective the advertisements are, for determining what to charge, and for implementing ads using advanced technologies like Java applets. You'll also see how you can use third-party intermediary services that will give you the advertisements (and the revenue) in return for the hits on your site.

**CAUTION:** You need to be especially sensitive about design considerations when you add advertisements to your Web pages. You want to make sure that the ads don't take away from the primary message of your own pages or are not presented in a manner that will turn off users to your pages or your company.

In this chapter, you learn the design tips and tricks you'll need to know to use Web page ads and how to turn visitors to your Web page into contributors to your bottom line ("if I had a penny for every time...").

# To Advertise or Not To Advertise?

The Internet was originally very hostile to any form of commercialization, which of course included advertising. However, in today's pop culture mecca that is the Web you'll probably find more sites (that people actually visit) with advertising than those with none. Advertising has been accepted on the Web (as it was on television) as a necessary evil for access to good quality and free content.

You can use advertising on your Web pages for a variety of reasons, but the big three reasons are

- To generate additional revenue
- To generate additional traffic to your site by trading advertisements with other sites
- To generate additional traffic to your other pages or sites

The second reason, to trade advertisements, is explored further in Chapter 20, "Marketing Your Web Pages."

No matter what reason you have for adding advertisements to your site, you'll need to follow the same sort of design considerations and track the success of your advertisements in the same way as you would for any other reason. Why you advertise in the first place will determine how much you advertise and where you place your advertisements.

**CAUTION:** Advertising on your Web pages is a not a get-rich-quick cure-all. You should think about it with a realistic view of the world. If you have ever monitored Web traffic on your site before, you can get a rough estimate of the upside potential of advertising by assuming $15 per 1,000 hits. You'll probably be able to generate only somewhat less than that, but it should give you an idea about whether revenue-generating advertising is an option worth your time in pursuing. For many sites, advertising will serve as only a partial offset to the cost of site development and maintenance.

# Advertising Basics: Placements, Charges, and Tracking

After you've decided to use advertising to support your site, you'll need to know some of the basics about where to put the ads and how much you charge when you sign up a client. The competition is fierce out there, and you need to know what you're doing going in.

## A Place for Every Ad and Every Ad in Its Place

Before you begin trying to sell people on advertising on your pages you'll need to be able to tell them what kind of placement their ads will receive on your pages. After all, you wouldn't just buy a commercial on NBC without knowing when they were going to broadcast it (hopefully during Seinfeld and not The Wonder Woman Reunion).

Ad placement will also affect the price you're able to charge for different ads. You could set up a multi-tier rate system in which banner ad placements at the top of a page are more expensive than banner ads placed at the bottom of the page.

Generally, you'll find that you are limited to placement at the bottom or top of pages. When you place a banner ad at the top of a page, be certain to place the banner ads so that the banner code comes immediately after the `</TITLE>` tag (or after the `</HEAD>` and `<BODY>` tags if you use them) so that it appears at the very top of the page, leaving maximum space for the page's actual content, as shown in Figure 17.1.

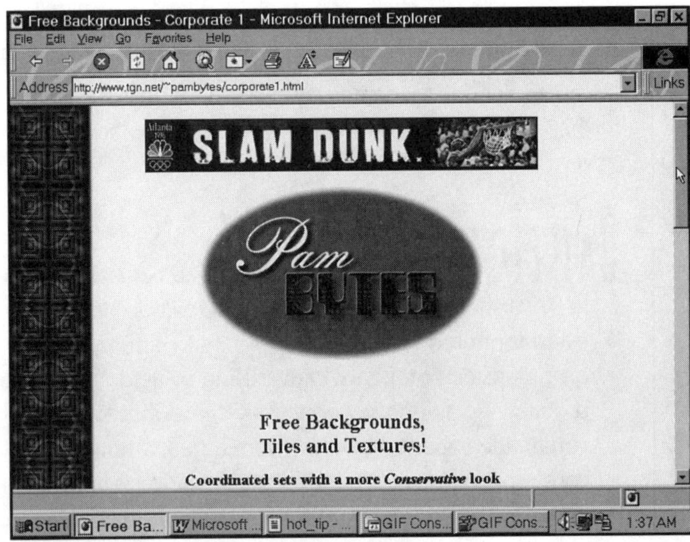


**Figure 17.1.**
*Placing a banner ad at the very top of the page leaves more room for the content.*

**TIP:** Some sites have begun integrating Web advertisements much more tightly into their content, such as the ads that appear to be almost part of MSNBC's menu bar, shown in Figure 17.2. Creative ad placement is probably best left to sites that can afford to experiment (such as any by Microsoft). By sticking with the basic and simple top/bottom placement you'll be offering the standard, but also not scaring any potential advertisers away.

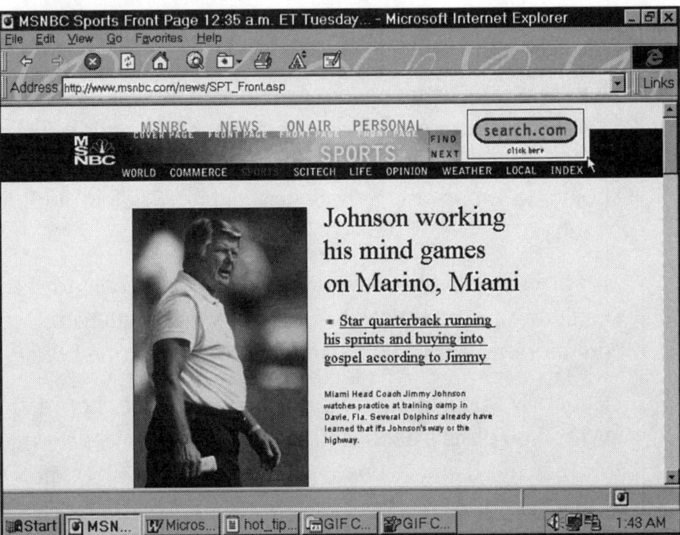


**Figure 17.2.**
*An example of a Web advertisement that is tightly integrated with the content.*

## Setting a Rate Scale

Deciding what to charge for a Web banner advertisement is probably a lot simpler than you might think. Because of the nature of the Web, and because you can precisely monitor traffic (as you'll see next), you can offer advertisers flexible rates that make even less-frequented pages as popular to advertisers as more visited rivals.

The structure of Web advertising is that you generally charge per hit or impression. Therefore, every time a page is accessed by a Web surfer, the advertiser is charged some very small amount. Advertisers are usually charged for every 1,000 times that a page with their ad is accessed on your server (sometimes called "price per M"). As a result, advertisers naturally pay less overall for less-frequented sites and more for popular sites, but the cost per user stays the same.

"Hits" are the raw number of times an ad is accessed. "Impressions" make adjustments for the same user accessing the same ad multiple times.

The beauty of the Web is that you can actually sometimes charge more to advertise on a less popular page. As a general rule, the price charged per 1,000 hits is normally between $10 and $15. However, if you can deliver a more carefully targeted audience (such as Web developers) to a company that wants to get a message to them (such as Microsoft) you can actually command a premium over a more general (and probably more popular) Web page.

**NOTE:** Another evolving model for setting rate charges is charging per *click-through*; that is, advertisers pay for each user who actually clicks on the banner ad to be taken to the advertiser's associated page. Click-through numbers will be dramatically lower than hit or impression numbers, but the cost per 1,000 is also dramatically higher for the advertiser. For now, you probably want to stick with charging per hit because click-through tracking can be more difficult, expensive, and unpredictable.

## Tracking Web Advertisements

You probably already have some tools for tracking Web usage on your site. If not, you can take this opportunity to not only get the tools you need to track your banner ads, but also to track overall usage of your pages in general.

To generate and sell Web advertising on your site, you'll need to have a Web access statistics program. Web statistics programs generate detailed reports about who accessed your pages, from where they accessed the pages, and the exact time they accessed the pages. The different programs have a variety of options for a broad range of data presentation options, including charts, such as those generated by the Statbot program in Figure 17.3.

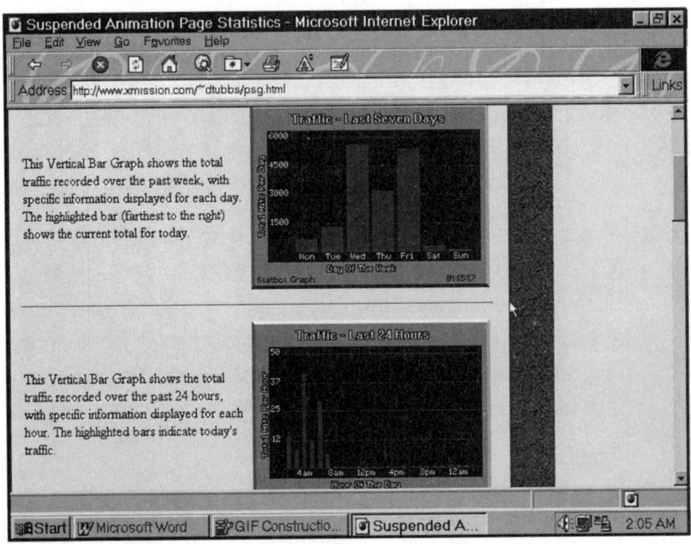


**Figure 17.3.**
*Statbot provides a variety of charting options for presenting your access data.*

Web statistics programs are available for any type of Web server on which your pages might be hosted. The following are some of the more popular programs from which you can choose:

- Statbot

  `http://www.xmission.com/~dtubbs/club/cs.html`

- WebTrends

  `http://www.Webtrends.com/download/wt_trial.exe`

- Access Watch

  `http://netpressence.com/accesswatch/download.html`

Grab any one of these shareware programs off the Web and you should be able to install them and start reviewing your access log in no time.

Now that you have the background necessary to start selling ads, you'll need to be able to create ads, as well. These can be ads for your advertising clients as well as your own pages so that you can tout them on other people's pages.

# Creating an Animated Banner Advertisement

If you have surfed the Web for even five minutes you have no doubt seen a Web page advertisement. The normal Web page ad is a horizontal banner at either the top or bottom of a page (often both) touting the products or services of a company. The ad is usually hyperlinked to that company's pages so that a user can simply click on the ad and be transported to the advertiser's site.

# The Animated GIF Format

The Web browsers that the vast majority of your users will be using, Netscape's Navigator and Microsoft's Internet Explorer, have the capability to display animated GIFs. A GIF file is the widely used format for displaying graphics and pictures on Web pages. The animated GIF file format enables you to create a series of pictures or graphics, store them in a single file, and then display them in an order and with a timing you specify.

Animated GIFs are similar to the flip books you created when you were a kid, where you'd draw a stick man in a different position on each page and then quickly flip the pages to give the illusion of animation.

Animated GIFs have become an almost universal element of banner advertisements. The format enables you to create banner ads that will be noticed by users and entertain them in the process. And you have all the tools necessary for making these animated ads on the CD-ROM.

# Using the GIF Construction Set

A wonderful program for creating animated GIFs is called the GIF Construction Set from Alchemy Mindworks, shown in Figure 17.4. You should install this program now so you can walk through the following steps for creating a sample animated banner advertisement.

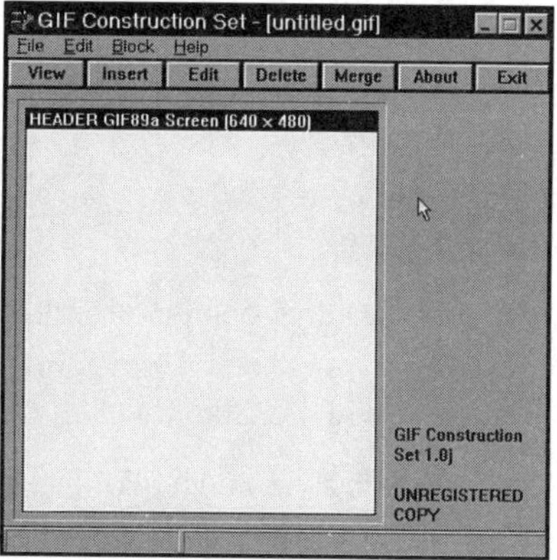


**Figure 17.4.**
*The GIF Construction Set program.*

## Preparing the Images

Before you begin this project, you must do an important preliminary task: You must gather together the images you want to include in your animation. When you create your ads, keep the following tips in mind when you put together the images to use:

- ❑ Images need not necessarily already be in GIF format; the program can import and convert images such as JPEGs, Windows BMPs, and others.

- All the images should be the same pixel width and height; for example, 300x75. Use a graphics editor such as Paint Shop Pro (also on the CD-ROM) to trim them all down to the same size if necessary.
- Create a storyboard (a step-by-step image layout, like a comic strip) either in your head, on paper, or on the PC of how you want the images to flow or to be animated within the file. Also, begin thinking about timing issues at this point (how long each image should appear).
- Create or find additional images that your storyboard reveals are needed to fill in any potential gaps in the animation.
- Rename each image file with a number to identify easily its place in the animate GIF order (for example, `ad1.gif`, `ad2.gif`, `ad3.gif`).

## Assembling the Animation

When you have all your images together and know the order in which you want them to appear, using the GIF Construction Set to assemble an animated advertisement that will be better than your average billboard is a snap. Remember, you can create animated GIFs to spice up the rest of your commercial Web pages as well.

The GIF Construction Set is available at `http://www.mindworkshop.com/alchemy/gifcon.html`.

**NOTE:** The ability to create eye-catching ads will give you a leg up on the competition when you are trying to attract advertisers to your site and when you are creating your own advertisements to include on other people's pages (or your own).

To assemble this animation, you'll need the following files from the CD-ROM: `buyad1.gif`, `buyad2.gif`, `buyad3.gif`, `buyad4.gif`, and `buyad5.gif`. And you'll need to fire up the GIF Construction Set. Next, here is what you do:

1. Create a new animation file by selecting File | New.
2. Select the Edit button from the top of the `untitled.gif` window and adjust the screen width and height properties to match the pixel dimensions of the ad images, in this case 280 for width and 80 for depth. Click OK.
3. Click the Insert button and then select Loop, this will make the animation play over and over again as users view the Web page. Click OK.
4. Click the Insert button again, and this time, select Control. Select Edit and choose Remove by: Previous image, as shown in Figure 17.5. You can use the options for each control element to set different timing and effects elements.

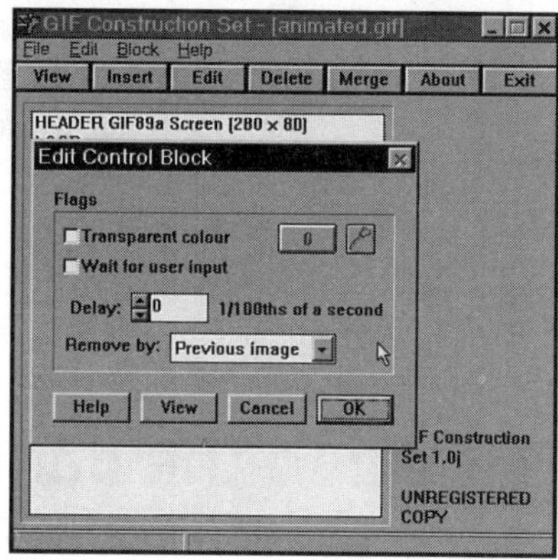


**Figure 17.5.**
*Editing the Control will enable you to set the properties for the animation within the file.*

5. Click the Insert button again and select Image. Choose the `buyad1.gif` image for the first image in this animated ad. If a user views the page with this ad using an old rickety browser that doesn't support the animated GIF format, they'll see just this image. Select Use a Local Palette for this Image, and then click OK.
6. Repeat steps 4 and 5 and insert `buyad2.gif`. Repeat again for `buyad3.gif`, `buyad4.gif`, and `buyad5.gif`, in that order. This establishes the playback order of the images, as shown in Figure 17.6.

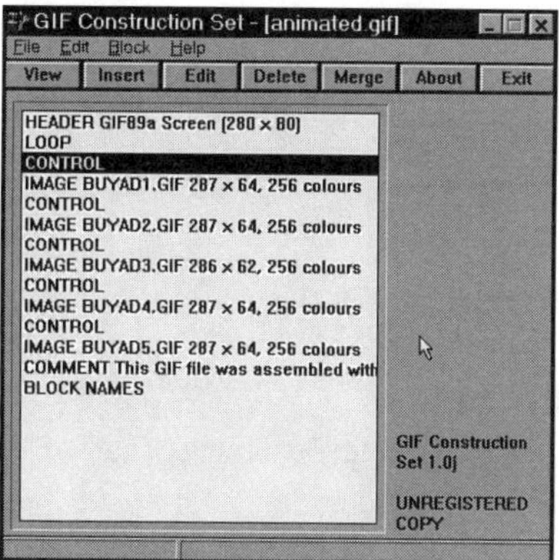


**Figure 17.6.**
*The GIF Construction Set lays out the playback order of the images.*

7. Save the animation as `animated.gif` by selecting File | Save as (you can use any name as long as it ends with the `.gif` file extension).
8. Click View to see the animation.

For maximum backward browser compatibility of ads, the first image of the animation should be able to stand on its own as a banner advertisement.

**TIP:** You can use the View button at any time to see the animation as a work in progress. Using this after you insert each image will enable you to more easily make adjustments as you go along.

You now have an animated advertisement to include on your (or someone else's) Web pages. Now you need to give the ad a home by actually integrating it into a page.

## Inserting the Banner Advertisement in Your Page

After you have created an ad for a client (or received one they have created), you'll need to place it on your Web page for the revenue to start flowing. The actual process of inserting a banner ad into one of your pages is extremely simple. The process is the same whether the graphic file is animated or static. All you need to do is go through the following steps:

1. Use an HTML editor such as HTMLed32 (included on the CD-ROM) to open the page on which the ad is to be placed.
2. Find the spot in the page's code where you want to place the ad, usually at the very top or very bottom of the page.
3. Insert an image reference tag `<IMG SRC>` pointing to the banner graphic. Often the graphic can actually be stored on the advertiser's server and not yours (for example, an image tag for a graphic on the advertiser's server could be `<IMG SRC="http://www.advertiser.com/banner.gif"`).
4. Place the appropriate link information `<A HREF>` to the advertiser's Web page that goes along with the ad.
5. Save the page, upload it to your server, and begin tracking hits.

Here's a simple example of some HTML code that inserts the animated banner graphic you created earlier:

```
<CENTER><A HREF="http://www.buythis.com/"><IMG SRC="animated.gif"
➥height=280 width=80></A></CENTER>
```

**TIP:** Banner advertisements offer an excellent opportunity to creatively use the ALT attribute of the image tag `<IMG SRC="ad.gif" ALT="Enter to Win Free Hosting for One Year! AOL Prime Host TEXT">`. Remember that

Microsoft's Internet Explorer displays the ALT attribute's text in a tooltip window when the mouse is passed over the image. For example, see Figure 17.7, which displays an advertisement that is supplemented by the tooltip.

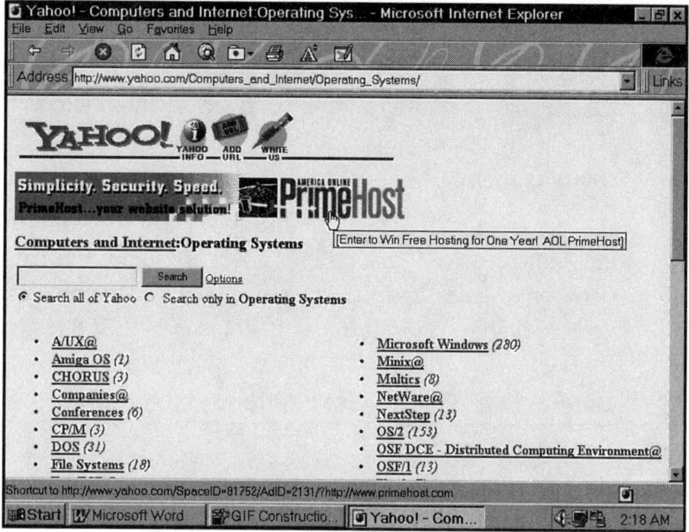


**Figure 17.7.**
*Microsoft's Internet Explorer enables you to squeeze even more information into a banner ad.*

# Creating Ads with the BillBoard Applet

You can use Java applets to make mundane advertising a little more exciting. A great applet for accomplishing just that is the Dynamic BillBoard applet, available on the accompanying CD-ROM and on the Web at

`http://www.jars.com/AppletBank/advertisements.html`

This applet is ideal when you want to advertise on your own page other sites or pages under your control. You can easily squeeze in several different rotating ads that generate more exposure for your various pages or products. The Dynamic BillBoard applet tool is relatively easy to set up and install and enables you to have different images rotated onto your Web page using a variety of transition special effects. Therefore, if you are selling ad space on your site, you can maximize your profits by rotating different sponsors' ads. If you watch an NBA game, you'll see a similar effect on the ad boards that surround the court. The Dynamic BillBoard applet also lets you associate an URL with each image so that a Web surfer can select an ad and jump to the related Web site for that advertiser.

The Dynamic BillBoard applet consists of the main `DynamicBillBoard.class` file and several additional class files that provide the necessary transitions between the images. You'll also need the graphic GIF images that you want to rotate using the billboard. All the class files and sample GIF images for this demonstration are available on the CD-ROM. Make sure that all the images you use for this applet are the same height and width in pixels.

For this example, assume that a bookstore owner has set up a Web page and wants to add a Java applet that will help sell some of his best titles. The GIF images on the CD-ROM contain seven different book covers, numbered 1 through 7 for this exercise. (The GIF images you use need not be numbered this way and can have any name you choose.)

The parameters available for this applet are the total number of billboards, the individual billboard images and associated URLs, the types of transitions available between images, and the delay between transitions. Listing 17.1 shows how the <APPLET> tag for the HTML document in Figure 17.8 looks.

### Listing 17.1. The Dynamic BillBoard example.

```
<HR SIZE=4>
<CENTER>Check Out All These Great Titles
<applet code="DynamicBillBoard" width="125" height="155" align="middle">
<param name="delay" value="2000">
<param name="billboards" value="7">
<param name="bill0" value="1.gif,http://www.mcp.com/samsnet/index.html,book 1">
<param name="bill1" value="2.gif,http://www.mcp.com/samsnet/index.html,book 2">
<param name="bill2" value="3.gif,http://www.mcp.com/samsnet/index.html,book 3">
<param name="bill3" value="4.gif,http://www.mcp.com/samsnet/index.html,book 4">
<param name="bill4" value="5.gif,http://www.mcp.com/samsnet/index.html,book 5">
<param name="bill5" value="6.gif,http://www.mcp.com/samsnet/index.html,book 6">
<param name="bill6" value="7.gif,http://www.mcp.com/samsnet/index.html,book 7">
<param name="transitions" value="6,ColumnTransition,FadeTransition,
➥TearTransition,SmashTransition,
UnrollTransition,RotateTransition">
<param name="bgcolor" value="#FFFFFF">
</applet> From Sams.net, The Internet Book Leader
</CENTER>
<HR SIZE=4>
```

The `height` and `width` values for this applet must match exactly those of the images being displayed. In this example, the images are 125×155 pixels. The `align=middle` element enables the tag line to be positioned in the center and on either side of the applet for a nice appearance. The `delay` value is in milliseconds, and it represents the lag time you want between images. The `billboards` parameter indicates the total number of images that will be used by the applet. The `billx` parameter is the individual images used by the applet. Note that the first parameter is `bill0`, and then it goes up to one less than the billboard's value, in this case, `bill6`. The `billx` parameter enables you to enter the image name, and then after a comma, a related URL. After the URL is another comma and text that you want to appear in the status bar when the mouse cursor is placed over the applet. The `transitions` parameter enables you to specify which transitions you want the applet to use by setting the number of transitions and the class files that contain them. Finally, the `bgcolor` parameter enables you to specify a backcolor for the applet in hexadecimal RGB color code.

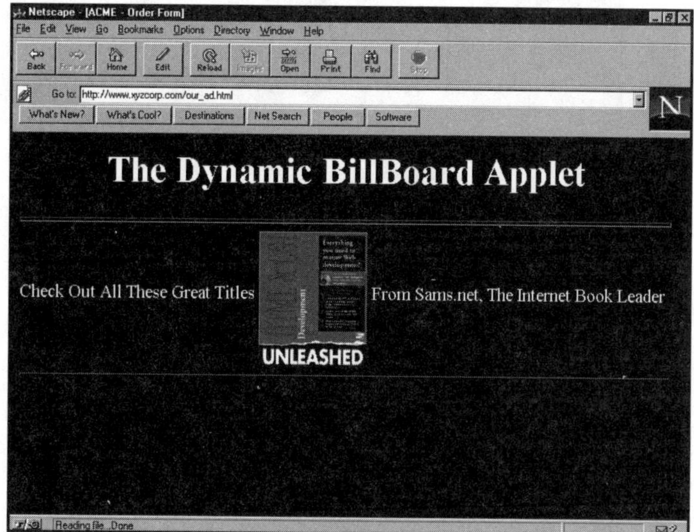


**Figure 17.8.**
*Advertising seven books in the space of one.*

The applet is centered and has horizontal bars at the top and bottom. It can be easily plugged into the bottom of the page on the bookstore owner's Web site. The orders should start pouring in any day now.

# Using the Commonwealth Network

Running a large Web site, or even a few Web pages, can take a lot of time and energy. Adding the additional responsibility of being an ad executive can be too much for you or your staff. After all, you'll need time to pay at least some attention to your business (and of course, to your family and friends). The task of finding and signing up advertisers can be a full-time job in and of itself.

Fortunately, there is a solution for those people who want to reap the benefits of Web page advertising but don't have the time (or know-how and contacts, for that matter) to sign up individual advertisers for their pages. Several companies have started Web advertising networks or co-ops. You become a member of the network and agree to place banner ads from the network on your pages. In return, you'll receive a royalty payment for each user who pulls up a Web page (a hit or impression) that contains one of the ads. One of the largest most popular of these companies is the Commonwealth Network at `http://commonwealth.riddler.com`, shown in Figure 17.9.

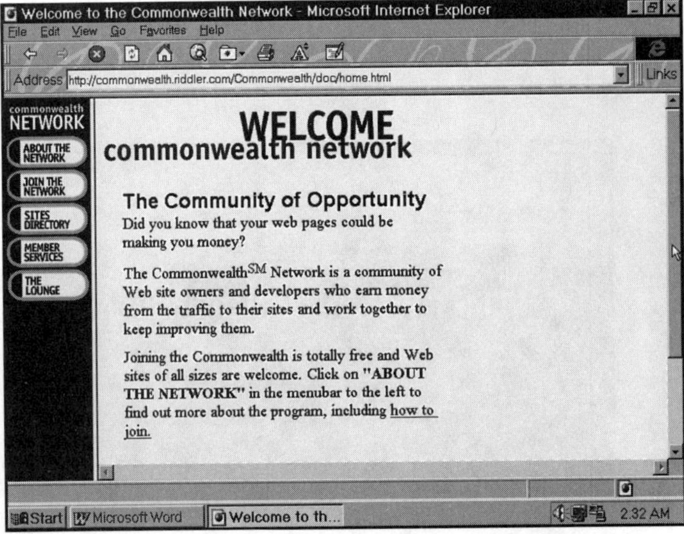


**Figure 17.9.**
*The Commonwealth Network will provide you with advertising (and revenue) for your Web pages.*

## What Is the Commonwealth Network?

The Commonwealth Network is an association of Web page affiliates that agree to carry network-provided advertisements on their pages in exchange for royalty payments based on the number of users that access your pages.

For many (if not most) Web sites, the Commonwealth Network is a simple and inexpensive yet profitable means to generate revenue from your pages without the hassle of dealing with advertisers on your own.

**CAUTION:** The Commonwealth Network must approve all pages you want to include as royalty-generating pages. The standard is that your site must contain material that would be suitable in a typical newspaper—not necessarily in quality, but in lack of offensiveness to the general public. After all, their advertisers probably don't want to be associated with Dan's Page of the Grotesque.

### How (and How Much) Do They Pay?

The Commonwealth Network pays you three-fourths of a cent for every impression (see the following caution) based on access statistics that are generated not on your server, but on the Network's computers. The actual ads that are included on your page are not stored locally, they are simply referenced in the HTML code. Thus, Commonwealth cannot only easily rotate ads on your pages, it can also carefully track accesses.

You'll receive a monthly royalty check if your pages generate a minimal amount of revenue ($50.00 per month). If you have a slow month, your royalties will carry over and you will be issued a check when the minimum transaction amount has been reached.

**TIP:** Before you become an advertising affiliate of the Commonwealth Network, be sure to sign up as a Level 1 or Level 2 member of Microsoft's Site Builder Network (SBN), a free service, at `http://www.microsoft.com/sbn`. Members of the Site Builder Network receive $.01 (a penny) per IP impression, an increase of 33 percent over Commonwealth's standard $.0075 (three-quarters of a penny). That increase in revenue is substantial enough to justify the short time it should take to become an SBN member (and there are some other great benefits, to boot).

**CAUTION:** Before you look at your latest Web server log and start making trips to Paris, note that the Commonwealth Network, like every other Web advertising network or co-op I have ever seen, pays not per hit, but per unique IP impression. Normally, you'll be paid for only one visit per day by a user from a specific IP address, no matter how many actual hits they will generate on your Web server in that period of time. Unique IP impression will be substantially lower in numbers than raw hits on your server.

## Joining the Commonwealth Network

The first step in actually joining the Commonwealth Network to generate ad revenue is to visit the Web site at `http://commonwealth.riddler.com`. You'll need to review the somewhat lengthy agreement and rules that apply. When you've decided that this advertising route suits your needs, you can register with the network and create a Commonwealth Portfolio.

**NOTE:** Although you can use ads from the Commonwealth Network on several different Web pages (or sites), you need to (and can) register and maintain only one affiliate identification. You will be paid for all the revenue generated by accesses to all the pages in your portfolio.

Filling out the actual registration form to join the network is very simple, but will require you to provide detailed information about yourself and your Web site. Specifically, the registration form, as shown in Figure 17.10, requires you to enter data in the following areas:

- Base Site Information

  Enter the location of your main home page here. Usually, this will be the `index.html` page at the root of your server.

- Contact Information

  Enter the name and contact information for the person primarily responsible for interfacing with the network.

- Address Information

  Enter your company's address.

- Account Access Information

  Create a new user name and password that you will use for administering your page portfolio on the Commonwealth Network. Be sure to jot down what you choose.

- Royalty Accrual

  Specify the minimum amount you want to accrue before being mailed a royalty check. The least you can select is $50 and is a good default to use.

- Referral Information

  Let them know how you found out about their program.

- ISP Information

  Enter general information about your ISP and the method through which you administer your pages.

## Managing Your Page Portfolio

When you finish filling out your registration form, you must enter your newly selected user name and password, and you'll be taken to the Portfolio Management section of Commonwealth's site, where you can begin the process of including pages that will display advertising.

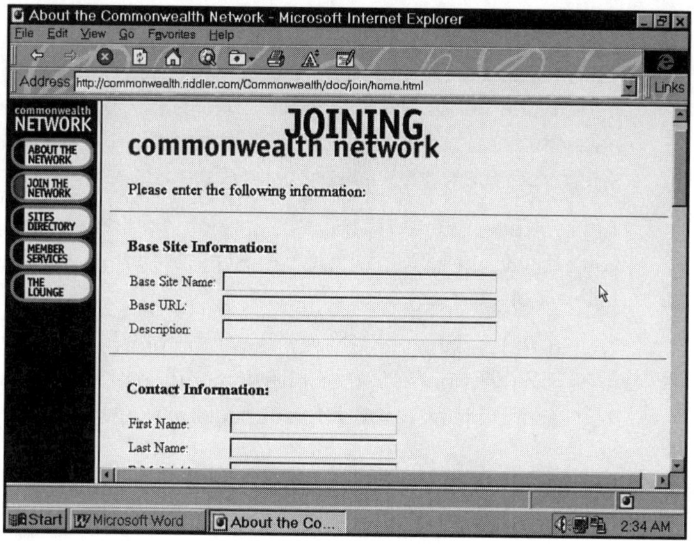

**Figure 17.10.**
*The registration form to become an affiliate on the network.*

When you first get to the Portfolio Management area, shown in Figure 17.11, you are presented with a drop-down menu with the following options:

- ❑ Add New Page
- ❑ Edit Existing Page
- ❑ De-Activate Page
- ❑ Re-Activate Page
- ❑ Content Change

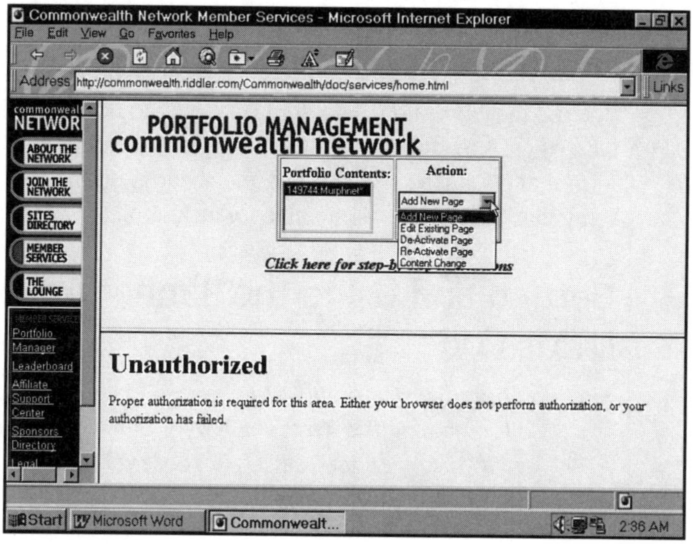

**Figure 17.11.**
*The Portfolio Management page is where you add and modify pages that include ads.*

### Adding a New Page

The first and most important step is to select Add New Page and enter detailed information about the first page on which you would like to include a banner advertisement. You'll need to specify an exact URL and also provide a description and select from the many available page categories.

After you have entered all the necessary information, select Submit, and in several days you'll receive the HTML code that must be inserted at the top of this page, which you'll take a look at in just a second.

To add additional pages, simply repeat this process. After a page is submitted it will appear in the window in the upper-left portion of the Portfolio Management screen. You can include as many different pages as you would like in your portfolio.

**TIP:** Commonwealth had been counting impressions on a per page basis, but they are starting to count on a per portfolio basis. However, you can still increase your revenue by placing advertisements on several pages in your site. By having more pages with advertisements, you increase the probability of visitors getting to a page with advertisements on it.

### Editing and Managing Pages

The remainder of the Portfolio Management menu enables you to edit and make changes to the status of current pages that you have registered for advertisement. Deactivating and reactivating pages enables you to decide when you want to remove ads from particular pages (and to put them back). An asterisk will appear next to pages that have been deactivated.

You use the last option, "Content Change," to notify the Commonwealth Network when there is a significant change in the content on your page. This is a simple e-mail form that permits you to describe the changes on the page. The network will then verify that the page is still suitable for inclusion in the program.

## Getting and Using the Banner Advertisement HTML Code

After you have registered and added pages to your portfolio, the final step in the process is to integrate the necessary advertisement code supplied by the Commonwealth Network. As discussed earlier, this code will automatically be sent to you when you have registered a new page.

Here is an example of how the snippet of HTML code you'll receive should look:

```
<!-- Interactive Imaginations Commonwealth Network Banner Tag v1.0 -->
<center>
<a target=_top
➥href="http://commonwealth.riddler.com/Commonwealth/bin/statthru?22206">
<img border=0 height=60 width=460
➥src="http://commonwealth.riddler.com/Commonwealth/bin/statdeploy?22206">
</a>
<br><font size=1><i>
<a href="http://commonwealth.riddler.com/Commonwealth/doc/bannersplash.html">
Commonwealth Network
</a></i></font>
</center>
```

The code needs to be inserted into your Web page. You have no discretion in ad placement for this one; it needs to be the first thing your users see on each page. Simply cut and paste the code you receive at the top of the page and save and upload the new HTML file.

Now you can sit back and let the cash start rolling in while you surf the Web yourself.

# Workshop Wrap-Up

Advertising support for your Web pages should be seen as a possible supplement to your overall business plan. Never let the advertising drive your pages or you're sure to lose users in the end.

Creating compelling Web advertisements can be simple and fun when you use formats like animated GIFs, created with the GIF Construction Set, or Java applets like the BillBoard example you worked with (both of which appear on the accompanying CD-ROM). Creative ads will sometimes garner as many kudos for your Web pages as the content itself.

Revenue-sharing ad networks like the Commonwealth Network are an excellent resource for developers who are either just starting out or small- or medium-sized businesses that are looking for a way to offset some of their Web development costs. You'll get paid a fair price for providing Web advertising without all the headaches that normally come with the territory.

## Next Steps

Now...

- If you want to see some real-life examples of advertising in action, turn to Chapter 19, "Real-Life Examples: Doing Business on the Web."
- A natural companion to advertising is marketing, so you might want to look now at Chapter 20, "Marketing Your Web Pages."

- In the next chapter, you will find out how to set up order and shipment tracking for your customers through your Web pages.

## Q&A

**Q: How can I compete for advertisers with big sites like CNN and ESPN out there?**

**A:** By providing a more targeted, specific audience for advertisers. It's true that you will never be able to match some of the big sites in raw numbers, but you can beat them for a small distinct segment of the market. As a result, you might be able to deliver more of the users a particular advertiser wants at a lower cost because they won't be paying for the vast majority of people they don't want from a general site like CNN.

**Q: What about using multimedia advertisements that incorporate video and audio?**

**A:** You might be able to get away with a small Macromedia Shockwave movie, but beyond that you need to be extremely careful about the size of the files that comprise your ads. People are impatient on the Web when it comes to "real" content, and they will be even quicker to hit the stop bottom when an ad is loading.

CHAPTER

EIGHTEEN

# Order and Shipment Tracking on the Web

## In this chapter, you

- Learn about customer order information.
- Learn inventory and order tracking.
- Learn shipping tracking options.

## Tasks in this chapter:

- Setting Up the Saletrak Program
- Using Indirect Database Input
- Using Stattrak for Providing Status

You have set up shop on the Net and are ready to start taking orders. What should you do with all the orders you are taking in? The obvious answer is, of course, collect payment and send the customers their merchandise. Fairly simple, right? Yes and no. The most important objective is to get the orders filled, but it is somewhat more involved than simply sending the ordered goods to customers.

With all the orders you will be taking in, you probably will want to

- Ensure that you receive payment.
- Ensure that you ship all the right merchandise.
- Notify customers of any problems with an order.
- Maintain inventory to fulfill orders.
- Keep customers abreast of the status of their orders.
- Adjust your inventory and your own ordering to meet demand.
- Adjust your line of merchandise to meet year-round and seasonal sales.
- Collect data for market analysis and planning.
- Ensure that all customer information is safeguarded.

Your online business will need much the same order processing, data handling, and bookkeeping as offline bussinesses, but by being online, you can handle almost all your information automatically. Even if an offline business uses the latest database and bookkeeping software, a person still has to manually enter the data. Your site can handle your order information automatically, without any human intervention.

# Customer Order Information

Remember the story of the three blindfolded men inspecting an elephant? One examined the tail, another a leg, and the third the trunk. All three thought the elephant was something different—a vine, a tree, and a snake. The story brings up an excellent point about things being much more than what they seem to be.

The order information you take in can be much more than "what to send to whom." Although the most important use of the information is to fulfill the customer request, other important aspects of the information are data that can be used for marketing analysis, sales promotion, customer relations, inventory control, and more.

## Order Data

Usually, you can use and analyze much of the online order information no differently than you would with offline order information.

Your order data typically consists of the customer who is making the purchase, the items being purchased, how and where to ship the items, and payment information for the purchase. You can use the order data to study and analyze your business, the products you offer, and your effectiveness in marketing those products and as a means to better establish your business with your customers.

From the order data, you can

- ❑ Determine how well products and types of products are selling, decide to adjust your selection of products offered, or change prices and terms.
- ❑ Build a targeted market for sale notices and literature. Customers who purchased certain types of products might be interested in similar or related new products or in a sale on those types of items.
- ❑ Evaluate the effectiveness of your site and possibly redesign your pages.
- ❑ Determine whether certain products have a particular market. For example, goods sent to addresses different from the customer's might be a gift. Some goods might move well at tradition gift giving times (Christmas, Mother's Day, Valentine's Day, and so on).
- ❑ Find that certain items are popular during part of the year or only in certain areas. An obvious example could be a winter coat. The coat would sell well at the beginning of winter, though probably not in Florida.

**TIP:** Periodically or at a particular selling season, you can send customers e-mail (provided they assented to receiving e-mail advertisements from you) or sales literature via the postal service. The messages/literature should thank them for their past purchases (besides being polite, it helps remind them of who you are) and invite them to visit your site again. Don't forget to give your site's address.

## Additional Customer Data

Your online survey can be like those on product resignation cards, in which customers tell the seller a little about themselves.

In addition to information directly related to and necessary for the order, you can request additional information that customers can optionally provide. This data can be helpful for market analysis and for making your business more effective in meeting the needs and desires of your customers. An online survey form can be useful for collecting additional customer data (see Figure 18.1). You can attach the survey form to the order reply (response) page or provide it as a separate Web page.

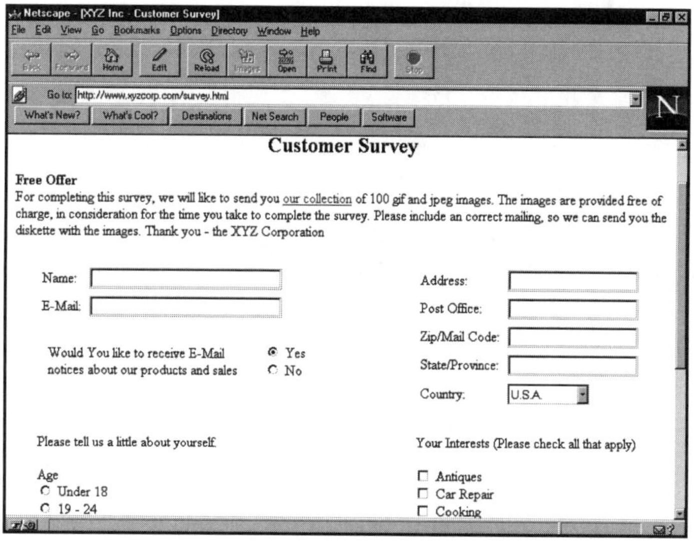

**Figure 18.1.**
*A sample survey form with a promotional incentive.*

Almost everyone prefers multiple choice over essay, and online surveys are no different. Use radio buttons, check boxes, and select menus, if possible.

**TIP:** Additional customer information from a survey or other means can be referenced to customer order information through a unique identifier field common to both sets of information (such as an e-mail address).

Possible data you might want to ask your customers for can include the following:

- Interests (sports, reading, gardening)
- Online purchasing habits (frequently, infrequently)
- Age
- Gender
- Marital status
- Income
- Occupation
- Other items that might be useful for your marketing studies

Be sure to check Chapter 20, "Marketing Your Web Pages," for information on how to effectively market your site. This will be useful in conjunction with marketing studies.

The more you identify who your clientele is, the better your business can serve them, and the more they will use your services. By requesting the appropriate information, you determine who your customers are and what their particular needs and interests are.

**TIP:** To help persuade customers to fill out and submit a survey, you can offer promotional prizes and other incentives in exchange for the additional information (see Figure 18.1).

**NOTE:** If you are collecting information for third parties, be sure to make the customer aware of this, as discussed in the "Customer Confidentiality" section later in this chapter.

## Collecting Customer Data

Offline businesses collect customer data in a variety of ways: register receipts, invoices, purchase orders, and so on. Many now tie their registers directly to a computer database or even use a terminal or a PC as the register. Of course, businesses that rely on telephone orders or a sales force (as opposed to a store) use computers almost entirely for inputting order information. They all need to have someone input the customer's order, however.

Your online site will be taking customer orders automatically for you. Your business will be open 24 hours a day, 7 days a week, taking orders and information from customers, but what do you do with the data your site so effortlessly collects? At some point, you or your staff will have to get involved with some of the data handling and analyzing. How involved you get depends a lot on your server and the software you have available.

A database report is a template developed to use predefined queries and calculations and is set up to present the results in a formatted content with text and possibly images (and other multimedia objects).

A database can be useful for processing and analyzing customer orders and other information. Prewritten reports can provide instant results for shipping, accounts receivable, inventory, accounting, sales, and other important information (see Figure 18.2). Businesses, whether online or off, are relying more on databases and other business software for data processing, storage, and analysis. By being online, you might be able to input your site directly to a back-end database.

If your site cannot access your database directly, you might use a script that receives processes and stores orders and other information for easy import into a database.

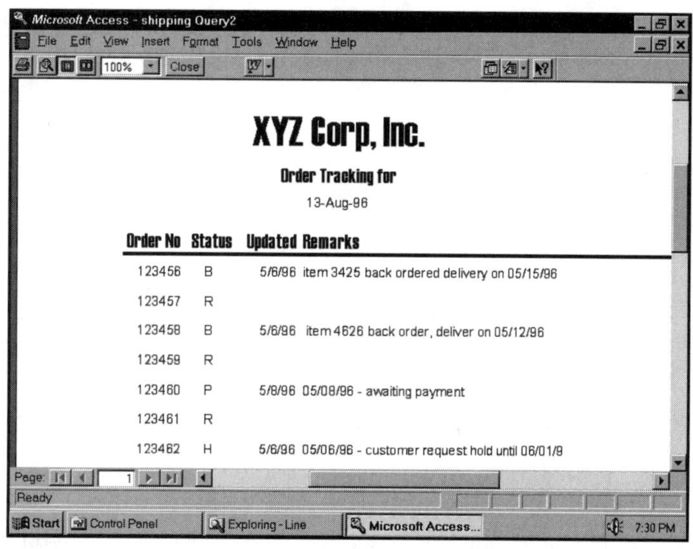


**Figure 18.2.**
*A database report showing order status for tracking purposes.*

## Direct Database Connection

One shareware database is mSQL, which has a C programming interface (you can use it in CGI programs) and is available at `hughes.com.au/product/msql/`.

You can establish a database for your Web site in a variety of ways. Microsoft's Internet Information Server can connect through an ODBC driver to your database. Netscape is offering Live Connect for its server to provide database connectivity. Other options are CGI scripts that have calls to an ODBC driver or to the database itself.

## Indirect Database Connection

Chapter 10 covers setting up and using a database with your Web site.

CGI scripts and programs can process and prepare your data to import into a database. This is sometimes the best method when direct connection to the database is not possible. Included on this book's CD-ROM is a C program, Saletrak, that can set up a variety of delimited text files and regular text and HTML files to your specification. It is rather simple to configure and use and it can prepare tables for relational databases or simply can be used to accept incoming orders.

Polyform is available at `polyform.ora.com`.

Other commercial and shareware software enables you to produce output files to import into databases. Polyform, one such program, can be set up to produce a delimited text file. Without a direct Web-to-database connection or the software to set up importable files, a business can also resort to what offline businesses do—enter the data manually.

**NOTE:** Not having business software, a database, or even a spreadsheet does not prevent you from collecting custom data. Although the software will certainly be quite beneficial to have, you can certainly take the order files, keep records manually, and perform tracking and analysis on the orders.

## Data Analysis

Sams and Sams.net publish numerous books on databases. Be sure to check `www.mcp.com` and nearby bookstores for titles.

You can create forms and reports with almost all modern databases. Forms provide a means to easily enter data without having to know anything about the structure or makeup of the database. Reports custom analyze and present the data, again without your having to know anything about the database. Using different reports, you generated the specific information for various parts and functions for your business. You can have a report for order status and tracking, for inventory, for accounts receivable, for analyzing order and survey information for market analysis, and more.

The following list details a procedure for setting up a database to handle your order information. If you do not have a relational database, simply ignore the reference to using a separate table and treat the guidelines as referring to just one database.

Of course, if your Web site can connect directly to your database, you will not have to be concerned with importing the text files.

A key field contains a value that uniquely identifies a record. No record in a table can have the same value as another record in the key field.

- ❑ Import the delimited text files into the database as separate tables, as shown in Figure 18.3.
- ❑ Specify the key field for each table (such as the order number and order e-mail address).
- ❑ Set field names and data types.
- ❑ Create the relationships between the tables.
- ❑ Write the queries and reports for routine analysis and data sorting.

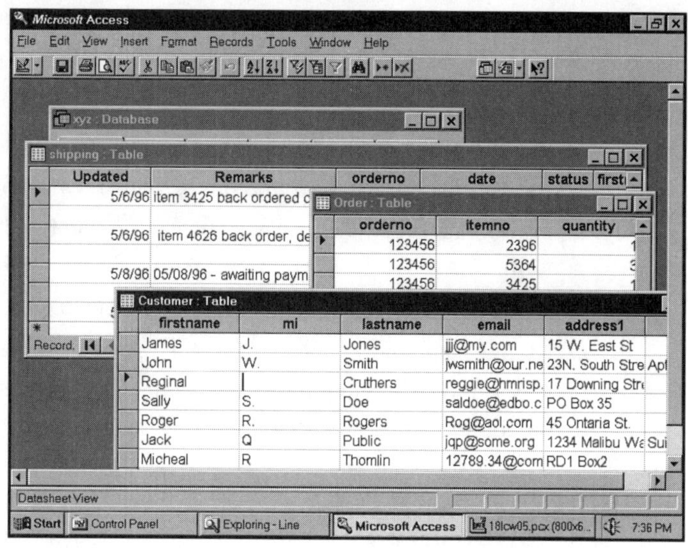

**Figure 18.3.**
*A database with separate tables for various types of order information.*

A short online customer survey form can be useful in obtaining additional data though you might want to offer an incentive for customers to fill it out (prizes, free software, promotional items).

Chapter 15, "Web Cash Registers: Taking and Making Money on the Net," covers various payment options for orders.

Examples of the queries and reports that you could write follow:

- Outstanding orders, orders more than a week old, or orders that are on hold
- Stock that isn't selling, stock that is selling very well, stock that is low
- Who is buying a certain product, that customer's age, interests, occupation, and so on (if you have this information)
- The different products particular types of customers have purchased
- E-mail addresses of customers who have purchased a particular product and requested information on similar new products
- The methods of payments people are using and what type of customer is using a particular form of payment
- The type of person who is the biggest consumer and repeat consumer

**TIP:** As important as it is to know who your customers are, you also should know who your customers are not. Are you appealing to and attracting as broad a market as possible? Granted, if your business is hunting supplies, you probably won't get many animal rights activists as customers. If your customer base isn't drawing from all segments of the online world, however, is there a reason for it and can that be corrected? Be sure to check out Chapter 20, "Marketing Your Web Pages," for information on how to effectively market your site. This will be useful in conjunction with marketing studies.

# Setting Up the Saletrak Program

Executable versions of Saletrak for 32-bit Windows and Linux systems are available on this book's CD-ROM. The source code is also available for compiling on other servers.

You can use the Saletrak program to do the following:

- Put orders and customer information directly into delimited text tables
- Specify which fields in what order to store in which files
- Incorporate order data (such as the invoice number) into a customer survey form
- Generate a custom response page for the customer
- Use the same program to process the customer survey data
- Import the customer information, along with order information, into a database (such as MS Access) for analysis

**NOTE:** Saletrak is not just for processing customer orders—you also can use it to process surveys and other input from customers and store the data in formatted files.

## Installation

Saletrak is fairly easy to install; only a few easy steps are required. The following are the steps needed to install Saletrak:

1. If needed, load the source code and compile it on your server.

**NOTE:** You might need your system administrator to perform the compiling.

**TIP:** The program can handle multiple users, so you can use one program for all the forms on one server.

2. Place the executable program in a directory were CGI scripts are allowed.

Web servers are typically configured to execute programs only in specified directories or with a special filename extension (for example, `.cgi`).

## Configuration

Saletrak requires a configuration file for each form that it processes. The configuration files instruct Saletrak on how to process the information received from the forms. The configuration process is as follows:

1. Create a configuration file for each form that the program will process.
   - ❑ The configuration file should be a plain ASCII text file.
   - ❑ You can give the configuration file any name that your operating system allows.
   - ❑ The configuration file needs to be accessible to and readable by Saletrak (running under the Web server's ID).

**NOTE:** The program runs under the Web server's user ID, so these user IDs must have permission to read the file. This is not the same as being able to serve the file to the Web. The Web server is typically restricted by its own configuration to serve files only from certain directories. However, through CGI scripts, the server can access files outside those directories (provided that file and directory permissions allow access by the server's user ID).

2. Build the configuration for each output file. In the configuration file
   - ❑ Use `#` at the very beginning of a line for a comment.
   - ❑ Use `file:` *`filename`* to list an output file. For example:

   ```
   file: order.txt
   ```

   - ❑ For files in different directories, use the full path for the file.

     For UNIX systems, this might be

     ```
     file: /var/order/input/order.txt.
     ```

     For Windows systems, this might be

     ```
     file: C:\order\info\order.txt.
     ```

**NOTE:** The program (the Web server) must have write permission to the files.

   - ❑ List all form field names to be written to the file, one field name per line.
   - ❑ Do not insert a blank line in the field name list or between the list and the `file:` line.
   - ❑ Include any of the special functions (`date:`, `host:`, `count:`) in the field name list.
   - ❑ List the field names and functions in the order that you need them to be listed in the file.
   - ❑ End each `file:` directive and its list with a blank line.
   - ❑ You can specify up to ten separate `file:` directives to create ten unique output files.

Host and agent are HTTP headers sent by the customer's browser and are obtained from the environment variables `HTTP_USER_AGENT` and `REMOTE_HOST`.

3. Special functions in the configuration file follow:
   - `date:` records the date and time of the transaction.
   - `host:` records the host name of the computer or service the customer is using.
   - `agent:` records the identification (make and model) of the browser used to place the order.
   - `count:` records a unique identifier for the order.

**TIP:**

Use `count:` in all files written by the program to serve as a key. Because `count:` is unique, you can use it to relate a record in one file to the record for the same order in another file.

4. Saletrak assigns a unique number to every order for each form. You need to specify a path or filename for a small text file Saletrak uses to store the next number to be assigned.
   - You can give the file any name allowed by your operating system.
   - The `count:` function can access the unique number assigned to the record in the output files and response templates.
   - The file must be readable and writeable by the program.

A response page acknowledges the receipt of the customer's input. For orders, the response page also should provide a tracking number, such as an invoice, customer, or order number.

5. Specify a response template with the directive `response:` ***path/filename***. The response template is optional for providing a custom response page. If not specified, Saletrak will output a generic response to the customer.
6. Specify a record template with the directive `record:` ***path/filename***. This record file is optional and stores the information in a plain text or HTML file.
   - After `record:`, specify the path or filename of the output file on the same line.
   - On the next line, enter the path or filename of the template for the record.

**NOTE:** For the `record:` directive, Saletrak appends new information to the end of the file. If you want to view the file as an HTML document, be sure not to include HTML, head, body, or title tags in the template.

A delimited text file separates data fields with a certain character as opposed to a fixed width file in which each field is a particular width in every record.

7. Specify the delimiter character to be used to separate the fields in the output file by the `delimiter:` character. The default delimiter is the tab but you can specify any character you want.

**TIP:** A customer might enter a character that also is used to delimit the data field, thus unintentionally rearranging the columns. Saletrak converts any incoming tabs to spaces, thus tabs can be safely used as the default delimiter. If you want to use the default, simply do not list the `delimiter:` directive.

8. To specify a particular file to be sent on an error, use `error:` *`URL`*, where *`URL`* is the Web address for the error page. Saletrak will generate a standard error message if a file cannot be opened and in the event of other problems.

**TIP:** Although errors are highly unlikely, they are still possible. A file removed, renamed, or without permissions correctly set can cause problems. If you use an error page, be sure to ask the customer to check his or her input and to try to resend it, if possible. Also include your e-mail address and any other contact information that will help the customer.

9. Keep directives separated.
   - ❑ Every single directive (including multiple instances of the same directive) must be separate from the other directive by at least one blank line.
   - ❑ Arguments to a directive (that is, the field name for the file) must be immediately below the directive line without any blank lines. Multiple arguments must be listed on their own lines without a blank line between them. The end of each directive and its list of arguments is signified by a blank line.

You can use Saletrak to process orders and apply shipping and tax costs based on customer location.

10. Other directives are included for use in the configure file. These include an `inventory:` directive, about which you learn later in the "Inventory and Order Tracking" section of this chapter.

**NOTE:** Other directives enable you to calculate shipping and tax, read a flat database of product descriptions, prices, weights, tax codes, and more. These other features are not needed to run Saletrak but are described in the `readme.txt` file that accompanies the program files on the CD-ROM.

Be sure to check Laura Lemay's *Teach Yourself Web Publishing with HTML in 14 Days* from Sams.net Publishing.

## Specifying the Configuration File

Saletrak is designed for multiple use and multiple users; each form can have its own configuration file. To tell Saletrak which form to use, include the path or filename in a hidden input file on the form. The name of the field must be `configure`, and the value is the path or filename. The path or filename is not a URL but a computer path file name for the configuration file. For example:

```
<INPUT TYPE="HIDDEN" NAME="configure" VALUE="configure.txt">
```

**NOTE:** Please remember that on many servers, case matters. If you use `Configure.txt` for a file named `configure.txt`, an error could result.

**TIP:** If you have several similar forms for which you want to use the same configuration file, simply insert a hidden field in each form. With the same field name but different field values you can uniquely identify which forms submit which records in the output tables.

You are now ready to use your Saletrak program. Enjoy.

## Customer Confidentiality

Customer trust is paramount to your business. If customers feel that they can trust you, they will be more willing to conduct business online. Treat all customer information as confidential. Especially protect credit card and other financial information, but also protect the customer name, address, phone, buying habits, and any other customer data you collect.

Let the customer know if you use the data for internal study and marketing, and ask for and receive customer permission before you release data to third parties. Never release any credit card or similar account information, but your customers might give you permission to release some information and might want other businesses to contact them about goods and services.

**NOTE:** Marketing studies that result from the analysis of order data can be released if there is no reference to the individual customer. For example, a report that states that 10,000 of product x and 5,000 of product y were sold in the month of May is quite all right because there is no connection or reference to any individual.

The following is a list of what you might do to maintain customer confidentiality (though not an all inclusive list):

- Respect customer confidentiality. Release customer information only with permission, and then only marketing information, not financial account data such as credit card or bank account information.
- Safeguard customer information. Protect files with customer data by
    1. Keeping them in password-protected directories.
    2. Encrypting files, if possible (especially account information).
    3. Setting file permissions so only you can read them.
- Ask for permission to release information.

  Include on the form a request to release marketing information, for example, near the order form Submit button, as shown in Figure 18.4.

  With the release request, include a check box for the customer to indicate permission to release the information.

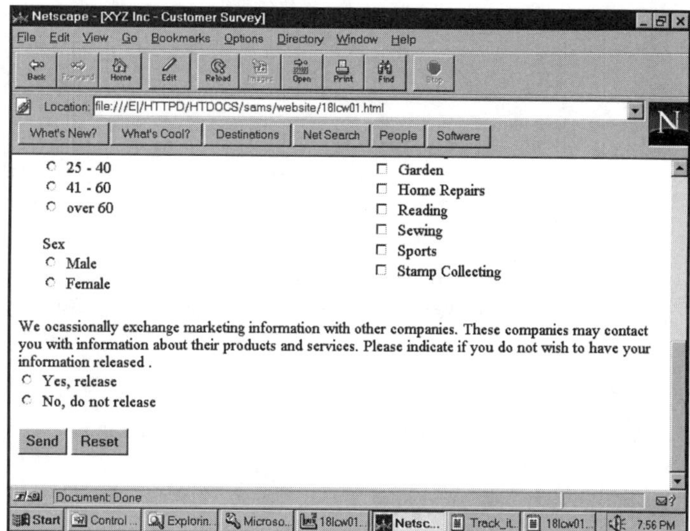


**Figure 18.4.**
*Information and release notice with request for customer permission.*

**TIP:** Customers who are indifferent to whether information is released might ignore the box or button and leave it at its default setting. It is OK to set the permission box or button to a default of checked, or permission granted. Customers who do not want their information to be released will deselect the box or button.

- Record customer permission as a separate field in the customer information database.
- Use the permission field to filter records for any reports generated for release to third parties, so that the reports do not include customer records without permission.
- Even with customer permission, never make any customer information available to the general public. Only release data to third parties that request it and have a valid marketing use for it.

**NOTE:** The preceding guidelines apply to customer order information. Customer testimonials and similar letters and messages, of course, can be displayed to the public for public relations purposes. You can also publicly disclose information when a customer agrees to your using him or her as a reference, such as appearing on a client or customer list (though disclose names and addresses only, not sales information).

# Inventory and Order Tracking

Making a sale is only part of doing business on the Net. The customer has done his or her part by placing the order and making the payment. The final part, delivering the merchandise to the customer, is yours. Non-delivery of ordered items will be a sore point in customer relations that you will want to avoid. Items can be out of stock or back ordered, you can have delivery problems with your own suppliers, an order might be overlooked or misplaced (hopefully you haven't charged the customer), a package can get lost in transit, and so on.

Most problems that you can apply to orders for an offline business can also apply to an online business.

Ensuring that orders are processed and carried out in a timely manner is perhaps the most important part of your business. It is not only a courtesy, but part of maintaining customer relations and your business's reputation to keep customers appraised of the status of the order.

Two main parts of fulfilling orders follow:

- Inventory tracking—ensuring that the needed merchandise is in stock to meet the expected demand
- Order tracking—following orders from receipt through delivery to prevent unnecessary delay in fulfilling any order

## Inventory Tracking

Perhaps the worst nightmare that you could have as a business person is receiving all the orders you could ever have hoped for and not being able to fill any of them because you are out of stock and your supplier can't make a delivery for a month. This probably won't happen, but it could happen to some of your orders. How can you prevent this?

Maintaining a large inventory can be rather expensive, especially with items that are not selling well. With good record keeping and tracking the items you're selling, however, you can maintain your inventory at a sufficient level to meet your demand. Your site can help with your inventory tracking by keeping track of orders and updating your database records to show stock depletion.

### Direct Database Connection

SQL stands for Structured Query Language, which is a standard for specifying data operation in conforming database software. Refer to the book *Teach Yourself SQL in 14 Days* by Jeff Perkins and Bryan Morgan, from Sams Publishing.

If your Web site can tie directly into your database, it automatically updates your inventory record with every order. An example SQL statement follows:

```
UPDATE STOCK
SET LEVEL = LEVEL - quantity
WHERE ITEM = product
```

`STOCK` is the table that contains your inventory, and `LEVEL` and `ITEM` are two fields (columns) in that table. The `quantity` and `product` variables are inserted by your CGI or interface program to represent the values of the order form fields for quantity and products ordered. On the Microsoft IIS Web server, they would be written in an `.idc` file as `%quantity%` and `%product%`. Your particular application can use different ways to specify SQL variables (for example, `@quantity`).

**NOTE:** You probably won't actually want to show the depletion until the order is actually shipped. You will need to indicate that the quantity is reserved for an order and not available for fulfilling other orders, however. You might want to use two-level fields, one for quantity in stock and another for quantity on order. You can set up a query or report to show the difference as the quantity available to fill other orders changes, as in Figure 18.5.

With the database constantly being updated with order information, you can frequently check your inventory levels, run a report to list items at or below their restocking levels, and order more stock as needed.

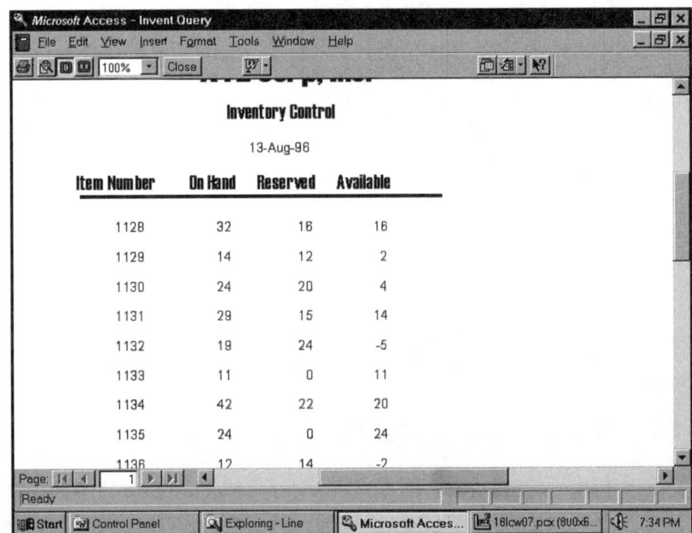


Inventory Control

13-Aug-96

| Item Number | On Hand | Reserved | Available |
|---|---|---|---|
| 1128 | 32 | 16 | 16 |
| 1129 | 14 | 12 | 2 |
| 1130 | 24 | 20 | 4 |
| 1131 | 29 | 15 | 14 |
| 1132 | 19 | 24 | -5 |
| 1133 | 11 | 0 | 11 |
| 1134 | 42 | 22 | 20 |
| 1135 | 24 | 0 | 24 |
| 1136 | 12 | 14 | -2 |

**Figure 18.5.**
*A report showing inventory information using an in-stock field and an on-order field.*

You can employ graphs and trending applications along with the inventory data to determine appropriate stocking levels and reorder points.

TASK

# Using Indirect Database Input

Even if your Web site is not connected to a database, you can use the order records to update your database or to update your books. If your order script produces a delimited text file for items ordered, you can import the data fairly easily into your database (see Figure 18.6).

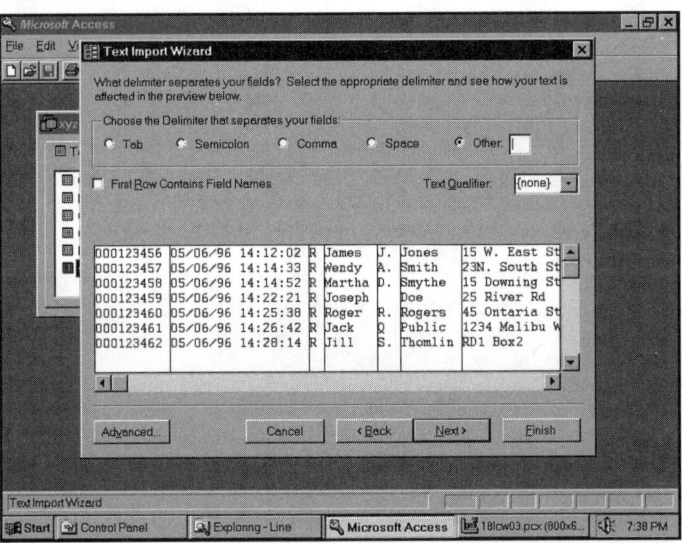


**Figure 18.6.**
*Saletrak generates a text table that can be easily imported into a database.*

Having all items in one field (column) makes queries easy and efficient. Instead of searching through an entire data-base, only one column is searched.

The Saletrak program on the CD-ROM can create a delimited file of items ordered. As you learned in the section, "Setting Up the Saletrak Program," you can set up Saletrak on your server to handle input for any number of forms and users. When you make the configuration file for your form, a special directive, `inventory:`, creates a table of the products ordered. This directive is different from the other directives in that a separate record (row) is created for each item in the order. Therefore, whether the customer orders two items or one hundred items, the fields for each item will be lined up in columns that will easily import into a database.

To set up the inventory option in Saletrak, follow these steps:

1. Start with the `inventory:` filename directive, where the filename is the path or filename of the inventory table.
2. List the fields you want to record in the order in which they should appear in the record.
3. The field names specified do not have to be complete field names; a partial name can be used. For example, `item` will match `item1`, `1item`, and `item`.

**CAUTION:** Be careful not to use a string that could match a part of a field name that you do not want in the record.

4. The fields will be separated with a tab unless you specify a different character with the `delimiter:` directive, as discussed in the "Customer Order Information" section.

**TIP:** The inventory table is the only table capable of storing each item ordered in its own record. You'll probably want to use this file to import the information of the items ordered into your database with other order information from different files. Use a unique identifier for the order, such as the `count:` function, so a relationship can be made between the items ordered and order information in other tables.

**NOTE:** The `inventory:` directive stores the fields for each item ordered in a separate record (row) because database records have a fixed length. Therefore, an order for two items would still have as many fields (columns) as an order for one hundred (though the one hundred item order will have more records). Having every ordered item in one record would create a lot of unnecessary fields for most records; and more important, order queries on the database would be almost impossible because criteria could be in any field (when the entire order is in one record).

**TIP:** Don't list fields that can appear only once on the form, such as a customer name or address.

Because a new record is written for each item ordered, redundant data can take up a lot of disk storage space. List only fields that will contain unique data for the record, such as items ordered and the quantity. The only exception would be an identifier used to relate items ordered to information in other tables.

## Order Tracking

Even though you have the best intentions, some orders might not be filled. Orders can be lost or misplaced or be on hold as back-ordered items and then forgotten. The better the business is, the more orders there are and the more likely that something could prevent some orders from being filled. How do you maintain a status on each and every order and ensure that it is promptly processed and shipped? You might already have a system in place to track orders using a database or bookkeeping. As in other sections in this chapter, a database is a powerful tool for taking care of orders.

A database of your order information can quickly provide information on orders and their status (see Figure 18.7). You can create database reports that list

- New orders that have come in
- Orders that are delayed (out of stock, awaiting payment, and so on)
- Orders that have been filled after a certain time

You can see an online order tracking page at `www.sparco.com/products/data/track.html`.

You also can provide your customer with an online update of their orders whether your database is online or offline. The next two sections discuss how to set up a custom order status update that can be accessed on the Web.

### Direct Database Connection for Status

With your database online, customers can query for their orders, receive an up-to-date status of the order, and note any remarks about problems with the order. A SQL statement that could be used in your interface for customer order status might look like the following code:

```
SELECT STATUS, REMARKS
FROM ORDERS
WHERE INVOICE=input
```

Chapter 10 provides information on making databases available online.

In this example, `ORDERS` is the table that contains your order status information and `STATUS` and `REMARKS` are two fields (columns) in that table. `INVOICE` is the field that contains the order numbers and `input` is a variable, the value of which is the order number entered by the customer. On the Microsoft IIS Web server, the variable would be written in an `.idc` file as `%input%` (the output `.htx` file will need to reference `%STATUS%` and `%REMARKS%`). Your particular application can use different means to specify SQL variables (for example, `@input`).

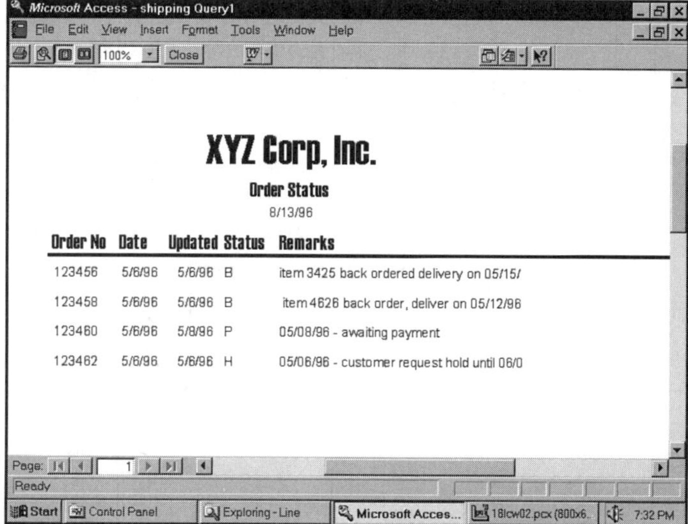


**Figure 18.7.**
*A report showing status of orders.*

# Using Stattrak for Providing Status

Stattrak, a program on the CD-ROM, is available to extract older status records. A customer simply inputs the order number (or other information you choose) and receives the status information you provide.

The following is a list of steps to perform to set up and configure Stattrak:

As with Saletrak, Stattrak is available as an executable file for Windows and Linux servers and as source code for other servers.

1. Place Stattrak in a directory that allows CGI programs.
2. Create a configuration file with the following directives:

   `file:` *`path/filename`*. The path or filename of the response page template used to generate the response page for the customer.

   `response:` *`path/filename`*. The path or filename of the order status table. Be sure to specify a full path name from the server's root directory (not the Web server's document directory) if the file is not in the same directory as Stattrak.

`Delimiter:` *`character`*. This character separates the fields.

`field:` *`number`*. This field indexes the table. Stattrak will search this field for the customer input and extract the record when it finds a match. The field number is used to specify the field. For example, the first field is 1.

`Error:` *`URL`*. The URL is the address of the page you want to have Stattrak serve, instead of a generic message, in the event of an error.

**NOTE:** Certain errors, such as not being able to access the configuration file, will always generate the standard message. Server errors will be handled by the server and not by Stattrak.

Please refer to `www.w3.org/pub/Protocols/` for information on HTTP methods, such `GET` and `POST` (see Section 5.1.1. of the HTTP 1.1 specification).

3. Create the response page template. This template is an HTML page that Stattrak reads and copies to the customer. The only difference between the template and a normal HTML page is that you put placeholders in the template for the fields to be listed.
   - ❏ The placeholders are enclosed in braces: `{}`.
   - ❏ Fields are designated by their number; the first field is 1, the second is 2, and so on. For example, to list the second, third, and fifth fields, use `{2} {3} {5}`.
4. Create an HTML form using the `GET` method.
   - ❏ Make a hidden field with the name `configure` and a value of the path or filename of the configuration file.
   - ❏ Make an input field named `invoice` for the customer to enter the invoice number. For example, the code for the form (Windows Servers use `stattrak.exe`) follows:

```
<FORM METHOD="GET" ACTION="/path/Stattrak">,
<INPUT TYPE="HIDDEN" NAME="config" VALUE="config1.txt">
<INPUT NAME="invoice">
<INPUT TYPE="SUBMIT" VALUE="Status">
</FORM>
```

   and the code for the configuration file would be

```
file: /var/order/track/status.txt
response: /var/order/track/update.txt
field: 2
delimiter: ¦
error: /~mycompany/status/error.html
```

**TIP:** For any orders that encounter a lengthy delay, notify the customer of the delay in filling the order.

## Shipment Tracking Options

Depending on where your business is located, you might be under legal obligation to fill orders within a specified time frame unless another time frame can be mutually agreed on.

Even after all the effort you put into ensuring that the goods are shipped to the customer in a timely manner, other problems can arise and delay getting the order to the customer. Although shipping companies and the postal service are very reliable, problems can occur—Murphy's Law.

United Parcel Service and Federal Express both provide online shipment tracking. See `www.ups.com` and `www.fedex.com`.

What can you do once you have turned the responsibility of delivering an order to a shipping company? Several shippers now provide Web pages in which customers can track a shipment right on the Internet. You simply enter your shipment or tracking number and receive almost instantaneous status of the package. Figure 18.8 shows a shipment tracking page.

**TIP:** You might want to include a postage paid card with each shipment, then the customer can hopefully return the card to acknowledge receipt. You can also include a brief survey on the card. Although not as handy as an online survey, it can help obtain additional customer information.

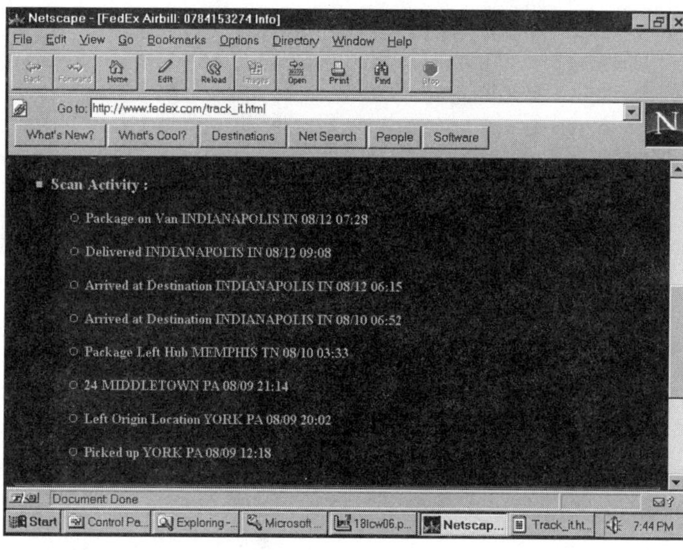


**Figure 18.8.**
*A shipping tracking page showing quite detailed information on a shipment.*

You can see a site that offers shipment tracking fields at `www.sparco.com/products/customer.html`.

You might want to consider adding a tracking form on your customer status update page. You would need to include the shipping or tracking number with the information the customer receives when you take his or her order, then the customer can not only see that the order was shipped, but can also track the shipment. The HTML for the forms could follow the form of the following code:

```
<FORM METHOD="GET" ACTION="/path/Stattrak">,
<INPUT TYPE="HIDDEN" NAME="config" VALUE="config1.txt">
<INPUT NAME="invoice"> Order Tracking
<INPUT TYPE="SUBMIT" VALUE="Status">
</FORM>

<FORM METHOD="GET" ACTION="http://www.fedex.com/CGI-bin/track_it">,
<INPUT NAME="trk_num">
<INPUT TYPE="SUBMIT" VALUE="Status">
</FORM>
```

To advance the idea of providing a form for tracking the shipment, you might want to include a shipment tracking form in the response page to the order status update form. For example, with Stattrak, if you use field number 4 for shipment tracking numbers, the response page template might include the following:

```
<FORM METHOD="GET" ACTION="http://www.fedex.com/CGI-bin/track_it">,
<INPUT NAME="trk_num" VALUE="{4}">
<INPUT TYPE="SUBMIT" VALUE="Status">
</FORM>
```

And of course, if your Web site can access your database, you would use the appropriate template, with similar code, to provide the customer with the easy-to-use shipment tracking form.

# Workshop Wrap-Up

In this chapter, you learned about several issues related to processing an online order. Although I did not go into the details of how a business should be run, you did learn how to apply and use your business practices with the Web. You learned the following:

- Customer order information: What you could do with and how to use information the customer sends. Also very important is the need to protect customer information and to safeguard customer privacy.
- Inventory and order tracking: How to implement online means to track your stock level and maintain your inventory and to track your orders to ensure that they are processed in a timely manner. You also learned how to provide customers with order status information online.
- Shipment tracking options: Although this section was rather short, it was no less important. Shipment is the phase of the order process not in your

control and is the final step in closing the order process. You can get updates on a delivery if needed through the shipping companies' online tracking programs.

## Next Steps

Now...

- Chapter 10, "Advanced Information Pages: Tying Data To The Web." You might want to review this chapter (or read if you haven't done so already) for information on setting and using databases on the Web.
- Chapter 14, "Web Shopping Carts." In this chapter, you learn to set up and use a shopping cart system for displaying products and taking customer orders.
- Chapter 19, "Real Life Examples: Doing Business on the Web." Find out about real Web sites that employ the techniques that you have learned.

## Q&A

**Q: What is the most important thing that you can do with the customer order information for your business?**

**A:** Although you can do many things with order information, such as conduct marketing studies, inventory control, and promotional mailing, the most immediate and important thing to do is process the order and ensure that the customer receives what he or she requested. By providing your customers with good and dependable service, you only further your reputation.

**Q: How can a business maintain inventory on the Internet?**

**A:** By maintaining a record of items that have been ordered and shipped, just as with offline businesses, you can determine how much has been used and how much is left. The main difference being online is that the record keeping can be performed automatically for you, instead of you or a staff member having to record the data manually.

**Q: What benefit does online ordering have over other traditional means of ordering?**

**A:** By taking orders online and using your Web site to write the order information into a database, there is no human intervention that might cause orders to be lost or misplaced. Other methods of taking orders, such as by mail or phone, require a person to process the order. Even if the order is entered directly into a database by the person who received the order, there is a chance that some of the information could be entered incorrectly. By using your site to handle the order data entry, all information is entered as the customer has actually entered it.

**Q: What kind of shipment status can be obtained online?**

**A:** Many shipping companies provide quite detailed online information on the shipment of a package. Every point at which the package is transferred or handled is recorded and the date and time is shown. When the package is delivered, the person signing for the package typically is identified. Their information is reliable and updated within several minutes of the time that the package information was recorded.

NINETEEN

# Real-Life Examples: Doing Business on the Web

## Examples in this chapter:

- Example 1: Jigowat Jewelry Catalog
- Example 2: Discovery Channel Catalog
- Example 3: Let's Talk Cellular Catalog
- Example 4: Steve Dahl & Company Catalog
- Example 5: NetBeat Catalog
- Example 6: SportsLine
- Example 7: Commonwealth Network Site
- Example 8: Package Tracking Services

Let's get down to business and see how other people are doing business on the Web today. Part IV, "Creating Commerce in Cyberspace: Online Ordering and Advertising Techniques," covers a lot of territory, so the examples in this chapter cover really only the highlights from each of the chapters in this section, but they should give you a firm understanding of how the information covered in Part IV can come together to help your business or company.

For more real-life examples, check out Chapters 7, "Real-Life Examples: Putting the Basics Together," 12, "Real-Life Examples: Advancing Your Site," and 22, "Real-Life Examples: Touting and Managing Your Site."

For each of these example pages, you see what advanced elements, techniques, and scripts are implemented and where you can locate the pages online. You'll also be referred to the appropriate chapter in which you can find more information about implementing similar code on your own pages.

# Example 1: Jigowat Jewelry Catalog

**Document title:** Jigowat Jewelry Catalog (Figures 19.1 and 19.2)

**Document URL:** `http://www.check-it.com/jigowat/`

**Description:** Jigowat Jewelry manufactures interesting and unique high-tech jewelry. The company's online catalog is as advanced as its products—it implements a variety of technologies including VRML and JavaScript in order to deliver a more effective catalog to its customers.

**Techniques and designs applied:**

> **Multimedia.** (See Chapter 13, "Advanced Catalogs.") The Jigowat catalog uses VRML to provide an advanced, interactive experience. In the upper-left corner of the screen, shown in Figure 19.1, you can see a graphic image of the current product being viewed in the catalog using VRML technology.

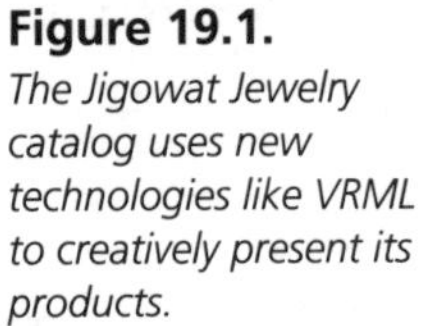

**Figure 19.1.**
*The Jigowat Jewelry catalog uses new technologies like VRML to creatively present its products.*

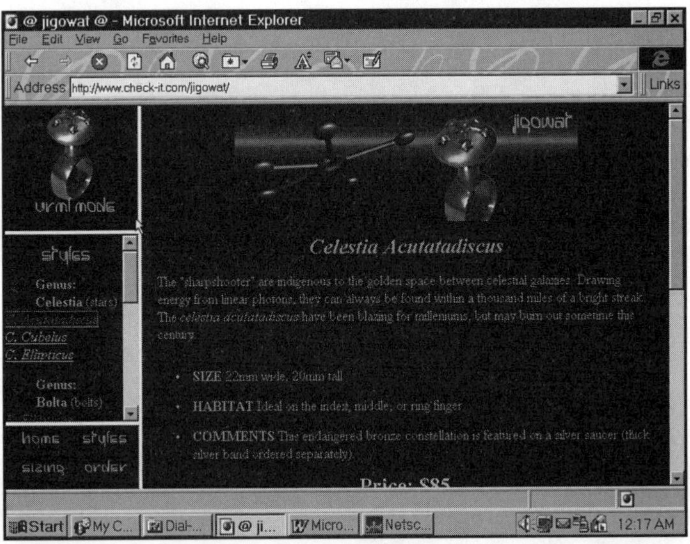

**Interaction.** (See Chapter 13.) The Jigowat catalog uses the interactive JavaScript language to enable users to pull up a small window containing a scrollable graphic listing of all the gemstones available in the company's product line, as shown in Figure 19.2.

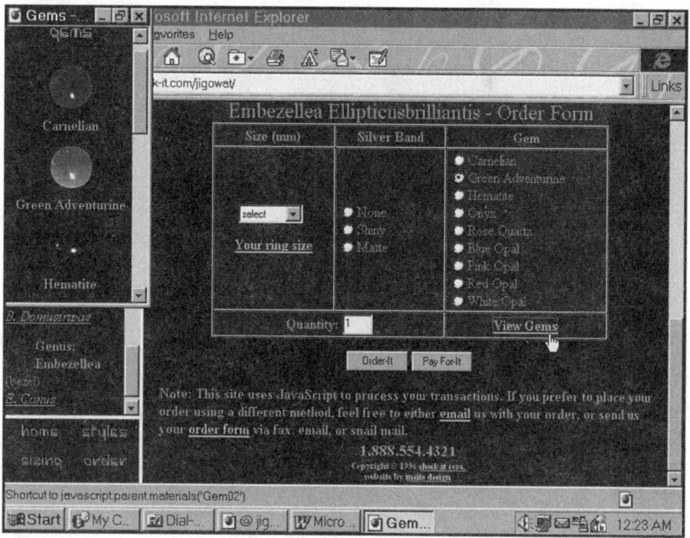


**Figure 19.2.**
*The Jigowat site combines interaction and multimedia using JavaScript and other technologies.*

# Example 2: Discovery Channel Catalog

**Document title:** Discovery Channel Catalog - Beer Hunter Video (Figures 19.3 and 19.4)

**Document URL:** `http://catalog.discovery.com/tours/details/beervid.html`

**Description:** The Discovery Channel has a fine reputation for providing excellent content in all its forms, whether it be on television or online, and its catalog is no exception. The Discovery Channel Catalog markets products such as CD-ROMs and videos that beg for the use of online multimedia in their presentation.

**Techniques and designs applied:**

**Multimedia.** (See Chapter 13.) The Discovery Channel sells many videos online. For example, you can pull up the description of the Beer Hunter video, shown in Figure 19.3, and see a brief narrative on the item along with a Download Video link. Selecting the link brings up a short video clip, as shown in Figure 19.4.

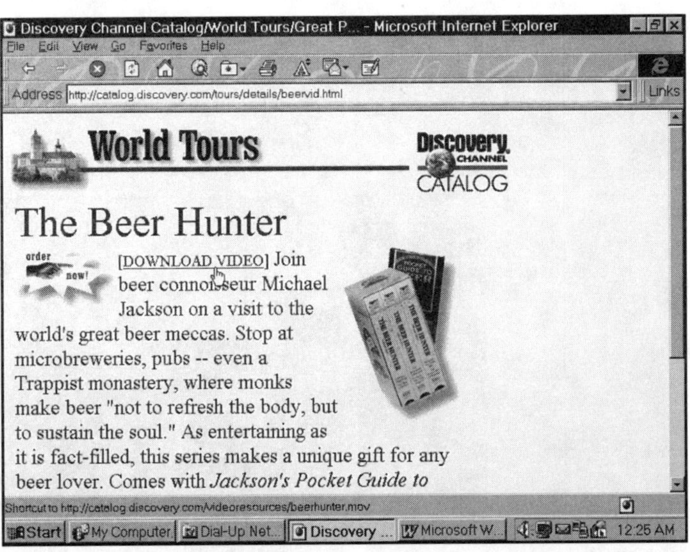


**Figure 19.3.**
*The Discovery Channel's product line is a natural fit for including online multimedia in its catalog.*

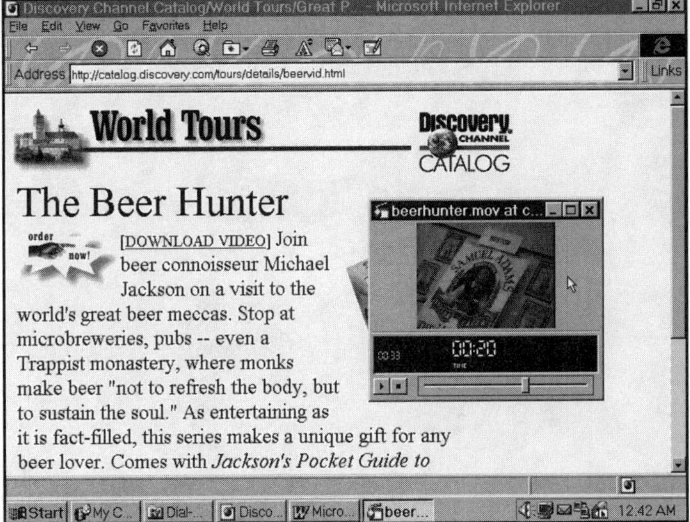


**Figure 19.4.**
*The Beer Hunter video clip launches a helper application while the catalog remains in the browser window in the background.*

# Example 3: Let's Talk Cellular Catalog

**Document title:** Let's Talk Cellular Catalog - Shopping Cart (Figures 19.5, 19.6, 19.7, and 19.8)

**Document URL:** `http://www.letstalk.com/`

**Description:** The Let's Talk Cellular Web site is one of the most extensive (and excellent) implementations of the OopShop shopping cart system. The company sells a wide variety of cellular, paging, and telephone accessories through its Web pages using the OopShop program.

**Techniques and designs applied:**

**Formulating Stores and Aisles.** (See Chapter 14, "Web Shopping Carts.") Creating separate virtual aisles for different product lines, as shown in Figure 19.5, is particularly important for a large catalog like Let's Talk Cellular's. OopShop makes the implementation of separate aisles for separate products extremely easy.

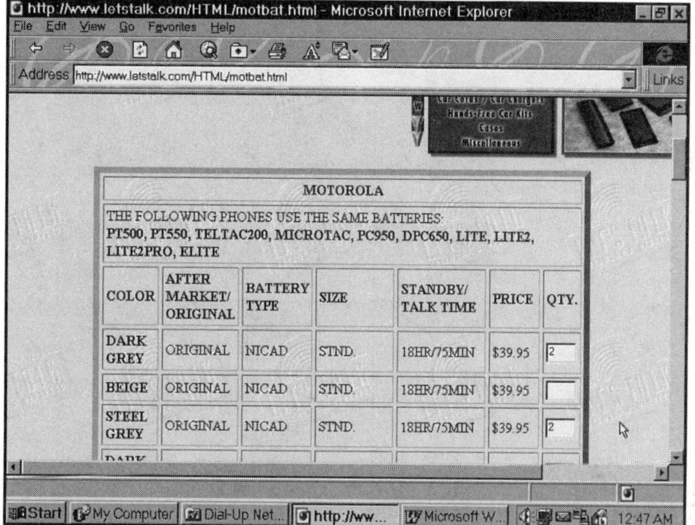


**Figure 19.5.**
*Just one of the many virtual "aisles" on the Let's Talk site, made possible by OopShop.*

**OopShop in Action.** (See Chapter 14.) You can see how the Let's Talk shopping cart (through OopShop) displays a user's cart contents as he or she adds products, shown in Figure 19.6. The Department designation helps identify the virtual aisle from which the product was selected online.

**Checking Out.** (See Chapter 14 and Chapter 15, "Web Cash Registers: Taking and Making Money on the Net.") When users have finished selecting products, they can select Check Out, and they will be presented with the summary information shown in Figure 19.7.

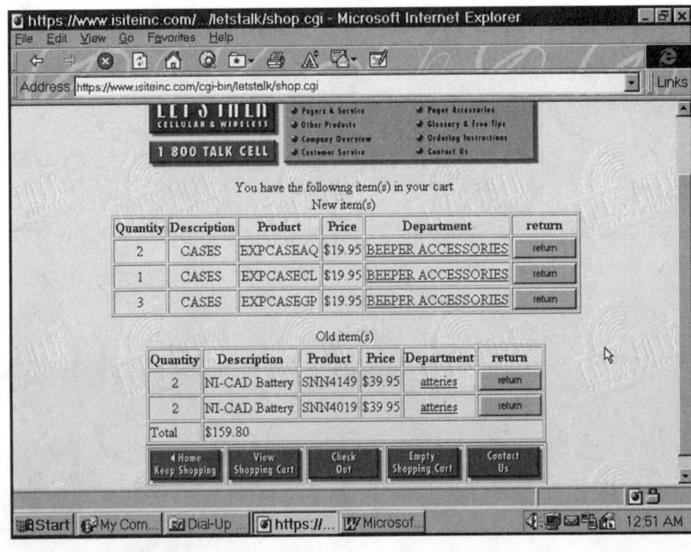


**Figure 19.6.**
*As products are added to the user's cart, OopShop updates the product information.*

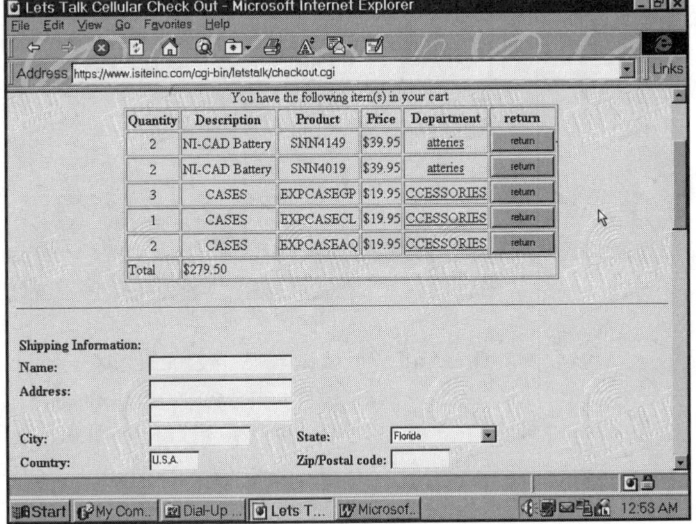


**Figure 19.7.**
*A summary of products purchased is generated by selecting the Check Out button.*

**Securing Transactions on Your Site.** Let's Talk uses a secure server in order to receive its customers' credit card information through the OopShop checkout procedure on its pages. You can see from the small padlock icon in the lower-right corner of the browser window that this is a secure submission page.

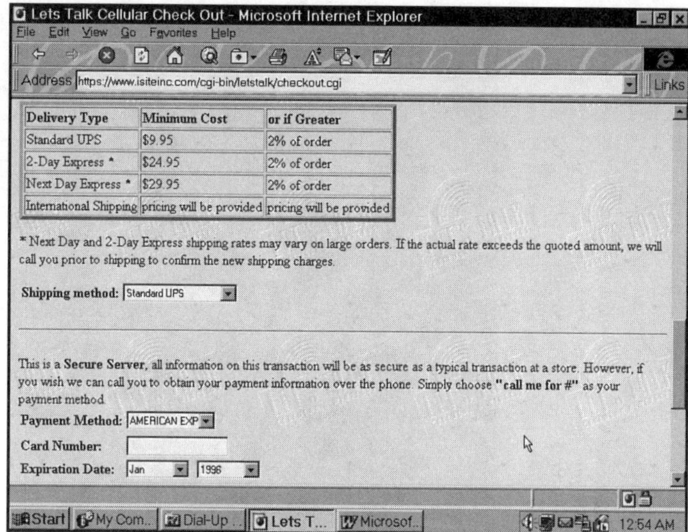


**Figure 19.8.**
*The Let's Talk shopping cart checkout pages are on a secure server to protect against credit card number theft.*

# Example 4: Steve Dahl & Company Catalog

**Document title:** Steve Dahl & Company Order Form (Figure 19.9)

**Document URL:** `http://www.dahl.com/order6.html`

**Description:** Steve Dahl is a Chicago radio personality and legend who offers for sale on the Web a variety of products including videos, tapes, CDs, and T-shirts. Users cannot only listen to his program using RealAudio, they can order his products through his Web pages as well, with a variety of payment options available.

**Techniques and designs applied:**

**Order Form Download.** (See Chapter 15.) Users are given many online and offline procedures for ordering merchandise from the Dahl site, as you can see from Figure 19.9. One of the most popular methods is to have users print out the page, fill in the blanks, and submit it via fax.

**Phone Orders.** (See Chapter 15.) Another simple but effective method is to simply provide a phone number (preferably toll-free) through which users can order merchandise after looking at your products on the Web.

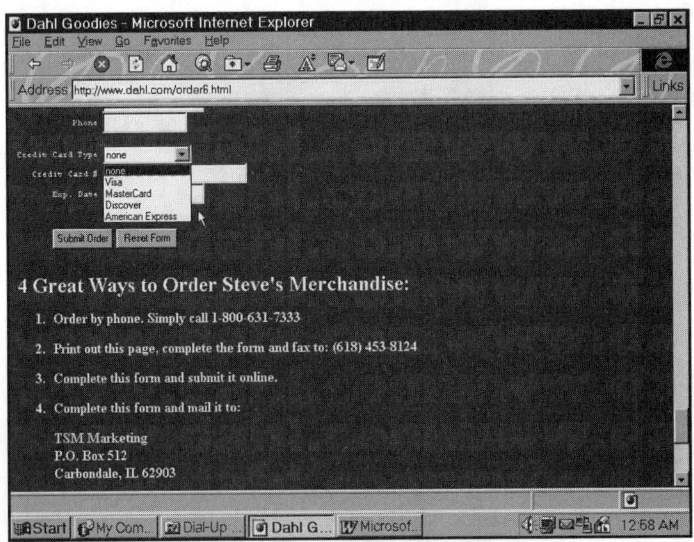


**Figure 19.9.**
*The Dahl site offers many online and offline ordering options.*

# Example 5: NetBeat Catalog

**Document title:** NetBeat Catalog and Order Form (Figures 19.10 and 19.11)

**Document URL:** `http://www.netbeat.com/`

**Description:** NetBeat is a hip online music store that sells and samples music online to people around the world. The company's Web catalog uses advanced multimedia and ordering technologies to make online buying as similar to a music store experience as possible, but without the drive to the store.

**Techniques and designs applied:**

> **Multimedia.** (See Chapter 13.) As you can see from Figure 19.10, NetBeat makes extensive use of RealAudio to enable users to sample different tracks from its inventory of albums online. RealAudio is particularly suitable for this task because it provides music virtually on demand with little or no waiting for downloading.
>
> **Ecash.** (See Chapter 15.) NetBeat also was one of the pioneering Web sites to accept ecash for products online, as shown in Figure 19.11. Ecash provides for secure anonymous transactions so that users can purchase ABBA CDs from NetBeat without fear of reprisals.

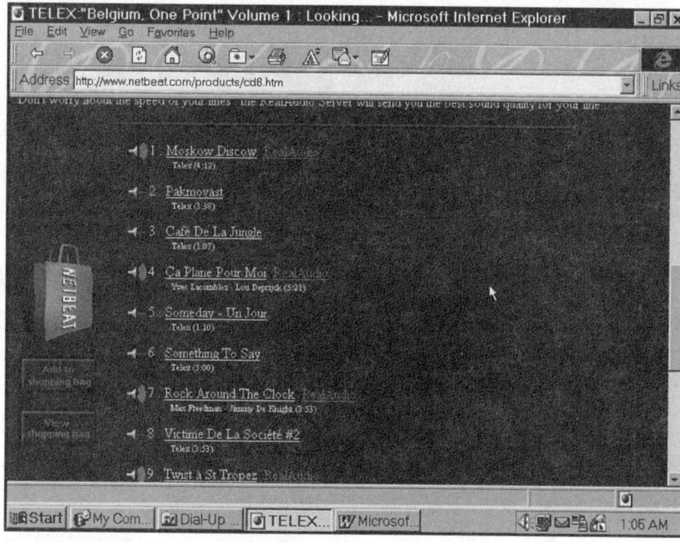


**Figure 19.10.**
*RealAudio is a natural match for online catalogs that sell music.*

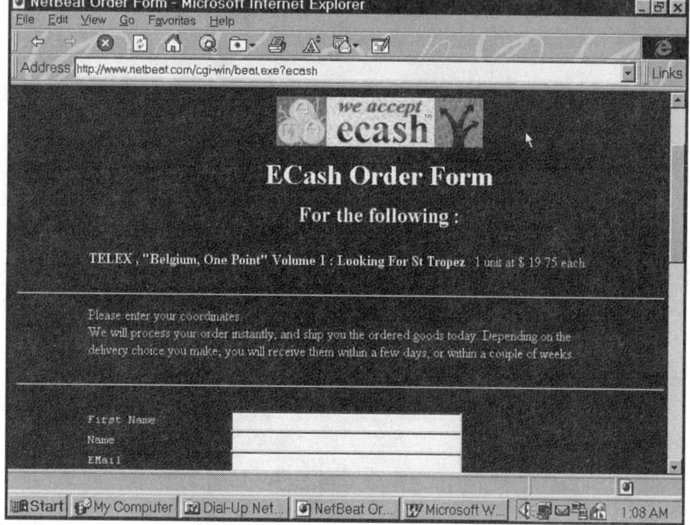


**Figure 19.11.**
*NetBeat accepts ecash so that purchasing music online is as secure and anonymous as doing it in person.*

# Example 6: SportsLine

**Document title:** SportsLine (Figure 19.12)

**Document URL:** `http://www.sportsline.com/`

**Description:** SportsLine is one of the most popular and comprehensive sports sites on the Web, subscription or otherwise. SportsLine provides a basic set of sports services to all Web surfers, with heightened access and privileges to those who pay a monthly fee and subscribe to the service.

**Techniques and designs applied:**

**Giving Content Away.** (See Chapter 16, "Providing Content for a Price on the Web.") What better way to draw people into your Web site than to give away valuable content for free? SportsLine does just that by providing a substantial amount of sports news and information without the need for a subscription, as shown in Figure 19.12.

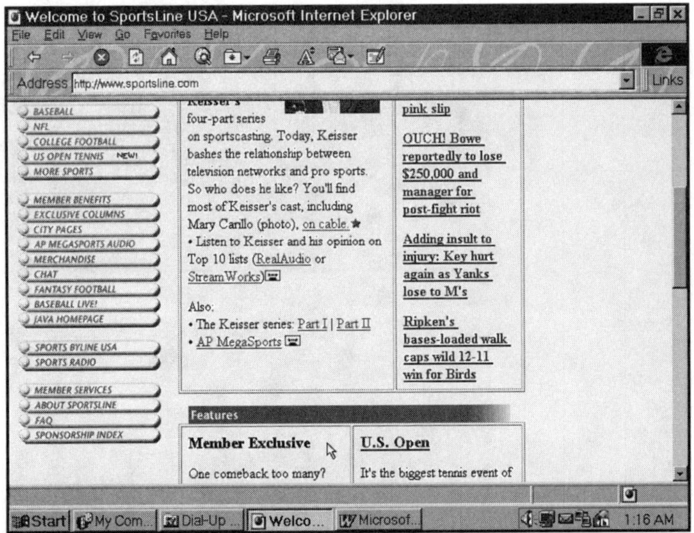


**Figure 19.12.**
*The SportsLine site provides many resources that lure prospective subscribers to its site.*

**Free Trials.** (See Chapter 16.) SportsLine also effectively uses a two-week trial period that enables potential subscribers to sample the benefits of a monthly membership to the service.

# Example 7: Commonwealth Network Site

**Document title:** The 3D Gaming Scene (Figure 19.13)

**Document URL:** `http://commonwealth.riddler.com/`

**Description:** The 3D Gaming Scene is just one of the many content sites that generates revenue by being a member of the Commonwealth Network, an advertising co-op. The site provides information on Doom-like games and is able to generate revenues by displaying ads provided by the Network.

### Techniques and designs applied:

**Using Advertisement HTML Code.** (See Chapter 17, "Setting Up Advertising-Supported Web Sites.") The ad at the top of the page for the site, shown in Figure 19.13, was provided by Commonwealth and involves a simple cutting and pasting of the appropriate HTML code into your pages.

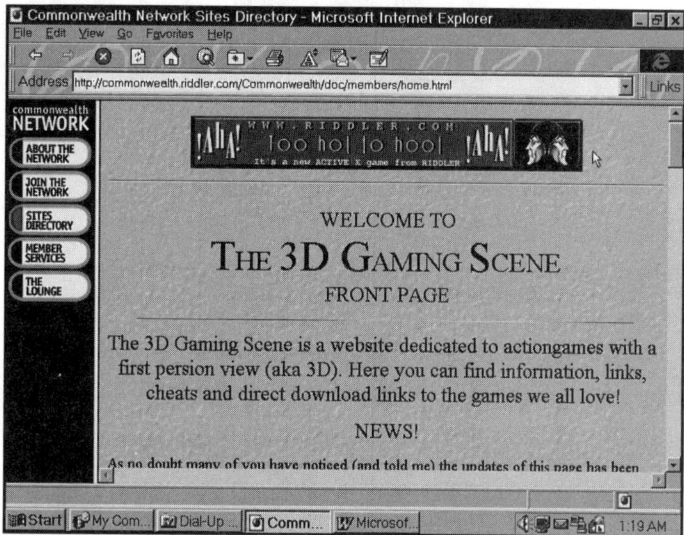


**Figure 19.13.**
*The HTML code that presents the banner ad at the top of the page can be implemented with a simple cut and paste operation.*

# Example 8: Package Tracking Services

**Document title:** FedEx and UPS Tracking Pages (Figures 19.14 and 19.15)

**Document URLs:** `http://www.fedex.com/track_it.html`, `http://www.ups.com/tracking/tracking.html`, and `http://www.starco.com`

**Description:** The two major package shipping services, FedEx and UPS, have excellent Web sites that enable you to track precisely any packages sent through their systems. You can link to or integrate these package tracking technologies into your own pages to further serve your customers.

### Techniques and designs applied:

**Shipment Tracking Options.** (See Chapter 18, "Order and Shipment Tracking on the Web.") Customers will probably find no service more useful than package tracking after they've ordered from you. As you can see in Figures 19.14 and 19.15, both FedEx and UPS provide an excellent means for tracking packages in their systems. Figure 19.16 shows how you can implement these tracking services within your own pages by simply cutting and pasting the appropriate form submission code.

**Figure 19.14.**
*The FedEx package tracking page.*

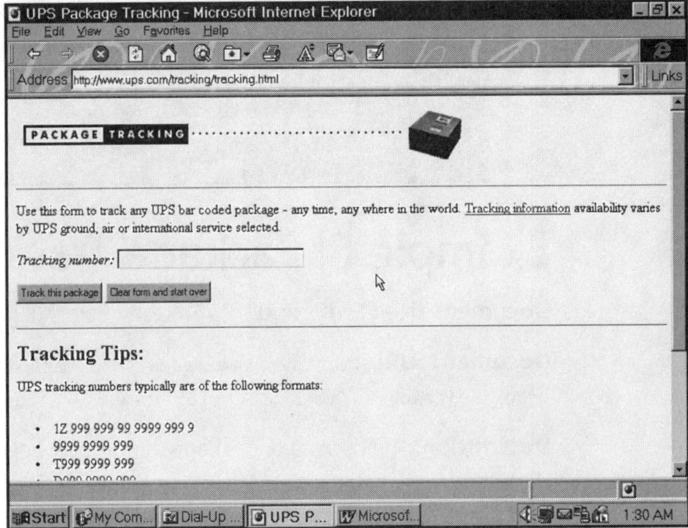


**Figure 19.15.**
*The UPS package tracking page.*

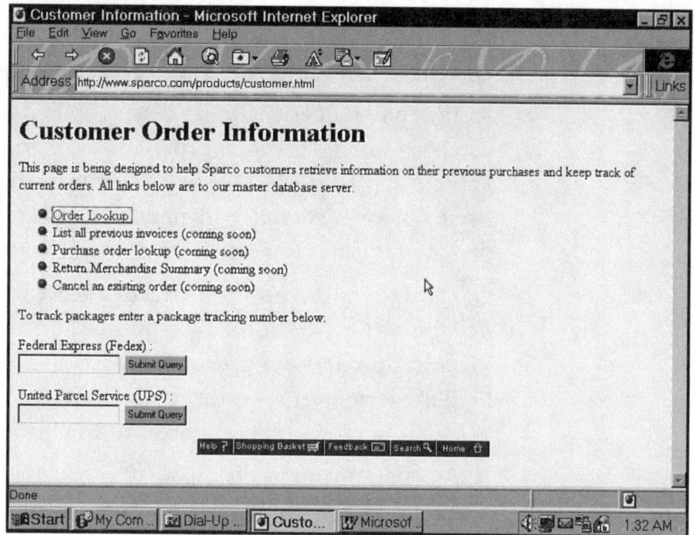


**Figure 19.16.**
*Integrating both FedEx and UPS package tracking services into your pages is extremely simple and useful.*

# Workshop Wrap-Up

Complicated commercial Web pages are becoming fairly commonplace. You'll need to keep on top of what other businesses are doing on the Net and how they're using the Web to get their message across. The examples in this chapter are a fine starting point for seeing how advanced elements can be used in a commercial Web page, but this is just scratching the surface. The Web is filled with excellent learning tools for Web design: other sites. Keep a careful lookout for pages that catch your interest and analyze why they made you stop and look. Chances are you can easily figure out some elements they used in creating their pages that you can use in your own page design.

## Next Steps

Now...

- In the next section, you'll see how to market and administer your Web site.
- If you want to see more real-life examples, you can turn to either Chapter 7, "Real-Life Examples: Putting the Basics Together," Chapter 12, "Real-Life Examples: Advancing Your Site, or Chapter 22, "Real-Life Examples: Touting and Managing Your Site," all of which contain more real examples for each section of the book.

# Q&A

**Q: Where can I find the code for these pages?**

**A:** The code for each of these pages can be found at the URL provided. All you need to do is use your browser's View Source command to pull up the appropriate HTML code for any Web page. Then you can copy the code and begin to work with it and identify more precisely how particular elements or designs were implemented on a page you found impressive.

**Q: I would like to add the UPS or FedEx tracking code to my site, but I don't want my customers to get lost once they enter their tracking information and are presented with a results page on either UPS's or FedEx's server with no direct link back to my site (other than the back button); is there any way around this problem?**

**A:** A good solution to this frequent problem is to set up a page with several frames and place the snippet of code that feeds into the package tracking service in its own separate frame. Then, when customers enter their information to track a UPS or FedEx package, their results will show up in the frame created for this purpose, and they'll still have access to other direct links on your site.

# PART V

# Putting It All Together


**Chapter 20** Marketing Your Web Pages

**21** Web Site Administration and Management

**22** Real-Life Examples: Touting and Managing Your Site

# CHAPTER TWENTY

# Marketing Your Web Pages

## In this chapter, you

- ❑ Learn about Netiquette for marketing
- ❑ Learn how to promote your Web page on Usenet
- ❑ Submit your Web page to indexes such as Yahoo!
- ❑ Make your Web page "search friendly"
- ❑ Start to generate links to your Web pages
- ❑ Use offline methods for online results
- ❑ Get media exposure for your site

## Tasks in this chapter:

- ❑ Getting Listed On Yahoo!
- ❑ Using Submit It!
- ❑ Create a Spider Web Page To Improve Search Results

If a Web page is put up and made available, but no users point their browsers to it, is it still a Web page or just a file on a computer somewhere?

Many people, including me, will tell you that the easiest thing about setting up a Web page is the actual task of designing the page and writing the necessary HTML code. The hardest part is getting at least some of the millions of Web surfers out there to point their browsers to your page and look at your slick, informative, interactive presentation. When you're dealing with commercial Web pages, this task can be especially difficult.

The Internet used to be a much more hostile place for commercial entities and interests than it is today. At one time, commercial use of the Internet and the Web was restricted by the National Science Foundation, which at that time provided significant support for the operation of the Internet's network infrastructure. As this book should make clear, however, such restrictions on commercial use of the Net are no more. However, you should bear in mind that many of your customers (and potential customers) might still be members of the old school in much the same way diehard baseball fans wince when they see a designated hitter come up to bat. As long as you keep that in mind while you market your site, you should be able to attract users to your site without stepping on any toes or making a *faux pas* that will hold your company (and you) up to ridicule and criticism.

This chapter shows you how to avoid the pitfalls of getting out the word about a commercial site on the Web. You'll walk through, step by step, how to go about making people aware that your Web page is up and where it's at and then getting those log files to start growing.

# Netiquette: Know It Now or Know It Later

If you were to open a McDonald's in an architecturally sensitive area such as Williamsburg, it is likely that you would receive a lot of resistance from locals who weren't exactly thrilled about having you as a new neighbor. If you were to add to that a plan to put up big billboards everywhere touting the new golden arches franchise, you would surely raise their ire even more.

In this situation, a prudent business person would take strides to ensure that the McDonald's was designed from an architectural standpoint to fit into its surroundings and to blend with the historical setting. Then he would be certain that his advertising worked in conjunction with this theme of assimilation in order to minimize the impact on the community and, more important, any potential negative publicity for the new venture.

When you set out to market and advertise your Web site, you should keep this example very much in the front of your mind. Make no mistake, you are setting up a business in a very real sense in a "community," even though it is an online one. Your attempts to market and advertise in this community are subject to the same kind of aesthetic and social considerations that come into play in any real neighborhood or community. If you get to know your new "neighbors," you'll have a better idea for what is and is not acceptable and what will be well received in your attempts to draw visitors to your Web pages.

The collective of neighborhood rules that are applicable to online behavior have become known as "netiquette." Netiquette once learned is never forgotten. You will find it well worth your time to learn as much information as you reasonably can digest. You'll find most of the generally accepted "rules" that have been accepted as a part of netiquette stem almost entirely from common sense and consideration. An investment in learning netiquette can be as good a one as you can make for your marketing endeavor.

**TIP:** There's probably no better way to learn what to avoid in marketing your Web pages than to look at others' mistakes. A Blacklist of Internet Advertisers who have committed a major *faux pas* on the Internet is maintained at `http://www.cco.caltech.edu/~cbrown/BL/`. The Blacklist, as shown in Figure 20.1, provides some useful real-world examples of how not to go about marketing on the Internet.

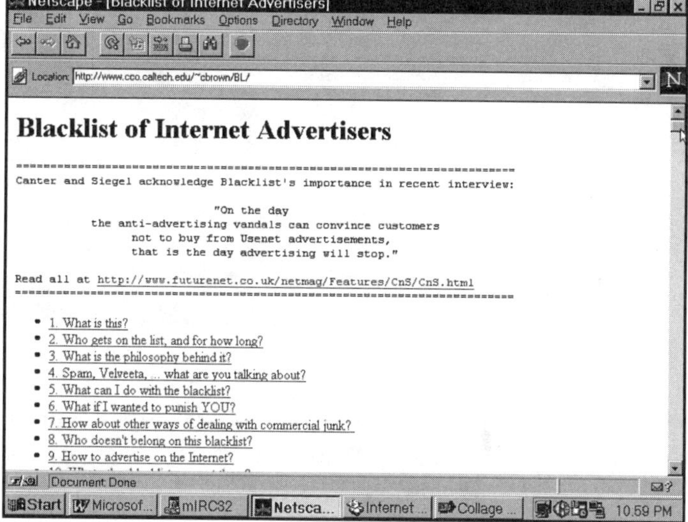


**Figure 20.1.**
*The Blacklist of Internet Advertisers can be used as a valuable lesson of what not to do on the net.*

## Where To Find the Online Rules of the Road

The most important piece of netiquette I can give you is to avoid any references or analogies to the "information superhighway." Having just violated that rule, I will give you some pointers to more detailed background that you should look at before undertaking any serious marketing campaign for your Web site.

Obviously, the best resources available for learning netiquette are on the Web. Throughout this chapter, you learn some of the major rules you need to be sure to follow, but a detailed exploration of the topic is beyond the scope of this book.

## The Netiquette Home Page

You can find the Netiquette Home Page, shown in Figure 20.2, at

```
http://www.fau.edu/rinaldi/netiquette.html
```

It gives you a good general background on a variety of netiquette subjects broken down into categories relating to the particular application.

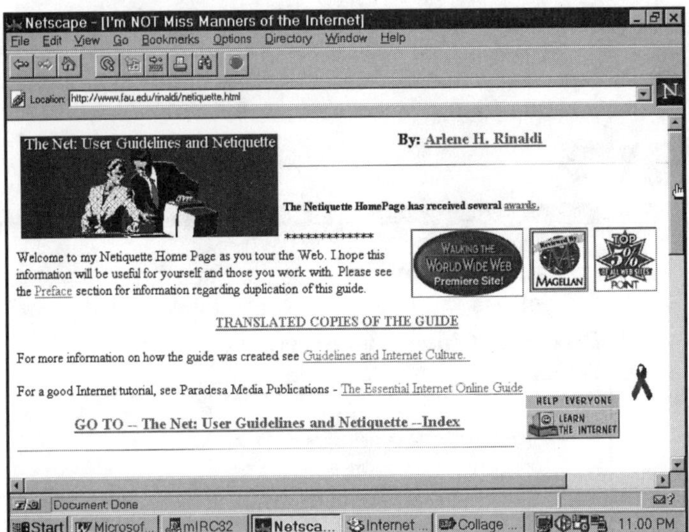


**Figure 20.2.**
*The Netiquette Home Page can be the ultimate flame retardant.*

The information you find on this page is probably broader than what is absolutely necessary for you to know in this area. A good starting point is to look at the discussion groups and World Wide Web subheadings to review guidelines that will be helpful as you start to use the techniques that follow in this chapter to make your Web pages pervasive on the Net.

### The Internet Marketing Resource

The Internet Marketing Resource is an excellent reference for online marketing. It provides a more targeted set of netiquette aimed at users like you who intend to use the Internet for commercial purposes to further the goals of their businesses. The site also provides some excellent pointers for maintaining your company's Internet image.

The netiquette portion of the Internet Marketing Resource is located at

```
http://edie.cprost.sfu.ca/~sigma6/image/netiquette/netiquette.html
```

You'll find not only general background on netiquette in commercial contexts, but there are also specific examples of how companies follow and breach netiquette and the resulting consequences of each example.

### *Web Workshop*: Creating Commercial Pages Online

As with the rest of this book, be sure to take a look at the latest resources available online at the Web pages dedicated to *Laura Lemay's Web Workshop: Creating Commercial Web Pages* at

```
http://www.murphnet.com
```

You will be able to find links to the sites discussed here, as well as other Web pages dealing with the topic of netiquette and the marketing of Web pages.

## Putting Your Page on a Web Index

The Web is filled with literally millions of pages. Many Web index sites have sprung up to help users deal with this information overload so that, at any time, they can find the sites they want to find. These indexing sites, like the popular Yahoo! site, are vital to your efforts to market your Web page and to attract Web surfers. Failing to have your Web page listed with at least some of the many Web indices is the equivalent of your business having an unlisted phone number.

There are two basic types of Web index pages that are important to know from a marketing perspective. There are sites like Yahoo!, shown in Figure 20.3, that break down Web pages into a topical hierarchical array that enables users to drill down through menu selections to find Web pages relating to a particular topic. On Yahoo!, a user looking for a place to buy records online can select Entertainment, then Music, then Companies, then CDs, Records, and Tapes, and be presented with a list of links to stores online that sell records.

The other major type of Web index page uses Web searching (called a *spider*) to generate an index of all the pages on the Internet. Such pages, like AltaVista, will find your site even if you fail to make any efforts to have it listed with its service. The downside to this is that although these search engines are more powerful than the hierarchical indexes, they can make it more difficult for users to find your particular pages through other Web noise.

For example, a search of AltaVista (shown in Figure 20.4) for records will yield 500,000 (yes, that's half a million) results with varying topics from computers to sports to video production to music. If you own a used record store, potential customers are much more likely to locate you out of the blue by accessing a topical index like Yahoo!. However, I'll show you some tricks to grab Web surfers who use even these search engines so that your site appears near the top of their search result pile.

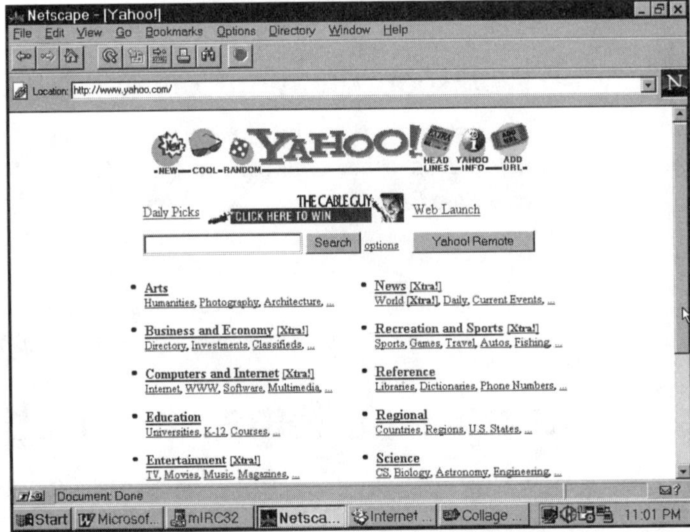


**Figure 20.3.**
*Yahoo! is a popular Web index that breaks pages down into easily navigable categories.*

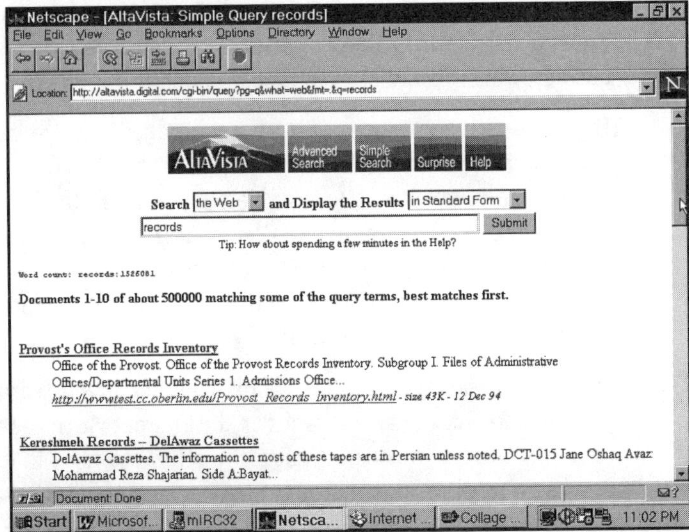


**Figure 20.4.**
*A search for "records" yielded this result on AltaVista.*

# Getting Listed on Yahoo!

The most important thing you must do after you complete your Web page is to make sure it is listed on Yahoo!, the most popular topical index of Web sites on the Net. Even if you do nothing else to market your Web page, this is the one simple task that must be completed and will at least make your Web site visible for those people who will be looking for you or a business in your particular specialty.

Yahoo! makes getting listed on its service as painless (and free) as possible. There are two easy ways to add your Web page to the index at Yahoo!

1. Select the Add URL icon at the top of the main page at `http://www.yahoo.com`.
2. Go directly to the URL submission form at `http://add.yahoo.com/bin/add?`.

As shown in Figure 20.5, filling out the form for Yahoo! is fairly simple and self-explanatory, but you will need to make sure that you know exactly under which categories you want your Web page to be listed. The best way is to explore the categories on Yahoo! and see what fits your business or the Web pages you're setting up. Another good place to start is by finding where your competitors, if any, have their pages listed under Yahoo!.

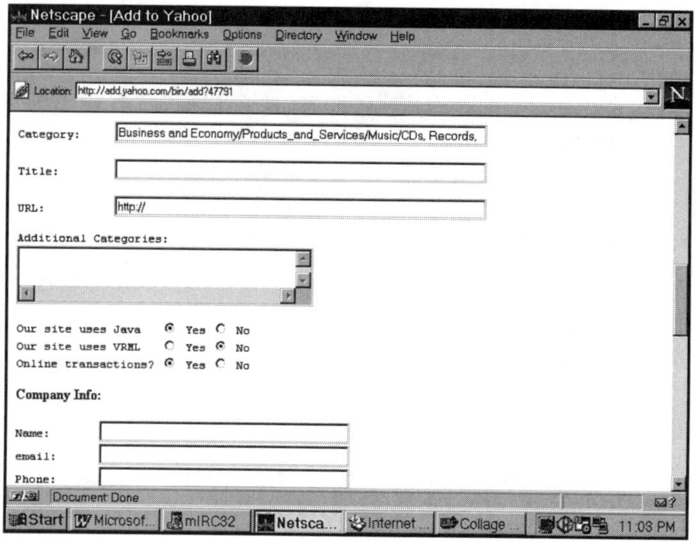

**Figure 20.5.**
*The Add URL submission form at Yahoo! is the easiest and most important marketing step you can take for your Web page.*

## Picking Your Categories

I'll be using the Old Dog Used Records example that we have talked about on many occasions in the previous chapters to show you how to fill out and submit a Web listing to Yahoo!.

**TIP:** If you explore the categories on Yahoo! and come across one that you find well suited to your Web page, simply click the Add URL icon on the menu bar at the top of the page, and Yahoo! will bring up a submission form with that category already filled in. Simply fill in the rest of the form and you're finished.

Also note that when you select the Add URL icon under a commercially related topic, you will be presented with the opportunity to enter much more detailed information about your company (including whether you offer online transactions) than with the standard Add URL form.

All commercial Web sites listed on Yahoo! must be placed in a Business and Economy subcategory, under either "Companies" or "Products and Services." Old Dog Used Records' Web page is used to sell its products—used records, tapes, and CDs—so fill in the main category as Business and Economy/Products and Services/Music/CDs, Records, and Tapes.

Yahoo! requires that all commercial or business Web page additions be limited to two categories, so you need to be selective with your next choice. At this point, I think about where my customers would be looking to find a site like mine. Usually this means working back from the end product or service that your business offers. In the case of Old Dog Used Records, it's records, tapes, and CDs.

I realize most Web surfers who will be interested in Old Dog's products will be looking for them under a Music-related category. If you search through Yahoo! under Entertainment, you can find the perfect match: Entertainment/Music/Companies/CDs, Records and Tapes. Add this to the Additional Categories portion of the form.

## Adding Title, Descriptions, and More

You also need to enter some basic information about your site so that Yahoo! can show its users a brief synopsis of your Web page.

1. First, fill in the title and use this as an opportunity to give your company name and the unique name of your Web site, if applicable. Fill in here "Old Dog Used Records—The Dawg House" to identify the store's Web page.

2. Next, add the all-important URL for Old Dog's Web page: `http://www.murphnet.com/bowwow`. Also, select the available options to indicate that this page uses Java and can use online transactions, thanks to the help of this book.
3. Finally, fill in all the important company and contact information and turn your attention to the final and extremely important step, filling out the brief description of the site.

Yahoo! asks that you submit a two-sentence description of your page sans marketing hype. You need to be as creative as you can to get as close to the "hype" line as you can without stepping over it. For Old Dog I wrote the following description for Yahoo!:

> *An online resource for buying, selling, and trading used CDs, vinyl, 8-tracks, whatever. We recycle music to avoid the trash.*

I think this will get across the point succinctly that this is a fun, laid-back site that should attract a customer base that's interested in buying used CDs. It's marketing, just without the hype.

## Using Submit It!

The best way to make sure that you take full advantage of the many indexes that are available on the Web is to visit each of them and fill out separate submission forms, tailoring your submission for each particular service. However, if you're in a hurry to get word of your Web page out there and would like an all-in-one efficient way to get it added to a lot of sites very quickly, you should use Submit It!, a free Web site submission service available at

`http://www.submit-it.com`

**NOTE:** Entering information for purposes of Submit It! is very similar to the process you use to submit a site to Yahoo!. The major difference is that although Submit It! enables you to reach more indices, it is somewhat limited in the degree of specificity that can be used for each of them. To make maximum use of the submission options of each index you'll need to visit their pages and do a submission directly.

Submit It! enables you to enter all the basic information about your Web page for submission to all the following Web indexing services:

- Yahoo (http://www.yahoo.com)
- Open Text (`http://www.opentext.com`)

- ❑ Infoseek Guide (`http://www.infoseek.com`)
- ❑ AltaVista (`http://www.altavista.com`)
- ❑ Lycos (`http://www.lycos.com`)
- ❑ WebCrawler (`http://www.Webcrawler.com`)
- ❑ New Rider's WWW Yellow Pages (`http://www.mcp.com/submit.html`)
- ❑ Apollo (`http://apollo.co.uk`)
- ❑ Starting Point (`http://www.stpt.com`)
- ❑ ComFind (`http://www.comfind.com`)
- ❑ BizWiz (`http://www.bizwiz.com`)
- ❑ Galaxy (`http://galaxy.einet.net`)
- ❑ What's New Too! (`http://newtoo.manifest.com`)
- ❑ METROSCOPE (`http://isotropic.com`)
- ❑ LinkStar (`http://www.linkstar.com`)
- ❑ Nerd World Media (`http://www.nerworld.com`)
- ❑ Mallpark (`http://www.mallpark.com`)

At the Submit It! site, you fill out the general information about your Web page—title, description, contact name, and so on. Then you move on to the submitting area, shown in Figure 20.6, where you can select to which of the Web services you want your site added. You can tailor your submission somewhat for each service.

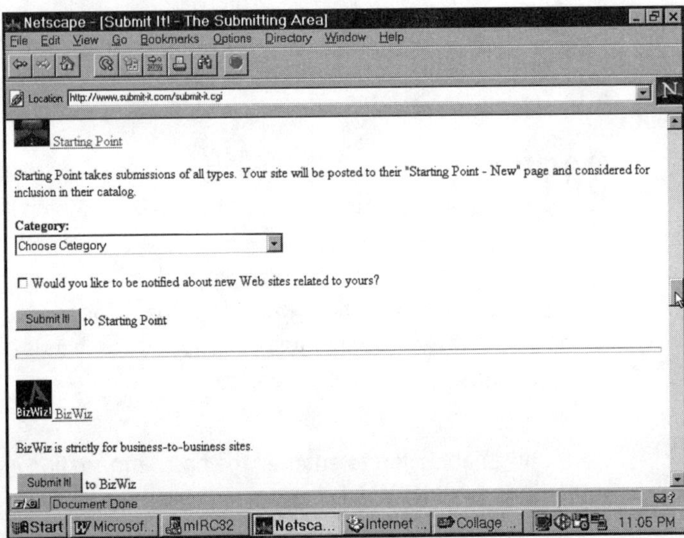


**Figure 20.6.**
*Submit It! enables you to choose which of the many services you want to submit your Web page to for indexing.*

The Submit It! site is extremely easy to use and has links to many commercial Web announcement and advertising services that can be used for greater exposure for your pages. It's definitely an excellent and broad springboard to get the word about your Web page out to as broad an audience as possible as quickly as possible.

# Making Your Commercial Web Pages "Search Friendly"

When you ran the sample search for `records` earlier in this chapter using AltaVista, the top result shown in Figure 20.4 was the Provost's office at Oberlin College. Internet search engines are powerful and useful, but sometimes they are not as helpful as they could be for Web surfers. Sometimes, you need to play a type of online shell game to make sure your site ends up at the top of every search result that your customers and potential customers run when they are looking for products in your area of expertise.

Web spiders such as AltaVista (`http://altavista.digital.com`), Lycos (`http://www.lycos.com`), WebCrawler (`http://www.Webcrawler.com`), and HotBot (`http://www.hotbot.com`) constantly search the Internet for Web pages and create indexes of the words that are contained on each page. Search results will generally be ranked according to those sites that have the most significant correlation to the words searched for by the end user. As a result, a site that has the word `records` on its page 10 times will be at the top of a search result list while a page with the word `records` on it only once will appear at the bottom of the list.

## Determine the "Key Words" for Your Page

The first step in making your commercial Web page "search friendly" is to determine what types of key words or phrases describe your site, your business, and your products. The goal here is to develop a list of about 20 to 30 words that you think most people might use when they are looking for a site like yours.

Create a master list of key words that you think best describe your site or describes the types of things for which your customers might be looking on the Web. The next step is to take this list and make it part of what I'll call a "spider Web page" so that you will be sure to capture all those Web search engines and convince them to put your site near the top of every list involving a search for your key words.

# Create a Spider Web Page To Improve Search Results

The first thing you need to do in creating a spider Web page is to create a separate Web page on your site for this task. For this example, I create a new Web document using HotDog called `spiders.html`, as shown in Figure 20.7. I'll be storing it in my root directory where the rest of the Old Dog Records Web pages are at `http://www.murphnet.com/bowwow`.

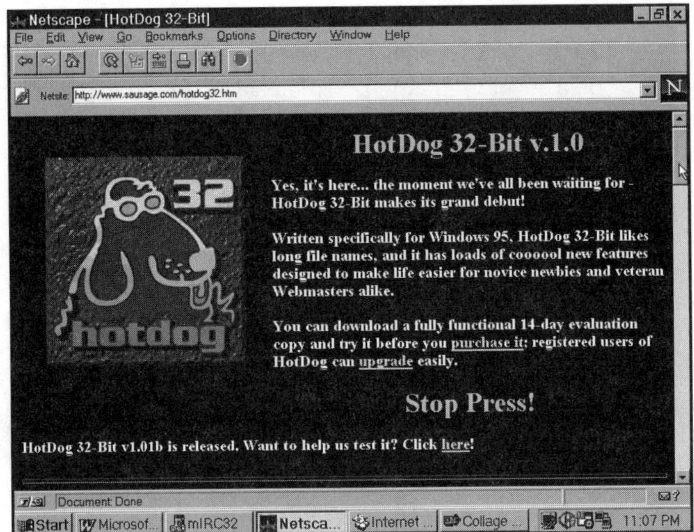


**Figure 20.7.**
*Use the HotDog Web editor included on the CD-ROM to create a page to help the Web search engines find your pages.*

At the top of the `spiders.html` page, place a link to Old Dog's main "The Dawg House" Web page and a small blurb about what the site is about and what users can find there. You want to make sure you design the top of this Web page so that it is readily obvious to Web surfers what its real intent is—to make it search friendly—so you should try to design it to look like a sort of front door entrance to your pages. For example, include a nice graphic of your logo and take the time to format the text using text elements that are centered and bold where appropriate.

You should then place your keyword list at the bottom of the Web page. Next, you can use the Copy and Paste commands to rapidly replicate your keyword list over and over. The ultimate goal is to have about 30 to 40 instances of each of your keywords appear on this spider Web page. When the Web spiders search the Internet for Web pages they will see all your keywords, and your chances of being near the top of a search result when a user searches for any of those words will be greatly enhanced.

The final trick in putting this spider Web page together is to make all your keywords "invisible" to the casual Web surfer, who might be confused by the purpose of the repetitive terms at the bottom of the page. In order to hide this text from the viewer (but not the search engines), use a solid color background and then format all of the text containing the keywords to be the same color. You can use HotDog, on the accompanying CD-ROM, to do this task. Simply use the Font selection under the Format menu and then check the font color box and select a match. Figure 20.8 shows the Old Dog Used Records' `spiders.html` with invisible search words.

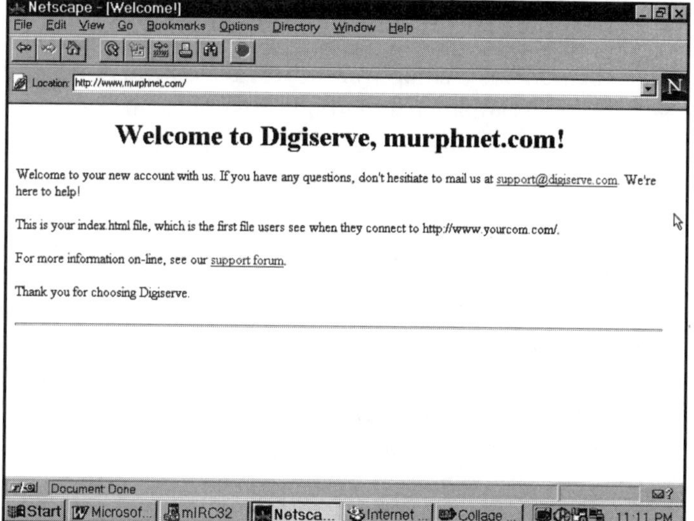


**Figure 20.8.**
*The search words are embedded in this page so that the user can't see them, but the search engines can.*

A sample template for a Web spider page that you can easily adopt for your purposes is available on the CD-ROM, and you can check out an online example of how a page like this works at the Website companion to this book, *Web Workshop: Creating Commercial Pages Online*, at `http://www.murphnet.com`.

# Spreading the Word Via Usenet

The audience for your Web page is primarily going to already be online and using the Internet. There are important tools beyond the Web that will enable you to effectively market your new Web page and to draw users to your site. One of the best of these potential tools is Usenet, the compendium of thousands of newsgroups on various topics. However, before you go using one of the newsreaders included on the CD-ROM to spam every available newsgroup, you need to be sure you understand what is and what is not a proper way to announce your pages to the Usenet world.

## Avoid the Flames

Before you post anything that could be perceived to be of a commercial nature to a Usenet newsgroup, be sure you locate and read the newsgroup's charter or FAQ. A polite posting requesting this information would probably be the best way to locate it quickly. Many, if not most, newsgroups prohibit unsolicited explicit commercial advertisements. Even a gentle reminder that you just started up a Web page for your company would violate these rules and subject you to serious roasting by the many flame throwers out there.

## Post Where You're Welcome

There are some groups in which announcements about new commercial Web pages are entirely appropriate and indeed encouraged. For example, `alt.biz` and the entire `biz.*` series of newsgroups are dedicated to discussions of commercial enterprises and won't object to the posting of an announcement regarding your new Web page.

## Helping Others Can Help Yourself

Many newsgroups that ban unsolicited advertising will tolerate commercial references where they come in response to a question or a query from a user. For example, it would be entirely appropriate to respond to a question about locating a rare Abba album from the 1970s by pointing out that the album is available from Old Dog Used Records at `http://www.murphnet.com/bowwow`.

You can also help draw users to your Web site by becoming (and encouraging your employees to become) an active participant and close follower of newsgroups that closely relate to the subject of your business and that might be of interest to your customers and potential customers. Such involvement can give you credibility far beyond any spamming of every newsgroup with a brash advertisement and will undoubtedly yield better results.

### Using Your Signature as a Web Page Ad

Another benefit of participating in Usenet newsgroups from a Web page marketing perspective is that you can plug your Web page via what is called your *signature* or *sig*. Signatures are customary on Usenet, and standard practice allows business plugs similar to what you would find on a business card. Most sigs take up a maximum of four lines and can include your name, your URL, and a brief description of your business or profession. Newsreader software, such as News Xpress, which is included on the CD-ROM, enables you to save your sig in a file and will append it to the bottom of every message you post to a newsgroup.

The sig can become a very helpful little billboard for your Web page. The following is an example of a sig I might use to promote the Old Dog Records example used extensively in this and other chapters:

> Brian K. Murphy
> Owner/Operator/Customer—Old Dog Used Records
> Visit "The Dawg House" at `http://www.murphnet.com/bowwow`
> You Can't Teach An Old Dog New Tracks

Now, every time I post a message to `rec.music.abba` I'll be able to draw visitors to my Web page without violating any of the prescribed rules for that newsgroup.

# Linking Your Pages

The Web was made popular in large part because of its capability to enable a user to traverse from one page to another to another while hopping all over the globe. Linking Web pages using HTML can help you make your site one click away from many other sites around the Web.

There are many approaches on how to go about getting people to link to your site. The best way is to simply produce an excellent set of Web pages that are exciting, informative, useful, or unique. Word of mouth and links spread quickly on the Net, and if you have a good site it is inevitable that fans of it will place links to it on their pages.

Another approach is to seek out Web pages that compile information relating to the business you're in or the products you sell and let them know about your page. Often, sites are established as a resource on a popular topic, and they welcome the chance to add another link so that they remain the comprehensive site in that area. You can also try to find Web pages of businesses that are related to yours and where linking to each others' sites can yield mutual benefits. McDonald's wouldn't put a link to Burger King on any of its pages, but it probably would put a link to Coca Cola or Disney. You might be able to trade links and build site exposure in this way.

## The Internet Link Exchange

Another alternative for trading links to Web pages has been established, and it's called the Internet Link Exchange at

`http://www.linkexchange.com`

The Internet Link Exchange is an innovative free service that is basically a cooperative of sites that have joined together and agreed that in return for placing an alternating ad banner on their pages, a banner ad touting their site will appear on other members' pages, as shown in Figure 20.9. The number of exposures your ad banner gets on other pages is directly proportional to the number of times your Web page is accessed and the ads on it are pulled up.

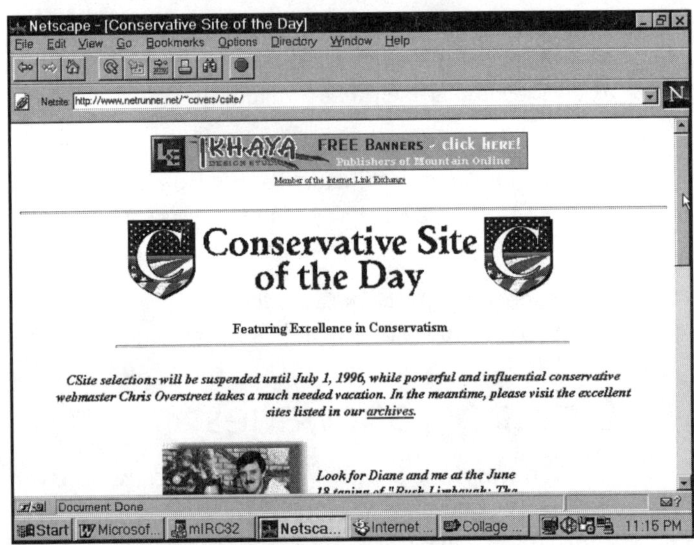


**Figure 20.9.**
*How a member of the Internet Link Exchange's Web page looks. An ad for their site will appear on other people's pages.*

The Internet Link Exchange is an excellent way to generate some initial traffic at no cost. The key is to design an effective banner ad, and there are links to many resources for that at the Internet Link Exchange, including many services that create banner ads free for Internet Exchange members, such as WebDesigns at

`http://www.execpc.com/Webdesigns/banners.html`

# Using Offline Techniques for Online Results

I knew the Web had become ubiquitous when I was driving by the mall the other day behind a delivery truck and on the back of the truck was the name of the company, its phone number, and its URL. Wherever you look today, you can see `http://` appearing everywhere, from television commercials to print ads to business cards.

You should embrace and integrate your Web page address into all your business and marketing activities. You should provide it in every medium at the same time and in the same way that you provide your phone and fax numbers. This means stationary, business cards, flyers, brochures, and yes, even delivery vehicles. You can be confident that the number of quizzical looks you will get regarding all those slashes and letters and dots will be minimal.

Another good idea is to mention your Web address on any voice recordings you have for playback either when callers are put on hold or when your voice mail or answering machine picks up after hours. Your Web page should be an asset not only to you, but to your customers, and you should take every opportunity to make them aware of it.

The possibilities for integrating your Web presence into your everyday activities are limited only by the nature of your business. Be creative, and look for new ways to get your www message across. Using the Old Dog Used Records example, you could add `http://www.murphnet.com/bowwow` to a sticker placed on every item in the store and also on the sales receipt given to the customers when they buy either at the store or through the mail (or the Web). The goal is to keep your Web page and your company in the front of your customers' minds as often as possible.

# Generating Media Exposure

The final, and probably most difficult, step is to try to generate some free publicity for your site by using traditional media outlets such as newspapers, television, and radio. Although the media is infatuated with the World Wide Web, grabbing media attention when it comes to new things on the Net is becoming more difficult.

A good starting point is local media outlets that, depending on the market, will be the most likely to do a story about your new Web pages. Make sure you have an angle on how to pitch it and what makes your Web page interesting for their readers or viewers.

Of course, many people involved with the popular media are online themselves and are accessible via e-mail. A comprehensive list of e-mail addresses for media contacts around the world is available at `http://www.ping.at/gugerell/media`, shown in Figure 20.10. If you're going to send unsolicited e-mail (a violation of netiquette that is somewhat more tolerable when you're dealing with the media) be sure to not simply spam the media list hoping anyone will do a story about your new commercial Web page for your cooking school. I guarantee that although *Gourmet* magazine might be interested in doing a story, *Car and Driver* and *Sports Illustrated* will simply be irritated.

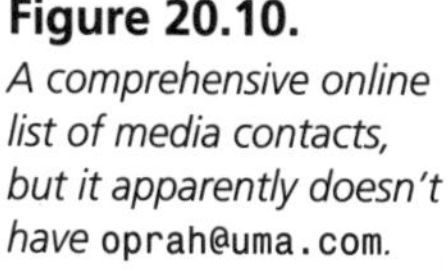

**Figure 20.10.**
*A comprehensive online list of media contacts, but it apparently doesn't have* `oprah@uma.com`.

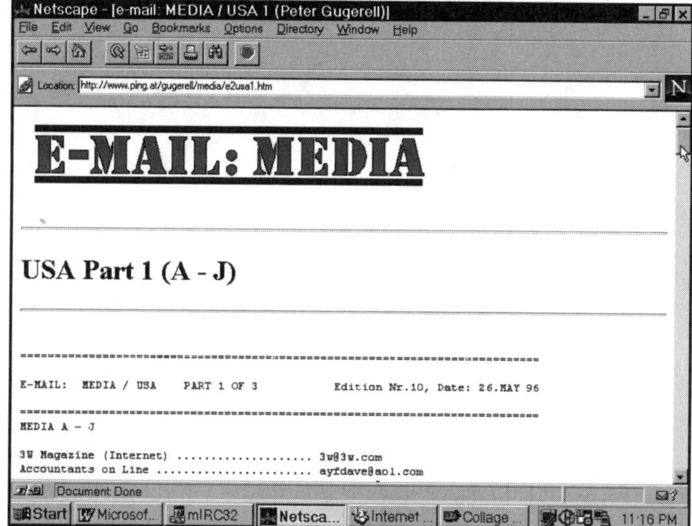

Don't be discouraged if you don't generate any media exposure right off the bat. It can take a while for your site to build in popularity, and at that point you can again try to get some good press for your pages.

# Workshop Wrap-Up

The two ingredients for successfully marketing a Web page are time and creativity. If you take the time to learn the techniques and areas you learned in this chapter and creatively apply the underlying concepts, you should have no problem generating traffic to your site almost immediately.

The Web is still a very young medium, so the rules of the game, particularly when it comes to marketing, are changing almost daily. On the Web, you can never be wed to the old familiar ways of doing business. You should always rely on your instinct when you are determining what might or might not be an acceptable marketing ploy to draw new users to your page.

I can't emphasize enough the importance of making sure that you have covered the basics. Get listed on Yahoo! and other Web indexes. Add your Web page address to your business cards and letterhead. Encourage your current customers to visit your page and to give you feedback about how to improve it.

## Next Steps

Now...

- In Chapter 21, "Web-Site Administration and Management," you learn how to manage your Web pages and to keep the content fresh and changing—the most important element to keep users coming back to your site after you've gotten them to take a first look using what you've learned in this chapter.
- Chapter 22, "Real-Life Examples: Touting and Managing Your Site," ties everything together with a look at some real-life examples of life after Web page creation—marketing and managing a Web site.

## Q&A

**Q: All these cost-cutting and guerrilla marketing techniques are fine, but my boss has given me a large budget to make this Web page fly and I want to get the word out at any price. Where should I go?**

**A:** Many places are ready, willing, and able to expose and link to your site all over their pages. Yahoo! runs a service called Web launch that will provide a great deal of exposure and tremendous initial traffic if you can afford the price of admission.

**Q: I don't really care about this netiquette stuff; I want everyone to know about my site. A guy sent me an offer for a software package that will enable me to send a million e-mail messages and post to ten thousand newsgroups with the push of a button. What's the worst thing that could happen—I get some flame mail in response?**

**A:** The worst thing that could happen is that your Internet service provider could shut down your Internet access and your Web page. Spamming is almost universally a violation of the terms of service you agreed to when you signed up for your Internet account, and providers won't hesitate to shut spammers down because it reflects badly on them as well as you. Good luck finding an account with someone else who will probably be personally aware of your disregard for netiquette by a message in his e-mail box or a post to his favorite newsgroup.

C H A P T E R

TWENTY-ONE

# Web Site Administration and Management

## In this chapter, you

- Set up and use Weblint to verify HTML code
- Use a Weblint gateway
- Use Doctor HTML to verify hyperlinks
- Organize your Web site for easier management
- Look at security considerations for Web site administration

## Tasks in this chapter:

- Using Weblint To Clean Your Pages
- Using a Weblint Gateway
- Organizing a Site

Imagine that you went out and bought a brand new cherry red Ferrari—and then never changed its oil. Your investment would quickly deteriorate and be wasted. Of course, that would never happen because you would take the time to care for and maintain the vehicle. Your Web pages require a high level of maintenance, administration, and management to prevent them from running out of gas and languishing on the Net.

The Ferrari would come with a handy owner's manual telling you to change the oil every 3,000 miles (and your gas probably every 30). Simply reading the manual and following its maintenance schedule should keep you out of trouble and keep your car on the road. Unfortunately, your Web pages don't come with an easy-to-follow owner's manual to guide you through this process. In many ways, you need to develop a manual and a plan for yourself. This chapter helps you develop that plan.

Your planning for site administration and management should be well underway even before you start creating your first page.

You might be amazed at how often people take the time, energy, and money to develop and create a Web page—or even an extensive Web site—and let the information or links become stale. Go to Yahoo! (`http://www.yahoo.com`) and click on some random links; I guarantee that it won't take you longer than five minutes to locate a site that hasn't been updated in months. If you had a television with 200,000 channels, would you watch the one playing reruns?

Entire books are written on Web site administration and management. The point of this chapter is to highlight some of the fundamentals that will preserve your time and financial investment in a commercial Web page. You'll see how to use some of the tricks and tools of the trade to make this process simpler and more effective.

A key to success is to make sure you devote sufficient resources, both in terms of people and finances, to the management of your pages.

# HTML Code and Link Verification

Nothing is more aggravating to users than to visit a site and find a broken image symbol, garbled layout or text, or possibly even a completely inaccessible page. Equally irritating can be hyperlinks that don't work when they are selected or that take you someplace unexpected. You shouldn't expect users to take the time to explore your pages if you don't take the time to make sure the pages work.

## HTML Verifiers

The simplest but probably most important of the tasks you need to conduct regularly in administering your pages is to verify the integrity of the HTML code for each page on your Web site. Although Netscape's Navigator and Microsoft's Internet Explorer are the dominant players on the Web, many other browser flavors are out there, and checking the integrity of your HTML code ensures that your document will function with anything a surfer can possibly use to view your pages.

**CAUTION:** It is vitally important to make sure that your page is compliant with HTML standards. Your page might appear to work properly with the latest version of Netscape, but it might contain code that causes ugly and problematic results in other browsers or even earlier or later versions of Netscape. Verifying that your pages are HTML compliant (regardless of version) opens up your potential Web viewing audience.

Of course, no one intentionally inserts non-conforming HTML code into his or her pages; it just happens sometimes. Sometimes, running a simple spell check reveals many of your coding problems, or the problems show up when you preview your page for the first time, as you can see in Figure 21.1. However, most Web designers and creators know that often you are made aware of a problem by a user who came across your page, couldn't make it work, and was kind enough to send an e-mail informing you that your page didn't work.

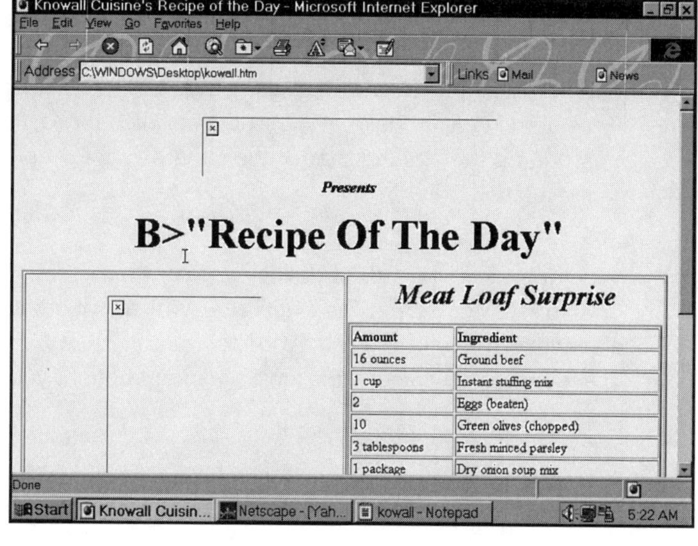


**Figure 21.1.**
*Incorrect HTML coding is readily apparent (and annoying) to many users.*

Non-compliant HTML code is an open invitation for flame-ready users to unload via e-mail. Think of HTML verification as a Web fire drill.

However, many options exist for nipping HTML coding problems in the bud. Let's take a look at some of the options you have available.

# Using Weblint To Clean Your Pages

Included on this book's CD-ROM is a very popular HTML validation program called Weblint. The Weblint program is actually a Perl script that you install on and run from your Web server. The Weblint program then generates a detailed listing of problems and potential problems with any Web page you specify.

Because of Weblint's popularity, you actually have two options for using the program: Either install and configure the script on your Web server, or simply use one of the many Weblint gateways on the Web to enter your URLs and have them checked for "lint." You'll see how you can use either of these methods. First, let's take a look at setting up Weblint on your own Web server.

## Setting Up Weblint on Your Server

You can find Weblint on the CD-ROM, and updated versions are available from `http://www.khoros.unm.edu/staff/neild/weblint`. Weblint is a Perl script and will work fine on your server as long as you have the appropriate Perl interpreter installed on your system. Most UNIX, NT, and OS/2 Web servers should have no problems working with this script.

**NOTE:** Don't be confused by the fact that Weblint is a Perl script but you don't need an HTML form to get it to run. Not all Perl scripts are necessarily to be used in the mode of a CGI script with Web forms. Perl scripts can simply be programs that are executed in the same way any simple DOS program can be executed.

Weblint is basically ready to go after you copy the necessary files from the CD-ROM drive to your Web server. The script comes with a configuration file that is ready to go, although you can customize it if you like. You configure Weblint in the `.weblintrc` file. The following are some of the most significant options you can configure in the file:

- `set message-style = lint`

  You can specify the style of the message warning that will be generated by Weblint. The options for this are `lint`, `short`, or `terse`.

- `extension Netscape`

  You can tell Weblint to recognize and accept advanced HTML tags that are specific to Netscape, Microsoft, or Java. To include all three, you simply change this to "extension Netscape, Microsoft, Java".

- `disable upper-case` and `enable obsolete`

  These options enable you to specify particular problem areas that you want Weblint to either pick up on or ignore. A complete list of the individual warnings that you can enable or disable is provided on the Weblint manual page at

  `http://www.khoros.unm.edu/ staff/neilb/weblint/manpage.html`

After you have copied Weblint to your Web server and you have your configuration settings to your liking, checking HTML code is fairly easy. Here is the syntax for executing Weblint from a typical UNIX prompt:

```
weblint [filename]
```

You can also add different command-line variables that will make the same types of changes or adjustments that you can generally find in your configuration file. For example, here's the command line you use to check a file called `index.html` and to show a short usage summary:

```
weblint index.html -U
```

If you don't want to go through the trouble of setting up and configuring Weblint on your server, you can always use one of the many Weblint gateways on the Web to check your pages for you.

# Using a Weblint Gateway

Many people have done you the valuable service of linking Weblint to simple Web-based interfaces that enable you to quickly and easily enter any URL on the Internet and have Weblint validate and generate a report, all in the context of a Web page.

One of the most comprehensive and easiest to use of these implementations is available from

```
http://www.fal.de/cgi-bin/WeblintGateway
```

As you can see in Figure 21.2, the gateway enables you to enter an URL and adjust all of the various options and warning messages that are available through Weblint.

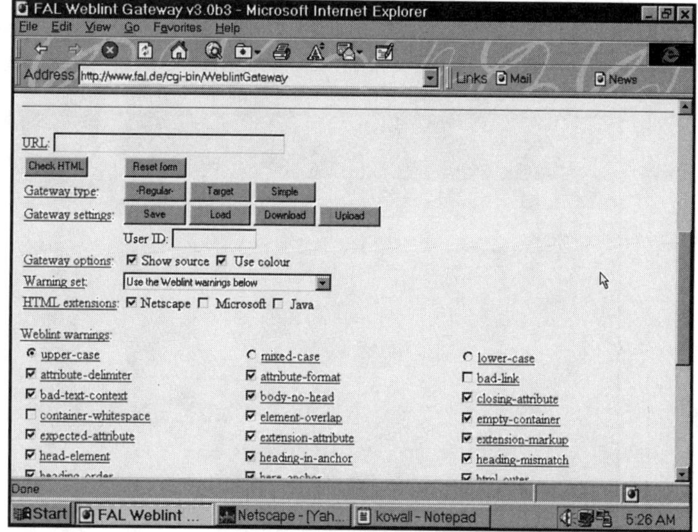


**Figure 21.2.**
*The Weblint Web gateway makes verifying HTML code even easier.*

**TIP:** Using a Weblint gateway enables you to more easily generate a hard-copy report of the problems with your pages. Simply use your browser's `Print` command when the results page is loaded.

After you enter the URL and make the appropriate selections, the Weblint gateway runs the HTML code through Weblint and then presents you with a Web-based report, as shown in Figure 21.3. To make this even more useful, each warning is tied to a specific line number within your HTML code. If you select the line number, which appears as a hyperlink, you are taken down the page to the color-coded source of the page with the appropriate Weblint warnings interspersed, as shown in Figure 21.4.

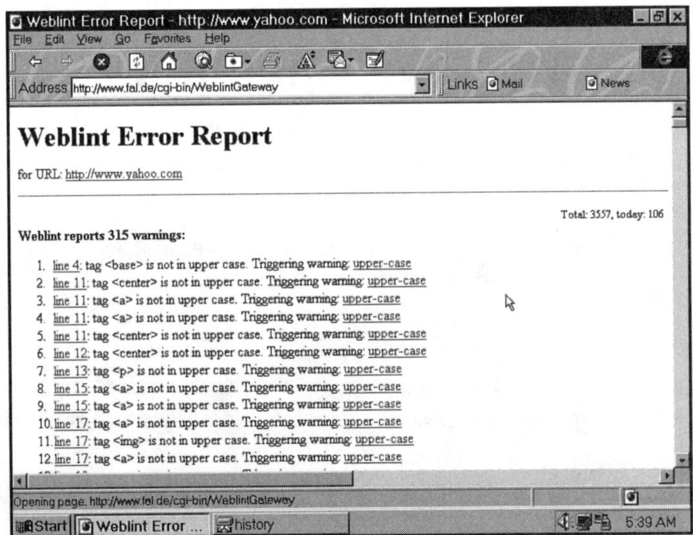


**Figure 21.3.**
*The Weblint report is brought up in your browser and can be printed immediately.*

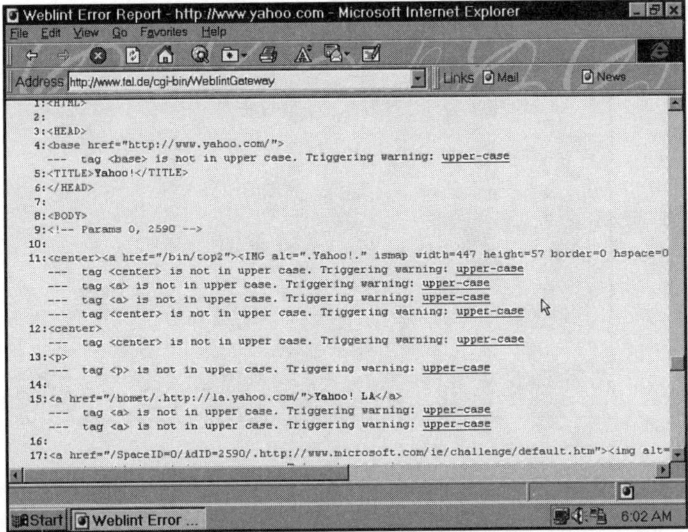


**Figure 21.4.**
*Your document's source code is interspersed with Weblint's warning messages.*

Don't forget to include the `http://` in the URL of the document that you want to run through the Weblint gateway.

# Link Checkers

Another type of validation that you need to run periodically on your pages is one to ensure that all of the hyperlinks in your HTML code are still working and operational. Just as broken HTML code annoys users, broken links annoy them even more.

## The Doctor Is In: Using Doctor HTML

Doctor HTML is another option that you can use for HTML validation. Doctor HTML is a valuable tool that goes beyond simple HTML code and verifies the integrity of images, tables, and (most important here) hyperlinks. Doctor HTML is a free Web-based service available from

```
http://www2.imagiware.com/RxHTML/
```

To use Doctor HTML, you simply enter the appropriate URL and then select all of the tests or specific tests to be done on the Web page (see Figure 21.5). The results are ready almost instantly, and a report is generated and loaded into your browser, as shown in Figure 21.6.

Doctor HTML is an excellent HTML verification tool in addition to Weblint. You should use it to verify your links on a regular basis to avoid the dreaded "URL Not Found" message that can send your users down a dead-end alley with nowhere to go.

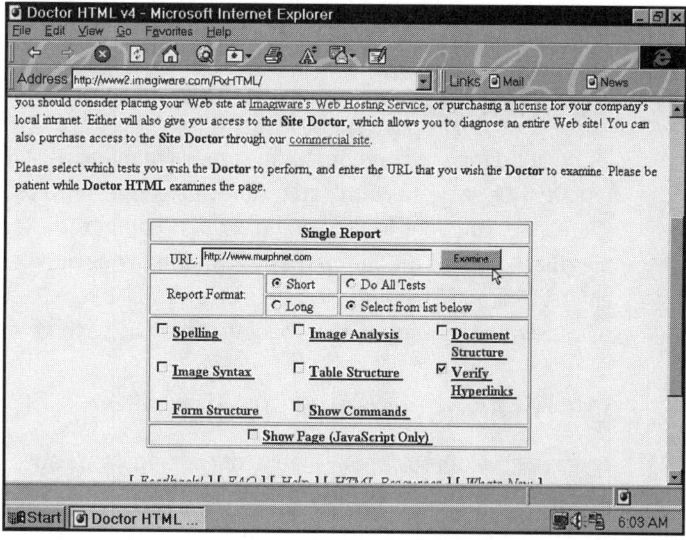


**Figure 21.5.**
*Doctor HTML enables you to specify which tests, including hyperlink verification, you would like it to run.*

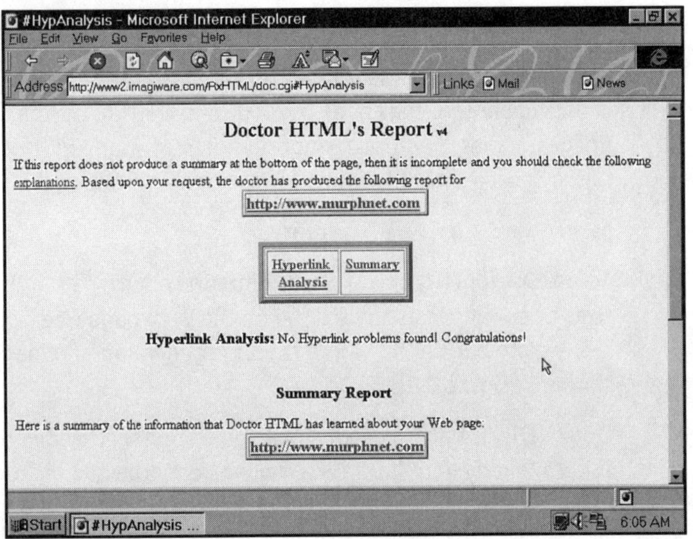


**Figure 21.6.**
*The Doctor's diagnosis on the hyperlinks looks good.*

# Managing Your Pages: Tools and Techniques

Often, it's difficult to prepare for the type of management that a large Web site might require. Normally, you don't start out with a huge, unruly Web site, but with a simple Web page. Thus, the idea of doing anything other than keeping all five of your basic files that comprise the various page elements in one directory seems unnecessary and almost foolish. However, in no time at all, you'll begin to add pages and add to your pages, and organizing and managing them will become a necessity.

## Web Management Tools

Just as a bevy of tools are available for creating Web pages, many more tools are also available for managing them. In fact, more and more Web creation packages come with site management features built in as a standard component. An excellent example of this trend is Microsoft's FrontPage, which encompasses an excellent WYSIWYG Web editor with a comprehensive site management tool, as shown in Figure 21.7.

**TIP:** You can download a time-limited version of FrontPage by becoming a member of Microsoft's Site Builder Network (which is free to join). For more information, go to

```
http://www.microsoft.com/sbn/
```

HomeSiteX can also be used as a pseudo site management tool. The program uses the Windows Explorer style of interface that appears on the left side of the program (see Figure 21.8) to make Web file management simple. In order to use this as a management tool, you need to either be using HomeSiteX on the computer that is your Web server, or upload your entire directory structure to your server after you make changes (which is actually an acceptable solution).

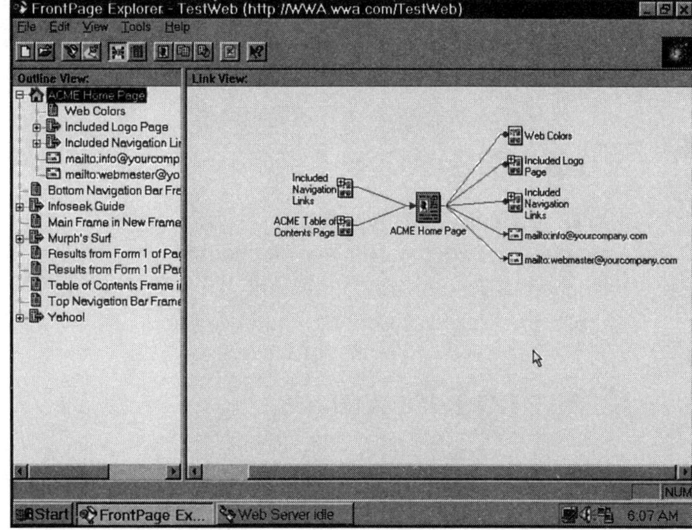


**Figure 21.7.**
*Microsoft's FrontPage has a built-in Web site management tool that provides visual organization.*

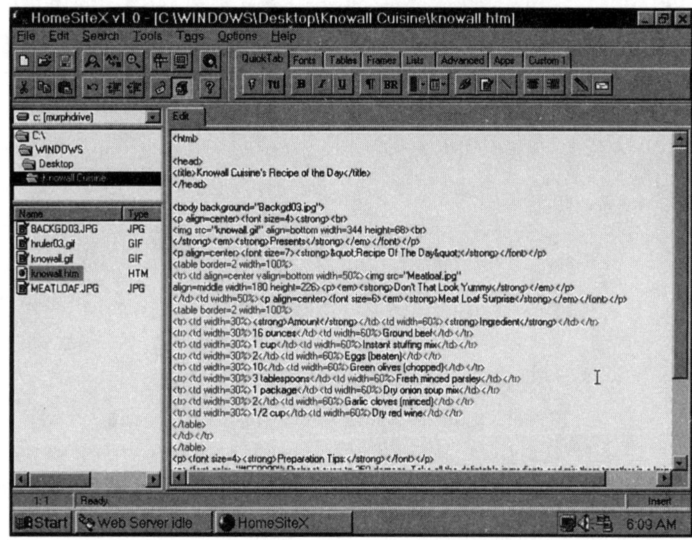


**Figure 21.8.**
*HomeSiteX can be used to manage Web sites with its built-in file explorer interface.*

## Management Techniques Without Tools

Some of the most fundamental Web management tasks can be implemented and accomplished with little more than your keyboard and a UNIX prompt. Your ability to manage a large Web site is directly related to your ability to organize. The chaotic and wide-open nature of the Web does not lend itself well to keeping your pages in proper order.

It's amazing how simple it can be to get your site into shape without expensive programs. With a few basic structural rules, you'll have your site under control in no time at all.

# Organizing a Site

As I've said time and time again, there is no better way to learn than by doing. I'll walk you step by step through the procedures for establishing a more organized and manageable Web presence. All of this is invisible to the Web user's naked eye, but it should help you to work with your pages and files.

## Creating Directories

A key to your organization is the directory structure of your Web site. Making sure that you have the proper layout and structure makes administration and updating of your site more efficient and effective. Here's how you should go about creating directories:

Depending on your Web hosting service, you might need to save your CGI scripts in a specialized directory, usually called `cgi-bin`, on their server.

1. Create a directory named `images`. You will use this directory to store all the inline GIFs and JPEGs you use on your pages. You might also want to create further subdirectories for individual pages—for example, `images/employees`.
2. Create a directory called `cgi-bin` for storing your Perl and CGI scripts and related files. You might want to create additional subdirectories for different scripts—for example, `cgi-bin/oopshop`.
3. Create a directory named `java`. You will use this directory to store and create more directories for Java applets used on your site.
4. Create individual subdirectories under `java` for each applet used on your pages—for example, `java/nervoustext`. Use a separate directory to store each applet.
5. Create a directory named `activex` if you utilize ActiveX controls on your site. Again, create individual subdirectories for each control—for example, `activex/marquee`.

Most UNIX-based systems follow the `mkdir` command for creating new directories.

6. If you use multimedia on your pages, create separate directories to store video and audio files. You should create one for audio and one for video for better organization.
7. Create a directory called `admin` in which to place all administration files or programs. You can use this directory for items such as log files. You should also create subdirectories for scripts such as Weblint.

## Moving Your Files

The next step is to move your files into the corresponding directory. The goal is to have only HTML documents in your base root directory. If you need to create an additional directory, even if it is just a `miscellaneous` directory to make the base directory clean (with only `*.htm` and `*.html` files), do that now.

**NOTE:** Many (perhaps even most) people organize their Web sites by individual pages. Thus, the base directory has the `index.html` file, all corresponding graphics, and so on. Then each significant page has its own directory, such as `employdir` for the employee directory. There are obviously many different competing and useful approaches for organizing your site. This section explains some of the benefits for using this scheme, but you should use what is best and most useful for your circumstances.

At this point, you should also create entirely separate directories for what you might consider to be different sites within your site. For example, you might run a Web server for a company that has four distinct businesses, each with its own "Web site" on the same Web server. You should create a directory for each business and then repeat the previous steps for all of the pages within each of these "sub-sites." This might also be wise if you have an extraordinarily complex set of pages within a commercial site, such as a catalog or shopping cart that takes up tens (or even hundreds) of separate HTML files.

## Resetting Links and Code

You often won't decide to organize your Web site until it is already to the point where it's a little out of control. Of course, it's best to do this up front, but if you're like me, you probably like to learn things the hard way.

The biggest downside to reorganizing your site after it is even mildly substantial in size is that you need to tweak your existing HTML code to reflect the changed locations of the files after you have gone through the previous steps.

**TIP:** Using the search and replace feature of your HTML editor (such as Hot Dog 32, which is on the CD-ROM) or even your word processor can speed up the time needed to accomplish this step. For example, you might reference your logo, `logo.gif`, at several places in your page. Simply do a search and replace for `logo.gif` with `images/logo.gif`.

The good thing is that you should be able to quickly identify which HTML documents need to be edited, because they now are all clearly identifiable in your main directory without the clutter of other files. When you have finished editing and putting in the new directory location references, be sure to use an HTML verifier and a link checker about which you learned earlier in this chapter.

## The Organizational Benefits: Easy Updating

Using Weblint and Doctor HTML at this point would be an excellent idea.

One of the key benefits to organizing your pages in this manner is that it allows you ready access to finding out when the pages were last changed. You want to make sure all of your pages are updated on a weekly basis at the very least. With all your Web pages by themselves in a single base directory, you can issue a simple `dir` command and look at the dates that all of your pages have last been changed. You can then easily spot pages that are becoming stale and need to be updated without trudging through a bunch of other files or directories to get this information.

# Security Considerations

I would be remiss if I didn't at least touch upon the issue of security in conjunction with administering and managing Web pages. Security on the Internet, and the Web in particular, is a popular topic in the media and on the Net these days. A growing number of Web sites have been victimized by Internet graffiti artists—hackers that get into a Web site and alter Web pages.

**CAUTION:** It's extremely important to ensure the security and integrity of your entire Web site and not just those pages where you need to facilitate online transactions. Hackers might find a way to alter your pages in subtle ways so that you end up losing real customers. Many users are unfamiliar with the Web graffiti spree that has taken place and might attribute outrageous or offensive comments on your pages to your company or business. Also, if your unsecured pages are exposed as vulnerable, the credibility of your secure, transactional pages is undermined.

Many security options are available in order to protect your site, your pages, and your business. Be certain you check your Web server documentation and use the proper `chmod`'s to ensure that not just anyone has write access to your server and can overwrite your pages. Also, be sure you change your server `admin` password on a weekly basis.

# Workshop Wrap-Up

Now you've seen what it takes to use the tools necessary to organize, manage, and administer the pages on your Web site. The one thing you need to do is develop a workable schedule by which you can regularly accomplish the tasks that were demonstrated in this chapter. Again, you should be updating and validating your pages on a weekly basis to be certain that the investment you've made in time and energy (and, of course, money) is protected.

## Next Steps

Now...

- Chapter 22, "Real-Life Examples: Touting and Managing Your Site," shows you some real-life examples for this section, covering marketing, managing, and administering Web pages.
- Appendix A, "Online Resources," contains a complete set of URL references for web resources cited in this chapter and throughout the book, broken down by topical categories.

## Q&A

**Q: I use Microsoft Word's Internet Assistant to code my HTML and I always run spell check, so do I really need to do anything else?**

**A:** Although it's good that you use spell check and it's true that spell checkers will catch some HTML coding problems, they won't catch them all. A spell checker won't be able to tell you that there is a `</B>` tag without a `<B>`. Also, a spell checker won't tell you that some of your links, although spelled correctly, are inoperational and outdated. You always need to make sure you run your pages through an HTML and/or hyperlink validation system.

**Q: Is there any foolproof security system that I could use to protect my Web site?**

**A:** Unfortunately, no. However, the lock on your door at home or the alarm at the office is not foolproof either. The key is just to make sure that you use the protections you have (lock your door, turn on the alarm, correctly configure your server and pages) so that you can minimize your risk of being victimized.

TWENTY-TWO

# Real-Life Examples: Touting and Managing Your Site

## Examples in this chapter:

- Example 1: Making Your Site "Findable"
- Example 2: Linking Up
- Example 3: Using Usenet To Spread the Word
- Example 4: Checking and Validating HTML
- Example 5: Checking Your Links
- Example 6: Management Techniques Without Tools

When you've made it this far, you're on the cusp of unleashing your creativity and energy out onto the Web. Before you do that, however, you should look at the final set of examples for this section. You should find these helpful for setting out to administer and manage your site and to generate enough Web traffic so that it even needs to be managed.

The examples in this chapter differ significantly from the ones you have seen in previous chapters. The areas just covered have less to do with Web design and involve more of the types of mental and managerial aspects of creating and maintaining a popular commercial Web page. The examples that follow highlight how some of the tools and techniques you just looked at can be used on the Net.

For more real-life examples, check out Chapters 7, 12, and 19.

# Example 1: Making Your Site "Findable"

The first step in trying to generate traffic to your Web pages is to get the word out that you even have Web pages. The importance of this proposition should be self evident, but you'd be surprised by how many people (and sites) fail to take this step. The following examples show you some excellent ways for making sure people know about your pages and know where to find them.

## Yahoo!

**URL:** `http://www.yahoo.com`

**Description:** Yahoo! is the undisputed king of the Web indexes. White Buffalo Trading & Handcraft Suppliers wisely took to Yahoo! to get listed and to provide a brief synopsis about the company and what they do (and sell).

**Techniques and designs applied:**

> **Getting Listed On Yahoo!.** (See Chapter 20, "Marketing Your Web Pages.") Just as every journey starts with the first step, every Web marketing effort starts with getting your page listed on Yahoo!. As you can see from Figure 22.1, White Buffalo's listing provides a concise and informative blurb about the company and its products. Just enough to get a click out of a potential customer.

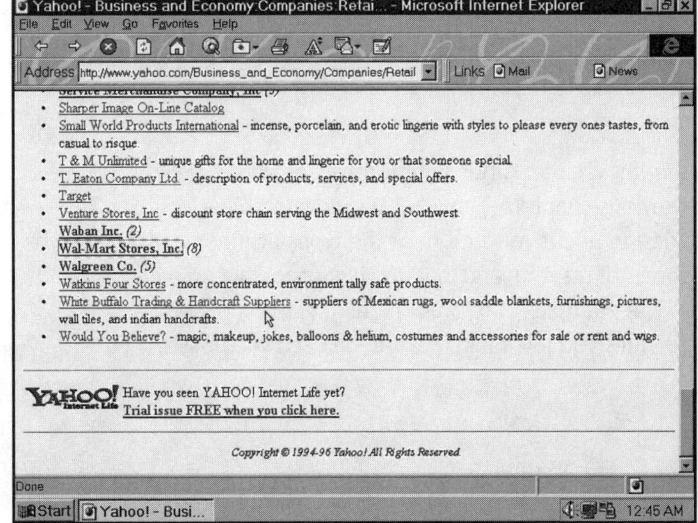


**Figure 22.1.**
*White Buffalo's listing as it appears on the Yahoo! Web index.*

**Picking Your Categories.** (See Chapter 20.) Getting listed on Yahoo! won't be as valuable as it can be if you don't correctly and carefully identify the appropriate categories under which your page should be listed in the index. You can see from Figure 22.2 that Yahoo!'s submission page enables you to specify the categories under which your pages should appear.

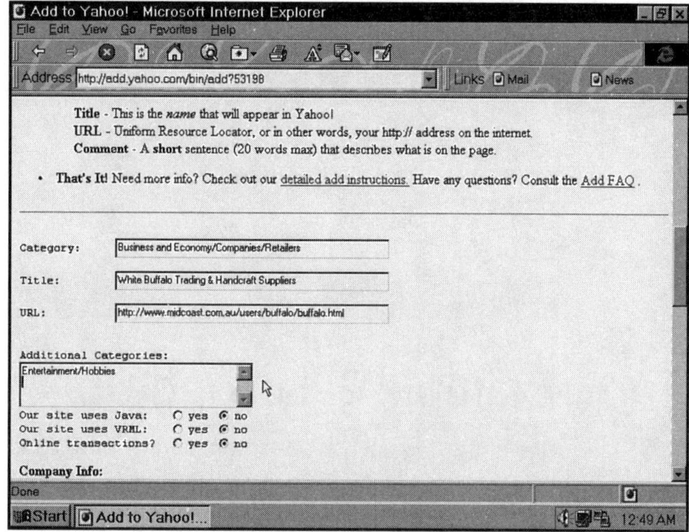


**Figure 22.2.**
*White Buffalo's submission page to Yahoo! could specify several different categories for its page.*

## Submit-It!

**URL:** `http:/www.submit-it.com`

**Description:** Submit-It! is the most cost-effective tool for getting your page listed on as many sites as possible. White Buffalo could turn to Submit-It! to garner even wider coverage for its page.

**Techniques and designs applied:**

**Netiquette.** (See Chapter 20.) One of the first netiquette mistakes you could make accidentally is to use Submit-It! to duplicate your submissions to some of the Internet announcement and index services. While such a faux pas will not get you blacklisted, such mini-spam could be annoying at the very least. As you can see from Figure 22.3, the Yahoo! box is not checked because the page is already listed on that service.

**Keywords and Search Terms.** (See Chapter 20.) As you can see from Figure 22.3, Submit-It! enables you to specify certain keywords for your submission to the various services. You should use the same keywords you utilize in the search-friendly page you learned how to create in Chapter 20.

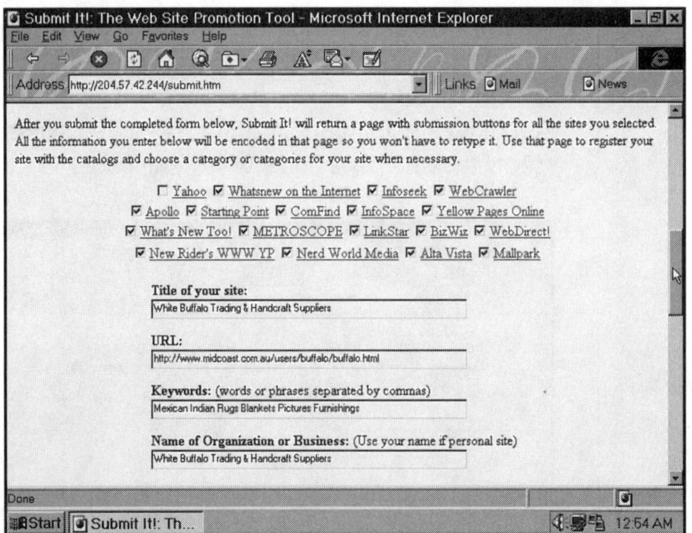


**Figure 22.3.**
*Submit-It! enables you to specify what service will—and won't—receive a request for listing your Web page.*

# Example 2: Linking Up

One of the original ways people generated traffic to their Web pages was by having their pages hyperlinked on other Web pages. This practice continues, albeit in a much more disciplined and commercial manner today. The following are some examples of services that provide links that help generate hits to your pages.

## Internet Link Exchange

**Description:** Internet Link Exchange provides an easy and inexpensive way to generate traffic by enabling you to barter ad space on your Web page for space on other pages. In this example, you see how this works for a Web page called the Photo Gallery, an advertiser-supported content site.

**Techniques and designs applied:**

> **Linking Your Pages.** (See Chapter 20.) The Photo Gallery is a member of the Internet Link Exchange, so it submitted a small banner ad that is placed on other Web sites, as seen in Figure 22.4. The banner ad touts the benefits of visiting the site and integrates graphics to enhance the presentation.
>
> **The Other Side of the Link.** (See Chapter 20.) Linking up is a two-way street, and you see that when you select the link in Figure 22.4 you are brought to the Photo Gallery's page shown in Figure 22.5, and you're immediately presented with a banner ad for another site. You have to remember that to get a link you'll need to give a link.

**Figure 22.4.**
*The Photo Gallery's banner ad appears at the bottom of this page courtesy of the Internet Link Exchange.*

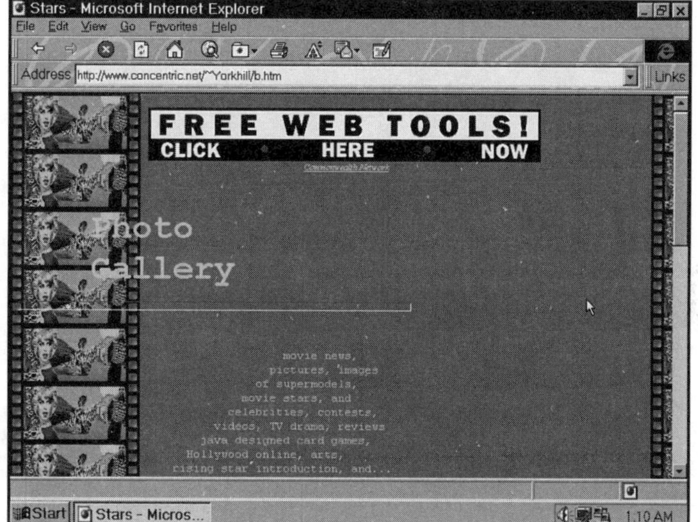


**Figure 22.5.**
*When you select a banner ad you'll be brought to the ad sponsor's page and you'll find further link ads.*

# Example 3: Using Usenet To Spread the Word

Usenet is one of the best ways to reach the most advanced and sophisticated Web users. Of course, to use it for marketing purposes means that your methods will need to be equally advanced and sophisticated or you risk being run off the Web. The following examples show how to use Usenet without getting burned.

## A Usenet Announcement

**Description:** The best place to spread the word on the Net is Usenet. You can target announcements and ads to reach a natural audience that is connected and has easy access to the Web. The best way to accomplish this is by targeting your page announcement in an appropriate forum, like `biz.marketplace`.

**Techniques and designs applied:**

**Choosing an Audience.** (See Chapter 20.) When you post to Usenet, you need to make sure your message will reach the right people. The posting shown in Figure 22.6 was posted to `biz.marketplace`, a general commercial posting area that is likely to draw people who are interested in buying on the Internet and who won't be averse to doing business on the Web.

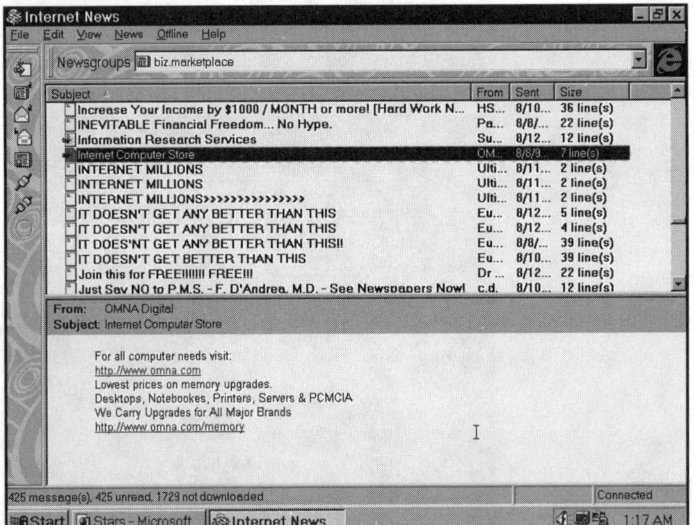


**Figure 22.6.**
*A simple and to-the-point Usenet posting is an effective way to spread the word about your pages.*

**Netiquette.** (See Chapter 20.) The posting in this example was posted to the `biz.marketplace` newsgroup, which has no restrictions on commercial postings like many groups do. Also, the posting was not spammed to many unrelated and irrelevant groups.

## A Signature Ad

**Description:** A newsgroup signature line, or sig, that appears every time the user posts to a particular newsgroup, in this example, `rec.video.satellite.dbs`.

**Techniques and designs applied:**

**Helping Others Can Help Yourself.** (See Chapter 20.) You should be able to tell from Figure 22.7 that this post came in response to a question someone placed on the newsgroup. By answering the question, the poster was able to include the signature line touting his satellite company's Web page in a subtle manner.

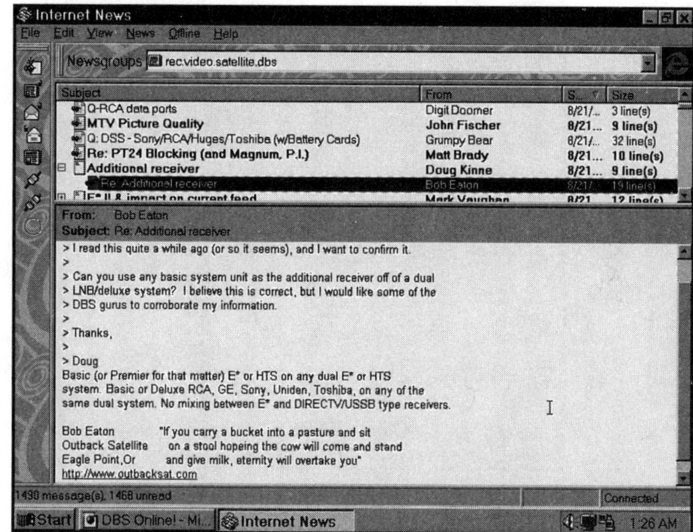


**Figure 22.7.**
*The signature line on a Usenet post can be a very useful billboard for your commercial Web pages.*

**Signature as a Web Page Ad.** (See Chapter 20.) The key to an effective signature is to keep it short and clean, and include the URL. Most news readers today will enable users to simply select your Web address and be instantly transported to your page through their Web browsers.

# Example 4: Checking and Validating HTML

Your Web page will only be as good as the HTML used to create it. The broad range of browsers that are available on the market, each with its own quirks in rendering HTML, can create major headaches for a Webmaster. Therefore, you need to check and validate your HTML to be certain that it complies with HTML standards, and the following examples show just how this is done.

## Weblint on Microsoft

**Description:** Even Microsoft's home page isn't free from errors. You see from Figure 22.8 that it's just as easy to check the HTML coding of Microsoft's pages as it is your own. And you might be surprised by the results this Weblint Gateway might give you.

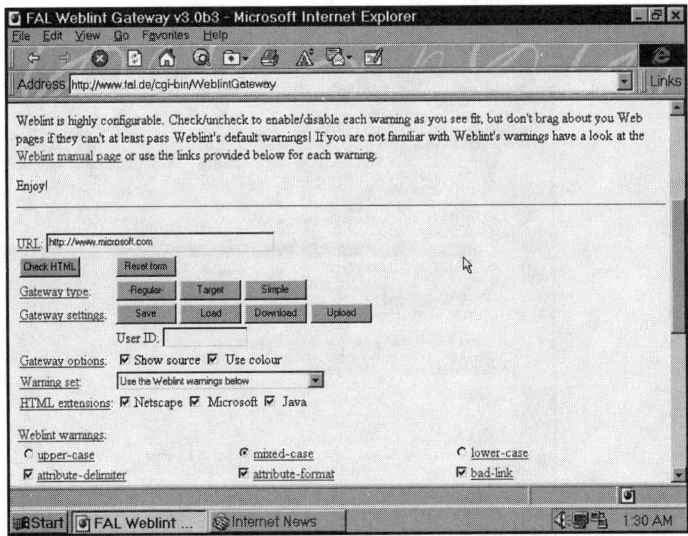


**Figure 22.8.**
*The Weblint Gateway provides an easy-to-use interface for checking HTML code.*

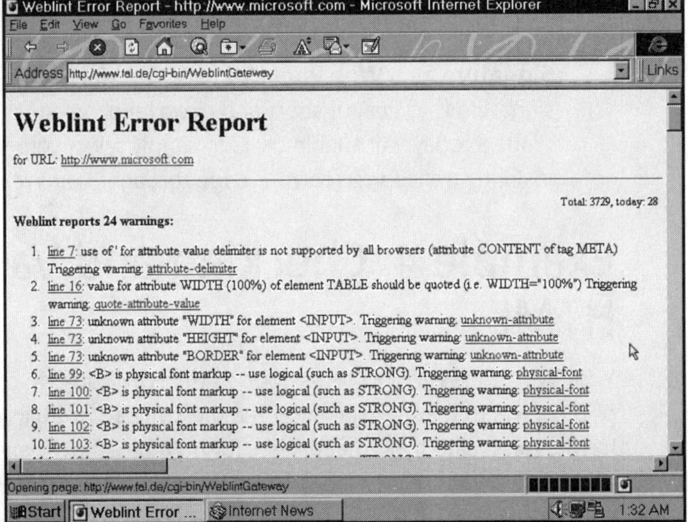


**Figure 22.9.**
*Weblint will point out HTML coding problems for even the best Web designers.*

**Techniques and designs applied:**

**Weblint Web Gateway.** (See Chapter 21, "Web Site Administration and Management.") The Weblint Gateway provides a prettier and more useful interface than the standard Perl script you could run from your UNIX server, as you can see from Figure 22.8.

**Looking at Results.** (See Chapter 21.) You might be surprised to see from the results in Figure 22.9 that Microsoft's page has some errors according to Weblint. Sometimes it can be a little too fastidious in its search for lint, but at least you can decide to disregard the problems if you want.

# Example 5: Checking Your Links

The Web is all about hyperlinking, that's what makes it a unique and exciting environment. Users get frustrated when they select links and think they're going somewhere exciting only to be presented with a "Page Not Found" error message. Verifying your links should be a weekly ritual, and this example shows how easy and useful this process can be.

## Doctor HTML

**Description:** Using Doctor HTML to verify the numerous links on the Jenner & Block home page, shown in Figure 22.10, takes only a few seconds whereas a manual check could take much longer.

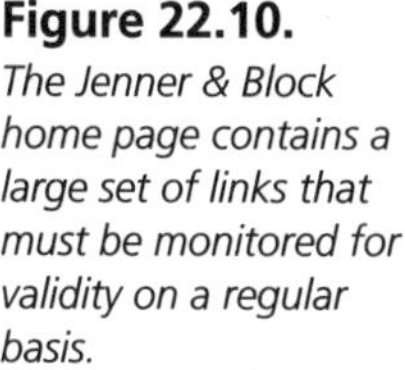

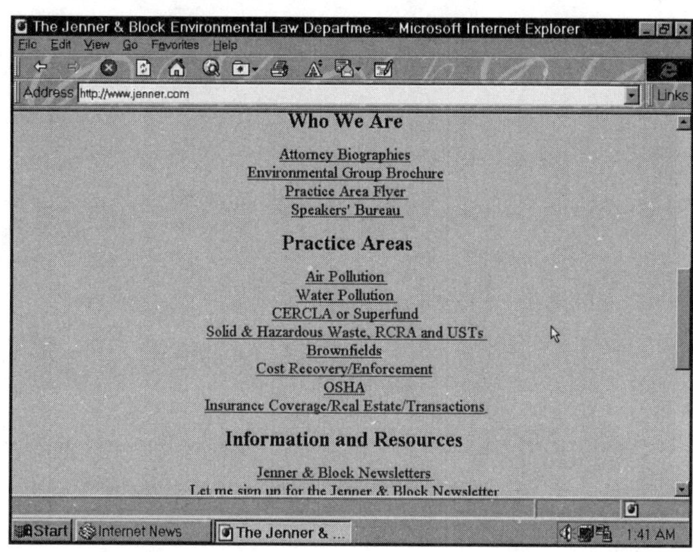


**Figure 22.10.**
*The Jenner & Block home page contains a large set of links that must be monitored for validity on a regular basis.*

### Techniques and designs applied:

**Using Doctor HTML.** (See Chapter 21.) Having the Doctor prescribe a solution to link problems is as simple as submitting the URL for examination on the form shown in Figure 22.11. As you can see, the `http://` must be included on the form.

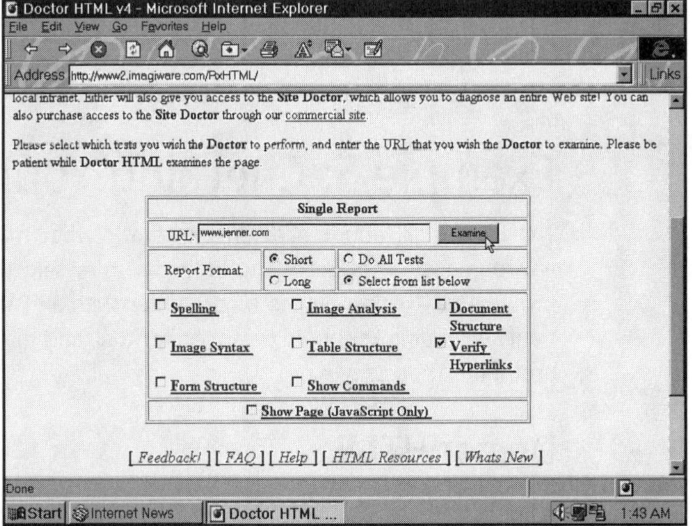


**Figure 22.11.**
*Limiting Doctor HTML to validating links can focus you in on the task at hand.*

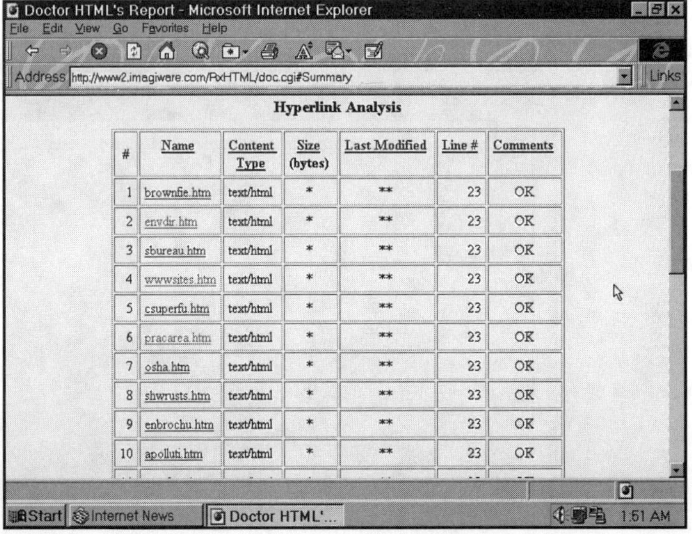


| # | Name | Content Type | Size (bytes) | Last Modified | Line # | Comments |
|---|---|---|---|---|---|---|
| 1 | brownfie.htm | text/html | * | ** | 23 | OK |
| 2 | envdir.htm | text/html | * | ** | 23 | OK |
| 3 | sbureau.htm | text/html | * | ** | 23 | OK |
| 4 | wwwsites.htm | text/html | * | ** | 23 | OK |
| 5 | csuperfu.htm | text/html | * | ** | 23 | OK |
| 6 | pracarea.htm | text/html | * | ** | 23 | OK |
| 7 | osha.htm | text/html | * | ** | 23 | OK |
| 8 | shwrusts.htm | text/html | * | ** | 23 | OK |
| 9 | enbrochu.htm | text/html | * | ** | 23 | OK |
| 10 | apolluti.htm | text/html | * | ** | 23 | OK |

**Figure 22.12.**
*The results of the link verification run on the Jenner & Block page.*

**Reading the Results.** (See Chapter 21.) For the example in Figure 22.11, Doctor HTML renders a diagnosis as shown in Figure 22.12. The page is in perfect health and all links are verified. If a problem had been found, the program would have flagged the item and Jenner's Webmaster could have quickly corrected the link.

# Example 6: Management Techniques Without Tools

Not all site management requires fancy and expensive software tools. Here's an example of how to manage your site without the need for anything other than your wits and a keyboard.

## Organizing Your Site

**Description:** An example that really hits home for me. The `www.murphnet.com` site needed to be prepared for the hosting of the Web page companion to this book, and following the organizational tips of Chapter 21 it was whipped into top shape.

**Techniques and designs applied:**

**Creating Directories.** (See Chapter 21.) You can see from Figure 22.13 that the directory structure for the site has been completely implemented in a clean and organized fashion. The only program used to accomplish this was the UNIX shell. The listing is displayed using WS_FTP.

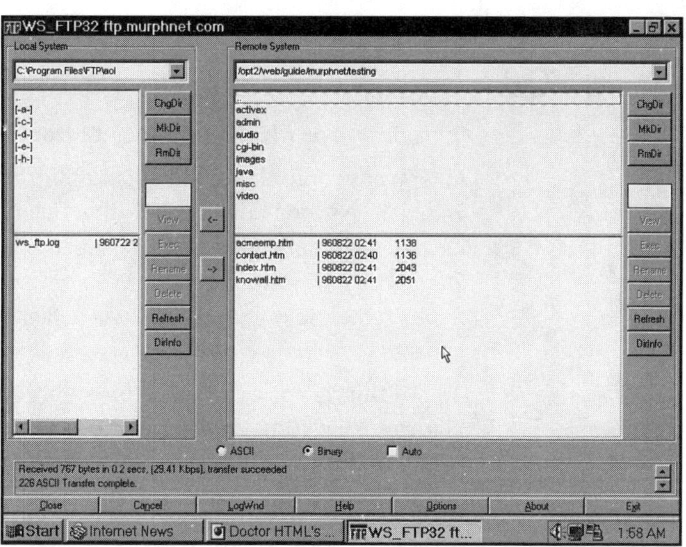


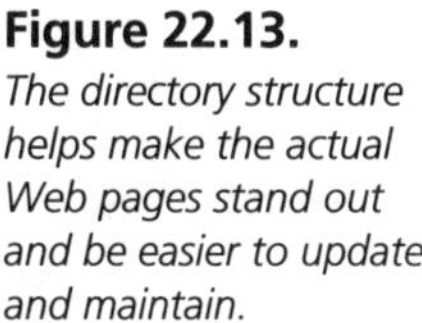
**Figure 22.13.**
*The directory structure helps make the actual Web pages stand out and be easier to update and maintain.*

**Moving the Files.** (See Chapter 21.) The files in this example have all been moved to their respective directories, leaving only the HTML files in the base directory. You can quickly identify from the date of the files the last time each page has been updated.

# Workshop Wrap-Up

Now is a good time to go back and refresh yourself on any items that might still be giving you trouble. Remember that this book is designed to be a reference in creating your commercial Web pages. Much of the information will be even more important (and more understandable) as you begin to actually create your pages. So code away, but keep this book close by.

## Next Steps

Now...

- ❑ There's a lot of information you can explore in the appendixes as well as the numerous software programs that are included on the CD-ROM. You can now start to experiment and play with designs for your own commercial Web pages and check back to this book periodically for a refresher as you need help through the process. Good luck; I can't wait to surf your pages.
- ❑ Appendix A contains a nice HTML 3.2 reference so that you can avoid some of the problems Weblint might find.
- ❑ Appendix B is a listing of all the online resources that were used throughout this book.

## Q&A

**Q: Is online or offline publicity better for promoting a Web page?**

**A:** The answer to this one gradually shifts as time goes by. A year ago I would have stated unequivocally that online publicity and advertising where much more important to generating site traffic than an ad in the Sunday paper. However, as the Web becomes much more broad-based in its reach the use of mass media will begin to have a greater and greater impact.

**Q: I'm thirsty for even more information on Web page design. I'd like to tackle some more advanced topics and features such as VRML and how to use some of the advanced Web editors. Where should I go?**

**A:** Go to another Laura Lemay *Web Workshop* title, that's where.

**Q: What do I do if I still have some questions?**

**A:** Send them to me at murph@murphnet.com and I promise I'll try to do my best to get you an answer or at least point you in the right direction.

# PART VI

# Appendixes


**A** Online Resources

**B** HTML 3.2 Reference

**C** What's on the CD-ROM

APPENDIX

# A Online Resources

## Graphics Sites

### Texture and Background Wonderland

http://netletter.com/cameo/hotlist/hotlist.html

### Clip Art

http://www.n-vision.com/panda/c/

### kira's icon library

http://fohnix.metronet.com/~kira/icongifs/

### Buttons, Cubes & Bars

http://www.cbil.vcu.edu:8080/gifs/bullet.html

### Imaging Machine

http://www.vrl.com/Imaging/

### Color Ramper

http://www.netcreations.com/ramper/index.html

### Randy's Icon and Image Bazaar

http://www.infi.net/~rdralph/icons

### Microsoft's Multimedia Gallery

http://www.microsoft.com/workshop/design/mmgallry/mmgallry.htm

### Color Browser

http://www.enterprise.net/iw/cbrowser.html

## General Business Reference

### Defining the Internet Opportunity

http://www.ora.com/gnn/bus/ora/survey/index.html

### 20 Reasons to Put Your Business on the Web

http://www.net101.com/reasons.html

### The Challenges of Electronic Commerce

http://www2000.ogsm.vanderbilt.edu/intelligent.agent/index.html

### The Internet Business Center

http://www.tig.com/cgi-bin/genobject/ibcindex

## HTML Authoring Tools

### HomeSiteX

http://www.windows95.com

### Sausage Software

http://www.sausage.com

### Microsoft

http://www.microsoft.com

### Netscape

http://home.netscape.com

### Stroud's Consummate Winsock Apps

http://www.cwsapps.com

### The Ultimate Collection of Winsock Software

http://www.tucows.com

### Cool Tool of The Day

http://www.cooltool.com

### Voice on the Net

http://www.pulver.com

### Statbot

http://www.xmission.com/~dtubbs/club/cs.html

### WebTrends

http://www.webtrends.com/download/wt_trial.exe

### Access Watch

http://net\pressence.com/accesswatch/download.html

## HTML Design and Authoring

### Webreference

http://www.webreference.com

### Cascading Style Sheets

http://www.microsoft.com/workshop/author/howto/css-f.htm

## HTML Authoring Newsgroups

comp.infosystems.www.html.authoring.html

comp.infosystems.www.html.authoring.cgi

comp.infosystems.www.html.authoring.images

### W3C HTML Standards Organization

http://www.w3c.org

## Web Searching and Indexes

### AltaVista

http://altavista.digital.com

### Yahoo!

http://www.yahoo.com

### InfoSeek

http://www.infoseek.com

### Lycos

http://www.lycos.com

### Excite

http://www.excite.com

### HotBot

http://www.hotbot.com

### Open Text

http://www.opentext.com

### WebCrawler

http://www.webcrawler.com

### New Rider's WWW Yellow Pages

http://www.mcp.com/submit.html

### Apollo

http://apollo.co.uk

### Starting Point

http://www.stpt.com

### ComFind

http://www.comfind.com

### BizWiz

http://www.bizwiz.com

### Galaxy

http://galaxy.einet.net

### What's New Too!

http://newtoo.manifest.com

### METROSCOPE

http://isotropic.com

### LinkStar

http://www.linkstar.com

### Nerd World Media

http://www.nerdworld.com

### Mallpark

http://www.mallpark.com

## CGI Scripts

### Selena Sol's Script Archive

http://www2.eff.org/~erict/Scripts

### Remote Software

http://www.remote.com

**Matt Wright's Script Archive (WWWBoard)**

http://www.worldwidemart.com/scripts

**OopShop Shopping Cart System**

http://www.ids.net/~oops/cart

# Subscription and Pay-Per-View Web Services

**Morph's Daily Spectrum**

http://www.morph.com

**Wall Street Journal**

http://www.wsj.com

**ESPN SportsZone**

http://espnnet.sportszone.com

**Solonian Journal**

http://www.solonian.org.

**Mark Twain Bank**

http://www.marktwain.com

# Web Page Marketing

**Commonwealth Network**

http://commonwealth.riddler.com

**The Internet Link Exchange**

http://www.linkexchange.com

**Microsoft's Site Builder Network**

http://www.microsoft.com/sbn

**The Netiquette Home Page**

http://www.fau.edu/rinaldi/netiquette.html

**Blacklist of Internet Advertisers**

http:// http://www.cco.caltech.edu/~cbrown/BL/

**The Internet Marketing Resource**

http://edie.cprost.sfu.ca/~sigma6/

**Media Contacts E-mail List**

http://www.ping.at/gugerell/media

# Multimedia

### RealAudio

http://www.realaudio.com

### VDOLive

http://www.vdolive.com

### Shockwave

http://www.macromedia.com

### QuickTime

http://quicktime.apple.com

### Java applets

http://www.jars.com

http://www.gamelan.com

APPENDIX

# B HTML 3.2 Quick Reference

This appendix is a reference to the HTML tags you can use in your documents. Unless otherwise noted, all of the tags listed here are supported by both Microsoft Explorer 3.0 and Netscape Navigator 3.0. Note that some other browsers do not support all the tags listed, and some of the tags listed as (MS) may also be supported in the final shipping version of Netscape 3.0.

The proposed HTML style sheet specification is also not covered here. Refer to the Netscape (`http://home.netscape.com/`) or Microsoft (`http://www.microsoft.com/`) Web sites for details on this and other late-breaking changes to the new HTML 3.2 standard.

## HTML Tags

These tags are used to create a basic HTML page with text, headings, and lists. An (MS) beside the attribute indicates Microsoft.

## Comments

| | |
|---|---|
| `<!- ... ->` | Creates a comment. Can also be used to hide JavaScript from browsers that do not support it. |
| `<COMMENT>...</COMMENT>` | The new offical way of specifying comments. |

## Structure Tags

| | |
|---|---|
| `<HTML>...</HTML>` | Encloses the entire HTML document. |
| `<HEAD>...</HEAD>` | Encloses the head of the HTML document. |
| `<BODY>...</BODY>` | Encloses the body (text and tags) of the HTML document. |

*Attributes:*

| | |
|---|---|
| `BACKGROUND="..."` | The name or URL of the image to tile on the page background. |
| `BGCOLOR="..."` | The color of the page background. |
| `TEXT="..."` | The color of the page's text. |
| `LINK="..."` | The color of unfollowed links. |
| `ALINK="..."` | The color of activated links. |
| `VLINK="..."` | The color of followed links. |
| `BGPROPERTIES="..."` (MS) | Properties of background image. Currently allows only the value `FIXED`, which prevents the background image from scrolling. |
| `TOPMARGIN="..."` (MS) | Top margin of the page, in pixels. |
| `BOTTOMMARGIN="..."` (MS) | Bottom margin of the page, in pixels. |

| | | |
|---|---|---|
| **<BASE>** | Indicates the full URL of the current document. This optional tag is used within <HEAD>. | |
| *Attributes:* | | |
| | HREF="..." | The full URL of this document. |
| **<ISINDEX>** | Indicates that this document is a gateway script that allows searches. | |
| *Attributes:* | | |
| | PROMPT="..." | The prompt for the search field. |
| | ACTION="..." | Gateway program to which the search string should be passed. |
| **<LINK>** | Indicates a link between this document and some other document. Generally used only by HTML-generating tools. <LINK> represents a link from this entire document to another, as opposed to <A>, which can create multiple links in the document. Not commonly used. | |
| *Attributes:* | | |
| | HREF="..." | The URL of the document to call when the link is activated. |
| | NAME="..." | If the document is to be considered an anchor, the name of that anchor. |
| | REL="..." | The relationship between the linked-to document and the current document; for example, "TOC" or "Glossary". |
| | REV="..." | A reverse relationship between the current document and the linked-to document. |

| | | |
|---|---|---|
| | `URN="..."` | A Uniform Resource Number (URN), a unique identifier different from the URL in `HREF`. |
| | `TITLE="..."` | The title of the linked-to document. |
| | `METHODS="..."` | The method with which the document is to be retrieved; for example, FTP, Gopher, and so on. |

**<META>** Indicates meta-information about this document (information about the document itself); for example, keywords for search engines, special HTTP headers to be used for retrieving this document, expiration date, and so on. Meta-information is usually in a key/value pair form. Used in the document `<HEAD>`.

*Attributes:*

| | |
|---|---|
| `HTTP-EQUIV="..."` | Creates a new HTTP header field with the same name as the attribute's value; for example, `HTTP-EQUIV="Expires"`. The value of that header is specified by the `CONTENT` attribute. |
| `NAME="..."` | If meta-data is usually in the form of key/value pairs, `NAME` indicates the key; for example, `Author` or `ID`. |
| `CONTENT="..."` | The content of the key/value pair (or of the HTTP header indicated by `HTTP-EQUIV`). |

| | |
|---|---|
| **<NEXTID>** | Indicates the "next" document to this one (as might be defined by a tool to manage HTML documents in a series). <NEXTID> is considered obsolete. |

## Headings and Title

| | |
|---|---|
| **<H1>...</H1>** | A first-level heading. |
| **<H2>...</H2>** | A second-level heading. |
| **<H3>...</H3>** | A third-level heading. |
| **<H4>...</H4>** | A fourth-level heading. |
| **<H5>...</H5>** | A fifth-level heading. |
| **<H6>...</H6>** | A sixth-level heading. |
| **<TITLE>...</TITLE>** | Indicates the title of the document. Used within <HEAD>. |

All heading tags accept the following:

*Attributes:*

| | | |
|---|---|---|
| | ALIGN="..." | Possible values are CENTER, LEFT, and RIGHT. |

## Paragraphs and Regions

| | |
|---|---|
| **<P>...</P>** | A plain paragraph. The closing tag (</P>) is optional. |

*Attributes:*

| | | |
|---|---|---|
| | ALIGN="..." | Align text to CENTER, LEFT, or RIGHT. |

| | |
|---|---|
| **<DIV>...</DIV>** | A region of text to be formatted. |

*Attributes:*

| | | |
|---|---|---|
| | ALIGN="..." | Align text to CENTER, LEFT, or RIGHT. |

## Links

| | |
|---|---|
| **<A>...</A>** | With the HREF attribute, creates a link to another document or anchor; with the NAME attribute, creates an anchor that can be linked to. |

*Attributes:*

| | |
|---|---|
| `HREF="..."` | The URL of the document to be called when the link is activated. |
| `NAME="..."` | The name of the anchor. |
| `REL="..."` | The relationship between the linked-to document and the current document; for example, `"TOC"` or `"Glossary"` (not commonly used). |
| `REV="..."` | A reverse relationship between the current document and the linked-to document (not commonly used). |
| `URN="..."` | A Uniform Resource Number (URN), a unique identifier different from the URL in `HREF` (not commonly used). |
| `TITLE="..."` | The title of the linked-to document (not commonly used). |
| `METHODS="..."` | The method with which the document is to be retrieved; for example, FTP, Gopher, and so on (not commonly used). |
| `TARGET="..."` | The name of a frame that the linked document should appear in. |

# Lists

|  |  | |
|---|---|---|
| **<OL>...</OL>** | An ordered (numbered) list. | |
| *Attributes:* | | |
| | TYPE="..." | The type of numerals to label the list. Possible values are A, a, I, i, or 1. |
| | START="..." | The value with which to start this list. |
| **<UL>...</UL>** | An unordered (bulleted) list. | |
| *Attributes:* | | |
| | TYPE="..." | The bullet dingbat to use to mark list items. Possible values are DISC, CIRCLE (or ROUND), and SQUARE. |
| **<MENU>...</MENU>** | A menu list of items. | |
| **<DIR>...</DIR>** | A directory listing; items are generally smaller than 20 characters. | |
| **<LI>** | A list item for use with <OL>, <UL>, <MENU>, or <DIR>. | |
| *Attributes:* | | |
| | TYPE="..." | The type of bullet or number to label this item with. Possible values are DISC, CIRCLE (or ROUND), SQUARE, A, a, I, i, or 1. |
| | VALUE="..." | The numeric value this list item should have (affects this item and all below it in <OL> lists). |
| **<DL>...</DL>** | A definition or glossary list. | |
| *Attributes:* | | |
| | COMPACT | The COMPACT attribute specifies a formatting that takes less whitespace to present. |

| | |
|---|---|
| **<DT>** | A definition term, as part of a definition list. |
| **<DD>** | The corresponding definition to a definition term, as part of a definition list. |

## Character Formatting

| | |
|---|---|
| **<EM>...</EM>** | Emphasis (usually italic). |
| **<STRONG>...</STRONG>** | Stronger emphasis (usually bold). |
| **<CODE>...</CODE>** | Code sample (usually Courier). |
| **<KBD>...</KBD>** | Text to be typed (usually Courier). |
| **<VAR>...</VAR>** | A variable or placeholder for some other value. |
| **<SAMP>...</SAMP>** | Sample text (seldom used). |
| **<DFN>...</DFN>** | A definition of a term. |
| **<CITE>...</CITE>** | A citation. |
| **<B>...</B>** | Boldface text. |
| **<I>...</I>** | Italic text. |
| **<TT>...</TT>** | Typewriter (monospaced) font. |
| **<PRE>...</PRE>** | Preformatted text (exact line endings and spacing will be preserved—usually rendered in a monospaced font). |
| **<BIG>...</BIG>** | Text is slightly larger than normal. |
| **<SMALL>...</SMALL>** | Text is slightly smaller than normal. |
| **<SUB>...</SUB>** | Subscript. |
| **<SUP>...</SUP>** | Superscript. |
| **<STRIKE>...</STRIKE>** | Puts a strikethrough line in text. |

## Other Elements

| | |
|---|---|
| **<HR>** | A horizontal rule line. |

*Attributes:*

| | | |
|---|---|---|
| | SIZE="..." | The thickness of the rule, in pixels. |
| | WIDTH="..." | The width of the rule, in pixels or as a percentage of the document width. |

| | | |
|---|---|---|
| | `ALIGN="..."` | How the rule line will be aligned on the page. Possible values are `LEFT`, `RIGHT`, and `CENTER`. |
| | `NOSHADE` | Causes the rule line to be drawn as a solid line instead of a transparent bevel. |
| | `COLOR="..."` (MS) | Color of the horizontal rule. |
| **<BR>** | A line break. | |
| *Attributes:* | | |
| | `CLEAR="..."` | Causes the text to stop flowing around any images. Possible values are `RIGHT`, `LEFT`, `ALL`. |
| **<NOBR>...</NOBR>** | Causes the enclosed text not to wrap at the edge of the page. | |
| **<WBR>** | Wraps the text at this point only if necessary. | |
| **<BLOCKQUOTE>...</BLOCKQUOTE>** | Used for long quotes or citations. | |
| **<ADDRESS>...</ADDRESS>** | Used for signatures or general information about a document's author. | |
| **<CENTER>...</CENTER>** | Centers text or images. | |
| **<BLINK>...</BLINK>** | Causes the enclosed text to blink irritatingly. | |
| **<FONT>...</FONT>** | Changes the size of the font for the enclosed text. | |
| *Attributes:* | | |
| | `SIZE="..."` | The size of the font, from 1 to 7. Default is 3. Can also be specified as a value relative to the current size; for example, +2. |
| | `COLOR="..."` | Changes the color of the text. |

| | | |
|---|---|---|
| | `FACE="..."` (MS) | Name of font to use if it can be found on the user's system. Multiple font names can be separated by commas, and the first font on the list that can be found will be used. |

**`<BASEFONT>`** Sets the default size of the font for the current page.

*Attributes:*

| | | |
|---|---|---|
| | `SIZE="..."` | The default size of the font, from `1` to `7`. Default is `3`. |

## Images, Sounds, and Embedded Media

**`<IMG>`** Inserts an inline image into the document.

*Attributes:*

| | | |
|---|---|---|
| | `ISMAP` | This image is a clickable image map. |
| | `SRC="..."` | The URL of the image. |
| | `ALT="..."` | A text string that will be displayed in browsers that cannot support images. |
| | `ALIGN="..."` | Determines the alignment of the given image. If `LEFT` or `RIGHT` (N), the image is aligned to the left or right column, and all following text flows beside that image. All other values such as `TOP`, `MIDDLE`, `BOTTOM`, or the Netscape only `TEXTTOP`, `ABSMIDDLE`, |

| | |
|---|---|
| | BASELINE, ABSBOTTOM determine the vertical alignment of this image with other items in the same line. |
| VSPACE="..." | The space between the image and the text above or below it. |
| HSPACE="..." | The space between the image and the text to its left or right. |
| WIDTH="..." | The width, in pixels, of the image. If WIDTH is not the actual width, the image is scaled to fit. |
| HEIGHT="..." | The width, in pixels, of the image. If HEIGHT is not the actual height, the image is scaled to fit. |
| BORDER="..." | Draws a border of the specified value in pixels to be drawn around the image. In the case of images that are also links, BORDER changes the size of the default link border. |
| LOWSRC="..." | The path or URL of an image that will be loaded first, before the image specified in SRC. The value of LOWSRC is usually a smaller or lower resolution version of the actual image. |

| | | |
|---|---|---|
| | `USEMAP="..."` | The name of an image map specification for client-side image mapping. Used with `<MAP>` and `<AREA>`. |
| | `DYNSRC="..."` (MS) | The address of a video clip or VRML world (dynamic source). |
| | `CONTROLS` (MS) | Used with `DYNSRC` to display a set of playback controls for inline video. |
| | `LOOP="..."` (MS) | The number of times a video clip will loop. (`-1` or `INFINITE` means to loop indefinitely.) |
| | `START="..."` (MS) | When a `DYNSRC` video clip should start playing. Valid options are `FILEOPEN` (play when page is displayed) or `MOUSEOVER` (play when mouse cursor passes over the video clip). |
| **`<BGSOUND>`** (MS) | Plays a sound file as soon as the page is displayed. | |
| *Attributes:* | | |
| | `SRC="..."` | The URL of the WAV, AU, or MIDI sound file to embed. |
| | `LOOP="..."` (MS) | The number of times a video clip will loop. (`-1` or `INFINITE` means to loop indefinitely.) |
| **`<OBJECT>`** (MS) | Inserts an image, video, Java applet, or ActiveX OLE control into a document. | |

**NOTE:** The full syntax for the `<OBJECT>` tag is not yet completely finalized. Check `http://www.w3.org/pub/WWW/TR/WD-object.html` and `http://www.microsoft.com/intdev/author/` for the latest attributes supported by the HTML 3.2 standard and implemented in Microsoft Internet Explorer.

| | |
|---|---|
| **`<EMBED>`** (Netscape only!) | Embeds a file to be read or displayed by a plug-in application. |

**NOTE:** In addition to the following standard attributes, you can specify applet-specific attributes to be interpreted by the plug-in which displays the embedded object.

*Attributes:*

| | |
|---|---|
| `SRC="..."` | The URL of the file to embed. |
| `WIDTH="..."` | The width of the embedded object in pixels. |
| `HEIGHT="..."` | The height of the embedded object in pixels. |
| `ALIGN="..."` | Determines the alignment of the media window. Values are the same as for the `<IMG>` tag. |
| `VSPACE="..."` | The space between the media and the text above or below it. |
| `HSPACE="..."` | The space between the media and the text to its left or right. |
| `BORDER="..."` | Draws a border of the specified size in pixels to be drawn around the media. |

| | |
|---|---|
| **<NOEMBED>...</NOEMBED>** (N) | Alternate text or images to be shown to users who do not have a plug-in installed. |
| **<OBJECT>** (MS) | Inserts an embedded program, control, or other object. (This tag was under revision when this book was printed—see the note at the beginning of this appendix.) |
| **<MAP>...</MAP>** | A client-side image map, referenced by <IMG USEMAP="...">. Includes one or more <AREA> tags. |
| **<AREA>** | Defines a clickable link within a client-side image map. |

*Attributes:*

| | | |
|---|---|---|
| | SHAPE="..." | The shape of the clickable area. Currently, only RECT is supported. |
| | COORDS="..." | The left, top, right, and bottom coordinates of the clickable region within an image. |
| | HREF="..." | The URL that should be loaded when the area is clicked. |
| | NOHREF | Indicates that no action should be taken when this area of the image is clicked. |

## Forms

| | |
|---|---|
| **<FORM>...</FORM>** | Indicates an input form. |

*Attributes:*

| | | |
|---|---|---|
| | ACTION="..." | The URL of the script to process this form input. |
| | METHOD="..." | How the form input will be sent to the gateway on the |

| | | |
|---|---|---|
| | | server side. Possible values are `GET` and `POST`. |
| | `ENCTYPE="..."` | Normally has the value `application/x-www-form-urlencoded`. For file uploads, use `multi-part/form-data`. |
| | `NAME="..."` | A name by which JavaScript scripts can refer to the form. |

**`<INPUT>`** An input element for a form.

*Attributes:*

| | | |
|---|---|---|
| | `TYPE="..."` | The type for this input widget. Possible values are `CHECKBOX`, `HIDDEN`, `RADIO`, `RESET`, `SUBMIT`, `TEXT`, `SEND FILE`, or `IMAGE`. |
| | `NAME="..."` | The name of this item, as passed to the gateway script as part of a name/value pair. |
| | `VALUE="..."` | For a text or hidden widget, the default value; for a checkbox or radio button, the value to be submitted with the form; for Reset or Submit buttons, the label for the button itself. |
| | `SRC="..."` | The source file for an image. |
| | `CHECKED` | For checkboxes and radio buttons, indicates that the widget is checked. |

| | | |
|---|---|---|
| | SIZE="..." | The size, in characters, of a text widget. |
| | MAXLENGTH="..." | The maximum number of characters that can be entered into a text widget. |
| | ALIGN="..." | For images in forms, determines how the text and image will align (same as with the <IMG> tag). |

**<TEXTAREA>...</TEXTAREA>** Indicates a multiline text entry form element. Default text can be included.

| *Attributes:* | | |
|---|---|---|
| | NAME="..." | The name to be passed to the gateway script as part of the name/value pair. |
| | ROWS="..." | The number of rows this text area displays. |
| | COLS="..." | The number of columns (characters) this text area displays. |
| | WRAP="..." (N) | Control text wrapping. Possible values are OFF, VIRTUAL, and PHYSICAL. |

**<SELECT>...</SELECT>** Creates a menu or scrolling list of possible items.

| *Attributes:* | | |
|---|---|---|
| | NAME="..." | The name that is passed to the gateway script as part of the name/value pair. |

| | | |
|---|---|---|
| | SIZE="..." | The number of elements to display. If SIZE is indicated, the selection becomes a scrolling list. If no SIZE is given, the selection is a pop-up menu. |
| | MULTIPLE | Allows multiple selections from the list. |

**<OPTION>** Indicates a possible item within a <SELECT> element.

*Attributes:*

| | | |
|---|---|---|
| | SELECTED | With this attribute included, the <OPTION> will be selected by default in the list. |
| | VALUE="..." | The value to submit if this <OPTION> is selected when the form is submitted. |

# Tables

**<TABLE>...</TABLE>** Creates a table that can contain a caption (<CAPTION>) and any number of rows (<TR>).

*Attributes:*

| | | |
|---|---|---|
| | BORDER="..." | Indicates whether the table should be drawn with or without a border. In Netscape, BORDER can also have a value indicating the width of the border. |
| | CELLSPACING="..." | The amount of space between the cells in the table. |

| | |
|---|---|
| CELLPADDING="..." | The amount of space between the edges of the cell and its contents. |
| WIDTH="..." | The width of the table on the page, in either exact pixel values or as a percentage of page width. |
| ALIGN="..." (MS) | Alignment (works like IMG ALIGN). Values are LEFT or RIGHT. |
| BACKGROUND="..." (MS) | Background image to tile within all cells in the table that do not contain their own BACKGROUND or BGCOLOR attribute. |
| BGCOLOR="..." (MS) | Background color of all cells in the table that do not contain their own BACKGROUND or BGCOLOR attribute. |
| BORDERCOLOR="..." (MS) | Border color (used with BORDER="..."). |
| BORDERCOLORLIGHT="..." | Color for light part of 3D-look borders (used with BORDER="..."). |
| BORDERCOLORDARK="..." (MS) | Color for dark part of 3D-look borders (used with BORDER="..."). |
| VALIGN="..." (MS) | Alignment of text within the table. Values are TOP and BOTTOM. |

| | | |
|---|---|---|
| | FRAME="..." (MS) | Controls which external borders will appear around a table. Values are "void" (no frames), "above" (top border only), "below" (bottom border only), "hsides" (top and bottom), "lhs" (left hand side), "rhs" (right hand side), "vsides" (left and right sides), and "box" (all sides). |
| | RULES="..." (MS) | Controls which internal borders appear in the table. Values are "none", "basic" (rules between THEAD, TBODY, and TFOOT only), "rows" (horizontal borders only), "cols" (vertical borders only), and "all". |

**<CAPTION>...</CAPTION>** The caption for the table.

*Attributes:*

| | | |
|---|---|---|
| | ALIGN="..." | The position of the caption. Possible values are TOP and BOTTOM. |

**<TR>...</TR>** Defines a table row, containing headings and data (<TR> and <TH> tags).

*Attributes:*

| | | |
|---|---|---|
| | ALIGN="..." | The horizontal alignment of the contents of the cells within this row. Possible values are LEFT, RIGHT, and CENTER. |
| | VALIGN="..." | The vertical alignment of the contents of the cells within this row. Possible values are TOP, MIDDLE, BOTTOM, and BASELINE. |
| | BACKGROUND="..." (MS) | Background image to tile within all cells in the row that do not contain their own BACKGROUND or BGCOLOR attributes. |
| | BGCOLOR="..." | Background color of all cells in the row that do not contain their own BACKGROUND or BGCOLOR attributes. |
| | BORDERCOLOR="..." (MS) | Border color (used with BORDER="..."). |
| | BORDERCOLORLIGHT="..." (MS) | Color for light part of 3D-look borders (used with BORDER="..."). |
| | BORDERCOLORDARK="..." (MS) | Color for dark part of 3D-look borders (used with BORDER="..."). |

**<TH>...</TH>** Defines a table heading cell.

*Attributes:*

| | | |
|---|---|---|
| | ALIGN="..." | The horizontal alignment of the contents of the cell. |

| | | |
|---|---|---|
| | | Possible values are `LEFT`, `RIGHT`, and `CENTER`. |
| | `VALIGN="..."` | The vertical alignment of the contents of the cell. Possible values are `TOP`, `MIDDLE`, `BOTTOM`, and `BASELINE`. |
| | `ROWSPAN="..."` | The number of rows this cell will span. |
| | `COLSPAN="..."` | The number of columns this cell will span. |
| | `NOWRAP` | Does not automatically wrap the contents of this cell. |
| | `WIDTH="..."` | The width of this column of cells, in exact pixel values or as a percentage of the table width. |
| | `BACKGROUND="..."` (MS) | Background image to tile within the cell. |
| | `BGCOLOR="..."` (MS) | Background color of the cell. |
| | `BORDERCOLOR="..."` (MS) | Border color (used with `BORDER="..."`). |
| | `BORDERCOLORLIGHT="..."` (MS) | Color for light part of 3D-look borders (used with `BORDER="..."`). |
| | `BORDERCOLORDARK="..."` (MS) | Color for dark part of 3D-look borders (used with `BORDER="..."`). |
| **<TD>...</TD>** | Defines a table data cell. | |
| *Attributes:* | | |
| | `ALIGN="..."` | The horizontal alignment of the contents of the cell. Possible values are `LEFT`, `RIGHT`, and `CENTER`. |

| | | |
|---|---|---|
| | `VALIGN="..."` | The vertical alignment of the contents of the cell. Possible values are `TOP`, `MIDDLE`, `BOTTOM`, and `BASELINE`. |
| | `ROWSPAN="..."` | The number of rows this cell will span. |
| | `COLSPAN="..."` | The number of columns this cell will span. |
| | `NOWRAP` | Does not automatically wrap the contents of this cell. |
| | `WIDTH="..."` | The width of this column of cells, in exact pixel values or as a percentage of the table width. |
| | `BACKGROUND="..."` (MS) | Background image to tile within the cell. |
| | `BGCOLOR="..."` (MS) | Background color of the cell. |
| | `BORDERCOLOR="..."` (MS) | Border color (used with `BORDER="..."`). |
| | `BORDERCOLORLIGHT="..."` (MS) | Color for light part of 3D-look borders (used with `BORDER="..."`). |
| | `BORDERCOLORDARK="..."` (MS) | Color for dark part of 3D-look borders (used with `BORDER="..."`). |
| **<THEAD>** (MS) | Begins the header section of a table. The closing </THEAD> tag is optional. | |

| | |
|---|---|
| **<TBODY>** (MS) | Begins the body section of a table. The closing </TBODY> tag is optional. |
| **<TFOOT>** (MS) | Begins the footer section of a table. The closing </TFOOT> tag is optional. |
| **<COL>...</COL>** (MS) | Sets width and alignment properties for one or more columns. |

*Attributes:*

| | |
|---|---|
| WIDTH="..." | Width of column(s) in pixels or relative width followed by a * ("2*" columns will be twice as wide as "1*" columns, for example). |
| ALIGN="..." | Text alignment within the column(s). Valid values are "center", "justify", "left", and "right". |
| SPAN="..." | Number of columns that the properties specified in this <COL> tag apply to. |

| | |
|---|---|
| **<COLGROUP>...</COLGROUP>** | Sets properties of a group of columns all at once (should enclose one or more <COL> tags). |

*Attributes:*

| | |
|---|---|
| ALIGN="..." | Text alignment within the columns. Valid values are "center", "justify", "left", and "right". |
| VALIGN="..." | Vertical alignment of text within the columns. Valid values are "baseline", "bottom", "middle", and "top". |

## Frames

| | | |
|---|---|---|
| **<FRAMESET>...</FRAMESET>** | Divides the main window into a set of frames that can each display a separate document. | |
| *Attributes:* | | |
| | `ROWS="..."` | Splits the window or frameset vertically into a number of rows specified by a number (such as 7), a percentage of the total window width (such as `25%`), or as an asterisk (`*`) indicating that a frame should take up all the remaining space or divide the space evenly between frames (if multiple `*` frames are specified). |
| | `COLS="..."` | Works similar to `ROWS`, except that the window or frameset is split horizontally into columns. |
| **<FRAME>** | Defines a single frame within a `<FRAMESET>`. | |
| *Attributes:* | | |
| | `SRC="..."` | The URL of the document to be displayed in this frame. |
| | `NAME="..."` | A name to be used for targeting this frame with the `TARGET` attribute in `<A HREF>` links. |
| | `<MARGINWIDTH>` | The amount of space to leave to the left |

| | |
|---|---|
| | and right side of a document within a frame, in pixels. |
| `<MARGINHEIGHT>` | The amount of space to leave above and below a document within a frame, in pixels. |
| `SCROLLING="..."` | Determines whether a frame has scrollbars. Possible values are `YES`, `NO`, and `AUTO`. |
| `NORESIZE` | Prevents the user from resizing this frame (and possibly adjacent frames) with the mouse. |
| `FRAMEBORDER="..."` (MS) | Specifies whether to display a border for a frame. Options are `YES` and `NO`. |
| `FRAMESPACING="..."` (MS) | Space between frames, in pixels. |

**`</NOFRAME>...</NOFRAME>`** Provides an alternative document body in `<FRAMESET>` documents for browsers that do not support frames (usually encloses `<BODY>...</BODY>`).

## Scripting and Applets

**`<APPLET>`** Inserts a self-running Java applet.

> **NOTE:** In addition to the following standard attributes, you can specify applet-specific attributes to be interpreted by the Java applet itself.

*Attributes:*

| | |
|---|---|
| `CLASS="..."` | The name of the applet. |

| | | |
|---|---|---|
| | `SRC="..."` | The URL of the directory where the compiled applet can be found (should end in a slash `/` as in `"http://mysite/myapplets/"`). Do not include the actual applet name, which is specified with the `CLASS` attribute. |
| | `ALIGN="..."` | Indicates how the applet should be aligned with any text that follows it. Current values are `TOP`, `MIDDLE`, and `BOTTOM`. |
| | `WIDTH="..."` | The width of the applet output area in pixels. |
| | `HEIGHT="..."` | The height of the applet output area in pixels. |
| **`<SCRIPT>`** | An interpreted script program. | |
| *Attributes:* | | |
| | `LANGUAGE="..."` | Currently only `JAVASCRIPT` is supported by Netscape. Both `JAVASCRIPT` and `VBSCRIPT` are supported by Microsoft. |
| | `SRC="..."` | Specifies the URL of a file that includes the script program. |

## Marquees

**<MARQUEE>...</MARQUEE>** (MS) Displays text in a scrolling marquee.

*Attributes:*

| Attribute | Description |
|---|---|
| WIDTH="..." | The width of the embedded object in pixels or percentage of window width. |
| HEIGHT="..." | The height of the embedded object in pixels or percentage of window height. |
| ALIGN="..." | Determines the alignment of the text *outside* the marquee. Values are TOP, MIDDLE, and BOTTOM. |
| BORDER="..." | Draws a border of the specified size in pixels to be drawn around the media. |
| BEHAVIOR="..." | How the text inside the marquee should behave. Options are SCROLL (continuous scrolling), SLIDE (slide text in and stop), and ALTERNATE (bounce back and forth). |
| BGCOLOR="..." | Background color for the marquee. |
| DIRECTION="..." | Direction for text to scroll (LEFT or RIGHT). |
| VSPACE="..." | Space above and below the marquee, in pixels. |
| HSPACE="..." | Space on each side of the marquee, in pixels. |

| | |
|---|---|
| `SCROLLAMOUNT="..."` | Number of pixels to move each time text in the marquee is redrawn. |
| `SCROLLDELAY="..."` | Number of milliseconds between each redraw of marquee text. |
| `LOOP="..."` (MS) | The number of times marquee will loop. (-1 or `INFINITE` means to loop indefinitely.) |

# Character Entities

Table B.1 contains the possible numeric and character entities for the ISO-Latin-1 (ISO8859-1) character set. Where possible, the character is shown.

**NOTE:** Not all browsers can display all characters, and some browsers may even display characters different from those that appear in the table. Newer browsers seem to have a better track record for handling character entities, but be sure to test your HTML files extensively with multiple browsers if you intend to use these entities.

**Table B.1. ISO-Latin-1 character set.**

| *Character* | *Numeric Entity* | *Character Entity (if any)* | *Description* |
|---|---|---|---|
| | �- | | Unused |
| | 	 | | Horizontal tab |
| | 
 | | Line feed |
| | - | | Unused |
| |   | | Space |
| ! | ! | | Exclamation mark |
| " | " | " | Quotation mark |
| # | # | | Number sign |
| $ | $ | | Dollar sign |

| *Character* | *Numeric Entity* | *Character Entity (if any)* | *Description* |
|---|---|---|---|
| % | % | | Percent sign |
| & | & | & | Ampersand |
| ' | ' | | Apostrophe |
| ( | ( | | Left parenthesis |
| ) | ) | | Right parenthesis |
| * | * | | Asterisk |
| + | + | | Plus sign |
| , | , | | Comma |
| - | - | | Hyphen |
| . | . | | Period (fullstop) |
| / | / | | Solidus (slash) |
| 0-9 | 0 - 9 | | Digits 0-9 |
| : | : | | Colon |
| ; | ; | | Semicolon |
| < | < | < | Less than |
| = | = | | Equals sign |
| > | > | > | Greater than |
| ? | ? | | Question mark |
| @ | @ | | Commercial "at" |
| A-Z | A-Z | | Letters A-Z |
| [ | [ | | Left square bracket |
| \ | \ | | Reverse solidus (backslash) |
| ] | ] | | Right square bracket |
| ^ | ^ | | Caret |
| — | _ | | Horizontal bar |
| ` | ` | | Grave accent |
| a-z | a-z | | Letters a-z |
| { | { | | Left curly brace |
| \| | | | | Vertical bar |
| } | } | | Right curly brace |

*continues*

**Table B.1. continued**

| *Character* | *Numeric Entity* | *Character Entity (if any)* | *Description* |
|---|---|---|---|
| ~ | ~ | | Tilde |
| | -   | | Unused |
| ¡ | ¡ | ¡ | Inverted exclamation |
| ¢ | ¢ | ¢ | Cent sign |
| £ | £ | £ | Pound sterling |
| ¤ | ¤ | ¤ | General currency sign |
| ¥ | ¥ | ¥ | Yen sign |
| ¦ | ¦ | ¦ or brkbar; | Broken vertical bar |
| § | § | § | Section sign |
| ¨ | ¨ | ¨ | Umlaut (dieresis) |
| © | © | © | Copyright |
| ª | ª | ª | Feminine ordinal |
| ‹ | « | « | Left angle quote, guillemot left |
| ¬ | ¬ | ¬ | Not sign |
| - |  |  | Soft hyphen |
| ® | ® | ® | Registered trademark |
| ¯ | ¯ | &hibar; | Macron accent |
| ° | ° | ° | Degree sign |
| ± | ± | ± | Plus or minus |
| ² | ² | ² | Superscript two |
| ³ | ³ | ³ | Superscript three |
| ´ | ´ | ´ | Acute accent |
| µ | µ | µ | Micro sign |
| ¶ | ¶ | ¶ | Paragraph sign |
| · | · | · | Middle dot |
| ¸ | ¸ | ¸ | Cedilla |
| ¹ | ¹ | ¹ | Superscript one |
| º | º | º | Masculine ordinal |

| *Character* | *Numeric Entity* | *Character Entity (if any)* | *Description* |
|---|---|---|---|
| › | » | » | Right angle quote, guillemot right |
| ¼ | ¼ | ¼ | Fraction one-fourth |
| ½ | ½ | ½ | Fraction one-half |
| ¾ | ¾ | ¾ | Fraction three-fourths |
| ¿ | ¿ | ¿ | Inverted question mark |
| À | À | À | Capital A, grave accent |
| Á | Á | Á | Capital A, acute accent |
| Â | Â | Â | Capital A, circumflex accent |
| Ã | Ã | Ã | Capital A, tilde |
| Ä | Ä | Ä | Capital A, dieresis or umlaut mark |
| Å | Å | Å | Capital A, ring |
| Æ | Æ | Æ | Capital AE diphthong (ligature) |
| Ç | Ç | Ç | Capital C, cedilla |
| È | È | È | Capital E, grave accent |
| É | É | É | Capital E, acute accent |
| Ê | Ê | Ê | Capital E, circumflex accent |
| Ë | Ë | Ë | Capital E, dieresis or umlaut mark |
| Ì | Ì | Ì | Capital I, grave accent |

*continues*

**Table B.1. continued**

| *Character* | *Numeric Entity* | *Character Entity (if any)* | *Description* |
|---|---|---|---|
| Í | Í | Í | Capital I, acute accent |
| Î | Î | Î | Capital I, circumflex accent |
| Ï | Ï | Ï | Capital I, dieresis or umlaut mark |
| Ð | Ð | Ð | Capital Eth, Icelandic |
| Ñ | Ñ | Ñ | Capital N, tilde |
| Ò | Ò | Ò | Capital O, grave accent |
| Ó | Ó | Ó | Capital O, acute accent |
| Ô | Ô | Ô | Capital O, circumflex accent |
| Õ | Õ | Õ | Capital O, tilde |
| Ö | Ö | Ö | Capital O, dieresis or umlaut mark |
| × | × | | Multiply sign |
| Ø | Ø | Ø | Capital O, slash |
| Ù | Ù | Ù | Capital U, grave accent |
| Ú | Ú | Ú | Capital U, acute accent |
| Û | Û | Û | Capital U, circumflex accent |
| Ü | Ü | Ü | Capital U, dieresis or umlaut mark |
| Ý | Ý | Ý | Capital Y, acute accent |
| Þ | Þ | Þ | Capital THORN, Icelandic |

| *Character* | *Numeric Entity* | *Character Entity (if any)* | *Description* |
|---|---|---|---|
| β | ß | ß | Small sharp s, German (sz ligature) |
| à | à | à | Small a, grave accent |
| á | á | á | Small a, acute accent |
| â | â | â | Small a, circumflex accent |
| ã | ã | ã | Small a, tilde |
| ä | ä | &aauml; | Small a, dieresis or umlaut mark |
| å | å | å | Small a, ring |
| æ | æ | æ | Small ae diphthong (ligature) |
| ç | ç | ç | Small c, cedilla |
| è | è | è | Small e, grave accent |
| é | é | é | Small e, acute accent |
| ê | ê | ê | Small e, circumflex accent |
| ë | ë | ë | Small e, dieresis or umlaut mark |
| ì | ì | ì | Small i, grave accent |
| í | í | í | Small i, acute accent |
| î | î | î | Small i, circumflex accent |
| ï | ï | ï | Small i, dieresis or umlaut mark |

*continues*

**Table B.1. continued**

| *Character* | *Numeric Entity* | *Character Entity (if any)* | *Description* |
|---|---|---|---|
| ð | ð | ð | Small eth, Icelandic |
| ñ | ñ | ñ | Small n, tilde |
| ò | ò | ò | Small o, grave accent |
| ó | ó | ó | Small o, acute accent |
| ô | ô | ô | Small o, circumflex accent |
| õ | õ | õ | Small o, tilde |
| ö | ö | ö | Small o, dieresis or umlaut mark |
| ÷ | ÷ | | Division sign |
| ø | ø | ø | Small o, slash |
| ù | ù | ù | Small u, grave accent |
| ú | ú | ú | Small u, acute accent |
| û | û | û | Small u, circumflex accent |
| ü | ü | ü | Small u, dieresis or umlaut mark |
| ý | ý | ý | Small y, acute accent |
| þ | þ | þ | Small thorn, Icelandic |
| ÿ | ÿ | ÿ | Small y, dieresis or umlaut mark |

APPENDIX

# C What's on the CD-ROM

On the *Laura Lemay's Web Workshop: Creating Commercial Web Pages* CD-ROM, you will find all the sample files that have been presented in this book along with a wealth of other applications and utilities.

**NOTE:** Please refer to the `readme.wri` file on the CD-ROM (Windows) or the Guide to the CD-ROM (Macintosh) for the latest listing of software.

## Windows Software

The following sections list all the Windows-compatible software on the CD. The section titles are functional area categories of software products and are mirrored in the directory structure of the CD to make things easier to find. Each section contains a list of demos, examples, or other items that appear on the CD. For the exact location and filenames of the products, please run the CD Guide interface or browse the CD yourself in Explorer or File Manager.

## ActiveX

- Microsoft ActiveX Control Pad and HTML Layout Control
- Sample controls

## CGI

- CGI*StarDuo and CGI*StarDuo95
- CGI PerForm command language interpreter for Common Gateway Interface (CGI) application design
- Several sample CGI scripts and libraries

## GNU

- GNU Licenses

## GZIP

- Gzip compression utility

## HTML Tools

- Web Transit—OEM version of HTML Transit
- Microsoft Internet Assistants for Access, Excel, Powerpoint, Schedule+, and Word
- W3e HTML Editor
- CSE 3310 HTML Validator
- Hot Dog 32-bit HTML editor
- HoTMeTaL HTML editor
- HTMLed HTML editor
- HTML Assistant for Windows
- WebEdit Pro HTML editor
- Web Weaver HTML editor
- ImageGen
- Sample icons and backgrounds

## Java

- Sun's Java Developer's Kit for Windows 95/NT, version 1.02
- Sample Java applets
- Sample JavaScripts
- JFactory Java IDE
- JPad Java IDE
- Jpad Pro Java IDE
- Javelin Java IDE

## Graphics, Video, and Sound Applications

- Goldwave sound editor, player, and recorder
- MapThis imagemap utility
- MPEG2PLY MPEG viewer
- MPEGPLAY MPEG viewer
- Paint Shop Pro 3.12 graphics editor and graphic file format converter for Windows
- SnagIt screen capture utility
- ThumbsPlus image viewer and browser

## Perl

- Perl 4
- Perl 5.002
- Perl 5 build 109 for Windows NT

## Explorer

- Microsoft Internet Explorer v3.0

## Utilities

- Microsoft Viewers for Excel, Powerpoint, and Word
- Adobe Acrobat viewer
- Microsoft Powerpoint Animation Player & Publisher

- Winzip for Windows NT/95
- WinZip Self-Extractor, a utility program that creates native Windows self-extracting ZIP files

## Electronic Books

- *Teach Yourself Web Publishing with HTML 3.2 in 14 Days, Professional Reference Edition*

# Macintosh Software

The following sections list all the Macintosh software on the CD. The section titles are functional area categories of software products and are mirrored in the structure of the CD to make things easier to find. Each section contains a list of demos, examples, or other items that appear on the CD. For the exact location and filenames of the products, please read the CD Guide file (located on the CD) or browse the folders of the CD.

## Java

- Sun's Java Developer's Kit for Macintosh v1.0.2
- Sample applets
- Sample JavaScripts

## HTML Tools

- HTML Web Weaver
- WebMap imagemap creator
- HTML.edit
- HTML Editor for the Macintosh

## Graphics, Video, and Sound Applications

- Graphic Converter
- GIFConverter
- Fast Player
- Sparkle
- SoundApp

## Electronic Books

- *Teach Yourself Web Publishing with HTML 3.2 in 14 Days, Professional Reference Edition*

# About Shareware

Shareware is not free. Please read all documentation associated with a third-party product (usually contained within files named `readme.txt` or `license.txt`) and follow all guidelines.

# INDEX


## A

**<A HREF> tag, 69-70**
**ACMEtplet.HTM document (listing 1.1), 17**
**advertising, 320-321**
- animated, 324
  - *banner graphics, 328*
  - *GIF format, 325-327*
  - *Java applets, 329*
- Commonwealth Network
  - *finding advertisers with, 331*
  - *joining, 333-334*
  - *page portfolio management, 336*
- links (Internet Link Exchange), 393-394
- offline media exposure, 394-396
- placement considerations, 321
- rate scale considerations, 323
- tracking, 323-324

**animated advertising, 324**
- banner graphics, 328
- GIF format, 325-327

**answer database, 161-162**
**Apache-SSL server Web sites, 288**
**API (Application Programming Interface), 176**
**Arachnid Worldwide (Web page), 124**
- content page, 127
- menu bar, 125
- reference page, 126

## B

**backgrounds (formatting for online catalogs), 114-118**
**banners (for animated advertising), creating, 26, 328**
**bgcolor attributes (site maps), 213**
**Blacklist of Internet Advertisers, 381**
**<BODY> tag, 32**
**bots (Microsoft FrontPage), 6-7**
**browsers (frameless), 97**
**bullet icons, creating, 28**
**bulletin boards**
- customer support bulletin board, 162-167
- setup, 167

**business references (online resources), 430**
**business transactions**
- data sniffers, 290
- Digicash, 291
- Ecash, 291
- form design items, 287
- Online ordering, 294-296
- payment options, 284-285
- Secure Socket Layers (SSL), 286
- security of, 286-289
- third-party transactions, 289-291

**buttons**
- navigational, 27
- on menu bars, 51-54

## C

**cart.conf configuration file (shopping carts), 271-272**
**catalogs (online), 103**
- background formatting, 114-118
- creating with database and CGI program
  - *index, 246*
  - *main menu, 246*
  - *templates, 248*
- design considerations, 102
- interactivity in, 260
- layering, 102
- multimedia in, 256-259
- nested tables, 118
- price information, 108
- product images, 120
- product information, 108
- product presentations, 252
- separate pages for, 245
- table formatting, 114-118
- tables, 104-108
- text in tables, 109-111
- text-only, 250

**CD-ROM**
- CGI spreadsheet, 195-196
- GIF Constructor Kit, 326-328
- indexer.exe program, 208-209
- research examples (Web pages), 124-134
- Weblint, 401-404

**CGI**
- CGI-based search engines, 214-220
- programs, online catalog creation with, 246-247

scripts (online resources), 432
spreadsheets, creating, 195-199
**CGI script (in HTML forms), 142, 295**
**cmap**
default file, 212
operating, 211
site maps, 211
**codes (HTML)**
error checking with Weblint, 420
verifying (Weblint), 400-404
**color**
assigning to links, 114
decreasing depth in graphics with Paint Shop Pro, 48
design issues, 30-33
hexadecimal values, 30
**colors, applying with bgcolor attributes, 213**
**configurations (cart.config file), 271-272**
**content pages, 75**
creating, 76
designing, 76-81
**cookies (with OopShop Shopping Cart System), 269**
**Cool Tool of the Day (Web site), 9**
**CoolTalk, 169**
**creating**
customer support bulletin board, 162-167
customer support FAQs, 157
FAQ pages, 157-161
links for Web pages, 170-171
site index files, 218
site indexes, 204-205
site maps, 210-213
table of contents, 204-206
**customer forms**
Competition Entry Form example, 226
Rolling Hills Guest Book example, 228
**customer support**
answer database, 161-162
formatting questions and answers, 160
service FAQs setup, 156-157
Web phones, 168-171
WWWBoard, 164
**customer support bulletin board**
setup, 162-167
Usenet, 162
**customer support FAQs, creating, 157**
**customer support pages, overview, 155-156**

## D

**data sniffers (for business transactions), 290**
**databases**
answer database, 161-162
of products, 174-175
*available interfaces, 176*
*creating with template, 180-181*
*Hawg's Harleys example, 175*
*ODBC databases, 189*
*shareware (mSQL), 182-188*
*SQL databases, 189-191*
*static pages, 177-178, 180*
**design, 21**
bullet icons, 28
color schemes, 30-33
*<BODY> tag, 32*
*hexadecimal value, 30*
content pages, 76-81
*Recipe of the Day page (listing 4.5), 79*
horizontal rule, 23-24
HTML forms, 148-150
menu bars, 51
*buttons, 51-52*
*links, 55*
*text for buttons, 54*
navigational buttons, 27
online catalogs, 102-103
*background formatting, 114-118*
*layering, 102*
*nested tables, 118*
*price information, 108*
*product images, 120*
*product information, 108*
*separate pages, 245*
*table formatting, 114-118*
*tables, 104-108*
*text in tables, 109-111*
press release archives, 67-68
theme, 22-23
**designing**
customer support FAQs, 157
Web sites, 221-222
**digital cash, 291**
Digicash (Web sites), 291
Ecash, 291
**directories**
moving files to, 409
of employees, 84
*default page creation, 91-93*
*frame layout creation, 85-86*
organizing Web sites with, 408-409
**Doctor HTML, link verification with, 405, 421**
**downloads**
order forms, 301-302
pay per view, 315-317
speeds, 45
**Dynamic Billboard applet, 330**

## E

**Ecash, 291**
payment options, 292
remote systems, 293

setting up, 292
setting up order links, 294

**editors**
HTML, 4
*Hot Dog, 4-5*
*Internet Assistant for Microsoft Word, 8*
*Microsoft FrontPage, 6-7*
*Netscape Gold, 7-8*
HTML editors, 207

**electronic commerce references (Web sites), 284**

**electronic mail addresses, posting on welcome page, 55**

**employee directories**
alphabetical list creation, 86-90
creating, 84
default page creation, 91-93
frame layout creation, 85-86

**employee Web pages, 93-94**

**Excel spreadsheets, creating Web pages from, 199-200**

**Excite for Web Servers (EWS), 219-220**

## F

**FAQ page**
formatting questions and answers, 160
internal links, 161
layout of, 159

**FAQ pages, creating, 157-161**

**FAQs (frequently asked questions), 156**
<UL> tag, 159
answer database, 161-162
creating a product catalog, 156-157
internal links, 161
layout of, 158
service FAQs setup, 157
using multimedia, 167-171

**files**
formats (for graphics files), 46
site index files, 218
types, 192-194
WWWBoard, 164

**flames (Usenet), 392**

**FONT FACE> tag, 109-111**

**form design items (security), 287**

**form processing (Web sites), 295**

**Formmail, 295-296**

**forms**
Competition Entry Form example, 226
customer support (Gaming Zone FAQs example), 229-230
downloading order forms, 301-302
Enteract example, 237-238
HTML, 140-148
*CGI scripts, 142*
*design considerations, 148*
*graphic links to, 145*
*mailto function, 141*
*mailto Manager program, 151*
*result management, 150*
*tables in, 149*
providing payment options, 286
Rolling Hills Guest Book example, 228

**<FRAME SRC> tag, 85**

**frameless browsers, 97**

**frames (Web site design), 221-222**

**<FRAMESET> tag, 85**

**FROM keyword (SQL), 190**

**FrontPage, 297**

**FrontPage (Web page management with), 406**

**FrontPage HTML editor, 164**

## G

**gateways, Weblint, 403-404**

**GIF Constructor Kit, 326-328**

**GIF format (for animated advertising), 325-327**

**graphics**
banners, 26
bullet icons, 28
color depth, decreasing, 49
for welcome pages, 42-44
*download speeds, 45*
*file formats, 46*
*image file activation, 47-48*
*image size considerations, 49-50*
*Microsoft Multimedia Gallery, 43*
*Paint Shop Pro, 44*
*shrinking, 45*
online resources, 429

## H

**HEIGHT parameter (<IMG> tag), 49-50**

**hexadecimal color values, 30**

**HomeSiteX (Web page management with), 407**

**horizontal rules, 23**
<HR> tag, 23-24

**Hot Dog (HTML Editor), 4-5**
ROVER (output viewer), 5
Sausage Software, 5

**<HR> tag (HTML), 23-24**

**HTML**
ACMEtplet.HTM document (listing 1.1), 17
authoring tools
*online resources, 430*
CGI scripts, 142
codes
*checking with Weblint, 420*
*verifying, 400-401*
*Weblint verification, 401-404*

design
*online resources, 431*
design considerations, 148-150
displaying spreadsheet data with, 195
editors, 4, 207
*Hot Dog, 4-5*
*Internet Assistant for Microsoft Word, 7*
*Microsoft FrontPage, 6-7*
*Netscape Gold, 7-8*
forms, 140-148
graphic links to, 145
mailto function, 141
mailto Manager program, 151
result management, 150
style sheets, 34
tables in, 149

## I

**IDC (Internet Database Connector), 192**
file types, 192-194
**<IMG SRC> tag, 54**
**<IMG> tag**
HEIGHT parameter, 49-50
WIDTH parameter, 49-50
**indexes**
creating site index files, 218
of Web pages, 383
online, 431
site indexes, 205
**indexing**
indexer.exe program (win32), 208-209
**INSERT INTO keyword (SQL), 190**
**INSERT keyword (SQL), 191**
**interactivity**
in online catalogs, 260
*customization, 261-262*
*ordering, 264*
*searches, 260*
**interfaces**
W3-mSQL, 184-186
*<! msql close> command, 184*
*<! msql connect host> command, 184*
*<! msql database name> command, 184*
**internet**
financial transactions, 286
**Internet Assistant for Microsoft Word (HTML editor), 8, 180-181, 199-200**
**Internet Database Connector, *see* IDC**
**Internet Link Exchange, 393-394, 416**
**Internet Marketing Resource, 382**
**investor relations pages, 200-201**

## J-K

**Java applets**
for advertising, 329
Dynamic Billboard, 330
**keywords (SQL)**
FROM, 190
INSERT, 191
INSERT INTO, 190
SELECT, 189-191
SET, 190
UPDATE, 190-191
VALUES, 190
WHERE, 190

## L

**layering information in Web sites, 102**
**<LH> tag, 72-73**
**<LI> tag, 73**
**linking**
Web pages, 393
*Internet Link Exchange, 393-394*
**links**
assigning color to, 114
creating for Web pages, 170-171
error checking with Doctor HTML, 421
in press release archives, 65-70
Internet Link Exchange, 416
Old Dog's 8-track sites (listing 4.3), 73
on menu bars, 55
reference pages of, 70-74
*graphics, 73-74*
*link creation, 73*
*list creation, 72-73*
*locating links, 71*
resetting (management technique), 409
verifying, 400-404
*Doctor HTML, 405*
**listings**
1.1 HTML document ACMEtplet.HTM, 17
4.1 Shamrock Software press release, 66
4.2 Shamrock Software press release header, 68
4.3 Old Dog's 8-track sites, 73
4.4 The 8-track reference list, 74-75
4.5 Knowall Recipe of the Day page, 78-79
10.1 Sample W3-mSQL template, 188
10.2 Sample htx file, 193
13.1 Sample W3-mSQL template for product description pages, 249
17.1 Dynamic Billboard applet, 330

## M


**Macromedia, Web sites, 168**
**mailto function (in HTML forms), 141**
**maintenance, 413**
**management**
- resetting links, 409
- security considerations, 410
- without management tools, 408

**management (Web page), 35**
**management tools**
- HomeSiteX, 407
- Microsoft FrontPage, 406

**Map This! (Web page creation tool), 10**
**marketing**
- online resources, 433

**marketing strategies, 380**
- advertising on Yahoo!, 385
- Internet Marketing Resource, 382
- Netiquette, 382
- Web page indices, 383

**Matt's Script Archive, 214**
**media exposure (offline site advertisements), 395-396**
**menu bars**
- buttons, 51-52
- creating, 50
- design considerations, 51
- links on, 55
- text for buttons, 54

**Microsoft FrontPage**
- bots, 6
- home page, 7
- HTML editor, 6, 164
- server extensions, 7
- wizards, 7

**Microsoft IIS server, Web sites, 288**
**Morph's Daily Spectrum (online newsletter), 307**
**<!msql free QueryHandle> command (W3-mSQL interface), 184**
**mSQL (shareware product databases), 182-187**
- installing on server, 183
- W3-mSQL interface, 184
  - *<! msql close> command, 184*
  - *<! msql connect host> command, 184*
  - *<! msql print "string" command>, 184*
  - *<! msql query "query string"> command, 184*
  - *<QueryHandle> command, 184*

**multimedia**
- in online catalogs, 256-259
  - *Shockwave, 257*
- online resources, 434

**multimedia files**
- customer support options, 167-171


## N


**navigational buttons, 27**
**navigational tools**
- for press release archives, 61-63
- menu bars, 50
  - *buttons, 51-52*
  - *design considerations, 51*
  - *links from, 55*
  - *text for buttons, 54*

**NeatBeat Catalog (online transaction example), 370**
**nested tables, 118**
**Netiquette home page, 382**
**NetMeeting, Web phones, 169**
**Netscape Gold, as an HTML editor, 7-8**
**Netscape servers, Web sites, 287**
**newsgroups**
- </NOFRAME> tag, 97
- HTML authoring, 431


## O


**offline advertising, 394**
- media exposure, 395-396

**offline ordering, 301-302**
**<OL> tag, 72-73**
**Old Dog's 8-track sites (listing 4.3), 73**
**online catalogs, 244**
- background formatting, 114-118
- design considerations, 102-103
  - *layering, 102*
  - *price information, 108*
  - *product information, 108*
  - *tables, 104-108*
- hyperlinks to product pages, 112
- interactivity in, 260
  - *customization, 261-262*
  - *ordering, 264*
- multimedia in, 256-259
  - *Shockwave, 257*
- nested tables, 118
- product images, 120
- product presentations, 252
- separate pages for, 245
- table formatting, 114-118
- text-only, 250

**Online ordering, business transactions, 294-296**
**online resources**
- CGI scripts, 432
- for business references, 430
- for graphics, 429
- for HTML authoring tools, 430
- for HTML design, 431
- for multimedia, 434
- HTML newsgroups, 431

indices, 431
pay-per-view Web services, 433
Web page marketing, 433

**online sales**
customer confidentiality, 350-352
order tracking, 339
*customer data, 341-342*
*data analysis, 344-345*
*indirect database, 354-356*
*inventory, 352*
*order data, 340*
*order status queries, 356-358*
*Salestrak program, 346-359*
*shipment tracking, 359-360*

**OopShop**
online ordering, 297

**OopShop Shopping Cart System, 268-281**
cookies, 269
footer, 274
header custom, 273

**operating**
CGI-based search engines, 214-220
cmap, 211

**order forms**
downloading, 301-302
providing payment options, 286

**order tracking, 339**
customer confidentiality, 350-352
customer data, 341-342
*collecting, 342*
data analysis, 344-345
direct database connections, 343
indirect database connections, 343-344
inventory, 352
*indirect database, 355-356*
*order status queries, 356-358*
*shipment tracking, 359-360*
order data, 340
Saletrak program, 346
*configuring, 347-349*
*installing, 346*
*orderqueries, 357-359*

**ordering systems**
offline ordering, 301-302
online/offline ordering, 294, 297
Polyforms, 300
shopping cart system, 297
telephone orders, 302
Webforms, 300

## P

**pages**
content
*pricing, 306-308*
*registration forms, 308-310*
free areas, 306-308

**Paint Shop Pro (Web page creation tool), 9**
color depth, decreasing, 49

**pay-per-view download services, 315-317, 433**

**Perl**
cmap, 211
Formmail, 295

**phones, Web phones, 168-171**

**Polyforms**
online ordering, 300

**<PRE> tag, 179-180**

**</PRE> tag, 179-180**

**press release archives, 60**
clickable headings, 63
designing, 67-68
links, 65-70
navigational tools, 61-63

**price information (in online catalogs), 108**

**pricing**
for page content, 306-308
*free trials, 314-315*
*registration forms, 308-310*

**product information (in online catalogs), 108**

**products**
content samples, 306-308
databases of, 174-175, 189-191
*available interfaces, 176*
*creating with template, 180-181*
*Hawg's Harleys example, 175*
*shareware (mSQL), 182-188*
*static pages, 177-180*
online catalogs, 254-256
*customization, 261-262*
*interactivity in, 260*
*multimedia in, 256-259*
*ordering, 264*
*presentations, 252*
pricing
*free trials, 314-315*
*registration forms, 308-310*

**ProMetrics, Inc. (Web page), employee pages, 131-132**

**purchases (online)**
shopping carts
*online store, 275-281*
*OopShop Shopping Cart System, 273-274*

## Q

**questionnaires**
online forms, 140-148
*CGI scripts, 142*
*design considerations, 148*
*graphic links to, 145*

*mailto function, 141*
*mailto Manager program, 151*
*result management, 150*
*tables in, 149*

## R

**readme file installation instructions, 214**
**reference pages (Arachnid Worldwide example), 126-127**
**reference pages (links), 70, 74**
graphics on, 73-74
link creation, 73
list creation, 72-73
locating links, 71
**registration forms, 309-312**
for trial offers, 314-315
**research**
Web page examples, 124-134
**ROVER (Hot Dog HTML editor output viewer), 5**

## S

**Salestrak program (online sales tracking), 346**
configuring, 347
installing, 346
**Sausage Software, 5**
**<SCRIPT> tag, 141**
**scripts**
Matt's Script Archive, 214
Web sites, 214, 295
**search engines**
CGI-based, 214-220
creating site index files, 218
Excite for Web Servers (EWS), 219-220
setting up, 214
spiders, 389
*page creation, 390-391*
Web sites, 204
Yahoo!
*categorizing pages on, 415*
*listing pages on, 414*
**search.html file (search queries), 214**
**searches**
Attachmate SupportWeb! example, 237
Enteract example, 237-238
Faxon Company example, 235-236
**Secure Socket Layers (SSL), 286**
**security, 410**
form design items, 287
Secure Socket Layers (SSL), 286
Web servers, 287-289
**SELECT keyword (SQL), 189-191**
**servers**
mSQL installation, 183
*W3-mSQL interface, 184-188*
Netscape server Web sites, 287
security of, 287-289
setting up Ecash, 292
setup bulletin boards, 167
Weblint setup, 401-402
**SET keyword (SQL), 190**
**setting up**
Ecash, 292
formmail, 296
search engines, 214
shopping cart system, 299
Web phones on Web pages, 169
**setup**
bulletin boards, 167
customer support bulletin board, 162-167
**shareware product databases (mSQL), 182-187**
**Shockwave (multimedia software), 257**
**shopping cart system**
online ordering systems, 297
setting up, 299
**shopping carts, 267-275**
creating, 268
OopShop Shopping Cart System, 268-281
*cart.conf configuration file, 272*
*cookies, 272*
*file/directory preparation, 272*
*header customization (head.html), 272*
**shrinking graphics for welcome pages, 45**
**signature ads (Web page advertisements with), 418**
**site indexes, 205**
creating, 204-205, 218
**site maps**
bgcolor attributes, 213
cmap, 211
creating, 210-213
table of contents alternative, 210
**sites**
Apache-SSL server, 288
business transaction payment options, 284-285
creating a table of contents, 204-205
design tips, 221-222
*multiple tables of contents, 221*
*providing links, 221*
*site search engines, 222-223*
*tables and frames, 221*
Digicash, 291
digital cash schemes, 291
electronic commerce references, 284

Excite for Web Servers (EWS), 219-220
form processing, 295
Macromedia, 168
Microsoft IIS server, 288
Netscape servers, 287
online checking, 285
online shopping malls, 301
scripts, 214, 295
search engines, 204
search overview, 204
Secure Socket Layers (SSL), 286
setting up search engines, 214
Solonian Journal, 316
SSL protocol, 286
third-party transactions, 289
URL encoding, 295
Web Developer's Virtual Library, 211

**Solonian Journal Web site, 316**

**spiders (search engines), 389**
page creation, 390-391

**SportsLine (online business transaction example), 371**

**spreadsheets, 194**
CGI, creating, 195-196
data display with HTML, 195
Excel, creating Web pages from, 199-200
static, 199

**SQL (Structured Query Language)**
FROM keyword, 190
INSERT keyword, 191
SELECT keyword, 189-191
SET keyword, 190
UPDATE keyword, 190-191
VALUES keyword, 190
WHERE keyword, 190

**SSL protocol (Web sites), 286**

**static database pages, 177**
creating with HTML editor, 177-180
creating with template, 180-181

**static spreadsheets, 199**

**Stroud's Consummate Winsock Apps (Web site), 9**

**Structured Query Language, *see* SQL**

**style sheets, 34**

**Submit-It!, Web site advertisement with, 387-388, 415**

**support options**
answer database, 161-162
formatting questions and answers, 160
overview, 156
service FAQs setup, 157
using multimedia, 167-171
Web phones, 168-171
WWWBoard, 164

**surveys**
Competition Entry Form example, 226
HTML design considerations, 150
Rolling Hills Guest Book example, 228

## T

**table of contents**
creating, 204-206
text editors, 206

**tables**
formatting for online catalogs, 114-118
in HTML forms, 149
in online catalogs, 104
*price information, 108*
*product information, 108*
*proportioning, 105-108*
*text formatting, 109-111*
nested, 118
Web site design, 221-222

**tables of contents (Faxon Company example), 235-236**

**tags**
<A HREF>, 69-70
<BODY>
*color and, 32*
<FONT FACE>, 109-111
<FRAME SRC>, 85
<FRAMESET>, 85
<HR>, 23-24
<IMG>
*HEIGHT parameter, 49-50*
*WIDTH parameter, 49-50*
<IMG SRC>, 54
<LH>, 72-73
<LI>, 73
</NOFRAME>, 97
<OL>, 72-73
<PRE>, 179-180
</PRE>, 179-180
<SCRIPT>, 141
<TD>, 105-108
</TD>, 108
<TITLE>, 181
</TITLE>, 181, 321
<TD> tag, 105-108
</TD> tag, 108
<TR>, 105-108
<UL>, 72-73, 159

**templates**
for Web pages, 14-17
*creating, 15*
*customizing, 18*
*graphics and, 15*
*saving, 17*
*text element determination, 15*

**text**
for menu bar buttons, 54
in online catalogs, formatting, 109-111

**text editors**
table of contents, 206

**text-only catalogs (online), 250**

**third-party transactions, 289-291**

**<TITLE> tag, 181**
**tools**
Doctor HTML (link verification), 405
for Web page management
*FrontPage, 406*
*HomeSiteX, 407*
navigational
*for press release archives, 61-63*
*menu bars, 50-55*
**tools (for Web page creation)**
Map This!, 10
online resources, 10-12
Paint Shop Pro, 9
**<TR> tag, 105-108**
**tracking**
orders (online sales), 339
*customer data, 341-342*
*data analysis, 344-345*
*indirect database, 355*
*inventory, 352*
*order data, 340*
*orderqueries, 356-358*
*Saletrak program, 346-359*
*shipment tracking, 359-360*

## U

**<UL> tag, 72-73**
**Ultimate Collection of Winsock Software (Web site), 9**
**UPDATE keyword (SQL), 190-191**
**URL encoding, 295**
**Usenet, 393**
customer support bulletin board, 162
flames, 392
site advertisement with, 391-393
*flames, 392*
Web page advertising with, 418
**utilities, 9**

## V

**VALUES keyword (SQL), 190**
**VRML (Virtual Reality Modeling Language), 257**

## W

**W3-mSQL interface, 184-186**
<! msql close> command, 184
<! msql connect host> command, 184
<! msql database name> command, 184
**Web Developer's Virtual Library, 211**
**Web pages, 93-94**
advertising, 320-321
*animated, 324-327*
*banner graphics, 328*
*Java applets, 329*
*media exposure, 395-396*
*offline, 394*
*placement considerations, 321*
*rate scale considerations, 323*
*tracking, 323-324*
*Usenet, 391-393*
advertising on Submit-It!, 387-388
advertising on Yahoo!, 385
advertising with Usenet, 418
Arachnid Worldwide, 124
*content page, 127*
*menu bar, 125*
*reference page, 126*
Autometric, Inc. press release archive, 128-129
basic creation overview, 12-13
bullet icons, creating, 28
by employees, 95-96
Commonwealth Network, joining, 333-334
content pages, 75
*creating, 76*
*designing, 76-81*
creating from Excel spreadsheets, 199-200
creating links for, 170-171
creation tools
*Cool Tool of the Day, 9*
*Map This!, 10*
*online resources, 10-12*
*Paint Shop Pro, 9*
*Stroud's Consummate Winsock Applications, 9*
*Ultimate Collection of Winsock Software, 9*
customer support overview, 155-156
design issues, 21
*color schemes, 30-33*
*hexadecimal color values, 30*
*theme, 22-23*
employee directories
*alphabetical list creation, 87*
*creating, 84*
*default page creation, 91-92*
*frame layout creation, 86*
*frameless browser considerations, 97*
for investor relations, 200-201
graphic banners, creating, 26
HTML, error checking codes with Weblint, 420
index of, 383
Internet Link Exchange, 416
linking (Internet Link Exchange), 393-394
maintenance, 413
management, 35, 408

management tools
*HomeSiteX, 407*
*Microsoft FrontPage, 406*
marketing strategies, 380
*Blacklist of Internet Advertisers, 381*
*Netiquette, 382*
*Yahoo!, 386*
organizing
*directory creation, 408-409*
*moving files to directories, 409*
*resetting links, 409*
*security issues, 410*
press release archives, 60
*clickable headings, 62-63*
*links, 65-66*
*navigational tools, 61-62*
ProMetrics, Inc. (employee page example), 131-132
reference pages (links), 70-74
*graphics on, 73-74*
*link creation, 73*
*list creation, 72-73*
*locating links, 71*
research examples, 124-134
search engines (spiders), 389-391
service FAQs setup, 157
signature ads, 418
site maps, 213
site organization, 423
Submit-It! listings, 415
templates, 14-17
*creating, 15*
*customizing, 18*
*graphics and, 15*
*saving, 17*
*text element determination, 15*
utilities, 9
welcome pages, 41-42
*creating, 44*
*download speeds, 45*
*electronic mail address on, 155*
*file formats for graphics, 46*
*graphics, 42*
*image file activation, 47-49*
*image size considerations, 49-50*
*Microsoft Multimedia Gallery, 143*
*Paint Shop Pro, 44*
*shrinking graphics, 45*
Yahoo! listings, 414-415

**Web phones, 168-171**
CoolTalk, 169
NetMeeting, 169
setting up on Web pages, 169

**Web servers**
security of, 287-289
setting up Ecash, 292
setup bulletin boards, 167

**Web sites**
Apache-SSL server, 288
business transactions (payment options), 284-285
creating a table of contents, 204-205
creating a site index, 204-205
design tips, 221-222
*multiple toc, 221*
*providing links, 221*
*separate toc pages, 221*
*site search engines, 222-223*
*tables and frames, 221*
Digicash, 291
digital cash schemes, 291
electronic commerce references, 284
Excite for Web Servers (EWS), 219-220
form processing, 295
Macromedia, 168
Microsoft IIS server, 288
Netscape servers, 287
online checking, 285
online resources
*business reference sites, 430*
*CGI scripts, 432*
*graphics sites, 429*
*HTML authoring newsgroups sites, 431*
*HTML authoring tool sites, 430*
*HTML design sites, 431*
*multimedia sites, 434*
*pay-per-view Web service sites, 433*
*Web page marketing, 433*
*Web search and indices sites, 431*
online shopping malls, 301
scripts, 214, 295
search engines, 204
search overview, 204
Secure Socket Layers (SSL), 286
setting up search engines, 214
SSL protocol, 286
third-party transactions, 289
URL encoding, 295
Web Developer's Virtual Library, 211

**Webforms (online ordering example), 300**

**Weblint**
gateways, 403-404
server setup, 401-402

**welcome pages, 41-42**
creating, 44
download speeds, 45
electronic mail address on, 55
graphics, 42
*file formats, 46*
*image file activation, 47-49*
*image size considerations, 49-50*
*Microsoft Multimedia Gallery, 43*

*Paint Shop Pro, 44*
*shrinking, 45*
**WHERE keyword (SQL), 190**
**WIDTH parameter (<IMG> tag), 49-50**
**Win32 (indexer.exe program), 208-209**
**wizards (Microsoft FrontPage), 7**
**WWW (World Wide Web)**
FAQs (frequently asked questions), 156
shopping carts, 267-281
*creating, 268*
*footer customization (foot.h), 274*
*header customization, 273*
*OopShop Shopping Cart System, 268-272*
**WWWBoard, 164**
customizing files, 164-166
**WYSIWYG (What You See Is What You Get), 4**

## X-Z

**Yahoo! search engine**
categorizing pages on, 415
listing pages on, 414
**Yahoo! search engines, advertising on, 385**

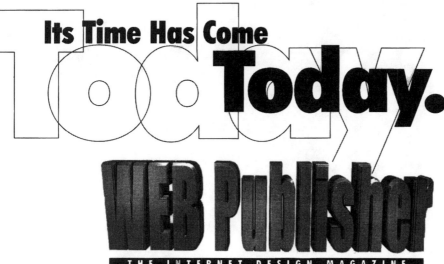

A VIACOM SERVICE

# The Information SuperLibrary™

Bookstore

Search

What's New

Reference

Software

Newsletter

Company Overviews

Yellow Pages

Internet Starter Kit

HTML Workshop

Win a Free T-Shirt!

Macmillan Computer Publishing

Site Map

Talk to Us

## CHECK OUT THE BOOKS IN THIS LIBRARY.

You'll find thousands of shareware files and over 1600 computer books designed for both technowizards and technophobes. You can browse through 700 sample chapters, get the latest news on the Net, and find just about anything using our massive search directories.

*All Macmillan Computer Publishing books are available at your local bookstore.*

We're open 24-hours a day, 365 days a year.

You don't need a card.

We don't charge fines.

And you can be as **LOUD** as you want.

The Information SuperLibrary

http://www.mcp.com/mcp/ ftp.mcp.com

## Laura Lemay's Web Workshop: Netscape Navigator Gold 3

*—Laura Lemay and Ned Snell*

Netscape Gold and JavaScript are two powerful tools to create and design effective Web pages. This book details not only design elements, but also how to use the Netscape Gold WYSIWYG editor. The included CD-ROM contains editors and code from the book, making the reader's learning experience a quick and effective one. You learn how to program within Navigator Gold's rich Netscape development environment and explore elementary design principles for effective Web page creation.

*Price: $39.99 USA/$53.99 CDN* *User level: Casual—Accomplished*
*ISBN: 1-57521-128-9* *400 pages*

## Laura Lemay's Web Workshop: Graphics and Web Page Design

*—Laura Lemay, Jon M. Duff, and James Mohler*

With the number of Web pages increasing daily, only the well-designed will stand out and grab the attention of those browsing the Web. This book illustrates, in classic Laura Lemay style, how to design attractive Web pages that will be visited over and over again. You learn beginning and advanced level design principles. The CD-ROM contains HTML editors, graphics software, and royalty-free graphics and sound files.

*Price: $55.00 USA/$77.95 CDN* *User level: Accomplished*
*ISBN: 1-57521-125-4* *500 pages*

## Laura Lemay's Web Workshop: JavaScript

LAURA LEMAY'S
WEB WORKSHOP
Add interactivity to your Web pages with JavaScript!
JavaScript
Laura Lemay
Michael Moncur


*—Laura Lemay and Michael Moncur*

Readers explore various aspects of Web publishing—whether CGI scripting and interactivity or graphics design or Netscape Gold—in greater depth than the Teach Yourself books. The book provides a clear, hands-on guide to creating sophisticated Web pages. The CD-ROM includes the complete book in HTML format, publishing tools, templates, graphics, backgrounds, and more.

*Price: $39.99 USA/$56.95 CDN* *User level: Casual—Accomplished*
*ISBN: 1-57521-141-6* *400 pages*

## Laura Lemay's Web Workshop: Microsoft FrontPage

*—Laura Lemay and Denise Tyler*

This is a clear hands-on guide to maintaining Web pages with Microsoft's FrontPage. Written in the clear, conversational style of Laura Lemay, it is packed with many interesting, colorful examples that demonstrate specific tasks of interest to the reader. You learn how to maintain Web pages with FrontPage. The CD-ROM includes all the templates, backgrounds, and materials needed.

*$39.99 USA/$56.95 CDN* *User level: Casual—Accomplished*
*ISBN: 1-57521-149-1* *400 pages*

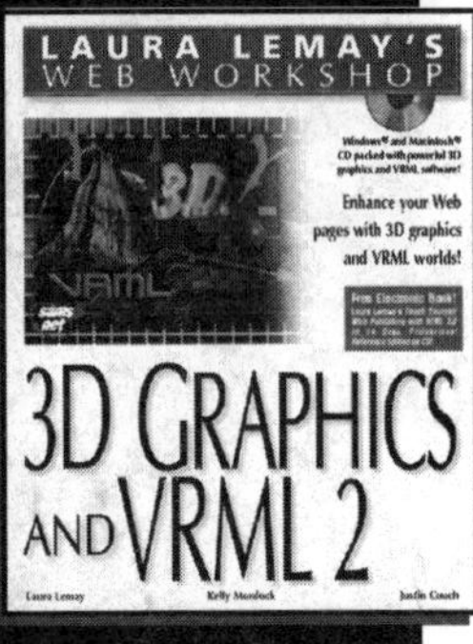


## Laura Lemay's Web Workshop: 3D Graphics and VRML 2

*—Laura Lemay, Kelly Murdock, and Justin Couch*

This is the easiest way for readers to learn how to add three-dimensional virtual worlds to Web pages. It describes the new VRML 2.0 specification, explores the wide array of existing VRML sites on the Web, and steps the readers through the process of creating their own 3D Web environments. The CD-ROM contains the book in HTML format, a hand-picked selection of the best VRML and 3D graphics tools, plus a collection of ready-to-use virtual worlds.

*Price: $39.99 USA/$56.95 CDN* *User level: Casual—Accomplished*
*ISBN: 1-57521-143-2* *400 pages*

## Teach Yourself Web Publishing with HTML 3.2 in 14 Days, Professional Reference Edition

*—Laura Lemay*

This is the updated edition of Lemay's previous bestseller, *Teach Yourself Web Publishing with HTML in 14 Days, Premier Edition.* In it, readers will find all the advanced topics and updates—including adding audio, video, and animation—to Web page creation. The book explores the use of CGI scripts, tables, HTML 3.2, the Netscape and Internet Explorer extensions, Java applets and JavaScript, and VRML.

*Price: $59.99 USA/$81.95 CDN* *User level: New—Casual—Accomplished*
*ISBN: 1-57521-096-7* *1,104 pages*

## Teach Yourself Web Publishing with HTML in 14 Days, Premier Edition

*—Laura Lemay*

This book teaches everything about publishing on the Web. In addition to its exhaustive coverage of HTML, it also gives readers hands-on practice designing and writing HTML documents. Readers learn how to upload their pages to a server and how to advertise. The CD-ROM is Mac- and PC-compatible and includes applications that help readers create Web pages using graphics and templates.

*Price: $39.99 USA/$53.99 CDN* *User level: New—Accomplished*
*ISBN: 1-57521-014-2* *840 pages*

## Teach Yourself Java in 21 Days

*—Laura Lemay, et al.*

Introducing the first, best, and most detailed guide to developing applications with the Java language from Sun Microsystems. This book provides detailed coverage of the hottest new technology on the World Wide Web and shows readers how to develop applications using the Java language. It includes coverage of how to browse Java applications with Netscape and other popular Web browsers. The CD-ROM includes the Java Developer's Kit.

*Price: $39.99 USA/$53.99 CDN* *User level: Casual—Accomplished—Expert*
*ISBN: 1-57521-030-4* *500 pages*

Book ISBN 1-57521-126-2

CD-ROM

# What's on the CD-ROM

The companion CD-ROM contains all the source code and project files developed by the authors, plus an assortment of evaluation versions of third-party products. To install the CD, follow these steps.

## Windows 95/NT 4 Installation Instructions

1. Insert the CD-ROM into your CD-ROM drive.
2. From the Windows 95 desktop, double-click the My Computer icon.
3. Double-click the icon representing your CD-ROM drive.
4. Double-click the icon titled setup.exe to run the CD-ROM installation program.

## Windows NT 3.51 Installation Instructions

1. Insert the CD-ROM into your CD-ROM drive.
2. From File Manager or Program Manager, choose Run from the File menu.
3. Type `<drive>\SETUP` and press Enter, where *<drive>* corresponds to the drive letter of your CD-ROM. For example, if your CD-ROM is drive D:, type `D:\SETUP` and press Enter.
4. Follow the on-screen instructions.

**NOTE:** Windows NT 3.51 users will be able to access those portions of the code with long filenames from the CD in either of two ways. You can run the source code installation program (`SOURCE.EXE`) located in the root directory or choose to unzip those elements separately. The zipped files are located in the `\WINNT351\BOOK\` directory.

Windows NT 3.51 users will be unable to access the `\WIN95NT4` directory because it was left in its original long filename state with a combination of upper- and lowercase letters. This was done to enable Windows 95 and Windows NT 4 users direct access to those files on the CD. All other directories were translated in compliance with the Windows NT 3.51 operating system and can be accessed without trouble. (Note: Trying to access the `\WIN95NT4` directory will cause no harm; it simply will not enable you to read the contents.)

## Macintosh Installation Instructions

1. Insert the CD-ROM into your CD-ROM drive.
2. When an icon for the CD appears on your desktop, open the disc by double-clicking its icon.
3. Double-click the icon named Guide to the CD-ROM, and follow the directions that appear.